Public Relations Theory

Public Relations Theory

Capabilities and Competencies

Jae-Hwa Shin
Robert L. Heath

Registered Office
John Wiley & Sons, Inc., 111 River Street, Hoboken, NJ 07030, USA

Editorial Office
111 River Street, Hoboken, NJ 07030, USA

For details of our global editorial offices, customer services, and more information about Wiley products visit us at www.wiley.com.

Wiley also publishes its books in a variety of electronic formats and by print-on-demand. Some content that appears in standard print versions of this book may not be available in other formats.

Library of Congress Cataloging-in-Publication Data

Names: Shin, Jae-Hwa, author. | Heath, Robert L. (Robert Lawrence), 1941-
    author.
Title: Public relations theory : capabilities and competencies / Jae-Hwa
    Shin, Robert L Heath.
Description: Hoboken, NJ : Wiley-Blackwell, [2021] | Includes index.
Identifiers: LCCN 2020021096 (print) | LCCN 2020021097 (ebook) | ISBN
    9780470659311 (paperback) | ISBN 9781119712961 (adobe pdf) | ISBN
    9781119712954 (epub)
Subjects: LCSH: Public relations. | Organizational change.
Classification: LCC HD59 .S454 2021 (print) | LCC HD59 (ebook) | DDC
    659.201–dc23
LC record available at https://lccn.loc.gov/2020021096
LC ebook record available at https://lccn.loc.gov/2020021097

Cover Design: Wiley
Cover Image: © akindo/Getty Images

Set in 9.5/12.5pt STIXTwoText by SPi Global, Pondicherry, India
Printed and bound by CPI Group (UK) Ltd, Croydon, CR0 4YY

10 9 8 7 6 5 4 3 2 1

Contents

Contents

About the Authors

Jae-Hwa Shin (Ph.D., University of Missouri-Columbia, 2003) is a professor at the University of Southern Mississippi. She has published numerous journal articles and book chapters, and co-authored *Public Relations Today: Managing Conflict and Competition* and *Think: Public Relations*, both widely adopted public relations textbooks. She is currently working on *Public Relations Strategies and Tactics*. Her research focuses on public relations from a strategic conflict management perspective. She is currently serving as the editorial board of the *Journal of Public Relations Research*. She previously worked as communication director at the Korea Economic Research Institute and the Center for Free Enterprise, affiliated with the Federation of Korean Industries in Seoul, Korea.

Robert L. Heath (Ph.D., University of Illinois, 1971) is professor emeritus of the University of Houston. He is the author or editor of 24 books, including handbooks and master collections, and 272 articles in major journals, chapters in leading edited books, and encyclopedia entries. In addition to strategic issues management, he has written on rhetorical theory, social movements, communication theory, public relations, organizational communication, crisis communication, risk communication, terrorism, corporate social responsibility, investor relations, engagement, public interest, and reputation management. He is on editorial boards and reviews for several major journals. His most recent books are the *International Encyclopedia of Strategic Communication* and the *Handbook of Organizational Rhetoric and Communication*.

Acknowledgments

The authors are grateful for the support and patience of the editorial team at Wiley-Blackwell, led by Todd Green, who took over from Elizabeth Swayze and Haze Humbert. We give our thanks for that team's perseverance through many iterations of this text. It has been a long journey, encompassing many evening hours, sleepless nights, weekends, and holidays. We thank our spouses and children for putting up with this project. I, Jae-Hwa Shin, appreciate the endless love and support from my spouse, Dr. Tony Lewis, and our children, Christian Shin Lewis and Colin Shin Lewis. I, Bob Heath, thank the ranks of dedicated academics who labor tirelessly to understand and foster public relations for its potential service to the strength of communities, which are the foundation of functional society. Finally, we both thank those who appreciate the value of this book's presentation of competing perspectives and acknowledge those who may criticize its incompleteness and shortcomings. We hope that the book represents one more step forward in our collective effort to capture the fullness of public relations theory. Once the discipline had only one academic journal, now it has many. Once those teaching graduate work relied on textbooks, now we have a library full of thought-provoking points of view—theory building in progress.

Introduction

Public Relations Theory: Capabilities and Competencies offers an overview of leading public relations theories that have been built up over the last four decades. With a combined experience of more than 50 years, we have worked to summarize each theory and provide insights into key themes such as risks, crises, issues, leadership, relationships, measurement challenges, and publics and stakeholders. While it is not possible to capture the fullness of each theory and each of the related topics, we believe that this book meets the challenge of describing the most salient and significant aspects of the discipline in its current state of theoretical and conceptual development. The field of public relations has been subjected to evolution, diversification, and merger of approach, spurred by rapid changes in society, cultural boundaries, technology, and media environments. As well as explaining the theories and key concepts, the book offers cases and challenges to help students bring theory and research to bear on solving the daily challenges of public relations practice.

Public relations practice, research, and theory building are organically interrelated and unchanging. Engagement of individuals and organizations in conflict, competition, and cooperation has defined human society since its very beginning, although how well power, control, material and symbolic resources, and quality of engagement are managed has varied throughout history. Public relations is often looked upon as a functional tool by which elites gain power and exert control. Throughout history, it has been both strategically and historically contingent on specific situations. Professionals (although not always going by the title of public relations practitioner) have employed their particular structures, tools, functions, and strategic processes to help individuals and organizations achieve their goals, missions, and visions. But as much as elites seek its service, others, including activists, have used public relations to reshape society. It can subvert public order and the will of the people (and even presume to convince the people as to what their "will" is). Private interests often have been sought at the expense of the public good, or in its name. Because the principles governing public relations practice and its roles in society are timeless, unique and ever-changing socioeconomic, cultural, media, and political conditions continue to affect professional practice.

The interaction of theory and practice is the central theme of this book: one cannot exist without the other. While the goal of both practitioners and theoreticians is to improve practice, it is clear that theory is no magic elixir that will overcome deficient practice, and even the most elegant execution cannot make up for a deficient conceptualization.

Given this history and context, Chapter 1 sets the stage by broadly asking whether public relations can be socially responsible, and if so, how. The term "public relations" is often associated with unsavory means and unethical outcomes. Yet, it is continually present in society as professional practice and socioeconomic, political influence. Theorists, as this chapter suggests, have worked with practitioners to define the practice, refine its application, and ensure that it serves the public good.

Chapter 2 explores the ways in which theory—and theoretical assumptions—operates to improve practice. While this necessarily means increasing organizational efficiency and individual efficacy, theory can help practitioners maintain focus on a social responsibility that goes beyond one's institutional role or organizational goals to make society as a whole more fully functioning. As Vision 2050, the Melbourne Mandate, and the Stockholm Accords propose, public relations must confront its place within global society to augment maximization of resources, foster communication on a level playing field, and augment sustainability. Fostering communicative interaction and augmenting the co-creation of meaning in order to enrich society at large is the laudable—if elusive—goal of public relations practice. This chapter identifies and explains theoretical assumptions that deserve to be kept in mind in order to improve practice, while guiding research and theory building.

Chapter 3 examines a major stream of public relations theory that emerged in the 1980s. Excellence theory, based on communication management, proposes that since each organization's actions affect its relationship with publics, conflicts stemming from those actions can be resolved by adjusting the organization's communication style or functions to bring it into alignment with the publics' expectations. This theory prompted research into which of several models best serves organizations and publics. Two-way symmetrical communication became the "gold standard" of this approach. Based on the theory's general systems theoretical underpinnings, behavioral adjustment—as opposed to symbolic or philosophical reexamination of relationships—was proposed as the means for resolving problems and building relationships. The key is that behavioral adjustment begins and ends with public relations being invested in management, so that the voice of critics can help define the qualitative dynamic of organization–public relationships.

Chapter 4 discusses the most strident challenge to excellence theory, known as contingency theory. Instead of proposing that there is a single means of correcting communicative behavior or that all publics have similar preferences and expectations, contingency theory argues that both individuals and organizations can take any number of positions along a continuum between advocacy and accommodation. The dynamics of the organization–public relationship depend on many factors and range from situations of pure agreement or alignment to ones of disagreement or conflict. Contingency theory begins as a description and mapping of the strategic choices made by the various parties involved. It then assesses the factors that can lead to changes of stance and strategic choices over time. It is expected that by developing models of greater precision, theorists can reach greater understanding of the cycle of conflict through proactive, strategic, reactive, and recovery stages. Unlike excellence theory, which reasons that mutual benefit is the universal goal, contingency theory proposes that some situations—such as interactions with irreconcilable groups—necessitate responses in which it is most ethical to adopt an asymmetrical response. The contingency theory of strategic conflict management includes game theory, coorientation, conflict, issues management, and threat appraisal model theories.

Chapter 5 examines rhetorical discourse in relation to public relations theory. Based on classical rhetorical theory, it explains how discourse and dialogue serve organizations' efforts to appeal to individuals in order to forge relationships, debate issue positions, defend propositions, interpret information, and resolve disagreement by co-creating concurrence. Rhetorical theory uniquely emphasizes how language, the most distinct human ability, creates opportunities to define and solve problems. While discourse and dialogue can facilitate democratic institutions, they can also serve to divide factions and augment conflict and competition. This chapter explores the history of rhetorical scholarship, which has served to define public relations practice and offers insight into the way that reality is socially constructed. Dialogue and language offer opportunities for the co-creation of meaning, but the theory acknowledges that bridging issues and value differences is not easy.

Chapter 6 examines the impact of critical theory on public relations, and even the concept of critical public relations. Critical theory argues that scholars and practitioners should be skeptical of the intellectual foundation and underlying rationale of a discipline. For instance, critical public relations theorists reason that practitioners and other theorists have avoided discussions of the relationship between capitalism and promotional campaigns: Who benefits? Who takes a disproportionate share of the resources? What strategic processes and ethical standards allow this to happen? A fundamental premise of critical theory is that each voice in an interaction should be heard, should be given just regard and opportunity to exercise power. While some may question the reasonableness of discussing a theory that seems to undercut much of the rationale for public relations as a discipline, it is important to consider that critical theory begins with the proposition that zeroing in on the areas of greatest ethical peril is beneficial to society as a whole, as opposed to a narrow segment—a hegemony. A fundamental premise of critical theory is that power differences conspire against the exercise of authentic dialogue and fairness. The goal of critical public relations is to identify and mitigate against privileged power in order to achieve a fairer, more fully functioning society and strengthen communities as a public good.

Chapter 7 looks at issues, crisis, and risk management in the context of public relations. Strategic issues management presumes the rhetorical nature of society and that organizations must be aligned with stakeholder interests if they want to gain and manage resources. Organizations, with various abilities and a sense of good will, identify issues that may have a negative impact on their ability to operate in ways that are legitimate in the eyes of stakeholders. They must use issues management to understand standards and dynamics of corporate social responsibility (CSR) as the strategic process of narrowing the legitimacy gap between what they want to do and what stakeholders believe is acceptable. This chapter emphasizes the interdependence of issues, crises, and risks as challenges to the management and motivation of strategic communication. Both avoiding and being prepared for a crisis are crucial to organizations. Public relations is at the forefront of using communication research to examine the environment and scan for potential opportunities and threats. Society can be viewed as "at risk," as can its members. Some risks are created by organizations; often, they are expected to help community members mitigate against associated harms.

Chapter 8 discusses the various dimensions of public relations measurement. Just as planning is essential to a successful public relations campaign, so too is measurement, a means–ends logic. Public relations relies on measurement to provide a rigorous means of comparing and contrasting inputs and outputs in order to understand how society functions. Measurement asks whether the objectives of a campaign or public relations program are met because of the strategic processes employed. This chapter examines methods and theories relevant to public relations measurement, cataloguing the terminology, practical insights, and pitfalls associated with it. Most importantly, it reinforces the central theme that ethical measurement is a responsibility that practitioners bear to their clients, and to the community and society in general.

Chapter 9 focuses on theories of public relations ethics. The discussion ranges from theories of professional ethics and the responsibility that management bears to junior colleagues to the meta-theoretical implication of issues management. The chapter also discusses the ethical issues associated with particular public relations theories, such as excellence theory and critical theory. The three strains of ethical theory that have most often been cited in connection with public relations theory are pragmatism, utilitarianism, and deontology. Their relative merits are weighed in connection to specific public relations perspectives.

Chapter 10 focuses on the public (as a mix of publics and stakeholders), and definitions thereof. During the late 1960s, theorists began to recognize that publics were not monolithic entities and that public opinion varied. Through the 1990s, however, public relations practitioners stressed the strategic role of organizations as disseminators of messages, focusing on targeting stakeholders according to their level of engagement. By the 2000s, scholars proposed that multiple and even marginalized publics had an important impact on organizations. Publics emerged on a footing co-equal with organizations, and theory began to stress the central role of democratic communication and dialogue beyond segmenting publics as a means for operationalizing strategies designed to achieve ends. The participation of multiple publics giving voice to their own opinions, information, beliefs, and values is seen as crucial to the concept of ethical public relations, contributing to a more fully functioning society.

Chapter 11 focuses on relationships. The concept of relationships has changed from a unidimensional one of organizations in relation to their stakeholder public, proposed in the 1920s with the formation of public relations as a discipline, to one characterized by multidimensional interrelationships. Multiple stakeholders and stake seekers are now considered in public relations theory. Drawing on interpersonal relationship scholarship, modern public relations theorists focus on a dialogic and co-creational model. In addition, the impact of theories drawn from economic, political, and social theory has cast the organization–public relationship in a broader theoretical context. The interaction of individuals and organizations is theorized rigorously in the context of power differences.

Chapter 12 looks at the radical transformation the role of the public relations professional has undergone in the last 40 years. An intense focus on ethics, pedagogy, and professional identification has remained constant, and debate continues over the distinction between licensing and accreditation and between the public relations technician and manager roles. But critical themes regarding gender, race, technology, and global identity have come to the fore, and the rise of globalism and multiculturalism—in tandem with changes wrought by new communication technologies—has emerged as a significant topic of theoretical debate. Likewise, the identity of the public relations practitioner as part of a larger movement in strategic communications has come to reshape or replace public relations as a practice.

Chapter 13 surveys salient emerging topics in public relations research. Meta-analyses conducted during the 2000s and 2010s reveal an enduring concern with the evaluation of public relations practice. Scholars have gravitated to issues of strategic communication and of ethics and social responsibility in diverse settings. For some, public relations has become increasingly defined as strategic communication, with the public relations practitioner serving as a kind of intermediary among different factions. The key is that public relations practitioners engage in deliberative, goal-oriented communication, yet play a role as social actors in a fully functioning society, beyond that of strategic managers in an organizational context. Other dominant areas of interest among theoreticians included dialogic theory, technology and new media, globalism, and diversity.

1

Public Relations: Socially Responsible or Work of the Devil

Introduction

Chapter 1 lays the foundation for the discussion that follows. It explores the nature and constructive role of public relations, examining its DNA and defining its professional practice—established as such in the nineteenth century. Such detective work looks for markers including purposes, strategies, functions, tools, tactics, impacts, structures, and justifying philosophies. It identifies the types of organizations, leadership roles, and contexts in which public relations is important.

In history, public relations can be seen as the means for achieving individual and organizational influence, as well as collective engagement among competing interests: strategic processes and efforts enacted by individuals, groups, organizations, and even nations in order that they can survive and thrive, enacted as forms of issues, risk, conflict, and crisis management. It searches for aligned interests, legitimacy, and the license to operate for reward. To discover what today is called "public relations" requires knowing what it does, what it is, where it occurs, and how it serves or confounds interests that encounter tensions of uncertainty and conflict. It can be a clash of perspectives, interests, identities, and identifications. It can be soothing words that allay differences of opinion. It can foster conflict and division.

Careful analysis of the discipline addresses the rationale for its professional practice as being invaluable to political economies, to the human condition, to the organizations that engage in its discourse. It looks at what defining conditions, contexts, and individual and organizational management requirements are needed to share ideas and co-create meanings, create divisions, identities, and identifications, and meet ethical challenges. Collective risk management, for instance, is the essence of public relations discourse and leadership strategies, whether in enacting emergency management or in debating contagion or unhealthy living conditions. It is inherent to clashes of interests, wrangles of ideas, and efforts to enlighten, compromise, collaborate, and accommodate.

Because of its prominence in human affairs, public relations must be subjected to descriptive, predictive, normative, and ethical discussion. Theory and research can lead to a better understanding and improved practice of public relations. Without a working definition—a detailed understanding of the practice coupled to normative theory—the profession will fail to add value to society and even decrease organizational effectiveness when trust is broken. Theory and research champion public relations as fundamental to the quality of relatedness that gives integrity to community.

Public relations is strategic (choice-driven), process-based, outcome-oriented, and guided by value-driven ethical choices. Supporters and critics debate what constitutes ethical principles, and

Public Relations Theory: Capabilities and Competencies, First Edition. Jae-Hwa Shin and Robert L. Heath.
© 2021 John Wiley & Sons, Inc. Published 2021 by John Wiley & Sons, Inc.

whether they are situational or universal. Public relations can make organizations (and causes) more effective (or less so), more capable, and more successful in achieving their missions and visions based on core values. It entails making ideas public and worthy of consideration, seeking concurrence, fostering reputation, building alliances, engaging in conflict, and being central to competition among ideas, products, and services. It includes attention to issues of public policy and organizational identity and reputation. Public relations deals with choices—those made by organizations and their stakeholders.

Much of the scrutiny of public relations since the late 1970s has seen it as an organizational function, but a competing sociological perspective has addressed whether, how, and how well organizations make society more fully functioning. The challenge is to see public relations from an organizational perspective without losing sight of the dynamics of engaged contests in issue arenas where the more expansive conception of societal good is debated. Public relations professionals must demonstrate to journalists and others that they ethically sort and process information in a chaotic universe, fraught with uncertainty. One of the greatest hurdles that they face is to convince critics that they behave responsibly and with the public interest at heart.

This inventory of topics poses a daunting challenge to public relations professionals, academics, and students. Dirty laundry must be sorted from clean, but both must be given due consideration. Iconic practitioners such as Ivy Lee, Edward Bernays, and John Hill recognized the pragmatic value, social responsibility, and ethics associated with public relations. They put their faith in the three legs of the public relations stool. It is pragmatic: it does something useful, and well. It is strategic: process-based, choice-driven, and goal-oriented. And it is ethical: serving the larger good of society and asking in whose interest the profession is practiced.

Public relations employs rhetoric, discursive text, persuasion, publicity, promotion, relationship building, conflict resolution, adjustive behavior, and issue, risk, conflict, and crisis management. It can be propaganda, spinning, and seeking to penetrate publics' mental defenses. It can be a means of engineering consent. It can foster relationships, and help stakeholders to make enlightened choices. It can help organizations to be "excellent" and reflective—or the opposite.

This opening chapter throws a lot of balls into the air, which will be caught and juggled throughout the book. It avoids the tendency to cherry pick by defining the discipline in glowing normative and aspirational terms while casting aside what does not fit that view as something else, something other—anything but public relations. It works to avoid demonizing definitions. It asks: can the beast be subdued by denying that it is in the garden?

Questions to Frame the Introductory Discussion

- What is public relations?
- Whose interests does it serve?
- Does it foster competing or aligned interests?
- What strategies, functions, purposes, tactics, tools, media uses, professional roles, reputation management techniques, and deliberative processes define its presence and value to society?
- Does public relations serve the collective management of risk and the social construction of shared meaning by which groups achieve sufficient concurrence and coordination to survive and thrive?

- Does public relations advance and result from the excellence of organizations, encourage a balance of advocacy and accommodation, employ discourse to advance and align interests, and engage in ethically critical battles?
- Is there evidence of the purposes, tools, tactics, and strategies of public relations in primitive—as well as sophisticated—societies?
- Can institutions such as commerce, church, and state advance without the service of public relations?
- What impact has globalization had on the practice and conceptualization of public relations?
- How have new technologies and changes in the media landscape affected public relations?

Questions such as these help students to act like detectives, identifying the fingerprints and DNA of public relations, knowing when it is on the scene, and determining how it contributes to or frustrates people's ability to get along, coordinate activities, and live in harmony. They suggest several important themes.

Key Themes

- Public relations is a timeless activity associated with the human condition and with the formation of societies, used to make individuals and groups effective in their endeavors.
- Public relations in a contemporary sense is more than press agentry and media relations; it includes all of the communications processes and symbolic actions by which groups seek to be efficacious.
- Attention to public relations as a function of (mass and social) media may be more a matter of its nature in a particular historical era than of that across all human history.
- History is replete with public relations functions, strategies, tools, and purposes, even though they may not have been named or conceived as such or be immediately apparent.
- The challenge for those who study and practice public relations is to emphasize social responsibility and collaborative decision making.
- Because public relations tends to center on controversy, conflict management, and matters of choice, it may be conceived both as socially responsible and as the devil's work, depending on context and one's subject position.

Opening Case: Socially Responsible or Work of the Devil

The title and overarching theme for this chapter come from a class designed primarily for senior-level public relations students, but which attracted students from other majors. The course was intended to prepare students, in a strategic and critical manner, to use discourse on behalf of clients and to benefit the community, and to understand the importance of social responsibility. It required them to write four papers. The first asked them to define public relations. Some took the easy route and used the definition they had learned from other courses, such as Principles of Public Relations. The instructor wanted them to go beyond that, however, and develop a definition in which they were intellectually and personally invested, or one that they could use during a job interview and to guide their professional careers. The final paper thus challenged them to explain, based on the readings and discussion, what public relations means to them—as a pre-professional, as a person, and as a member of society. It challenged them to consider from a personal ethical perspective why they wanted to practice public relations, what responsible service to a client or employer meant to them, and what roles public relations plays in society. Can it serve the "public interest" in a socially redeeming manner? Thus, they were challenged to defend public relations as a positive force in the world.

One student, an aspiring journalist, expressed the opinion that "public relations is the work of the devil." So much did he believe this proposition that he had written an editorial with that title for the campus newspaper. He was proud of the editorial, and distributed copies to the professor and other students. The instructor recognized this as a teachable moment. Practitioners, the student reasoned, thrive by spin, propaganda, and outright lying to serve a client's interest. To heck with the public interest; practitioners don't care about truth and honesty, only self-interested outcomes.

In contrast, he argued, journalists are committed to discovering the "truth" and bringing it to the public's attention, despite practitioners' efforts to the contrary. For this student, the entire field of public relations was built on deception, "lies, and damned lies," pitted against journalists' unselfish commitment to "truth, beautiful and just." The student maintained his binary thinking: public relations represents the *bête noir* of professional communication—spreading falsehood and deceit—kept in check by vigilant journalists cast as white knights. His argument was compelling—evidence of spin and deception by public relations professionals is easy to find.

Most of the other students were quiet, perhaps timidly reconsidering their career choice. A few mounted defenses of the field, pointing to journalists who have deceived readers, viewers, listeners, and users—generically, "the public." Some reasoned that quite possibly public relations practitioners have a greater incentive to be truthful (the first and best sources of information) than do journalists. Hyperbole and distortion can be good for sales of newspapers and magazines, and of television, radio, and Internet advertising. Tactics that increase media attention and coverage can be unyielding pressure points that lead to public relations crises resulting from irresponsible journalists' behavior.

Others pointed out the good that practitioners do, the facts and opinions they provide. They raise money for the arts. They attract students to universities and colleges, easing their transition into higher education. They advocate for conservation, saving the wolves and the whales. They encourage people to contribute to cure diabetes, help children suffering from complex health needs, and convince the public and politicians that climate change is real. Nonetheless, the dissenting student was strident in his assertion that public relations meant a midnight meeting at the crossroads to make a deal with the devil.

This chapter—this entire book—challenges students to consider what they believe public relations is and whether it (and they as practitioners) deserves to be seen as a positive force in society or as a tool of the devil.

However good or bad its reputation, the practice of public relations is evident in the dynastic work of Chinese, Japanese, and Korean emperors. Was the building of the Great Wall of China a public relations statement designed to foster identification among the Chinese people, while rejecting outside influence and protecting their "superior" culture? Were emperors' temples a statement about their magnificence and invincibility, calling for the loyalty of their subjects?

Similar questions could be asked about ancient Persia's military, political, and agricultural might. Was the promulgation of Hammurabi's Code a public relations strategy intended to bring order to a chaotic and lawless society, a high point in Babylonian self-governance? No study of ancient Egypt can ignore the use of symbols and pageantry, canonical wall paintings and public sculptures,

---

Ancient Rome as "Public Relations"

The Roman Empire was built with the aid of public relations, including the famous discipline of its legions, technological advances, and systems of self-government. The Empire became an idea; Roman leaders created an ideology that promoted, promulgated, and translated it into a coordinated worldview of institutionalized government. Huge armies, monuments, edifices, and statues were a mighty physical force and a metaphor used to communicate Rome's power (Beard, 2015), even as Romans failed to achieve sustainable self-governance (Duncan, 2017).

Modern Europe reveals the infrastructural legacy of the Roman Empire. Forums, theaters, bridges, aqueducts, roads, and arenas dot the countryside, as do baths. These structures not only served basic utilitarian needs, but also had enduring symbolic value. Roman infrastructure represented the rhetorical enactment of an orderly "global" power. News of victory provoked spectacles, including battles among gladiators, wild animal shows, chariot races, and public executions (Meijer, 2003). These moments of pomp and circumstance played out in in arenas across the Empire, including the Colosseum in Rome itself—the Indianapolis Motor Speedway of its day.

Romans became master image builders. As relationship managers, they strategically used treaties and marriages to foster alliances. They polished the discourse of self-government and the means for promulgating Roman law, order, and administration. Relationships were forged among the Roman people, by class and occupation, as well as within and among the legions. Economic arrangements became relationship management. Symbolic representation, rhetoric (oratory and writing), and propaganda were used to shape opinions, forge attitudes, create culture, and influence behavior. The Romans sought to reinforce the legitimacy of their government through public art, installing portrait busts of military and political leaders in public spaces. They recognized the salience of local customs and mores, tailoring their message to accommodate tropes familiar to those they conquered. Such is the stuff of public relations.

This discussion uses several terms that are part of the lexicon of public relations. It illustrates not only the role of public relations in society, but also the elements of it that form the basis for the theory and research to be discussed in subsequent chapters. These foundational elements are vital to understanding, studying, and practicing public relations. This example asks whether the public relations efforts of ancient Rome were socially responsible or the devil's work.

---

and mammoth edifices constructed to honor the "human gods" who ruled the country. Though not defined as such, public relations was vital to the promulgation of effective governance in ancient Syria (Xifra & Heath, 2015). Centuries later, it was in no small part involved in Martin Luther's Protestant Revolution, as well as in the Catholic Church's response, the Counter Reformation.

This rest of this chapter offers a historical and definitional overview of the purposes, strategies, roles, functions, and ethics of public relations. It provides grounding for what this book proposes to study. It does so without sanitization, in order to show the roles public relations plays on behalf of individuals, institutions, communities, and societies. Only by knowing some of the history of the practice can students appreciate why theory is developed in the way it is. What factors explain the innovation, development, and roles (functions and purposes) of public relations? The study of theory begins with knowing what concepts matter and what patterns of behavior reveal the presence of public relations. The societal motivators of the practice set the tone, scope, and purpose of its study today.

Origins of Public Relations

The examples of Rome, Egypt, Persia, and China highlight key moments in the origination of public relations. It was not the specific innovation of some individual or group, but seems to have flowed from the natural tendency of peoples to communicate "formally" within their group and to or with members of other groups in order to co-manage relationships. It may thus be central to human beings, as group-oriented, social animals seeking to manage relatedness as the essential purpose of communication (Cobley, 2008).

The markers for historical study, then, are (a) the sorts of communication tools and strategies that are characteristic of the practice; (b) the strategic rationale for such communication, which seems basic to organizational, individual, and societal efficacy (the rationale for public relations is inseparable from the need by groups of people to collectively manage risks of survival; Douglas, 1992); (c) the purposes, structures, functions, and discourse engagement typical of the practice—central to this are terms such as "reputation," "image," "brand," "relationship" (quality, purpose, and type), "power" (both as structures/functions and socially constructed meaning), "interests," "awareness," "efficacy," and "influences" (of behavior, as well as the results from or impact of behaviors)—conflict and competition are motivators, as are achievement and success; (d) how all of what organizations do, as they enact "management" philosophies, affects relationships, reputations, and societal efficacy. In all, however, a lot of public relations work is not actually public, but either occurs behind the scenes, is masked, or is triggered—as in the case of media relations and event planning.

DNA markers are often used to pinpoint the origins of public relations in nineteenth- and early twentieth-century America and Europe. The Americentrism in this view emphasizes key personalities and moments in modern practice. P. T. Barnum, for example, has been heralded and vilified as perfecting the art of celebrity promotion. But image, reputation, and event management are timeless. So too is financial communication—between company and stockholder, between university and students, faculty, and parents. Reputation and promotion support the practice of different religions and international sporting events such as the World Cup and Tour de France. This section examines whether public relations might be fundamental to the human condition.

Antiquity and Inherency in Human Relatedness

Looking back into history is like exploring the cluttered attic of a timeless public relations practitioner. In every nook and cranny, evidence can be found of the activities, purposes, tools, strategies, discourse processes, and tactics of public relations.

One can imagine, for instance, how the experiences of the Comanche in North America and the Vikings in Europe demonstrated sophisticated strategic processes of resource management, including communication. Gwynne (2010) notes how the Comanche slowly began to dominate the Great Plains through their skilled horsemanship and ferocity. This tribal nation used strategic relationships and reputation management with other tribes, as well as sheer intimidation, to control the source of their food, lifestyle, and wealth. To reinforce social formations, they made images documenting their structural and kinship relationships. Their motive was simple: collective management of risk through relatedness—they fought to control their survival. In that regard, they negotiated with other tribes and European settlers to exchange staples and expand their gene pool. Collective myths and legends, as Claude Levi-Strauss (1978) has shown, emerged as a means of building social consent as a form of social control.

The control that the Comanche sought was no different from that of Europeans, especially the Plains setters, who wanted land. They wanted eternal access to buffalo. They used events (raids), treaties (with other nations), image and reputation (through apparel and appearance, as well as massacre and torture), and culture as a social glue to vanquish others to their own benefit. Modern academics might call this something other than public relations. But, for several generations, their communication, identity building, identification, and conflict management ability made them highly successful. Then a society that was stronger and even more property hungry forced them into asymmetrical negotiation and submission (by many of the same tactics that they had used to their own ends).

Ferguson (2009) tells a similar story of the Vikings—Scandinavian sea warriors. They mastered the arts and sciences of intimidation, even in the ferocious names their leaders adopted and the religion they developed. Their cultural artifacts reinforce two themes: survival and conquest—best expressed in the fearsome sea monster figureheads that adorned their raiding vessels. They managed risk by developing and mastering superior weapons and means of assault. They attacked only when they were reasonably sure of victory.

The Vikings developed a religion that accounted for their existence and for their relationships to one another and to outsiders—identity and identification. This gave them vision and purpose. It explained the mysteries that puzzled them. It helped them deal with the uncertainties of death and birth, as well as self-identity. It justified their power. It served as the means and rationale for events, treaties, associations, and adventures. It included ritual and speeches, laws and punishments, ceremonies and tributes. It offered purposeful means for the collective management of risk.

The Comanche and Vikings offer examples emphasizing not how public relations is associated with violence and pillage (which accounts for much of human history), but how it empowers a people and gives them the rationale and strategic processes for managing their affairs and associating with others. It focuses attention on the need for ritual, identity, resource management, power, symbolism, textuality, and other elements vital to organizational success. Chapter 2 will argue that various management theories are fundamental to public relations theories. Such interconnection is borne out not only in research, but also in the scope of history, as people press themselves on and form relationships with one another.

In ways too complex to easily unpack here, the Comanche and Viking stories repeat those in ancient Persia, China, India, Japan, Korea, and Africa. They reflect Polynesian exploration, European emigration to the Americas, the Moors' advancement (and retreat) in Spain. Today's news plays similarly, whether in politics, economics, war, peace, harmony, or violence. This narrative has implications for governance and for commerce. Similar instances involve non-profit organizations and social movements. All of this institutionalization has implications for public relations.

Such history is never separate from the science of the time, or from the culture and religion which give character, purpose, and destiny to a people. The means, rationale, and discourse of commerce, government, religion, war, peace, love, and wickedness are universal. As societies mature, so too do their management and communication systems, including public relations. Yet, the basic functions of symbolic representation remain constant. Are the ancient temples and government buildings in Persia, China, India, and elsewhere any different in function and purpose than modern examples in Washington, DC, London, Paris, Berlin, Beijing, or Tokyo? The iconographic sculpture and other adornments of ancient sites have parallels across time and space. Recall for a moment the pageantry of the 1936 Olympic Games in Berlin, designed to exalt the Third Reich, as captured on film by Leni Riefenstahl. Was this not similar to the spectacle of Roman legions parading through the capital following a military victory?

In many ways, the communications and technological sophistication of our ancestors rivaled that of the Facebook and Twitter generation. Pyramids, built in Egypt and across Central and South America, were symbolic reflections of complex and highly coordinated societies, as were Buddhist temples in Asia. The iconography of totem poles in the northwest of the United States and the carved ornamentation of Polynesian boats represent a complex language of symbolic form related to social organization aimed at reinforcing messages to specific publics.

Strategic management and communication provide the rationale and tools for government (and government relations), religion, self-identity/identification, and commerce. Museums around the world collect, categorize, and research cultural artifacts in order to understand how people used them to define themselves and organize societies. The concept of lobbying, so crucial to government relations today, is a new name for the timeless art of striking an inside deal. Relationship management is essential to politics. Marriages among European royalty were diplomatic public relations efforts aimed at establishing alliances and thereby collectively managing risk.

Without exception, the same sorts of strategies, tactics, purposes, and structures/functions can be found throughout history around the world. As Heath (2005) notes:

> The ceremonial burial of leaders, even as deities, is part of the history of public relations. Throughout ancient societies, statues and other carved figures were widely used to capture the personas and personalities of government and religious leaders. Coins often carried some logo of the visage of some leader as a way of uniting that person or image with the national identity of a people. (p. 33)

So, too, were commercial events such as fairs a timeless public relations effort. How were they any different in purpose than Apple's announcement of its latest product line?

Military symbolism, such as Roman victory spectacles, is also timeless. Is Arlington Cemetery in Washington, DC any more or less of a military public relations effort than the loading and firing of a Viking vessel to give a leader his last moment at sea? As Heath (2005) observes:

> Once Philip II of Macedonia had subdued the regions of the Hellenic peninsula, he commissioned the creation of gold and ivory statues of himself to adorn the temples. He taught his son, Alexander the Great, similar techniques of power display. (p. 34)

Colors such as England's red and France's blue were carefully developed and used to communicate the character of a nation's military, governmental, and commercial might. Recently, President Donald Trump and Supreme Leader Kim Jong-un met, greeted one another, and embraced in symmetrical harmony against alternating US and North Korean flags. Similar displays of power and prestige appear in advertisements for products ranging from Nike to Pampers. With copyrighted logos and color combinations, corporations assert their image and brand equity, crafting an identity to build loyalty and so affect people's behavior.

Games are events, means for people to challenge others and assert their prowess. Were the ancient Olympic Games in Greece any less a matter of public relations than the modern Olympics today? National, regional, and scholastic sporting contests offer people a sense of identity and relationship. More than 34 million Germans (over one in three) tuned into the 2014 World Cup Final against Argentina.

Songs such as the "Star Spangled Banner" capture the identity of U.S. citizens, as "La Marseillaise" symbolizes modern France and "God Save the Queen" Great Britain. The chronicler, the balladeer, the wood or stone carver, the master architect—all were pressed into public relations service. Artifacts on display at the National Palace Museum in Taiwan underscore the role that artists play in imperial glory.

Contemporary analysis of the origin of public relations associates it with media, particularly mass media. Certainly, the history of the Roman Catholics, and their creation of propaganda as a means for proselytizing the faith and saving souls, is one of media. Monks created Bibles through patient artistry. One marker of media history is the creation of moveable type by Johannes

Gutenberg in the fifteenth century. Bibles and other religious texts constituted the great bulk of production during the first two hundred years following its invention. This made Bibles more readily available, although they were still tethered to churches. Later, roving ministers carried them in their packs and saddlebags. Was John Wesley, founder of the Methodist church and one of the greatest writers of Christian hymns, a public relations practitioner? Is his modern equivalent the writer of advertising jingles?

During the seventeenth century, the term "propaganda" became forever associated with efforts to communicate church doctrine. In 1622, Pope Gregory XV created the *Congregation de Propaganda Fide* (Sacred Congregation for the Propagation of the Faith) in response to the Protestant Revolution. It was designed to organize missionary work under the rubric of evangelism, presenting a dramatic challenge through art and rhetoric to the more staid message of Luther, Wesley, and other reformers. The intent was to strengthen the faith of Catholics and convince non-Christians to convert (albeit often under pain of torture or death). In 1627, Pope Urban VIII augmented this effort by creating a training college to strengthen the communication skills of the missionaries. From this came the word "propaganda," or speech designed to build faith and convince. This organizational function of the Catholic Church continues today, although it was given a new name by Pope John Paul II in 1982.

Brown (2003) argues that much the same strategies, whether one wishes to call them propaganda or public relations, were used by the apostles. None was more prolific or had a greater impact than St. Paul, a contemporary of Jesus. Noting his influence, Brown writes:

> Historians of early Christianity actually regard Paul, author and organizer, rather than Jesus himself, as the founder of Christianity. Writing his epistles as much as 20 years before the authors of the New Testament's four gospels, Paul's influence transformed not only religion but history itself. (p. 1)

Such claims perplex those who work to define public relations. Some conclude that it and propaganda are the same. Others define it more narrowly, in an effort to claim the "good ground" in the battle to make it (and strategic communication) respectable, above reproach. This effort has led to a distorted sense of history and of the profession, and even to the development of models designed to differentiate "ethical" from "unethical" public relations. Sometimes, this strategy is strained, because the cases for (and against) public relations as a positive force end up on contested ground—in the tension between social responsibility and the work of the devil.

In a similar manner, the history of commerce is inseparable from what eventually would be called public relations by some, and marketing communication by others. Bazaars, fairs, and other commercial events involved a degree of publicity and promotion. Announcements were promulgated, and people were employed to spread the word. Such efforts made certain ports and cities both famous locally and far away. They created and advanced the interests of companies such as the Dutch West India Company, which, in concert with governments and their military might, implemented and sustained global colonialism and the exploitation of indigenous populations.

With analysis broadly drawn, many find the origins of public relations to be far more ancient than nineteenth-century America. Explicitly from a management science perspective, Croft, Hartland, and Skinner (2008) advise that those who see public relations only as a business activity miss the importance of church and government communication. Adopting narrative analysis as their historical methodology, they find evidence of communication fostering revenue streams, building military power, and getting an important segment of a population on the same narrative, leading to coordinated and purposeful activities—so-called relatedness.

Without any stretch of the imagination, this encompassing view of the precedents of modern public relations sees it as vital to humans' timeless techniques. Croft et al. reason that this analysis extends that of Watson (2008), who finds during the Dark Ages "practitioners ... engaging in political communication, brand extension and brand creation, managing stakeholder engagement with word-of-mouth, music and publications" (Croft et al., 2008, p. 302).

Other researchers have marked the origins of public relations with great civil events. Cutlip (1995) chronicles part of its history as connected to events in North America from the seventeenth through the twentieth centuries. Analysis of the eighteenth would be incomplete without serious attention to the role and purpose of the Declaration of Independence. This was a public relations gambit, placing blame for the "crisis" in the colonies on the shoulders of George III, King of England, rather than on parliament. It was an extraordinary moment in the practice of public relations on behalf of a people seeking to sustain and advance their self-government. Thomas Paine's pamphlet "Common Sense" was a further stroke of genius, justifying the American Revolution and laying the foundation for the one in France.

Public relations historians are wise to ponder Cutlip's (1994) comments on the unseen power of public relations in society. On one hand, he is aware of the *socially responsible* role that it has to play, but on the other he is equally cognizant that it can be the *work of the devil*:

> I held, and still hold, that only through the expertise of public relations can causes, industries, individuals, and institutions make their voice heard in the public forum where thousands of shrill, competing voices daily re-create the Tower of Babel. I did not and do not deny the harm done by the incompetent, the charlatan, and those who serve dubious causes. (p. ix)

> Public relations strategies and tactics are increasingly used as weapons of power in our no-holds-barred political, economic, and cause competition in the public opinion marketplace, and thus deserve more scholarly scrutiny than they have had. (p. xi)

> Propagandist, press agent, public information officer, public relations or public affairs official, political campaign specialists, lobbyist—whatever their title, their aim is the same: to influence public behavior. (p. xi)

The objective of such efforts is to make a group of people or an organization more effective in accomplishing its mission, vision, and core values.

"Bread or Blood"

Scholarship on public relations often overlooks how it serves ordinary citizens. Too often, it is incorrectly reserved for the work of businesses or governments. The following example indicates (a) how ordinary citizens use it to help them solve problems, (b) that it is used universally to address issues, and (c) that scholars who are not in public relations can recognize its presence.

During the U.S. Civil War (1861–1865), food became scarce and prohibitively expensive in Confederate states. By 1863, merchants' prices, especially for corn, were so high that most families could not afford to eat. Women organized into small groups to bring attention to their problem, petitioning the governors of their states, but to no avail. They framed their case around the fact that because their husbands and older sons were serving in the military, they could not raise and harvest crops, and so their families could not be fed.

Eventually, the women armed themselves and went to the stores to demand lower food prices. They coined a slogan: "Bread or Blood." The shopkeepers did not honor their demands, so the women brandished their weapons, took the food, commandeered wagons, and drove off. Some were arrested and sentenced to as small a punishment as 4 hours in jail. Most were not. Governors responded. Food subsidies were created. The problem was addressed as well as was possible given the general resource conditions in the South.

A historian of the Civil War writes of the food protestors in Richmond, Virginia: "The women had guns, but like the mobs in Atlanta (Georgia) and Salisbury (North Carolina), they had a public relations strategy" (McCurry, 2011, p. 40). This strategy entailed organizing on a common cause and creating a compelling rationale for their demands. In that sense, the women were willing to accommodate the wishes of the governors and shopkeepers. Once accommodation failed, they upped the ante to pure advocacy, making more pointed demands by brandishing pistols, knives, and hatchets.

McCurry observes how one woman, Mary Jackson, organized her food protest in Richmond, the capitol of the Confederacy:

> Her strategy for the riot confirms how she regarded the action as a culmination of a process of protest. By insisting that the rioters first make an offer to pay government price for the goods they planned to seize—and in first seeking an audience with the governor before taking to the streets—she and the others showed their deep investment in the ideas and practices of Southern white women's new wartime political culture. (p. 40)

The point is not that public relations requires extreme measures, but that extreme measures can become public relations' compelling rationale. The women, as argued by contingency theory (discussed in detail in Chapter 4), considered the options of accommodation and advocacy public relations solutions to a real-life problem.

These cases and examples demonstrate that public relations is timeless, not some product of Roman emperors, popes, P. T. Barnum, colonials protesting British rule, or the railroad industry offering free land to immigrants. Sometimes, theorists shun certain activities as not being public relations so that they can define what they want to study rather than being objectively honest, encompassing, and candid in the subject of their investigation. It will become clear in subsequent chapters how scholars and practitioners have defined and defended various public relations strategies, purposes, and roles. Without doubt, various applications and approaches to public relations could and did help advance interests, sometimes to the ruin of others. It is interesting to speculate whether media—and, eventually, mass media—developed to provide news and information or to serve as tools of propaganda. Did the commercial incentive to call favorable attention to goods and services and to serve the interests of government lead to, rather than merely employ, news media? Are mass media a defining moment in public relations history or merely tools relevant to an eternal practice? Modern public relations is, as in earlier times, involved in commerce, business administration, management, government, religion, social movements, and grassroots activism.

The next section explores some subtle but compelling changes in the practice, which, to some historians and theorists, suggest that if public relations did not begin in the nineteenth century, that was at least the dawn of the modern version. It was during this period that public relations was named as such.

The Nineteenth and Early Twentieth Centuries: The Origins of "Modern Public Relations"

Those who do not see public relations as inseparable from the origins of organized society tend to place its benchmark later—much later. They often insist that a society cannot have the practice of public relations until it has been industrialized, developed sophisticated means of reaching large audiences, and adopted "public relations" as a professional title. They reason that the modern version of public relations was driven by the growth of mass media, starting in the nineteenth century. This mass-mediated bias tends to conclude that it is the product of the Industrial Revolution, the era of modern mass production and mass consumption. And, similarly, public relations has been defined as a separate discipline and art for only a little more than a century, even though publicity, promotion, and communications designed to affect public policy have an ancient history.

Modern public relations features four P's: publicity, promotion, and public policy. It is conceptualized through the logics of commerce, business administration, management, government, religion, and social unrest (social movements and activism). It is associated with political philosophy, sociology, and civil society. It is treated as a topic relevant to media, media effects, and media practices—even media impact. And it is seen as an academic discipline subordinate to journalism.

Journalism faculty have sought to make public relations useful to journalism, perhaps fearing the opposite dynamic, that journalists should serve the purposes of public relations professionals. The eighteenth-century *Philadelphia Gazette*, for example, offered as much shipping news (notices of articles that had arrived by ship and were offered for sale) as other reporting, if not more. Thus, press agentry and media relations were—and perhaps continue to be—the keys to defining public relations, and enriching publishers. Such a view is far too journalistic-centric, and this is ever more true with advances in social media, and its connection to advertising. Implicit also in the nineteenth-century history of American public relations is a faith in codes of ethics based on accuracy, openness, and fairness—an ethical standard shaped by journalists.

A media bias and historical association with publicity and promotion features businessmen such as P. T. Barnum as exemplars of modern American public relations. But by Barnum's time (1810–1891), others had already used press agentry (or "puffery" as it was called) and events to attract attention, often for commercial ends (Papinchak, 2005). This was common practice by the time Barnum issued a pamphlet narrating the life of Joice Heth. Claimed to be the 161-year-old former slave and nurse of George Washington, Heth attracted audiences enthralled by the stories they had read about her life. Was she a hoax? Did these promoters do more than just bend the truth? It did not much matter—the excitement generated, even as myth, was enough to attract widespread attention.

Although Barnum and other businessmen of his era have been tarred with the brush of hucksery (just as public relations has been tarred with the moniker of hackery), he contributed huge sums to charity, supported his performers with better-than-average compensation, and provided a valuable service—entertaining the masses. Barnum hired those who might not otherwise be employable, because of their small size or atypical features. And customers were free to enter his show or spend their money in some other way.

Coincidental to the timeframe of Barnum's enterprises was one of the most important eras of social movement activism. From the early 1830's until the Civil War, activists mounted a rhetorically designed issue campaign against slavery. Hundreds of abolition groups arose in the United States and many other countries. The American Anti-slavery Society (1833–1870) was just one such organization. International societies often combined their efforts, representing one of the first coordinated communications initiatives on a global scale. They spawned newspapers and speakers bureaus. They used publicity to draw attention to the issue, and promoted resistance to it.

They created events and helped publish books such as *Uncle Tom's Cabin* (1852) by Harriet Beecher Stowe, in order to dramatize the horrors and suffering of "the peculiar institution."

Frederick Douglass spoke at one such event on July 5, 1852 to condemn the traditional claims made on July 4 that America was the land of the free. Douglass' statement can be interpreted as pointing out the paradox of the positive. That paradox is made evident by the public relations celebrations of July 4 that lauded the "freedom" gained through the Declaration of Independence. Douglass used rhetorical devices to demonstrate that the Declaration was overly praised for accomplishing liberty in a land with legalized slavery and racist restrictions on African Americans (Heath & Waymer, 2009).

Although invaluable to social movement activism, public relations is largely shaped by its association with the organizational and societal effectiveness of commercial enterprise. Public relations practitioners and "newsmen" touted railroads as being vital to the United States. Starting with George Washington, national leaders realized that transportation was the lifeblood of their vast nation. This took on new dimensions when people began to worry that such a large and unpopulated land could easily be lost to other nations. One such was Abraham Lincoln, who helped create the transcontinental railroad as the soul and glue of the sprawling nation. Hordes of publicists promoted the western frontier and railroad connections in order to sell land to raise money to build more railroads. Immigrants from all parts of the world arrived to build, advance, and use them. Thus was the heartland populated—by publicity and promotion.

During the age of industrial revolution, commerce often employed public policy to achieve competitive advantage. Here, public relations not only publicized the new electricity industry businesses, but helped define them and make them legitimate. During the Battle of the Currents, George Westinghouse and Thomas Edison used every available public relations tool at their disposal to have the public and government choose between direct and alternating current. Westinghouse had science on his side, as he reasoned that alternating current was more efficient and useful. In response, Edison argued that it was unsafe and pointed to all of the people who had been killed by it. To up the argumentative ante, he directed that alternating current be used in stunts to kill stray cats and dogs, as well as unwanted cows and horses; he has been erroneously linked to the electrocution of an elephant named Topsy. He even lobbied the state legislature of New York to use alternating current as a form of execution; William Kemmler was the first to be killed by the application of high voltage. That might have convinced people it was too dangerous to have in their homes and businesses, but Westinghouse's science won the advocacy battle— although the war waged for years (Hearit, 2005).

This was just one of many public relations struggles to define the rationale for and limits on the burgeoning industrial power in the United States and elsewhere. Public policy, promoted by grassroots advocates, sought to use higher standards of corporate social responsibility to constrain and correct business practices thought to be unjust and even ruinous.

Dawn of Modern Public Relations

Without doubt, the practice was searching for an identity, rationale, and name by the time of World War I. Emerging as a leading economic and political power, the United States became a primary driver of the practice and its theory-based justification as vital to the democratic process. Some milestones marking the dawn of public relations as a discipline include:

- The foundation of agencies, primarily for the purposes of publicity and media relations.
- Practitioners joining the executive management team.

- Practitioners beginning to advertise specialization in public relations, including media and government relations.
- Practitioners beginning to conceive of their work as a specialized discipline.
- Large corporations creating specialized public relations departments with the stated purpose of fostering communications on their behalf.
- The foundation of professional organizations to forge the identity and identification of practitioners.
- The offering of courses and degree programs in public relations at colleges and universities.
- The beginning, by the 1950s, and even more robustly by the 1970s, of academic writing about the discipline.
- The hiring of public relations specialists by state, local, and federal governments to serve key roles in the public interest.

Some of the items in this list will be featured in the discussions that follow, but the establishment of the Committee on Public Information (CPI) during World War I to generate support for the war effort at home and abroad is a good place to start the discussion of the contrasting views of public relations that arose during the twentieth century. A great deal of attention has been devoted to this government program, which, in many respects, opened the door to decades of discussion about the nature and limits of public relations (especially propaganda) in the United States and elsewhere. The CPI sought to understand what constitutes propaganda and how it can serve socially responsible purposes. In this regard, it served as a training ground for a new generation of practitioners interested not only in tactics and strategy, but in theory and ethics as well. It also spawned young communicators for the war effort, who carried on such professional activities after the war ended.

The Committee on Public Information

President Woodrow Wilson created the CPI on April 3, 1917 with Executive Order 2594. Advisors had recommended that he create a government agency to address the need for U.S. involvement in the war. Thus, the Committee began a publicity campaign to condemn the enemy, justifying U.S. entry.

One of the proponents of using publicity to sell the war was George Creel. Over time, his name became associated with the effort, and the CPI became known as the Creel Committee. As Lubbers (2005a) notes, this was probably the "earliest example of a large-scale promotional campaign" (p. 155). Its purpose was to use information to a persuasive end. However, some of the information it put out was distorted and embellished, characterized by hyperbole, or even concocted. For instance, it developed a poster depicting German soldiers skewering Belgian babies on their bayonets.

Other forms of communications available at the time were film, press relations, and public speaking. A speakers bureau offered inspirational talks by staff who came to be known as the "Four-Minute Men" (Lubbers 2005b). The Four-Minute Men were trained and scripted through a series of bulletins that explained the Committee's goals and structure in a matter of minutes. Other messages asked audiences to contribute funds to the war effort, increase agricultural production, conserve food and other resources, or enlist and serve in the military. In total, thousands of men, women, and children—organized into Junior Four-Minute Men school groups—contributed to this communication effort, which reached millions, raised far more money than it cost, and built consent for the war effort.

Is it socially responsible or the work of the devil to "sell" a war (see Hiebert, 1991)? President George W. Bush "sold" the invasion of Iraq as a means for combatting terrorism, removing a ruthless dictator from office, and destroying weapons of mass destruction. Is it socially responsible if the characterization of the enemy is dramatically false? Is the characterization necessarily "false" if it creates resolve and focused energy to combat that enemy? These are the kinds of questions raised about such campaigns. Distortion, information, persuasion, effectiveness, motivation, and social responsibility have all been invoked in discussing the roles of "publicity" and promotion. A by-any-means-necessary rationale has been part of the battleground that has served as the foundation for the work-of-the-devil argument—but does it tell the whole story?

The CPI sparked a generation-long battle regarding the nature of propaganda and whether it is the same as public relations. John W. Hill, co-founder and co-principal of Hill & Knowlton, took a firm stance on this issue. One of the most successful and influential public relations executives in the mid-twentieth century, he worked to provide intellectual and ethical justification for and set boundaries on the field. Reflecting on the matter of public relations and propaganda, he observed in eloquent terms:

> Public relations in its controversial usage is sometimes dubbed "propaganda." Actually propaganda was a "good" word until brought into disrepute when Hitler and the Communists began to pollute the airways with their "Big Lies," and made it a "bad" word. In a public relations battle in a free country it is important that there be no lies. Different interpretation of the facts is possible, and each side is entitled to present its views, leaving it to public opinion to decide which to accept. The purpose of public relations in its best sense is to inform and to keep minds open. The purpose of "propaganda" in the bad sense is to misinform and to keep minds closed. (Hill, 1963, p. 6)

Hill recognized the rhetorical and ethical problems and the impact potential associated with propaganda to define the practice of public relations and its role in society. He justified the practice by examining its rhetorical role and legitimacy, as well as its need to educate the public. He observed, "Good corporate public relations depend, first, upon sound policies truly in the public interest and second, upon clear and effective communication, explanation, and interpretation of policies and facts to the public" (Hill, 1958, p. 163). Sound policies, he argued in ways that are similar to our contemporary call for reflective management and corporate social responsibility, require that companies serve the public interest and be good neighbors. Public relations, therefore, starts with sound management: "Big companies, if they are properly managed, have a keen sense of public responsibility. They guide their policies in keeping with the public interest and make sure that each of their plants is a good neighbor in its respective community" (Hill, 1958, p. 39). For Hill, sound public relations begins with reflective management, followed by clear and effective communication to explain policies and present facts to the public.

Reasoning such as that championed by Hill reflected thinking that had emerged at the dawn of the twentieth century. Corporate lack of self-restraint was challenged during the Progressive Era. At the same time, public relations provided a means by which presidents such as Theodore Roosevelt could sell sound public policy such as creating and managing national forests. Government and corporations could push agendas that represented the interests of a large segment of the public or catered to the interests of a few (Ponder, 1990).

The sorts of battles Hill and others waged to justify, define, and rein in public relations were picked up by academics. The following section reviews some of their theory-laden investigations of modern public relations.

Theorists Weigh In on Public Relations

Starting in the Progressive Era, according to reasoning advanced by Gower (2008) and Curtin (2008), discussions of public relations evolved from merely focusing on press agentry to incorporate public information, two-way communication, and symmetry—the four-part model made famous by Grunig and Hunt (1984). Their theory proposed that practitioners seek excellence, manage communication for their organizations, and achieve high ethical standards. This sparked a raging battle among practitioners and academics (Gower, 2008, p. 305).

The broad sweep of how business, government, and public relations serve or deny the betterment of society is an intrinsic theme in discussions of the history of the twentieth century. Like Stoker and Rawlins (2005), Gower reasons that Progressive reformers (including social movement activists) used public relations tactics and strategies to build support for the reform and regulation that reshaped U.S. business culture in the early twentieth century. This view assumes that publicity on behalf of the "public interest" is good, whereas that used to marginalize the public is bad. Such reasoning suggests that the ethics is not inherent to a communication style but a matter of intent and consequences. Also, if management changes so as to become committed to the public interest, so too will public relations. If management does not change, neither will public relations. Thus, there is nothing inherent nor linear about the ethical development of public relations independent of management theory.

Voicing similar criticism, L'Etang (2008) doubts that the development of public relations theory and practice represents a normative progression toward an excellence model of ethics. She points out that such a view implies that the field has been historically deficient and dysfunctional from the vantage points of practice, research, and theory. But the evolutionary model is misguided in its focus on how and why the practice began, developed, and became what it is today. Viewing its history and theory under a critical lens, L'Etang challenges practitioners and academics to "determine whether the symmetrical notions (in their various formulations) are any more than a mantra and myth for practitioners and academics alike—a way of justifying to themselves the ethics of their practice and educational legitimacy" (p. 333).

Much of the attention given by historians who rely too heavily on twentieth-century practice, and that associated with the United States in particular, may focus overmuch on business and business ethics—themselves matters of ethical debate. During the Middle Ages, guilds played a large role in publicizing business activities, as well as goods and services. The latter were touted as the work of skilled craftsmen, and publicized by parades and fairs. In the twentieth century, trade unions and trade associations took on the same role.

Examining the battle between brewers and prohibitionists, Lamme (2009) finds that multiple voices engaged in variously proactive and reactive strategies as they used persuasion campaigns to debate the fit between business practices and public policy. The workers who brewed beer were as likely as the owners to advocate responsible drinking. Both had a common interest in managing the risk of prohibitionist arguments, which could destroy their work and business. Public relations served many conflicting interests. Which arguments were socially responsible, and which were the work of the devil? Can the answer to that question be boiler plated into a model, or must it always be contextual?

Thus, consideration of the theme of social responsibility squarely focuses on the complexity of the practice. What is it, how does it operate, and by what standards is it judged? And, what does the evidence of the practice and what do the interpretive frames of historians and critics have to do with the conclusions drawn? These sorts of questions are central to the discussion in the next section, which features additional theory-based investigations.

Public Relations Through the Squinted Eyes of Historians

Historical analysis and theory development are old friends. History entails more than reporting facts; the real task is interpreting them. Theory provides an interpretative frame, and history offers evidence to support or revamp it. Theory building and application in public relations require that we wrestle with the beast of the socioeconomic role of business and public relations. The socioeconomic perspective preferred by a particular theorist influences the conclusions as to which approaches are best.

Conducting a comparative review of several historians' approaches, Pearson (1990) analyzes Ray E. Hiebert's *Courtier to the Crowd: The Story of Ivy Lee and the Development of Public Relations* (1966), J. A. R. Pimlott's *Public Relations and American Democracy* (1951), Richard S. Tedlow's *Keeping the Corporate Image: Public Relations and Business, 1900–1950* (1979), Dallas W. Smythe's *Dependency Road: Communication, Capitalism, Consciousness and Canada* (1981), and Marvin Olasky's *Corporate Public Relations and American Enterprise: A New Historical Perspective* (1987). Each author, Pearson asserts, provides a unique and contrasting explanation of the social, political, and commercial roles of public relations. Setting up his review, he muses: "These historians come to historical texts with different philosophies of history, different social, political and moral philosophies, and even different assumptions about epistemology and ontology" (Pearson, 1990, p. 28). He wonders whether and how the profession should be regulated, "to what set of values should public relations adhere" if it is to be legitimate. Throwing what may be the most important ball into the air, he asks, "in whose interest should public relations be practiced" (p. 27). As will be seen in the rest of this chapter, the matter of interests is a telling factor in how scholars and practitioners view the legitimacy of public relations.

Pearson's review begins by investigating Hiebert's thoughts about Ivy Lee, often considered one of the fathers of modern U.S. public relations. Addressing the interests to be served by public relations, Hiebert focuses on Lee's belief that public relations was a response to the twentieth century's fondness of democracy. Hiebert's analysis sets up polar brackets to judge "good" versus "bad" public relations. If public relations is to support democracy, the items on the right side of the list must prevail.

Fiction, lies	vs.	Truth
Secrecy	vs.	Openness
Partisan	vs.	Neutral
Persuasion	vs.	Understanding
Image	vs.	Reality
Propaganda	vs.	Education
Publicity	vs.	Public relations
Muckrakers	vs.	Gentlemen of the press

Hiebert stresses the tensions of democracy, an interpretative frame that is quite comfortable with media studies, public policy battles, and rhetorical influences over enlightened choices. He conceives of the press as a pillar supporting democracy. Public relations undermines democracy if it violates journalistic principles of truth, accuracy, and fairness. Democracy functions well as long as citizens have sound information to make enlightened choices, and it is "the task of public relations to assist in supplying that information" (Pearson, 1990, p. 29). Hiebert champions Lee as an example of socially responsible public relations, "a strategic response to the problematic environment" (p. 31).

Pimlott, the second historian Pearson puts under his historiographic microscope, conceives public relations' rise as a natural response "to the growth of the mass media" (Pearson, 1990, p. 31). As business became more complex, public relations emerged as a means for explaining business decisions to citizens through mass media. Public relations was citizens' window into industry.

1) As industry became larger and more complex, various "publics" desired information. Specialized publics, such as employees, customers, and shareholders, called for specialized communication efforts.
2) This complexity created a communication (understanding) gap. Business needed to explain and justify itself.
3) Mass media emerged as a major force in this education process, and public relations entered the scene.
4) Fundamental to the democratic process, public relations "is highly functional for the smooth functioning of society and supportive of American democratic ideals" (p. 32).

According to Pimlott's "change management" rationale for public relations, it helps business adapt to citizens and citizens adapt to business.

Tedlow, Pearson's third author, a business historian at the Harvard School of Business Administration, attacks "one of the most revered beliefs of public relations—the belief that business, prior to the coming of public relations, was secretive and insensitive, indeed contemptuous, of public opinion" (Pearson, 1990 p. 32). Contrary to that theme, Tedlow contends that businessmen have always solicited public approval. "Only politicians have rivaled them in the use of publicity to further their enterprises" (p. 32). In Tedlow's opinion, the role of public relations changes as does business's sense of social responsibility. In many ways, his is a "defense against anti-business sentiment" (p. 33).

Up to this point in his analysis, Pearson has featured pro-business advocates who reinforce the notion that public relations plays a useful (and ethical) function because it serves to help complex organizations manage and defend their images, as well as to explain their role in and contribution to society. The role of public relations, therefore, is to make business more effective in a free-market economy, which itself needs constant public relations care.

A vastly different perspective is offered by Smythe, who examines public relations though "a materialist-realist theory of mass communication" (Pearson, 1990, p. 34). His Marxist view, instead of bending business to the public interest, reasons that the objective of public relations is to bend customers to serve businesses' interests. This purpose is accomplished through language: practitioners socially construct a rationale by which customers see themselves as served by the marketplace. By using professional communicators (such as advertising and public relations), business conceives or creates "audiences as commodities which are marketed to business organizations which want to advertise consumer goods, and establish a daily agenda of news, entertainment, and information which defines 'reality' for the people" (p. 34). Whereas Lee, for instance, believes the tension between business and citizens constitutes an understanding gap, Smythe reasons that the crisis is due not to a failure to understand on the part of consumers, but rather to the deep-seeded belief that business has failed to serve the public interest, and that businesses by nature are inclined to subvert the social good.

The fifth voice in Pearson's analysis is that of Olasky, who condemns what he believes to be a steady progression of a sort of public relations totally dependent on press agentry. From this critical perspective, Olasky reasons, public relations serves industry by masking its intent and role in commerce. The conflict between business and the public centers on tensions between self-interests. Business seems to be working in the "public interest," but this masks that it only operates in its own.

In fact, business deplores free markets. As criticism mounted against business, public relations helped create regulation that actually buffered and protected business, not the public interest.

With these historians' views of business, the free market, democracy, and public relations, Pearson explores the latter's theoretical rationale. Is public relations the servant of democracy, a champion and means for increasing transparency? Does it bend industry to serve the public interest? Does it justify and foster free-market activity? Or does it merely seem to be socially responsible, while serving a narrow private interest? Is it dependent on media, media relations, media effects, publicity, and press agentry?

Pearson's analytic lenses, through which he understands, critiques, and justifies public relations, are shaped and polished by each historian's assumptions about social ideology, democracy, media practices, and businesses' roles and contributions. Whether public relations serves society or the devil depends on whether it subverts democracy, creates false images, or serves to better society and improve the lives of citizens. Pearson points out how definitions of public relations are never free from ideological assumptions. This lesson is vital to those who study and add to public relations theory. A quick glance at some leading definitions of public relations offers the opportunity to examine their theoretical underpinnings.

Definitions of Public Relations

Forty years ago, senior practitioners and a few academics sought systematically to define public relations. Harlow (1976) drew on such discussions, surveys of the literature, and thoughtful speculation to offer this definition:

> Public relations is a distinctive management function which helps establish and maintain mutual lines of communication, understanding, acceptance and cooperation between an organization and its publics; involves the management of problems or issues; helps management to keep informed on and responsive to public opinion; defines and emphasizes the responsibility of management to serve the public interest; helps management keep abreast of and effectively utilize change, serving as an early warning system to help anticipate trends; and uses research and sound and ethical communication techniques as its principal tools. (p 36)

Harlow aspired to link practice with concepts and theory, and sought a positive role for public relations — although he recognized it could violate such aspiration. He situated it as connected to management, community, public interest and opinion, and the strategic means by which issues are managed, monitoring occurs, trends are anticipated, harmony is sought, and communication occurs through sound and ethical techniques.

Seen through a similar lens of practice and theory, one of the most influential definitions is offered by Cutlip, Center, and Broom (2006): "Public relations is the management function that establishes and maintains mutually beneficial relationships between an organization and the publics on whom its success or failure depends" (p. 5). This definition embraces both internal and external public relations and features publicity, advertising, press agentry, public affairs, lobbying issue management, and investor relations. On its view, public relations serves a social need "by mediating conflict and by building the consensus needed to maintain social order" (p. 25). The origins of this definition reach back to the 1950s, but it remains today as it was first stated in 2006 (Broom & Sha, 2013).

Taking a values-driven approach, Guth and Marsh (2017) define public relations as "the values-driven management of relationships between an organization and the publics that can affect its success" (p. 11). Reasoning that all choices and actions are driven by values, they argue that the challenge for public relations practitioners is to find agreement between an organization's values and those of the entities that the hold resources it needs and desires; in other words, stakeholders. Values-driven alignment, however difficult to achieve, can satisfy the relationship between organization and resource holder.

Similarly resource oriented, Heath and Coombs' (2006) comprehensive definition features a complex set of challenges:

> Public relations is the management function that entails planning, research, publicity, promotion, and collaborative decision making to help any organization's ability to listen to, appreciate, and respond appropriately to those persons and groups whose mutually beneficial relationships the organization needs to foster as it strives to achieve its mission and vision. (p. 7)

Like many others before them, Heath and Coombs ask public relations to use strategic processes to aspire to a society based on mutual benefit and aligned interests achieved through collaborative engagement.

Roles and functions are key themes of relevance to organizational change and society as arbiter and partner. In this vein, Lattimore, Baskin, Heiman, and Toth (2012) stress the dynamism of relationships between an organization and its public:

> Public Relations is a leadership and management function that helps achieve organizational objectives, define philosophy, and facilitate organizational change. Public relations practitioners communicate with all relevant internal and external publics to develop positive relationships and to create consistency between organizational goals and societal programs that promote the exchange of influence and understanding among an organization's constituent parts and publics. (p. 4)

Cameron, Wilcox, Reber, and Shin (2007) conceive of public relations as managing conflict and competition. The goal has an ethical component, as "the strategic management of competition in the best interests of one's own organization and, when possible, also in the interests of key publics" (p. 35). For organizations competing for limited resources or managing inevitable conflicts, public relations professionals can organize communication efforts and offer mediation.

Communication and management functions unique to public relations play a central role in all these definitions. Newsom, Turk, and Kruckeberg (2000) emphasize many public relations specializations: (a) publicity; (b) communication; (c) public affairs; (d) issues management; (e) government relations; (f) financial public relations; (g) community relations; (h) industry relations; (i) minority relations; (j) advertising; (k) press agentry; (l) promotion; (m) media relations; and (n) propaganda.

Rather than offering a simple definition, Hallahan (2018) points to various approaches that are used to analyze public relations. He emphasizes how it is an organizational activity; however, definitional emphasis on "organization" must acknowledge that activism, social movement, and even single individuals engage with others in relation to important matters. Public relations is a professional practice requiring unique management activities, strategies, functions, tactics, and tools and is performed strategically. It can be discussed, studied, and practiced from many approaches: managerial/functional, behavioral/relational, rhetorical, constructionist/sociocultural, comparative/cross-cultural, and social/critical. The chapters that follow will opt for special emphasis on one or more of these approaches as the grounding for public relations theory.

All of these definitions feature key themes: management function, evolving and wide-ranging sets of practices (roles and functions), ethical concerns in service to the public interest, symmetry, mutual benefit, social responsibility, resource management, and textuality. Distinguishing public relations from related disciplines such as marketing, advertising, and strategic communication causes anxiety in answering a basic question: What is the unique essence and societal value of public relations? Does it really make a difference, and to whom?

Recent Thoughts on Old Problems: Competing Logics of Public Relations

This chapter is dedicated to identifying and examining the phenomenon of public relations in order to build a foundation for discussing various theories that have been proposed to explain, enact, and improve its practice. Theorists must know what phenomena they address in their studies, otherwise they cannot adequately construct theory that sheds valuable light on the subject. Just as detectives must understand what clues solve a crime, so must theorists critically judge the evidence that they put under the lens for analysis. For that reason, this chapter lays the foundation for Chapter 2.

To know what we study, before discussing how to study it, we must pay attention to the conceptualization and evidence of what the discipline is and what it does. Vos (2011) focuses on three logics—functionalist, institutional, and cultural—which he uses to understand public relations, how it came about, and how it evolved—if it has. He begins his discussion by examining publicity, one of the dominant themes in the cases and analyses offered in this chapter. He notes that "some historians have questioned whether it is even valid to posit publicity seeking as an evolutionary ancestor of PR" (p. 121). In support of that conclusion, Vos cites Gower (2008), Lamme (2009), and Russell and Bishop (2009). Part of the rationale for this cautious approach is that "although public relations practitioners would sometimes create publicity, their duties were more expansive." Those duties include mediating between the public and clients—"shaping the public's views of the client and the client's view of the public" (Vos, 2011, p. 121). Even though public relations is more than publicity (and publicity is valuable), it still plays an important role in creating awareness and fostering idea engagement.

The first of the three logics Vos features is *functionalism*. Based on systems theory, functionalism argues that organizations put public relations into action when they sense imbalance between systems. This view parallels the logic of biological systems: systems constantly use adjustment to achieve balance—restore harmony—between one another and their environment. All aspects of an ecosystem, for instance, are interrelated; what affects one part affects all. This paradigm applies to social systems such as business and government as well. If tensions arise between parts of larger systems, then public relations, so the argument goes, intervenes to achieve balance or restore harmony.

Thus, reasons Vos, public relations helps organizations adjust to and achieve equilibrium with one another. Since criticism and opposition to what an organization is doing serve as negative feedback, according to systems theory and its companion cybernetics, organizations are motivated to adjust and solve problems, and thereby gain the positive feedback needed to balance their relationships. Critics urge businesses to be responsible and responsive to the interests of others; public relations is necessary to meet this strategic challenge in socially responsible ways or to deny, negotiate, or deflect them (as the work of the devil). To some extent, herein lies the rationale for "spin."

Vos' second logic is *institutional theory*, which reasons that organizations create rituals that guide their employees to behave as they do. Businesses likewise create rituals of consumption that influence customer preferences and behaviors. As evidence for this, Vos focuses on how the CPI—discussed earlier—offered a strategic response to the need for stronger public support of U.S. involvement in World War I. The question is how public relations, as a strategic practice that coordinates communication, can get information out, create images, motivate behavior, and achieve defined outcomes. As Vos describes it, institutions realize how a "rhetorical strategy that works well in one setting might be adapted to another institutional setting" (p. 128). A lingering problem is to discern whether the strategies used produce advantages for some interests at the disadvantage of others.

Vos' third logic is *cultural logic*, which traces the origins and rationale of public relations back to the Progressive Era in the United States; as such, it can be seen as a constructive reaction to the abuses of big business. This era witnessed a battle to create and implement regulation to constrain the excesses of industry. This battle was an expression of the democratic process, whereby the power of industry was rebalanced by public outrage. Vos points to the significant role Ivy Lee's "Declaration of Principles" played in helping bring about openness and transparent decision making (see Gower, 2008). Reformers understood the power of public relations as well, taking "a culturally legitimated practice and put[ting] it to use for their own ends and the ends of their clients" (Vos, 2011, p. 131).

In these ways, scholars such as Pearson (1990) and Vos (2011) (along with others introduced in this chapter) dig deeply into historical evidence and apply theoretical perspectives to explain what public relations is and how it emerged to be part of commerce, controversy, politics, socioeconomics, and the adjustments between systems in varying degrees of conflict and harmony. Such discussion is frustrated by many problems, one of which is the mercurial nature and role of the practice and the ability of theory to account for and improve it. Do systems inherently seek balance when interests compete? Do institutions use trial and error to ritualize and implement complex strategies and functions in order to achieve defined ends? Does culture inexorably move toward positive states? Are other explanations of the origins, nature, and impact of the practice possible?

Conclusion

Such questions motivate practitioners and academics to study public relations by using theory in their detective work. A recurring theme in the discussion of public relations centers on the efforts individuals and organizations make to engage one another in varying degrees of competition, conflict, and cooperation. It seems persistent to matters of power, resource distribution, risk management, and the quality of community. Many agree that public relations is strategic, operating through identifiable structures, strategies, functions, tools, and tactics to help organizations and other entities achieve their missions, visions, and operations. It operationalizes the human need collectively to manage risks, distribute resources, and align interests. However, it is possible that public relations can also subvert equilibrium, destabilize community, and augment risk to a less powerful audience in the pursuit of promoting selfish, private interests as opposed to the public good. In that pursuit, is it socially responsible or the work of the devil?

Using a historical approach to public relations practice to understand its identity and quality, Salcedo (2008) asks whether public relations is inherent to human nature and society. Did it exist prior to its being named and becoming a profession? There are many answers. For example, Salcedo argues, using Spain as a case study, that it existed there as a practice prior to its became a named profession after World War II.

Public relations is nothing new. It is a social phenomenon, capable of being a professional practice. This is so, Raucher (1990) concludes, because of (a) each society's unique socioeconomic, cultural, and political environments, (b) the nature of the media industry, and (c) "the vulnerability and needs of large institutions, especially business corporations" (p. 19). These conditions suggest that even if public relations is timeless, substantial tensions continue to motivate those who study and seek to improve its practice through theory, research, and critical judgment.

Chapter Summary

Practitioners, theorists, and researchers obsess over the basic question: What is public relations, is it socially responsible or the work of the devil? No definition is accepted universally, and so the search continues—although we have come up with some major agendas and key terms associated with the field over the last several decades. All parties are devoted to "improving" the practice, but they don't agree on how, or on what constitutes improvement. No magic wand is available to bring this wrangle to a comfortable and agreeable conclusion.

This observation not only justifies the scope and purpose of this book, but also suggests the robust health of the discipline in practice and theory. Over time, study peels back each layer of the public relations onion to eventually arrive at its core. Toward that end, Chapter 2 suggests how theory operates as theory, how it interacts with practice, and how systematic inquiry based on philosophic assumptions can advance the discipline.

As a foundation for subsequent chapters, this one has focused on three themes: (a) that which is called public relations seems to be timeless and iteratively inherent to the human condition; (b) to unlock this mystery requires examining the nature of societies, communities, and organizations as struggles for collective efficacy and aligned interests in the face of uncertainty and continuous changes, as well as the need for individuals and organizations to be communicative in pursuit of relatedness; and (c) the study of public relations is not only descriptive—seeking to explain what public relations is—but also centers on contests of social responsibility beyond institutional role—whether it is constructively valuable.

Discussion Questions

1 What is public relations? Is it timeless or a product of mass media and the business contexts of the nineteenth century? Has the definition changed over time? If so, what defines the current practice?
2 Is public relations exclusively the tool of business commerce, or does it serve the interests of other types of organizations, as well as individuals and groups?
3 What evidence should a detective theorist look for to solve the mystery of the identity, role, purpose, discourse, and institutional and social value of public relations?
4 Is public relations a strategic tool, a means, or an outcome—or all three?
5 For what reasons has public relations become vital to human society?
6 Is being a good communicator inseparable from moral judgments of management?
7 How do answers to these questions help construct and test theory?

References

Beard, M. (2015). *SPQR: A history of ancient Rome*. New York: Liveright Publishing.
Broom, G. M., & Sha, B.-L. (2013). *Cutlip and Center's effective public relations* (11th ed.). New York: Pearson.
Brown, R. E. (2003). St. Paul as a public relations practitioner: A metatheoretical speculation on messianic communication and symmetry. *Public Relations Review, 29*, 1–12.
Cameron, G. T., Wilcox, D. L., Reber, B., & Shin, J. H. (2007). *Public relations today: Managing conflict and competition*. Boston, MA: Pearson.

Cobley, P. (2008). Communication: Definitions and concepts. In W. Donsbach (Ed.), (Editor in Chief).*The international encyclopedia of communication* (pp. 660–666). Malden, MA: Blackwell Publishing.

Croft, R., Hartland, T., & Skinner, H. (2008). And did those feet? Getting medieval England "on-message." *Journal of Communication Management, 12*, 294–304.

Curtin, P. A. (2008). Fred Harvey Company public relations and publicity (1876–1933). *Journal of Communication Management, 12*, 359–373.

Cutlip, S. M. (1994). *The unseen power: Public relations. A history.* Hillsdale, NJ: Lawrence Erlbaum Associates.

Cutlip, S. M. (1995). *Public relations history: From the 17th to the 20th century. The antecedents.* Hillsdale, NJ: Lawrence Erlbaum Associates.

Cutlip, S. M., Center, A. H., & Broom, G. M. (2006). *Effective public relations* (9th ed.). Upper Saddle River, NJ: Pearson.

Douglas, M. (1992). *Risk and blame.* London: Routledge.

Duncan, M. (2017). *The storm before the storm: The beginning of the end of the Roman Republic.* New York: Hachette.

Ferguson, R. (2009). *The Vikings: A history.* New York: Penguin Group.

Gower, K. K. (2008). US corporate public relations in the progressive era. *Journal of Communication Management, 12*, 305–318.

Grunig, J. E., & Hunt, T. (1984). *Managing public relations.* New York: Holt, Rinehart, and Winston.

Guth, D. W., & Marsh, C. (2017). *Public relations: A values-driven approach* (6th ed.). New York: Pearson.

Gwynne, S. C. (2010). *Empire of the summer moon: Quanah Parker and the rise and fall of the Comanches, the most powerful Indian tribe in American history.* New York: Scribner.

Hallahan, K. (2018). Public relations. In R. L. Heath & W. Johansen (Eds.), *International encyclopedia of strategic communication* (pp. 1192–1207). Hoboken, NJ: Wiley-Blackwell.

Harlow, R. F. (1976). Building a public relations definition. *Public Relations Review, 2*, 34–42.

Hearit, K. M. (2005). Battle of the currents. In R. L. Heath (Ed.), *Encyclopedia of public relations* (pp. 68–70). Thousand Oaks, CA: Sage.

Heath, R. L. (2005). Antecedents of modern public relations. In R. L. Heath (Ed.), *Encyclopedia of public relations* (pp. 32–37). Thousand Oaks, CA: Sage.

Heath, R. L., & Coombs, W. T. (2006). *Today's public relations.* Thousand Oaks, CA: Sage.

Heath, R. L., & Waymer, D. (2009). Activist public relations and the paradox of the positive: A case study of Frederick Douglass' "Fourth of July Address." In R. L. Heath, E. L. Toth, & D. Waymer (Eds.), *Rhetorical and critical approaches to public relations II* (pp. 195–215). New York: Routledge.

Hiebert, R. E. (1991). Public relations as a weapon of modern warfare. *Public Relations Review, 17*, 107–116.

Hill, J. W. (1958). *Corporate public relations: Arm of modern management.* New York: Harper & Brothers.

Hill, J. W. (1963). *The making of a public relations man.* New York: David McKay.

Lamme, M. O. (2009). The brewers and public relations history, 1909–1919. *Journal of Public Relations Research, 21*, 455–477.

Lattimore, D., Baskin, O., Heiman, S. T., & Toth, E. L. (2012). *Public relations: The profession & the practice* (4th ed.). New York: McGraw-Hill.

L'Etang, J. (2008). Writing PR history: Issues, methods and politics. *Journal of Communication Management, 12*, 319–335.

Levi-Strauss, C. (1978). *Myth and meaning*. Abingdon: Routledge & Kegan Paul.

Lubbers, C. A. (2005a). Committee on public information. In R. L. Heath (Ed.), *Encyclopedia of public relations* (pp. 154–157). Thousand Oaks, CA: Sage.

Lubbers, C. A. (2005b). Four-minute Men. In R. L. Heath (Ed.), *Encyclopedia of public relations* (pp. 337–338). Thousand Oaks, CA: Sage.

McCurry, S. (2011). Bread or Blood. *Civil War Times*, *49*(3), 36–41.

Meijer, F. (2003). *The gladiators: History's most deadly sport* (trans. Liz Waters). New York: Thomas Dunne.

Newsom, D., Turk, J., & Kruckeberg, D. (2000). *This is PR: The realities of public relations* (7th ed.). Belmont, CA: Wadsworth/Thompson Learning.

Papinchak, K. M. (2005). Barnum, P. T. In R. L. Heath (Ed.), *Encyclopedia of public relations* (pp. 62–65). Thousand Oaks, CA: Sage.

Pearson, R. (1990). Perspectives on public relations history. *Public Relations Review*, *16*(3), 27–38.

Ponder, S. (1990). Progressive drive to shape public opinion, 1898–1913. *Public Relations Review*, *16*(3), 94–104.

Raucher, A. R. (1990). Public relations in business: A business of public relations. *Public Relations Review*, *16*(3), 19–26.

Russell, K. M., & Bishop, C. O. (2009). Understanding Ivy Lee's Declaration of Principles: U. S. newspaper and magazine coverage of publicity and press agentry. *Public Relations Review*, *35*, 91–101.

Salcedo, N. R. (2008). Public relations before "public relations" in Spain: An early history (1881–1960). *Journal of Communication Management*, *12*, 279–293.

Stoker, K., & Rawlins, B. L. (2005). The "light" of publicity in the progressive era: From searchlight to flashlight. *Journalism History*, *30*, 177–188.

Vos, T. P. (2011). Explaining the origins of public relations: Logics of historical explanation. *Journal of Public Relations Research*, *23*, 119–140.

Watson, T. (2008). Creating the cult of a saint: Communication strategies in 10th century England. *Public Relations Review*, *34*, 19–24.

Xifra, J., & Heath, R. L. (2015). Reputation, propaganda and hegemony in Assyriology studies: A critical view of public relations historiography. *Journal of Public Relations Research*, *27*, 196–211.

2

Role of Theory: Affirming and Advancing Professional Practice

Introduction

Chapter 2 explains the nature and importance of theory and research, especially their contribution to the study and practice of public relations, including its institutionalization and societal impact. Public relations is more than random communications or routinized media reports designed to provide information to some undifferentiated audience. That audience, or public, might be defined as the readers, listeners, viewers, or users of information and value judgments provided through a medium.

Public relations is purposeful, goal-directed, programmatic, managerial, and strategic; it is expected to have impact. Strategy is informed and intuited choice-making regarding the defined and understood processes, functions, tactics, and tools used to achieve particular goals. Research couples with strategy insofar as it helps explain and predict means–ends, if-this-then-that outcomes, and relationships. In brief, theory-driven research improves professional practice.

Best practices are strategic processes typically learned through mentored experience, common sense, and tested applications to achieve desired effects. They assume that through trial and error (which actually is a research protocol), professionals can generate insights to predict which strategies are likely to be more or less successful as they are used in a variety of contexts and within various ethical guidelines. Skilled practitioners acquire over time a firm sense of best practices, which, based on experience, are routinely applied to have an effect. In their routine activities, practitioners thoughtfully consider programs and strategies to learn which work best and do the most good.

Public relations practices, however originally intuitive and innovative, can be tested and refined through theory and research. Professional practice requires both understanding and skilled application of best practices and research-based theory. Professional best practices and academic theory-based conclusions should be partners, not enemies. Although academics spend a lot of time developing and testing theory, their effort should never obscure that leading practitioners add their own intellect, experience, and voice to improving practice. Conferences, institutes, journals, books, and foundations bring academics and practitioners together to collaboratively solve practical and ethical challenges facing the profession. Through joint efforts and diligence, theory and research can help professionals learn what approaches and strategies are most effective and ethical.

To help affirm or disconfirm best practices as insightful strategies, academics develop theory to explain and improve practice through systematic research. Sound theories of public relations can help solve problems by elucidating the logic of which concepts in the best relationship produce the desired outcome. As best practices and theory work together in common interest, a synergy builds that keeps the discipline focused on how to add value to society, making it a better place to live and work.

Public Relations Theory: Capabilities and Competencies, First Edition. Jae-Hwa Shin and Robert L. Heath.

Building on that premise, Chapter 2 sets the foundation for later chapters by continuing to discuss themes set out in Chapter 1 explaining how public relations practice arises from the natural desire individuals have to make themselves, their organizations, and their communities effective. It explains the nature and role of theory and sets out the conceptual underpinnings that ground the discipline and guide its improvement. Leaders in the field, observing success in other professions, know that professional practice requires continual, thoughtful modification and refinement. Organizations' successes—even their survival—create the rationale for knowing how management and communication processes help achieve specific, valued outcomes.

For that reason, this chapter adopts a theme regarding the education of public relations students on which working professionals and academics agree: today's public relations students should learn to practice in ethical, reflective, responsible, strategic, programmatic, and managerial ways. Such an education is built on knowledge of best practices, refined and supported by theory and research.

By the end of the chapter, readers should understand the nature of theory, appreciate how central it is to professional practice, and recognize some of the specific ways that it can improve practice.

Questions to Frame the Discussion of the Role of Theory

- How do best practices and theory intertwine?
- What is theory—along with companion terms such as concept, construct, variable, and hypothesis?
- How do theory and its companions, hypothesis and research questions, add clarity to the strategic performance of public relations?
- What philosophic perspectives ground and enrich public relations theory?
- What assumptions are foundational to and perplexing for the development of public relations theory?
- How useful is public relations theory for solving public relations problems—as process, generation of meaning, and ethics?
- How well do the major theories discussed in this book reflect the standards for creating and testing theory? (Note: This question introduces the notion of different and even competing theories, which will be explained and evaluated in the following chapters.)

Key Themes

- Theory is an intellectual tool used to observe and understand concepts and patterns and to predict and judge how the patterns of specific phenomena lead to outcomes.
- Theory and its partner concepts—variables, constructs, hypotheses, and research questions—are means for understanding observable and measurable patterns, which can be examined through formal research and time-tested practice.
- Theory can guide researchers to investigate further research directions.
- Public relations theories should help make the practice useful and socially responsible.
- Theory can help practitioners develop and implement strategic policies, practices, programs, plans, functions, tactics, and tools effectively and ethically.
- Theory aids the profession's ability to help create the shared meaning needed for collective, value-driven behavior.
- Theory can enrich the strategic ability of practitioners, as it explains how organizations can and should engage with publics and stakeholders.

Case Study: The Stockholm Accords—Blending Theory and Best Practices

Perhaps no challenge to human survival and quality of life is greater than the need to achieve resource sustainability, to be able to develop, apply, and protect the resources needed to sustain life, and to support desirable life styles. Scientists project the world population will reach 9 billion by 2050. A population of that size challenges the best efforts of businesses, governments, and nongovernmental organizations (NGOs) to meet people's basic resource needs. It calls on science, social science, management, humanities, liberal arts, and communication to imagine and achieve a sustainable world. Sustainability presumes that once used, some resources cannot be replaced or restored.

As one of many initiatives to help achieve global sustainability, the World Business Council for Sustainable Development (WBCSD) met in Stockholm, Sweden in 2010 to lay out a plan called Vision 2050: The New Agenda for Business. It offered a blueprint for the coordinated strategic change management of populations, organizational (managerial) performance, basic animal and plant needs, and available resources, both sustainable and unsustainable. One of the sponsoring organizations was the Global Alliance for Public Relations and Communication Management.

Senior public relations practitioners and academics realized that global sustainability planning will fail if the organizations involved cannot communicate effectively. Organizations (commercial, governmental, and nongovernmental) need to help change opinions, attitudes, and behaviors both internally and externally regarding how organizations and societies plan for and achieve change. Motivated practitioners and academics thus worked together to draft and maintain a plan to define and guide what they called the "communicative organization" as a means to lead global society to achieve sustainability.

Through the effort of 985 public relations/communication management industry leaders from 32 countries, a companion document to Vision 2050 was drafted: the Stockholm Accords (World Public Relations Forum, 2010). The Accords were endorsed at the World Public Relations Forum in Stockholm, Sweden on June 15, 2010 and have been discussed and refined at Forum meetings in Melbourne (2012), Madrid (2014), Toronto (2016), and Oslo (2018).

The Accords are grounded in theory, research, and best practices in order to define, recommend, and promulgate performance guidelines, strategies, and standards to help leading organizations be communicative. They were designed to enable associations, managers, consultants, students, educators, and researchers "to administer [their] principles on a sustained basis and to affirm them through the profession, as well as to management and other relevant stakeholder groups" (p. 1). They propose that a communicative organization is one that "assumes leadership by interpreting sustainability as a transformational opportunity to improve its competitive positioning by pursuing and constantly reporting on the achievement of its sustainability policies across the economic, social, and environmental 'triple bottom line'" (p. 2).

The Accords feature concepts vital to communicative organizations: engagement, interpretation of expectations, ensuring stakeholder participation, transparency, authenticity, governance of stakeholder relationships, trustworthy behavior, verifiable representation of community, license to operate, a listening culture, open systems, two-way communication, legitimacy, reputation management, internal and external communication, and consistency and accuracy of message content. They emphasize relationship management as (a) a means to communicate effectively with stakeholders and (b) a goal to be achieved through communication. In addition to relationship building and leadership development, they offer advice for conflict resolution, public discourse that seeks to support and guide change management, and critical perspectives that bring ethical considerations to bear on solving challenges of sustainability. The Accords encourage organizations to become communicative partners with identifiable stakeholders in search of wise solutions to common problems. Inspired leadership is required in this effort. If humans are to accomplish their goals, how can they do so without the defining and evaluating power of language?

The Accords were superseded in 2012 by the Melbourne Mandate (see https://smith.queensu.ca/insight/system/files/Melbourne-Mandate-Text-final.pdf), which calls upon public relations and communication professionals to:

- define and maintain an organization's character and values;
- build a culture of listening and engagement; and
- instill responsible behaviors by individuals and organizations.

These roles are essential and interconnected: an organization must understand its character and responsibility if it is to have meaningful engagement with its stakeholders. Taken together, they form an essential contribution to organizational strategy—and to society. Note that the word "engagement" is prominent in the Mandate.

The WBCSD works to set templates and offer leadership, because sustainability requires policy development and organizational communicativeness focused on building positive stakeholder relationships relevant to economic, social, and environmental success. Thus, practitioners work to help organizations be communicative by identifying and building productive relationships with stakeholders, resolving conflict, using public discourse to support and guide change management, and bring ethical considerations into solving problems of sustainability. Those goals are rich with the need to know how to accomplish such outcomes using best practices, research, and theory.

Projects such as the Accords and the Mandate demonstrate why students need to know, understand, and be able to apply theory, as well as understand how it is conceptualized, grounded, and examined. Practitioners often are given outcome-driven assignments and guidelines. The question is in what way can best practices and theory achieve such ends within those guidelines (see Gregory, 2015). In conjunction with this question, the purpose of this chapter is to help students understand and appreciate how the formation and discussion of theory guide and enrich its strategic professional application. With specific regard to the Accords and the Mandate, key questions need to be addressed:

- What makes an organization communicative?
- What theory would you draw on to advise others on how to increase an organization's communicativeness and ability to engage with stakeholders?
- What would you like to know about public relations theory in order to write and implement a document such as the Accords or the Mandate?
- What assumptions are sound and how can theory help organizations avoid mistakes as their managements work to make them more communicative?
- What best practices and theoretical insights are valuable for achieving sustainability?
- What philosophies and theories are available to guide and enrich public relations theory, in order to answer questions such as those listed here?

Theory as a Companion to Practice

This section discusses the partnership, even tug-of-war, between theory and practice. One grave mistake that academics can make is to conclude that best practices are devoid of or indifferent to theory. Practitioners similarly make a mistake if they believe that theory and research have no place in their "best practices." This section explains the nature and role of theory—its challenges and solutions—in order to create a clear and coherent statement about which practices truly are best, and how public relations theories explain them.

Theory's Role in Academic Study

Throughout their academic life, students learn what professionals do and how, on a day-by-day, project-by-project basis. Such best practices are passed from one generation to another, as the instructor tells the students, "Do X; this is how and what practitioners do." By this logic, students receive guild or craft training. A curriculum might, for instance, offer courses that introduce students to "public relations principles."

Basic public relations texts often rely on practitioner traditions, with some research and theory sprinkled on top to support the advice and prescriptive guidelines. These books offer cases as "research" and practitioner guidelines based on experience as tests of "theory." Such study is typically skewed toward a discussion of public relations roles, strategies, functions, tactics, and tools. It can slight strategic communication management decision making. Consequently, teachers and employers often observe that students are not taught to think and act in strategic ways. They might know something about the tools of public relations, but can they use them strategically? Such criticisms force the question of whether a grounded understanding of theory helps make students effective, strategic, and ethical practitioners.

Theory's Role in Professional Practice

Theory offers insight into the rational, grounded strategies needed to achieve outcomes through "if–then" reasoning. Using if–then logic, theory is an intellectual tool that connects strategies, processes, functions, tools, and tactics with outcomes. It both guides and reflects observation and interpretation of patterns of action–outcome relationships. It can be purely objective (observant) or normative (heavy on prescriptive guidelines, which may include moral judgment). Professional practices often reflect if–then reasoning, which can be supported, enriched, and focused by knowing theory and research.

By that logic, for example, aeronautical engineers know it would be unwise to design an airplane without understanding the theory of aerodynamics. By contemporary standards, the early airplanes were laughably clumsy; their airworthiness was tested by trial and error. Based on a century of theory and research, engineers now design planes that fly safely in excess of the speed of sound and carry hundreds of passengers, items of luggage, and pieces of freight. Over time, airplane design has become informed through testing and retesting, or by supporting or rejecting a theory based on real experience.

Similarly, medical students learn that it is unwise to practice medicine without knowing theories relevant to diagnosis and therapy, including medication. For that reason, they study endocrinology and physiology. Advances in medical theory and research augment physicians' ability to diagnose, treat, and heal. The practice of medicine has come a long way from the time when quackery was the standard and treatment could be more dangerous than disease. Now, major medical teaching colleges and massive research facilities ensure that the practice is more science-based.

In all professions, best practices are innovated and tested through trial and error. Theory and research support, correct, and enhance professional practices. Research can refine, prove or disprove, and challenge specific conclusions on which theories rest. Theory and research help practitioners make strategic choices regarding how they influence their organizations, enact their leadership roles, create and implement problem-solving approaches to "public relations" problems, and advise management.

The more completely academic research and theory are able to support, refine, and critically guide management decision making, the more important a discipline is to organizational decision makers. Thus, engineering and physical science researchers routinely refine businesses' organizational practices. The same is true of disciplines such as finance, economics, psychology, organizational communication, marketing, human resources, and legal counsel. To be taken seriously by others in the management team, experts representing the disciplines needed for an organization to succeed are expected to call on relevant theory and research to make sound, well-informed decisions and recommendations.

Because of the clarity of purpose and insight achieved through theory and research, professionals in all disciplines thirst for insights that add value to their performance and leadership service to others.

Practitioner Thirst for Sound Theory

During the first part of the twentieth century, leading practitioners explicitly and aspirationally drew on theories to decide which strategies, plans, and programs best served their clients' missions, visions, and core values. Theory helped them understand the positive role public relations could—and should—play in society.

Chapter 1 explained how democratic theory guided Ivy Lee's sense of how public relations serves society. Democracy requires an informed public. Similarly, John W. Hill's ideas about public relations drew on journalism, the theory of deliberative democracy, and management theory to demand of business leaders that they never presume to operate at odds with public opinion—explicitly, that they never act against the public interest. He championed citizens' right to criticize business when they found commercial practices offensive—a principle of democratic theory. Thus, he believed management practices are inseparable from public relations.

Another leader in the development of twentieth-century public relations was Edward L. Bernays. Although Bernays and Hill were contemporaries, each based his work on quite different theoretical foundations. Bernays called on psychology, the study of how people think and act as they do. In 1923, he wrote *Crystalizing Public Opinion*. Five years later, he published an article entitled "Manipulating Public Opinion" and a book on propaganda. By 1955, he argued that the purpose of public relations was to "engineer consent." All these works featured the public relations expert as being uniquely able (even gifted) to shape (crystalize or engineer) consumer opinions to the benefit of client businesses. Such uses of theory would ultimately anger many practitioners and academics as being manipulative.

A major difference between the perspectives of Hill and Bernays was not a matter of psychology, but rather of openness, transparency, and regard for the intellectual capability of citizens to make enlightened choices. Bernays thought that companies had the right, even the responsibility, to engineer consent, whereas Hill thought they should facilitate or enlighten choice.

Since the 1950s, the theory developed by leading practitioners and academic researchers has struggled to understand what communication processes and kinds of discourse are effective and socially responsible. Therein lies the call for ever better theory. It can be seen as a means of shaping and controlling thought and action. It can respond to the desire to understand how organizations—especially businesses—thrive by aligning their interests and the public interest.

As this discussion continues, it is reasonable to ask a probing question related to the case analyzed in this chapter: Does the theory of democracy, with its underpinning principles of information, openness, transparency, and responsiveness to public opinion and public interest, help practitioners know what is required to make organizations communicative?

This emphasis on democracy does not suggest that undemocratic cultures, sociopolitical systems, and organizations do not use public relations. Contrasting theories based on competing socioeconomic systems were explained in Chapter 1. For example, Vos (2011) reasoned that theory variously addresses, or exhibits, at least three logics: functionalism, institutionalism, and culturalism. These logics can be described as having layers (more to less general) or as overlapping with other theories—a cross-fertilizing influence. Keeping such contextual influences in mind, the next section explains the "theory" of theory.

Theory Is as Theory Does

Hansen-Horn and Neff's (2008) book on public relations theory and practice opens with the following adage: "There is nothing as practical as a good theory" (p. xvii). A theory must be useful, helping to solve complex, practical problems and informing the conduct of additional research. It must give practitioners practical advice on how to shape public relations programs and strategies relevant to the scope and purpose of the organizations, causes, and issue positions that it serves.

Theory Defined

A theory can help people understand specific phenomena—in this case, the practice, process, and role of public relations in organizational and societal effectiveness. Theory grows from observing and postulating to explain what can be seen and interpreted as "public relations." For this reason, a theory is a skilled way of looking at some matter; the key elements or aspects—what we call "concepts" and "variables"—of that matter are framed as premises, propositions, and paradigms that capture its essence. In the case of public relations, theory requires a shared understanding of what the phenomenon of public relations entails—the key theme of Chapter 1.

Theories are generalized statements about identifiable relationships among concepts and constructs relative to some phenomena. They are systematic, coherent, and plausible sets of statements that explain those phenomena: rigorous analyses of some set of observable and measurable facts. They use concepts and specified relationships among these facts to generalize about them so as to predict that as conditions occur, and as concepts play out, certain outcomes will result. For this reason, Hazleton and Botan (1989) observe that "a theory consists of at least two concepts and a statement explaining or predicting the relationship between those concepts" (p. 7). Similarly, Sha (2018) reasons that theory expresses a "set of related propositions that presents a systematic view of phenomena by specifying relationships among concepts" (p. 1).

This definition does not clearly distinguish between theory and hypothesis. Theory is a "bigger," broader, and more generalized kind of conclusion about concepts, their relationships, and their influences on outcomes. Fretwurst (2008) advises always thinking of theory and hypothesis in tandem. A hypothesis is a testable proposition. Thus, a theory in relationship to a hypothesis "is a system of (few) basic propositions and a large number of logical derivations" (p. 2155).

To be coherent, a theory must be logical; it must explain, predict, and offer insights that can be examined by research and applied in practice. Other researchers must be able to understand and follow its logic so they can generate hypotheses to test and propose research questions to answer, and so that they can prove (or disprove), dispute, or revise it. Finally, a theory is plausible to the extent that it "makes sense": that it can define and express the essence of the patterned relationships among concepts in a few words; that it is capable of being expressed as an encompassing principle or premise. Such a relationship should reflect one or more paradigms, and may in and of itself constitute a paradigm. A paradigm is a conceptual perspective that is foundational to a theory, "the entire constellation of beliefs, values, techniques, and so on shared by members of a given community" (Kuhn, 1970, p. 175).

In communication studies, two major paradigms contrast how the process works: information flow versus stimulus–response. A transmission model presumes that information flows, as meaning, between sender and receiver. Stimulus–response presumes that the response, as interpretation, determines what the source's message is. Because they are foundational, paradigms shape how theorists see and interpret data. They serve as lenses through which practitioners and academics interpret phenomena; here, the phenomenon of public relations

Theory building is both an inductive and a deductive process. Conceptualizing and theorizing are patterns of reasoning from practice to theory or of building from theory to practice in a circular manner. Such reasoning requires (a) conceptual development, (b) operationalization, (c) confirmation or disconfirmation, and (d) application. As application is observed, the process can reverse by asking whether practice (as theorized) confirms or disconfirms theory in ways that affirm or challenge operationalization, leading to conception (re)development and refinement (Lynham, 2002).

The next section poses the conditions of a definition of public relations. That definition, relevant to the case featured in this chapter, provides insight into what makes an organization communicative.

The Phenomenon Called Public Relations

Academics and practitioners—as well as students—need to share a definition of public relations. If they study different phenomena or interpret the same phenomenon differently, this will confuse theory building. Relevantly to the case used to open this chapter, they must have a shared sense of what makes an organization communicative if they are going to advance the cause of achieving sustainability.

As discussed in Chapter 1, socioeconomic and cultural perspectives shape what researchers view as public relations, which has led to two competing paradigms. One is corporate-centric, viewing public relations from a "dominant" organizational point of view. The other views it from a community, society, or even cultural perspective.

Do we view public relations as an organizational activity or a community activity? What boundary conditions, for instance, might distinguish it from advertising or other forms of marketing communication? Is activism public relations? Is emergency management communication (risk and response awareness, which alerts people to a risk and then guides their response to it) an aspect of public relations? Does public relations include publicity, promotion, reputation building, crisis recovery, and image management? Is public relations the actions and statements that affect the quality of the relationships between an organization and its publics and stakeholders? Can it strengthen the relationships that motivate publics to support/favor or oppose an organization? Is it strategic processes, a flow of cross-currents of influence, or merely campaigns? Is it the rationale for effective discourse, whereby the interests of organizations and publics are brought into alignment? How does practice relate to ethics?

Chapters 3–6 present and discuss four major theories of public relations, in order to improve our understanding and practice of it. Those same four theories will be previewed later in this chapter, highlighting their unique views (principles or premises) of the subject. First, however, the following thoughts on public relations can help frame its definition for the purposes of discussion.

Query to Student

How do you define public relations? Beyond those provided in this book, what definitions can you find? How do different definitions of public relations confirm or confound your efforts to develop a theory of how it should best be practiced? Is it necessary to understand public relations in order to help organizations be more communicative in the cause of sustainability? Can you name any specific public relations theory? Can you suggest a public relations theory explaining some public relations phenomena, or a public relations practice relating to a public relations theory?

Theory is only meaningful if those seeking to understand and evaluate it agree on what phenomena are being considered. One of the tricky challenges when defining a term such as "public relations" is not to confuse the phenomenon with the practice. The same is true of engineering, medicine, psychology, nutrition, accounting, finance, marketing, advertising, and so on.

By this reasoning, for instance, it would be a misnomer to define medicine as the practice of medicine, or as doing what doctors do. It might also be unhelpful to define it as an outcome: helping people to be well, or not be sick. Accounting might thus be defined as the process of calculating and reporting on the financial health of some person or organization. Engineering might be the process of solving problems, making decisions, and providing and implementing designs to achieve orderly and safe operations (specific to the particular discipline; thus, chemical engineering differs from mechanical engineering).

A definition of public relations might focus on function, strategy, role, impact, or outcome. What happens if public relations is defined as spin, manipulation, or propaganda? These concepts focus on what practitioners do, the role the field plays in society, and the impact it can have.

Impact is important, as is process. These themes will be elaborated on in Chapter 8, which looks at how the impact of the practice is measured. One could define the impact of public relations as the degree of positive or negative regard people pay to what an organization is, does, and accomplishes; its impact on the interests of others, both internally and externally. According to John Hill (1963), an observer might conclude that an organization such as a business has "public relations" whether or not anyone is actually overseeing or managing how it operates in the public interest. Hill reasons: "I say 'organized' public relations advisedly. Every business, and for that matter, every activity with public overtones, has public relations whether or not it recognizes the fact, or whether or not it does anything about it" (p. 259). Practice is defined as the professional manner in which activities and functions are brought into the service of an organization and of society. In that sense, consequence (impact, influence) is an important aspect of the definition of public relations.

Public relations theory can address means, activities, philosophy, practice, strategies, processes, functions, programs, plans, tactics, and tools. The means used to achieve certain ends characterize or define how the profession serves organizations, individuals, communities, and society. Such an analysis focuses attention on the rationale for the practice—what is accomplished, in what way, and whether it should be.

To set the stage for further discussion of theory, the following definition is offered for consideration: *Public relations entails practices, strategic processes, and meaningful enactments used to listen to others, build and wield relationships, co-create meaning, and bring ethical (values-driven) judgments to guide how organizations work to enact themselves in association with and to align their interests with those of stakeholders.* Recall the definitions offered in Chapter 1, and consider the definitional aspects of the Accords and Mandate.

However acceptable this definition is, it points to certain key concepts and the relationships among them and offers an organizing perspective regarding some unique phenomena. The worth of a theory depends on its ability to focus attention on and explain the relationship among concepts that are unique and foundational to what is under study, or what is being practiced. That is true of aerodynamics, of medicine, of accounting—and of public relations.

The next step toward understanding how theory sheds light on a particular matter is to understand concepts—the topic discussed in the next section. Of relevance to the opening case, by what concepts might one define a communicative organization?

Theory Based on Concepts

A good theory is able to define phenomena and, based on that definition, predict "if–then" outcomes. It can do so because the theorists carefully and wisely observe, explain, and seek to understand concepts and the relationships between them. This intellectual process can be called conceptualization. It is the reasoning process by which concepts are developed in association with one another to formulate a theory.

Concepts are the building blocks of theory. They characterize the phenomena vital to the matter under consideration. As Hazleton and Botan (1989) observe:

> Concepts are descriptive in purpose and function. They reference the fields of human experience. Concepts vary principally in their degree of abstractness. Level of abstractness is a function of the number of differentiated exemplars that constitute instances of a concept, as well as the extent to which exemplars are directly/indirectly observable. (p. 7)

For aerodynamics, materials, airflow, and thrust are key concepts. Accounting builds upon the nature of and ratio between debits and credits. Audiology (the study of hearing) features structures and functions (normal and abnormal/functional and dysfunctional) of the body, including the receiving mechanism, the mechanism that transmits sound to the brain, and the ability of the brain to receive and interpret sounds.

In the discussion of theory in the chapters that follow, many concepts will be featured. Each theory makes reasoned, logical claims by linking concepts to one another. Each linkage between concepts is captured by some organizing principle, an encompassing premise, or a paradigm. Such conceptualization can be addressed by answering research questions and testing hypotheses. Importantly, each theory builds on or incorporates specific concepts even as it slights, ignores, or even rejects others. To understand and evaluate any theory requires knowing and considering the concepts that are its foundation.

Concepts are vocabulary builders. Without a shared vocabulary, theorists cannot hope to capture and express the insights needed to make their theories understood—and useful. Such vocabulary represents the terms used in the specific discipline. Relevant concepts are those uniquely central to the strategic processes of public relations and the measurement of its impact and role in society.

With that in mind, the next section considers what makes any theory sound. By what criteria are theories judged and evaluated?

Theory Kinds and Qualities

Theories are a way of reasoning about the relationships among concepts. There are several kinds of theories, as there are many criteria by which to judge them. McQuail (1987) suggests four. *Social scientific theories* are developed through systematic observation and reasoning; they are formally tested through rigorous procedures. *Normative theories* propose better ways of behaving and communicating (being communicative). *Working theories* are like houses under construction; they exist under various stages of development. *Commonsense theories* seem intuitively correct, or are rooted in the collective experience of practitioners. That does not mean that all theory does not need to be "intuitively correct." It is often a problem to develop and advance a theory that is counterintuitive. But commonsense theories are taken at face value, and may, in the sense already discussed, be "best practices."

The following criteria are used to judge the quality of a theory. A good theory must:

- be internally consistent and not contradict or argue against its own conclusions.
- explain the relationship between key variables in such a way that practitioners and researchers can make use of it; the "if–then" relationship between concepts must describe and predict.
- be useful; its heuristic purpose presumes that it is capable of being applied to solve some real-life problem; it must help generate research and additional theory.
- guide research while supporting and correcting practice.
- explain general patterns of practice over time.

To satisfy these "musts," a theory should be examined using hypotheses and research questions.

The next section explains how concepts become variables that facilitate hypothesis testing. Can we define what makes an organization communicative?

Variables Used in Hypotheses and Research Questions

A variable is a concept that takes on different values, such as measurable values. It can be varied, operationalized, and measured. For instance, speed of travel is a concept. As a variable measured by a speedometer, a driver might go 10 miles per hour or 60 miles per hour—or any speed in between or above. It can be operationalized to avoid a traffic ticket and to ensure safety. Likewise, heat is a concept. As a cook prepares to heat food in an oven, they set the desired temperature. Temperature is a variable; it can be cold, cool, hot, or very hot. It is measured in degrees by using a thermometer.

The nature of a variable can be examined by how and why it varies (or changes) in relationship to another concept/variable. A simple, practical example is the way heat is applied to a tea kettle. As the temperature rises, the water in the kettle will boil. The relationship between temperature and the boiling point of water can be tested, as can relationships between concepts relevant to the practice of public relations. Research tests how well a theory explains and predicts the phenomenon under consideration.

Hypotheses are the workhorses of theory building and testing, and of the strategic thinking needed for public relations practice. As practitioners work to solve a public relations problem, they are testing a hypothesis that certain strategies will be effective under a certain set of circumstances with certain stakeholders whose opinions and behaviors can affect the success of the organization, or help solve a problem such as achieving sustainability. To understand that point, the first step is to revisit the topic of concepts, and view them as variables.

In public relations, a practitioner might be interested in the concept (as a variable) of shared meaning. The strategic question is how well individuals agree or disagree on some matter. Researchers can measure the degree (strong/weak) of agreement/disagreement (variable). They might postulate that stakeholders grant resources to stakeseekers as they believe this will lead to conditions of favorable reward management. Thus, an environmental organization (stakeseeker) might ask supporters to donate to the organization so it can use the money to litigate to protect wildlife, and perhaps challenge corporate or government agency behavior.

Research can measure the degree to which stakeholders believe (yes/no) their interests align with those of an organization, whether a business, a nonprofit, or a government agency. Practitioners can work to build a relationship (a variable), repair one, or use one to engage in collaborative decision making. Do people better work together, toward collaborative agreement, if they have a positive rather than a negative relationship and are more willing to trust than to distrust an organization? Do they have a stronger relationship if they collaborate rather than compete to achieve outcomes?

A hypothesis is a conjectural statement regarding the relationship between two or more variables that can be tested through empirical observation. A research question asks about such relationships. In research, and in practice, a hypothesis is used when the researcher or practitioner has an educated guess (conjecture) regarding how certain changes in key variables (such as openness/transparency) will lead to desired outcomes. Contextual and mediating variables can affect how well hypotheses lead to sound conclusions.

One everyday example of formulating and testing a hypothesis begins when a driver inserts an ignition key and turns it (or presses start in the presence of a FOB). The turning of the key is one variable—an independent variable. The ignition of the engine is another—a dependent variable. Each time the driver turns the key, they test the hypothesis that the car will start. If it does not, then other hypotheses become relevant to determining why ignition failed.

Analysis of variables depends on the social science logic of variable analytic research. Such research presumes that, given enough time and with enough experiments, nature will be fully explained and all matters can be reduced to scientific (even social scientific) prediction. McKie (2001), an advocate for critical approaches to public relations, was one of the first public relations scholars to voice doubts about this level of certainty. He emphasized the need for critical, subjective judgment in matters of organization–stakeholder relationship building. He cautioned that scholars and practitioners might use data to draw quite wrong conclusions, that researchers might ask and address the wrong questions. Statistics, a means of positivistic reasoning, can be used to test hypotheses, but some researchers can create studies or conduct experiments that are flawed, in which randomness, chaos, and uncertainty prevail despite alleged statistical certainty. Even advocates of positivistic social science research worry that statistical analysis can lead to incorrect conclusions. For example, two economists at the University of Warwick recently overturned years of research claiming that winning the lottery was not correlated with increased happiness, showing that previous studies had been poorly designed and reached unsupported conclusions (Oswald & Winkelmann, 2019).

As a best practice of media relations, the hypothesis tested might be this: If a practitioner can get the right reporters to receive the information contained in a press release and comment favorably on it, the sponsoring organization can generate favorable publicity for some product or service, or increase its own reputation. This hypothesis relates to one that states that favorable news coverage attracts readers', listeners', viewers', or Internet/social media end-users' attention so that they become informed, and favorably so. The end-users will thus become motivated to think about and even act in a manner desired by those who designed the press release. This sort of logic, framed as hypothesis, is a routine aspect of public relations practice.

A related hypothesis might be framed to capture negative outcomes. As such, drawing on crisis communication, one might reason that as people learn about some problem with the steering or braking function of a brand of automobile, they will formulate a negative opinion of it, and not want to own one; the company's reputation will thus be harmed. These examples suggest the logic of kinds of variables and what this means for hypothesis testing and strategic planning.

Independent variables (such as heat) affect *dependent variables* (such as the molecular agitation in a pan of water). The logic is that as independent variables change, so do dependent ones—and proportionately so. In public relations, the more (variable) high-quality (variable) information is provided to a public, the more it should feel it is knowledgeable on some particular matter.

Mediating variables affect the degree to which independent variables affect dependent variables. Thus, water boils at a lower temperature the lower the atmospheric pressure: at sea level, it boils at 212 °F, but on top of a mountain the boiling point will be lower. In public relations, a public's perception of a company's crisis reputation mediates how it will interpret statements about the company in a current crisis.

This section has presented a working vocabulary so that students of public relations theory know the basics required to understand, judge, and apply theory. Strategic thinking, whether for professional application or for research, requires insightful understanding of concepts and variables (along with their relationships) in order to solve public relations problems.

The next step in this discussion is to ask why and how theories come about. Consequently, the following section addresses the conceptualization roles of induction and deduction.

Inductive and Deductive Approaches to Theory

Earlier, the point was made that theory grows out of observation, a kind of detective work. A detective solves a crime by observing facts and developing a comprehensive reason to explain how they fit into a theory of how the crime was committed and by whom. Induction and deduction are the modes of analysis needed to build theory.

Induction is the process of looking for relevant facts and posing explanations (generalizations) that shed light on some unsolved matter. By this process, theorists try to identify factors that are relevant to aspects of the practice. Thus, an observer might notice that a practitioner responds to critics in argumentative ways. Say critics claim that a company's product is unsafe. The company might counter-advocate that the product is safe because it meets relevant engineering standards. This process of induction could lead a theorist to postulate that one public relations strategy is advocacy.

The same theorist may note that another company, suffering similar complaints of product safety, accommodates its critics. It might quickly acknowledge, for instance, that its ground meat contains levels of *E. coli* sufficient to make customers sick and even lead to death. Accompanying that statement, the company could initiate a formal and systematic recall of the product. The recall might contain an apology and a statement that the company will implement higher standards of meat processing.

By the process of induction, observation, and generalization, the theorist might postulate that two (at least) response strategies are typical of public relations practice in situations such as this.

Once that conclusion is seemingly sound, can and should the theorist formulate a more complex and meaningful theory? Yes. That is when deduction becomes important. The theorist has two competing explanations of how companies respond to criticism. Can both be true? That is a matter for the role of deduction.

As a detective looks at facts and deduces who could, who could not, and who did commit a crime, so the process of deduction looks for a theme that accounts for all the facts. Deduction connects the dots.

The public relations theorist, having observed advocacy and accommodation, might conclude that which strategy is most effectively used will depend on one or more contingencies. Thus, the researcher might argue, developing a line of thought that is now known as contingency theory, that the response used depends (is contingent) on the character of the company, the strength of the facts regarding guilt or innocence, and the character of the critics. It is worth noting, for subsequent discussion, that effect is separate from ethics.

Thus, by applying induction and deduction, a theory is born. Those who work to develop a new theory often draw on the logics of other theories to stimulate conceptualization and achieve insight. This process is also typical of police detectives, who might use personality theory to narrow the list of suspects to those most likely to think and act as did the person who committed the crime.

After a good deal of research, the processes of induction and deduction lead to refinements in a theory. Theorists capture the essence of the theory in one or more key premises that help others to understand and buy in or reject it. These framing premises are extremely helpful to practitioners.

The next section expands this line of discussion by previewing how the public relations theories discussed in the following chapters build on specific variables (and concepts) and their relationships to explain and predict effective and ethical public relations. Such analysis can also explain what makes an organization communicative.

Premises of Public Relations Theories

Close examination of each theory reveals the key theme or premise that captures its essence. As already noted, a good theory ought to be capable of being stated in a few sentences. Those previewed in this section will be discussed in detail in the chapters that follow. Here, each is defined and discussed briefly to highlight its key premise—its characteristic theme.

Excellence Theory

Chapter 3 discusses excellence theory and the closely related situational theory. The premise of excellence theory is that excellent organizations empower public relations practitioners by bringing them into the dominant coalition, where they can participate in the decisions by which each organization adjusts itself best to its publics. The theory reasons that excellent organizations benefit from two-way symmetrical communication facilitated by management as they interact with key publics. Such interaction is most productive when it produces satisfying organization–public relationships (OPRs). Effective communication depends on providing information each public wants in order to solve some problem it is facing. If the relationship that results is strong and positive, the public is satisfied and extends its good will to the organization.

Contingency Theory

Chapter 4 discusses contingency theory and the concepts of conflict, conflict management, and leadership. It features two basic premises. One is that organizations must skillfully and strategically manage conflict if they are to succeed. The other is that conflict can be managed by choosing strategies from a continuum with pure accommodation at one end and pure advocacy at the other. The public relations practitioner must choose the stance, on that continuum, that will best serve the interest of the organization by resolving conflict. The stance adopted by the organization is subject to shift as the situation (variables) changes.

Practitioners should be leaders in managing conflict by exerting contingent leadership. Contingency leadership theory reasons that skilled leaders know alternative communication strategies that can be applied to manage conflict, as well as when and how to effectively marshal a particular strategy in a particular situation. Leadership includes knowledge of and ability to use various conflict resolution strategies contingent on the situation. The key is to use the most effective strategy given the nature of the problem and the persons involved, and to be willing to adjust as the situation evolves.

Rhetorical Theory

Chapter 5 discusses rhetorical theory and the roles that discourse and shared meaning play in human affairs. It rests on the premise that in the communicative process, meaning matters. Individuals and organizations assert themselves into a community of interested parties through what they do and say, where it is meaningful to and has impact on others. Individuals and organizations of all types manage their affairs and align their interests through varying degrees of deliberative democracy, which implies a struggle between agreement and disagreement. This view of democracy reasons that each society is organized for the collective management of risk; as people manage risks collectively, they use discourse to co-create meaning, which makes societies good places to live and work—a theme central to communitarianism and neo-institutionalism. Through discourse, ideas become stronger and actions more ethical as they are contested, refined, and aligned. Organizations are limited in what they can accomplish by whether they encounter support or resistance (e.g., agreement/disagreement).

What the theory lacks in social scientific precision, it makes up for in scope and importance, because of its relevance to the discourse processes that influence choices based on fact, value, policy, identity, and identification.

Critical Theory

Chapter 6 discusses critical theory, which proposes the key premise that purely informative and rational discourse is impossible because reality is unstable and disorderly, language is never neutral, and choices always have moral implications. Not only does chaos prevail, but language confounds understanding. Power disparities fracture societies as members variously battle to empower and marginalize one another (Edwards, 2006). Key premises of this theory are that language is the basis of influence, maintenance of order is based on privileged interests, and society is contestable ground framed through socially constructed meaning.

The theory presumes that since the world (physical and sociopolitical) and behavior are disorderly, humans work to impose order and structure (control) through language because they cannot tolerate disorder. Critical public relations theory sees the human condition as being essentially sociological (the search for order in society) and political (the struggle for power, dominance, control, hegemony, or harmony). As one means for increasing public relations literacy and a commitment to ethical practice, "critical theory has provided a much needed call for reflection on the practice of public relations" (Holladay & Coombs, 2013, p. 126). The search for order is self-interested and distorts strategies needed to achieve truth and ethics.

In summary, excellence and contingency theories feature variable analytical functions and processes of communication relevant to the role that public relations plays in relationship management and conflict resolution. Even though rhetorical and critical theories do not deny the importance of precisely testable processes, they reason that meaning trumps process. Social construction of shared meaning and conflicts of interests are never separate from the meaning people use as they engage in conflict, negotiation, engagement, adjustment, and collaboration. Ethics is fundamental to questions of behavior and the crafting of societal arrangement, and of collective efficacy as social, relational capital. These theories are multidimensional and multilayered, and the latter two presume that the human condition is multitextual.

To further examine the foundations of these four theories, the following subsections examine how they emerged from other, earlier theories. This will help public relations theorists and practitioners to develop, refine, and implement their own theories.

Related Theories that Feature Functions and Process

The poem "The Rime of the Ancient Mariner" by Samuel Taylor Coleridge (1797–1798) contains this passage:

> Water, water everywhere,
> Nor any drop to drink.

Theorists and students may have a similar feeling as did the crew of that fated ship, adrift at sea and suffering from thirst. Theory, theory everywhere, but which is truly useful? Not only are students of public relations confronted with competing public relations theories, but they are asked to understand and weigh the usefulness and ethics of them, resulting in an often perplexing intellectual matrix.

In these matters, organization (managerial) effectiveness is a central theme in public relations; the discipline is expected to help make organizations effective. Some theories are devoted to knowing the options and strategies by which managements can plan and operate to make organizations effective. Simply stated, an agentic organization is one that can establish its legitimacy and sustain itself by gaining the resources it needs by what it *does and says* in a competitive environment.

Given that challenge, practitioners and scholars ask how theory can help organizations, through public relations, to be effective and ethical. Such thinking is called upon to consider how an organization can be effective, by bending society to serve it, or by working to serve society.

Cheney and Christiansen (2001), among others, critique public relations theory based on what it draws from management theories. They reason that "like its cousins of advertising and marketing, public relations grew out of a highly practical context and subsequently developed a theoretical apparatus to support the analysis and legitimation of its professional activity" (p. 167). These authors worry that advocates for pragmatic effectiveness (utilitarianism) will shape the ethics of public relations work by cloaking the discipline in democratic attire to make it look better than it is. This means that public relations theorists are obsessed with developing theory that is not only practical but also morally justifiable.

Continuing their critique, Cheney and Christiansen warn against a commitment to helping organizations, especially businesses, to achieve their mission and vision by whatever means necessary. To avoid that perilous commitment to pragmatism, public relations theory needs to be critically reflective, devoted to collaboration, and willing to embrace organizational theory that questions Western *management theory's* emphasis on power and control as means for efficiently serving any organization's self-interest. Sensitive to such critiques, public relations theorists desire a normative explanation of the discipline. Can public relations make society more fully functioning, rather than merely making organizations more influential, self-interestedly agentic?

To wrestle with such challenges, scholars have gravitated to established theories on which to build. Thus, sparked by *information theory*, *systems theory* is used to explain the dynamic processes by which organizations and publics (stakeholders) functionally adjust to and achieve balance with one another. Systems theory postulates that organizations, entities, and groups seek balance with one another because they cannot tolerate or exist for long in imbalance.

As a parallel to human systems, which depend on information to survive, biological systems depend on energy exchanges. Biology features efficiency of energy exchange as the rationale for effective biological systems. A species' (a system's) success depends on its ability to interact with its environment through such exchanges. Thus, cattle eat grass and give back to the environment in the form of nutrient-rich material, including waste. Notwithstanding questions of the ethics and efficiency of the meat industry, cattle provide food (energy) for other systems. In terms of human systems, such as businesses, some theorists have reasoned that symmetrical efforts, through OPR, increase the flow of information, decrease costly controversy, and facilitate efficient accomplishment of goals. That principle has been a rationale for openness and transparency—knowing what information publics want and providing it.

Systems theory, drawing on *cybernetics*, reasons that systems seek to be in harmony with one another through strategic information sharing and strategic behavioral adjustment. This preference for harmony motivates advocates for this theory to reason that a symmetrical approach to communication management and behavioral adjustment is the preferable, excellent state of cybernetic existence.

Some public relations theorists reason that general systems theory inherently brings ethics into public relations theory and practice. They even argue that systems theory provides the only ethical rationale for public relations. A brief example suggests that systems theory, based on information (energy) flow and cybernetic adjustment, is actually aethical. That means it is inherently incapable of intrinsically offering ethical judgment.

For example, imagine a loaded tour bus that stops on its route in Alaska so the tourists can take pictures of a mother moose and her two calves grazing. While the tourists are happily snapping pictures, a grizzly bear crashes from the brush and kills the calves. Then, her cubs come to eat them (energy flows from one system to another). Without the food, the bears would perish. The attack was clearly "asymmetrical." The mother bear was strong and ferocious. The calves, and their mother, were defenseless. Was the act of the bear, in all of its violence, an ethical violation of the lives of the calves?

Some of the tourists think so. They complain that the bus driver should not have stopped and subjected them to nature's brutal side. They argue that the mother bear had no "right" to kill the defenseless calves. In this case, the tourists impose ethics on the system; morality is not inherent in it. The natural system of survival is aethical.

Such is also the case when theorists argue that systems theory is inherently ethical. It features information flow and behavioral adjustment of systems to one another, but it has no inherent means for determining what information is functionally better or worse. The logic of efficiency and balance reasons that bears cannot consume more food than is available to them. If they should try to do so, they would be starved into balance with the food sources. There is no logic to the ethical judgment, except in the dysfunction of one system being pragmatically out of balance with others.

This reasoning informs the logic of relationship development. The assumption is that high-quality relationships produce benefits to both parties whereas low-quality relationships benefit only one, and may even disadvantage the other. Thus, customers can be encouraged to bank with company A because they have a good relationship with it, while activists are less likely to punish such companies. But balance can be static, whereas dissensus motivates systems to change and improve.

Institutional theory is used to explain how organizations (and their members and other stakeholders) become agentic (effective in goal-motivated ways) through structures, functions, rituals, rules, routines, narratives, and other strategic processes. Communication allows members to know which roles and functions to enact to make gains and avoid losses. It helps them organize, based on established and appropriate beliefs and attitudes, so that they can perform in a coordinated, communicative manner.

Institutional theory follows the logic that sound management results from rational efforts by managers to figure out what internal structures and functions best contribute to their organization's success. That logic, reasoned by public relations theorists, can be applied as the rationale for communication with persons outside of the organization. Structures and functions are created and put into place so customers know how to do business with the organization.

In contrast to institutional theory, *neo-institutional theory* focuses on the meaning that allows both members and outsiders to have a sense of which actions are preferred and rewardable. This theory advocates the appealing premise that "communication sustains institutions" (Lammers & Barbour, 2006, p. 364). It reasons that instead of organizing to communicate, organizations communicate to organize.

Such logic explains how stakeholding publics learn the standards and expectations that they use to judge which organizations perform in ways that are preferable to others. Thus, public relations can be conceptualized as how an organization manages communication in ways that helps (at least ostensibly) it to know and understand the whims and wishes of those whose goodwill it needs in order to be successful.

Resource-dependency theory starts with the stark reality that organizations are resource-dependent, as are humans, grizzly bears, and moose. Humans need food, water, and air. Organizations need revenue, reputation, and goodwill. Without resources, organizations fail to survive and thrive.

Based on this premise, resource-dependency theory reasons that the organization that operates best is the one most likely to get the resources it needs with the least amount of effort. This can be a zero-sum game. Thus, it can be the basis for conflict, and even deceit. According to the resource-dependency perspective, this is where public relations enters the picture. Which business is likely to thrive? Perhaps the answer is the one most willing and able to use deceit and trickery to get those who hold resources (stakeholders) to yield them to its benefit.

If stakeholders believe that stakes are falsely obtained and ill-gotten, they are likely to look for other organizations to reward with the resources they hold, and to punish those that offend them. So, consumers switch companies. Activists protest activities, such as mining or oil production, that they believe cause damage which either mitigates or outweighs the organization's benefit to society. They are motivated to withhold the resources the company needs, such as drilling or mining permits, until its practices and policies change. If companies create risks for community residents (e.g., toxic emissions or mining safety), those residents are likely to protest, lobby for regulation, or work to harm the business. In these ways, resources and their granting/withholding become the rationale of organizational effectiveness; enter public relations.

Social exchange theory offers a parallel justification to explain relationship quality. It presumes that rules (norms of exchange) govern resource exchange between relational partners. It reasons that people are "accountants." They realize, for instance, that the "benefits" of friendship come with "costs." If one relational partner does something nice for another, is the other obligated to make a comparable "social exchange" by doing something in kind as an appropriate response? Is such interaction the rationale, or even narrative ritual, for each person's successes and actions as a relational partner? This theory reasons that relational partners know that they have to give a little to get along. They must reward others in order to get rewards in return. They negotiate, cooperate, and align interests as social exchange. This logic applies equally to organizational success, and opens the door for public relations practice and theory. Monarchs presume that all of a country's resources are their resources. Democracy presumes that resources are co-managed.

John Dewey's theory of pragmatism, publics, and processes of problem solving was quite influential throughout the twentieth century. Dewey believed that humans constantly recognize and solve problems. For that reason, he concluded that education and social arrangement are best when they help people adequately meet the challenge of identifying and resolving problems in an efficient, effective manner.

Dewey argued that persons (and organizations) who are better problem solvers are more successful. To help people be better problem solvers, he proposed the process of reflective thinking, which features the following steps:

1) defining problem;
2) analyzing problem;
3) recognizing possible solutions;
4) developing/applying criteria by which to solve problems; and
5) implementing the solution that best solves the problem.

As well as being useful as a foundation for public relations theory, pragmatism became a backbone of many other communication plans and strategies—as well as the curriculum by which they are taught.

For decades, public speaking instructors have used this logic, as have those in communication studies who teach strategies of group dynamics. The logic of designing a public speech is that it flows from gaining the audience's attention by pointing to a problem, suggesting possible solutions, offering criteria by which to enact them, demonstrating which is the best one, and providing the rationale for actuation—taking action to solve the problem. Public speaking skill presumes that the speaker will help audiences solve problems. Groups make better decisions, so the logic goes, if they can quickly and effectively engage in motivated, collaborative problem solving.

As theorists advanced understanding of the processes of problem solving as the rationale for human choice and action, they helped public relations theorists solve the problem of knowing how to make organizations (as well as members and publics) agentic, or capable of achieving their missions. That synergism between public relations and process theories is well established and enduring.

Such reasoning presumes that human (and organizational) behavior and interaction transpire primarily, even exclusively, to solve problems. This reasoning is comfortable with process approaches to public relations that feature the processes of problem solving. But theorists and practitioners also draw on Dewey as they ponder the shared, co-created meaning that helps people recognize, define, evaluate, decide, and act to solve problems.

Communitarianism adds another layer of analysis relevant to organizational management and public relations. Starck and Kruckeberg (2001) discuss the normative value of this theory.

Communitarianism emphasizes the paradoxes of relatedness, as societies and communities consist of multiple collectivities—people living and working in groups with varying degrees of agreement, permeability, trust, power, and interdependence (see Hallahan, 2004).

Communitarianism is closely related to *reflective management theory*, which counters traditional management theory by arguing for normative reflection about the role the organization plays in the community as a means for earning its license to operate (legitimacy). Emphasizing legitimacy theory, Holmstrom (2010) reasons that reflection is required for an organization to see itself from the outside—a powerful rationale for public relations: "Reflective decision making views the organization within a larger interdependent societal context and leads to the approach that the environment is to be respected instead of managed" (p. 262).

Relevant Theories that Feature Meaning

Public relations theory and research must never lose sight of the importance of discourse and dialogue, the need to understand how meaning is created, shared, and co-enacted. The legendary public relations scholar Scott Cutlip (1994) underscores the importance of discourse and meaning as he justifies the field: "I held, and still hold, that only through the expertise of public relations can causes, industries, individuals, and institutions make their voice heard in the public forum where thousands of shrill, competing voices daily re-create the Tower of Babel" (p. ix). This view suggests that individuals and organizations speak their minds in the public arena.

Such a view of public discourse reaches back 2500 years to the golden age of Greece. Today, the *Western heritage of rhetoric* continues its keen interest in meaning and language, the role of text in human affairs. This heritage focuses on all forms of symbolic action in which people engage for social, political, and commercial purposes: public debates, ceremonial speaking, and statements by monarchs, church leaders, political activists, and business people. It addresses the role of ideas, contested by advocates for and against various points of view, as the foundation of society. Such discourse includes words, pictures, pageantry, and even statuary and accouterments of state.

In the twentieth century, no louder and clearer voice called attention to the centrality of language—and all symbolic action—in human life than did Kenneth Burke's (1934, 1973). His *dramatistic theory of language* reasoned that the fundamental characteristic of humans, and therefore of human society, is the fact that people are symbol users—and misusers. In this way, they live and organize themselves with varying degrees of merger and division through language. Society is a wrangle, a textual marketplace of ideas.

All of the problems of human existence can be attributed to language and other symbolic systems by which individuals variously create cooperation and competition. Humans, "wordy people" (Burke, 1973), decide matters through statements and counter-statements (words, discourse, dialogue, engagement, all forms of meaning co-creation). Looking as he did so often and so well for the chinks in the armor of society, Burke (1934) warned: "If language is the fundamental instrument of human cooperation, and if there is an 'organic flaw' in the nature of language, we may well expect to find this organic flaw revealing itself through the texture of society" (p. 330).

Another important theory of meaning is *social construction of reality*, "a theoretical perspective to explain how humans account for their worlds" (Gordon & Pellegrin, 2008, p. 104; see Tsetsura, 2010). This theory stresses the proposition that reality—the collective and individual sense and understanding of it—results from definitions that shape human understanding and affect relatedness.

This theme does not argue against the reality of nature being what it is. Calling snow "hot" does not make it so. But calling an animal "cow" can lead to its being raised for slaughter or being given the protection of the Hindu religion, which advocates vegetarianism. The animal is what it is, but the language that "stands between" the human mind and reality predicts how that reality will be understood and what actions are likely or unlikely to occur based on particular definitions and the perspectives or outlooks that they imply. Even social power is largely derived from language, and the definitions and motivations it provides. As the critical organizational communication scholar Stanley Deetz (1982) reasons, "Meaning structures are filled with privileged interests" (p. 139). This problem is one of the many key points discussed by those invested in rhetorical and critical studies.

According to social construction theory, humans "create" the world they live in by the definitions they impose on physical and social reality. Language is inseparable from customs, norms, preferences, laws, rules, and obligations. Without language, there could be no ethics, no preferences of better and worse, right and wrong. Recalling the example of the mother grizzly bear, was what she did morally wrong, or merely nature? Humans use language to construct answers to quandaries of this kind.

Discourse analysis is a sociopolitical theory of language that has been quite influential on the critical theory of public relations. It draws on two lines of thought that have been especially important in Europe since World War II. One is the power of language, which reasons that language is never neutral or purely descriptive, but is always a matter of how power is developed and implemented in society. The other is discourse analysis, which centers on factors that support or impede the quality of dialogue in society (Foucault, 2002). It examines how well people, through their institutions, communicate on matters of shared concern. Is the dialogue wholesome or dysfunctional; is it distorted to serve some and harm others?

One important contributor to discourse analysis is Fairclough (1989, 1992), whose *critical language study* (CLS) has helped support critical theory. His insights add clarity and insight to the understanding of the role meaning plays in the power dynamics of society. He seeks "to help correct a widespread underestimation of the significance of language in the production, maintenance, and change of social relations of power" (Fairclough, 1989, p. 1). Of special interest is the desire "to help increase consciousness of how language contributes to the domination of some people by others, because consciousness is the first step towards emancipation" (p. 1) Public relations requires theory that helps practitioners and academics understand the dynamics of power (note the title of Cutlip's, 1994 book, *The Unseen Power*). CLS reasons that "discourse is the site of power struggles" (Fairclough, 1992, p. 74). Popular discourse often asks: What's in a name? CLS reasons: Often, everything.

Applying this logic to power dynamics inside as well as outside and on behalf of organizations, Clegg, Courpasson, and Philips (2006) call attention to this meaning-centric approach: "organizations and individuals use discourses purposefully to shape the political situation in and through which they can act and perform" (p. 17). Managements use language to shape the power resources that govern operations and employees. Externally, language shapes the power conditions of a business, and even industry, for instance. Thus, it was not surprising that the banking industry came to the George W. Bush administration in 2008 looking for a bailout, which it leveraged because it was "too big to fail."

Public relations theory, in these ways, draws on theories of language to understand how people co-create the meaning that defines and empowers social arrangement and relatedness. At its best, dialogue is fair, open, informed, value-centric, and collaborative. Through discourse, people make enlightened choices and wise decisions in the community interest. As such, theorists are committed to the quality of discourse, transparency, and mutuality of interest and conclusion.

Theorists emphasize how society consists of many voices, in competition to champion ideas through narrative; thus, the role of public relations is to help shape the understanding and motives that empower an organization and ensure its position in society. Customers and other stakeholders may be bent toward the interest of the organization through the effective use of the language of commerce. An important ethical question is whether the organization is also receptive to be bent to the interest of the consumers, in appropriate social exchange and the alignment of interests under conditions of corporate social responsibility (CSR).

Framing theory grew out of mass media theory to explain how reporters socially construct a story, as do public relations professionals. Gitlin (1980) defines frames as "persistent patterns of cognition, interpretation, and presentation, or selection, emphasis, and exclusion, by which symbol-handlers routinely organize discourse" (p. 7). Hallahan (1999) reasons that framing is paradigmatic, a key to "examining the strategic creation of public relations messages and audience responses" (p. 205). The theory explains how vocabularies (even idioms) are skillfully selected and used—by reporters, for instance, to "slant" stories, or by practitioners, to "pitch" them. Thus, in politics, it is easy to find news reporting and commentary that frames stories in conservative terms, liberal-progressive terms, or more centrist terms.

Stakeholder theory, as well as theories of stakeholder participation, offers robust and useful lines of analysis featuring the role of relationships as essential to resource dependency. Freeman (1984) makes this theory central to management and public relations when he argues that managements are likely to fail if they do not consider stakeholders and their impact on the success and failure of an organization's business plan.

Freeman warns that stakeholders are motivated to grant or withhold the stakes that organizations need for success. For that reason, how seriously an organization takes stakeholding into consideration and how it participates constructively with stakeholders can have a substantial impact on its success or failure. As de Bussy (2010) observes, public relations is a discipline that helps organizations engage, through discourse, with their stakeholders to align their interests.

Relevant Theories that Feature Ethics

Chapter 1 asked whether public relations can be socially responsible. That question hinges on whether or not public relations theory must necessarily consider ethics. Critical theory is the closest thing to a coherent statement that organically connects organizational performance to ethical principles, but all other theories are liable to fail to thrive if they are indifferent to ethics. For that reason, several theories of ethics have been used to bolster public relations theory.

Pragmatism, especially as advanced by John Dewey, offers a major ethical underpinning for public relations theory. It reasons that what works (what solves problems) is "good." But is this universally true? One does not have to look far back into history to find examples of effective public relations campaigns in the service of nefarious purposes. Pragmatism is used to determine how "what works" can be improved, made more effective. It asks whether, at least at this moment, people have the best solution to any given problem under consideration—as was discussed earlier in this chapter.

The ethics of pragmatism can be situational. For instance, in the slaughter of cattle, each animal must be killed. Advocates for humane slaughter (which, by the way, is a public relations issue campaign) call for the quickest and most effective killing method, and in many places this is the one required by law. But this logic becomes problematic when applied to public relations. It might advocate, for instance, that the most effective lobbying effort is the one that most quickly and cleanly achieves a preferred end in some controversy. This might fit with one sense of pragmatic ethics, but it flies in the face of the ethics of collaborative pragmatism.

A companion theory of pragmatism, *utilitarianism*, features the ethical quality of an expected outcome as the essence of ethics. Outcomes typically are not sought for themselves; rather, the quality of being utilitarian results from achieving a desirable one. The problem is in getting all parties to agree on outcomes and their relative desirability. For instance, an outcome of war might be peace, which will satisfy the victor but may infuriate the vanquished. Without doubt, utilitarianism has its place in human life and decision making. Radical surgery, for instance, can remove cancerous tissue and save the patient's life, while taking the cars keys from someone too drunk to drive can prevent a fatal accident.

A third theory of ethics is *deontology*. Bowen (2008, 2010), a scholar insightfully engaged in ethical discussions, advocates deontology as the strongest ethical position because it focuses on the ethical principle that guides the practice, rather than the moral principle that justifies its outcome. This theory of ethics reasons "that there are moral principles that are right and wrong independent of their consequences" (2008, p. 169).

This ethic features moral duty—the responsibility and expectation that practitioners and the organizations they represent will enact "the right act" rather than "the effective act." This theory is guided by the ethic of achieving positive regard and goodwill by adhering to principles that are morally just. This ethic features the societal value of what is done. Public interest is a key standard and the rationale for justifying the practice and its role in society based on being and doing what is good.

The topic of *CSR* originated from a robust discussion among business management ethicists and economists in the latter half of the twentieth century. The question they asked is what ethical standards of performance businesses must follow if they are to deserve their license to operate and be legitimate brokers of the public interest. Issues management, spawned during the turbulent 1970s, was founded on business ethics decisions that were pushed by social movement activists from all moral points of the compass relevant to organizational legitimacy.

The question is, what should an organization do and say to meet or exceed community standards—the ethical expectations held by stakeholders. CSR is the rationale for ethical performance; as Ihlen, Bartlett, and May (2011) observe, "Corporate activities are increasingly scrutinized for their effect on society and the environment" (p. 3).

Analysis of the ethics of public relations has argued that senior practitioners must be the ethical conscience of the organizations they represent and help manage. As such, ethical theory must inform public relations theory, research, and best practices. This logic seems quite relevant to publicity and promotion. The next section offers brief insights into the theoretical foundations of this part of the practice.

Relevant Theories that Support Publicity and Promotion

Modern public relations theory and research often slight publicity and promotion. Despite the prominence of these strategic options in the toolbox of practitioners, they are often treated as marketing communication (and not "true" public relations) or shunned because they do not fall within theoretical boundaries of some public relations scholars. And, some worry, they are based on questionable ethics, such as spin.

The rationale for publicity is the need by organizations, and even individuals, to make some matter public (Hallahan, 2010). This can be accomplished with information about a product or service, but it might be a cause or a problem that needs public policy attention—as Picasso's mural "Guernica" gave to the Nazi bombing atrocity of the Basque city in 1937 (Xifra & Heath, 2018). Promotion is a companion to publicity; it sustains publicity efforts over time as a campaign. It starts with gaining awareness, perhaps helping publics to recognize a problem that deserves to be solved.

Hallahan (2010) describes in great detail how publicity is grounded in persuasion theory, relationship theory, public policy and dispute theory, and crisis management and communication theory. Throughout the discussion runs a steady and informed commitment to ethical responsibility, because calling attention to and promoting some matter requires ethical oversight.

Many of the theoretical foundations for public relations mentioned in this section are relevant to publicity. It draws on theories of process and meaning, as well as rhetorical, critical, and ethical judgment. Because of this extensive theoretical foundation, publicity must be justified, rather than dismissed, as a vital part of the public relations arsenal.

Summary

The point to be drawn from the various theories discussed in this section is that the discipline of public relations is built on fertile ground. It requires ongoing work to solve important intellectual problems with practical consequences. The groundwork draws from insights about strategic processes, the co-creation of meaning, and the enactment of ethical principle. Such theoretical discussions are mined to understand and improve best practices.

Theories that feature strategic process, meaning, ethics, and even publicity/promotion can serve to create and guide communicative organizations—the case used to open the chapter. Without doubt, many systems need to work together to achieve the balance required for resource sustainability. No effort can be successful in the absence of socially constructed and widely shared definitions, especially ones regarding sustainability. The battle to achieve sustainability is an ethical, deontological one, and one with pragmatic and utilitarian implications. In this endeavor, excellence theory—as well as contingency, rhetorical, and critical theories—offers insights that are relevant to making organizations sufficiently communicative to advance the cause of sustainability as achievable through change management. Organizations exerting leadership on sustainability need to set examples and to inform and inspire others to work together to achieve sustainability.

Given this summary, on what specifics might a student of this topic call in the effort to define and implement a communicative organization?

Conclusion

Theory can inform, confirm, and correct best practices, as well as challenge the entire profession to consider new directions and approaches. Theories constitute a focused and systematic effort by researchers and professionals to collaborate in order to make organizations more reflective, communicative, and socially responsible.

As this chapter closes, the reader is encouraged to think back to the opening case. Vision 2050 gave practitioners and academics the incentive to call on best practices and public relations theory in order to draft the Stockholm Accords. The Accords in turn challenged them to advise organizations on how to support communicatively the goal of achieving global sustainability. This is not trivial to human destiny.

Challenge to the Reader

Consider how well the Stockholm Accords and the Melbourne Mandate draw on best practice and public relations theory to help organizations be sufficiently communicative to achieve sustainability. Other disciplines also engage in meeting this challenge. Management theories help organizations better manage themselves to that end. Engineers are asked to know and apply theory to create and improve products; sustainability requires new products and services, and improvements to existing ones. Agriculture experts call on soil and plant science to refine farming techniques to produce more and healthier agricultural products for a huge and growing population.

The discussion that resulted in the Accords laid the foundation for another attempt at operationalizing organizational communicativeness. Reflecting on how the Melbourne Mandate improved the Stockholm Accords, Gregory (2015) acknowledges that "public relations was still struggling to be taken as essential to business and society in any more than a tactical role" (p. 601). Theory and research can help achieve and justify the normative role that public relations professionals may play in changing global and local societies to achieve sustainability. What drives organizational change is a constant monitoring and awareness of the performance standards required to earn the license to operate. Such a license derives from the value an organization creates for its stakeholders, and to the benefit of society at large. Organizations must use their ability and resources to benefit others.

To accomplish these outcomes, theory inspired the authors of the Mandate to recommend that public relations and communication professionals do the following:

- Shape organizational character by enhancing, maintaining, and protecting their organization's authenticity—its reputation for consistently communicating truth and meriting trust.
- Be guardians of the organization's character and values by providing feedback on how they are being judged and received, and communicating this to the stakeholders.
- Ensure organizational values guide decisions and actions internally, and that externally they are recognized and understood by stakeholders.
- Evaluate the organization against these values by monitoring stakeholder views and discussions of it.
- Help leaders uphold and communicate these values to inspire stakeholders to follow, support, or change behavior.
- Help leaders understand where they need to change, and ensure they are equipped to be effective communicators and to embrace communication responsibilities.
- Work with senior managers, human resource professionals, and other management functions to ensure that structures, processes, and ways of working reflect the claimed organizational character and values.
- Research and create initiatives that bring the culture to life, recommending the most appropriate communication channels, content, and tone. (Gregory, 2015, p. 602)

Reflection on the challenges introduced in this chapter—and on the Accords and Mandate—should demonstrate to the reader the value public relations can bring to organizations, stakeholders, and society. Good outcomes require a thorough understanding and wise consideration of what value theory adds to professional practice. Central to this discussion is the reality that communicativeness is both a management and a communication challenge, the two disciplines being inseparable.

Chapter Summary

Chapter 2 has discussed the nature and role of theory, both in general and as they relate to improving public relations by enriching its contributions to society. The discussion featured a definition of theory along with its companion and component terms, concept, variable, and hypothesis. The chapter reasoned that public relations theory does not grow out of thin air, but is crafted from case observations and knowledge of theories related to organizational and societal efficacy and agency.

Some theories supporting public relations feature process; others call attention to the importance of language, other symbol systems, co-created meaning, and the social construction of reality. But neither process nor meaning can advance the discipline without a consideration of ethics. However intellectually enriching this discussion, its ultimate value lies in its ability to inform, shape, and confirm best practices—a profession at work.

Discussion Questions
1   What is theory? Why is it important to the practice and study of public relations?
2   What terminology is needed to understand and appreciate theory and its component parts as a means for thinking and acting strategically?
3   How and why does public relations draw inspiration and analysis from related theories?
4   Is it good that the theories relevant to public relations feature process, co-created meaning, and ethics?
5   How can the theories that support public relations combine to help organizations be communicative?

References

Bowen, S. A. (2008). Foundations in moral philosophy for public relations ethics. In T. L. Hansen-Horn & B. D. Neff (Eds.), *Public relations: From theory to practice* (pp. 160–180). Boston, MA: Pearson.

Bowen, S. A. (2010). The nature of good in public relations: What should be its normative ethic? In R. L. Heath (Ed.), *SAGE handbook of public relations* (pp. 569–584). Thousand Oaks, CA: Sage.

Burke, K. (1934). The meaning of C. K. Ogden. *New Republic, 78*, 328–331.

Burke, K. (1973). *The philosophy of literary form* (3rd ed.). Berkeley, CA: University of California Press.

Cheney, G., & Christensen, L. T. (2001). Public relations as contested terrain. In R. L. Heath (Ed.), *Handbook of public relations* (pp. 167–182). Thousand Oaks, CA: Sage.

Clegg, S. R., Courpasson, D., & Phillips, N. (2006). *Power and organizations*. Thousand Oaks, CA: Sage.

Cutlip, S. M. (1994). *The unseen power: Public relations. A history*. Hillsdale, NJ: Lawrence Erlbaum.

de Bussy, N. M. (2010). Dialogue as a basis for stakeholder engagement: Defining and measuring the core competencies. In R. L. Heath (Ed.), *SAGE handbook of public relations* (pp. 127–144). Thousand Oaks, CA: Sage.

Deetz, S. A. (1982). Critical interpretive research in organizational communication. *Western Journal of Speech Communication, 46*, 131–149.

Edwards, L. (2006). Rethinking power in public relations. *Public Relations Review, 32*, 229–231.

Fairclough, N. (1989). *Language and power*. London: Longman.

Fairclough, N. (1992). *Discourse and social change*. Cambridge: Polity Press.

Foucault, M. (2002). *The archeology of knowledge*, trans. A. M. Sheridan Smith. London and New York: Routledge.

Freeman, R. E. (1984). *Strategic management: A stakeholder approach*. Boston, MA: Pitman.

Fretwurst, B. (2008). Hypothesis. In W. Donsbach (Ed.), *The international encyclopedia of communication* (pp. 2154–2158). Malden, MA: Blackwell Publishing.

Gitlin, T. (1980). *The whole world is watching*. Berkeley, CA: University of California Press.

Gordon, J., & Pellegrin, P. (2008). Social constructionism and public relations. In T. L. Hansen-Horn & B. D. Neff (Eds.), *Public relations: From theory to practice* (pp. 104–121). Boston, MA: Pearson.

Gregory, A. (2015). Practitioner-leaders' representation of roles: The Melbourne Mandate. *Public Relations Review, 41*, 598–606.

Hallahan, K. (1999). Seven models of framing: Implications for public relations. *Journal of Public Relations Research, 11*, 205–242.

Hallahan, K. (2004). "Community" as a foundation for public relations theory and practice. In P. J. Kalbfleisch (Ed.), *Communication yearbook 24* (pp. 233–279). Mahwah, NJ: Lawrence Erlbaum.

Hallahan, K. (2010). Being public: Publicity as public relations. In R. L. Heath (Ed.), *SAGE handbook of public relations* (pp. 523–546). Thousand Oaks, CA: Sage.

Hansen-Horn, T., & Neff, B. D. (2008). Preface. In T. L. Hansen-Horn & B. D. Neff (Eds.), *Public relations: From theory to practice* (pp. xvii). Boston, MA: Pearson.

Hazleton, V., Jr., & Botan, C. H. (1989). The role of theory in public relations. In C. H. Botan & V. Hazleton, Jr. (Eds.), *Public relations theory* (pp. 3–15). Hillsdale, NJ: Lawrence Erlbaum Associates.

Hill, J. W. (1963). *The making of a public relations man.* New York: David McKay.

Holladay, S. J., & Coombs, W. T. (2013). Public relations literacy: Developing critical consumers of public relations. *Public Relations Inquiry*, *2*, 125–146.

Holmstrom, S. (2010). Reflective management: Seeing the organization as if from the outside. In R. L. Heath (Ed.), *SAGE handbook of public relations* (pp. 261–276). Thousand Oaks, CA: Sage.

Ihlen, O., Bartlett, J. L., & May, S. (2011). Corporate social responsibility and communication. In O. Ihlen, J. L. Bartlett, & S. May (Eds.), *Handbook of communication and corporate social responsibility* (pp. 3–22). Chichester: John Wiley & Sons.

Kuhn, T. S. (1970). *The structure of scientific revolutions* (2nd ed.). Chicago, IL: University of Chicago Press.

Lammers, J. C., & Barbour, J. B. (2006). An institutional theory of organizational communication. *Communication Theory*, *16*, 356–377.

Lynham, S. A. (2002). The general method of theory-building research in applied disciplines. *Advances in Developing Human Resources*, *4*(3), 221–241.

McKie, D. (2001). Updating public relations: "New science," research paradigms, and uneven developments. In R. L. Heath (Ed.), *Handbook of public relations* (pp. 75–91). Thousand Oaks, CA: Sage.

McQuail, D. (1987). Functions of communication: A nonfunctionalist overview. In C. R. Berger & S. H. Chaffee (Eds.), *Handbook of communication science* (pp. 327–349). Thousand Oaks, CA: Sage.

Oswald, A. J., & Winkelmann, R. (2019). Lottery wins and satisfaction: Overturning Brickman in modern longitudinal data on Germany. In M. Rojas (Ed.), *The economics of happiness: How the Easterling Paradox transformed our understanding of well-being and progress* (pp. 57–84). Cham: Springer.

Sha, B.-L. (2018). Editor's essay: Thoughts on theory. *Journal of Public Relations Review*, *30*, 1–4.

Starck, K., & Kruckeberg, D. (2001). Public relations and community: A reconstructed theory revisited. In R. L. Heath (Ed.), *Handbook of public relations* (pp. 51–60). Thousand Oaks, CA: Sage.

Tsetsura, K. (2010). Social construction and public relations. In R. L. Heath (Ed.), *SAGE handbook of public relations* (pp. 163–176). Thousand Oaks, CA: Sage.

Vos, T. P. (2011). Explaining the origins of public relations: Logics of historical explanation. *Journal of Public Relations Research*, *23*, 119–140.

World Public Relations Forum. (2010). The Stockholm Accords. Available from http://web.archive.org/web/20100714103439/http://www.wprf2010.se/wp-content/uploads/2010/05/Stockholm-Accords-final-version.pdf (accessed May 20, 2020).

World Public Relations Forum. (2012). The Melbourne Mandate. Available from https://www.globalalliancepr.org/s/Melbourne-Mandate-Text-final.pdf (accessed May 20, 2020).

Xifra, J., & Heath, R. L. (2018). Publicizing Atrocity and Legitimizing Outrage: Picasso's Guernica. *Public Relations Review*, *44*, 28–36.

3

Excellence Theory: Public Relations as Strategic Communication Management

Introduction

Excellence theory was spawned in the 1960s as the defining work of a research team led by James and Larissa Grunig. Since then, and through many iterations, it has become a pillar of public relations theory and research. Offered as the foundation for a general theory of public relations as a strategic management function, excellence theory proposes standards, dimensions, practices, and benchmarks that differentiate "excellent" public relations from less normatively sound explanations of what the practice should be and its role in the success of organizations. It has evolved to empower public relations professionals to normatively guide managers' strategic, situational responses as sound relationship management between them and key publics so as to mitigate conflict. Thus, excellence has become the defining concept of the behavioral, strategic management paradigm.

Reflecting on the trajectory of the theory, James Grunig (2006) concluded that "the greatest challenge for scholars now is to learn how to institutionalize strategic public relations as an ongoing, accepted practice in most organizations" (p. 151). To meet this challenge, excellence theorists built a normative rationale, featuring situationally relevant problem-solving processes and championing the role of relationship quality in organizational success. In order to support this general theory, they presented research to justify the organizational position and decision-making role of public relations practitioners in the corporate, strategic management structure. Metaphorically, the theory is the forest and several other mid-range theories constitute the trees (Kim & Ni, 2010). It is currently featured as "the behavior, strategic management approach to public relations" (Kim & Ni, 2010, p. 54; see also Kim & Grunig, 2011; Grunig, 2018).

The key to achieving professionalism is the ability of research and theory to empower "public relations managers to negotiate with clients to change organizational behavior—helping organizations to rise above the 'wrangle in the market-place' to consider the interests of publics as well as their own interests" (Grunig, 2000, p. 23). By 2018, according to James Grunig, this discussion had formulated a paradigm: "The strategic behavioral paradigm resulted from a research tradition that conceptualizes public relations as a strategic management function rather than as a messaging, publicity, and media relations function—that is, a symbolic-interpretive paradigm" (2018, p. 1457).

Early in his academic career, Grunig (1966, 1968) applied ideas drawn from microeconomics and behavioral economics that had been advanced by John Dewey. He reasoned that Dewey's pragmatism provided support for the development of an efficient, cost-effective, and normative approach to communication. To that end, he worked to reconcile two of Dewey's themes: "Although the

Public Relations Theory: Capabilities and Competencies, First Edition. Jae-Hwa Shin and Robert L. Heath.
© 2021 John Wiley & Sons, Inc. Published 2021 by John Wiley & Sons, Inc.

microeconomic theories assumed rationality, the behavioral economic theories did not" (Kim & Grunig, 2011, p. 124). This tension required the support of a theory of problem solving, decision making, and communication management. The roles of information exchange, communication management, problem solving, and organizational strategic (behavioral) adjustment became hallmarks of excellence theory.

The theory draws on institutional theory "to identify how an organization's structure, environment, history, size, and technology affect the practice of public relations" (Grunig & Grunig, 2008, p. 328). In the tradition of institutional theory, public relations excellence was conceptualized and researched with the purpose of helping managements (members of the dominant coalition) to organize to behaviorally adjust to publics' expectations. This corporate-centric theory looks for strategic and ethical means by which organizations can increase their return on investment through building relationships and minimizing conflict.

Development of this theory began with James Grunig's research-based efforts to communicate improved agricultural practices to Colombian farmers. That research led him to consider how institutions and any public can work together (collaborate) to solve problems, including the factors that hinder and facilitate cooperation. Such challenges led conceptually to the situational theory of publics and eventually to the situational theory of problem solving. On this foundation, excellence theory came to conceive public relations as a management function, which at its best helps organizations and publics—as well as stakeholders—to adjust to one another in order to achieve harmony and goodwill (Dozier & Grunig, 1992). This reasoning justified a strategic management approach to public relations enacted as strategic planning and implementation through a strategic technician, tactical approach.

James Grunig and Todd Hunt laid the cornerstone statements of this theory when they published *Managing Public Relations* (1984), exploring the history of strategic practices and the measures organizations need to apply to be effective. This work helped create a vibrant era in the development of public relations research and theory. Its legendary four-dimension model became a dominant template for detailed attention by academics and practitioners for the next decade. The model compared one-way asymmetrical, one-way symmetrical, two-way asymmetrical, and two-way symmetrical communication as rationalized by general systems theory.

Public relations' strategic communication management role in society is to help some entity achieve its mission and vision. Serving to make individuals and organizations more able to achieve their goals, academics ask in various ways how the practice can do more to earn organizations the right to operate without dominating and manipulating customers, neighbors, and other publics and stakeholders.

By the end of this chapter, readers should understand the logic and concepts that characterize and support the excellence theory of public relations and communication management. In a fundamental sense, this normative theory guides the practice of public relations as a strategic, behavioral adjustment rather than merely a symbolic process. In addition, situational theory advises practitioners to improve the quality of communication and relationship as bridging rather than buffering between the organization and its key publics.

Questions to Frame the Discussion of Excellence Theory

- What assumptions and key concepts support excellence theory?
- What are the four models of excellence theory and its modification based on criticism?
- What is the strategic advantage of being excellent? What are the costs of not being excellent?

- Why does excellence theory consider two-way symmetrical communication superior to its alternatives? Are there circumstances where any of the other options is superior?
- What organizational management positions should practitioners hold and what roles should they perform in the decision-making processes of an organization?
- Are the situational desire for information, the ability to solve problems, and the ability to act as desired in the face of constraint among the key characteristics of humans? If so, why is this the case and what are the implications for public relations?
- How can managements use publics' desires for information to solve problems in order to increase the efficiency and effectiveness of their communication?
- Does the strategic use of a public's involvement, problem recognition, and constraint recognition affect its ability to receive and process information?
- What are organization–public relationships (OPRs)? What dimensions affect the quality of relationships, and can they be used to measure it?

Key Themes

- Excellence theory conceptualizes public relations as a normative and strategic behavioral, communication management function.
- Excellence theory has sought to replace a symbolic management, persuasion approach to public relations as image building with one that champions proactive action such as information sharing, behavioral management, and relationship building.
- Excellence—a broad, general theory—begins with the general premise that public relations adds value to organizations and to the society where they operate.
- To add value, two-way symmetrical communication is preferred in comparison to the alternatives: one-way symmetrical, one-way asymmetrical, and two-way asymmetrical, which are identified as less effective and less ethical for building useful relationships.
- By featuring problem solving as a core concept for communication management, middle-range theories explain the factors that influence how people obtain and use information to solve problems.
- As one of its core conceptualizations, excellence theory features humans as problem solvers who organize themselves (based on relationship quality) and communicate to seek, acquire, and process information to that end.
- Situational theory can guide practitioners' ability to identify publics based on their recognition of a problem and level of involvement, as well as on constraint recognition as a precursor to their being active communicators who seek information and attend to and process it.
- Through adjustive behavior, organizations should avoid the tendency to buffer themselves from criticism and instead build bridges with stakeholder critics through open, cooperative, and collaborative communication.
- The behavioral, strategic management approach advocates that public relations advance from being a mere occupation to being a profession that creates strategic management value. Public relations benefits society by building and strengthening relationships through mutual adaptation among social actors.
- Public relations theory, based on research, should help the field of public relations advance in terms of professional, managerial status.

Excellence Theory: Public Relations Through Communication Management

Excellence theory developed from a keen desire to know how organizations should communicate effectively and help publics get the information they want and need to solve problems expeditiously. As they encounter organizations that affect their lives, publics become aware of problems; such awareness motivates them to share their concerns with others, and even to punish organizations by withholding goodwill. Left unsolved, problems can escalate into conflict and crisis.

These hallmark themes guided James and Larissa Grunig's (Grunig & Grunig, 2008; Grunig, Grunig, & Ehling, 1992) definition of excellence theory to specify "how public relations makes organizations more effective, how it is organized and managed when it contributes most to organizational effectiveness (i.e., when it is excellent), the conditions in organizations and their environments that make organizations more effective, and how the monetary {value} of excellent public relations can be determined" (p. 27). Rather than taking a logical positivistic approach to theory as the description of reality, this definition was built on the normative rationale for theory building as a way to improve organizational performance. Normatively, excellent public relations can reduce the likelihood of conflict by engaging in research to determine whether publics believe that problems exist and, if so, how these problems can be solved by supplying information and making strategic behavior adjustments to please or at least mollify the publics—whose goodwill each organization needs for its success.

If these norms are essential to organizational success, more than one theory is capable of advancing them. As James Grunig (2006) acknowledged, other theories can offer insights in order to strategically solve problems. For that reason, excellence has its merits, but other theories need not be proposed to tear down this edifice before, or as a means for, building another theory: "Multiple edifices can exist side by side, and all can be useful for solving the same or different problems" (p. 153). This conclusion is possible because public relations theory is normatively prescriptive, rather than a logically positivistic description of "what is."

Exploring this reasoning, Chapter 3 explains the principles of organizational excellence as a strategic behavioral paradigm. This exploration begins by noting how excellence is grounded in systems theory, augmented by institutional theory's interest in structures, functions, and rituals. Systems theory features the positive impact achieved when information flows easily and efficiently within and between systems, so that people get the information they want when the want it. Various systems use this information to adjust to one another and so be in harmony, or balance. Building on systems theory, institutional theory features the structures, functions, and rituals of adjustment and communication management that help each organization and its publics know how best to interact with and adjust to one another. (Both of these supporting theories are discussed in Chapter 2.)

Excellence theory formed around a commitment to key publics' satisfaction by understanding how to achieve organizational goals by fostering goodwill. Central to that effort is the strategic need to adjust an organization's policies and performance so they align with various publics' needs to solve problems that, if left unresolved, can confound relationships. By coming into symmetry, the organization and its publics benefit one another. Excellence theory addresses the conditions that encourage the alignments needed for a symmetrical relationship.

Such reasoning supports what excellence theorists call a general theory of public relations (see Grunig, 2006). First, public relations managers need to be part of each organization's dominant coalition—those organization members who either are in or have the ear of upper management and are respected for their knowledge of communication management. Second, excellent organizations use situationally adjusted, strategic communication to help publics receive and process the information they need to solve problems effectively and take actions with minimal constraint. Third, two-way symmetrical communication can help organizations build and maintain sound relationships with constituent publics, both internal and external to the organization. Fourth, organizations can increase relationship quality by behaviorally adjusting to their publics.

Case Study: A Regional Bank in Texas—Success Through Excellent, Two-Way Symmetrical Public Relations

Effective businesses engage in public relations to gauge and adjust (strategic management) to the nuances of their publics' interests. This adjustive sensitivity is designed to increase business effectiveness.

The following case highlights these principles by examining the strategic planning and operations of a regional bank in Texas. Operating through multiple branches in several cities, the bank's mission and vision proclaim that its success will be achieved by offering competitive banking products and high-quality service tailored to small and medium-sized businesses.

The Executive Vice President for Public Relations and Marketing Communications is part of the bank's executive team, the dominant coalition. As a member of that team, in conjunction with external financial and public policy/legal counsel, this senior public relations professional conducts an ongoing, multifaceted research program to study customer satisfaction and public sentiment toward banking. The team monitors the comparative level of satisfaction expressed by individual and small-business customers in the communities where the bank operates. These customers are the targets of the organization's decision-making process.

The adjustive process requires strategic community relations, which for this bank is more than a symbolic polishing of its image. It works to use community relations to build a stronger business environment in the community, one that fosters the small-business interests and activities of its customers. The bank's executives believe that what is good for the communities where it operates is good for the small businesses who need a bank with competitive products and excellent, customer-focused service. Thus, the bank supports the arts in ways that elevate the quality of life in these communities (which has business advantages). It offers free seminars on small-business success and helps fund business curricula in high schools and universities, especially coursework to help entrepreneurs. And it lobbies for city services that will help small businesses.

Another aspect of its research agenda addresses its competitive positioning versus other banks in regard to customer service, banking products, and fees. Ongoing research reveals that customer service quality tends to be a stronger predictor of customer satisfaction, loyalty, and brand equity/reputation than are products per se. This means that the quality of the relationship with the bank's primary customers—small and medium-sized businesses—is the best predictor of their loyalty. A key measure used in this research asks respondents to judge whether the bank's products and customer service help their businesses to survive and prosper. This sort of measurement is vital, since the bank believes that it must add value to its customers' businesses by having knowledgeable and responsive bankers who can help them solve their business problems.

Because anticipating customer needs and delivering timely service is a primary factor in customer loyalty and satisfaction, constant monitoring of these activities helps increase the bank's responsiveness and efficiency. This banking service conforms to systems theory, since the bank asks its bankers to provide information easily and efficiently on an as-needed basis in an open system. Such measures are included in employee reward, especially for the "professional bankers" who are expected to build and maintain a personal, professional relationship with each of their clients. These bankers, assigned to individual small-business customers, are a crucial part of the bank's public relations. They are educated and motivated to build and maintain effective and aligned interests with customers. Small-business customers want to know who to call when questions need answers and for advice on how to tailor banking services to their specific needs. They do not want to be told, "We'll call you back," or to talk to an answering machine. They believe that banking should not be a chore, but a service that adds value to their efforts to be successful. In keeping with the norms of excellence theory, bankers are required and trained to look for problems, especially those encountered by small-business customers. They are required to help solve the banking and finance problems of their customers and to remove or lessen constraints between banker and customer.

Questions for Consideration

- Is the senior public relations practitioner a valued member of the bank's senior decision makers? If so, why does this status benefit the bank, its customers, and the community in which it operates?
- Does this person help the bank to listen to and understand the communities where it operates, public policy and opinion, and its customer satisfaction? Do they help strategically plan effective communication that makes information easy to obtain for customers in order that they can efficiently solve their banking and operational problems? Does it help create the internal structures and functions needed to educate and motivate bankers to make the bank's mission and vision a reality through customer relations?
- Is the communication two-way and symmetrical with customers and the community at large?

Excellence as a Rationale for Public Relations

The term "excellence" was adopted by the team that assembled in the 1980s to help define and focus a research project funded by the International Association of Business Communicators (IABC). The team consisted of communication professionals and academics, primarily associated with the University of Maryland. During planning discussions, it drew inspiration for the title— "excellence"—and key theme of its project from the 1990s' robust commitment to improving institutions' productivity and quality. This analysis, built on foundations laid in the 1980s, featured two-way symmetrical public relations as ethical, effective, and thus excellent public relations.

Throughout the 1990s, senior executives, consultants, and academics wondered which productivity and quality factors best predicted why some organizations achieved management excellence. Although particularly interested in improving business management, this discussion did not neglect strategies to improve government agencies and nonprofit organizations, and even activists (Grunig, 2000, 2008). Applying productivity and quality standards, the IABC project reasoned that excellent organizations had excellent public relations that produced measurable benefit.

Drawing on the spirit of the time, excellence was defined "as a set of characteristics of a public relations function that were correlated with organizational effectiveness." Framed as the attributes and practices needed to "build quality, long-term relationships with strategic constituencies," excellence theorists reasoned that organizational effectiveness occurs "when an organization achieves goals chosen in consultation with stakeholders—goals that serve the interests of both the organization and these strategic constituencies" (Grunig & Grunig, 2008, p. 328; see also Grunig, 2018). The virtue of excellent public relations is reduced cost—an accounting measure of success—due to unresolved or protracted conflicts.

As the "excellence" team explored this strategic management challenge from a public relations perspective, it concluded that several factors falling under the purview of public relations managers can contribute to an organization's success. Thus, public relations became conceptualized and studied as one of several strategic functions and structures organizations need to be effective. Two foundational concepts associated with this theory are symmetry and linkages between an organization and its publics.

Four Models (Dimensions): Symmetry to the Rescue

James Grunig and Todd Hunt offered the four-part model, the signature of their theory, in 1984. Each of the four models (later called dimensions) of public relations featured the flow of communication (one-way out from the company or two-way interaction) and the qualitative balance of the interaction (asymmetry or symmetry).

With these four dimensions, Grunig and Hunt launched the tradition of parsing out the normative functionality of public relations by using the models as independent variables. Excellence theorists reasoned, then, that each of these dimensions produces an outcome (dependent variable) that is more or less superior to those of the others. This logic was framed as normative theory such that each of the four models can be scaled as a hierarchy based on norms of effectiveness and ethics. With that reasoning, proponents differentiated four options:

- *One-way asymmetrical:* Press agentry/publicity.
- *One-way symmetrical:* Public information.
- *Two-way asymmetrical:* Scientific persuasion.
- *Two-way symmetrical:* Cooriented, mutual adjustment and influence.

The model captures the ethical battle regarding forms of communication: information dissemination and exchange, propaganda, persuasion, advocacy, and conflict resolution. It addresses the challenge of control, based on whether a model of public relations favors the organization or serves the mutual benefit of both parties.

Press agentry/publicity (one-way asymmetrical) is linked to propaganda, which involves one-way dissemination of information and not necessarily scientific or truthful information. Practitioners who use this option sometimes treat truth as unessential, even trivial, to achieving an organization's goals. It employs half-truths and incomplete and distorted information.

Public information (one-way symmetrical) is featured when organizations disseminate information to publics; truth is important and serves a valuable purpose for both entities. Information is provided to influence, but without a persuasive (propaganda) intent. The quality of information determines how well people can use it to make judgments and solve problems.

Scientific persuasion (two-way asymmetrical) leads to unbalanced effects whereby an organization uses communication appeals to benefit itself more than its publics. It is normatively less excellent because the organization strategically affects (persuades) the publics but is unaffected by them. The theme of scientific persuasion underscores the problem of using research to determine what ideas a public will accept or resist, rather than listening to (often through research on) that public as a first step toward being influenced by it. With such insight, practitioners can present messages that are accepted and change publics' opinions without encountering resistance. Practitioners who employ this model presume that the attitudes they prefer are better than those held by publics.

Finally, cooriented, mutual adjustment and influence (two-way symmetrical) aspires to produce mutual understanding and balanced (mutual) influence/effects between an organization and its publics and stakeholders. This option presumes that each public—the positions and concerns it holds—can affect the organization. Through research, the organization can strategically change its policies and practices to behaviorally adjust to its publics' concerns. It can respond to their information needs. To avoid or eliminate conflict, it can adjust its behavior and correct how it operates to fit more comfortably within their expectations. Thus, symmetrical two-way communication builds and enhances relationships.

Through such reasoning, the four-dimension model has been refined, including by adopting a mixed-motive perspective that allows for conflict resolution. By 2008, it would be stated thus: A symmetrical and two-way public relations is that strategic approach which relies on "collaboration and public participation." Arguably less effective and less ethical, the other three options exhibit the following characteristics:

> press agentry (emphasizing only favourable publicity), public information (disclosing accurate information but engaging in no research or other form of two-way communication), or two-way asymmetrical (emphasizing only the interests of the organization and not those of publics). (Grunig & Grunig, 2008, p. 337)

In these ways, the theory was designed to cover an array of communication and relationship tensions, objectives, and strategic options.

As rational and ethical as excellence theory is presented to be, it is not without its challengers. For example, critics wonder whether two-way symmetry is always the best option. What about when we are dealing with an individual or matter that is morally and socially reprehensible? Under such conditions—say, in dealing with Somali pirates—should practitioners opt for a two-way symmetrical solution? One of the tensions between admirers and critics of the model lies in whether this four-part parsing of public relations options has sufficient ethical grounding to advise practitioners in knowing when and how asymmetry—even advocacy—may be (or is) ethically superior.

To use another example, what should excellent management do if its policy of hiring people of color and buying agricultural products from them—as well as selling products to them—is opposed by activist groups such as the Ku Klux Klan? One perplexity of the four-dimension model is its ability to guide practice when community opinions and interests (those of several publics) are divided or even quite at odds. For instance, what if Hitler and the members of his dominant coalition requested favorable relationships with a company—and recommended exclusion of Jews as part of the bargain? So, we have one challenge to the model: Can and when should asymmetry be preferred to symmetry? Stated in a different way, do all publics deserve a symmetrical two-way relationship, or in important instances is one-way or two-way asymmetry preferred? If so, what is the rationale for the strategic and ethical choice? Because excellence relies on systems theory, there is no inherent reasoning for an ethical solution to such quandaries. Toth (2009) argues that under such conflict situations, if a "Hiltler" does not reciprocate an organization's two-way symmetrical approach, the organization may engage in advocacy.

Of related interest is the following question: What if, in the face of efforts to engage two-way and symmetrically, key activist or governmental publics refuse to reciprocate in a manner that frustrates collaborative decision making? In short, does symmetry demand compromise and negotiation, even in the face of a win–lose-oriented adversary? When committed to being socially responsible, what are the standards by which social responsibility is calculated?

Making an important contribution to the normative quandary of asymmetry and symmetry, Toth (2009) reasons that relations are excellent if they are dialogic. She notes how Grunig (2001) conceptualized symmetry as "a process oriented experience of collaboration, of mixed motives, collaborative advocacy, and cooperative antagonism" (Toth, 2009, p. 56). With these paradoxes to consider, Grunig (2001) averred that he might have been more conceptually correct to use an alternative term to "symmetry" as he sought to define and study the tensions that arise when efforts are made to balance "self-interests with the interests of others" as "a give-and-take process that can waver between advocacy and collaboration" (p. 28). As this dialogic approach to symmetry aspires, practitioners:

> must listen as well as argue. This does not mean, however, that they do not argue or attempt to persuade. Rather they must consistently remind themselves and management that they might not be right and, indeed, that their organizations might be better off if they listen to others. (p. 28)

As the theory rests on the tensions between asymmetry and symmetry, analysis along these lines adds clarity to the strategic management and communicative role of organizations through public relations. Such paradoxes, however, lend support to the efforts of proponents of other theories of public relations, to be explored in subsequent chapters.

As such, these two dimensions may not be the best when approached as binary and mutually exclusive but strategic options given the ethics and moral implications of a particular situation. Such analysis "supports the notion that asymmetry and symmetry (or advocacy and collaboration) work in tandem in excellent public relations. Therefore, we now seem to have a much better developed theory of symmetrical (dialogic, collaborative advocacy) public relations that should serve well as a model for research, teaching, and practice of public relations during the 21st century" (Grunig, 2001, p. 30).

By 2010, two-way symmetry was advocated as setting the standard by which other approaches should be judged: "The attempts of two-way symmetrical public relations to balance the interests of the organization and its publics are based on research and use communication to manage conflict and cultivate relationships with strategic publics" (Kim & Ni, 2010, p. 38). This preferred approach to the practice not only resulted from (or required that) public relations persons participate in the management team, but also produced greater engagement and professional job satisfaction. As the theory reasoned, such practitioners "are loyal to both their employers and the publics of their organizations" (p. 38).

One dimension has continued to feature communication directionality: one-way versus two-way is typically conceptualized as information flow—information sharing—leading to mutual understanding. This dimension is complemented by purpose: "a continuum from an asymmetrical to symmetrical *purpose* of public relations" (Kim & Ni, 2010, p. 39; italics in original). Given the process emphasis in this theory, it is not entirely clear how purpose substitutes for and provides the definition or critical guidelines by which practitioners and others judge the quality and underlying ethics of an interaction between organization and publics that is strategic and adjustive.

Keen to understand and recommend two-way approaches, the theory matured to focus on the communication context or channels of mass-mediated, interpersonal (whether complementary or at odds), and ethical dimensions (Grunig, 2001). Thus, by 2010, theorists proposed that we have "two continua indicating the frequency of using mediated or interpersonal *techniques* or both, depending on the situation and public" (Kim & Ni, 2010, p. 39; italics in original).

Facing critiques of his work on the idealism of symmetrical public relations, Grunig (2001) suggested a modified yet equatable version of symmetric communication on a continuum, which he called a mixed-motive model. Continuing to feature the relevance of models—or dimensions—symmetry has proved to be both a staking point and a point of attack. Thus, excellence researchers "changed their conceptualization of symmetry by proposing a new model of symmetry as two-way practice that recognizes the potential strategic influence of both organizations and publics in seeking to resolve problems toward a possible win–win zone" (Toth, 2009, p. 56).

One response to the ethics paradox of when and why asymmetry and even advocacy might be strategically superior depends on the worldview of practitioners. This led to a judgment that the asymmetrical worldview is more closed, more self-affirming, and less responsive than the symmetrical, and that the incentive toward asymmetry is one of self-interest. Thus, when self-interest, which is justified by opinions on the part of key publics, is shared with others, the effort to achieve agreement requires resisting that which seems to violate societal "interests." This line of reasoning can justify those instances when some public advocates positions that violate a collective ethics as the interest of a community.

Organizations' managements, even with ethical practitioners playing influential advisory roles, may not be the best judges of which ideas and values benefit the various interests that make up a community. Dialogue in the broadest sense is important, but its nature and conditions cannot be universally determined by a preference toward a boiler-plated application of the four-part model. The outcome of discourse should be the value it adds to the community, rather than the narrow implementation of one model in preference to others.

To partially solve such quandaries, excellence theory addresses how linkages serve as a basis for OPRs.

Linkages, Systems, and Organization–Public Relationships (OPRs) as Rationales for Excellence Theory

Based on systems theory, excellence theory emphasizes the strategic management of communication between an organization and its publics and stakeholders. How that occurs, the theory reasons, depends on the presence and quality of functional and structural linkages with all such publics and stakeholders. These linkages are the basis for relationships that lead to mutual benefit. Although Chapter 11 explains relationship theory (as OPR) more fully, here it is discussed as a pillar of excellence theory.

Accordingly, public relations can help create and maintain strong linkages between an organization and the parties that can provide the goodwill it needs to be successful. Grunig and Hunt's 1984 explanation of this condition was that relationships result from the linkages by which organizations and publics interact with and affect one another.

Systems theory provided Grunig and Hunt with the foundation for discussing linkage, and relationships. As discussed in Chapter 2, systems theory, a theory of adjustment, arose from the theory of cybernetic realignment and information flow. It postulated that networks exist as structures and functions by which subsystems adjust to one another through the flow of information. The adjustment of one system to another was conceptualized as a cybernetic system.

For example, a thermostat monitors and adjusts the temperature of the air in a room by controlling the operation of a heating and cooling system. Monitoring occurs when information is obtained, processed, and output regarding the desired temperature. As the room warms (or cools, as the case may be), the thermostat reads the change in temperature (input) and engages the air conditioner (process) to cool it (output) (or the furnace to warm it). Thus, information-driven cybernetic cycles go on serving specific functions—in this case, heating and cooling.

Cybernetics helped Grunig and Hunt (1984) differentiate two-way asymmetrical and two-way symmetrical communication, as systemic adjustment. Feedback, as used for two-way asymmetry, "is communication that helps a source control a receiver's behavior" (p. 23). A message—an independent variable—is provided to a public. When the public accepts or rejects it, feedback tells the source whether the communication was successful or unsuccessful. The two-way flow is based on (a) the information flowing from the organization and (b) the feedback used to determine whether the message "controlled" the public's behavior. This control is the rationale for differentiating asymmetry and symmetry.

In contrast to this "mediating role," whereby a furnace is controlled, for instance, but does not influence the temperature setting of the thermostat, a symmetrical system is two-way and balanced. The difference between asymmetry and symmetry lies in human intervention to define the temperature setting (or, in the case of this theory, the quality of the relationships), bringing a balance between the heating/cooling system and people's preferences regarding the ideal room temperature. Symmetry thus presumes that people discuss what temperature is preferred rather than deferring that question to one particular person, a decision-making elite.

Excellence theory emphasizes this mediating role for public relations. Symmetry occurs if the influence between the organization and its public is mutual; if so, excellence prevails: "If persuasion occurs, the public should be just as likely to persuade the organization's management to change attitudes or behavior as the organization is likely to change the publics' attitudes or behavior" (Grunig & Hunt, 1984, p. 23). The preference for symmetry presumes mutual control rather than one entity controlling another.

Such engagement serves to link organizations with other organizations and publics in varying degrees of balance or harmony. As systems, organizations functionally and structurally link with one another and the components of the environment in which they operate. Structures and functions are needed to achieve balance—equilibrium—between systems. As Grunig and Hunt (1984) reasoned, "'function' is a concept that describes what the system or subsystem does to affect the equilibrium of the larger system of which it is a part" (p. 96). Based on this premise, excellence theory postulates that public relations helps (strategic management) the members of the dominant coalition recognize and plan for disruptions in the equilibrium needed for successful linkages.

Public relations managers are expected to know the strategic options for creating and restoring balance between an organization and its environment (supra system). They do this by sharing information, achieving understanding, and addressing any problems recognized by each external system (each public). In this way, linkages, as relationships, advance or impede an organization's efforts as it interacts with other systems.

As a subsystem, public relations structures and functions are defined and justified by the strategic management each organization needs in its efforts to be successful. Excellent public relations, as part of the management system, serves to meet the needs and advance the interests of other systems inside and outside the organization. Thus, public relations is a means for increasing the efficiency and effectiveness of information flow from and into any system. It satisfies the need for information sharing and processing to facilitate mutual understanding. It helps build positive relationships. As a means for increasing the efficiency and effectiveness of information flow from and to a system, public relations serves a boundary-spanning function.

Related to functions are structures: the positions and ranks (and leadership) held by the members of an organization, who can come from various disciplines. The structures and functions relevant to accounting, general counsel, and manufacturing, for instance, connect in different ways with those vital to public relations. What public relations does is to participate in information flow, conceptualized by systems theory as input, processing/throughput, and output. These are the process aspects of organizational structures and functions by which practitioners and academics can address who does what, how, and why—the dynamics of institutional development.

For these reasons, advocates of excellence champion the research role of public relations. Such research is valuable to an organization because it guides the cybernetic adjustment it needs to be successful. As organizations exert themselves toward the systems around them, they require feedback to understand how effective they are, how favorably their actions are received, and whether behavior adjustment is needed. Feedback can evaluate the success of a program in order to build effective linkages and help predict the most effective course of action in the future.

Linkages may be of various kinds—functional, diffused, enabling, and normative—depending on how organizations and publics relate to one another. So, linkage is strategic and situational. Public relations should help determine how well each individual linkage operates. Based on that feedback, it serves to create, sustain, and repair challenges to the equilibrium in the relationships between an organization and each of its publics.

Building on such conclusions, excellence theory postulates that the quality of relationships is evidence of the quality of public relations and a key to the ability of an organization to succeed, to be effective (Grunig, Grunig, & Ehling, 1992). This hypothesis has been the subject of substantial theory and research. For instance, Huang (2001) finds that excellent public relations helps build positive relationships that benefit an organization's efforts to reduce conflict with its key publics. Of particular importance, good relationships tend to result in integrative rather that distributive conflict resolution. Integrative conflict resolution leads to shared benefits from engagement and mutually acceptable solutions. Distributive conflict resolution relies on compromise and trade outs.

As this section draws to a conclusion, the discussion of excellence theory can be used to explain the success of the bank examined in the case study. Its public relations team is intimately connected with its senior management's decision-making processes. Key outcomes of that process include hiring and training bankers to be ambassadors who use banking knowledge to help customers grow their businesses. The business rationale is that bankers are the crucial point of contact with key publics, especially small-business clients. Bankers are rewarded for their relationship-building abilities as constructive, collaborative problem solvers. Ideally, conflicts are used constructively to improve strategies that produce shared benefits for customers and the bank. Consequently, customers tend to be extremely loyal, reducing the need for the bank to replace them. Happy customers attract more of the same. Positive OPR advances the bank's reputation. Two-way information flow, including constant and focused research, measures customer's needs and the bank's ability to meet them.

This reasoning opens excellence theory to continuing consideration of relationships, relationship quality, and situational approaches to problem solving—a topic that will be further developed in Chapter 11. In the meantime, the next section focuses on the evolution and centrality of situational theory to excellent public relations.

Situational Theory as the Foundation for Excellent Public Relations

Although Chapter 10 explains situational theory in comparison to other theories on publics, stakeholders, and voices, here it is discussed as the foundation of excellence theory. Early in the formulation of excellence theory, the concept of "situational" became a hallmark. This concept presumes that many contingent options can be used to affect an organization's success either favorably or unfavorably. The nature and quality of linkages (relationships) and the type of model relevant to excellent communication management offer two such options. A third is the situationally sensitive design and delivery of information. In this third option, situational variables predict how individuals receive and process information, as well as how they utilize it in their problem solving, both individually and collectively. These themes will be discussed in this section, focusing first on publics and then on problem solving.

Situational Theory of Publics

Situational theory, as it originated in the 1960s, was based on "communication theories of media effects," as well as "attitude theories from social psychology." To focus that body of literature, researchers addressed "the characteristics of press releases most often used by editors" (Grunig & Grunig, 2008, p. 328).

These concepts were used to determine which research-based practical strategies could be employed to increase the ability of organizations to communicate with various publics. From a focus on the effectiveness of press releases, the theory matured to address "when and why individuals become active in communication behaviors such as information seeking" (Kim & Grunig, 2011, p. 120).

What factors influence how an organization can communicate successfully with its publics as a means for improving its strategic management? This question was central to James Grunig's dissertation, which examined how experts could best communicate with Colombian farmers in order to increase their yields. Such research helped give meaning to the concept of "public," and thereby launched the situational theory of publics.

One of the first advances was in differentiating between types of publics: active/activist, aware, latent, or not affected/nonpublic. Publics differ in how involved they are; for instance, whether they are interested in many or a few issues, and how important any one issue is to them. Thus, publics may be hot-issue, all-issue, single-issue, or apathetic.

The situational theory of publics reasoned that communication effectiveness depends on three independent variables—publics' problem recognition, their level of involvement, and their constraint recognition—as well as two dependent variables that differentiate active and passive communication as information acquisition—information seeking and attending/processing (Grunig & Hunt, 1984, pp. 147–154; Grunig, 1997, 2003). Such analysis is fundamental to classic systems theory, which is based on the premise that information flow efficiency and ease (i.e., openness; thus, open systems) are the hallmarks of excellent systems and are essential to the quality of OPR.

The concept of *problem recognition* is intimately associated with the concept of problem solving, as discussed in Chapter 2. Problem solving has a long history in U.S. culture, including the communication discipline. Drawn from the philosophy of pragmatism championed by John Dewey, it has been addressed as a key human characteristic. Prior to solving a problem, people must recognize some matter as constituting it. Communicators can help them perceive and understand problems as matters that long for a solution. Situational theory predicts why people seek and process information once they perceive a problem.

The second independent variable, *level of involvement*, predicts whether people will seek and process information. High (as opposed to low) involvement can be conceptualized as the importance or relevance of some matter—a problem, for instance—to different publics. Involvement results when individuals recognize that their self-interests are affected by that matter. It rises as individuals are confronted with choices they see as being relevant to their interests. If a choice is seen as relevant, they will seek information to form the opinions they need to make the best choice and thereby solve the problem.

The third independent variable, *constraint recognition*, can mitigate the effects of problem recognition and involvement. If an individual or public perceives there is little they can do about a problem, they have less reason (motive) to communicate about it. Constraint recognition can be an impediment to communication effectiveness and efficiency.

These three independent variables predict the two dependent ones: *information seeking* and *attending/processing*. High problem recognition and involvement with low constraint recognition predicts that people will seek information, be open to receiving it, and use it to solve problems. Increased processing—thinking about the information—can help in solving them.

With this sort of reasoning, the situational theory of publics provides a cornerstone for excellence theory. Applied to the banking case, it predicts that people are interested in solving the problem of which bank is best for their personal and small-business interests. They have a problem, it relates to them and their business success, and they appreciate it when communicators put minimal constraints between them and the information they require in order to make an informed decision. Thus, a client's banker must be responsive to their needs regarding business and personal banking problems.

When people obtain information, they use it to solve the problem that set them looking for it. Thus, situational theory predicts that if a bank employs a customer and community relations effort to share information and solve problems—especially ones related to business education and community enrichment—it will enjoy increased customer appeal. A community with good education (including technical skills) and arts will provide the employees and customers needed for small business success. This is a mutual benefit (Heath & Ni, 2010).

Situational Theory of Problem Solving

Over the years, the situational theory of publics became the foundation for understanding how publics communicate collectively to solve problems. The situational theory of problem solving, on the other hand, focuses not just on seeking/reception and processing, but more specifically on problem solving on an individual and collective basis. In addition to the three independent variables of the situational theory of publics, this theoretical advance offers one new one: *situational motivation in problem solving* (Kim & Grunig, 2011). This variable explains why individuals are situationally motivated to solve problems and to communicate among themselves to that end.

Thus, a bank's customers are likely to communicate not only with one or more banks, but also with those who share similar problems. The shared sense of the world is more than a definition of a public—it serves to explain how and why members of a public communicate with one another. Each public collectivity experiences life as continuous problem solving. To that end, it engages others of like mind as communication partners. One of the situational consequences of relationship quality (satisfaction and continuation) is positive or negative megaphoning. Megaphoning is a chain network effect whereby individual voices amplify positive or negative comments to others in the same network, based on the quality of their relationship and their experience with the target of commentary (Tam, Kim, & Kim, 2018).

Thus, public relations theory is enriched by John Dewey's work on the public and problem solving. Dewey's (1910, 1922, 1927, 1938) theory of pragmatism supported his theories of education, economics, democratic society, and collective behavior. For Dewey, human thought (including communication) and action center on problem solving. Quality of life depends on how well people learn to solve problems ranging from the menial to those of a democratic society.

With this intellectual foundation, situational theory matured to feature macro- and micro-level analyses of problem solving (Kim & Grunig, 2011; see also Grunig, 1966, 1968, 2003). Problem solving is communication-centric and cognitive, and has implications for organization–public communication. Consequently, Kim and Grunig (2011) explain this advance in the excellence theory of public relations thus:

> In a situation in which an organization and a public have a conflict, public relations managers can set situational variables as communication objectives and track and assess their changes as they implement programs. The theory of problem solving suggests that active problem solvers have a tendency toward higher information selectivity and sharing; thus, as an organization plans and implements conflict resolution programs, it can track and assess the changes in problem recognition, motivation about the problem, and information forefending and forwarding. (p. 142)

This problem-solving logic matured to postulate that in its first stage "people tend to search for information that can enhance problem-solving potential" (p. 126).

Of particular relevance to communication, and to the situational theory of problem solving, is that "information consumption becomes systematic when people find that information matches their subjective life problems" (p. 122). What is one of the most important factors in solving problems? Kim and Grunig answer that it is a referent criterion, which they define "as *any knowledge* or *subjective judgmental system* that influences the way in which one approaches problem solving" (p. 131; italics in original).

People tend to share information in order to help others solve a shared problem. Through this process, publics create collective opinions. These serve individual and collective needs for problem solving. By determining what information is needed for such problem solving, the situational theory of publics can help public relations practitioners use research to monitor and shape the future of an organization.

The situational theory of problem solving helps achieve that end because it expands the original dependent variables (information seeking and attending/processing) to embrace and support "a more generalized dependent variable (*communicative action in problem solving*), which itself integrates several communication behaviors" (Kim & Grunig, 2011, p. 123; italics in original).

By this logic, the concept of referent criterion is a decision-making heuristic that recurs in each similar problem situation. This means that people learn, as reasoned by pragmatism, to use referent criteria to solve various problems, then use that history to solve others. Each referent criterion is relevant to making decisions in the face of those same problems. Prior experience is relevant to current problem solving.

In this way, decision makers improvise, but they do so by recalling and testing referent criteria that have been employed before. After seeking and processing information about relevant referent criteria, individuals set about solving each specific problem with varying degrees of insightfulness. The degree to which they have or find a satisfying referent criterion predicts whether and how they continue to seek information and engage with others in the process. Such success is defined as a measure of cognitive satisfaction regarding how relevant the available referent criterion is to the problem at hand.

This theory is useful for understanding how individuals, both alone and with others as publics, recognize, solve, and engage the problems they confront. The conceptual impact of this theoretical advance helps public relations practitioners expand the explanatory power of the situational theory of publics and add variables to monitor and explain the problem solving and communicative behaviors relevant to the environment in which public relations occurs.

In summary, the situational theory of problem solving features six information-relevant variables. In the information-acquiring domain:

1) information seeking (active communication behavior); and
2) information attending (passive; unplanned discovery of problem-relevant information).

In the information-selecting domain:

3) information forefending (active; forefending refers to problem solvers' efforts to judge the value and relevance of information before considering it);
4) information permitting (passive).

In the information-transmitting domain:

5) information forwarding (active; passing information to others confronted with the same problem); and
6) information sharing (passive).

These factors predict how and whether individuals will share problem-relevant information in varying degrees of activity and passivity. Situational theory helps practitioners understand how and why problem solvers are thoughtful about information, willing to share it, and systematic in its use.

Again, the case of the communicative bank helps illustrate this theory. Small business owners have many problems relevant to the successful running of their operations. Bankers can help or hinder them in their information-seeking, high-involvement, and constraint-recognition behaviors. Based on the six variables just listed, banking customers are liable to seek, attend to, and share information with others. Part of the activity of sharing entails checking the information, whether through direct experience or by seeking the judgment of others. Such sharing may be passive or active. It may occur through conversation or online. Thus, in various ways and to varying degrees, people with a common sense of some problem engage in information sharing and evaluation in an effort to individually and collectively reach the best possible solution to it.

Public discourse is important to the bank's success. It recognizes customers as problem solvers. This is especially important for owners of small businesses, but is not irrelevant to regular customers. People look to banks to solve an idiosyncratic array of problems. They seek information, share it, discuss it, and utilize it. Their decision criteria are dynamic and likely to change. The bank wants, using research, to understand the decision criteria customers use. Some of those criteria may need to be changed. Others determine the sorts of information the customers require in order to make decisions. Public relations can play a sensitive and constructive role in this communicative action.

Stressing the importance of information and problem solving as defining ingredients of excellent public relations, the next section emphasizes behavior adjustment (strategic management) as the paradigm of public relations.

Excellence Theory (Behavioral, Strategic Management)

Excellence theorists have come increasingly to advocate a "behavior, strategic management paradigm of public relations" (Kim & Ni, 2010; see also Grunig, Ferrari, & França, 2009; Grunig, 2018). On this point, Kim and Ni (2010) reason that:

The behavioral, strategic management approach will assist and accelerate the evolutionary process of public relations from a mere occupation to a profession that creates value for its users (organizations and publics alike) and value for a society that recognizes the importance of mutual adaptation among its social actors. (p. 54)

This conceptualization emphasizes the need for organizations to use professional and research-based guidance to adjust themselves to key publics, rather than to (a) convince or teach publics that their expectations of the organization are incorrect and that it deserves a better image than they hold of it or (b) engage in symbolic communication that seeks merely to manage image rather than to earn it through constructive problem solving and adjustment of the expectations that publics have of it.

Applying this reasoning, excellence theory poses a choice between two paradigms: the interpretive, symbolic approach to public relations and the behavioral, strategic management one (Kim & Ni, 2010; see Grunig, 1993). The latter "focuses on the participation of public relations executives in strategic decision making to help manage the behaviors of organizations" (p. 35). Thus, the behavior of the organization is the triggering variable that leads to either a positive or a negative reaction in a given public. In contrast, "the symbolic-interpretive perspective sees such concepts as organizations themselves, their environments, and the behavior of managers as subjective enactments of reality—enactments that can be negotiated through communication" (Grunig, 2018, p. 1458).

Actions speak more loudly than words. Images are earned through actions, not concocted through words. Meeting this challenge requires specialized public relations functions performed with others on the senior management team.

Public Relations and Decision Making

An employer-centric approach to public relations emphasizes how the success of an organization results from its ability to cooperate with others for mutual benefit. Such symmetry occurs, so excellence theory reasons, when public relations professionals perform specialized functions for the mutual advantage of organizations and their publics.

Practitioners can best help organizations meet this challenge by being a key part of each management's strategic decision-making team. Their arguments for inclusion can fail if others in senior management do not recognize and appreciate what public relations can offer for this decision-making process, in terms of improved relationships. Thus, to empower public relations managers, excellence theorists have defined which key public relations roles are vital to organizational success.

Excellence theory reasons that organizations are excellent when they are able to adjust to conditions and demands specific to the interests and problem-solving needs of publics. Excellence requires organizational structures and functions that make such adjustment and adaptation possible, in order to build, maintain, and restore the goodwill needed for organizational effectiveness.

To advance this theme, excellence theory differentiates four levels of analysis: program, functional, organizational, and societal (Grunig, 1992). Each offers a research opportunity to explore the role and impact of public relations and a normative opportunity to advance the social responsibility of the profession.

The *program level* addresses topics relevant to public relations specialties, such as media relations, community relations, and customer relations. These traditional public relations initiatives result from the structures—even linkages—by which the organization engages its stakeholders. Each program employs technical strategies and tactics to bring about successful public relations.

The *functional level* compares the structure and function of public relations units to other managerial-level units both within the organization and in organizations in general. Each function calls for specific actions and specialized knowledge regarding what makes organizations effective.

The *organizational level* addresses how public relations thinks about the organization as a whole and in relationship to other organizations and publics. In the case of public relations, excellence theory reasons, it brings to bear research and theory on OPR and situational communication. In this way, public relations can add to the bottom line by creating goodwill.

The *societal level* focuses on how organizations contribute to society through public relations. Public relations serves an organization best by helping it be socially responsible and successful.

At each level, excellence theory reasons, organizational culture shapes how and why public relations is practiced—both in general and in each specific instance. If the organization's culture promotes excellence, public relations can help deliver it. If the organization's culture frustrates efforts to achieve excellence, public relations is limited in its ability to help the organization be effective. To have an impact on an organization, public relations must be instrumental in changing the organizational culture.

Excellence theory postulates that authoritarian, elitist, and reactive cultures lead to asymmetrical practices. In contrast, symmetry is likely to be fostered by "participative, integrative, liberal, and interactive" cultures (Grunig, 1992, p. 25–26). By this reasoning, in order to improve the quality of public relations, how it is practiced, and its strategic management, an organization must adopt and implement a constructive culture.

Participative Decision Making

Organizations are more excellent when they empower people internally and externally, exhibit an organic rather than a rigid structure, innovate with an entrepreneurial spirit, engage in participative leadership, and effect strategic planning by identifying opportunities and recognizing legitimate constraints. To this list can be added a high commitment to social responsibility, support for women and minorities (diversity), commitment to high-quality performance, effective operations, and collaborative approaches to societal problems (Grunig, 1992).

According to excellence theory, public relations serves an organization and its publics best when its managers are part of the executive decision-making team—the dominant coalition. Thus, the top person in public relations should be a manager. Within the public relations structure, technicians implement the strategies planned and prescribed by senior management. Senior members need to be managerial decision makers rather than simply committed to implementing management's communication policies and strategies.

Key functions define excellent public relations. These include the ability to scan environments and identify and understand publics and their problem-solving approaches and information needs. Public relations managers help other executives to "think out loud" by engaging in scenario building. In this regard, they are wise to pose what-if scenarios in order to help others recognize, weigh, and accommodate environmental exigencies that might affect the organization's ability to acquire and use resources.

Excellence theorists advocate that practitioners should constantly engage in ethical decision making; as such, senior practitioners should be ethics managers and should help others to manage ethically. Ethical decision making is situationally strategic, with relevance to specializations such as employee relations, community relations, and government relations (Grunig & Grunig, 2008).

Public relations managers can bring a stakeholder approach to executive decision making. A stakeholder approach is important because it "makes it possible to integrate economic performance and the achievement of social goals into a definition of effectiveness" (Grunig et al., 2006, p. 34). Public relations' impact can be measured by the organization's success—its economic performance.

This point of view is not new, but every generation of theorists and practitioners needs to be reminded of its virtue. At least since the writings of John W. Hill (1958; co-principal and founder of Hill and Knowlton), excellent managers have realized the need to connect an organization's interests with those of various groups, individuals, and other organizations who are affected by and capable of affecting it. More recently, this spirit of adjustment has been termed an "organic approach" to stakeholder participation.

The opinions of key publics—what excellence theory calls "reference criteria"—set the standards by which organizations are judged. For that reason, well guided performance and excellent communication management counts—especially when it conforms to standards expressed in these criteria.

Excellence theory reasons that well-managed organizations that are well adjusted to society have societal value. As Kim and Ni (2010) continue, public relations adds "value to society by encouraging organizations to practice social responsibility and helping reduce societal conflicts" (p. 36).

By emphasizing the impact organizations can achieve through strategically adjusting to stakeholders, excellent theorists work to empower the role and status of public relations as benefiting organizations and society. This topic is further explored in the next subsection.

Strategic Adjustment as Relationship Building

This chapter has already explained the role of OPR as a principle of organizational excellence. The quality of its relationships depends on cooperation between an organization and its publics. To that end, an organization needs to operate in ways that advance the community in which it operates. Excellent organizations are willing and able to adjust their behaviors in ways that build, maintain, and repair relationships with key publics who hold stakes necessary to their success.

Conditions call for specific public relations efforts that support a behavioral, strategic approach. These can be conceptualized as four segmentable stages of adjustment: stakeholder, public, issue, and crisis.

In the *stakeholder* stage, adjustment requires insights into how "behaviors of the organization or of a stakeholder have decisional or behavioral consequences on the other" (Kim & Ni, 2010, p. 40). The nature and quality of the relationships between an organization and its stakeholders depend on the decisions of each party and their subsequent impacts. Stakeholders can grant, withhold, or otherwise use resources to force organizations to change.

In the *public* stage, certain publics develop as people share a problem–solution approach to some matter. When they determine that problems exist, publics work to solve them. They employ the resources they hold to advocate and push for changes regarding how the organization operates. They seek and can achieve behavioral adjustment, whereby the organization changes in ways that reduce the problem.

During the *issue* stage, publics recognize and analyze problems as issues. These issues are used to address problems that need solutions. As issues arise and publics form, practitioners have several options: they can segment the publics and use mass media and interpersonal communication to engage them, or they can negotiate to resolve conflict.

In this same stage, the relationship can be changed and rehabilitated by corrective behavioral adjustments. If the adjustments and changes satisfy the public, the problem is solved. If not, it may become more severe and lead to the *crisis* stage. If issues are not handled satisfactorily, excellence theory reasons, they become crises.

Engagement over issues, and on many other matters, requires effective OPR. Relationship development, maintenance, and repair require strategic management relevant to three conditions: antecedents to the issue and crisis, maintenance and cultivation strategies for use in such conditions, and commitment to achieve outcomes that result from and build relationship quality.

As Grunig (2018) compares stakeholders and publics, he emphasizes that they are similar in many ways but that "'stakeholder' is a broader concept than 'publics'. Different types of publics arise within a single stakeholder category and can be segmented into activist, active, latent, and nonpublics" (p. 1460). Actions by publics, based on problem recognition, can create issues and crises, "which typically lead to programs of issues management and crisis communication" (p. 1460). How managers evaluate and respond to such pressures can entail task and societal orientations.

Excellence theory recognizes that the quality of problem recognition and problem solving becomes crucial to how public relations responds to the need for interdependent relationships with publics. As organizations and publics affect one another, public relations' success depends on how adjustive each party is to the other, the satisfaction that arises from the relationship and adjustment, the trust that grows or is destroyed during the process, and the mutual benefit that occurs.

Broadly, then, the public relations option is to change behavior that is problematic or to communicate in ways that resolve the problem or the conflict associated with it. "Public relations as communication management thus engages in communicative efforts of seeking, selecting, and sharing problem-relevant information from the problem-causing entities (e.g., organization) and for problem-solving opportunities (e.g., resource or power holders)" (Kim & Ni, 2010, p. 48).

Such reasoning emphasizes the need to choose between symbolic image management and behavioral adjustment. The latter is more rational and information-driven. The former is more subjective and evaluative. The symbolic rests on the assumption that messaging can be used to change publics' knowledge, assessment, and satisfaction regarding an organization. This approach, excellence theorists reason, depends on changing publics to look favorably on organizations rather than behaviorally adjusting organizations to satisfy publics' problem-solving preferences and so resolve conflict.

Following this line of reasoning, Kim and Ni (2010) point out that the symbolic approach to public relations "uses only the press-agentry, public information, and two-way asymmetrical models to negotiate those interpretations" (p. 49). Of the four models, two-way symmetry is preferred because it is more focused on solving problems and adjusting the organization to the public. The other models tend to favor efforts to adapt a public to the interests of the organization.

Excellence depends on how problems are solved in ways that foster and sustain relationships rather than manipulate them. Excellent communication balances organizational self-interest with the interests of others. Such adjustment can employ "a give-and-take process that can waver between advocacy and collaboration" (Grunig, 2001, p. 28). Such communication is strategic and adjustive to mutual interests and sound OPRs, as competing perspectives set against one another in honest and reflective dialogue. Thus, "mixed motives, collaborative advocacy, and cooperative antagonism all have the same meaning as does symmetry" (Grunig, 2001, p. 28).

During mixed-motive engagement and advocacy, organizational communication requires that practitioners and others in management "must listen as well as argue." Excellence allows communicators to advocate, but they must acknowledge that if they listen carefully to what is said, it can lead them to conclude they are wrong. Such discourse needs to be socially responsible and other-centered, without losing "the uniqueness of one's self-interest" (Grunig, 2001, p. 28).

In these ways, public relations should engage in bridging strategies, which are excellent, rather than buffering strategies, which are not—the topic of the next subsection.

Excellence as Bridging, Not Buffering

Excellence theory emphasizes the efficacy of building relationships—bridging—as opposed to crafting messages to buffer an organization against its critics. That theme supports a behavioral, strategic management approach to public relations.

To develop the rationale for this premise, excellence theorists drew upon the work of institutional management theorists and organizational sociologists Scott (1987) and Van den Bosch and van Riel (1998). Scott (1987) reasoned that protective boundaries lead systems to become closed and therefore dysfunctional and inorganic. Executives employ such strategies on the assumption, Scott reasoned, that buffering gives them more opportunity for rational choices and actions. They try to avoid the subjective criticisms of publics, which they believe distract them from their mission and vision. Van den Bosch and van Riel (1998) recommended against buffering: "Buffering strategies are used by management to help seal off the firm from disturbances in the business environment due to, for example, the environmental impacts of a firm's activities" (p. 24). Such efforts block external stakeholders from "interfering in internal operations" and "amplify the organization's protective boundaries" in ways that reduce planning and adjustive uncertainty. In contrast, "bridging strategies seek to adapt organizational activities in such a way that they conform to the expectations of external stakeholders regarding, for instance, environmental aspects of a firm's activities" (p. 24). Like a moat around a castle, buffering can protect organizations from attack, but it does nothing to abate the incentive to attack them.

According to systems theory, bridging results in boundary spanning. Key players, including public relations professionals, create the means by which an organization interacts with its key publics. Such efforts actually add to the security of the organization, because it will be more in tune with the forces that shape its future and success. Bridging, theorists reason, can reduce uncertainty concerning the preferences and evaluations held by stakeholders. Knowing such preferences can help develop options by which to avoid collisions with stakeholders. An open organization is best because it is capable of growth and change as it adjusts to its stakeholders. Bridging offers the rationale for negotiated engagement. Such efforts add to the security of the organization, because the information obtained allows management to be strategically in tune with the forces that shape its future and success.

Recommending openness and negotiated engagement, Kim and Ni (2010) reason that both concepts become informed choices by applying the logic of two-way symmetry. A two-way asymmetrical approach to negotiation presumes that an organization's management seeks to understand the preferences of its stakeholders. That is the first step toward creating strategies "to create favorable interpretations of an organization's behaviors to buffer those behaviors from public opposition or negative public behaviors—thus allowing the organization to behave the way it wants and still receive public approval of that behavior" (p. 49). Buffering as two-way asymmetry seeks to defeat or coopt publics rather than engage them symmetrically.

In contrast to buffering, bridging is two-way and symmetrical. It aspires to dialogue and interaction rather than defense and deflection. Symmetry, Kim and Ni (2010) reason, gives key publics a "voice in management decisions" (p. 49). The challenge is to adjust organizational and individual interests through problem resolution. As such, bridging communication increases the quality of relationships.

In this way, excellence theory helps explain why the bank's management was wise to incorporate principles of excellent public relations in senior management decision making. It believes that bridges, primarily created through bankers and other personnel, attract and keep customers, especially small business owners. Such customers confront many problems in their efforts to run successful businesses. Senior management realizes this, and creates a culture in which bankers are expected to know their customers and to work with them to solve their problems before they become issues and crises. The bank relies on bridges, not buffers, to build its reputation, attract and keep customers, and operate in a collaborative, problem-solving mode.

Ongoing Research

The situational theory of problem solving is discussed further in Chapter 10, while OPR is discussed in Chapter 11. The bulk of the research on these topics has been devoted to refining and extending excellence theory.

Addressing the tensions between symmetry and asymmetry, Deatherage and Hazleton (1998) find that the two concepts are best understood and used not as polar opposites, but as situational or contingent options. These options reflect different worldviews that are not inherently ethically different. The authors confirm the role of worldview as a predictor of how and why practitioners prefer one approach to another, and they consider how worldview leads to strategic options rather than merely enacted categorical preferences such as two-way symmetry.

Similarly, Leichty and Springston (1993) argue that the four models should not be assumed to be categorically superior or inferior to one another. Emphasizing the need for situational sensitivity, they reason that analysis should consider what strategy is best under given circumstances. This suggests that excellence theory needs a rationale to reconcile how and why the strategies that are chosen must reflect a commitment to social responsibility (as aspects of contingency theory; see Chapter 4).

Many authors outside of public relations use Dewey's framework. For instance, Pratkanis and Turner (1996) draw on Dewey in a way that does not play up information and downplay persuasion. They reason, using the logic of pragmatism, that discourse is motivated by people's need for efficacy. People must use discourse to be effective problem solvers, or to solve problems in a pragmatic way. Persuasion and information (if the two concepts can be separated) are vital to decision making.

For Pratkanis and Turner, the challenge is in the quality of public debate, which is vital to democratic decision making. They observe that "Dewey felt the public could rise to the occasion if two changes occurred: (a) social structural changes to improve the methods of public discussion and (b) public education in the skills of democracy" (p. 201). (These discourse challenges are discussed in Chapter 5, while the infrastructural challenges are discussed in Chapter 7.)

Worrying that citizens today are less skilled in the principles and practices of persuasion than were those in Greek and Roman democracies, Pratkanis and Turner advocate that citizens require increased "cognitive capacity about persuasion" so that they can "evaluate the merits of a persuasive appeal," and that they must develop their "own skills so that they can take meaningful action" (p. 202). They also need skills in group dynamics and increased self-efficacy as decision makers.

Extending the behavioral, strategic management paradigm, Kim and Ni (2013) combine the challenges of formative and evaluative research with two sorts of problems: public-initiated and organization-initiated. Research can alert management to the first type as it senses problems between an organization and some publics; these problems are controversial and policy issue-related. Organizational response options need to acknowledge that such problems result when active, involved publics seek a solution to a problem relevant (including conflict) to an organization's strategic behavior. Organization-initiated problems are those that have implications for the interests of the organization and at least one public. They can motivate nonprofit organizations, for instance, to engage with publics to support a fund-raising program aimed at resolving some shared problem.

As well as shaping external insights, this line of research has been applied internally to theorize strategic internal communication (Men, 2014). Following the threads of excellence and behavioral strategic management theory, transformational leadership can make an organization's internal communication more symmetrical, leading to greater employee relational satisfaction.

Reasoning that excellence theory provides a solid platform for refining public relations practice, Steyn (2007) adds detailed elaboration on strategies of planning and implementation. Acknowledging weaknesses in practitioners' preparation for engaging in strategic communication management, she emphasizes how strategic management, situated at the macro, meso, and micro levels of an organization, must monitor the societal context of the organization and feed such intelligence "into the organization's strategic formulation process ... with regards to strategic stakeholders (and their concerns or expectations), societal issues, and the publics that emerge around the issues" (p. 139). She goes on: "By acting socially responsible and building mutually beneficial relationships with the organization's stakeholders and other interested groups in society on whom it depends to meet its goals, an organization obtains legitimacy, garners trust, and builds a good reputation" (p. 139). Emphasizing situated strategic challenges, Steyn translates these management challenges into specific strategic communication management practice. Her highly detailed explanation of strategic communication management principles is influenced by research and theory in support of best practices for strategic planning and implementation. In order both to critique the theory and to advance it, robust analysis addresses excellence theory as the rationale for behavioral, strategic management.

Conclusion

Proponents of excellence theory in its various stages of development reason that if problems result because of an organization's actions, they can be corrected by adjusting its communicative behavior to publics' and stakeholders' preferences and expectations. Communicative action can change the understanding of a problem so that management can help publics to solve it (behavioral adjustment). Failing to meet a public's expectations results in conflict and can discourage management from taking corrective action to achieve the organization's mission or goals. This public relations option sees virtue in problem solving through behavioral adjustment rather than symbolic buffering.

OPR helps an organization to engage, resolve conflict, earn a positive reputation, and gain its publics' goodwill. This view of public relations, excellence theorists argue, is preferable to a symbolic interpretativist approach that relies on messaging to polish an organization's reputation and even deny the legitimacy of any problems with the organization that publics believe exist.

Chapter Summary

Supporters of excellence theory reason that it offers the conceptual framework necessary to engage in problem recognition, relationship building, and strategic management choices. The theory seeks to empower public relations managers by giving them strategic options to benefit their organization by helping others in management to understand its societal context. Excellent public relations strives to identify, understand, and resolve problems through constructive engagement.

Key Terms

Bridging: Building constructive linkages between an organization and its publics or stakeholders, to their mutual benefit; contrast with buffering.

Buffering: Protecting the image or reputation of an organization; contrast with bridging.

Dominant Coalition: Those organization members who either are in or have the ear of upper management and are respected for their knowledge.

Excellence: Best practices that correlate with organizational success and effectiveness.

One-Way Asymmetrical Communication: Information flows from an organization to its publics without opportunity for meaningful response from the latter.

Publics: Identifiable individuals who share a problem–solution approach to some matter.

Strategic Behavioral Paradigm: Public relations as a strategic management function rather than as a messaging, publicity, and media relations function—that is, a symbolic-interpretive paradigm.

Situational Theory of Problem Solving: A focus not only on seeking/reception and processing, but more specifically on problem solving on an individual and collective basis. In addition to the three independent variables of the situational theory of publics, this theoretical advance offers one new one: situational motivation in problem solving.

Situational Theory of Publics: The idea that communication effectiveness depends on three independent variables—problem recognition, level of involvement, and constraint recognition—as well as two dependent variables that differentiate active and passive communication as information acquisition—information seeking and attending/processing.

Stakeholder Relationship Management: The idea that the behaviors of an organization or a stakeholder have decisional or behavioral consequences for the other.

Systems Theory: The idea that the structures, functions, and rituals of behavioral adjustment and communication management help an organization and its publics know how best to interact with and adjust to one another.

Two-Way Symmetrical Communication: Information flow between an organization and its publics that fosters cooriented, mutual adjustment between them based on collaboration and public participation.

Discussion Questions

1 What reasoning does excellence theory use to explain how public relations can help organizations achieve productive relationships with their publics or stakeholders?

2 What are the four models of excellence theory on the two dimensions? What is the modified model based on criticism?

3 Excellence theorists reason that communication needs to be two-way and symmetrical if stakeholders, publics, and organizations are to form positive relationships. What arguments justify this conclusion?

4 What are the situational theories of publics and of problem solving? What are the key variables of both, and how do they predict the rise of activist publics as they use information and referent criteria to identify, understand, and seek solutions to problems? How can you connect them to excellence theory?

5 What organizational culture conditions are necessary for excellent public relations and how can public relations help form cultures that are optimally amenable to organizational excellence?

6 What are the implications of buffering versus bridging for excellent public relations?

References

Deatherage, C. P., & Hazleton, V. (1998). Effects of organizational worldview on the practice of public relations: A test of the theory of public relations excellence. *Journal of Public Relations Research, 10,* 57–71.

Dewey, J. (1910). *How we think.* Boston, MA: D. C. Heath.

Dewey, J. (1922). *Human nature and conduct.* New York: Modern Library.

Dewey, J. (1927). *The public and its problems.* Chicago, IL: Swallow.

Dewey, J. (1938). *Logic: Theory of inquiry.* New York: Holt, Rinehart & Winston.

Dozier, D. M., & Grunig, L. A. (1992). The organization of the public relations function. In J. E. Grunig (Ed.), *Excellence in public relations and communication management* (pp. 395–417). Hillsdale, NJ: Lawrence Erlbaum.

Grunig, J. E. (1966). The role of information in economic decision making. *Journalism Monographs, 3.*

Grunig, J. E. (1968). Information, entrepreneurship, and economic development: A study of the decision making processes of Colombian Latifundistas. Unpublished doctoral dissertation, University of Wisconsin.

Grunig, J. E. (1992). Communication, public relations, and effective organizations: An overview of the book. In J. E. Grunig (Ed.), *Excellence in public relations and communication management* (pp. 1–28). Hillsdale, NJ: Lawrence Erlbaum.

Grunig, J. E. (1993). Image and substance: From symbolic to behavioral relationships. *Public Relations Review, 19,* 121–139.

Grunig, J. E. (1997). A situational theory of publics: Conceptual history, recent challenges and new research. In D. Moss, T. MacManus, & D. Vercic (Eds.), *Public relations research: An international perspective* (pp. 3–46). London: ITB Press.

Grunig, J. E. (2000). Collectivism, collaboration, and societal corporatism as core professional values in public relations. *Journal of Public Relations Research, 12,* 23–48.

Grunig, J. E. (2001). Two-way symmetrical public relations: Past, present, and future. In R. L. Heath (Ed.), *Handbook of public relations* (pp. 11–30). Thousand Oaks, CA: Sage.

Grunig, J. E. (2003). Constructing public relations theory and practice. In B. Dervin, S. Chaffee, & L. Foreman-Wernet (Eds.), *Communication, another kind of horse race: Essays honoring Richard F. Carter* (pp. 85–115). Cresskill, NJ: Hampton Press.

Grunig, J. E. (2006). Furnishing the edifice: Ongoing research on public relations as a strategic management function. *Journal of Public Relations Research, 18*, 151–179.

Grunig, J. E. (2008). Public relations management in government and business. In M. Lee (Ed.), *Government public relations: A reader* (pp. 21–62). Milwaukee, WI: CRC Press.

Grunig, J. E. (2018). Strategic behavioral paradigm. In R. L. Heath & W. Johansen (Eds.), *International encyclopedia of strategic communication* (pp. 1457–1463). Hoboken, NJ: Wiley Blackwell.

Grunig, J. E., & Grunig, L. A. (2008). Excellence theory in public relations: Past, present, and future. In A. Zerfass, B. van Ruler, & K. Sriramesh (Eds.), *Public relations research: European and international perspectives and innovations* (pp. 327–347). Wiesbaden: VS Verlag.

Grunig, J. E., & Hunt, T. (1984). *Managing public relations.* New York: Holt, Rinehart & Winston.

Grunig, L. A., Grunig, J. E., & Ehling, W. P. (1992). What is an effective organization? In J. E. Grunig (Ed.), *Excellence in public relations and communication management* (pp. 65–90). Hillsdale, NJ: Lawrence Erlbaum.

Grunig, J. E., Grunig, L. A., & Dozier, D. M. (2006). The excellence theory. In C. H. Botan & V. Hazleton (Eds.), *Public relations theory II* (pp. 21–62). Mahwah, NJ: Lawrence Erlbaum.

Grunig, J. E., Ferrari, M. A., & França, F. (2009). *Relações públicas: Teoria, contexto e relacionamentos.* São Paulo: Difusao Editora.

Heath, R. L., & Ni, L. (2010). Community relations and corporate social responsibility. In R. L. Heath (Ed.), *SAGE handbook of public relations* (pp. 557–568). Thousand Oaks, CA: Sage.

Hill, J. W. (1958). *Corporate public relations: Arm of modern management.* New York: Harper & Brothers.

Huang, Y.-H. (2001). Values of public relations: Effects on organization–public relationships mediating conflict resolution. *Journal of Public Relations Research, 13*, 265–301.

Kim, J.-N., & Grunig, J. E. (2011). Problem solving and communicative action: A situational theory of problem solving. *Journal of Communication, 61*, 120–149.

Kim, J.-N., & Ni, L. (2010). Seeing the forest through the trees: The behavior, strategic management paradigm in public relations and its future. In R. L. Heath (Ed.), *SAGE handbook of public relations* (pp. 35–57). Thousand Oaks, CA: Sage.

Kim, J.-N., & Ni, L. (2013). Two types of public relations problems and integrating formative and evaluative research: A review of research programs within the behavioral, strategic management paradigm. *Journal of Public Relations, 25*, 1–29.

Leichty, G., & Springston, J. (1993). Reconsidering public relations models. *Public Relations Review, 19*, 327–339.

Men, L. R. (2014). Strategic internal communication: Transformational leadership, communication channels, and employee satisfaction. *Management Communication Quarterly, 28*, 264–284.

Pratkanis, A. R., & Turner, M. E. (1996). Persuasion and democracy: Strategies for increasing deliberative participation and enacting social change. *Journal of Social Issues, 52*, 187–205.

Scott, W. R. (1987). *Organizations: Rational, natural, and open systems* (2nd ed.). Englewood Cliffs, NJ: Prentice-Hall.

Steyn, B. (2007). Contribution of public relations to organizational strategy formation. In E. L. Toth (Ed.), *The future of excellence in public relations and communication management* (pp. 137–172). Mahwah, NJ: Lawrence Erlbaum.

Tam, L., Kim, J., & Kim, J.-N. (2018). The origins of distant voicing: Examining relational dimensions in public diplomacy and their effects on megaphoning. *Public Relations Review*, *22*, 407–418.

Toth, E. L. (2009). The case for pluralistic studies of public relations: Rhetorical, critical, and excellence perspectives. In R. L. Heath, E. L. Toth, & D. Waymer (Eds.), *Rhetorical and critical approaches to public relations II* (pp. 48–60). New York: Routledge.

Van den Bosch, F. A. J., & van Riel, C. B. M. (1998). Buffering and bridging as environmental strategies of firms. *Business Strategy and the Environment*, *7*, 24–31.

4

Contingency Theory: Strategic Conflict Management

Introduction

The contingency theory of conflict management explains the dynamics of public relations practice as choosing the stance that best serves the interests of an organization, while at the same time following strategies that are dependent on the given situation—one that is often unfolding or in flux. This theoretical perspective suggests that public relations professionals adopt an "it depends" approach, defined as the most strategic response to changing circumstances. Contingency theory may be defined as analysis of the dynamic interplay of parties on a continuum in a given set of internal and external circumstances over time.

Contingency theory has roots in observations about the behavior of individuals in corporate roles tracing back to the late nineteenth century. It developed at a time when serious scientific analysis of labor and management was undertaken in an attempt to understand work and supervision and make it a science. Later, following World War II, contingency theory became vital for analyses of various management styles. Most notably, the clinical psychologist Fred Fielder (1958, 1964, 1967) developed a sophisticated measurement system for assessing perceptions of common ground and psychological distance among coworkers. Fielder's contingency model of leadership showed how the interplay of multiple variables affected productivity in the workplace.

In essence, Fielder proposed that effective managers change their leadership style to suit the situation at hand. His analyses suggested that work behavior could be described meaningfully only when combined with factors that were contingent—for example, how a manager addressed subordinates, or subcultures within working teams. This research countered the predominant "one size fits all" approach to management and organizational leadership. Fielder reasoned that management leadership style was an independent variable (one that is changed or controlled), with contingency as a mediating variable and worker satisfaction as an outcome/dependent variable (the one being tested or examined). This frame became the basis for the contingency theory of public relations.

Derived from organizational theory, contingency theory represents a challenge to excellence theory, which also derives at least some assumptions from organizational and management theory. But excellence and contingency theories draw contrasting conclusions and make divergent recommendations for public relations practice regarding the quest to advance the profession and develop the discipline. The mission of contingency theorists has been to focus on strategic, managerial, and contingent practices of public relations as they encounter issue, conflict, and crisis with key publics.

Public Relations Theory: Capabilities and Competencies, First Edition. Jae-Hwa Shin and Robert L. Heath.
© 2021 John Wiley & Sons, Inc. Published 2021 by John Wiley & Sons, Inc.

Pure Advocacy -- Pure Accommodation

Figure 4.1 Continuum between pure advocacy and pure accommodation.

The dynamics of the contingencies outlined in contingency theory are conceptualized as falling on a continuum that ranges from "pure" advocacy to "pure" accommodation as possible stances defining an organization's position. Pure advocacy means arguing for or supporting a thing or idea without qualification. Pure accommodation, on the other hand, means completely conceding a point or adjusting a position in response to a counterargument.

The continuum is composed of hybrid points of advocacy and accommodation. The logic of the theory reasons that an organization is strategically best advised to think in terms of where on the continuum its engagement is most likely to be productive in solving each instance of conflict with each key stakeholding public in a particular instance, at a particular time, and given the specific context. This theory also reasons that the first choice or selection of a strategic point on the continuum may or may not lead to conflict resolution. Thus, the continuum offers a range of options—requiring ancillary variables—which the organization, as well as the engaged publics, can use to determine various strategic options. This theory, therefore, offers contingent options, well defined on this continuum, by which an organization can strategically interact with its public and best reach its goals. The continuum is composed of hybrid points of advocacy and accommodation (Figure 4.1).

A number of factors are involved in the decision-making process, in order to—ideally—serve both the organizational and the public interest in fostering effective communication. This emphasis on multiple factors dynamically affecting the continuum is a key aspect of contingency theory and represents one of the hallmarks of strategic communication management.

Contingency theory qualifies key themes advanced by excellence theory. For example, a key theme of excellence has been a focal point for the comparison of excellence and contingency theories. As Pang, Jin, and Cameron (2010a) observe:

> The contingency theory of strategic conflict management ... began (by) questioning excellence theory's positioning of symmetrical communication as normative theory on how organizations should be practicing public relations that was regarded as the most ethical and effective. (p. 17)

As such, it might have matured to serve "as an elaboration, qualification, and extension of the value of symmetry" (p. 17). What occurred instead, however, was a substantial reconceptualization of strategic communication based on empirical testing, which revealed that its complexity could not be reduced to a handful of variables. By the early 2000s, contingency theory had developed into a separate theory of public relations, with its own rationale and research grounding.

What, then, is the essence of contingency theory, as focused on conflict resolution as a basic rationale for public relations? According to Pang et al. (2010a):

> The alternative view pioneered by contingency theory of how strategic communication ought to be practiced, that communication could be examined through a continuum whereby organizations practice a variety of stances at a given time for a given public depending on the circumstance. (pp. 17–18)

Rather than relying on the possibility that symmetry alone offers a solution to public relations challenges, this theory reasons that practitioners should—and do—select wisely and ethically, as well as strategically, from options on a continuum contingent to the conditions and challenges present in each specific public relations moment.

Overall, this chapter will address the key assumptions of the contingency theory of public relations as a form of strategic conflict management. It will examine the qualifications of excellence theory and tie contingency theory to other theoretical orientations, in order to understand it on a macro level. Overall, contingency theory can best be illuminated from the perspective of strategic conflict management. Conflict inherently exists in the relationship between an organization and its public. Depending on the issue, conflict or crisis will form, develop, and deteriorate through a cycle of conflict. Thus, it is crucial for a public relations professional to manage conflict strategically.

Questions to Frame the Discussion of Contingency Theory

- What are the main assumptions of the contingency theory of public relations?
- How do an organization and its publics change their stances on a continuum between pure accommodation and pure advocacy?
- What are the contingent variables that affect the decision to advocate a position or attempt to accommodate the other side?
- How does contingency theory add to the ongoing efforts to develop an effective and ethical approach to the study and practice of public relations?

Key Themes

- The principle of the contingency theory of strategic conflict management in public relations is an "it depends" approach.
- Contingency theory suggests a continuum between pure advocacy and pure accommodation of organization–public relationships (OPRs). The stances taken or strategic choices made by public relations professionals move on this continuum, being sometimes advocating and sometimes accommodating.
- The dynamics of OPR in a given situation depend on a number of internal and external factors. Public relations professionals are influenced by factors on the individual, organizational, and societal levels in terms of their decision-making process.
- Contingency theory embraces dynamic and complex processes among the parties involved in a conflict in meeting its strategic goal over time.

Case Study: Toyota Weathers the Storm

Several spectacular cases of Toyotas accelerating out of control dominated media coverage in March 2010. The issue of automobile safety and the company's reputation for excellent engineering and manufacturing became the focal point of controversy and conflict. Toyota at first defended itself by demonstrating that most of the nearly 80 cases of runaway acceleration were the result of incorrect floor mats, not an electronic glitch. Its internal investigation concluded that either the floor mats were improperly designed or that they were used in a manner whereby they interfered with the operation of the gas pedal.

Cases of individual accidents became central to the technical assessment of the reason for the sudden and uncontrolled acceleration. One of the most remarkable incidents involved the death of California Highway Patrol Officer Mark Saylor, who was killed with his family in a borrowed Lexus. In another case, Belent Ezel and his wife plunged off a cliff after their 2005 Camry accelerated suddenly. Shortly after this, live news coverage followed Jim Sikes' Prius accelerating out of control to 94 miles per hour on a freeway near San Diego—a claim later proved not to be the result of a defect. Unintended acceleration played into the public's deepest fears. With sensational headlines like, "Terror of the Roads: Runaway Toyotas," media outlets channeled anxiety about loss of control over machinery. For the company, as an observer noted, "It took forty years to build a reputation and a few days to cut it in half" (Evans, 2010).

Media coverage, public opinion, and Toyota's response illuminate several dimensions of crisis communication and set the groundwork for our explanation of how contingency theory applies in a real-world situation. The evolution of the crisis shows how Toyota continually reassessed and renegotiated its stance—ranging from advocacy (putting the interest of the organization first) to accommodation (considering first the interests of its audience or constituents).

Toyota's communication team was initially silent, as a form of nonaccommodation. Silence as a strategy can be a form of taking an advocacy stance. Silence on the part of a company can be interpreted as advocating continued confidence that its first explanation—including denial—"settles" the matter. As such, silence lets public opinion, including that expressed in online forums and blogs, drive the story. Toyota's nonaccommodation offended many, leading Jim Lentz, President of Toyota Motor Sales in the United States, to issue an apology for its poor communication and a promise to do better. Without directly attacking its accusers, the company adopted a stance of advocacy, suggesting that nothing was wrong with its vehicles. Only after the crisis had reached a critical stage did it react with more accommodating communication strategies.

As a key part of its advocacy, Toyota exposed faults in the research of a Southern Illinois University professor who had captured headlines by creating unintended acceleration in a Toyota Avalon. In dramatic fashion, before Congress, Toyota countered by replicating the glitch in several rival vehicles. This advocacy seemingly convinced key members of Congress, but definitely did not win the day in the court of public opinion.

The company presumed that the scientific battle, won by its argument and conceded by Congress, would settle the matter (Cole, 2011). It did not, and therefore, reacting to negative public opinion and media coverage, Toyota's stance quickly shifted from advocacy to accommodation. First, it stopped production and suspended sales of the affected models—nearly 8 million vehicles in total were affected. Second, it encouraged all owners to bring their cars in for an inspection. Third, it hired the public relations firms GolinHarris and Robinson Lerer & Montgomery—with strengths in crisis communication and conflict management—and government relations specialists including Glover Park Group and Quinn Gillespie & Associates. Through counseling and strategic communication, these agencies enlarged the range of stance options available to the company. Toyota seemed unfamiliar with the public opinion arena in the United States, where distrust is often associated with corporate defensive statements. One operating assumption there is that powerful organizations will make claims that they believe settle a matter without fully, responsibly, or ethically responding to consumer concerns. Once consumer concern became the point of conflict—as contingency theory predicts—the company picked a different communication solution.

An apologetic television commercial, aired shortly after the congressional testimony, struck an accommodating tone, suggesting that Toyota had failed to live up to its reputation for safety, quality, and excellence. Near the end of 2010, it announced on its corporate website that it had "taken major steps to become an even more responsive, customer-focused organization—and to strengthen our leadership in automotive quality and safety." In this case, accommodation meant putting the public interest first, even if the statements were rhetorical. The company's president, Akido Toyoda, issued a rare public appeal, again stressing the interest of Toyota's constituents: "We are putting our customers and the values on which our company was founded, front and center" (Toyoda, 2010).

Did Toyota's process of crisis management—the shift in stance from advocacy to accommodation—work? It seems at first to have failed to react with messages that were timely and targeted. Piotrowski and Guyette (2010) find that 57% of 72 college business majors and 37 other adults believed that Toyota had handled the crisis poorly, moving too slowly to address perceived public concerns. A similar number perceived little corporate transparency and expressed little confidence in the company's ethical stance.

Later, however, Toyota effectively engaged in reputation restoration through positioning tending toward accommodation on a moving continuum. By December 2010, the crisis appears to have been abated, and the provision of information on its responsiveness and consumer commitment seems even to have strengthened the company's reputation. Toyota eventually agreed to settle a class action court case for $1.2 billion. The *Wall Street Journal* estimated that the issue cost Toyota at least $3 billion in direct costs, including recalls and not counting potential lost sales and damage to its reputation (Del Valle, 2019; Ramsey, 2012). But Toyota actually saw an increase in sales of between 30 and 35% compared with the previous year following the congressional testimony and its proactive public relations campaign, according to Jim Lentz.

The company faced a rebuilding of its reputation. In 2012, it regained its position as the global leader in automotive sales, moving 10.2—about 18%—of the total 63 million vehicles produced. While Volkswagen eclipsed it in total volume in 2017, as of late 2019 the Japanese manufacturer retained a strong second-place position and maintained healthy profits by focusing on just-in-time manufacturing processes. Toyota has also taken proactive steps to enhance vehicle safety, such as the creation of the Collaborative Safety Research Center in 2011. Its efforts extend to direct outreach to potential customers, including installing displays showing how changes in design have made its cars safer (Greimel, 2017; Kelly, 2012).

Questions for Consideration
- Do you think Toyota responded effectively to the crisis? If so, was the first response as good as its subsequent ones? What could Toyota have done differently in dealing with the crisis situation and the conflict it generated?
- What are some of the factors that Toyota may have considered as its conflict and crisis management positioning evolved over time?
- What is the aftermath of Toyota recall case? Do you think the company will be able to regain or even strengthen its reputation using the accommodative strategies of responding to and listening to consumer concerns? If so, what efforts can it make from a public relations theoretical standpoint?
- Did Toyota appropriately and fully explain the lessons learned from the crisis in ways that built customers' confidence in its commitment to their safety?
- Can a company use a strategy that in one context is effective but in another is not? If so, what does that tell us about the need to have and use an array of strategies ranging from "pure" advocacy to "pure" accommodation as means for resolving a crisis through effective and ethical conflict management?

Contingency Theory: Public Relations Through Strategic Conflict Management

As already noted, the contingency theory of management initially began more as a system of measurement than a full theory. It was intended to determine how contingent, as opposed to regimented, leadership and management practices are in the success of companies. Later, theoretical speculation based on practical observations expanded the system of measurement into a theory. The reasoning focused on contingent behaviors, sensitive to preferred outcomes. Such behaviors and outcomes could be measured, but no theory had emerged to explain and predict selection based on outcome. Fielder's proposition that effective managers change their leadership style to suit the situation at hand is one of the bases of the contingency theory of public relations. For example, management style is considered a contingency variable with influence on how a public relations professional makes a decision. In this way, the conceptual foundation had been established for a contingent approach to leadership as being effective for management and supervision.

While Fielder concentrated on contingency associated with leadership at the individual level, other scholars refined and expanded the theory to describe interactions at the organizational level. Woodward (1958), for example, found that no consistent pattern or common workplace variables defined success among about 100 manufacturing plants in South Essex, England. The correlation between organizational structure and performance was significantly related to the contingent variable of how technology was employed. Although she has been criticized for developing a rather blunt instrument, Woodward challenged the idea that successful organizations operated according to principles that were universally applicable—in other words, that the success or failure of organizations depended on contingencies. Hersey and Blanchard (1972) expanded the contingency theory of management by adding a situational—or readiness—component. They suggested that there is no *one* way to lead; rather, effectiveness is based on a contingent leadership style, defined as the amount of task behavior and relationship behavior matching with the working group's level of maturity, defined in turn as the ability to understand and complete tasks.

Hersey and Blanchard's emphasis on flexibility and situational variability provided an important precedent for the contingency theory of management, organizational success, and leadership. By this advance, theorists aspiring to the usefulness of contingency were now able to apply it to public relations. To do so, they would need to be able to explain not only how and why contingency led to preferred organization–stakeholder relationships, but also what variables were needed to understand and solve the mysteries of contingency. Without a systematic research-based explanation, contingency could not be considered as a theory of public relations.

The roots of that advance again came from work by management theorists. The contingency theory of management represented a challenge to earlier, modernist theories of management, such as Max Weber's (1930) Marxist concept of bureaucracy as a system corrupted by the interests of powerful public officials and Frederick Taylor's (1911) concept of scientific management. These approaches focused exclusively on internal factors—often in excruciating detail, such as Taylor's measuring with a stopwatch the time it took a worker to shovel coal. Taylor, in particular, expressed a normative faith that if each function could be measured with enough precision, it would be possible to devise a system for improving efficiency that benefited both labor and management and that could be applied in all situations. Weber's conception, too, is a one-way street, where managers universally exert dictatorial control over their subordinates and tend to be unresponsive to the various publics that they serve. By Taylor's logic, applied to the skills of a baseball pitcher, the manager would seek to perfect "pitching" so that all pitchers performed in exactly the same way.

Knowledgeable fans understand that exactly the opposite is the key to a pitcher's success. Individual differences make it more difficult for batters to predict the next pitch, which is to the pitcher's advantage.

Early contingency theorists such as Fielder (1958), Woodward (1958), and Thompson (1963) challenged the notion that there was a single best way to perform a function—that external or situational factors affected actions and outcomes. Contingency theory management researchers have championed the virtue of varying degrees of flexibility in response to changing situations and conditions. For public relations professionals, the theory suggests the crucial role of accurate assessment of these contingencies, the ability to anticipate the move and stance of the contending party, nimbleness, and uncertainty. Instead of treating variability and uncertainty as whimsy or caprice, the contingency theory of public relations attempts to provide a systematic account of how these variables interplay in actual practice.

Within the logic of contingency, the decisions made by managers and leaders are not derived from mere whimsy, inconsistency, or uncertainty. How, the reasoning goes, is management strategically programmatic? How does being able to react to "contingency" define leadership style? Is it possible to predict what strategies lead to the best performance outcomes? The contingency theory of public relations suggests that a degree of flexibility, in contrast to the more formulaic answers provided by excellence theory, can help organizations reach their goals more effectively. In the case of Toyota, as customer complaints began to surface, management worked with public relations professionals to address them in a serious manner and develop strategic options based on evidence, engineering science, and customer satisfaction. Toyota needed to be less sure that its response was self-satisfying than that it selected response options that bolstered customer satisfaction and preserved its reputation, particularly its cherished reputation for safety. Thus, we have the foundation for applying the contingency theory of management to the practice and research of public relations.

Contingency Theory in Public Relations

The contingency theory of public relations shares many premises with the contingency theory of organizational studies. Both suggest that there is no best way to manage, organize, lead, communicate, or make a decision in all situations. Thus, each management or public relations situation or moment requires a strategic, rather than a fixed, response that is sensitive to it. As excellence theory is associated traditionally with a research agenda that developed at the University of Maryland, so contingency theory has been primarily associated with work at the University of Missouri. In the early 1990s, Cameron and his colleagues developed this contingency perspective for public relations theory building to explain the complexity and dynamism of public relations practice. Contingency theory urges public relations professionals to consider the influences of internal and external factors and make a decision in facing a situation of conflict or dealing with the public in their routines.

Cancel, Cameron, Sallot, and Mitrook's (1997) study provided a foundation for the central assumptions of theory. They argued for a theory based on a continuum from pure accommodation to pure advocacy, moderated or mediated by 87 variables antecedent to the degree of accommodation undertaken by public relations or the degree of advocacy taken by the professional. They assumed that a hybrid of stances, with some degree of accommodation and some degree of advocacy, would provide the degree of contingency required to most strategically, effectively, and even ethically respond to a given situation. For example, a public relations professional facing a situation affected by certain contingency variables should be able to identify the most salient factors among these in a given situation and react to bring about the best positioning leading to a resolution. This contingency approach is not normative but positive and realistic, in order to meet the needs of an organization and possibly also the public's interest. Contingency theory reasons that the first strategic choice might not be the best, but that it will be tested in operation. If it is found to be inadequate, or unhelpful to conflict management, other hybrid options are available. Thus, the logic of contingency in public relations, as in management, is that having a fixed-option solution to fit or solve all problems is limiting. The narrowness of a fixed option, as was the case with Taylor's scientific management (see earlier), can frustrate efforts and produce less than optimal outcomes for both the organization and its stakeholders.

This theory, with its commitment to contingency, represents a challenge to the "normative" model of two-way symmetrical communications—an ideal espoused by Grunig's (1992) excellence theory or four models of public relations (see Chapter 3). Instead of relying on a limited set of normative models, Cancel et al. (1997) argued that a dizzying variety of factors (variables) affected whether or not a practitioner should adopt a stance of accommodation:

> Is the public reasonable or radical? Are the public's beliefs or behavior morally repugnant? Do I have support from top management to make the call? How enlightened is my boss about accommodation's benefits to all parties? How much of a threat is the public? (p. 32)

By "the" public, advocates of this theory mean some undifferentiated beast, or "the" in the sense of each depending on the circumstances of each conflict. Cancel et al. also suggested that "public relations is too complex, too fluid, and impinged by far too many variables" (p. 32) to be forced into narrow categories—in this case, a seemingly limiting binary choice between symmetry and asymmetry. Contingency theory has been developed and refined in an attempt to account for the complexity, multiplicity, and subtlety of public relations practice. Assessing the weight of each factor, and its relative importance, represents a major challenge for public relations professionals. The central question is, "What is the best way to practice public relations?" The answer, invariably, is, "It depends."

As a response to excellence theory, contingency theory also responds to the situational theory of publics and of problem solving (see Chapter 3). Given contingencies, symmetry can limit rather than empower organizations to respond and react in ways that may be responsive and responsible to other publics in each case. Excellence theory, with situational theory, seems to focus on one public at a time, and not to presume the reality that many players may be involved in each conflict. Thus—and this is crucial—what is appropriate to solving the problem in mutual interest may in fact require that some interest—one less deserving—be communicated about differently than other interests. While advocacy might be reasonable and ethical with some publics, accommodation might be unreasonable and unethical with publics in the same contingent situation.

In their literature review, Cancel et al. (1997) identified several forerunners of the assumptions of the contingency theory of public relations. Hellweg (1989) argued that the relationship between two-way symmetrical and asymmetrical communication was not binary, but existed on a continuum. Likewise, Murphy (1991) demonstrated how the positions advocated by contending sides (organizations and external publics) tend to reach equilibrium through a process described as "mixed-motive games," or more simply, the process of negotiation. Organizations and publics, Murphy contended, generally bargain for an "uneasy and precarious" balance situated on a continuum, suggesting that game theory may help describe how contending parties reach a level of accommodation. The work of Cancel et al. (1997) represents a specific challenge to the four models of public relations. The data supporting these models, they contend, is weak, with seven studies yielding low reliability among items specific to each. They further discuss the complexity of mixed motives arrayed on a continuum.

Contingency theory does not ignore the fact that excellence theory has also acknowledged the mixed-motives option, although it is not the same notion of hybrid points of advocacy and accommodation. A key—one central to a comparison of excellence and contingency theories—is to identify the factors or variables that predict and guide the strategic choices. This central concept has motivated contingency theorists to entertain multiple options. At the same time, researchers have guarded against committing to a dimension that might be limiting or less serviceable given the range of strategic response options. Contingency theorists have also considered the implications of multiple interests, as well as scientific bases and theoretical justification, in selecting factors and variables.

The initial contingency study provided a synthetic definition of the operational stances of public relations professionals along an advocacy–accommodation continuum. Cancel et al. (1997) developed a set of internal and external variables. Broad categories included the public's perception of its own power, potential threats to an organization, organizational characteristics, economic concerns, public relations practitioners' experience levels, individual characteristics such as tolerance of uncertainty, and personal ethics. However, the study was based on qualitative observations, which required quantitative analysis to further develop its theoretical basis.

A follow-up study conducted by Cancel, Mitrook, and Cameron in 1999, "Testing the Contingency Theory of Accommodation in Public Relations," was based on in-depth interviews of 18 public relations professionals and educators. The objective was to conceptualize and define public relations practice with regard to degree of accommodation. The results helped ground the contingency theory of public relations by seeing if public relations professionals would independently validate a number of variables affecting stances of or tensions between accommodation and advocacy.

To help set the foundations for this theory, Cancel et al. (1999) observed the following key themes: (a) the validity of the advocacy–accommodation continuum as an organization's stance; (b) potential variables affecting an organization's stance; and (c) the degree of support of each variable. They concluded that the interviewees were "quite sophisticated in considering a welter of factors affecting accommodation of publics" (p. 171), and that there was strong support for several predisposing variables. For example, several of the public relations professionals interviewed cited the importance of corporate size, corporate culture, corporate business exposure, public relations access to the dominant coalition, the dominant coalition's decision power, and enlightenment and individual characteristics as supportive of accommodative positions. Also, several predisposing variables were identified with weak support of accommodative positions. For instance, the age of the company, whether or not value or tradition was important, and the product/service environment seemed to have little to do with whether an accommodative stance would be adopted.

These variables, Cancel et al. (1999) argued, are predisposing in the sense that they affect where a corporation's opening stance sits along the continuum from advocacy to accommodation as a given situation arises and continues. The situational decisions made by a public relations professional, in concert to a greater or lesser degree with other members of executive management, depend on a highly complex and shifting set of situational variables. Situational variables such as the urgency of the situation, threats, and the external public's power to positively impact the organization interact with predisposing variables to affect whether the organization is accommodative of or advocating with the public at a given point in time.

Later, Cameron, Cropp, and Reber (2001) presented an even greater variety of variables, which they reasoned operated on external and internal levels as a refinement of the proposed predisposing and situational ones: threats, industry environment, general political/social environment/external culture, external public, issue under question, organization characteristics, public relations department characteristics, dominant coalition characteristics, internal threats, individual characteristics, and relationship characteristics. They also assessed the salience of six proscriptive factors that justify the continuum between advocacy and accommodation:

1) moral conviction;
2) multiple publics;
3) regulatory constraints;
4) management pressure;
5) jurisdictional issues; and
6) legal constraints.

For example, an organization cannot satisfy multiple publics with conflicting interests simultaneously, so a public relations professional must be accommodating with one public but advocating with another.

In 2003, Reber and Cameron further tested the robustness of the contingency scale, including factors such as external threats, organizational characteristics, public relations department characteristics, and dominant coalition characteristics within an organization. They found a strong relationship between the move toward accommodation and the characteristics of executive management. The goal was to establish a simple matrix of contingent variables using factor analysis. Later, Shin, Cheng, Jin, and Cameron (2005) showed through content analysis that the 86 contingent variables, which were thematically created as 87 variables in the initial contingency study, were associated with stances taken along the continuum between accommodation and advocacy during the conflict management process. Shin, Cameron, and Cropp (2006) provided further validity for contingency theory and simplified the relationships among a number of variables. They conducted a national survey of public relations practitioners, refining the associations with the 86 variables, which they divided into five external categories (threats, industry environment, political/social/cultural environment, public power, and public relationships), and seven internal, organizational ones (development, structure, independence of the public relations department, governance of the public relations department, top management characteristics, individual characteristics, and individual capabilities). This was the first attempt to quantify all the contingency variables previously identified into 12 factors with strong reliability. The central arguments of contingency theory remain prescriptive in the sense that they seek to ground theory in field tests or the insights of practitioners, thereby using research and theory to validate current best practices. The goal of the theory is to improve the practice of public relations and guide research. It offers a set of practical implications, such as convincing management that the role of public relations goes beyond deontological two-way symmetrical communication.

Qualifications of Excellence Models

As discussed in Chapter 3, excellence theory features four models of public relations: press agentry, public information, two-way asymmetrical, and two-way symmetrical. It proposes that two-way symmetrical public relations is an ideal to which all public relations professionals should aspire in their practice. According to Cameron, Cropp, and Reber (2001), excellence theory does not so much describe what public relations is as what it should be: "dialogue and trade-offs between an organization and a public," where each side negotiates from a more or less equal footing (p. 253). In this case, communication and negotiation hold promise of being successful because each side

| Theory in Practice: Shifting Stances—The 1996 Olympic Games |

Contingency theorists have argued that it is not always ethical for, or in the best interest of, an organization to accommodate all audiences in all situations or at all times. Organizations often shift their stances based on emerging factors, or variables, that affect their position as a conflict or controversy unfolds. Stances change as situational factors introduce new information, different publics, or responses to changed strategies by other participants in the conflict. This aspect of the contingency theory of conflict management was examined in 1998, based on the experience of C. Richard Yarborough, the Managing Director-Communications for The Atlanta Committee for Olympic Games. The case shows how the ACOG shifted its position from accommodation to advocacy in response to changing conditions (Yarbrough, Cameron, Sallot, & McWilliams, 1998).

In January 1994, beginning with the Super Bowl, the ACOG announced that Cobb County (one of three counties making up Atlanta) would be the site of preliminary rounds of the volleyball tournament. John-Ivan Weaver, a prominent and vocal gay activist, objected to this on the grounds that Cobb County had recently passed a resolution designed to discourage gay couples from moving there. He advocated moving the games out of the county if it did not rescind the resolution. Billy Byrne, representing Cobb County, refused to do so, but he did agree to negotiate. At this point, the ACOG merely observed—engaged in nonaccommodation—until the situation could be evaluated thoroughly.

The lines were drawn sharply when Weaver organized a small parade that garnered nationwide attention. He was joined by organizations such as the Cobb Citizens Coalition, a human rights' group with broad interests. The ACOG received letters from people across the nation, including congressmen, in support of rescinding the resolution or moving the games. Media, for the most part, came out in support of the gay activists. As a result, and through pressure from the ACOG and sponsors of the Olympic Games, Byrne agreed to introduce a substitute resolution that was less odious. The moderates were disposed to accept this compromise.

However, after being booed roundly at an Atlanta Braves game, Bryne announced he had withdrawn the new resolution. At this point, Yarborough recommended a course of pure advocacy, arguing that the ACOG should move out of Cobb County because the cost to defend against protests and other issues would far exceed the $4 million committed to the project. The volleyball tournament was moved to Athens, Georgia, with little further protestation.

But the life cycle of the issue was not over; it reemerged in the form of anti-homosexual resolutions in Spartanburg and Greenville, South Carolina. The ACOG adopted stances of both accommodation and advocacy to handle the conflict. In the end, it enlisted sponsors such as BMW to bolster its position and help negotiate a compromise in Spartanburg, and held its ground by driving the Olympic torch through Greenville when attempts to reach a compromise there failed.

It was important that the ACOG acted consistently on the continuum, based on the precedent it established in Georgia.

has a good sense of the arguments and expectations of the other. Excellence theory recognizes that organizations and publics engage in and enact a process of adaptation as problem solving occurs.

Cameron and his colleagues admitted that excellence theory offers a "compelling" and useful model of public relations, but nevertheless offered contingency theory as a substantial qualification, elaboration, and refinement of it. Contingency theory challenges excellence theory through what may be seen as a subtle (or profound) refinement, but one that threatens its very core. Three principal arguments are advanced against excellence theory: (a) organizations take stances with their publics along a continuum ranging from advocacy to accommodation; (b) a variety of internal and external factors affect where an organization positions itself along the continuum at any given time; and (c) the strategic stance is not the same as the specific tactics used by an organization. In short, whereas excellent theory offers a well-defined set of stances and strategies, contingency theory recognizes the many shades of gray and shifting positions that characterize the practice of public relations. This acknowledgment suggests that the contingency approach may lead to a more effective way of managing relationships between organizations and publics in real-world settings.

It may be illuminating to see how contingency theory differs from excellence theory regarding the six proscriptive factors identified by Cameron et al. (2001):

- First, it challenges James Grunig's (1989; Grunig, Grunig, & Dozier, 2002) contention that two-way symmetrical communication and accommodation are always necessarily ethical. For instance, it may not be ethical to engage in accommodation when dealing with a segment of the public that engages in libelous, racist, or slanderous utterances.

- Second, there are usually multiple publics engaged in an issue, and a public relations professional cannot practice a single model to satisfy all of these at the same time and in the same way. Often, these publics do not share the same interests and points of view. In fact, using the logics of the situational theory of problem solving (discussed in Chapter 3), one can easily reason that different publics will see matters differently in terms of problems, degree of involvement, constraint recognition, and, particularly, referent criterion.

- Third, regulatory constraints may prevent one company from engaging in dialogue or negotiation with another—for example, due to anti-trust regulations.

- Fourth, management often resists accommodative stances or the adoption of two-way symmetrical communication because they are perceived as showing weakness or conflicting with the organization's interest.

- Fifth, jurisdictional issues can interfere with the smooth flow of two-way communication—such as when union rules dictate what may or may not be discussed in a given situation.

- Sixth, legal constraints may inhibit dialogue—for example, the limits placed on certain speech in foreign countries.

Key Assumptions of Contingency Theory

A brief overview of some of its key assumptions will further establish contingency theory's contribution to public relations theory and practice:

- Contingency theory postulates that the stances of organizations and their publics move in dynamic relationships depending on (a) the adoption of an initial position along a continuum between accommodation and advocacy and (b) situational variables. This cycle of conflict and incremental adjustment of stances suggests that strategic conflict management is a core function of the public relations process. An organization and its publics may change their stances many times before a resolution is reached, or not. As the cycle of ongoing strategic conflict management unfolds, dozens of variables influence the position taken by the organization and its publics. Cameron and his colleagues identified 87 variables, but the number, character, nature, and significance of these are constantly revised, refined, and developed.

- Public relations professionals play a crucial role in the cycle of negotiation and conflict management, dealing with the matrix of contingent factors influential to their stances and defining their respective strategies. In practice, it is difficult to establish a fixed, stable point on the continuum between advocacy and accommodation, since stances are dynamic and evolve in response to a variety of internal and external variables. At the same time, these stances may not be in line with the strategies chosen to respond to a given situation. Cameron et al. (2001) gave the example of an environmental activist group that initially adopted a stance of pure advocacy against a plastics manufacturer. When the manufacturer improved its environmental record, engaging in a sustained recycling initiative, the environmentalists became much more collaborative, but not necessarily accommodating. Both the company and the environmentalists embraced collaborative strategies—the company, by changing its behavior, likely at the initial expense of its bottom line, and the group, by compromising at least to a degree, and demonstrating a commitment to engage in negotiation. But each party essentially held to its stances.

- Strategies and tactics used by public relations professionals are not necessarily in line with their stances of advocacy or accommodation. Thus, collaborative advocacy or cooperative antagonism is common.

Theory in Practice: Who's Getting the Best Piece of the Pie?

One of the major assumptions of contingency theory stresses the dynamics of decision making. To set the context for this theme, let's think about how a buyer and seller might negotiate the price of a historic automobile, something for which no value is set (imagine a 1959 Ferrari driven by legendary driver Juan Fangio at Monaco). The seller has an obvious interest in getting the highest price possible. Naturally, the buyer tries to discover the lowest they will accept. Buyer and seller try to reach consensus, but rarely without going through some measure of conflict or disagreement. The resulting negotiation often involves shifts in position, from advocacy to accommodation. For example, the seller might feign disinterest in making a deal and then suddenly announce a one-time, limited window of opportunity. Or perhaps the potential buyer will be intentionally abrupt at first, waiting for the right opportunity to reveal a gentler personality in an effort to win the seller over.

Similar shifts and changes of position and strategy will occur in the many and various relationships between an organization and its publics. Organizations have a natural interest in advocating their positions and defending their reputations. These interests do not always square with those of their publics. Depending on the situation, contending parties reach consensus by moving on a continuum between advocacy and accommodation, according to their respective goals and interests. This contingency approach describes the efforts of each to get the best piece of the pie—that often allusive coordination between an organization and its public by which each interest group believes it is receiving the best possible—or, at least, a good—deal. To reach a state that is acceptable to each party requires clear and effective communications, often managed by a public relations professional who understands situational contingencies.

The boxed text makes an important point of relevance to contingency: communication strategies change as interaction and responses occur. This illustration highlights the continuum between advocacy and accommodation; it is defined by these polar ends in order to capture the dynamics of the communication between an organization and its various publics. Strategic adjustments and tensions, driven by a number of factors, affect the strategic positions chosen by each. Public relations practitioners can influence such choices by affecting how the organization approaches the challenge. Given the range of options, contingency theory emphasizes "an organization's possible wide range of stances taken toward an individual public, differing from the more prescriptive and mutually exclusive categorization necessarily found in a limited set of models of communication" (Cancel et al., 1999, p. 172). Hellweg (1989), Murphy (1991), and even Dozier, L. Grunig, and J. Grunig (1995) all suggest the variables involved in the strategic management of conflict fit into a continuum. They further confirm that the notion of a continuum represents the varying stances that individual public relations professionals find themselves adopting in an accurate and useful sense. This wide range of options available to public relations professionals is, in a realistic sense, evidence of mixed motives between the polarities of advocacy and accommodation.

A public relations professional can constantly assess whether to adopt a response that is accommodating or advocating toward a certain public around a particular issue. Generally, the response represents a hybrid point of advocacy and accommodation, or a compromise between some set of organizational goals and some degree of the perceived interests of the public. Often, what the professional expects the other party's stance will be affects these decisions (see coorientational analysis and game theory). Similarly, in discourse, an entity's design and execution of a message (and message strategy) are selected for effect, and to achieve some outcome that is contingent. Inauthentic statements can be made because of the assumption that in some contexts, they may be more successful than authentic ones. For this reason, discourse can be less transparent, authentic, and responsive—simply because of the problem of foretelling outcomes.

Contingency theory can also be illustrated in the following way. The communications strategy used by a small nonprofit dedicated to ending offshore drilling would be different with a U.S. Senator from Louisiana than with one from Minnesota. It is reasonable to expect that Louisiana has a greater economic interest in the issue, in the form of a tax windfall, than does Minnesota, a state without offshore oil reserves. The advocacy group might emphasize the short-term threat to wildlife and fishing to the Senator in Louisiana, while using the long-term environmental impact of drilling to reach the one in Minnesota.

Neither organization nor public is limited to a particular position, but moves to choose the best strategies and tactics to accomplish its goals. Imagine if a public relations professional were to question what would be the best approach in a given situation with the public at a given point in time. No doubt, the answer would be, "It depends."

A crucial aspect of the concept of stance is dynamism as it moves on a continuum. To identify any fixed point at any given time is difficult, and likely to be relevant only for a short period—particularly in a crisis situation. Once a stance is identified, it tends to shift, and requires further specification and examination. In a sense, it is like Zeno's arrow—before it can travel a certain distance, it must travel halfway, and halfway before that, in infinite regress. Identifying stances may also be qualified by the quantum Zeno effect, discovered in 1977 by E. C. G. Sudarshan and B. Misra: the motion of a quantum system can be affected by the very act of observation. It is also like a punctuated equilibrium, or uneven a distribution of changes, which is drawn from recent theory of evolutionary biology.

The assumption of dynamic adjustment highlighted by contingency theory offers insights into the source–reporter relationship, which has many of the characteristics of OPR. In this relationship, public relations professionals and journalists represent an organization and the media, respectively. Shin and Cameron (2003) discuss the dynamic between journalist and public relations professional as a "love–hate relationship," no matter how much camaraderie or cooperation may exist between them. Journalists rely on public relations professions for information (news subsidies), but tend to be suspicious of the power they exert in the newsgathering process. Public

---

Case Study in Accommodation: Domino's Mea Culpa

Domino's Pizza launched a campaign in early 2010 that was remarkable for its conciliatory tone. The company appeared to be taking a stance of near pure accommodation. One commercial featured a clip of a Domino's executive reading comments such as, "Worst excuse for a pizza I ever had," along with footage from a focus group in which a woman stated that, "Domino's pizza crust to me is like cardboard." The message in the ad was: (a) the company has done a poor job in the past; (b) we understand your complaints; and (c) we promise to do better. The company's incoming CEO, Patrick Doyle, stated that no one factor had motivated the campaign. Rather, Domino's was "brutally accepting the criticism that's out there" in order to demonstrate responsiveness to its customers.

The same accommodative strategy had been used 6 years earlier when Hardee's fast food sought to encourage customers to try an improved hamburger. Its frank admission of its problems led to improvement in customer satisfaction scores, if not overall sales. But a stance of pure accommodation may backfire. According to William Benoit, a leading scholar on crisis communication, in an interview with *The Washington Post*, the public may hear only one aspect of an accommodative stance ("we made bad pizza") without understanding the full apologetic message (Fahri, 2010). The strategy also risks alienating loyal customers who liked the old recipe. For the most part, however, according to Benoit, the public tends to respect organizations that candidly admit their mistakes.

"Mea culpa" has been an effective strategy in other cases. After suffering negative reactions when it blamed a passenger who was forcibly removed from his seat in 2017, United Airlines learned its lesson. In 2018, when a dog died because a flight attendant insisted it travel in an overhead bin, the company was quick to issue an apology:

> We assume full responsibility for this tragedy and express our deepest condolences to the family and are committed to supporting them ... We are thoroughly investigating what occurred to prevent this from ever happening again. (Ascierto, 2018)

By admitting fault and outlining the steps taken to prevent further incidents, United took a proactive step toward regaining stakeholder trust.

---

relations professionals, on the other hand, are eager to have journalists interested in making news from the contents of their information subsidies, but are wary of a process driven by journalists' commitment to the public's right to know. Although journalists do not readily admit the influence of public relations sources, research suggests that nearly 80% of print news stories originate from news subsidies.

The relationship between journalists and public relations professionals—and their cooriented views of one another—may be characterized by mixed views: sometimes adversarial, sometimes cooperative. They are always skeptical of one another's motives and outlooks. Journalists and public relations professionals tend to disagree based on their inherent roles as source and reporter. Journalists harbor negative impressions of public relations professionals—but they inaccurately predict public relations practitioners' true views.

Shin and Cameron (2003) characterize the mixed relationship between reporters and sources as an "endless dance" or "tug-of-war" marked by "mutual distrust," but also "mutual dependency" (p. 318). The relationship can be understood from the perspective of contingency theory: each side engages in some degree of conflict with the other, and such tension is inherent in their professional relationship. Depending on the conflict within a particular situation, and using conflict management strategies, both parties will come to a more or less uneasy and time-dependent cooperation based on their respective interests. Conflict often exists in their perceived differences of roles, values, rules, and interdependency.

The contingency theory of conflict management can be exemplified by the source–reporter relationship as it moves toward "a punctuated hybrid point of advocacy and accommodation on a continuum" (Shin & Cameron, 2003). Often, taking a stance of accommodation or advocacy is represented as a strategic choice on the part of both professions. For example, public relations practitioners may present themselves as more accommodative or strategic to gain the attention of a journalist, who in turn might adopt a more conflicting or skeptical approach to gain some power in the relationship.

Case Study in Advocacy: The National Rifle Association

Historically, the National Rifle Association (NRA) has adopted pure advocacy in the face of challenge from publics. It is unwavering in its mission to promote unfettered, responsible gun ownership. Concerned about the so-called "slippery slope," the NRA vigorously argues that *any* gun regulation represents a fundamental challenge that will ultimately, step by step, destroy the Second Amendment to the Constitution: "A well-regulated militia, being necessary to the security of a free State, the right of the People to keep and bear arms, shall not be infringed." Using this logic, it has defended the sale of assault weapons, concealed-carry permits for most members of the public, open-carry laws, bullets designed to inflict maximum damage, and high-capacity ammunition magazines. Similar pure advocacy positioning is found also among activist groups that may be defined by their "whatever it takes" approaches. Akin to the NRA's support for unfettered gun rights, groups such as Greenpeace and PETA work purely in the interest of furthering their cause, at the expense of missing what more moderate citizens would call the "big picture." Public challenges to the NRA's advocacy often follow tragic shooting events, such as the Columbine High School and Virginia Tech shootings, or, more recently, the shooting at Marjory Stoneman Douglas High School in Parkland, Florida on February 14, 2018. In this incident, a gunman murdered 17 students and wounded another 14 using an AR-15 assault rifle (CBS, 2019).

The advocacy characterizing the two sides of the gun-control debate establishes strong relationships with each of their target stakeholder groups. However, the positions of the opposing forces have remained irreconcilable, as neither side has demonstrated willingness to engage in accommodation. Calls for "common-sense" gun laws are met with vigorous, even intractable defense of the Second Amendment by the NRA, while organizations such as Brady/ United Against Gun Violence and the Parkland Students have argued for a complete ban on the sale of automatic weapons and high-capacity magazines at a minimum, as well as pressing for other restrictions such as waiting (or "cooling-off") periods and limiting the number of guns a person can buy to one per month. The suggestion that gun owners are by and large law-abiding and responsible citizens is met with a barrage of statistics showing how much higher the murder, accidental death, and suicide rates are in the United State compared to other countries with strict gun-control legislation.

The contradiction is framed as protecting lives versus preserving the absolute and inviolable Second Amendment right to keep and bear arms. For the NRA, this right is a metaphor for individual freedom and a bulwark against potential tyranny by the government. For the Parkland

Students, gun control is intimately connected to the most basic human right, that to life. In the conflict between these absolute rights, from the perspective of both activist groups, there can be no accommodation and no middle ground. The closest thing to accommodation offered by the NRA is the explanation that schools need to allow more guns to protect students, because the only way to protect against a "bad guy with a gun" is to have more "good guys with guns." As Heath and Waymer (2009) observed, this argument puts a positive spin on the issue that masks or occludes a contrary reality. As the Parkland Students counter, even the presence of a trained and armed security guard failed to protect them during their shooting incident.

The two sides operate from two different worldviews. The NRA pro-gun stance is based on the absolutist faith that a gun in the hands of a "good guy" will always make people safer, and gun-rights advocates firmly believe that ordinary citizens are naturally inclined to behave responsibly. Gun-control advocates, on the other hand, argue that there are too many continent variables, too many situations that can have negative outcomes, to permit unfettered access to weapons, including assault rifles with large-capacity ammunition magazines. They argue that gun ownership without limitation represents a danger to society. Assessing who is responsible and who might be prone to violence is impossible, and thus society should place restrictions on access to the most lethal weapons.

The public seems to support "common-sense" gun control, such as banning high-capacity ammunition magazines, assault rifles, and "bump stocks," which turn semiautomatic weapons into automatic ones, by a margin of about 70%, while more than 90% favor universal background checks (Cohn & Sanger-Katz, 2019). Given the political reality, however, the NRA holds more power than public opinion, and it is unlikely that substantive gun-control measures will be enacted. Unless the fundamental gulf narrows and one or both side acquiesce or concede, the pattern will continue. Support for gun control tends to rise temporarily in the immediate wake of tragedies such as the Parkland shooting, only to recede again as the news cycle moves on. The most substantive action of organizations such as the NRA is to redouble the defense of firearms and reaffirm individual rights, while offering their "thoughts and prayers" to the victims.

Which Variables Influence Contingency?

As in all theory and research, academics and practitioners are confronted with identifying and selecting key variables to explain the phenomena under consideration. For contingency theory, this is daunting. Its proponents have reasoned that its purpose is to consider all of the variables, rather than a limited few, that realistically come into play during conflict management between an organization and various key publics.

In this exploration, a matrix of contingent variables was developed based on an extensive review of the literature, discussions with public relations professionals, and personal experience, as already discussed (see Cameron et al., 2001). This review identified approximately 87 variables that affected the options along the continuum between accommodation and advocacy, divided among external and internal variables.

The external variables were:

1) *Threats:* Litigation, government regulation, potentially damaging publicity, scarring of organization's reputation in community, legitimizing activists' claims, industry environment, changing or static industry environment, number of industry competitors, richness or leanness of industry resources in the environment.

2) *General political/social environment/external culture (level of constraint/uncertainty):* Degree of political support of business, degree of social support of business.

3) *The external public (group, individual, etc.):* Size or number of external public members, degree of powerful members or connections, past successes or failures of public to evoke change, amount of advocacy practiced by organization, level of communication of public's members, whether the public has PR counselors or not, whether the community's perception of public is reasonable or radical, level of media coverage the public has received in past, representatives of the public know or like, representatives of the organization, public's willingness to dilute its claim, public's moves or countermoves, public's relative power over organization.

4) *Issue under question:* Issue size under question between the organization and its public, issue stakes under question between the organization and its public, issue complexity under question between the organization and its public.

While the internal variables were:

1) *Organization characteristics:* Open or closed culture of organization, dispersed geographically widely or centralized, level of technology the organization uses to produce its product or service, homogeneity or heterogeneity of employees in your organization, age of your organization, speed of growth in the knowledge level your organization uses, economic stability of your organization, existence or non-existence of issues management personnel or program in your organization, organization's past experience with its public, distribution of decision-making power in your organization, number of rules defining the job descriptions of employees in your organization, hierarchy of positions in your organization, existence or influence of legal department on PR department, business product and customer mix, corporate culture.

2) *Public relations department characteristics:* Total number of PR practitioners and number with college degrees in your organization, type of past training of employees (PR practitioners, ex-journalists, marketing, etc.) in your organization, location of PR department in hierarchy in your organization, representation in top management of your organization, your experience level in dealing with conflict, general communication competency of the PR department in your organization, autonomy of the PR department of your organization, physical placement of the PR department in your organization's building, your knowledge or experience in research methods, PR department's amount of funding available for dealing with external publics, percentage of female upper-level staff in the PR department in your organization, potential of the PR department to practice various models of public relations in your organization, characteristics of dominant coalition (top management), conservative or liberal political values of the top management in your organization, whether the management style is dominating or not in your organization, general altruism level of the top management of your organization, top management's support and understanding of PR in your organization, top management's frequency of external contact with its publics in your organization, PR department's perception of your organization's external environment, whether the top management of your organization calculates potential rewards or losses caused by using different strategies with external publics, degree of your line manager's involvement in external affairs, internal threats (how much is at stake in situation), economic loss or gain from implementing various stances of your organization, marring of employees' or stockholders' perception of your organization, marring of the personal reputation of your organization's decision makers.

3) *Individual characteristics (public relations practitioner, dominant coalition, and line managers):* Whether PR practitioners are trained in PR, marketing, journalism, engineering, etc., or not, your ethical value, your tolerance of ability to deal with uncertainty, your comfort level with conflict or

dissonance, your comfort level with change, your ability to recognize potential and existing problems, extent to which you are open to innovation, extent to which you can grasp others' worldviews, whether your personality is dogmatic or not, your communication competency, your ability to handle complex problems, your predisposition toward negotiation, your predisposition toward altruism, your familiarity with external public or its representative, how you receive, process, and use information, whether you like external public and its representative or not, your gender.

4) *Relationship characteristics:* Level of trust between organization and external public, dependency of parties involved, ideological barriers between organization and public (Cameron et al., 2001).

A subsequent quantitative study of the influence of the 87 variables, led by Shin et al. (2006b), regrouped them into 12 quantified factors and added parsimony to the theory. Each factor, individually and in combination, affected a public relations professional's degree of accommodation at a specific point in time along a continuum.

Five external factors were produced:

1) External threats (litigation, government regulation, potentially damaging publicity, scarring of organization's reputation in community, and legitimizing activists' causes).
2) Industry environment (changing or static industry, number of industry competitors/competition, and richness or leanness of industry resources in the environment).
3) Political/social/cultural environment (degree of political support of business, degree of social support of business, and degree of powerful members or connections).
4) Public power (size or number of external public members, organization's advocacy, and public's communication).
5) Public relationships (past successes or failures of public, whether the public has public relations counselors, community's perception of public, past media coverage of public, whether the public representatives know/like organization's representatives, public's willingness to dilute its cause, and public moves and countermoves).

Along with seven internal factors:

1) Organization's development (geographical dispersion/centralization, organization's use of technology, employees' homogeneity/heterogeneity, organization's age, and organization's knowledge growth).
2) Organization's structure (distribution of decision-making power, job rules of employees, and hierarchy of positions).
3) PR department independence (past training of employees, hierarchical location of PR department, representation in top management, practitioners' experience in handling conflict, PR department's communication competency, and PR department autonomy).
4) PR department governance (PR department funding, top management support, and PR department of external environment).
5) Top management characteristics (political value of top management, management style, and management altruism level).
6) Individual characteristics (personal ethical value, tolerance with uncertainty, comfort level with change, comfort level with conflict, ability to recognize potential or existing problems, openness to innovation, grasp of others' world-views, dogmatic personality, and predisposition toward negotiation).
7) Individual capabilities (individual communication competency, ability to handle complex problems, how to receive, and process and use information) (Shin et al., 2006b).

Shin et al. (2005) noted the most crucial variables within these categories: litigation, government regulation, threat of damaging publicity, fear of loss of reputation, degree of stability in the industry environment, degree of political support for an organization or business, number and strength of industry competition, and industry resources. Important organizational-level variables include top management support of public relations, public relations department's communication competency, representation in top management, top management's frequency of external contact, PR department's perception of external environment, department funding, and organization's experience with the public. Some external variables were assessed as highly significant: scarring of organization's reputation, potentially damaging publicity, and marring of the personal reputation of the company decision makers.

Among these variables, Shin et al. (2006a) found that individual-level ones, especially those related to individual qualifications, were perceived as most influential and predominant by public relations professionals. Such variables included individual communication competency, personal ethical value, ability to handle complex problems, ability to recognize potential or existing problems, familiarity with external public or its representatives, openness to innovation, how to receive, process, and use information, grasp of others' world-views, tolerance with uncertainty, and experience in handling conflict. Shin et al., however, also found that public relations professionals' stances were influenced by organizational variables such as top management support of public relations, public relations departments' communication competency, public relations representation in top management, top management's frequency of external contact, public relations department's perception of the external environment, department funding, and the organization's experience with the public. Shin et al. confirmed the perceived influence of organizational-level and individual-level variables on their practice.

"Taming" the complicated array and interaction of variables is an ongoing project for contingency theorists working toward revision and parsimony. The contingency approach attempts to avoid tautological or reductivist validation of current practice as ideal or "best" practice. The notion of "it depends" suggests a certain degree of flexibility. However, contingency theory does not exclude a sense of stability, or commonality, in that it presents a set of preexisting or predisposing factors that affect the initial stance of an organization in its relationship with a public. These predisposing factors come into play *a priori*, before the organization engages in interactions with the public. They also serve as cues or predictors of how likely the organization is to accommodate the public in a conflict or disagreement.

Other Theories Associated with the Contingency Theory of Public Relations

Contingency theorists work to establish the integrity of their theory. In doing so, they note how it works with and complements or is complemented by other theories. This section features brief discussions of such interrelationships.

Coorientational Theory

Coorientational theory, an important frame related to contingency theory, was defined by Pearson in 1989. Coorientation postulates how parties engaged in strategic negotiation interact as the result of three factors: (a) degree of agreement between one's beliefs and the other's; (b) how congruently one assesses the other's beliefs and actions; and (c) how accurately one predicts the other's actual belief or actions. Broom and Dozier (1990) examined the interaction between dominant coalitions within organizations and their publics by featuring four coorientational states:

1) true consensus (both groups actually share the same view);
2) dissensus (each group is aware of holding differing views);
3) false consensus (one or both groups misinterprets the other's position as consensus); and
4) false conflict (one or both groups misinterprets the other's position as dissensus).

The important connection between contingency theory and coorientational theory is the realization that the interaction between an organization and its publics is fluid, malleable, and contingent; such interaction depends on how one perceives the other in choosing accommodative strategies. Similarly, Dozier and Ehling (1992) argued that public relations professionals play an important role in reorienting the direction of discussion, particularly when false dissensus, or misperception of the other's position, arises. Using environmental scanning of issues, they can influence the outcome through "truthful communication," thereby correcting misperceptions.

Game Theory

Game theory is a way of understanding how people make choices. It underlies contingency theory, if in a general way. Organizations use game theory to weigh the benefits and costs of various strategic options. Like contingency theory, game theory examines the interrelationship of discrete variables as they unfold in time and space. Both attempt to explain and predict how changing one factor (or multiple factors) affects the process and outcome. Originating in the 1950s in the field of mathematics, game theory seeks to describe the behaviors of individuals operating in strategic situations. It holds that a person's choices are conditioned by those of their opponent, as well as the expectation of the opponent's behavior. In a zero-sum game, for example, one player wins only if the other player loses. In real life or actual practice, things are rarely so simple. The American mathematician John Nash offered a more subtle description of the complexity of behavior with the prisoner's dilemma. In this game, two prisoners held separately must decide whether to remain silent or testify against one another. If both snitch, both get a five-year sentence. If neither snitches, both get a six-month sentence. If one snitches and the other does not, the snitch goes free while the silent prisoner gets 10 years. This model suggests the importance of one's predictions and expectations of one's opponent. Game theory attempts to predict and measure the effects of decisions made along a continuum—suggesting that each individual decision affects subsequent decisions among parties and, ultimately, the outcome. The perceived or relative power of each party often plays a role—especially in terms of one's prediction of the other's behavior.

Game theory has been embraced by a variety of social sciences since the late 1950s. In the early 1980s, scholars examined its usefulness in describing the interaction of organizations and publics. For instance, Folger and Poole (1984) suggested that the promise of reward governs behaviors or stances. Pavlik (1989) posited that asymmetry is defined by the relative power difference between organizations and their publics. Drawing on game theory, Murphy (1991) introduced into public relations theory the concept of mixed motives to explain its complexities. Despite providing many of the terms used in this discussion, game theory has not had robust theoretical development among public relations scholars.

Conflict Theory

Conflict theory represents an attempt to describe how individuals behave when faced with tension or disagreement. It assumes that conflict is inevitable, is based on differences of power or resources, and can be a positive force. The key, as suggested by game theorists, is not necessarily to reach a state of equilibrium among interdependent parties, but rather to obtain a relative balance of interests serving both sides at once. Conflict theory assumes that both parties interact through moves and countermoves.

Blake and Mouton (1964) identified five styles of conflict: competitive, accommodative, avoiding, collaborative, and compromising. They further categorized each of these dimensions according to whether they were assertive or unassertive. Keltner (1987) stressed the importance of managing conflict to reach resolution. His "struggle spectrum" proceeded through six stages: difference, disagreement, dispute, campaign, litigation, and violence.

Offering a synthetic definition of conflict, Hocker and Wilmont (1991) argued that parties in conflict make two sets of strategic choices: (a) whether to engage or avoid conflict; and, if they engage, (b) where they will position themselves along a continuum ranging from competition to collaboration. Avoidance tactics range from denial to noncommitment, whereas tactics of engagement can be either competitive or collaborative. Competitive techniques are usually based on self-interest or advocacy, while collaborative techniques involve accommodation.

Conflict theory suggests that organizations are more likely to accommodate groups that advance their interests. For example, an organization might more readily accommodate a regulatory body with oversight powers than an activist group holding relatively little power. By the same token, a group that gains greater relative power—such as one advocating gun control in the wake of a shooting incident—is likely to influence the stance of an organization that is affected by public perception. Like contingency theory, conflict theory also presupposes that the organizational climate affects the interaction among organizations and publics. For example, Druckman and Broom (1991) suggested that parties engaged in conflict tend to be accommodative when they perceive familiarity and liking—in other words, when they empathize with their adversaries.

Issues Management Theory

Growing out of a robust era of conflict between activists and businesses that emerged in the 1960s, *issues management theory* shares contingency theory's perspective on helping an organization understand and satisfy the demands of one or more of its external publics, who are constantly changing on a continuum. Writing the first academic book devoted to issues management, Heath and Nelson (1986) provided a synthetic definition of it as a strategy to "help organizations fit themselves to long-term shifts in the climate of public sensitivity, whether by changing corporate policy, shaping legislation, or influencing public opinion" (p. 51). Public relations practitioners accomplish these goals by scanning the environment, selecting and organizing significant data, suggesting courses of action in line with the interests of their employers, and taking into account public opinion. The goal is to inform the management team about external threats and opportunities, and thereby provide a means of accommodating, or advocating against, the position advocated by each public. Issues management is seen as a means of forging positive relationships by resolving conflicts by both sides through building consensus or leveling the playing field.

Issues management is concerned with predicting and "strategically adapting" to changes in the external environment. Heath and Nelson (1986) put it this way: "Much as a driver with quick reaction time has a better chance of avoiding a traffic accident, successful issues monitoring affords companies the alternative of accommodating rather than colliding with public opinion" (p. 14). It is an important precursor to contingency theory because it takes into account a great number of variables arrayed in shifting constellations of interaction and interdependency, depending on an evolving situation. Miles' (1987) theory of corporate social performance, although assessing a limited set of circumstances related to an insurance company's relationships to numerous external publics, provided an important validation of the shifting positions, influenced by social constraints, that are essential to contingency theory. In his pioneering practitioner book on issue management, Chase (1984) identified three strategies that characterize interactions with an external public: reaction or opposing, adapting or accommodative, and dynamic or creative.

Drawing on these established and growing bodies of related research and practice, contingency theory has continued to address the dynamics of conflict resolution. This can be conceptualized as a cycle of strategic conflict management.

Cycle of Strategic Conflict Management

Conflicts are an ever-present aspect of OPRs and emerged as an area of focus in contingency theory. They result from perceptions of differences in roles, values, goals, or interests among two or more parties. Interactions bring about changes, both positive and negative, in OPRs over time in ways that are modeled as the life cycle of conflict (see Figure 4.2).

For public relations professionals, the life cycle of a conflict involves four general phases: proactive, strategic, reactive, and recovery. It is easy to see how these phases are in constant flux, interacting on multiple levels simultaneously. Public relations professionals can increase the likelihood that they will resolve or reduce a conflict between their organization and its publics by managing the proactive, reactive, and strategic phases.

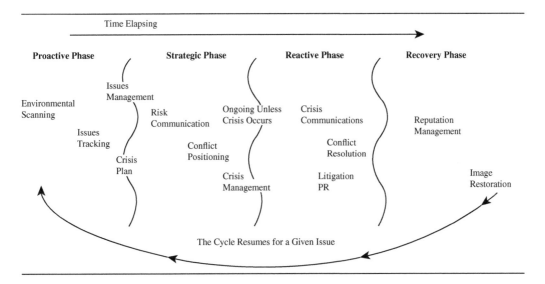

Figure 4.2 The life cycle of conflict. Depicts the four phases in conflict management experienced by public relations professionals, as well as a few of the numerous strategies they can employ to deal with conflict. Cameron, Wilcox, Reber, & Shin (2007).

The phases featured in Figure 4.2 can be defined and explained in the following ways:

- The *proactive phase* may be seen as planning and preparing to either prevent or effectively handle an emerging issue. Environmental scanning—monitoring the state of affairs on issues related to the organizational interests—is a crucial first step. This is usually done through analysis of print, broadcast, online, or social media and allows the assessment of potential issues—notably, threats and conflicts. Many crises or conflict may be averted through close attention to proactive measures, and preemptive monitoring helps organizations prevent escalation of conflict.
- The cycle enters the *strategic phase* once an emerging conflict has been identified. Coordinated action is then required on the part of public relations professionals, who must provide their organization with an assessment of risk and suggest strategies to position it for possible litigation, regulation, legislation, or similar conflict. Crisis management plans can be designed to be actively prepared for potential crises.
- When a conflict is emergent, the cycle enters the *reactive phase*. Practitioners are responsible for crisis communication, including implementing the crisis management plan. If it is not a full-blown crisis, public relations professionals may suggest negotiation or alternative dispute resolution techniques to bring the conflict to a successful resolution without resort to the courts. If a conflict results in litigation, they play the crucial role of developing communication and publicity strategies that support the organization's interests. A public relations professional's stance in this regard may change dramatically as the situation unfolds.
- Finally, the cycle enters the *recovery phase* once the crisis is over or the conflict has been resolved. This phase is especially important if the conflict has affected public perception of the organization. Public relations professionals are then called upon to implement strategies to restore its reputation. When a crisis is severe, the organization will go through a process of change in this phase. The effective management of the recovery phase leads to a successful proactive phase in ongoing cycles of conflict management.

Given the array of variables identified as being central to contingency, efforts such as the differentiation of those relevant to internal and external conditions help make them more strategically manageable. In addition, conceptualizing themes into phases of conflict management serves to improve theoretical coherence. Such analysis is part of ongoing development, as described in the following section.

Ongoing Research

Cameron, Cropp, and Reber (2001) expressed concern that it was difficult to manage so many variables in "any useful way" (p. 247). Assessing the relative salience and usefulness of dozens of variables has been an ongoing project of contingency theorists. Recent studies have examined how contingent variables constellate, and how they are influential in different contexts. One of the most focused efforts to explain contingency factors centers on refining the understanding of external threats. Jin, Pang, and Cameron (2005) differentiated between "fear," "conflict," and "risk." They developed a threat appraisal model, taking into account cognitive, affective, and conative aspects, to show how a public relations professional is forced to consider a variety of variables in order to address a threat. In a follow-up study (Jin, Pang, & Cameron, 2006), they tested this model by examining differences in assessment of threat level among Department of Homeland Security (DHS) agents and conservative and liberal members of the public. The results suggested improving internal consistency in threat communication within the DHS would increase effectiveness.

The threat appraisal model of crisis management examines two dynamics: the seriousness or severity of a threat and what resources are needed to meet it (Jin, Pang, & Cameron, 2005). Threats are appraised according to their cognitive, affective, and conative dimensions (Kim & Cameron, 2016). Just as contingency theory focuses on the dynamic nature of organizational stances conditioned by external and internal factors along a continuum ranging from pure advocacy to pure accommodation, so the threat appraisal model proposes that a combination of situational factors and organizational demands conditions an organization's response, and that this response can change as the threat evolves. The appraisal of threats takes place first as a primary assessment of the situational variable from the perspective of the potential danger and degree of uncertainty, followed by an appraisal of available resources, time, and level of support from a dominant coalition or locus of control (Jin, Pang, & Cameron, 2007). The cognitive level associated with threat appraisal is connected to individual perception of threat type, duration, and potential resource allocation. The affective level focuses on the feelings that an individual has about the threat, including tone, intensity, and perception of importance. The conative level refers to the particular stance taken during a crisis and its relationship to past and future stances taken as the situation evolves (Jin et al., 2007; Kim & Cameron, 2016). Jin et al. (2007) point to the importance of examining an organization's locus of control and how it affects decisions about communication strategies.

Exploring the cognitive and affective aspect of threat, Jin et al. (2007) surveyed 116 strategic communication professionals about the effects of different threat types and threat durations and the stances they would take in response to each. They found that external, long-term threats led to increased emotional arousal and higher situational demands. Strong affective response and high cognition were related to accommodating stances. Following an external threat, public relations professionals tended to take an accommodative stance characterized by qualified-rhetoric mixed accommodations or action-based accommodations. The qualified-rhetoric mixed stance is characterized by a willingness to accept blame and express regret. According to Pang, Jin, and Cameron (2007, 2010a, 2010b), the rhetorical approach places an emphasis on qualification—a willingness to accede to public demands, for example—and even posturing. An action-based stance, on the other hand, promises action by providing concrete steps toward a solution. Publics can also predict the stance of an organization that affects them or that they can affect or influence. Hwang and Cameron (2008a) demonstrated that situational factors—especially external threat, external public characteristics, and the characteristics of each dominant coalition—were associated with the general public's estimation of the stance taken by their government during a nuclear crisis between North and South Korea. A subsequent paper by the same authors (2008b) showed how perceptions of leadership style affected public estimation of an organization's stance during crisis.

Another external dimension of contingency theory has cross-cultural relevance. Shin, Park, and Cameron (2006) examined public relations practice in South Korea. Their results demonstrated that when a dominant coalition governed public relations practice in conflict situations, it constrained the release of negative information. Likewise, a survey by Li, Cropp, and Jin (2010) found that contingent external variables such as political-social-environmental culture affected public relations practitioners' understanding of crises in China. Xie (2017) undertook a cross-cultural study of the public relations strategies used by the Confucian Institutes in China. A key finding was that the organization used a variety of stances ranging along the continuum from advocacy to accommodation, and the contingent variable of external publics could be divided into several categories, such as prohibitive, administrative, and authoritative, according to the power that those publics wielded. Choi and Cameron (2005) identified the salience of fear as a contingent factor affecting whether or not multinational corporations in South Korea adopted accommodative stances. This fear, they argued, was rooted in an important cultural concept based on *cheong*, a sense of social harmony and belonging to the inner group. Korean multinational corporations tend to accommodate the public, fearing that negative media framing might upset the sense of "we-ness," which differentiates in-group from out-group and affects how multinational corporate messages and behaviors are interpreted by Korean publics.

Several studies have also examined internal variables. For instance, organizational-level variables have been shown to be most significant in affecting stances. Shin, Cameron, and Cropp (2006) grounded this observation in a national survey of public relations professionals concerning their evaluation of the relevant weight of contingency variables in their daily practice. Park (2008) showed how organizational characteristics such as corporate size and characteristics were related to Apple's move toward accommodation when faced with lawsuits over hearing loss in early 2006. Similar to what was found by other studies, a dominant coalition's degree of enlightenment was found to either facilitate or hinder a public relations professional's effectiveness. Pang, Cropp, and Cameron (2006) conducted a case study of a Fortune 500 company, which demonstrated that conservative and less enlightened dominant coalitions tended to not allow public relations representation in management decisions. This exclusion provided a barrier to effective public relations initiatives.

Organizations are more likely to engage in dialogue and accommodation when public relations professionals are represented within the dominant coalition. This conclusion was demonstrated by Reber, Cropp, and Cameron (2003), who examined the case of Norfolk Southern Corporation's hostile bid to purchase Contrail Inc. Public relations initiatives filled the lacunae left by legal and jurisdictional constraints. Strategic communication with the legal department, coordinated by public relations professionals, opened dialogue and served, in essence, as the "constructive creator of antecedent conditions" necessary to bring resolution (p. 17).

On the other hand, when public relations professionals are excluded from representation within the dominant coalition, negotiation and accommodation tend to be proscribed. Zhang, Qiu, and Cameron (2004) showed a dominant coalition's sense of moral conviction limited dialogue and conciliation during a crisis after a U.S. military jet collided with a Chinese fighter in April 2001.

Beyond the investigation of the relationship between contingent factors and an organization's stance, there has been an effort to connect organizations' stances along the advocacy/accommodation continuum with their strategies. Shin et al. (2003, 2005) found that parties in high-profile conflicts favored advocacy and employed contending strategies associated with it. Later, Shin (2008) found a strong relationship between internal contingent factors—such as relationship, organizational, and management characteristics—and more accommodative strategies—such as concession and corrective action, as well as reducing offensiveness strategies such as bolstering and minimization. On the other hand, external contingent factors such as political, social, and cultural environments or external threats involved more contending strategies, such as denial and shifting the blame, and evading responsibility strategies, such as good intentions, accident, defeasibility, and provocation.

Conclusion

As is evident from the studies featured in the previous section, the themes and assumptions of contingency theory continue to be researched, and the theory to be reinforced and refined. This in itself demonstrates the theory's central premise of realistic dynamism. Such research supports the logic of featuring strategic options along a continuum conceived as a wide range of possible stances available to an organization in relation to different publics. This differs from the limited set of categories proposed by previous models of public relations theory, such as excellence theory (Cancel et al., 1999). Accounting for the wide range of positions taken by public relations professionals represents, in a realistic sense, the mixed motives of advocacy and accommodation. OPRs are driven by a number of variables that affect the strategic position on this continuum at any given time during crisis and conflict. The theory further shows that the stances and strategic approaches chosen by a professional often evolve over time, as a situation changes.

Starting from a criticism of normative models such as excellence theory, contingency theory provides a refined description of the interactions between organizations and publics, and of the practice of public relations. The complicated interrelationships between organizations and publics—rife with relational, organizational, and societal conflicts—may remain always elusive, owing to this complex interplay of contingent variables on different levels. This situation does not suggest that the task is impossible or futile. On the contrary, quantification and qualification of the varying dimensions of OPRs with increasing degrees of precision hold the promise of leading to greater understanding of the ongoing cycles of conflict.

Chapter Summary

The contingency theory of conflict management focuses on the dynamics of public relations strategies by proposing that the stance taken by public relations practitioners working for organizations depends on the particular internal and external variables associated with a given situation. The "it depends" approach accommodates change over time as stances shift according to how the situation unfolds and evolves. Contingency theory suggests that practitioners operate on a continuum between pure advocacy and pure accommodation in dealing with a conflict with a given public. In situations of disagreement, various hybrid points along this continuum are adopted in an effort to reach resolution. If the first strategic choice proves ineffective, the practitioner moves to another from the range of options along the continuum. The contingency theory of strategic conflict management suggests an ongoing cycle of conflict with proactive, strategic, reactive, and recovery stages, in which a public relations professional is likely to adopt different strategic choices on the continuum.

The contingency theory of public relations evolved from the contingency theory of management, which served as a system for measuring the effect of leadership decisions on outcomes. However, contingency theory rejects the modernist supposition that external and internal factors can be measured in such a way that predictable outcomes can be devised. Instead, it presupposes that every situation is unique and that no formula can be applied universally. It is rooted in the idea that mutual benefit is a goal, as advocated by excellence theory, but questions the proposition that symmetrical communication is the best strategy in all situations. In some conflict situations, it suggests, it is most ethical to adopt an asymmetrical stance.

Cameron and his associates have been credited with developing the contingency theory of strategic conflict management in public relations since the 1990s. They initially proposed 87 variables that mediate the degree of accommodation or advocacy adopted by public relations professionals. The theory has since been tested through both qualitative and quantitative studies in order to group these variables into 11 or 12 factors on internal and external dimensions and to add parsimony. Ongoing testing in non-Western contexts indicates that the number of factors could be expanded, suggesting that cultural variables such as *cheong* are influential in public relations practice.

Other theories associated with contingency theory include coorientation, game theory, conflict theory, issues management theory, and the threat appraisal model. Coorientation proposes that parties engaged in strategic negotiation consider degree of agreement with one another, how they assess one another's beliefs and actions, and how congruent or accurate their predictions are. Game theory is a mathematical model seeking to understand how people make strategic choices by weighing the benefits and costs of particular actions. Conflict theory represents an attempt to understand how and why people behave in situations of disagreement or tension. Issues management theory focuses on how organizations meet the needs of external publics by understanding their environment or context. The threat appraisal model analyzes crises through their cognitive, affective, and conative dimensions. What each of these theories shares with contingency theory is the idea that interactions are dependent on the context, situation, or environment and that as situational variables shift, so too do the strategic approaches of those who are involved.

Key Terms

- *Accommodation:* The act of adjusting the views of an organization to harmonize with the views of the public or the process by which an organization changes its behaviors in the interest of given public.
- *Advocacy:* The act of supporting an organization, individual, or idea for the purpose of persuading targeted audiences to see it in a favorable light or accept its point of view.
- *Conflict:* Differences in roles, values, beliefs, rules, identity, etc. among different parties. Entails interdependency between them.
- *Conflict Cycle:* An ongoing process of managing conflict or competition. The cycle shows a process of issue, conflict, and crisis development and how a public relations professional can manage it.
- *Contingency:* Public relations professionals are influenced by a number of internal and external variables, determining what stances or strategies they should undertake in dealing with a given public at a given time. The essence of contingency is moving stances between advocacy and accommodation to strategically and effectively meet the best interests of an organization, and possibly the public.
- *Continuum:* An organization's possible range of stances taken toward an individual public. A point of stance on a continuum is often a hybrid between degrees of advocacy and accommodation. Effective public relations may result from taking the most appropriate stance along the continuum that best fits the current need of the organization and its public.
- *Dominant Coalition*: The site of power governing an organization—those individuals or groups who have influence or power over its actions, decisions-making process, and outcomes. The dominant coalition can be fluid, but in most organizational situations it represents top management.
- *Mixed Views*: A hybrid point of advocacy and accommodation. Similar terms include "collaborative advocacy" and "cooperative antagonism," which suggest that a party may be willing to accommodate another to some degree, while at the same time advocating its own interest.

Discussion Questions

1 Assume that you are asked to release your company's position by your boss, but you are certain that the information released will do harm to the public based on research you have conducted. What will you do? Why?
2 How does contingency theory represent a criticism of excellence theory?
3 Describe some of the circumstances in which it might not be in the best interest of an organization to make attempts to accommodate a given public.
4 Distinguish between internal and external factors affecting the organization's stance in the 1996 Atlanta Olympics case.
5 What are some of the reasons why a public relations professional might suggest accommodating an external public or advocating an organization's interest?
6 How does the National Rifle Association use advocacy to advance its goals? Why would it be reluctant to accommodate those who disagree with its position?
7 What are the four phases of the strategic conflict management cycle? What is the role of a public relations professional in each?

References

Ascierto, J. (2018). United's latest mea culpa shows lesson learned from dragging incident. *PR Newswire*, March 3. Available from https://www.prnewsonline.com/united-learns-crisis-communications-lessons (accessed May 20, 2020).

Blake, R. R., & Mouton, J. S. (1964). *The managerial grid*. Houston, TX: Gulf.

Broom, G. M., & Dozier, D. M. (1990). *Using research in public relations: Application to program management*. Englewood Cliffs, NJ: Prentice-Hall.

Cameron, G. T., Cropp, F., & Reber, B. H. (2001). Getting past platitudes: Factors limiting accommodation in public relations. *Journal of Communication Management*, 5(3), 242–261.

Cameron, G. T., Wilcox, L., Reber, B. H., & Shin, J. H. (2007). *Public relations today: Managing conflict and competition*. Boston, MA: Allyn & Bacon.

Cancel, A. E., Cameron, G. T., Sallot, L. M., & Mitrook, M. A. (1997). It depends: A contingency theory of accommodation in public relations. *Journal of Public Relations Research*, 9(1), 31–63.

Cancel, A. E., Mitrook, M. A., & Cameron, G. T. (1999). Testing the contingency theory of accommodation in public relations. *Public Relations Review*, 25(2), 171–197.

CBS. (2019). Florida school shooting ranks among America's deadliest. *CBS News*, January 2. Available from https://www.cbsnews.com/news/florida-school-shooting-ranks-among-americas-deadliest (accessed May 20, 2020).

Chase, W. H. (1984). *Issue management: Origins of the future*. Stanford, CT: Issue Action Press.

Choi, Y., & Cameron, G. T. (2005). Overcoming ethnocentrism: The role of identity in contingent practice of international public relations. *Journal of Public Relations Research*, 17(2), 171–189.

Cohn, N., and Sanger-Katz, M. (2019). On guns, public opinion and public policy often diverge. *The New York Times*, August 10. Available from https://www.nytimes.com/2019/08/10/upshot/gun-control-polling-policies.html?auth=login-email&login=email (accessed May 20, 2020).

Cole, R. E. (2011). Who was really at fault for the Toyota recalls? *The Atlantic*, May 1. Available from https://www.theatlantic.com/business/archive/2011/05/who-was-really-at-fault-for-the-toyota-recalls/238076 (accessed May 20, 2020).

Del Valle, G. (2019). Boeing is in the middle of a safety-related PR nightmare. Can it recover? *Vox*, May 27. Available from https://www.vox.com/the-goods/2019/3/27/18284285/boeing-737-max-crash-safety-public-relations (accessed May 20, 2020).

Dozier, D. M., & Ehling, W. P. (1992). Evaluation of public relations programs: What the literature tells us about their effects. In J. E. Grunig (Ed.), *Excellence in public relations and communication management* (pp. 159–184). Hillsdale, NJ: Lawrence Erlbaum Associates.

Dozier, D. M., Grunig, L., & Grunig, J. (1995). *Manager's guide to excellence in public relations and communication management*. Mahwah, NJ: Lawrence Erlbaum Associates.

Druckman, D., & Broom, B. J. (1991). Value differences and conflict resolution: Familiarity or liking? *Journal of Conflict Resolution*, *35*, 571–593.

Evans, S. (2010). Runaway Prius round-up: Latest incidents raise questions. *Motortrend*, March 10. Available from https://www.motortrend.com/news/runaway-prius-roundup-latest-incidents-raise-new-questions-7265 (accessed May 20, 2020).

Fahri, P. (2010). Domino's mea culpa ad campaign. *The Washington Post*, January 13. Available http://www.washingtonpost.com/wp-dyn/content/article/2010/01/12/AR2010011201696.html (accessed May 20, 2020).

Fiedler, F. E. (1958). *Leader attitudes and group effectiveness*. Urbana, IL: University of Illinois Press.

Fiedler, F. E. (1964). *A contingency model of leadership effectiveness*. *Journal for Advances in Experimental Social Psychology*, *1*(12), 149–190.

Fiedler, F. E. (1967). *A theory of leadership effectiveness*. New York: McGraw-Hill.

Folger, J. P., & Poole, M. S. (1984). *Working through conflict: A communication perspective*. Tucker, GA: Scott Foresman.

Greimel, H. (2017). Toyota keeps its big recall alive. *Automotive News*, June 11. Available from https://www.autonews.com/article/20170611/OEM11/170619965/toyota-keeps-its-big-recall-alive (accessed May 20, 2020).

Grunig, J. E. (1989). Organizations, environments and models of public relations. *Public Relations Research & Education*, *1*(4), 6–29.

Grunig, J. E. (1992). Communication, public relations, and effective organizations: An overview of the book. In J. E. Grunig (Ed.), *Excellence in public relations and communication management* (pp. 285–326). Hillsdale, NJ: Lawrence Erlbaum Associates.

Grunig, L. A., Grunig, J. E., & Dozier, D. M. (2002). *Excellent public relations and effective organizations: A ctudy of communication management in three countries*. Mahwah, NJ: Lawrence Erlbaum Associates.

Heath, R. L., & Nelson, R. A. (1986). *Issues management*. Newbury Park, CA: Sage.

Heath, R. L., & Waymer, D. (2009). Activist publics and the paradox of the positive: A case study of Frederick Douglass's Fourth of July Address. In R. L. Heath, E. L. Toth, & D. Waymer (Eds.), *Rhetorical and critical approaches to public relations* (2nd ed., pp. 195–215). New York: Routledge.

Hellweg, S. A. (1989). The application of Grunig's symmetry–asymmetry public relations models to internal communications systems. Paper presented at the International Communication Association annual conference, San Francisco, CA.

Hersey, P., & Blanchard, K. H. (1972). *Management of organizational behavior: Utilizing human resources* (2nd ed.). Upper Saddle River, NJ: Prentice Hall.

Hocker, J. L., & Wilmont, W. W. (1991). *Interpersonal conflict* (3rd ed.). Dubuque, IA: Brown.

Hwang, S., & Cameron, G. T. (2008a). The elephant in the room is awake and takes things personally: The North Korean nuclear threat and the general public's estimation of American diplomacy. *Public Relations Review*, *34*, 41–48.

Hwang, S., & Cameron, G. T. (2008b). Public's expectation about an organization's stance in crisis communication based on perceived leadership and perceived severity of threats. *Public Relations Review, 34*, 70–73.

Jin, Y., Pang, A., & Cameron, G. T. (2005). *Explicating threats: Towards a conceptual understanding of the faces and fabric of threat in an organizational crisis.* New York: International Communication Association.

Jin, Y., Pang, A., & Cameron, G. T. (2006). Scale development for measuring stance as degree of accommodation. *Public Relations Review, 32*, 423–425.

Jin, Y., Pang, A., & Cameron, G. T. (2007). The effects of threat type and duration on public relations practitioner's cognitive, affective and conative responses in crisis situations. *Journal of Public Relations Research, 19*(3), 255–281.

Kelly, A. M. (2012). Has Toyota's image recovered from the brand's recall crisis? *Forbes*, March 5. Available from https://www.forbes.com/sites/annemariekelly/2012/03/05/has-toyotas-image-recovered-from-the-brands-recall-crisis/#358e79324dff (accessed May 20, 2020).

Keltner, J. W. (1987). *Mediation: Toward a civilized system of dispute resolution.* Annandale, VA: Speech Communication Association.

Kim, J., & Cameron, G. T. (2016). When cousins feud: Advancing appraisal and contingency theory in situations that question the essential identity of activist organizations. *International Journal of Communication, 10*, 1934–1949.

Li, C., Cropp, F., & Jin, Y. (2010). Identifying key influencers of Chinese PR practitioners' strategic conflict management practice: A survey on contingent variables in Chinese context. *Public Relations Review, 36*(3), 249–255.

Miles, R. H. (1987). *Managing the corporate social environment: A grounded theory.* Englewood Cliffs, NJ: Prentice-Hall.

Murphy, P. (1991). The limits of symmetry. A game theory approach to symmetric and asymmetrical public relations. *Public Relations Research Annual, 3*, 115–131.

Pang, A., Cropp, F., & Cameron, G. T. (2006). Corporate crisis planning: Tensions, issues, and contradictions. *Journal of Communication management, 10*(4), 82–96.

Pang, A., Jin, Y., and Cameron, G. T. (2007). Building an integrated crisis mapping (ICM) model: Organizational strategies for a publics-driven, emotion-based conceptualization in crisis communication. Paper presented at the Association for Education in Journalism and Mass Communication, Washington, D.C.

Pang, A., Jin, Y., & Cameron, G. T. (2010a). Strategic management of communication: Insights from the contingency theory of strategic conflict management. In R. L. Heath (Ed.), *SAGE handbook of public relations* (pp. 17–34). Thousand Oaks, CA: Sage.

Pang, A., Jin, Y., & Cameron, G. T. (2010b). Contingency theory of strategic conflict management: Directions for the practice of crisis communication from a decade of theory development, discovery, and dialogue. In W. T. Coombs & S. J. Holladay (Eds.), *The handbook of crisis communication* (pp. 527–549). Boston, MA: Wiley-Blackwell.

Park, S.-A. (2008). Consumer health crisis management: Apple's crisis responsibility for iPod-related hearing loss. *Public Relations Review, 34*(4), 396–398.

Pavlik, J. V. (1989). The concept of symmetry in the education of public relations practitioners. Paper presented at the meeting of the International Communication Association, San Francisco, CA.

Pearson, R. (1989). Beyond ethical relativism in public relations: Coorientation, rules and the idea of communication symmetry. *Public Relations Research Annual, 1*, 67–86.

Piotrowski, C., & Guyette, R. W. (2010). Toyota recall crisis: Public attitudes on leadership and ethics. *Organization Development Journal, 28*(2), 89–97.

Ramsey, M. (2012). Toyota in $1.1 billion gas-pedal settlement. *Wall Street Journal*, December 27. Available from https://www.wsj.com/articles/SB10001424127887324669104578203440990704994 (accessed May 20, 2020).

Reber, B. H., & Cameron, G. T. (2003). Measuring contingencies: Using scales to measure public relations practitioner limits to accommodation. *Journalism and Mass Communication Quarterly*, *80*(2), 431–446.

Reber, B. H., Cropp, F., & Cameron, G. T. (2003). Impossible odds: Contributions of legal counsel and public relations practitioners in a hostile bid for Conrail Northfolk southern corporation. *Journal of Public Relations Research*, *15*(1), 1–25.

Shin, J. H. (2008). Contingency, conflict, crisis: Strategy selection of religious public relations professionals. *Public Relations Review*, *34*, 403–405.

Shin, J. H., & Cameron, G. T. (2003). The potential of online media: A coorientational analysis of conflict between PR professionals and journalists in South Korea. *Journalism & Mass Communication Quarterly*, *80*(3), 583–602.

Shin, J. H., Jin, Y., Cheng, I. C., and Cameron, G. T. (2003). Tracking messy organization-public conflicts: exploring the natural history of conflict management through the news coverage of unfolded cases. Paper presented at the International Communication Association conference, San Diego, CA.

Shin, J. H., Cheng, I. H., Jin, Y., & Cameron, G. T. (2005). Going head to head: Content analysis of high profile conflicts as played out in the press. *Public Relations Review*, *31*(3), 399–406.

Shin, J. H., Cameron, G. T., & Cropp, F. (2006a). Occam's razor in the contingency theory: A national survey of PR professional response to the contingency model. *Public Relations Review*, *32*(3), 282–286.

Shin, J. H., Park, J., & Cameron, G. T. (2006b). Contingent factors in public relations practice: Modeling generic public relations in South Korea. *Public Relations Review*, *32*(2), 184–185.

Taylor, F. W. (1911). *The principles of scientific management*. New York: Harper & Brothers.

Thompson, J. (1963). *Organizations in action*. New York: McGraw-Hill.

Toyoda, A. (2010). Back to basics for Toyota. *Wall Street Journal*, February 23. Available from https://www.wsj.com/articles/SB10001424052748704454304575081644051321722 (accessed May 20, 2020).

Weber, M. (1930). *The Protestant ethic and the spirit of capitalism*, trans. T. Parsons. New York: Allen and Unwin.

Woodward, J. (1958). *Management and technology*. London: Her Majesty's Stationary Office.

Xie, N. (2017). "It depends" on power: A case study of China's Confucius Institute as public relations function abroad. *China Media Research*, *13*(3), 99–108.

Yarbrough, C. R., Cameron, G. T., Sallot, L. M., & McWilliams, A. (1998). Tough calls to make: Contingency theory and the Centennial Olympic Games. *Journal of Communication Management*, *3*(1), 39–56.

Zhang, J., Qiu, Q., & Cameron, G. T. (2004). A contingency approach to the Sino-U.S. conflict resolution. *Public Relations Review*, *30*, 391–399.

5

Rhetorical Theory: Shared Empowerment Through Discourse

Introduction

Rhetoric is the rationale of strategic discursive action. It is inherent to humanity's ability to use text. Meaning matters. Ideas count. Rhetoric is voice. People and organizations have different opinions, factual interpretations, values, policy preferences, identities, and identifications. Consequently, shared and contentious meanings constitute the range of appeals humans use as they engage in collective decision making. Ideally, meaning and ideas are supported strategically by fact and reasoning and framed by competing, cooperative, and collaborating voices, both individual and organizational. Rhetoric occurs in many structures and forms, and is essential to the relationships needed for organization, society, and community.

Rhetoric is inherent to all contexts of human relatedness under the principle of self-governance. Humans use text strategically to craft relationships, however harmonious or contentious; to discuss issues and make choices about them; and to influence and be influenced by others' judgments on a panoply of matters. Relationships involve strategic adjustment—all forms of association (and dissociation) are possible through propositional and invitational discourse.

Adjustive behaviors become meaningful via textual interpretations. Rhetoric takes its power from the fact that humans live in a world that they define and attitudinize through language; it provides the rationale for how and why they (through organizations, of course) strategically enact themselves in association with one another via words and other symbolic actions. Rhetorical theory helps position the strategic management and communication roles of public relations as normatively argumentative. Rhetoric is the rationale for translating communication as information flow into strategic communicativeness. Such agency occurs through debates over interpretations and evaluations (recall the discussion of the communicative organization in Chapter 2). By this reasoning, public relations is increasingly informed by bringing it into the rhetorical tradition, as a meaning-based view of media studies.

As is true of excellence theory and contingency theory, the rhetorical theory of public relations provides insight into the processes by which organizations, individuals, and groups strategically, contingently, emergently, and situationally manage relationships, infrastructures, interests, and power/control issues as means for normatively moving from discord to concurrence, and even consensus, then back to discord. This theory, like critical theory, offers the rationale required for societies to be fully functioning, because of the power of text. In regard to internal matters, organizational discourse is oriented to making organizations better places to work. In external matters,

Public Relations Theory: Capabilities and Competencies, First Edition. Jae-Hwa Shin and Robert L. Heath.
© 2021 John Wiley & Sons, Inc. Published 2021 by John Wiley & Sons, Inc.

such as public policy and even consumer affairs, rhetorical theory supplies the textual strategies and ethical choices societies need to be good places to live.

Rhetoric is inseparable from the culture or enactment of citizenship. Citizens (natural and artificial) engage in rhetorical arenas when they publicly consider, for instance, matters of military defense, principled norms of citizenship, conditions and processes of commerce and labor, and even whether an individual's or an organization's reputation should be celebrated (or condemned). They contest the quality of society, the environment, and all values-based decisions.

Today, voices engaged in public and private dialogues tend to be those of organizations: business, activism, nongovernmental organizations (NGOs), nonprofits, and government officials and agencies. Publics' and stakeholders' interests are given voice, debated, aligned, and translated into relationships (see Chapter 10 on publics and stakeholders, Chapter 11 on relationships, and Chapter 12 on leadership challenges—all relevant to rhetorical theory).

Organizations strategically frame their ideas in language (rhetoric, discourse, text) and justify them as good—discursive processes of collective problem solving and choice making. The communicative challenge of democratic engagement—deliberative democracy—justifies the study and professional practice of public relations as the strategic actions, processes, and discourse-bound means required to achieve civil society through engagement (Taylor, 2009; see also Johnston & Taylor, 2018).

Perhaps the most important rhetorical theorist of the twentieth century, Kenneth Burke (1969a), reasoned that rhetoric naturally grows out of division, courtship, merger, and other permutations of humans' relatedness. He posed the following irony: "How can a world with rhetoric stay decent, how can a world without it exist at all?" (Burke, 1946). He might have asked: How can a society with public relations stay decent, how can a society without it exist at all? Burke devoted his long career to examining how people—symbol-using and misusing animals—enact their lives through symbolic action.

By this rationale, ethical public relations can help make society more civil, more fully functioning, and a better place to live (Heath, 2011; Heath et al., 2006; Taylor, 2009). Society advances through dialogue (Buber, 1965; Conrad, 2011; Kent & Taylor, 2002; Heath et al., 2006). Value judgements are inherently rhetorical, and, conversely, rhetoric addresses matters of ethical choice.

This rhetorical view of public relations began to take shape in the 1970s, and was more fully developed in the 1990s, as scholars studied how and why activists pressured businesses and governments to change policies fundamental to the nature and quality of society. Topics such as environmental quality, race relations, fairness, equality, gender politics, consumer and workplace safety, and national security were subjected to robust scrutiny. Articles and books such as those by Toth and Heath (1992), Elwood (1995), Brummett (1995), and Heath, Toth, and Waymer (2009) built on policy and reputation tensions to link rhetoric, critical studies, and public relations.

Scholars and others examined three competing views of rhetoric as they sought a solid grounding for public relations. One view, which sees discourse as "just or mere rhetoric," asserts that it consists of hollow, vacuous, and even deceitful statements: the art of lies and spin. Another is that rhetoric is used by large, powerful organizations and other elites to gain power by bending public opinion to their own interests. The preferred view, however, is that rhetorical theory addresses the quality of propositional discourse by which people become informed, develop the evaluative criteria needed to make reasoned and ethical choices, and so formulate policy and behavioral preferences. Rhetorical statements influence citizens' identities and identifications so that they can forge relationships through textual association/disassociation.

Rhetorical theory encounters the critical reservation that it is harmful to the reputation of public relations because the field itself has had a bad reputation historically, being often associated with manipulation, persuasion, and vacuous statements devoid of action (Ihlen, 2010). Does rhetoric inherently incline toward one-way or asymmetrical communication? Is it too complex to be useable, or too simplistic to account for what is, should be, and should not be said and done strategically in rhetorical situations to best serve individual and collective interests through deliberation of rhetorical problems?

By addressing such questions in order to theorize public relations from the perspective of rhetorical heritage, readers can examine the strategic, emergent discourse resources that may be employed to enlighten choices, or confound them. By the end of this chapter, they should understand rhetorical theory, its connection with public relations, its normative principles contributing to academic research and professional practice, and its strategic, emergent role in human deliberation.

Questions to Frame the Discussion of Rhetorical Theory

- How and why are the structures, forms, and strategic processes of dialogue and discourse important to human affairs, and thus public relations?
- What is a rhetorical problem and why is it the focal point for discourse engagement?
- In the practice of public relations, how do discussants choose when and how to engage in public discourse as they adjust ideas to people and people to ideas?
- What best-case rhetorical principles help professionals to understand and enact the discourse strategies, techniques, and purposes of public relations?
- What role does the character of the source of discourse play in its impact? Is character revealed by what communicative individuals and organizations say and do?
- If community is a context, motive, and source of substance for the discourse of public relations, can the profession help make society more fully functioning, a better place to live and work?

Key Themes

- Rhetoric, the rationale for effective discourse and dialogue, provides theoretical and critical grounding for public relations because both deal with strategic, emergent, contingent decision making, problem solving, and social identification under conditions of uncertainty.
- Competing voices, including those relevant to public relations, have access to various decision-making infrastructures, including media, political arenas, and commercial venues where opinions are socially constructed through give and take: debate, competition, collaboration, and concurrence.
- Rhetorical theory enriches public relations as a professional practice and an academic discipline by examining and explaining the dialogic and discursive processes by which individuals and organizations co-create the meaning needed for community as a comfortable fit between the interests and ideas of organizations, publics, and stakeholders.
- Practitioners are expected to understand compelling rhetorical problems and to know the strategic and ethical means for addressing them.
- Rhetorical theory emphasizes the important role that character, facts, values, policies, identities, and identifications play in public dialogue. Character depends on an organization's commitment to co-creating enactable meaning that aligns its interests with those of others as they negotiate concurrence and seek consensus.

Rhetorical Theory: Public Relations Through Problem-Solving Discourse

The rhetorical heritage began when struggles for self-governance in Greece about 2500 years ago motivated philosophers to search for the rationale and means for citizen-driven collaborative decision making. To replace a reign of tyranny, citizens began to use rhetoric to create deliberative, democratic self-governance. They participated in policy-formulating discourse.

The oldest theory relevant to public relations arose from the cultural heritage of public citizenship and self-government, which originated in the golden age of Greece and continued into the Roman Republic and Empire, and over the centuries to today. Philosophers have examined how citizens' speaking and writing skills, as well as their character, could sway debates regarding contestable matters of public importance—issues, relationships, reputations, policy, character, and values as change management. They realized that fact, reasoning, appeals, motives, language, message structure, and character account for how some statements have more influence than others. Rhetoric is inherently coupled with choice, relational association, and rationale for individual and collective problem solving in the face of uncertainty. With no choices, no uncertainty, no disagreement, no need for identification, there is no need for rhetoric.

The preferred classical paradigm contends that ideas become better (at least, they have that potential) through public examination. People become more committed to ideas because they take part in decision processes. This better version of rhetoric occurs when propositional statements are pitted against one another. Stakeholders in context, faced with rhetorical situations and problems, argue their cases and make enlightened choices to improve their society.

Today, rhetorical theorists, among many other intellectual pursuits, work to conceptualize public relations as the clash of competing and collaborating voices in search of enlightened choices for organizational relatedness. In such clashes, deep-pocket organizations—power elites—may distort and at least partially control public policy dialogue, organizational culture, and commercial activity. By these processes, they may be countered, blunted, circumscribed, diverted, and defeated.

Individuals employ and yield to rhetorical appeals in endless kinds of collective arrangements—merger as well as division. Public relations enacts strategic dialogic adjustments as people seek to achieve agency in public, private, nonprofit, and commercial marketplaces by contesting issues and influencing choices related to resource acquisition and management. In private and public spheres, people textually relate to one another in varying degrees of association/dissociation, merger/division, conflict/agreement, and harmony/disharmony. Communal empowerment is deliberative democracy, whereas disempowerment occurs when dominance exerts control in service of narrow and particular interests.

This clash of ideas demonstrates the virtue of advocacy and counter-advocacy—statement and counter-statement. By such process, Lentz (1996) reasoned, "Truth should prevail in a market-like struggle where superior ideas vanquish their inferiors and achieve audience acceptance" (p. 1). Even powerful organizations compete to contest and weigh ideas. Propositions are set against one another to examine which is better and which inferior. Over time, deep-pocket organizations—and even tyrants—give way as competing voices advance their own answers to the problems facing them and their communities.

Antecedents

This perspective of society as a means for self-governance and self-agency took root in the writing of Aristotle (384–322 BCE), who was keenly interested not only in what was said, but also why, and especially how. As he listened to debates, he noted the structures, forms, strategic processes, purposes, linguistic nuances, and contents of the discourse, as well as the appearance and manner of the speakers. The character of each told him a lot about the strategic purpose and substance of public address as a collective means for solving problems, setting standards of character, and aligning interests (see Kennedy, 1991).

Rhetorical theorists have recognized that discourse is purposeful; it addresses matters of importance. In ancient Greece, discourse was strategically associated with three kinds of assembly, or forum, each of which raised a different kind of rhetorical problem. Each required its unique set of propositions to address specific kinds of questions: forensic (guilt or innocence), deliberative (politics and public policy issues of expedience, what should be done and why), and epideictic (praise and blame, consideration of whether a citizen might deserve an award or censure). Rather than mere image, epideictic questions contested the moral value of public actions and affirmed values essential to the quality of communities. The most important aspect of such proceedings was the faith that citizens, through discourse, could enlighten judgments on important matters. Self-rule is advanced through public trust built upon statements and actions that lead individuals and organizations to enjoy the license to operate and the right to reward: a rationale of legitimacy.

The rationale for such discourse is motivated by problems and questions that require answers. What a person (or organization) does and says constitutes a response to some undecided, often emergent, contested matter. A statement or action raises issues that prompt other voices to become engaged. These undecided matters are rhetorical problems.

The Rhetorical Problem

The concept of a rhetorical problem, resulting from some unknown or unresolved matter, became one of the most useful contributions of twentieth-century rhetorical theory. Vital to the practice of public relations, a rhetorical problem is an exigency that both motivates and constrains why something must be done or said, by whom and to whom, how it should be framed, when it must be addressed, and to what end it must be deliberated. Such exigencies occur for many reasons, including:

- naturally occurring events, such as disaster (e.g., forest fires, hurricanes);
- concerns voiced and issues raised about some organizational or public policy (e.g., food or worker safety);
- the character of some leader or organization (e.g., whether the banking industry deserves respect or censure);
- public health problems (e.g., child obesity, opioid addiction, type-one diabetes);
- choices regarding the quality of a product or service (e.g., cell phone coverage);
- matters of wise policy (e.g., whether to raise taxes on rich people to help pay for school construction and renovation);
- facts and evaluations needed to make decisions (e.g., whether a major pipeline should be approved);
- risks that seem badly managed (e.g., oil-field drilling engineering, the formulation of pharmaceuticals);
- the willingness and ability to be responsive to a crisis (e.g., whether a company took prudent measures to protect customers from product tampering that led to deaths).

Such rhetorical problems inherently make discourse propositional—consisting of assertions calling for sound proof and good reasons through iterative dialogue (Lane & Kent, 2018).

Rhetorical problems can be framed as outcomes that are desired or required to solve problems and serve a social need:

- Need to increase or decrease awareness of an organization, problem, issue, product, service, issue advocate, action, fact (information), value, policy, identity, identification, and so forth.
- Need for understanding or agreement on the part of an organization, stakeholders, or stakeseekers regarding fact (information), value, or policy position, as well as identification and relationship quality.
- Need to build, repair, or maintain relationships that serve the public interest or the integrity of community.
- Need to align multiple interests.
- Need to create, repair, and maintain a clear, coherent voice for an organization.
- Need to understand and implement appropriate standards of corporate social responsibility (CSR) as organizational legitimacy.
- Need to accept stewardship of some community or relationship imperative to build social capital.

The nature and role of rhetorical problems serve as the rationale for human society; strategic dialogue and discourse become the energy of societal agency.

Form, content, context, and structures of discourse have been examined as strategic processes for co-enacted problem solving for centuries. Close attention to rhetoric was crucial to the flourishing of Europe during the Renaissance and the Enlightenment. The disputatious rationale for the British parliament inspired other democratic countries. In the United States, departments of speech communication, and then of communication studies, continued this rhetorical heritage. Millions of public speaking students learned the principles of effective speaking, which championed propositional matters of fact, value, policy, and identification as means for shared problem solving. Public speaking texts emphasized the persuasive power of joint problem solving based on convincing audiences—through an examination of key premises—that some solutions are better than others.

Rhetorical Themes and Cultural Values

The rhetorical themes familiar to twentieth-century teachers and practitioners of public relations—principles, contexts, strategies, and ethics—are the same as those that interested ancient students of rhetoric. Over the years, rhetorical theory has focused attention on the processes of dialogue and discourse, as well as on rhetoric's ability to socially construct opinions and influence individual judgment as collective processes. The substance of discourse relies on facts, evaluations, and recommendations of policy and behavior. This triad parallels psychology's efforts to explain how knowledge, attitude, and behavior interconnect. The deliberative decision-making heritage seeks to explain how discourse creates personally and socially relevant meaning. Reflecting on the substance of this discourse, Campbell (1996) observed: "The issues it [rhetoric] examines are social truths, addressed to others, justified by reasons that reflect cultural values. It is a humanistic study that examines all the symbolic means by which influence occurs" (p. 8).

Intellectual inquiry in the twentieth century witnessed many innovations in thought, including the role of identification and rhetorically powerful idioms. Vocabulary creates—socially constructs—an understanding of social and physical reality. It allows people to forge identities and identifications. Even though they are not identical in thought and action, people can identify with (and separate from) one another as fans, supporters of various charities or political parties, advocates of various causes, and users of various products. Such identification results when people use terms—labels—to define their identity and name themselves. Every weekend in the fall, supporters divide themselves by allegiance to college football teams, don the appropriate apparel, and shout competing chants.

To justify that view, perhaps no singular statement is more profound than Burke's proposition that words serve as terministic screens—powerful social constructions. He invented this concept when he viewed photographs at an art show that were of the same subject but "looked" different because they were taken through different colored lenses. Each lens, like a different "tribal vocabulary," inspired a different view of the same scientifically ascertainable facts:

> We must use terministic screens, since we can't say anything without the use of terms; whatever terms we use, they necessarily constitute a corresponding kind of screen; and any such screen necessarily directs the attention to one field rather than another. (Burke, 1973, p. 50)

Each terministically-framed perspective constitutes an idiosyncratic way of thinking and acting.

For people and organizations to work and live together, they must agree on many matters in order to align their preferences and coordinate their activities. Worldviews developed and shared through language allow people to think and act collectively—a community of aligned interests through shared meaning—and even to disagree vehemently.

By adopting idiomatic or terministic screens, stakeholders' perspectives support or challenge the views and actions preferred by organizations. For instance, activists might complain about soot emitted from a manufacturing facility, which the company calls unharmful and standard operating practice. The activists will call for higher standards of environmental responsibility, including reduction of carbon emission, while the industry says that such changes are unnecessary or will raise costs and produce unemployment. Such discourse might include letters to opinion leaders, speeches and rallies, and lobbying efforts with appropriate regulators. Disgruntled customers vote with their feet—and their credit cards. They support one business by making a purchase from it, simultaneously expressing a lack of support for its competitors. Similarly, whereas some people are indifferent to natural resource exploitation and depletion, others champion sustainability. Such battles invariably pit one set of interests, values, ideas, and policies against another. Such battles are the fodder of public relations.

Under these pressures, rhetoric in ancient times became a highly developed symbolic action (or interlocking sets of symbolic acts) that divided and bound people together with the dialogic threads of the social fabric of contested and coordinated beliefs and acts. Using such discourse resources, citizens of ancient Greece spoke in forums before a relatively small and homogeneous body of privileged men to address one or more well defined rhetorical problems. Decision making was the heart and soul of Greek civil society—as it is in all others.

Today, both small and massive organizations address rhetorical problems, answer media inquiries, react to events, and report on an array of topics (e.g., environmental responsibility, product safety). Although rhetorical public relations can be narrow and self-serving, its strategic processes empower citizens to participate in the give-and-take competition of the marketplace of ideas. Through clash and collaboration, "the wrangle" of statement and counter-statement, they socially construct the identities and identifications needed to form communities (Heath, 2009). This occurs when family members gather around the kitchen table to discuss the family budget or college tuition. It occurs when someone mounts a soapbox (literally or figuratively) or engages in a battle of editorials, and in the back-and-forth exchange of social media. It occurs whenever ideas are set forth, supported, contested, refined, and rejected. It occurs in legislative arenas, judicial settings, administrative proclamations, and diplomatic dialogue. This wrangle of voices is sometimes a cacophony, but it is one that moves into forums through a myriad of media and non-media channels, and even into daily conversation.

This symbolic action composes the constitutive meaning by which people judge whether to support or oppose some organization. Opposition can affect product/service purchases and decisions regarding whether the organization is welcome to operate in the community or should be constrained through regulatory, legislative, and judicial oversight. This discourse creates and harms reputation, and identity.

The most basic premise connecting rhetorical theory to public relations theory and practice is that rhetoric, as discourse and dialogue, co-creates the meaning by which people judge organizations, products, and services—and policy proposals. Processes of consent and dissent formulate and implement the ideas that executives use to manage organizations, whether commercial, nonprofit, or governmental.

The 2010 blowout of a well in the Gulf of Mexico belonging to British Petroleum (BP) offers an excellent case to examine how and why rhetorical problems occur when rhetorical situations require public relations attention. The blowout, which released approximately 5 million barrels of crude oil, required BP to answer questions on employee safety and its operational ability to skillfully and responsibly produce oil. Voices questioned the soundness of public policy oversight regarding drilling science and engineering, employee and environmental safety, and the financial impact of BP's decisions on people's lives. Rhetorical problems arose for the federal and several state governments. Activist and trade groups, such as shrimpers and vacation property owners, got into the action.

As will be discussed in Chapter 7, the BP case illustrates the issue controversy that can result when a risk became a crisis—the rhetorical situation of an environmental rhetorical problem.

Case Study: BP's *Deepwater Horizon* Disaster—Public Relations and a Contestable Matter

On April 20, 2010, there was an explosion on board BP's drilling vessel, *Deepwater Horizon*, in the Macondo Prospect of the Gulf of Mexico, resulting in 11 deaths. The world watched crude oil spew from the ocean floor, rise to the surface of the Gulf, and harm wildlife and livelihoods. From day one, startling pictures of the fire and the knowledge that the drilling vessel had sunk—a rhetorical problem, or many rhetorical problems—consumed the attention of the company, the industry, the nation, and the world.

Media accounts tracked BP's struggle to cap the well and stop the flow, and documented the far-reaching environmental damage resulting from the blowout. Advocates sought to assign responsibility to the several companies working to finish the well so it could go into production. The battle raged in the media, in court, in Congress, and in other public venues. It pitted BP against other major oil companies, oil field service companies, government officials and agencies, fishing industry representatives, environmental groups, and citizens who lived and owned businesses along the Gulf Coast from Florida to Texas.

The dialogue around the *Deepwater Horizon* disaster addressed many issues. Public relations practitioners working on behalf of BP and affiliated companies designed and issued public statements. They were joined by legal counsel, engineers, senior managers, and other corporate and governmental agency voices. BP worked to speak to the world with one voice in explaining the reason for the blowout, how it would be stopped, and how containment and cleanup should proceed.

Debate weighed legal liability—how much, and in what ways, should liability be shared by the various companies involved, and even by government agencies? This further raised the issue of the amount of oil being released, and of how best to stop the flow once the blowout preventer failed. The controversy had public policy implications regarding whether current legislative and regulative oversight was sufficient to reduce the recurrence of such events. It also had reputational impact regarding BP's brand equity at the gas pump; on the other hand, oilfield services companies' reputations and marketing were unlikely to be affected in such visible ways.

Questions for Consideration

- Why did the blowout occur, and who was to blame? Could it have been prevented?
- Did the workers die because of engineering and operational errors?
- How much oil contaminated the Gulf and how much damage resulted from this contamination?
- Did chemical dispersants harm birds, fish, and vegetation?
- How credible was BP's judgment on these matters, and how sound was the information it provided? How did its response to the crisis affect its reputation and its relationships with stakeholders?
- How competent was BP to cap the well, track the damage, and engage in cleanup?
- Did BP executives engage with people who were affected by the disaster, including those advocating for the environment?

Rhetorical Theory as Rationale for Problem-Solving Discourse

As a foundation for examining principles of rhetoric, and thus the rhetorical theory of public relations, this section digs more deeply into rhetoric to understand and appreciate its strategic norms and principles. If rhetoric is vacuous speech, how can it provide intellectual rationale for the principles and strategies of public relations? If it is merely a tradition of deceit, lying, and spin, could it help salvage the reputation and social importance of public relations? These questions call for a solid understanding of the constructive role discourse can play if it is to support a valid theory of public relations.

This investigation returns to the culture of ancient Greece; there, citizens believed politics, ethics, and rhetoric were intertwined. Aristotle made that point in his *Rhetoric*: "Rhetoric is useful because things that are true and things that are just have a natural tendency to prevail over their opposites" (Aristotle, 1952, p. 594). The criticisms against rhetoric—and public relations—serve ironically to be its justification. At the polar ends of a continuum, either some power elite's strategic management imposes its judgment upon and makes decisions for people—and thereby guides and even dominates their consideration of such matters—or the people have the means to achieve self-efficacy. Advocates of rhetoric—discourse-based public relations—see rhetorical enactment as the rationale for public as well as corporate empowerment.

By its nature and purpose, rhetoric presumes that individuals and organizations manage their affairs and align their interests through the struggle between agreement and disagreement. Addressing that theme, Gaines and Gronbeck (2008) observed that the "rhetorical impulse may be conceived as the desire to express one's thoughts in a way that affects the thoughts of others"

(p. 4382). Discourse allows humans to live in various amounts of harmony and disharmony. Ideas become stronger and actions more ethical the more they are contested and refined through public discourse. This desire for individual and societal self-efficacy is the rationale for deliberative democracy (Palazzo & Scherer, 2006; Scherer & Palazzo, 2007).

Such conclusions were not easily reached in ancient times, nor are they today. Greek thinkers were not universally convinced that discourse and citizenship could produce a fully functioning society. Among the several philosophers weighing in on the matter, Plato (428/427–348/347 BCE) had the most uncomplimentary thoughts on rhetoric and the greatest fondness for elite decision making. He recognized how persuasion could be useful—but he condemned rhetoric for its potential to distort or deceive. One of the reasons such distortion could occur was the bad character of some individuals (today, entities) engaged in public discourse.

To partially counter that view, Aristotle reasoned that three criteria were imperative regarding the communicative character of speakers: "good sense, good moral character, and goodwill" (Aristotle, 1952, p. 623). Standards of each "good" were basic to rhetoric, which "exists to affect the giving of decisions" by listeners (readers or viewers), who then decided among the positions presented to them (p. 622). Credibility and trust, its companion, were vital to public relations, which in modern parlance requires organizational managements to be reflective. In that regard, CSR standards have become essential to ethical decision making as public relations. Managements have learned to consider others' ideas, perspectives, interests, and such as they create the policies by which they aspire, constitutively, to organizational success.

Notwithstanding Plato's skeptical view of rhetoric, Greek philosophers assumed that good argument and appeals, linked to "good moral character," would ultimately prevail against unsound, unreasoned, unethical, or dishonest alternatives. Today's public relations similarly is concerned with character, reputation, and image. That is not only the case in terms of how organizations are perceived and judged, but also in the extent to which they are believed. Character counted in matters of rhetoric in ancient Greece; that logic set the stage for current discussions of CSR and legitimacy, key themes facing managerial public relations. The character of an organization is judged by what it does and says; character affects people's willingness to believe and trust it.

Isocrates (436–338 BCE), like Aristotle, believed that rhetoric was essential to self-governance; citizens needed to take responsibility for maintaining the state apparatus, its decision-making abilities and integrity. To help them accomplish that goal, he challenged them to be effective rhetors committed to the good of society, not merely to winning individual arguments (see Isocrates, 1929). Following that line of reasoning, Marsh (2010) advocated using Isocrates' thoughts on rhetoric and citizenship to give solid footing to ethical, effective public relations theory.

According to Isocrates, citizens were expected to understand, appreciate, and reflect on the larger societal context for their actions and statements. The challenge was to use discourse to live together in harmony. That was not to dispute the value of individual instances of advocacy and debate, but it recognized that what would today be called engagement—collaborative decision making—is the glue of society. Such insight laid a foundation for today's commitment to reflective management, by which managements consider the impact of their decisions on the well-being of others. In Isocrates' time, citizens were challenged to understand the citizenship consequences of their words and deeds for the good of society; so, too, does today's public relations theory build on reflectiveness—responsible citizenship.

Isocrates and Aristotle were not alone in their efforts to link rhetoric and citizenship. For the Roman Quintilian (35–100 CE), the connection was obvious: the essence of citizenship is the good person speaking well. In an era deeply engaged in understanding the role of public relations ethics, CSR standards, and stakeholder participation, Quintilian's ideal could easily be restated:

The essence of public relations is the good organization communicating well. Here is the call for reflective citizenship as a forerunner to reflective management (see Quintilian, 1951).

By this logic, several key themes were championed by the ancient theorists, as they continue to be today: Communicators must have good character—be ethical—as the basis for legitimacy. They must be committed to high-quality discourse that enlightens choices. To that end, they must be willing and able to attack ideas that they believe to be faulty. They need to defend their own ideas with facts, sound reasoning, value judgments, and policy justifications that align interests and resolve uncertainty as much as is possible. They need to yield to superior arguments by others.

At its best, rhetorical discourse is founded on the assumption that open and vigorous debate can make society better for all. At its worst, it can encourage deception, manipulation, slander, character assassination, distortion, misinformation, and disinformation. Such motives result when some interests seek to privilege themselves at the expense of others. Champions of the rhetorical heritage believe that free and open examination of good reasons is the best answer to the misuse of the art. The compelling rhetorical problem is not only what one party believes, but what several voices joining in dialogue create together.

As is evident in the BP *Deepwater Horizon* case, companies and governmental agencies are called on to get to the bottom of matters, seek and examine facts, and resolve controversies. Risks must be managed in the public interest. Discourse, fairly contested, is one means by which the best individual and collective decisions are made.

To emphasize this point, the chapter now returns to the BP case, to examine the public relations teams (with allies from other disciplines, such as engineering, accounting, and general counsel) that contested a key rhetorical problem: Who or what was responsible for the blowout? Answers to that question are important for several public relations reasons. The first is the need for society to epideictically assign blame (thus requiring risk and crisis responses). Another is the ability of society to work to reduce the likelihood that a similar engineering and management/operational failure will recur during future oil drilling and production.

Keeping the issue of responsibility for the blowout on the front page, Rep. Henry Waxman (D-Calif.) framed BP's rhetorical problem by calling the CEOs of major oil companies to testify before the House Energy and Commerce Committee, which he then chaired. First, he asked them for their judgment on whether BP had been wisely responsible in how it handled a difficult stage in the development of the well. They unanimously said they did not believe it had. Then, he called on Tony Haywood, BP's CEO, the same question, set in the context of peer judgment.

What makes public relations honest and useful for organizations and those whose support they need? The answer is that individuals and organizations are constantly being judged, supported, and opposed. They encounter and create rhetorical problems, which foster discourse. As each voice asserts itself in dialogue, it stands the risk of counter-statement, a justification for honest transparency. Advocacy—propositional discourse as the rationale for public relations—is a means by which ideas can be tested to make them better, and therefore to enlighten decisions. Rather than the ethics of a single voice being empowered to answer such public contests, the conceptual and physical space where discourse occurs serves to motivate clear, responsible, and ethical discourse.

Thus, the rhetorical theory of public relations is affirmed and guided by the principle that many engaged voices are useful and, indeed, necessary when some matter requires discussion and when transparency is valued (Conrad, 2011; Heath, 2009; Ihlen, 2011). To support that conclusion, the following section features some timeless principles of rhetorical theory that can guide the practice of public relations.

BP and the Debate Over Responsibility

At some point, BP had to answer Waxman's question. On September 8, 2010, it issued a detailed report to explain why the event had happened and who was responsible for it. Although it was almost alone in the hot seat from April to September, its report claimed it had played "only a limited role in the disaster" (Clanton & Dlouhy, 2010, p. A1). Its report asserted that the blowout resulted from a complex series of failures of interrelated equipment operated by subcontractors. In response, "key contractors quickly dismissed BP's report as inaccurate and one-sided" (p. A1).

BP put forward eight reasons for the explosion, alleging that its personnel were directly involved in only one. For instance, it blamed Halliburton for providing poor-quality cementing services in the well's completion. In response, Halliburton argued that it was "confident in the work it did on the Macondo well, noting it was done according to BP specifications and criticized the report for 'substantial omissions and inaccuracies'" (p. A11). According to Transocean, the company that provided the drilling vessel, "BP made a series of cost-saving decisions that increased risk—in some cases, severely" (p. A1). Meanwhile:

> at the end of the day, BP can only blame others so much for the accident, said Nansen G. Saleri, CEO of Houston-based Quantum Reservoir Impact, an oil and gas industry consultant. "The elephant in the room," he said, "is that collectively and ultimately the responsibility lies with BP." (p. A11)

Through such processes of assertion and rebuttal, the debate was a rhetorical contest to set out and weigh the facts and reasoning needed to apportion responsibility for the blowout.

Other voices entered the fray. Kent Moors, professor at the Graduate Center for Social and Public Policy at Duquesne University and president of ASIDS, an international oil and gas consulting firm, drew the following conclusion: "BP has set the battleground, now Transocean, Halliburton, and Cameron are going to have to respond initially on the turf BP has selected" (Hatcher, 2010, pp. D1, D4).

Setting the tone of debate by defining how issues need to be resolved is a traditional rhetorical strategy; framing influences how issues are debated. For that reason, BP's strategy of diffusing responsibility may have prompted Rep. Waxman to conclude that its report "raises many questions" (p. D4). In response, Mark Bly, BP Safety and Operations Chief, said at the briefing on the report: "We wanted to understand what happened and why" (p. D4). During this controversy, the influential American Petroleum Institute and International Association of Drilling Contracts, both trade associations, made no comment as to liability.

On September 14, 2011, the U.S. Bureau of Ocean Energy Management, Regulation, and Enforcement set out the federal government's answers regarding the issue of blame. Its findings determined that the crew of the *Deepwater Horizon* should have stopped work as key problems began to occur. BP needed to have better contingencies in place to prevent such blowouts. Its desire to cut costs and save production time increased the likelihood that a blowout would occur. It did not exert full supervision and accountability over the activities that led to the blowout. Thus, the Bureau observed:

> While it is not possible to discern which precise combination of these decisions and actions set the blowout in motion, it is clear that increased vigilance and awareness by BP, Transocean and Halliburton personnel at critical junctures during operations at the Macondo well would have reduced the likelihood of the blowout occurring. (p. 200)

Despite these decisions, dialogue regarding the Macondo event continued. Over many years, it transpired in litigation, and in regulatory and legislative debates. Many more voices joined the deliberations. Interests argumentatively pitted facts against facts. Millions, even billions, of dollars were at stake, as were the quality of the environment and the livelihood of citizens affected by the disaster. Various voices used rhetorical structures and forms in their collective efforts to bring closure to the disaster. One—that of U.S. Bureau of Ocean Energy Management, Regulation, and Enforcement—clearly performed vital public relations activities on behalf of the federal government, and of the citizens of the nation. Its narrative defined the public interest. Such debates also offer insights into the nature and quality of the relationships that existed among the many interests at various key points in the controversy.

The release of BP's report opened the floor for questions regarding the quality of its reasoning and character. This case demonstrates how statements invite counter-statements. In this manner, do judgments and decisions become more sound?

Questions for Consideration

- Did BP demonstrate good character by issuing its report?
- How much of the impact of the report depended on BP's character, on the strength of its argument, and on the quality of its relationships with those involved?
- Can one voice control discourse on important matters, or does it merely become grist for the decision-making process?
- Should BP have adopted a collaborative engagement decision-making approach rather than assigning blame?
- Did the public relations strategy of deliberative democracy serve the government agency's assessment of responsibility?
- Did the rhetorical positioning in the decision process demonstrate that the government agency exhibited good character and presented sound arguments?

Principles of Dialogue: Foundation for Public Relations

Rhetorical theory reasons that discourse is not some random and nonstrategic aspect of human life; its rationale and strategic options can inform and normatively guide public relations, as well as justify the profession's contributions to management decision making, stakeholder alignment, and fully functioning societies (Kent & Taylor, 2002). This section features some strategic options that can be used to make discourse—and organizations—effective.

Public Relations as Enlightening Choice

The first principle to be discussed is that discourse can enlighten choices (Nichols, 1963). Enlightened choice results when one point of view is tested and determined to be superior to others. Rhetoric offers a much more specific, sound, and complex view of human communication than that limited to information sharing. Enlightened decisions require information, but information becomes relevant as it serves as fact-based, reasoned discourse.

This principle suggests that it is insufficient, for instance, for practitioners to be told that they should transparently provide or share information. Three questions are central to this principle: What facts does the organization want and need to provide? What facts do decision makers seek?

List of Rhetorical Principles

Taken together, the following principles offer a coherent and comprehensive theory for the effective and ethical practice of public relations:

- enlighten choices;
- adjust organizations to people and people to organizations;
- advocate sound solutions based on good reasons;
- build relationships through strategic courtship;
- create identifications through shared perspectives;
- align narratives;
- implement efforts to build community; and
- advocate responsible, reflective strategic management.

What facts are ultimately essential to contesting issues, reducing uncertainty, enlightening choices, and solving problems?

In the case of the *Deepwater Horizon*, society adheres to the ideal that public debate (rational, disputational inquiry) can clarify and establish the responsibility of various parties for that disaster. As already noted, BP's report allotted responsibility, but its unilateral discourse was dysfunctional because it was self-serving. It framed information—fact—to narrowly support the decisions it championed. In order to enlighten choices, all voices need to be empowered to have sway in each rhetorical arena. When some—especially those coming from the organizations most likely to be responsible—cannot fully collaborate in decision making, government as the voice of the people is obligated to step in—to make and justify the necessary choices.

Discourse allows industry, government, and citizens to understand what flawed equipment and procedures led to a disaster. Companies such as BP are likely to share information that will prove their point, but will this lead decision makers to the best decision, the most enlightened choice?

Public Relations as Adjusting Organizations to People and People to Organizations

The rhetorical theory of public relations assists organizations in adjusting themselves to the ideas of individuals and other organizations and in inviting individuals and other organizations to make corresponding adjustments to theirs. Justifying that principle, Bryant (1953) reasoned that the primary role of discourse is to adjust ideas to people and invite people to adjust to ideas. Such adjustments occur when ideas and key terms create a common ground for shared problem-solving collaboration (Heath, 2007a). These adjustive ideas and terms are valuable for the understanding of relationships, including their imbalances.

A case in point occurred during the 2008 banking crisis. As the U.S. housing market collapsed, and with banking executives having put profits and bonuses before sound financial practices, the banks asserted that they were "too big to fail." Using that adjustive terminology, they engineered a government bailout and encouraged citizen support for it—in the public interest. Rather than adjusting themselves to calls for better regulation, these financial institutions expected the public, government, and other organizations to adjust to them. The banks refused to call for or accept mutual adjustment—a true alignment of interests. They sought to end the financial crisis without reciprocating by adjusting to serve the public through revised banking practices.

Whether leading to good or bad outcomes, adjustment and alignment can occur as different sides explore the reasons for collaborative decision making. The rhetorical theory of public relations advocates that achieving those ends requires that ideas can create strategic alignments when they are supported by good reasons; choices need to be shared and fully justified.

Public Relations as Discourse-Based Good Reasons

People expect practitioners to give them good reasons for adopting some product or service, preferring one issue position to another, supporting the cause advocated by a nonprofit, encouraging a policy, or liking an organization because it does good or has a good reputation. To be good requires practitioners to demonstrate reasons and associate their preferences with values that endure over time, and to bring praise for the value they add to the quality of life.

Advocates of rhetoric champion discourse as a strategic means for achieving enlightened choices and responsible, reflective adjustment—reflective management. Supporting such a view, Wallace (1963) reasoned that "the basic materials of discourse are (1) ethical and moral values and (2) information relevant to these" (p. 240). The ideal substance of rhetoric is good reasons.

Dialogue enriches society when it sheds light on which reasons are truly best for the choices at hand. Decision making is fraught with uncertainty; important decisions are not clear-cut. As uncertainty persists—a rhetorical problem—dialogue must strategically test competing points of view to determine which is supported by the best reasons. Give and take tests which reasons best solve rhetorical problems.

Rhetorical discourse seeks to reveal and weigh ideas that truly reflect the interests of the people in society and champion what is good for them. The character of each individual or organization depends on the quality of the values that drive its choices and underpin the reasons proposed for or against any contested decision or action. Dialogue investigates what advice can normatively be brought to bear on the choices people are asked, want, and need to make.

Rhetoric occurs contextually in polyvocal (more than one voice) arenas where uncertainty abides and different opinions are pitted against one another. Discourse arenas, as rhetorical situations, arise in infrastructural and intellectual spaces where interests become issue-driven rhetorical problems that are asserted textually to empower and frustrate decision making that affects relatedness. Zones of engagement produce zones of meaning, whereby people share topic-specific knowledge, values, policy preferences, and identifications (including identities). Arenas are shaped by arguments/advocacy, the to and fro of voices seeking to influence and being influenced— including during crises (Frandsen & Johansen, 2017).

Industry voices in the BP case worked to assign and deflect blame and responsibility. As was evident in the decision by the U.S. Bureau of Ocean Energy Management, Regulation, and Enforcement, some neutral agency was needed in this rhetorical arena to obtain and assess the facts required to draw wise conclusions. The purpose of such deliberative inquiry was not inherently to vilify one party, but rather to make citizens the benefactors of the rhetoric of good reasons. Thus, the quality of discourse can build or harm relationships.

Public Relations as Invitation and Courtship Through Shared Perspectives

Character and the ability to build strong relationships are imperative for rhetorically effective public relations. With an invitation for others to consider one side of a matter, however, comes the obligation for the inviting party to consider other points of view and interest alignments. Such strategies lead some critics to worry that rhetoric is nothing more than a clever and deceitful trick deep-pocket organizations use to cloud judgment and manipulate relationships. Being open, willing to engage, and taking constructive positions on important matters can align the interests needed for constructive relationships; false flattery and fake identifications in normal circumstances have dire consequences.

Strategic invitation is part of public relations. Practitioners can ask others to contribute (e.g., to support research, treat breast cancer, and defeat childhood diseases), to visit (e.g., museums, parks, and vacation locations), or to sponsor (e.g., runners raising money for some charity). Such invitations can align interests by asking supporters to be a breast cancer advocate, a technology leader, or an advocate of some public interest (e.g., highway safety: "Don't text and drive"). Organizations, including companies, invite customers to identify with them through brand equity: Try our product. Identify with our team. Be a loyal arts supporter. Recommend us to your friends. The list of invitations is long and valuable to the relationships that assure the quality of society.

Rather than opting for a philosophy that empowers one advocate to the disadvantage of others, rhetorical theory helps public relations practitioners by providing insights regarding the invitational power and implications of the statements they make and the actions they take. It requires as well the realization that asking others to accept an invitation to form a relationship requires the inviting organization to be reflective, responsible, and capable of understanding and yielding to other points of view—a dance that may be likened to courtship.

As one of the advocates for featuring courtship as the paradigm of rhetoric—and therefore of public relations—Burke (1969b) argued that rhetoric is based on appeals to identification. Discourse invites individuals to identify with key terms (such as those associated with brands), important points of view (based on good reasons), products, services, organizations, causes, identities, or policies. By stating its mission and vision, for instance, an organization invites publics to consider identifying with it through a shared vision of how it can serve society.

Justifying this courtship view of rhetoric, Burke (1969b) wrote: "persuasion ranges from the bluntest quest of advantage, as a sales promotion or propaganda, through courtship, social etiquette, education, and the sermon" (p. xiv). In this sense, rhetoric is "the use of language as a symbolic means of inducing cooperation in beings that by nature respond to symbols" (p. 43). Cooperation and alignment of interests result from identification—shared meaning—through which people associate with causes, products, and organizations.

Association presumes dissociation. To prefer one brand of computer or automobile is to not prefer others. For this reason, rhetoric deals with "the ways in which the symbols of appeal are stolen back and forth by rival camps" (Burke, 1937, p. 365). Such discourse is similar to a bazaar, where vendors invite customers to check out their wares.

A courtship approach to identification rests on the subtle but powerful influence of terms, such as terms of identity: geographical, race, religion, gender, age. Black Lives Matters courts supporters through terministic identifications, as does the Tea Party. Football clubs and associations invite fans to support teams by using colors and chants to express identity. Diseases and health issues become defined by the language of courtship: breast cancer, children's health, Alzheimer's. So too have the arts: opera, rap, R&B, country, visual, graphic, digital.

Invitation appeals are so alive and well that they go unnoticed and often are used uncritically. Terms relevant to audiences, customers, publics, markets, stakeholders, followers, and supporter/ opponents are central to the lexicon of public relations. Internal organizational rhetoric invites employees to bond with the company and one another. By this rationale, workers are not "employees": they are "associates" and "team members." Doesn't it sound better and more empowering to be an "associate" than a mere "employee"? Likewise, people identify with products and those who use them: "Oh, I see you also have an iPhone." And identifications can lead to loathing, such as the rivalry between Red Sox and Yankee fans. (More discussion of relationship occurs in Chapter 11.)

All in the Way it's Worded

Through appeals to identification, public relations inspires people to champion sports teams, buy products, purchase services, support and oppose political candidates, give to charities, and live their lives in all of the ways that can be influenced by words. They might support nonprofits that solicit funds to combat one specific disease but show little regard for other causes.

Words influence people's judgments, forge relationships, and build a sense of community. One can imagine, for instance, how we respond to "our team," "our candidate," "our car," "our clothes," and "our causes." A key aspect of "our" is simply imagining the breadth of its inclusiveness. By knowing these terms and responding to them as propositions, people's actions are prescribed by the shared meaning associated with the relevant sports star, political candidate, or product. Through such means, people coordinate, seek what is mutually and individually beneficial, and relate positively (identify) to some organizations, actions, and issues—and not to others.

Burke's (1969b) insights into human identity and the identificational power of language led him to reason that "A character cannot 'be himself' [or herself] unless many others among the dramatic personae contribute to this end, so that the very essence of a character's nature is in a large measure defined, or determined, by the other characters who variously assist or oppose him [or her]" (p. 84). Companies employ this narrative principle when they proudly announce, through public relations, that a new movie is coming soon. The same is true of nonprofit supporters of environmental quality or the fight to end childhood diabetes. It helps identification if volunteers receive T-shirts or coffee mugs bearing logos or announcing how much blood they have donated. By this logic, organizations are rhetorically enacted to become an integral, even taken-for-granted, part of culture.

Through identification, relationships develop and social order is made possible; rewards are dispersed, identities shaped, and relationships developed and maintained—and terminated. Public relations practitioners use discourse to bring people together, to have them identify with one another. Such coming together and separating are universal shifts in the ebb and flow of society. Identification and aligned interests, as well as adjustive behavior, are not random but influenced by identifications made possible through language. Thus, community is linguistically born and sustained.

As BP suffered endless days when customers could see the flow of crude oil from the broken wellhead, it called on supporters to stick with it as it worked to solve the problem. It demonstrated its character by espousing its ability and responsibility to take the lead in cleaning up the Gulf and in developing equipment and practices that would protect the environment in the future. It wanted people to stick with it, and to return to vacation spots and work in affected areas.

Public Relations as Narrative

The BP case illustrates the narrative drama (continuity) of oil bubbling out of the wellhead, reaching shore, and coating wildlife. Ultimately, the narrative turned toward a happy ending (at least, an acceptable resolution), but not without substantial damage to the industry's reputation and to the wildlife and people along the Gulf Coast.

The disaster played out as a series of episodes. Characters came on to the scene, spouted lines (scripts), and left the stage. For instance, Tony Hayward, BP CEO, said he "wanted his life back" and was recalled to England once he became a lightning rod of controversy. Various voices, such as the U.S. Coast Guard, competed to impose comprehension of an achievable outcome on to a seemingly never-ending moment.

The event began with the theme that "once upon a time" companies were drilling for oil. Then, the blowout occurred. Each day, people longed for a happy ending, but they were frustrated when that ending eluded the industry's containment and recovery engineering skills, demanding governmental efforts to assist and force an effective response. One narrative asserted that by applying skilled engineering and strategic operations, the drama would end happily. A competing one foretold years of disaster and BP's ruination because of its operational ineptitude.

This case shows how people develop and enact narratives as a means of coordinating thoughts, identities, and actions as a community of shared interest. What Fisher (1985b) called the narrative paradigm assumes that "there is no genre, including technical communication, that is not an episode in the story of life" (p. 347). Conceptualizing people as storytellers—as co-authors of the drama of their enacted lives—Fisher (1987) reasoned that, "A narrative perspective focuses on existing institutions as providing 'plots' that are always in the process of re-creation rather than existing as settled scripts" (p. 18; see also Gergen, 1994). For this reason, "all forms of human communication need to be seen fundamentally as stories—symbolic interpretations of aspects of the world occurring in time and shaped by history, culture, and character" (p. xi). This view is akin to the argument that human beings are essentially narrative creatures—the *Homo narrans* perspective (Fisher, 1985a, 1985b). Disharmony, by extension, assumes that if people see reality differently, they enact competing and even conflicting life narratives, or counter-narratives.

Since narrative depends on language, practitioners are wise to avoid as best they can the perils of flawed thinking and communicating. Burke (1934) challenged critical scholars to spot the flaws that make language use for deliberation dysfunctional or dehumanizing. Looking for the chinks in the armor of sound reasoning, he warned that "if language is the fundamental instrument of human cooperation, and if there is an 'organic flaw' in the nature of language, we may well expect to find this organic flaw revealing itself through the texture of society" (p. 330). One such flaw is the paradox of the positive, along with its companion, the paradox of the negative. Each poses a flaw in thinking, often encountered by public relations professionals who overly praise or overly denigrate some particular matter. For example, a Volkswagen owner pleased with their vehicle's reliability and performance is more likely to believe the company's explanations of the 2014 emissions cheating scandal than someone who is not similarly invested in the product.

Narrative substance states good reasons. For example, once hydrocarbons were cheap and abundant. Today, that narrative collides with one focused on diminishing resources (sustainability) that are increasingly difficult, costly, and dangerous to produce. This again clashes with hydraulic fracturing (fracking), another narrative of controversy (Smith & Ferguson, 2013).

Narratives open public relations professionals to an infinite array of challenges and opportunities. News reports use narrative form and content. If a report creates a crisis, it poses a rhetorical problem that requires a narrative explanation of what happened, why, and what will be done to prevent its recurrence.

Narratives offer opportunities. For instance, public relations events have narrative form and content, which serve the purposes of publicity and promotion—and identification and relationship building. Practitioners use narratives in publicity to invite consumers to pay attention to see who is doing what, why, how, when, and where.

Large organizations and activists engage in publicity battles, advocacy, and counter-advocacy by contesting narrative views of the future—such as procedures for environmentally sound oil production. NGOs reason that their targets' narratives harm society, or some part of it. The rhetorical problem asks whether certain products or services, as well as management operations and even stakeholders' lifestyles, will lead to a tragic end or a "happily ever after" outcome. For that reason, some products are indicted as being harmful or unhealthy. Statements invite consumers to adopt a particular narrative vision of the future in order to make "enlightened" choices.

Public relations can assist organizations' narrative enactments—those relevant to strategic management and communication (Heath, 1994; Weick, 1987). Through narrative form, discourse gives people a sense of who creates the scripts that narrate society, how characters act, why plots develop, and which enactments are appropriate or inappropriate. Narrative continuity predicts which outcomes are preferred and which scripts define a fully functioning society.

In the case of the oil industry, the narrative of oil production asks what risks will be tolerated (paradox of the positive?). Whose interests can be harmed? What narratives put Humpty Dumpty back together again? It assumes the potential for oil spills and releases that will result in environmental and economic damage. Nevertheless, at least in the United States, political candidates periodically cry, "Drill, Baby Drill." These narrators see domestic oil production as the answer to virtually every economic problem: raising employment, lowering the cost of living, weakening adversarial foreign governments, and enacting an exceptional national character (identity and identification).

The questions raised and debated by competing voices, as illustrated by the BP case, demonstrate how rhetorical judgments arise from and center on the narrative quality of community sought by citizens.

Public Relations as Community Building

Community (a complex of relationships) is a context, motive, meaning, narrative, and rationale for the good reasons that enlighten choice. It is a place, idea, and narrative by which people align, contest, and weigh interests. It consists of venues, relationships, and infrastructures. It is where dialogue transpires and interests collide: "The role of opposition is by no means negligible in the shaping of society" (Burke, 1968, p. 71). As Hallahan (2004) concluded, "Indeed, healthy conflict is possible only within the context of supportive community" (p. 263).

Justifying this discursive view of community, George Herbert Mead (1934) reasoned that society is a blend of mind, self-identity, and social interests:

> Our society is built up out of our social interests. Our social relations go to constitute the self. But when the immediate interests come in conflict with others we had not recognized, we tend to ignore the others and take into account only those which are immediate. The difficulty is to make ourselves recognize the other and wider interests, and then to bring them into some sort of rational relationship with the more immediate ones. (pp. 388–389)

Mead's insight positions the discursive role of rhetorical public relations in the context in which it transpires and the role that it plays.

People act in the name of community. How they communicate (verbally and nonverbally) socially constructs and enacts that community. Communities seek members' loyalty, but appeals to loyalty can stifle change and prolong negative conditions such as racial discrimination (paradox of the negative?). It is a rationale for good reasons that feed decision-making processes with shared incentives to collaboratively engage for the greater good. Thus, McKerrow (1989) cautioned, discourse is about power "as it serves in the first case to maintain the privilege of the elite" and "to maintain social relations across a broad spectrum of human activities" (p. 91).

In context and cognitive space, shared meaning defines and allots power resources, as words bend reality to serve interests. Mead (like Foucault) reasoned that three concepts account for this human experience: mind/ideation, self/identity, and society/relationships (Heath, Motion, & Leitch, 2010). *Mind/ideation* refers to any socially constructed sense of reality. *Self/identity* refers to individual and group personhood. *Society/relationships* consists of interlocking relationships. These concepts can be defined by terms such as marriage or implemented through structures such as the hierarchy of courts. Power results from the rhetorical ability to privilege ideas regarding these matters and thereby to define societal relationships. Rhetorical theory enriches the discussion of topics such as trust, legitimacy, CSR, and rectitude. Rhetoric connects personal interest, economics, power, and class.

Such interlocking and even circular themes emerged in the discussion of public relations theory in the 1980s (Kruckeberg & Starck, 1988; Starck & Kruckeberg, 2001). Society cannot function without language and other forms of symbolic interaction. Yet, the discourse resources of a community can lead either to fully functioning or to variously dysfunctional societies.

Communitarianism, as noted in Chapter 2, challenges organizations to add value to the communities in which they operate, rather than presuming and communicating to prove that communities are obligated to serve them. This rhetorical problem asks whether organizations work successfully to bend community to their interests or to bend themselves to community interests. Such tensions are relevant to the rights of the organization to be rewarded, to operate, and to achieve legitimacy. Definitions of "contribution" and "community" often embrace contractions such as whether communities must endorse and support banks and other financial institutions that are "too big to fail."

Community incentives lead rhetorical theorists to champion the spirit and principles of deliberative democracy, free speech, and transparency. The right to speak is testimony that public discourse can play a positive role in society; voice strengthens and enlivens competing points of view. Community consists of socially constructed relationships that align interests. Bosses exchange money and workspace for labor. Regulators implement standards of operation, which businesses must accede to or oppose. Governments tell taxpayers where their tax dollars are spent. Charities show donors where their contributions go.

Community informs the discussion of the BP blowout. BP and the other companies involved were expected to serve the community and thereby earn the right to operate and deserve reward. When properly executed, drilling technologies produce oil and gas, to the benefit of consumers. But neither these nor the cleanup activities can be assessed independent of the myriad interests examined and contested by multiple voices in varying degrees of harmony and cacophony. Organizations that presume to benefit by managing risks need to demonstrate their ability to live up to that commitment. By so bending to serve the community, they are legitimated and become deserving of reward.

Public Relations as Advocacy

The term "advocacy" has a checkered place in the theory of public relations, but an understanding of rhetoric helps set it as a solid foundation on which public relations builds. To some, advocacy is seen as mind control, intimidation, and manipulation. To others, it can illuminate and enlighten choices. Some contend that rhetoric is vacuous, or spin. But both spin and empty statements can be examined and rejected as voices engage in propositional discourse. The truly worthy advocate knows that as much as one seeks to influence, there is also much to be learned from what is said by others. Thus, rhetorical theory accounts for how its nature results from and counters its inherent flaws—through advocacy.

Advocacy is inherent to controversy that enlightens choice. Do advertising, publicity, and promotion "advocate" the merits of a product or service? Through rhetoric, ideas clash. Harmony is possible because words allow us to reconcile opposites, which when viewed from "another point of view ... cease to be opposites" (Burke, 1961, p. 336). Advocacy relies on or occurs through propositional statements; it asserts facts, evaluations, and other good reasons to justify the superiority of one conclusion over its alternatives (Heath, 2007b). By asserting points of view, voices strive to influence one another, and likewise respond to counter-influence. In this way, rhetoric is "the art of describing reality through language" (Cherwitz & Hikins, 1986, p. 62). Similarly, Scott (1976) reasoned that rhetoric is "a way of knowing not *the way*" (p. 259). Thus, "reality is socially constructed" (p. 261).

What merit is there in what others say? Skilled and mature public relations professionals listen to the advocacy of others and use it to help manage their own organizations and engage in strategic communication. Using issues monitoring, public relations can help management become more reflective by knowing, considering, and appreciating the merit of claims made by other voices. Management can reflect on (consider and weigh) the discourse (facts, evaluations, identifications, and policies) of voices in the community.

Such reflection can help management to become good, as the first requirement for an organization to be ethical and effective. The objective of such internal analysis should not be simply to determine how arguments can be refuted, but rather should look at how the merits of such arguments can be incorporated into dialogue toward collaborative problem solving (Heath, 2007a; Johnston & Taylor, 2018; Marsh, 2010, esp. pp. 373–374).

During and after the time when the oil was flowing out of control, BP asserted facts to convey the impact and assign responsibility for the disaster. Each of its claims was subject to agreement or rebuttal. Forums (rhetorical arenas) where discourse occurs become vessels in which the soup of public discourse simmers, boils, and becomes resolved into something that can be consumed and shared. Thus, after the crisis, as BP issued its report in an attempt to parcel out responsibility, it had to realize that other voices and interests would either agree or advocate counter-positions.

Rather than merely making an organization effective, advocacy can make society stronger. BP advocated points of view that it believed were useful for understanding the crisis—its causes and consequences. Sometimes, its statements were self-serving, and accordingly they suffered counter-advocacy. As it asserted its estimates of the amount of oil flowing from the broken wellhead, some agreed, but others advocated other amounts, often higher than those it claimed. Likewise, experts took sides on the efficacy of various dispersants and their toxicities—a contestable issue regarding environmental impact.

However much it expressed regret and responsibility, BP longed to be out of the mess. Instead of being the only voice on such matters, it slowly realized that it was one of many examining facts, weighing ethical choices, evaluating, and determining which policies were wisest. Aligned and competing interests fostered and frustrated the efforts of the community to deal with the disaster. As the rhetorical problem shifted and twisted, those affected hoped for their interests to be wisely addressed and not to be damaged by the business plans of oil companies. They wanted to be able to receive facts, judge them, and draw enlightened conclusions.

As this section demonstrates, the strategic options of rhetoric are limitless. Discourse quality can be judged by focusing on principles capable of guiding the ethical practice and study of public relations.

Ongoing Research

Now into its third millennium, the marriage of rhetoric and public relations continues because both are central to the human condition. Rhetoric, now firmly connected to public relations, continues to generate research and reveal strategic options, flaws, and paradoxes.

Heath and Waymer (2009) examined the paradox of the positive (and negative) through abolitionist Frederick Douglass' "Fourth of July Address." This was delivered on July 5, 1852 in Rochester, New York as part of a fund-raising event by the Rochester Ladies' Anti-Slavery Society. The address countered the positive "spin" associated with the celebration of July 4 in honor of the Declaration of Independence, which ignored, and thereby marginalized, the millions held in slavery. Thus, such paradoxes are not only the motive but also the substance of advocacy. Similarly, Boyd and Waymer (2011) concluded that organizational messages, as well as those of external stakeholders, inherently represent a clash of interests.

Examining outlaw versus activist discourse, Boyd and VanSlette (2009) contrasted traditional activism against the postmodern view of the "outlaw rhetor." As much as activists speak to change the norms of society, they often do so within established power infrastructures. Outlaws advocate change outside of such infrastructures and in ways that may challenge the power establishment. On the other side of the equation, Baker, Conrad, Cudahy, and Willard (2009) examined "big pharma" to determine how industries influence not only the regulatory system that oversees their activities, but also the standards by which they are regulated.

Examining the proposition that strategic management and communication are ethically able to achieve comfortable fit with the communities in which they operate, Heath, Waymer, and Palenchar (2013) asked whether the universes of democracy, rhetoric, and public relations are inherently entwined or wholly separate. Ihlen and Heath (2018) assembled a group of leading thinkers on organizational rhetoric and communication to produce a handbook on the subject. Their analysis focused on the history of rhetoric in organizations and in society, looking at big-picture issues such as strategic processes of influence, including dialogue and discourse. On this analysis, organizations are a context for and constituted by rhetoric. Words matter, as meaning matters. The authors examined topics of theoretical importance, including identification, truth, myth, stasis, topoi, ethos, metaphors, tropes, and persona. The search for legitimacy is a motivation for strategic discourse, which includes verbal and visual elements. Context matters as a rationale for strategic approaches to relationship building and assaults on relationships. However stodgy rhetoric seems, given its classical origins, it continues to examine emergent strategy through contests of issues, risks, and crises.

Such studies pursue the question of whether society can survive rhetoric or exist without it. That question empowers a critical examination of public relations. Reflecting this paradigm, the rhetorical theory of public relations explains and guides the professional practice as a discursive means of achieving concurrence and coordination for strategic change management. Public discourse can help create and empower (or disempower) individuals, organizations, and societies. The dialogic view of public relations contrasts with one that conceives society as being put into place by powerful elites in furtherance of their own interests. It moves beyond the assumption that organizations can use (share) information via managerial problem-solving tactics to instrumentalize publics and stakeholders.

Conclusion

Discourse socially constructs perspectives that guide human behavior through propositional statements, dialogue, advocacy, evaluative appeal, invitation and rejection, and argument and engagement. With discourse, organizations appeal to workers and craft the purposeful relationships necessary for organizational effectiveness. Individuals appeal to one another to take positions on propositions, make decisions, share and interpret information (facts), weigh values, craft policies, define identities, formulate identifications, create and resolve tensions arising from differences of opinion, and allow for agreement, concurrence, and even consensus. Voices call for others to join this organization, support this cause, adopt this identity, buy this product or service, read and act on this statement, and so on for all forms and structures of discourse and choice-driven action.

Rhetorical theory empowers public relations to address how discursive strategies help individuals and organizations make the enlightened choices required for fully functioning societies. The long tradition of rhetorical dialogue is the means by which people and organizations solve problems, make decisions, and press for the collaborative processes fundamental to democracy. Such discourse empowers civil society (Taylor, 2009, 2011) and builds social capital (Ihlen, 2005).

Chapter Summary

To examine connections between rhetorical theory and public relations, this chapter revisits the robust rhetorical heritage to appreciate how meaning and ideas matter. They are improved through public examination, where many voices compete in various rhetorical arenas. Public discourse, however cordial or contentious, serves the public interest as voices compete to answer an infinite variety of rhetorical problems. Noting how ideas matter in human affairs, the chapter argues that public relations helps make them better—more enlightened—as statements are subjected to counter-statements. This theory defines how public relations can play a productive role in society, as well as pose a potential danger to it. Rhetorically, public relations is a rationale for the social construction of change management.

Key Terms

Co-created Meaning: View of communication as democratic, interactive, and participatory process in which meaning is constructed and exchanged by involved parties at all levels.

Dialogue: Iterative statements that take various positions on issues relevant to some matter.

Discourse: Language-rich, ongoing, and enduring interpretations that have the potential to become lived perspectives.

Fully Functioning Society: As an aspirational and functional concept, presumes that civil society processes and discourse strategies are best when they make communities good places to live and work.

Narrative: A story that symbolically interprets aspects of the world as occurring in time and shaped by history, culture, and character.

Rhetoric: Entails the strategic textual logics and discourse processes by which communities think out loud in search of the relatedness needed for shared governance through individual, group, organizational, and societal agency.

Rhetorical Character: A rhetor's good sense, moral character, and good will, empowering a free and open examination of good reasons relevant to choices.

Rhetorical Problem: Some unknown, unresolved, contestable matter; an exigency that results from pressures salient to a rhetorical situation proceeding from some unknown or unresolved matter.

Rhetors: Those who give voice to some matter or decision that needs to be made.

Terministic Screens: The defining and attitudinizing impact words have on interpretations of reality as the reflection and deflection of meaning.

Discussion Questions

1 Why did rhetoric arise as a system of collective decision making in ancient Greece and Rome? In what ways is this relevant to public relations theory and practice today?

2 What is the justification for enlightened decision making? How does a commitment to discursive strategies that improve ideas blunt the allegation that public relations is a stealth activity used to manipulate outcomes so that some interests gain at the disadvantage of others?

3 What six terms best define the principles of discourse that constitute responsible and legitimate rhetorical public relations?

4 How do concepts such as enlightened choice, dialogue, civil society, community, social construction of reality, terministic screens, identity, identification, good reasons, advocacy, engagement, and social capital pose critical challenges and opportunities for the professional practice and academic research of public relations?

References

Aristotle (1952). *Rhetoric,* trans. W. R. Roberts. R. M. Hutchins (Ed. in Chief)In *Great books* (Vol. *2,* pp. 593–675). Chicago, IL: Encyclopaedia Britannica.

Baker, J. S., Conrad, C., Cudahy, C., & Willyard, J. (2009). The devil in disguise: Vioxx, drug safety, and the FDA. In R. L. Heath, E. L. Toth, & D. Waymer (Eds.), *Rhetorical and critical approaches to public relations II* (pp. 170–194). Thousand Oaks, CA: New York: Routledge.

Boyd, J., & VanSleet, S. H. (2009). Outlaw discourse as postmodern public relations. In R. L. Heath, E. L. Toth, & D. Waymer (Eds.), *Rhetorical and critical approaches to public relations II* (pp. 328–342). Thousand Oaks, CA: New York: Routledge.

Boyd, J., & Waymer, D. (2011). Organizational rhetoric: A subject of interest(s). *Management Communication Quarterly, 25,* 474–493.

Brummett, B. (1995). Scandalous rhetorics. In W. N. Elwood (Ed.), *Public relations inquiry as rhetorical criticism: Case studies of corporate discourse and social influence* (pp. 13–23). Westport, CT: Praeger.

Bryant, D. C. (1953). Rhetoric: Its function and its scope. *Quarterly Journal of Speech, 39,* 401–424.

Buber, M. (1965). *Between man and man,* trans. R. G. Smith. New York: MacMillan.

Burke, K. (1934). The meaning of C. K. Ogden. *New Republic, 78,* 328–331.

Burke, K. (1937). Synthetic freedom. *New Republic, 89,* 365.

Burke, K. (1946). Letter to Malcolm Cowley, October 22. Burke File, Pennsylvania State University.

Burke, K. (1961). *Attitudes toward history.* Boston, MA: Beacon.

Burke, K. (1968). *Counter-statement.* Berkeley, CA: University of California Press.

Burke, K. (1969a). *A grammar of motives.* Berkeley, CA: University of California Press.

Burke, K. (1969b). *A rhetoric of motives.* Berkeley, CA: University of California Press.

Burke, K. (1973). *Language as symbolic action.* Berkeley, CA: University of California Press.

Campbell, K. K. (1996). *The rhetorical act* (2nd ed.). Belmont, CA: Wadsworth.

Cherwitz, R. A., & Hikins, J. W. (1986). *Communication and knowledge: An investigation in rhetorical epistemology.* Columbia, SC: University of South Carolina Press.

Clanton, B., and Dlouhy, J. A. (2010). BP spreads blame for deadly blowout. *Houston Chronicle,* September 2. Available from https://www.chron.com/business/energy/article/BP-spreads-blame-for-deadly-blowout-1695116.php (accessed May 20, 2020).

Conrad, C. (2011). *Organizational rhetoric*. Malden, MS: Polity Press.

Elwood, W. N. (Ed.) (1995). *Public relations inquiry as rhetorical criticism: Case studies of corporate discourse and social influence*. Westport, CT: Praeger.

Fisher, W. R. (1985a). The narrative paradigm: In the beginning. *Journal of Communication, 35*, 74–89.

Fisher, W. R. (1985b). The narrative paradigm: An elaboration. *Communication Monographs, 52*, 347–367.

Fisher, W. R. (1987). *Human communication as narrative: Toward a philosophy of reason, value, and action*. Columbia, SC: University of South Carolina Press.

Frandsen, F., & Johansen, W. (2017). *Organizational crisis communication*. Thousand Oaks, CA: Sage.

Gaines, R. N., & Gronbeck, B. E. (2008). Rhetorical studies. In W. Donsbach (Ed.), *International encyclopedia of communication* (pp. 4382–4395). Malden, MA: Blackwell.

Gergen, K. (1994). *Realities and relationships*. Cambridge, MA: Harvard University Press.

Hallahan, K. (2004). "Community" as a foundation for public relations theory and practice. In P. J. Kalbfleisch (Ed.), *Communication yearbook 28* (pp. 232–279). Mahwah, NJ: Lawrence Erlbaum Associates.

Hatcher, M. (2010). BP report sets probe agenda—for now. *Houston Chronicle*, September 9, pp. D1, D4.

Heath, R. L. (1994). *Management of corporate communication: From interpersonal contacts to external affairs*. Hillsdale, NJ: Lawrence Erlbaum Associates.

Heath, R. L. (2007a). Management through advocacy. In E. L. Toth (Ed.), *The future of excellence in public relations and communication management: Challenges for the next generation* (pp. 41–65). Mahwah, NJ: Lawrence Erlbaum Associates.

Heath, R. L. (2007b). Rhetorical theory, public relations, and meaning: Giving voice to ideas. In T. Hansen-Horn & B. D. Neff (Eds.), *Public relations: From theory to practice* (pp. 208–226). New York: Allyn & Bacon.

Heath, R. L. (2009). The rhetorical tradition: Wrangle in the marketplace. In R. L. Heath, E. L. Toth, & D. Waymer (Eds.), *Rhetorical and critical approaches to public relations II* (pp. 17–47). Thousand Oaks, CA: New York: Routledge.

Heath, R. L. (2011). External organizational rhetoric: Bridging management and sociopolitical discourse. *Management Communication Quarterly, 25*, 415–435.

Heath, R. L., & Damion, W. (2009). Activist public relations and the paradox of the positive. In R. L. Heath, E. L. Toth, & D. Waymer (Eds.), *Rhetorical and critical approaches to public relations II* (pp. 195–215). New York: Routledge.

Heath, R. L., Motion, J., & Leitch, S. (2010). Power and public relations: Paradoxes and programmatic thoughts. In R. L. Heath (Ed.), *SAGE handbook of public relations* (pp. 191–204). Thousand Oaks, CA: Sage.

Heath, R. L., Pearce, W. B., Shotter, J., Tayler, J. R., Kersten, A., Zorn, T., ... Deetz, S. (2006). The processes of dialogue: Participation and legitimation. *Management Communication Quarterly, 19*, 341–375.

Heath, R. L., Toth, E. L., & Waymer, D. (Eds.) (2009). *Rhetorical and critical approaches to public relations II*. New York: Routledge.

Heath, R. L., Waymer, D., & Palenchar, M. J. (2013). Is the universe of democracy, rhetoric, and public relations whole cloth or three separate galaxies? *Public Relations Review, 39*, 271–279.

Ihlen, Ø. (2005). The power of social capital: Adapting Bourdieu to the study of public relations. *Public Relations Review, 31*, 492–496.

Ihlen, Ø. (2010). The cursed sisters: Public relations and rhetoric. In R. L. Heath (Ed.), *SAGE handbook of public relations* (pp. 59–70). Thousand Oaks, CA: Sage.

Ihlen, Ø. (2011). On barnyard scrambles: Towards a rhetoric of public relations. *Management Communication Quarterly*, *25*, 455–473.

Ihlen, Ø., & Heath, R. L. (Eds.) (2018). *Handbook of organizational rhetoric and communication*. Malden, MA: Wiley.

Isocrates (1929). *Antidosis*, trans. G. Norlin. In *Isocrates* (Vol. *2*, pp. 182–365). Cambridge, MA: Harvard University Press.

Johnston, K. A., & Taylor, M. (Eds.) (2018). *The handbook of communication engagement*. Malden, MA: Wiley.

Kennedy, G. (1991). *Aristotle: A theory of civic discourse*. Oxford: Oxford University Press.

Kent, M. L., & Taylor, M. (2002). Toward a dialogic theory of public relations. *Public Relations Review*, *28*, 21–37.

Kruckeberg, D., & Starck, K. (1988). *Public relations and community: A reconstructed theory*. New York: Praeger.

Lane, A., & Kent, M. (2018). Dialogic engagement. In K. A. Johnston & M. Taylor (Eds.), *The handbook of communication engagement* (pp. 61–72). Malden, MA: Wiley.

Lentz, C. S. (1996). The fairness in broadcasting doctrine and the Constitution: Forced one-stop shopping in the "marketplace of ideas." *University of Illinois Law Review*, *271*, 1–39.

Marsh, C. (2010). Precepts of reflective public relations: An Isocratean model. *Journal of Public Relations Research*, *22*, 359–377.

Mead, G. H. (1934). *Mind, self, and society*. Chicago, IL: University of Chicago Press.

McKerrow, R. E. (1989). Critical rhetoric: Theory and practice. *Communication Monographs*, *56*(2), 91–111.

Nichols, M. H. (1963). *Rhetoric and criticism*. Baton Rouge, LA: Louisiana State University Press.

Palazzo, G., & Scherer, A. G. (2006). Corporate legitimacy as deliberation: A communicative framework. *Journal of Business Ethics*, *66*, 71–88.

Quintilian, M. F. (1951). *The Institutio Oratoria of Marcus Fabius Quintilianus*, trans. C. E. Little. Nashville, TN: George Peabody College for Teachers.

Scherer, A. G., & Palazzo, G. (2007). Toward a political conceptualization of corporate responsibility: Business and society seen from a Habermasian perspective. *Academic of Management Review*, *31*, 1096–1120.

Scott, R. L. (1976). On viewing rhetoric as epistemic: Ten years later. *Central States Speech Journal*, *27*, 258–266.

Smith, M. F., & Ferguson, D. P. (2013). "Fracking democracy": Issue management and the locus of policy decision-making in the Marcellus Shale gas drilling debate. *Public Relations Review*, *39*, 377–386.

Starck, K., & Kruckeberg, D. (2001). Public relations and community: A reconstructed theory revisited. In R. L. Heath (Ed.), *Handbook of public relations* (pp. 51–59). Thousand Oaks, CA: Sage.

Taylor, M. (2009). Civil society as a rhetorical public relations process. In R. L. Heath, E. L. Toth, & D. Waymer (Eds.), *Rhetorical and critical approaches to public relations II* (pp. 76–91). Thousand Oaks, CA: New York: Routledge.

Taylor, M. (2011). Building social capital through rhetoric and public relations. *Management Communication Quarterly*, *25*, 436–454.

Toth, E. L., & Heath, R. L. (1992). *Rhetorical and critical approaches to public relations*. Hillsdale, NJ: Lawrence Erlbaum Associates.

U.S. Bureau of Ocean Energy Management, Regulation, and Enforcement. (2011). *Report regarding the causes of the April 20, 2010 Macondo Well blowout.* Washington, D.C.: U.S. Government.

Wallace, K. R. (1963). The substance of rhetoric: Good reasons. *Quarterly Journal of Speech, 49,* 239–249.

Weick, K. E. (1987). Theorizing about organizational communication. In F. M. Jablin, L. L. Putnam, K. H. Roberts, & L. W. Porter (Eds.), *Handbook of organizational communication: An interdisciplinary perspective* (pp. 97–122). Newbury Park, CA: Sage.

6

Critical Theory: Critiquing Discourse Processes, Meaning, and Power

Introduction

By the mid-1990s, social scientific methodologies and variable analytical logics had become routine tools in the development of public relations theory. The influence of the rhetorical tradition steadily added breadth and depth to the literature. Critical theory was beginning to question how and why public relations should be practiced—what roles it should play in organizational success and societal quality. It challenged those who work for hire to understand the implications of discourse beyond the advantage it can produce for their employers and to be cognizant of the harm that can result when some interests are privileged to the disadvantage of others. Community became an agentic forum for shared decision making toward the forging of moral political economy. Critical theorists deconstructed textual, language-based meaning to reveal perspectives that created and recreated power resources. Emphasizing organizational legitimacy and hegemony, critical theory reasoned that the quality of society—community—is the ultimate criterion for successful public relations.

By the dawn of the twenty-first century, advocates had laid a foundation for a critical theory of public relations, and even a theory of critical public relations. This chapter features topics and themes that define and support that body of theory. Its primary contribution to public relations theory is its ability to help shift the focus from an analysis of how to make organizations effective to strategies that make society an ever-better place to live and work. Theorists believe that normative outcomes require penetrating insights into the weaknesses of corporate-centric approaches to public relations, especially those that feature structures, functions, and adjustments that ultimately favor corporate interests and empower the strategic ability of corporations to instrumentalize publics to serve those interests.

These advances in the critical theory of public relations have been published in *Public Relations Inquiry* and *The Routledge Handbook of Critical Public Relations* (L'Etang, McKie, Snow, & Xifra, 2016). Slowly, a coherent theory is advancing a moralized sociological perspective by which to critique other theories. To justify their approach, critical theorists draw on ideas proposed by several intellectuals, most notably Michel Foucault (1926–1984), Pierre Bourdieu (1930–2002), Norman Fairclough (b. 1941), Jürgen Habermas (b. 1929), Antonio Gramsci (1891–1937), Jacques Derrida (1930–2004), and George Herbert Mead (1863–1931). Characterizing this line of discussion crisply is not easy: it centers on the quality of society, openness of communication, fairness of discourse, transparent language, and a political economy that raises the quality of community; and it investigates norms of marginalization and empowerment.

Public Relations Theory: Capabilities and Competencies, First Edition. Jae-Hwa Shin and Robert L. Heath.
© 2021 John Wiley & Sons, Inc. Published 2021 by John Wiley & Sons, Inc.

Such ideas helped inaugurate the critical theory of public relations in the mid-1990s. Moffitt (1994) explored the impact of professional communication on publics' socially constructed worlds. Motion and Leitch (1996) used Fairclough's views to enlighten discourse practices during the transformation from one dominant view of sociocultural practices to another. In the same year, Leeper (1996) drew on the work of Habermas to address discourse ethics that advance a communitarian approach to public relations.

Public relations traditionally has been associated with the strategies, theories, and philosophies required to make organizations—especially businesses—effective. Critical theory shifts the focus from organizations, however adjustive, to the requirements needed to make society more effective and individuals more empowered. It reasons that organizations do best when they engage with others to solve collective problems and manage collective interests rather than focusing narrowly on problems and interests from their own point of view and to their own advantage. For that reason, critical theory examines discourse in search of values and conditions such as control, power, and egalitarianism. It believes that words—often, only a few—can embed power/knowledge implications that favor some interests and marginalize others.

This theory features several themes. One is the daunting question of power. Another is the nature of legitimacy. On such matters, critical public relations cautions against being too positive that good outcomes will come easily, if at all, from the simple application of a strategic formula. It claims that strategy is best when all interests are treated appropriately and ethically. To guide its standards, it critically interprets the economics, human relations, and language resources by which ideologies compete to define political economy.

Rhetorical and critical theories are more philosophically humanistic than those featuring variable analytical approaches; humanists can profoundly distrust statistical analysis (positivism). Critical theorists challenge the ability of empirically-based social science to ask and answer the right questions in the best manner to further the cause of humanity. Rather than statistical methodologies, they apply conceptualization, philosophical discussion, and case examination to disclose ironies, paradoxes, inconsistencies, power struggles, critical turns, and ideological battles. Ethics is an inherent critical problem, rather than a seasoning added to make a theory socially palatable. For that reason, critical theory offers normative guidelines for professional practice based on the proposition that meaning counts substantially in the success of an organization or community. Meaning is best when it is the product of thoughtful, open discourse whereby interested parties engage in a principled investigation of what actions and ideas enjoy support or suffer opposition.

Taking the concept of "critical" seriously, supporters of critical theory examine the critical turns that justify management decisions, including strategic public relations. Such criticism of organizations, especially doubts about modern (rather than postmodern and critical) management theory, can lead critics of this theory to believe that its intent is to deny or destroy organizations—especially businesses—as being seriously flawed on principle.

Critical theory does not propose to make organizations less effective, but draws on economics, anthropology (culture), politics, and sociology to help them to be effective by being mindful of, responsive to, and responsible for the interests of a broad range of stakeholders. It looks for the ways in which strategic communication constructs meaning that guides and results from marginalized voices and interests. If marginalized, a voice is muted, its interests trivialized, and its role in society diminished. If, on the other hand, a voice loudly dominates discourse to favor a narrow set of interests then critical judgment is needed. Since empowerment counterbalances marginalization, critical public relations seeks to learn how interests are marginalized and empowered in order to avoid the former and champion the latter.

Worried that economics and politics are logics by which power is imposed linguistically on segments of society, critical theorists champion a more empowering approach to management and communication. Discourse is a tool of interested parties. Language (textuality) is never neutral, but always expresses power and defines legitimacy through economics, politics, and culture. Wording privileges some interests and disadvantages others because discourse ideologically expresses preferred ethics (McKie, 2001, 2005).

Sensitive to paradoxes of power and legitimacy, Cheney and Christensen (2001) asked whether modern, Western management philosophies couple with public relations theory to obscure the values of humanity. Modern management philosophy seeks to understand how to make organizations effective, often by increasing efficiency in quite self-interested ways. Consequently, the purpose of public relations may be to foster good will that relieves organizations—primarily businesses—from criticism leading to public policy and reputational constraints.

The premise of critical theory is that what advances society also advances organizational existential interests. This draws on themes of legitimacy, resource dependency, power (including hegemony and imperialism/colonization), control, language as enactment, the public sphere, *communitas* versus *corporatas*, narrative, globalization, reflective management and corporate social responsibility (CSR), intersectionality, identity, interests, paradoxes, ironies, ecology, sustainability, and more. Civil society is dedicated to rigorous humanization, transparency (in terms of power and legitimation), and a quest for authenticity. By understanding these themes' implications for the alignment of interests between people and organizations, students can learn how to manage and communicate for organizations by using discursive strategies to humanize social reality.

This chapter addresses the quality of the context in which discourse (discursive strategies) occurs, outcomes from discourse, and meaning as a way of thinking and acting in concert. Critical perspectives reveal the distortions and injustices that language and argument bring into problem solving. Dedicated to the formation of morally principled society, critical theory, like rhetorical theory, is keenly interested in how meaning is created and whom it privileges or marginalizes.

By the end of the chapter, readers should understand critical theory, its connection with public relations, its normative principles contributing to academic research and professional practice, and its strategic, emergent role in human deliberation. Mastering its terminology and reasoning can untangle complex thought, clarify ethical judgment, and empower self-reflection.

Questions to Frame the Discussion of Critical Theory

- Can a modern organization, using Western managerial philosophy, communicate well?
- Can public relations help to make managerial decision making reflective?
- Which language hegemonies privilege some interests while disempowering others?
- Which hegemonies foster or hamper efforts to increase the quality of society and the success or failure of organizations and individuals seeking collectively to solve problems, make decisions, and manage risks?
- What concerns do critical theorists have regarding the "arenas" or "spheres" in which discourse occurs?
- If the quality of the public arena affects the quality of discourse, what criteria should be applied to improve discourse quality?
- What makes some discourse better than other discourse?
- Do interests embedded in language hamper the quality of discourse?
- Do public relations and the organizational interests it serves do best with a commitment to *corporatas* or *communitas*?
- If power is the universal struggle, community the context, and language the means, can public relations advance the ability to make each community a good place in which to work and live?

Key Themes

- Critical theory asks management teams to be mindful of the hegemonies they support, often uncritically, through the policies they develop and implement and the discursive strategies and messages they champion.
- According to critical theory, public relations practitioners should be ethically cautious to avoid dominating the news agenda for their employers in ways that mute important voices in public debate.
- Critical theory claims public relations is integral to the social hierarchy of power resources. Its identity and role in society interconnect with its ability to promote interests and generate voice on behalf of its organizational employers. However, it needs to be ethically committed to aligning the interests of others with those of the organization it represents.
- Public relations' sense of purpose can too narrowly (too insularly) be that of its organization, rather than being aligned to higher-order community benefits such as environmental quality, sustainability, and inclusive egalitarianism.
- Too often, public relations seeks to tell publics what and how to think. Critical theory urges it to welcome stakeholders as equal participants in public discourse.
- Much public relations theory and many best practices address the functionality of the profession—why it does what it does. As a counterforce to such functionality, critical public relations adopts an anthropological approach based on understanding and supporting cultures to benefit people's lives, beliefs, values, and knowledge.
- To be integral to management, critical theory argues that public relations must avoid any self-interested hegemony that narrowly privileges its own interests.

Critical Theory: Public Relations Through Sociocultural Discourse

Critical theory arose from the concern that economics, politics, sociology, and culture come to life through discursive strategies and the shared meaning that they create. Unlocking this problem requires understanding the distorting and privileging capacity of language, which critical theorists seek to explain using the concept of hegemony. As Roper (2005) observes, *"[h]egemony* can be defined as domination without physical coercion through the widespread acceptance of particular ideologies and consent to the practices associated with those ideologies" (p. 69). Critical theorists are intent on disclosing how idioms express taken-for-granted perspectives that impose power structures, identities, and identifying relationships on to members of society.

Critical theorists reason that any textual hegemony that privileges some to the disadvantage of others ultimately frustrates societal decision making and thereby leads organizations to be less successful than they desire. Key words become crucial to key turns in society: free enterprise, democracy, liberty, and equality. A hegemony gains power when it becomes a "taken-for-granted" way of thinking and acting.

"Hegemony" refers to the sociocultural power of language to influence collective thought and behavior. It results when a power elite uses discursive strategies to impose itself on to society. "Organizational" hegemony occurs when management shapes organizational culture. Parents work for a hegemony by connecting phrases such as "good boy" and "good girl" with the expected, rewarded behavior of their children. Businesses do the same as they engage in internal ("organizational") communication that defines employees' importance based on their rewardable work for the organization. Thus, when once employee loyalty was the essence of the corporate contract, internal newsletters featured employees' milestones by reporting how long they had worked for the company. When layoffs became the rationale for senior management cost-cutting, longevity was no longer a useful hegemony. Similarly, marketing communication defines the brand-loyal consumer, while political discourse defines people by political party and issue position. Such discursive strategies can seem quite harmless, or even useful to social order. But critical theorists wonder whose sense of order is served by a given hegemony.

Language, the voice of hegemony, is the site of discursive struggle; idioms (specialized vocabulary) socially construct a worldview—a set of perspectives that is lived and enacted because it specifies conditions of reward, relationship, allegiance, identity, and social hierarchy. Those voices that shape textual meaning control action.

Critical theorists are convinced that public relations can be a tool for creating the web of meaning that snares people into one way of thinking and acting to the advantage of an elite. Consequently, they encourage practitioners to voice dissent and caution regarding the ethics of managerial policies and communicative positioning (Holtzhausen, 2002). Theorists ask whether audiences, publics, or stakeholders control, yield to, or help co-create the ideological perspectives that shape the culture they enact.

Does control result singularly from management's voice? To help understand the power of hegemony, this chapter's case study examines statements on climate change.

Case Study: Climate Change—Functional Science and Moral Judgment

The critical relationship in the climate change battle is that among climate scientists (Le Treut et al., 2007) who Arte in a position to use scientific conclusions in the public interest. For climate scientists, no relationship seems more relevant than that with the Intergovernmental Panel on Climate Change (IPCC). This carefully self-vetted group engages in peer review of scientific studies and collectively shapes the funding protocols for climate change research. That fact, however, is used by climate change deniers to discredit the organization, with the claim that once funding protocols come into being, they tend to lead to the funding only of studies that appear likely to support the interests of the sponsoring body, to the detriment of those who would argue against it.

According to Le Treut et al. (2007), climate-focused scientific conclusions led to the IPCC's first report on climate change in 1990. The scientific method presumes the fundamental standard of scientific research: the testing and falsifiability of theory-based observations and conclusions. Related to this presumption, peer review defines and expresses the relationship standard among scientists: within or among cadres of scientists, "peers" create specific standards for testing context-relevant hypotheses; if the data do not justify rejection, then the veracity of a hypothesis will stand until they do. But as much as this is the gold standard of scientific research, it is also the point on which climate science is contested as being political ideological self-fulfillment.

Two broad questions guide climate change research: Is the climate changing in some predictable way? and Can the causes of such change be demonstrated so that knowable outcomes or ends can be identified and predicted to occur in ways that allow for actions to be taken to abate the effects? Further, is human activity contributing to such change, and are its consequences severe?

As much as causation is an aspirational goal—as is true of most science—correlation is the standard assessment of the strength of a hypothesis (Cook, 2019; see also Cook, Lewandowsky, & Ecker, 2017; de Witt, Funke, Haberreiter, & Matthes, 2018).

The IPCC doesn't simply monitor reports in scientific publications, but directly "contributes to science by identifying the key uncertainties and by stimulating and coordinating targeted research to answer important climate change questions" (Le Treut et al., 2007, p. 95). This simplifies the multidimensional complexity of climate science research. Two facts are important here. One is that as snow and ice melt, the surface of the earth attracts more heat from the sun. The other is that carbon has an insulating effect that traps heat in ever-increasing feedback loops: "There are many feedback mechanisms in the climate system that can either amplify ('positive feedback') or diminish ('negative feedback') the effects of a change in climate forcing ... Detecting, understanding and accurately quantifying climate feedbacks have been the focus of a great deal of research by scientists unravelling the complexities of Earth's climate" (p. 97). That conclusion would seem, on face value, to serve the interests of all who live on earth.

In April 2014, the IPCC expressed substantial concurrence (often wrongly expressed as "consensus") regarding climate science conclusions, and thus issued a report on the matter, which was endorsed by 1250 scientists and nearly 200 governments. Sufficient scientific concurrence existed to justify striving to reduce carbon emissions and even to decarbonize the environment (Rowell, 2014). Scientists, acting on their sense of public interest, worked with public policy leaders dedicated to ever more encompassing, interdependent, and structured responses to carbon emissions.

The Kyoto Protocol was proposed in 1992 to extend the United Nations Framework Convention on Climate Change; it was adopted in 1997 and went into force in 2005. Some countries embraced the protocol; others withdrew from it (e.g., Canada and the United States). The science behind it pointed to an adverse impact of CO_2, methane, nitrous oxide, hydroflourocarbons, perfluofocarbons, and sulfur hexafluoride.

Next came the Paris Agreement (2015), which asked member nations to address "greenhouse" emissions in terms of mitigation, adaptation, and finance. While there is overwhelming scientific agreement on climate change, the public become polarized over fundamental questions such as whether global warming had a human cause. Communication strategies to reduce polarization rarely address the underlying issue: "ideologically-driven misinformation" (Cook, 2019, p. 281). Polarization is often a reality in what can be called mutually beneficial relationships, but information and reasoning should be corrective rather than disorienting factors.

Companies and countries (through governmental agencies) set out to make a difference. Norway and Sweden undertook emission reduction and remediation, combined with aspirational sustainability. Others made some commitment, while others still may have engaged in false commitment. The United States withdrew from and put into place policies that conflict with the Paris Agreement. Such policy decisions gave critics like Aitken (2019), Heath and Waymer (2019), and Heath and McComas (2015) reason to emphasize that hydrocarbon discourse is inherently public-interest discourse.

Climate denial is robust, asserting critiques of science (as mistaken or merely tainted wish-fulfillment), arguments for sun temperature variability and cyclical natural trends (with periods of glaciation and warming temperatures), and the position that climate change is simply God's will. Books such as *Climate Change* (Abbott et al., 2015) point out scientific flaws in data gathering and interpretation, alternative interpretations of observable phenomena, and the extraordinary cost of carbon abatement, which would be squandered if based on bad science. This book, first published by the Institute of Public Affairs (IPA) in Melbourne, Australia brought together the voices of scientists, public policy discussants, politicians, and media commentators. The IPA, a conservative public policy think tank, was founded in 1943 to offer an alternative to what was then the progressive voice in Australia. Funded by industry groups, it champions conservative, limited-government, deregulatory causes. Climate change skepticism is a key theme.

Critics such as those writing in *Climate Change* ask whether a full list of potential causes has been identified and whether each has been properly explored to determine if it really is a cause (correlate)—and if so, how much of one. Companies, especially those engaged in carbon emission, voice caution. The cost of change is huge. The impact on society is dramatic. And if the analysis is flawed, both will be wasted.

Skepticism in decision making is desirable. However, if groups approach science with different worldviews, polarization may increase rather than decrease. "Cultural worldviews which contribute to politically polarized beliefs about climate were predictive of perceptions of sea level rise risk" (Akerlof, Rowan, La Porte, et al., 2016, p. 314). Fostering one hegemony, conservative think tanks communicate with individuals who are uncertain and persuadable in ways that account for decreases in poll results regarding expressed confidence in climate change data and the human causes of climate change (McCright & Dunlap, 2000).

Enter climate change activists. Their voice reasons that either enough science exists for a call to action or action is unwise because the science so far has been inadequate. Emphasizing the persuasive effects of collective response efficacy, researchers have found "that efforts to increase citizen activism should promote specific beliefs about climate change, build perceptions that political activism can be effective, and encourage interpersonal communication on the issue" (Roser-Renouf, Maibach, Leiserowitz, & Zhao, 2014; Roser-Renouf, Atkinson, Maibach, & Leiserowitz, 2016). Collective efficacy is a defining rationale for activism: together, we prevail.

Much to the point are activists such as Greta Thunberg (born in Stockholm in 2003), who has become the moral (critical) voice of climate change. In her *New York Times* bestseller, *No One Is Too Small to Make a Difference* (2018), she voices moral outrage that she, a young person, must call on adults to act as adults and take the positive steps needed so that they do not leave a wrecked world for her generation to inherit. She calls on scientists, companies, politicians, and deniers to prove her wrong. She speaks to the world, but specifically to Sweden:

> In Sweden, we live our lives as if we had the resources of 4.2 planets. Our individual carbon footprint is one of the worst in the world. This means that Sweden steals 3.2 years of natural resources from future generations every year. Those of us who are part of these future generations would like Sweden to stop doing that. (p. 2)

She emphasizes the point: "Right now." She speaks for young people, especially, as inheritors of a damaged world.

Such a voice addresses what Aitken (2019) calls a dysfunction of climate science in the public interest: "Ultimately the dominant framing of climate change as an issue of universal public interest has had detrimental effects on the extent to which strategies for addressing climate change in fact reflect or serve public interests" (p. 72). She continues:

> While in some countries (notably the United States) climate change policy remains highly politicized, resulting in debate regarding the veracity of claims about the realities or causes of climate change, the concept itself is depoliticized as the nuances and complexities of what climate change means, how it is investigated and whose voices are heard in debates regarding approaches for addressing climate change are consistently overlooked. (p. 72)

For that reason, writing comprehensively and with deep insight is challenging. Thus, it is reasonable to ask whose interests are served by the positions taken by various voices—and whose are harmed. What are the benefitting arguments of the case: cost, scientific fact, variability versus stability of climate impact, and harm burden versus reward? Such battleground decision making points to the embracing notion of climate justice. Consequently, Aitken presumes that the quality of dialogue—the dialectics of public-interest controversies (Heath & Waymer, 2019)—avoids facilitating self-interests that speak for others:

> Questions around how climate science is framed and interpreted, what its implications are within particular geographical, social, political or cultural contexts, and how policymakers should respond to the challenges that it poses could all benefit from the inclusion of diverse voices and interests. (p. 87)

As Thunberg (2018) reflects on the quality of the discourse arena, "Our civilization is so fragile it is almost like a castle built in the sand. The facade is so beautiful but the foundation is built from sand" (p. 46).

Critical Theory as Rationale for Sociocultural Discourse

What critical principles strengthen public discourse and commercial activity? Like other theories of public relations, critical theory asks whether publics receive the information they want intellectually and deserve morally in order to make enlightened decisions. Information seeking is only part of the process. Statements that express ethical and public policy positions are a crucial facet of discourse, as in the case of Thunberg.

The traditional role of critical theory is to ask questions that may be awkward and unpopular. According to Downing, Mohammadi, and Sreberny-Mohammadi (1995), critical inquiry "means not merely taking information for granted, at face value, but asking how and why these things come to be, why they have the shape and organisation they do, how they work and for whose benefit" (p. xx). Awkward and unpopular questions probe management's planning and operational decisions and discursive strategies. The goal is to understand the power incentives of management and illuminate how professionally generated messages work to support them. Questions become unpopular and awkward when they address power—especially power disparity (Motion & Weaver, 2005).

What the critical theory of public relations brings to the table is structured insight beyond the apparent factual and moral meaning of statements. Since public relations engages in discursive strategies, critical theorists reason, practitioners are obligated to understand and avoid distorting and unethical strategic communication that ends with some interests being privileged and others marginalized.

This logic, as the climate change case illustrates, means that an industry—especially when engaged with government—has an incentive and textual ability to create a sociocultural justification for its place in the economy that moralizes its business practices. This hegemony privileges it to make decisions—including setting safety standards—that are appropriate to a return on investment. The hegemony of free enterprise is such that when laborers, landowners, or city officials oppose safety standards or environmental regulations, they are swimming upstream against the political and economic power marshalled by the industry. Industry advocates can claim that activist complaints harm the industry and the economy, as well as the way of life they provide.

That's a powerful hegemony. Not only is it a major theme in its own right, but it also justifies or denies the sorts of premises and decision criteria that are allowable in public debate on such issues. Those premises are used to interpret and weigh facts. They are the foundations for the ethical evaluations central to public-interest communication (Johnston & Pieczka, 2019). Critical premises contest public and private policy, as well as citizens' identities. Thus, for instance, workers are not an oppressed group being asked to put their lives on the line for corporate greed; they are economic warriors whose noble labor produces a strong economy and an enviable quality of life for the nation. Work in coal mines is noble, however dangerous and potentially harmful to the environment, because it serves a high master: public interest.

In the sections that follow, these themes come to life, because the critical theory of public relations asks questions that are awkward and unpopular. Do statements such as those used in the climate change case result from dialogue whereby all voices are genuinely heard and considered? A similar question can be posed in an attempt to understand the merit of organizational mission and vision statements: What do they mean, what implications do they hide, and what unmet promises do they make? Does the text used in discourse highlight and illuminate conflicts and competing interests or mask them in order to give the appearance of consensus? What key words and competing meanings are central to the narrative of society by which organizations and citizens seek to coordinate behaviors (relatedness)? Do idioms represent the hegemony of narrow interests resulting from misinterpreted conflict and disingenuous differences of opinion? Hegemony is about power first and foremost, and about honest misinterpretation or genuine differences of opinion only a distant second.

Questions of this kind can be raised by practitioners in management discussions in order to understand the rationale for operations and discourse—the topic of the next section.

Critical Theory and Reflective Management

Much of what has been discussed in previous chapters presumes that public relations grows out of and advances management's decision making—a corporativist perspective. Similarly, critical theory reasons that an unwise, unreflective organization can narrowly seek to justify its self-interest through actions and choices made by others—such as customers, voters, legislators, regulators, or employees. That view of the role organizations play in society, so critical theory reasons, can position the management team in an unethical and unfruitful relationship with other interests.

Critical theory aspires to help practitioners think from the outside in, in order to help management teams position their organizations on sustainable, shared senses of reality. Critical public relations seeks to understand the ideologies and interests of others, rather than merely to bend them to support the efficient implementation of an organization's business plan.

A managerial-oriented approach to public relations can work to understand how relationships and communication processes make an organization continually worthy of stakeholder support. Powerful organizations can see opposition and opinion differences as something to be defeated rather than as offering an opportunity to learn and grow. However, this view may suffer from an agentic bias that treats public relations practice (and shapes its theory and research) as a tool for making organizations effective by getting others to accommodate to them.

Since chaos can be bewildering and unproductive, modern management presumes that carefully crafted ideology is the oil of business efficiency. Public relations, so this logic progresses, serves best by minimizing differences of opinion to maximize efficient business practices. Enormous industry-wide marketing, advertising, and publicity/promotion budgets shape and reshape market structures, consumer preferences, and standards of brand equity.

Reflective management presumes that lessons must be learned through robust engagement in order to critically moralize business practices. The question is whether managements, through public relations, can listen and appreciate others' opinions or will unwisely use their deep-pocket advantage to work to crush opposition.

McKie (2001) challenge critical theorists to reexamine the management assumptions that define public relations. To keep public relations theory and practice from becoming insular, he call for an expanded list of authors to help shed light on the perplexities of power in society and the means by which power could be used constructively for a broad array of interests, beyond merely finding an efficient marketplace for those with the deepest pockets. He deplore "the sheer range of missing thinkers and ideas, and their currency in other disciplines" and was concerned that "the so-called discursive, or linguistic, turn in knowledge remains underexplored in public relations" (p. 76).

Similarly, Holtzhausen (2002) reason that "most traditional and contemporary formulations of public relations" are "parochial, utilitarian, and insufficiently self-reflective" (p. 179). Such critique acknowledges the need "to become even more intellectually expansive, more critically reflective, and more cognizant of the diverse forms of organizational activity in today's world" (pp. 179–180). This search requires having fewer "imperialistic pretensions" while dealing with three biases: "the illusion of symmetrical dialogue, explicit and implicit corporatism, and Western managerial rationalism" (p. 180).

A call for symmetry can be used by management to deny critics' ideological foundations for challenging the status quo (Brown, 2010; Roper, 2005). Discourse defines, at a community level, the standards by which organizations need to build effective relationships in the communities where they operate. Rather than a discourse variable, symmetry can be viewed as an adjustive variable that can actually privilege corporate interests, on the assumption that symmetrical moves by an organization necessarily produce reciprocally accommodative adjustment.

Sociocultural perspectives reflect and support multiple interests, not just those of an organization using public relations to achieve its mission and vision. Critical theory presumes that discourse is ideological—language is never neutral. The crucial problem occurs when an organization works discursively to make its interests the same as those of others, rather than reflecting on others' interests along with its own. Such positioning can deny conflict and differences of opinion instead of dealing with them in a constructive manner. The climate change battle has substantial policy development implications for management decision making, especially on the part of carbon-generating industries.

Challenging the efficiency pillar of management planning, critical theorists prefer the political economy ideology of economic democracy. Ideological battles build on themes of identity, place, rights, privilege, power relationships, power in general, and types, structures, and functions. Modern management theory likes to presume that these need to be orderly, efficient, and fair for engagement. Public relations is expected uncritically to help create needed orderliness.

Rather than being merely "informed" and efficient, modern management philosophies build on the means by which power elites create and impose hegemony on others as social order. Serious attention to ideology assumes that it is the ultimate level of engagement. In discourse, information is vital—but as facts to be interpreted, debated, and weighed, rather than as neutral "data" that magically come into play free of the need for interpretation and moral judgment.

Such reasoning cautions against a narrow cybernetic, adjustive paradigm of corporate public relations. However useful that paradigm might be for understanding and correcting tensions between an organization and its publics, it is inadequate for understanding and correcting more daunting challenges and relationship dynamics. Postmodern analysis challenges the scope of operations captured in mission and vision statements, especially since issues of globalization and sustainability have become and will continue to be daunting. Critical theory presumes that publics can be instrumentalized against their own interests and the interests of others.

Such analysis does not so much start with a different vision of public relations as presume a reflective management philosophy (Holmstrom, 2004, 2010) as the rationale for a critically advanced understanding of the societal, community-building role of public relations (Heath, 2006). Reflective management entails constructive efforts to understand and judge an organization from the outside in and reflect upon its role in and impact on each political economy in which it seeks its needed social capital.

Critical reflection about what is good for society builds on two related themes. First, humans are communal animals that by nature engage in individual and collective decision making in order to work out individual and collective interests. The meaning that unites and divides such efforts becomes a shared sense of physical and sociocultural reality. Second, human decisions fundamentally address risk management, especially the uncertainties that characterize a risk's existence and impact. As will be expanded upon in Chapter 7, discourse addresses what constitutes a risk, who suffers it, and whether measures are needed to correct or mitigate its occurrence and impact fairness.

Based on that reasoning, management theory is inherently risk management. A corporativist view of business—and of public relations—presumes that commercial entities can benefit as other entities absorb and become committed to preventing and solving the harms that befall them (e.g., climate change). A reflective management approach assumes that how risks are managed for the good of society is the basis for judging what is good for an organization. This is the position of critical public relations.

Modern, efficient management philosophy seeks to institutionalize and privatize public opinion and public interest. Critically motivated reflective management asks whether the tipping point of interdependence makes the community dependent on the organization and therefore marginalized to support it. It considers whether the adage, "You can't make an omelet without breaking a few eggs," captures the central premise in discourse such as that surrounding climate change. Reflective management works to avoid an ideology that unbalances interests, costs, and rewards; it demands that an organization adds value to its community and customers, for instance, rather that calling for the community, workers, and customers to make the organization successful.

For these reasons, the critical theory of public relations thinks from the outside in rather than working to impose the organization on to the community by generating consent. Critical theory reasons that two conditions lead to constructive management planning and high CSR standards. One is the quality of the infrastructures whereby decisions are made through engagement. The other is the quality of the sociocultural ideology: the shared meaning produced by engagement. The next two sections explore these themes, starting with the quality of the public sphere as the location for discursive strategies.

Critical Theory and the Public Sphere

Critical theorists use ideologically-based analysis to judge public relations theory and practice. They do not share a tight-knit set of universally agreed upon principles but base their evaluative perspective on principles that focus a critical eye on the conditions that affect collective decision making through discourse, language, and power resource management. For that reason, the critical theory of public relations cautions against predictive (button-pushing) guidelines based on variable analytic research, which can make mistakes, including approaching matters as neutral, aethical, and being invariant when they are insensitive to biased privilege.

Theorists seek insights into the quality of the arenas where discourse occurs. Such arenas can be intellectual (conceptual) as well as physical, including company conference rooms, legislative halls, media, and even citizens' homes. Critical theorists believe it is "just as important to consider ... the sociopolitical context that surrounds the organization and the notion that power exists in other sites beside the dominant coalition" (Moffitt, 2005, p. 3; see also Brown, 2010). Arenas serve best when multiple voices can make their cases in ways that are heard and given proper responsive consideration. Thus, critical theorists reason that best thoughts cannot result when infrastructures privilege some voices and marginalize others.

Rhetoric is closely linked to the rise of democracy as a form of government and to places where democratic discourse co-creates shared meaning (Heath & Frandsen, 2008). Prior to the American War of Independence, British officials closed the coffee shops and taverns in which their critics raved. But the arenas simply moved, and criticism continued until it spread on to the street.

The quality of any arena where ideas pound against one another is highly relevant to reflective management and ethical public relations. Intellectual life spaces approve and disapprove of ideas and their accompanying discursive strategies. To judge the quality of a place where discourse occurs, critical theories are disposed to disfavor predetermined conditions (such as symmetry/ asymmetry or even advocacy/accommodation).

Specific venues are essential to the formalization of the purpose, form, and content of public voices. Venues constitute relational infrastructures of public policy formulation as risk management. Places where discourse occurs may at important times be remote from and even indifferent to general discourse. For instance, scientists working far from the public sphere investigate hypotheses regarding climate change. The key concept is discourse "place."

In recent decades, critical theory has explored how well formally established places of discourse actually produce engagement that is robust enough to bring interested parties together to resolve fundamental issues and sort out important matters. The ability to create and pick the place for discourse can be a power move (as in the case of funding climate research). Corporate voices, through public relations, can control place and thereby distort dialogue to the disadvantage of community citizens. To avoid such problems, critical theorists delve into the conditions that foster or impede discourse.

By the mid-twentieth century, place had become known conceptually as *the public sphere*, or *die Öffentlickkeit*. In some European countries, it became especially "relevant to the theory, teaching, and practice of public relations because it forces attention and gives substance to efforts to understand the form and content of the public arenas where practitioners do their work and academics conduct research" (Bentele, 2005, p. 707). In Germany in the 1950s, public relations was spoken of as *Öffentlickkeitsarbeit*. Since then, "the term 'public relations' has become an acceptable word in colloquial speech and is used as a synonym for Öffentlickkeitsarbeit. It is no longer regarded as a threat to German culture" (Nessman, 2000, p. 220). This history of the term positively links various conceptions of the public: relations, sphere, and interest.

The shift of the locus of discourse from a place where elites make decisions to one where communities make them is central to the critical theory of public relations. In his seminal work, *The Structural Transformation of the Public Sphere*, Jürgen Habermas (1991) proposed a historical account and normative theory of the "grandeur," and especially the "fall," of the formation of public opinion in the twentieth century. In the eighteenth century, he argued, during a period of revolutionary ferment in Europe, voices in the community began to question and evaluate social conditions and the policies produced and implemented by the state. In coffee houses, clubs, and salons in England, and then in France and Germany, discussions transformed into a critical forum, supported by a growing free press. These discursive places gave birth to contests to reshape public opinion. Thus, Habermas (1991) conceived the public sphere as "the sphere of private people come together as a public" (p. 27). Power was relocated to the "people."

Over time, the role and societal value of public relations was revisited. The issue was one of rights, and the ability of people to voice opinions on matters of self- and public interest. As Leeper (2005) synthesized the discussion of the public sphere, it:

> mediates between the realms of the private and the state, and the guarantees of the basic rights of citizens in the liberal state depend on the demarcation between the two. For such mediation to be effective, discourse in the public sphere must be critical and rational. Above all, such discourse must rise above simply aggregating individual interests and form a bridge between self-interest and common good. (p. 711)

Tensions between individual and organizational interests become the grist for the public relations mill.

How can individual ideas be synthesized into collective ideas? The question doubts the ability of professional communicators to tailor individual rights to serve organizational ones. Discussion of ideas does not easily or always achieve a co-created meaning that perfectly synthesizes all competing opinions and interest. Nor does it reconcile differences that are deeply held.

Habermas' (1976, 1981) normative theory of the public sphere and public opinion informed his exploration of the dialectic of private versus public discourse and the realms in which each transpires. These necessary conditions come in the form of four universal validity conditions, which communicators are expected to observe:

- comprehensibility (the expression level of the message);
- truth (the content level or propositional level of the message);
- sincerity (the intention behind the message); and
- rightness (the normative background for interpersonal relations).

These validity conditions constitute the basis for discourse ethics—and an ethically critical rationale for public relations.

Pressing to understand such themes, Bentele (2005) contrasted two versions of the public sphere. First, Habermas' *discourse model* focused on universal and rational dimensions of citizens' public debate, outside the private sphere and detached from private interests, to produce a public opinion. Second, a *mirror model*, proposed by Niklas Luhmann, emphasized the "mirror" function of the public sphere, in which communicators can observe both themselves and others (including their observations about the others' contributions to the dialogue). Luhmann's ideas opened the discourse to consider the nature, role, and advantages of reflective management (Holmstrom, 2004, 2010).

Thus, critical theory draws on the logic of where and how discourse occurs to advise professional communicators—and the organizations they serve—to look at themselves in the mirror of others' opinions. Are such opinions something to learn from, refute, or accommodate to? Public relations professionals must monitor issue-based opinion and learn from what they discover, rather than aspire to control and dominate others' opinions. How well an organization communicates depends on its ability to engage in self-reflection, learning from other voices. This condition of discourse is central to the discussion that follows.

Community as Discourse Conditions

Critical theorists address how the place and resultant quality of dialogue lead to conclusions and actions that achieve legitimacy. They reason that it is not enough for public relations practitioners to understand how a discourse arena works and thus can be navigated; they must also know how to help that arena work in the interests of others, whose voices might otherwise go unheard and be unheeded.

Efforts to make organizations appropriately responsive to community interests are likely to fail if they reduce power relationships to only addressing neutral concepts and championing transparency as information sharing. A constructive approach to engagement presumes that competing ideas are not inherently destructive to the ideology needed for organizational effectiveness; dissent, argument, and conflict can constructively change management. But as Roper and Motion caution (in Heath et al., 2006), "dialogue is often described uncritically as a panacea without questioning, for example, its potential to disguise covert agendas or power relations" (p. 342).

The basic paradigm of dialogue, statement and counterstatement, can illuminate or mask the peril of various discussants' predispositions to frame statements that strategically predict outcomes—however intentional or unintentional—which are narrowly favorable to them. Thus, discourse can lack legitimacy as engagement because, or if, it is designed to seek and achieve agreement and influence as the prelude to advancing one interest against others. True dialogue, however propositional, works to avoid an ends-justify-the-means design and calls on each participant to both exert and yield control over the outcome.

Dialogue should be driven by the agency of the community in which it occurs, what Martin Buber (1965) called "between." Derived from the Greek word *dialogos*, "dialogue" blends *logos* ("word") and *dia* ("through" or "across"). Taken this way, dialogue is:

> [B]oth a quality of relationship that arises, however briefly, between two or more people and a way of thinking about human affairs that highlights their dialogic qualities. Dialogue can identify the attitudes with which participants approach each other, the ways they talk and act, the consequences of their meeting, and the context within which they meet. (Cissna & Anderson, 1998, p. 64)

Buber's (1965) standard of dialogue depends on whether participants have "in mind the other or others in their present and particular being and turn to them with the intention of establishing a living mutual relationship between" themselves and the others (p. 19).

In order to better understand the conditions that lead to legitimacy through dialogue, Roper (2005) drew insights from Habermas:

> Legitimation, according to Habermas, is provided by civil society for institutions of the political sphere when their policies and actions are considered to be rational because they coincide with existing social norms. The same applies to policies of institutions of the economy when they affect civil society. Ideally, public opinion, which establishes social norms, is formed through open discussion within the public sphere of civil society and is based on full information regarding issues of public importance. (p. 75)

Discourse quality is important; the outcome should be a shared, co-created meaning that reflects multiple interests in varying degrees of alignment. In discourse, compromise can be accommodative without leading to sufficient change to produce true harmony as public interest. Otherwise, participants in civil society are motivated to continue to battle over policy positions and struggle to define legitimacy as contested interests.

Whether in physical or conceptual space, discourse arises from and reveals conflicting and compatible interests. Critical public relations is keenly interested in how interests are inherent, and likely asymmetrical, in the conditions that motivate discourse. Relevant to climate change statements, it is important to understand the arena in which voices speak. Do statements promote and result from dialogue that is genuine and open to learning, or are they driven by predetermined hegemonic outcomes that shape not only their content but also the strategic process that produces them?

Community as Discourse Outcomes

Community can be conceptualized as the relationships that produce and result from discourse. Such means–ends conceptualization champions reflective management as a means, not an end in itself. Engaged collaboration acknowledges and supports collective interests. Adding to this analysis, Bentele (2005) weighed theories of political communication, public opinion, and public arenas in his search for a more empirical approach to the field. This investigation motivated critical theorists to examine the substance of discourse, discursive strategies, by understanding that discourse outcomes indicate improved management and society as supportive rather than oppositional relationships.

Exploring communicative action, Leitch and Neilson (2001) and Leitch and Motion (2010) argued for ensuring that publics' voices are constructively brought into public relations practice and research. Similar thinking connects public relations and civil society (Taylor, 2010) and justifies stakeholder participation in the repertoire of public relations practices (de Bussy, 2010). Given the tensions between discourse that is private and discourse that is public, critical theorists confront the challenges of pursuing discourse through levels (layers) to see how the fabrics of private and public policy preferences merge and divide, compete and collaborate. They do so not only because of dialogue patterns and qualities but, even more importantly, because of what language can reveal and conceal.

Discourse can open the "window" through which concerned interests come to know and understand one another. As a salve for the dysfunctional separation of the private and the public, the term "transparency" became a slogan, one that was often uncritically used to open discourse or to paper over misunderstandings, perplexities, and paradoxes. But the ideal of transparency can easily collide with reality (Christensen & Langer, 2009).

Making organizations an open book is aspirationally sound but unrealistic. One reason is the public relations decision regarding how much information needs to be shared in order to achieve transparency. Can the aspiration to disclose *all* information actually lead to less transparency if kernels of thought get hidden by chaff? And, since information necessarily requires interpretation, are the standards of interpretation inherent and universal? True transparency is always in the eye of the beholder (Christensen & Langer, 2009). Does disclosure merely seem to be transparent because it puts out some information, as though that were all that was relevant? Does providing information fail to appreciate how competing voices variously interpret details? Does industry hegemony govern its communicativeness?

Critical theory, along with rhetorical theory, wonders whether voices that are not encouraged to participate in the public sphere nevertheless are prone to assert themselves, sometimes quite loudly, in other venues (other configurations of the public sphere). For that reason, public relations practitioners have a critical incentive to include voices reflectively into private management decision making, as well as in public discourse.

Critical Theory and Language and Meaning

The critical theory of public relations wrestles with paradoxes of power based on the proposition that language is never neutral and always a power resource. For that reason, power results as voices define (assign meaning to) the physical and societal resources by which each community collectively manages risks (Beck, 1992, 1999).

This conclusion acknowledges the definitional nature of language, and its hegemonic role in human perception, thought, and behavior. Public relations theory can see language as a vehicle for making reports—sharing information. It can be the means for solving problems, making decisions, and resolving conflicts. But the fundamental issue is whether words add (hegemonic) value to how physical and sociocultural reality is perceived, and how such perception affects behavior. Language (text) is not only the tool of discourse, but also its rationale and grist.

Anthropologist-linguists demonstrated the foundational as opposed to purely technical role of language in human affairs. One such pioneer was Edward Sapir, who explained more than 60 years ago how language, thought, and action are intertwined:

> Human beings do not live in the objective world alone, not in the world of social activity as ordinarily understood, but are very much at the mercy of the particular language which has become the medium of expression for their society. We see and hear and otherwise experience very largely as we do because the language habits of our community predispose certain choices of interpretation. (Quoted in Whorf, 1956, p. 134)

This conclusion agrees with Kenneth Burke's view that language forms terministic screens, as discussed in Chapter 5.

The critical theory of public relations reasons that the roots of power and its disparity reside in assumptions made salient through textuality. Assumptions are embedded in idioms relevant to the interdependence between organizations and stakeholders. "Market," for instance, is a term of interdependence, as are "employment/work" and "gross state product." Idioms can express consent by key stakeholders to support or oppose some matter simply (the term here is used ironically) because of the terministic screens expressed in some ideology. Critical theorists worry that such ideology and its soft power can be manufactured by power elites, and through public relations become the means and rationale for relationships.

This observation recognizes the potential peril of problem-solving strategies. It cautions against theoretical assumptions that organizations should take the lead to solve publics' problems. It prefers civil society, where dialogue genuinely occurs; statements are responded to for their merit, with self-interest present but not preventing aspirations to co-achieve decisions in various parties' favor (Taylor, 2010).

The impact of language results from power achieved through social construction of meaning (Gordon & Pellegrin, 2008). Clegg, Courpasson, and Phillips (2006) press theorists to consider the challenges of this meaning-centric approach to thought and action: "organizations and individuals use discourses purposefully to shape the political situation in and through which they can act and perform" (p. 17). In the sense discussed here, "political" can refer to the discourse conditions inside a business as well as in the public policy arena that defines political economy.

Language's power has substantial implications for management theory. Some such theories reason that the systems, functions, and structures by which organizations operate are neutral and therefore efficient. A neo-institutional approach, on the other hand, reasons the opposite: that the nature, dynamics, and functions of structures—no matter how seemingly neutral—are envisioned not merely as "natural," but as politically rich, powerful meanings. Meanings are created, defined, and used to empower specific structures and functions, which in turn deliver and reinforce an organization's power to achieve its desired outcomes.

Critical theorists share a deep interest in how discourse generates meaning. What can loosely be called "public opinion" can be measured as the meaning that is shared by various groups on an array of topics. Such meaning, whether held or rejected, becomes widely or even narrowly used as the premise for additional discourse and for individual, state, and corporate actions. In this way, critical theorists center their attention on the normative quality of the textual meaning generated and shared as a precursor to how terms guide behavior—which includes definitional legitimacy.

Discourse and the meaning it produces create the windows through which to view the operational quality of society. The critical theory of public relations underscores the peril for research, theory building, and professional practice if meaning is taken for granted rather than as the fundamental condition of the relationships between people and organizations. Thus, "female" and "climate activist" can both be "descriptive" terms, but they are also normative, prescriptive, and relational. How does this principle apply to Greta Thunberg?

Advancing this idea, Norman Fairclough (1989), one of the founders of discourse analysis, articulated two themes relevant to the use of a linguistic lens in examining society:

> The first is more theoretical: to help correct a widespread underestimation of the significance of language in the production, maintenance, and change of social relations of power. The second is more practical: to help increase consciousness of how language contributes to the domination of some people by others, because consciousness is the first step towards emancipation. (p. 1)

These are precisely the conditions for empowerment/disempowerment, as well as for instrumentalizing publics. One of the clearest strategies in this direction occurs when "job killer" or "job creator" is used descriptively, and also evaluatively and preferentially.

If a public is relevant to the success or failure of an organization, merely defining it as such can be a power move. It means that the organization views the public as an instrument by which it can increase its success. In the best-case scenario, such a definition sees the public in terms of the voice and position it champions; alternatively, it might be viewed as something to be managed, accommodated to, or moved out of the way. Seen in this way, publics are inconvenient means to be managed to the advantage of the organization (as opposed to the organization working to the advantage of the public).

This is especially true in the case of marketing. A market can be defined as a power resource useful to the economic success of a company. Individuals, when defined as specific consumers (e.g., students, workers, etc.), serve the company's need for money (resources/stakes). Employees are often expected to advocate for their company or industry.

Various publics thus become either an instrument of an organization's success or an inconvenient bump in the road. This hegemony suggests why the concept of "public" is so important and so problematic for the critical theory of public relations. How and to what ends stakeholders are approached and engaged reveals a great deal about the kinds and qualities of relationships a company has and the sense of engagement it holds. Commitment to the ideal of dialogue and shared sense making reasons that "publics are not just a means to an end. Publics are not instrumentalized but instead are partners in the meaning-making process" (Botan & Taylor, 2004, p. 652)—but under what conditions?

Instrumentalized publics are treated as problematic means by which an organization achieves, or does not achieve, its mission and vision in line with its core values. Thus, are voters to be taxed without receiving the public administration benefit of those taxes? Are customers to be instrumentalized to serve as revenue resources for businesses? If conflict resolution and publics' and stakeholders' goodwill are the essential goals of public relations, are publics instruments to be used to achieve goodwill through relationship quality? Is the language that defines such relationships more a means of creating obligation than one of reflectively aligning interests to serve publics? What safety standards and working conditions, for instance, do mine owners/operators owe their workers in exchange for their labor? Or, are miners obligated to suffer unsafe conditions because "at least they have a job"?

As such, the critical theory of public relations can be predicated on the ability and incentive managements have (or lack) to listen and respond to publics in ways that appear to be reflective. The problematic occurs when such accommodation leads these publics to believe they have influenced the private sector when in fact they have been instrumentalized by it.

By examining conditions of power and obligation, discourse analysis can unravel the role stakeholders play in public relations theory and practice. Are their opinions and choices a reflection of a management's communication efforts, or are they independent voices engaged in the co-creation of meaning, the shared knowledge by which societies and communities organize themselves?

This sort of thinking reveals the resources that can be used to marginalize and even instrumentalize the stakeholders who possess the goodwill and other resources desired by organizations. In these ways, discourse analysis reveals how much resource dependency theory requires language to define the quality of resources and the conditions relevant to an entity's deserving them. The satisfaction of stakeholders' expectations is not only the relational sense of CSR but the rationale for an organization's legitimacy.

This linguistic interpretation presumes that the resources required to achieve success go beyond "purely" economic challenges to the conditions of resource exchange captured in the language unique to each political economy. For instance, can carbon-based companies presume that governmental regulation will not offend their sense of "fair and wise regulation"? In matters of environmental quality, are companies' definitions of "fair and wise" the same as those of stakeholders worried about environmental harm? If carbon consumption is essential to the economy, does environmental or safety regulation harm it? Is "in the interest of the economy" the linguistic trump card that carbon-based companies can always use to achieve the regulatory environment they prefer?

Discourse can rationalize each political economy so that advantage for some players becomes a zero-sum game, requiring that certain interests be marginalized to empower others. Power, as expressed though discourse, may be both the rationale for and a means of enacting infrastructures of influence; it is the bending of interests and realities to serve competing wills. This is the case because language shapes ideas, identity, and relatedness (Heath, Motion, & Leitch, 2010).

Discourse is anchored by the imperative to acquire resources; this imperative shapes discourse outcomes. As tradition has it, such thought was embodied by the CEO of General Motors when he claimed: "for years I thought what was good for our country was good for General Motors, and vice versa." In the case of climate change, is what is good for the carbon-using economy good for the nation, or the globe? This blatant confusion of corporate self-interest with public interest presses critical theorists and practitioners to seek the motive for the advantage gained and interests served by discourse.

Critical theory treats power as the ability/inability of persons (and organizations) to be influential members of each society's power infrastructure. Further, membership includes access to the hierarchies of decision-making structures and their discourse rights and responsibilities, which terministically shape hegemonies. Thus, access to the Supreme Court or any legislative body is "merely" a structural matter. The key to understanding power is insight into the definitions of those systems that include or deny the privilege of access. For that reason, the functioning of the public sphere can never adequately be reduced to a systems/structure and functional explanation of power; power resource is the vocabulary that defines systems, including access and barricades against entry and meaningful involvement—conditions of empowerment and marginalization.

Power Resources: Systems and Meaning

Power resources have two dimensions: system structures and functions and language resources. The issue of marginalization—and its counterpart, empowerment—begins with an examination of system structures and functions (Monge et al., 1998) and socially constructed meanings of power (Courtright & Smudde, 2007; Heath et al., 2010; Leitch & Neilson, 2001; Motion & Leitch, 2007).

Exploring networks of power, Monge and Contractor (2000) and Shumate, Fulk, and Monge (2005) argued that social capital is created through the systemic quality of organizations and relationships, as well as the kind and quality of communication they facilitate. A similar analysis of global regimes, including the role of nongovernmental organizations (NGOs) (Stohl & Stohl, 2005), helped Taylor (2009) explain the structural/functional and rhetorical resources needed for civil society. This view of power presumes that systems are naturally occurring forces of information flow and adjustment, as well as the operant dynamics of inclusion/exclusion and interpretation.

Critical theorists assume that power structures and functions are continually shaped to the advantage of powerful interests. Influence results when discursive strategies are put into play by professional communicators. Insofar as meaning matters—and defines as well as trumps process—meaning, as the rationale for power, is essential to empowering the empowered, and marginalizing the marginalized. One of the deepest concerns of critical theorists is that the language used to define systems becomes ingrained in discourse as "neutral," "natural," and "truthful." Opinionated speech privileges some interests to the disadvantage of others. Hegemonies define and empower structures and functions as they justify how power resources are defined, discussed, and allotted.

Critical theorists opt for an agentic approach to management in order to investigate how organizations employ their public relationships to gain self-interested advantage. These theorists prefer a sense of agency that arises from community dialogue (Motion, 2005). The critical challenge lies in whether corporate hegemonies instrumentalize publics or publics as stakeholders define themselves through shared meaning regarding reality, identity, and relationship (Heath et al., 2010; Leitch & Motion, 2010; Motion & Leitch, 2007).

Publics as Emergent Meaning

Publics are often conceptualized as groups that are identifiable and motivated by shared concerns and united by a shared awareness of, concern for, and approach to decision making. Shared meaning gives publics identity, purpose, and power. As such, the critical theory of public relations investigates whether stakeholding publics are a construction of management or self-defining (and therefore not the instruments of organizations).

Sparking a controversy, Leitch and Neilson (2001) argued that publics were self-defining. This conceptualization brought publics into the public relations process in constructively empowered ways. The question of when—and, indeed, whether—publics "come into existence" becomes relevant when they are identified and treated as part of power systems recognized and authenticated by management decisions. A critical question is whether workers are publics instrumentalized by managements in order to defend their industry, achieve profits, and so bolster the economy.

The rationale for such a conceptualization results from Habermas' (1991) distinction between system and lifeworld and Fairclough's (1992, 1995) discourse theory:

> A lifeworld organization may be distinguished from a system organization to the extent that, in the former, organization develops as an artifact of the communicative interaction of a public. That is, lifeworld organizations grow out of the debates that take place within the sphere. (Leitch & Neilson, 2001, p. 132; see also Leitch & Motion, 2010)

Lifeworlds are the products of shared belief, evaluation, and knowledge systems, as zones of meaning. That vantage point is important to critical theorists because it does not approach public relations from the orientation of the organization but as the language-bound sociocultural context in which organizations and publics meet and engage.

Private-sector organizations, and their counterparts in government, "embody the strategic goals and rationality of the state and economy" (Leitch & Motion, 2010, p. 101). Meaning surrounds organizations and is used, sometimes reflexively (as opposed to reflectively; see Holmstrom, 2004), to define them.

Competing voices become key to power structures and ideologies. Engagement centers on tensions of change and resistance, on matters of knowing, identity, and relationship. The power resource of language shapes reality as what the mind knows, who people are, and how they relate to one another. Carbon is thus perceived cognitively through various sociocultural lenses. One is as a black lump of hydrocarbon that has financial value, a foundation of "coal country's" economy. Another is as a source of carbon-based pollution that contributes to climate change both directly and as an essential insulator in the feedback loop of global climate. The identity of industry (and individual companies) can collide or be compatible with the identities—senses of self—of the citizens of the state. Every carbon-based society exhibits harmony and tension, resulting from the relationships between citizens, workers, and industry.

Coal advocates reason that what is good for coal companies is good for West Virginia, for instance. How can advocates (including public relations professionals working for the industry and for the state) allow full and free dialogue with key publics without compromising their corporate interests and the bottom line? Is the voice of any public one that might say, "coal is king, but..."? That premise is foundational to the relationship identity of the state and its citizens.

Publics as Isms, Interests, and Identities

In the debate over the language used by climate advocates and climate deniers, those who protest carbon may be labeled as traitors to the public interest of carbon use. Should critics of coal mining, for instance, expect to be treated as heroes or as villains (by arena)?

Critical theorists caution against conceptualizing language (text) as neutral. Even in seemingly pure descriptions of individuals or economic resources, terms are likely to contain evaluation, preference, and prescription. This is important for discussions of place and identity in public relations.

Identity is inseparable from discourse systems and the text that serves as their grist. Edwards (2010) explores that point as she investigates hierarchy as role definition in public relations agencies (or any other corporate entity). She reasons, for instance, that race is a social construction of hierarchy and role definition. How the owners and employees of an agency or company are defined by power-laden language can determine the roles they play within hierarchies of power. Identities can be grounded in gender, race, age, and national origin—even religion. Practitioners implement boundaries and privileges based on the sociocultural construction of identity.

Questions arise, in both research/theory and practice, as to the civility of roles and discourse conditions: gender, sexuality, age, disability, and so on. As Vardeman-Winter and Tindall (2010) reason, "[i]dentities like race, gender, class, and sexuality/sexual orientation can act together, simultaneously, to place groups in distinct situations of power," including power disparity. If public relations is "to be defined as an ethical advocacy function that serves publics' interests" then theory and practice must appreciate the intersectionality of the human condition (pp. 223–224). In these ways, critical theory inquires into the impact that text-based identifiable identity traits have on power and privilege.

Many issues that become part of the discursive strategies of public relations arise because of identity. Issue orientations such as advocacy for environmental quality, gender equality, sexuality equality, fair wages, race identity, and wealth equity become motives and foundations for dialogue. In ideologically-charged political discourse, identity battles are inseparable from issues battles. For this reason, scholars ask questions such as, "does public relations scholarship have a place in race" (Waymer, 2010, p. 237) and gender (Wrigley, 2010)? What about national origin, religion, sexuality, and other identities? Similarly, critical theory addresses the textuality of owner, manager, and worker. Discourse occurs among kinds of people and about kinds of people. Does the language of relevant discourse privilege or marginalize discussants (climate advocate vs. denier)?

By addressing such questions, critical theory asks whose interests managements serve—including through public relations. Why are they interests, and who cares? This theme is relevant to the analysis of CSR, one of the foundational tensions in public relations theory. CSR is central to questions regarding relationship.

Linguistic Constructions of Corporate Social Responsibility

CSR is central to organizational legitimacy and relationship quality. Critical theorists evaluate an organization's legitimacy by judging whether it is able to meet or exceed the normative performance standards expected by its stakeholders. In that way, CSR, judged critically, is a key to the quality of the relationships organizations have with others. Thus, publics are linguistic, value-laden constructions of CSR.

CSR is a sociocultural construction. Of relevance to climate change, CSR necessarily implies standards of environmental impact. The CSR standards preferred by industry (or individual companies—even the state) may differ from those of key publics. Environmental impact may range from local impact, such as an individual's automobile emissions, to the national carbon footprint.

In discussions of business ethics, CSR constitutes a political and economic battle over the role of businesses (and other organizations) in society. Critical consideration of CSR standards resulted from activism in the late 1950s and the decades that followed, when critics examined every aspect of society: civil rights (first race, then more broadly gender, age, and disability—and beyond), human rights, war (and peace), environmental quality, working conditions (including workplace equity), fairness, safety, product safety, and now sustainability—to mention only a few key highlights.

The identity of advocates for and against issue positions is central to their self-definition and relationships and to the social constructions that occur as organizations respond to critics. Thus, stakeholders who call for higher environmental impact standards define themselves as advocates for clean air and water. Based on critics' self-identity, mining companies' CSR identity involves environmental quality.

Some discussants engaged in the CSR dialogue doubt the genuineness of private-sector CSR efforts in principle (see, e.g., May, 2008; Reich, 2008). They see CSR as a charade used communicatively by companies to divert attention from abuses of power and a flaunting of standards. CSR claims may mask outright corporate malfeasance, justify brand equity, or reduce the impact of legislation and regulation.

By addressing such themes, critical theory aspires to establish principles that guide managerial decision making and public relations practice—a topic that is expanded in the next section.

Community, Civil Society, Humanization, Authentication, and Legitimation

Viewed through the lens of critical theory, public relations is not a management topic *per se*, but a sociocultural topic with implications for management. Theory can blind researchers and practitioners to the challenges, goals, omissions, advantages, and dysfunctions that make the profession useful, powerful, or threatening. Thus, theorists such as McKie and Munshi (2009) aspire to broaden the range of topics used to improve the practice and the organizations it counsels by making it better aligned with community values and needs.

Such broadening can draw on anthropology, according to L'Etang (2010), who is interested in "human activities that share overlapping communicative characteristics and the functions of agency, representing interests through advocacy" (p. 145). To facilitate that exploration, she reasons, "Anthropology can help us understand public relations and related occupations (at various points in the human story) as a unique feature of human culture" (p. 145).

Investigating the limitations of a corporativist approach to public relations, Vujnovic and Kruckeberg (2010) caution that "the traditional understanding of public relations ... originates from the functionalist and organization-centric perspective in which the practice is seen as a managerial, strategic, and highly structuralized function that is easily quantifiable in its processes, albeit not so easily in the more elusive measurements of 'effectiveness'—however this effectiveness may be conceptualized and operationalized" (p. 671). Critical analysis should recognize and chart "the proliferation of different cultural identities, as well as organizational identities" as "a consequence of the globalization processes" (p. 675). The goal is to understand, appreciate, and foster the identities of multiple publics for their own advantages, not merely that of management systems.

Anthropology informs the eternal tension that the critical theory of public relations explores: that between *communitas* and *corporatas* (Trujillo, 1992). *Corporatas* features the agencies and interests enacted by organizations. The question is whether community decision making favors corporate interests by supporting its hegemony. *Corporatas* demands that decisions, actions, and shared meaning be devoted to raising the quality of the community in which an organization operates.

Such tensions allow critical theorists to ponder how much and in what ways carbon-based energy is the basis for corporate legitimacy (*corporatas*), and beyond that the nation and the world. Are industry advocates playing in the same discourse lifeworld as those who demand the industry operate according to higher CSR standards regarding the health and safety of the climate? In that regard, can public relations for the energy industry be seen as a "neutral" practice, or is it one that is inherently politicized and ethically obligated? Can assessments of benefit mutuality avoid bias via sociocultural interests and identities relevant to carbon footprints, climate change, and climate denial?

Ongoing Research

L'Etang et al.'s (2016) comprehensive analysis of the critical theory of public relations aspires to develop the discipline of critical public relations. This discipline not only focuses on ethical questions facing the practice, but investigates how public relations should improve organizations and the societies in which they operate.

In critical theory, "turns" have become a vital line of analysis. Molony and McKie (2016) reason that one of the most important critical turns in the unpacking of language used in many disciplines and organizational settings involves understanding the embedded politicization of ostensibly neutral analysis. Thus, power is a sociocultural turn, often masked in ostensibly neutral texts.

Also interested in critical turns, Torp (2018) concludes: "The organization is not merely a 'container' within which or from which one communicates; the organization comes into existence through communication" (p. 43). Participation and organization are not only means, but outcomes. The same can be said for society and community. In that regard, rather than noting a reconciliation of opinion differences, critics such as Cook (2019) point to the polarizing perils of misinformation regarding the impact of carbon on global warming (see also Cook et al., 2017; McCright & Dunlap, 2000; Painter & Gavin, 2016; van der Linden, Leiserowitz, Feinberg, & Maibach, 2015). Scientific data and conclusions, engaged discourse, and personal and public policy change can be compromised by uncomfortable points of view. "Mounting evidence from across the behavioral sciences has found that most people regard climate change as a nonurgent and psychologically distant risk—spatially, temporally, and socially—which has led to deferred public decision making about mitigation and adaptation responses" (van der Linden, Maibach, & Leiserowitz, 2015, p. 1). Given shifts in opinions measured by pollsters and the influence of groups seeking to speak for those with whom they have functional relationships, it is important to realize that reflective discourse, however complex and dynamic, is appropriate for determining what strategic issues management intelligences are at work. "Given the political stakes involved, the scientific findings specific to global warming have been selectively interpreted in ways that fit the political goals of elected officials, interest groups, and even scientists" (Nisbet & Myers, 2007, p, 444).

Conclusion

The critical theory of public relations asks vital questions not to make organizations (such as businesses) less effective, but to ensure that their effectiveness is earned through constructive practices that serve rather than colonize the communities in which they operate. Cheney and Christensen (2001) aspire for public relations to be "a vibrant discipline." Constant reexamination is required to create "a vision of what it wants and ought to be" (p. 167). Thus, they reason, "it is important that a discipline's theoretical agenda not simply be beholden to trends already present or incipient in the larger society. Otherwise, a discipline can fail to exercise its own capacity for leadership on both practice and moral grounds" (p. 167).

Although critical theorists seem to work against the viability of public relations practice, they should be seen as exerting the intellectual leadership that is necessary to meet critical challenges. Critical theorists challenge other theorists' assumptions. Sometimes they do not have better answers for daunting questions, but they worry that assumptions that go unquestioned can become dysfunctional to the value of an academic and professional discipline.

For that reason, the critical theory of public relations—and critical public relations—is intended to help practitioners serve many interests by enabling them to know when and how to ask questions that are awkward and unpopular. Such questions can help managements to be reflective, the discourse arena to be wholesome, and discursive strategies to be beneficial because meaning is co-created.

Critical theorists reason that if the foundations of a discipline are flawed, then so too is its theory. They presume that all theory begins with ethical concerns, and works to identify where ethical peril occurs.

Chapter Summary

This chapter summarizes the contribution of structured critical inquiry into the conditions relevant to the discourse foundations of public relations theory and practice. Among the awkward and unpopular questions critical theory asks is whether text privileges—empowers—some interests over others while seeming and even scheming to disguise or avoid exactly such conditions. A fundamental premise of this theory is that every voice (private and public—and the eventual blending of the two) *should be* heard and given fair and just regard.

Power differences can make justice and fairness rare. Voices can frame the human condition by setting a tone in texts that predispose specific outcomes and privilege certain interests. A fundamental premise of true dialogue is that statements are made, as propositional discourse, in ways that should not presume and predict concurrence but merely give each perspective the best chance of influencing final outcomes.

Critical theory can create a vocabulary and formulate systematic analysis to help organizations avoid instrumenalizing stakeholder publics for their own interest. In these ways, practitioners can address hegemony as the DNA of public relations. They can investigate sociocultural discourse, shaped by language, to foster reflective management.

Key Terms

- *Agency:* The ability to produce desired results, the quality of that ability.
- *Corporate Social Responsibility (CSR):* An emerging view holding that organizations should consider the impact of their decisions, actions, and communication on multiple stakeholders and on society as a whole.
- *Discourse:* According to Foucault (2002), a sequence of signs that form the basis of written or spoken conversation.
- *Hegemony:* The domination that occurs without physical coercion when people accept particular ideologies and consent to the practices associated with them.
- *Power:* The ability to bend reality—especially social reality—to serve one's interests.
- *Reflective Management:* Involves holding others' interests as inseparable from those of an organization's resource management.
- *Social Capital:* The value created by the systemic quality of organizations and relationships, as well as the quality of communication they facilitate.
- *Text:* An object or sign that can be read in different ways in order to transmit information, the meaning of which is contingent on the subject position of the person perceiving and interpreting it.

Discussion Questions

1 What is the rationale for the rise of critical theory? To what outcomes does it aspire, especially in the case of public relations theory and practice?

2 What assumptions need to be explored to make public relations effective and enduring rather than self-serving?

3 What conditions make public relations a positive, even noble contributor to civil society?

4 What aspirations guide inquiry into the public sphere?

5 How do biased, privileging aspects of language serve or hamper the relationships between organizations and society?

6 What six terms best define one's ability to unlock privilege and marginalization as a precursor to correcting discourse to serve various communities of interest?

7 What contributions can critical theory make over the coming years to enhance the practice of public relations and give it a noble role in society?

References

Abbott, J., Armstrong, J. S., Bolt, A., Carter, R., Darwall, R., Delingpole, J., et al. (2015). *Climate change: The facts*. Woodsville, NH: Stockade Books.

Aitken, M. (2019). Climate change and the public interest: Science, legitimacy and diversity. In J. Johnston & M. Pieczka (Eds.), *Public interest communication: Critical' debated and global contexts* (pp. 72–91). Oxford: Routledge.

Akerlof, K. L., Rowan, K. E., La Porte, T., Batten, B. K., Ernst, H., & Sklarew, D. M. (2016). Risky business: Engaging the public on sea level rise and inundation. *Environmental Science & Policy*, *66*, 314–323.

Beck, U. (1992). *Risk society: Towards a new modernity*. London: Sage.

Beck, U. (1999). *World risk society*. Cambridge: Polity.

Bentele, G. (2005). Public sphere (*Öffentlichkeit*). In R. L. Heath (Ed.), *Encyclopedia of public relations* (pp. 707–710). Thousand Oaks, CA: Sage.

Botan, C. H., & Taylor, M. (2004). Public relations: The state of the field. *Journal of Communication*, *54*, 645–661.

Brown, R. E. (2010). Symmetry and its critics: Antecedents, prospects, and implications for symmetry in a postsymmetry era. In R. L. Heath (Ed.), *SAGE handbook of public relations* (pp. 277–292). Thousand Oaks, CA: Sage.

Buber, M. (1965). *Between man and man*, trans. R. G. Smith. New York: Macmillan.

Cheney, G., & Christensen, L. T. (2001). Public relations as contested terrain: A critical response. In R. L. Heath (Ed.), *Handbook of public relations* (pp. 167–182). Thousand Oaks, CA: Sage.

Christensen, L. T., & Langer, R. (2009). Public relations and the strategic use of transparency: Consistency, hypocrisy, and corporate change. In R. L. Heath, E. L. Toth, & D. Waymer (Eds.), *Rhetorical and critical approaches to public relations II* (pp. 129–153). New York: Routledge.

Cissna, K. N., & Anderson, R. (1998). Theorizing about dialogic moments: The Buber-Rogers position and postmodern themes. *Communication Theory*, *1*, 63–104.

Clegg, S. R., Courpasson, D., & Phillips, N. (2006). *Power and organizations*. Thousand Oaks, CA: Sage.

Cook, J. (2019). Understanding and countering misinformation about climate change. In I. Chiluwa & S. Samoilenko (Eds.), *Handbook of research on deception, fake news, and misinformation online* (pp. 281–306). Hershey, PA: IGI Global.

Cook, J., Lewandowsky, S., & Ecker, U. (2017). Neutralizing misinformation through inoculation: Exposing misleading argumentation techniques reduces their influence. *PLoS ONE*, *12*(5), e0175799.

Courtright, J. L., & Smudde, P. M. (Eds.) (2007). *Power and public relations.* Cresskill, NJ: Hampton Press.

de Bussy, N. M. (2010). Dialogue as a basis for stakeholder engagement: Defining and measuring the core competencies. In R. L. Heath (Ed.), *SAGE handbook of public relations* (pp. 127–145). Thousand Oaks, CA: Sage.

de Witt, T. D., Funke, B., Haberreiter, M., & Matthes, K. (2018). Better data for modeling the sun's influence on climate. *EOC: Earth & Space Science News*, September 4. Available from https://eos.org/science-updates/better-data-for-modeling-the-suns-influence-on-climate (accessed May 20, 2020).

Downing, J., Mohammadi, A., & Sreberny-Mohammadi, A. (1995). Preface. In J. Downing, A. Mohammadi, & A. Sreberny-Mohammadi (Eds.), *Questioning the media: A critical introduction* (pp. xv–xxix). Thousand Oaks, CA: Sage.

Edwards, L. (2010). "Race" in public relations. In R. L. Heath (Ed.), *SAGE handbook of public relations* (pp. 205–221). Thousand Oaks, CA: Sage.

Fairclough, M. (1992). *Discourse and social change.* Cambridge: Polity.

Fairclough, M. (1995). *Critical discourse analysis.* London: Longman.

Fairclough, N. (1989). *Language and power.* London: Longman.

Foucault, M. (2002). *The archeology of knowledge*, trans. A. M. Sheridan Smith. New York: Routledge.

Gordon, J., & Pellegrin, P. (2008). Social constructionism and public relations. In T. L. Hansen-Horn & B. D. Neff (Eds.), *Public relations: From theory to practice* (pp. 104–121). Boston, MA: Pearson.

Habermas, J. (1976). What is universal pragmatics? In J. Habermas (Ed.), *Communication and the evolution of society.* Toronto, ON: Beacon Press.

Habermas, J. (1981). *Theory of the communicative action.* London: Beacon.

Habermas, J. (1991). *The structural transformation of the public sphere: An inquiry into a category of bourgeois society*, trans. T. Burger and F. Lawrence. Cambridge, MA: MIT Press.

Heath, R. L. (2006). Onward into more fog: Thoughts on public relations research directions. *Journal of Public Relations Research*, *18*, 93–114.

Heath, R. L., & Frandsen, F. (2008). Rhetorical perspective and public relations: Meaning matters. In A. Zerfass, B. van Ruler, & K. Sriramesh (Eds.), *Public relations research: european and international perspectives and innovations* (pp. 349–364). Wiesbaden: VS Verlag.

Heath, R. L., & McComas, K. (2015). Interest, interest, whose interest is at risk? Risk governance, issues management, and the fully functioning society. In U. F. Paleo (Ed.), *Risk governance: The articulation of hazard, politics, and ecology* (pp. 117–133). Dordrecht: Springer.

Heath, R. L., Motion, J., & Leitch, S. (2010). Power and public relations: Paradoxes and programmatic thoughts. In R. L. Heath (Ed.), *SAGE handbook of public relations* (pp. 191–204). Thousand Oaks, CA: Sage.

Heath, R. L., Pearce, W. B., Shotter, J., Taylor, J. R., Kersten, A., Zorn, T., ... Deetz, S. (2006). The processes of dialogue: Participation and legitimation. *Management Communication Quarterly*, *19*, 341–375.

Heath, R. L., & Waymer, D. (2019). Terministic dialectics of individual and community agency: Co-creating and co-enacting public interest. In J. Johnston & M. Pieczka (Eds.), *Public interest communication: Critical debate and global contexts* (pp. 32–51). Abingdon: Routledge.

Holmstrom, S. (2004). The reflective paradigm of public relations. In B. van Ruler & D. Vercic (Eds.), *Public relations and communication management in Europe* (pp. 121–133). Berlin: Mouton de Gruyter.

Holmstrom, S. (2010). Reflective management: Seeing the organization as if from outside. In R. L. Heath (Ed.), *SAGE handbook of public relations* (pp. 261–276). Thousand Oaks, CA: Sage.

Holtzhausen, D. R. (2002). Towards a postmodern research agenda for public relations. *Public Relations Review, 28*, 251–264.

Johnston, J., & Pieczka, M. (Eds.) (2019). *Public interest communication: Critical debates and global contexts*. Abingdon: Routledge.

Le Treut, H., Somerville, R., Cubasch, U., Ding, Y., Mauritzen, C., Mokssit, A., ... Prather, M. (2007). Historical overview of climate change. In S. Solomon, D. Qin, M. Manning, Z. Chen, M. Marquis, K. B. Averyt, et al. (Eds.), *Climate change 2007: The physical science basis. Contribution of working group I to the fourth assessment report of the intergovernmental panel on climate change* (pp. 93–128). Cambridge: Cambridge University Press.

Leeper, R. V. (1996). Moral objectivity, Jurgen Habermas's discourse ethics and public relations. *Public Relations Review, 22*, 133–150.

Leeper, R. V. (2005). Public sphere discourse. In R. L. Heath (Ed.), *Encyclopedia of Public Relations* (pp. 710–712). Thousand Oaks, CA: Sage.

Leitch, S., & Motion, J. (2010). Publics and public relations: Effecting change. In R. L. Heath (Ed.), *SAGE handbook of public relations* (pp. 99–110). Thousand Oaks, CA: Sage.

Leitch, S., & Neilson, D. (2001). Bringing publics into public relations: New theoretical frameworks for practice. In R. L. Heath (Ed.), *Handbook of public relations* (pp. 127–138). Thousand Oaks, CA: Sage.

L'Etang, J. (2010). "Making it real": Anthropological reflections of public relations, diplomacy, and rhetoric. In R. L. Heath (Ed.), *Handbook of public relations* (pp. 145–162). Thousand Oaks, CA: Sage.

L'Etang, J., McKie, D., Snow, N., & Xifra, J. (Eds.) (2016). *The Routledge handbook of critical public relations*. London: Routledge.

May, S. (2008). Reconsidering strategic corporate social responsibility: Public relations and ethical engagement of employees in a global economy. In A. Zerfass, B. van Ruler, & K. Sriramesh (Eds.), *Public relations research: European and international perspectives and innovations* (pp. 365–383). Weisbaden: VS Verlag.

McCright, A. M., & Dunlap, R. E. (2000). Challenging global warming as a social problem: An analysis of the conservative movement's counter-claims. *Social Problems, 47*(4), 499–522.

McKie, D. (2001). Updating public relations: "new science," research paradigms, and uneven developments. In R. L. Heath (Ed.), *Handbook of public relations* (pp. 75–91). Thousand Oaks, CA: Sage.

McKie, D. (2005). Critical theory. In R. L. Heath (Ed.), *Encyclopedia of public relations* (pp. 226–228). Thousand Oaks, CA: Sage.

McKie, D., & Munshi, D. (2009). Theoretical black holes: A partial A to Z of missing critical thought in public relations. In R. L. Heath, E. L. Toth, & D. Waymer (Eds.), *Rhetorical and critical approaches to public relations II* (pp. 61–75). New York: Routledge.

Moffitt, M. A. (1994). Collapsing and integrating concepts of "public" and "image" into a new theory. *Public Relations Review, 20*, 159–170.

Moffitt, M. A. (2005). Comments on special issue: Public relations from the margins. *Journal of Public Relations Research, 17*, 3–4.

Molony, K., & McKie, D. (2016). Changes to be encouraged: Radical turns in PR theorization and small-step evolutions in PR practice. In J. L'Etang, D. McKie, N. Snow, & J. Xifra (Eds.), *The Routledge handbook of critical public relations* (pp. 151–161). London: Routledge.

Monge, P. R., & Contractor, N. S. (2000). Emergence of communication networks. In F. M. Jablin & L. L. Putnam (Eds.), *The new handbook of organizational communication* (pp. 440–502). Thousand Oaks, CA: Sage.

Monge, P. R., Fulk, J., Kalman, M. E., Flanagin, A. J., Parmassa, C., & Rumsey, S. (1998). Production of collective action in alliance-based interorganizational communication and information systems. *Organization Science*, *9*, 411–433.

Motion, J. (2005). Participative public relations: Power to the people or legitimacy for government discourse? *Public Relations Review*, *31*, 505–512.

Motion, J., & Leitch, S. (1996). A discursive perspective from New Zealand: Another world view. *Public Relations Review*, *22*, 297–309.

Motion, J., & Leitch, S. (2007). A toolbox for public relations: The *oeuvre* of Michel Foucault. *Public Relations Research*, *33*, 263–268.

Motion, J., & Weaver, C. K. (2005). A discourse perspective for critical public relations research: Life sciences network and the battle for truth. *Journal of Public Relations Research*, *17*, 49–67.

Nessman, K. (2000). The origins and development of public relations in Germany and Austria. In D. Moss, D. Vercic, & G. Warnaby (Eds.), *Perspectives on public relations research* (pp. 211–225). London: Routledge.

Nisbet, M. C., & Myers, T. (2007). Trends: Twenty years of public opinion about global warming. *Public Opinion Quarterly*, *71*, 444–470.

Painter, J., & Gavin, N. T. (2016). Climate skepticism in British Newspapers, 2007–2011. *Environmental Communication*, *10*, 432–452.

Reich, R. B. (2008). *The case against corporate responsibility*. Berkeley, CA: Goldman School of Public Policy, University of California.

Roper, J. (2005). Symmetrical communication: Excellent public relations or a strategy for hegemony? *Journal of Public Relations Research*, *17*, 69–86.

Roser-Renouf, C., Maibach, E. W., Leiserowitz, A., & Zhao, X. (2014). The genesis of climate change activism: From key beliefs to political action. *Climate Change*, *125*, 163–178.

Roser-Renouf, C., Atkinson, L., Maibach, E., & Leiserowitz, A. (2016). The consumer as climate activist. *International Journal of Communication*, *10*, 4759–4783.

Rowell, A. (2014). Exxon's 25 year "drop dead" denial campaign. *Oil Change International*, April 14. Available from http://priceofoil.org/2014/04/14/exxons-25-year-drop-dead-denial-campaign (accessed May 20, 2020).

Shumate, M., Fulk, J., & Monge, P. R. (2005). Predictors of the international HIV/AIDS NGO network over time. *Human Communication Research*, *31*, 482–510.

Stohl, M., & Stohl, C. (2005). Human rights, nation states, and NGOs: Structural holes and the emergence of global regimes. *Communication Monographs*, *72*, 442–467.

Taylor, M. (2009). Civil society as a rhetorical public relations process. In R. L. Heath, E. L. Toth, & D. Waymer (Eds.), *Rhetorical and critical approaches to public relations II* (pp. 76–91). New York: Routledge.

Taylor, M. (2010). Public relations in the enactment of civil society. In R. L. Heath (Ed.), *SAGE handbook of public relations* (pp. 5–16). Thousand Oaks, CA: Sage.

Thunberg, G. (2018). *No one is too small to make a difference*. London: Penguin.

Torp, S. M. (2018). The strategic turn of communication science: On the history and role of strategic communication science from ancient Greece until the present day. In D. Holzhausen & A. Zerfass (Eds.), *The Routledge handbook of strategic communication* (pp. 34–52). New York: Routledge.

Trujillo, N. (1992). White knights, poker games, and the invasion of the carpetbaggers: Interpreting the sale of a professional sports franchise. In E. L. Toth & R. L. Heath (Eds.), *Rhetorical and critical approaches to public relations* (pp. 257–278). Hillsdale, NJ: Lawrence Erlbaum Associates.

Van der Linden, S. L., Leiserowitz, A. A., Feinberg, G. D., & Maibach, E. W. (2015). The scientific consensus on climate change as a gateway belief: Experimental evidence. *PLoS ONE*, *10*(2), e0118489.

Van der Linden, S., Maibach, E., & Leiserowitz, A. (2015). Improving public engagement with climate change: Five "best practice" insights from psychological science. *Perspectives on Psychological Science, 10,* 758–763.

Vardeman-Winter, J., & Tindall, N. T. J. (2010). Toward an intersectionality theory of public relations. In R. L. Heath (Ed.), *SAGE handbook of public relations* (pp. 223–235). Thousand Oaks, CA: Sage.

Vujnovic, M., & Kruckeberg, D. (2010). The local, national and global challenges of public relations: A call for an anthropological approach to practicing public relations. In R. L. Heath (Ed.), *SAGE handbook of public relations* (pp. 671–678). Thousand Oaks, CA: Sage.

Waymer, D. (2010). Does public relations scholarship have a place in race? In R. L. Heath (Ed.), *SAGE handbook of public relations* (pp. 237–246). Thousand Oaks, CA: Sage.

Whorf, B. L. (1956). *Language, thought, and reality.* Cambridge, MA: MIT Press.

Wrigley, B. J. (2010). Feminist scholarship and its contributions to public relations. In R. L. Heath (Ed.), *SAGE handbook of public relations* (pp. 247–260). Thousand Oaks, CA: Sage.

7

Issues, Crisis, and Risk Communication and Management

Introduction

During the late 1970s and 1980s, new conceptual directions for public relations came from management studies, risk studies, and crisis studies, all of which focused attention on planning, relational, and performance issues. Major books and new topics changed the conceptual and practical landscape of public relations, most particularly strategic issue(s) management (SIM), crisis communication and management, and risk communication and management. Emphasis on management does not mean that communication is irrelevant or unimportant. It means that the concept of management is the vital challenge for organizational legitimacy in its many configurations. For that reason, issues, crises, and risks are interlocking lines of legitimacy analysis.

All three disciplines can be seen as corporate-centric management, but they inherently reflect concerns over interests sought both inside and outside a given organization because communities legitimate organizations. Some who write about public relations theory ignore these disciplines or treat them as minor parts of a general theory of public relations. In fact, they are both overarching matters and contribute to mid-level theory. Writers treat risk management as a profound—perhaps the most profound—sociopolitical challenge facing human society.

Issue contests are not new, nor are crisis or risk management challenges. Discussions of issues had become central to nascent public relations by the 1870s, often intertwined with the analysis of risk and crisis. By 1900, work in mines, mills, forests, and railroads had become notoriously unsafe. Crises occurred as workers were harmed. Risk of toxic exposure from unsafe food, medicine, and cosmetics became commonplace. Seventy years later, these disciplines reflected widespread criticism that included the military (industrial complex), advances and failures in civil rights, efforts to increase safety in the face of scary technologies such as nuclear power, and protests over environmental quality and risk equity. On this point, Jaques (2006) notes:

> Professionalism of activism is in some respects a direct response to the growth of stakeholder participation as a key element of issue management. Processes such as community consultation or corporate social responsibility or stakeholder engagement have accelerated and formalized participation by external parties. (p. 414)

By the 1990s, these lines of research and practice had become professionally prominent and conceptually interdependent. Analysis centered on helping organizations defend themselves through skilled management of issues, well-crafted crisis responses, and transparent risk assessment.

Criticism fanned crises, such as when scientists discovered an association between health problems and smoking and asbestos. Led by medical scientists, the tobacco/health battle heated up in 1953, while asbestos became a massive risk controversy in the 1960s and 1970s, leading to highly punitive legislation, including the creation of trusts to compensate victims; lawsuits forced well-known companies into bankruptcy. These battles expanded to include chemicals (and processes for manufacturing them) in the environment, as well as industrial practices such as clear-cutting timber.

Iconic events such as Three Mile Island (1979) and Chernobyl (1986) led thousands of people around the world to focus attention on health and safety issues related to the use of nuclear energy to generate electricity. Oil spills/releases began to receive attention in the United States in 1969 with the Alpha rig blowout off Santa Barbara, California, followed by the Exxon Valdez (1989) oil transportation disaster in Prince William Sound, Alaska. Legislation was enacted during the last three decades of the twentieth century to solve issues, punish crises, and reduce risk (for a list, see Heath & Palenchar, 2009, see p. 76), both in the United States and in Europe. Corporate criticism continues to characterize the global policy battlefield in the twenty-first century.

Academic and professional study of the role of public relations in issues, crises, and risks led to a bounty of articles and books. In 1984, W. Howard Chase (see also 1977, 1982) produced his seminal work, *Issue Management: Origins of the Future* (note that some authors prefer this concept without an "s" after "issue"). This was followed by other practitioner treatises and the first academic book, *Issues Management: Corporate Public Policymaking in an Information Society* (Heath & Nelson, 1986). The Public Affairs Council added SIM to its portfolio; the Issue Management Council was formed in 1988.

Crisis communication was launched as a topic of serious discussion following the iconic Johnson & Johnson Tylenol case (1982), when someone replaced the ingredients in Tylenol capsules with cyanide and left them on store shelves. The deaths that resulted caused great anxiety and spawned a cottage industry: crisis communication. Out of this furor emerged the first book on crisis: Fink's (1986) *Crisis Management: Planning for the Inevitable*.

The first discussants of crisis were from management science. Later, communication scholars began to use the topic as a context and condition for research into the processes and statements that precede (pre-crisis), occur during, and follow (post-crisis) a crisis event. Public relations scholar W. Timothy Coombs' *Ongoing Crisis Communication* was published in 1999. Crisis as an academic topic earned handbook status in 2010, with the publication of Coombs and Holladay's *Handbook of Crisis Communication*. By then, other books on the topic had reached professional and academic libraries. Some thought crisis was a public relations topic and could be explained as a failure of effective communication management. Others saw it more as a management topic. Still others viewed it as a separate topic, or even one that overshadowed a substantial amount of the territory claimed by public relations.

Risk analysis, management, and communication are central to the human experience, as old as humans' struggle for survival—including the need to deal with the unknown. Years of thought eventually framed this discipline with the caveat that societies (communities) organize to collectively manage risk. Those that best understand and adapt to risks increase their chances for societal survival and success. Tobacco, alcohol, chemicals, and natural events such as hurricanes, tornadoes, earthquakes, and tsunamis gave rise to the modern discipline of risk management and communication, including emergency planning and response. Quintessential events that launched recent trends in the discipline included Three Mile Island (nuclear radiation) and Union Carbide's 1984 massive methyl isocyanate (MIC) leak in Bhopal, India, which killed, blinded, and produced sustained respiratory damage in thousands. But disasters had happened before these events, and they will happen again. In the last half of the twentieth century, the stars aligned just right to bring together tensions over corporate social responsibility (CSR) standards and government intervention and planning in support of professional practices that engaged many disciplines and much academic research largely in order to make communities better places to live and organizations safer places to work.

Drawing together scientists, social scientists, and policy experts, the National Research Council (1989) published *Improving Risk Communication*. Ironically, what had been and continues to be a discipline heavily dependent on science and management emerged as a communication topic. Other books quickly followed: Douglas' (1992) *Risk and Blame*; Beck's (1992) *Risk Society: Towards a New Modernity*, Krimsky and Golding's (1992) *Social Theories of Risk*; Friedman, Dunwoody, and Rogers' (1999) *Communicating Uncertainty*; and Morgan, Fischhoff, Bostrom, and Atman's (2002) *Risk Communication: A Mental Models Approach*. Later, Heath and O'Hair (2009) edited the *Handbook of Risk and Crisis Communication*. Such treatises centered on science, management, ethics, social sciences, and communication.

Major topics featured in this chapter call upon communication and public relations theory and research to partner with management studies and the ideology that defines the quality of community and society interest alignment. These topics are interdependent. Issues mature into crisis. Crisis can be defined as a risk manifested. Risks produce issues and become crises themselves.

This overview of key events, streams of analysis, and major publications is intended to establish the integrity of SIM, crisis management and communication, and risk management and communication. By the end of the chapter, readers should understand the nature of issue contests, the challenges of crisis prevention and response, and the reality that risk management and communication define the agency of communities, small, national, and global.

Questions to Frame the Discussion of Issues, Crisis, and Risk Communication and Management

- How does society, through multiple voices, create, debate, implement, and refine private and public policy that supports and constrains not only the missions and visions of large organizations, but also entities of society affected by those organizations?
- What role does resource dependency play in organizations' successes and failures and society's agency?
- What theories help explain the role organizations play in the successful use of SIM to acquire and distribute tangible and intangible resources in the public interest?
- What theories of crisis management and communication have developed? What does each offer to understanding how organizations can, do, and should respond during trying times? In what ways is organizational self-defense adequate, and when does crisis management require change, improvement, and renewal?
- Is risk management and communication a rationale for understanding how society organizes for the collective management of risk?
- What theories best support the research and practice of risk management and communication?
- How do issues, crisis, and risk interrelate and why?
- How do these topics, as researched and theorized, draw on, challenge, and add to excellence theory, contingency theory, rhetorical theory, and critical theory?

Key Themes

- Jaques (2010) provides an enlightened definition, scope, and purpose for SIM: "*Issue management is not about how to manage an issue, but how to manage because of an issue*" (p. xx, italics in original)
- According to Ulmer, Sellnow, and Seeger (2009), "Organizations that are willing to view from a balanced perspective including both threat and opportunity have a much greater potential for experiencing renewal. Despite this potential, we observe a persistent bias toward viewing crises solely from the perspective of threat" (p. 317).
- Coombs (2010) reasons that crisis communication by necessity depends on an understanding of crises and crisis management: "The three are inextricably interconnected and must be considered in a progression from crisis to crisis management to crisis communication" (pp. 17–18).
- Renn, Webler, and Wiedemann (1995) caution that "Without public involvement, environmental policies are doomed to fail" (p. xiii). Concerns about sustainability, CSR, social marketing, and community relations make stakeholder participation an important topic for management and operations; this topic requires theoretical examination, monitoring processes, and understanding of negotiation and collaborative decision making, as well as an examination of the ethics of community engagement.

Case Study: Issues, Crises, and Risks Associated with Japan's Fukushima No. 1 (Daiichi) Plant

The nuclear disaster at Japan's Fukushima No. 1 (Daiichi) Plant in 2011 resulted from an earthquake so strong that it moved the entire island of Honshu and caused a tsunami that overwhelmed the plant's science and engineering. The event became iconic, "one for the books." As late as 2016, Herman reported: "Experts say Japan's nuclear energy problems are worsening." Fukushima demonstrates not only the conditions relevant to issues, crisis, and risk management separately, but also these topics' interdependence.

This case did not begin in 2011; it started much earlier, through the interconnected dynamics of nuclear energy, earthquakes, tsunamis, and public health and safety. Perhaps no country in the world knows more than Japan about and has a better intellectual and emotional response to the devastating power of nuclear energy, to say nothing of the country's experience with earthquakes. The Fukushima event, a crisis that occurred when several risks manifested and amplified one after another, is part of an ongoing, larger dialogue about nuclear power facility safety, design, and operation. The event provides motive and substance for rhetorical dialogue on earthquakes and tsunamis, and their interaction with nuclear power generation. It demonstrates how such events can focus analysis on the nexus of human risk management planning and "mother nature." It is central to the need for organizations and communities to wisely seek and manage resources for individual and collective agency.

On March 10, 2011, an 8.9 magnitude earthquake off the eastern shore of Japan produced a 23 ft tsunami that killed thousands, damaged homes and other properties, caused a fire at a petrochemical facility, and overwhelmed the defenses that had been engineered and constructed at the Fukushima Daichi nuclear power electricity-generating plant. This event angered the plant's near neighbors, and some far away, who worried about the radiation release and doubted whether they had been fully, transparently, and strategically informed. Crops and cropland were devastated. Communication infrastructures were ruined. International manufacturing supply lines were affected. The response efficacy of government officials and the experts and operators at the nuclear facility was tested in real time.

The plant's defenses had been designed to withstand a tsunami breach, but the containment wall proved not to be built high enough. Internal technologies were in place to sustain safe operations. The specific breach—magnitude of the risk—overwhelmed the defenses, and the generating facility's nuclear power technologies were unleashed. Engineering and operations emergency response planning was inadequate because of the complexity of the event. Explosions and releases at the generating facility continued for months. Issues regarding the design of the plant and the nature of nuclear energy will be debated for years.

A full presentation of the details of this case is too extensive to include here. Crucial to this chapter, however, is that it demonstrates not only issues, risks, and crises, but also their interlocking nature. The event revived the debate over the safety of nuclear power around the world. It emphasized the dangers posed by natural events (these had been considered before, and were part of the hesitation to support the building of facilities near high-probability earthquake zones). It brought back into the public agenda discussions of events such as that at Cherbnobyl (which is relevant to both design and long-term recovery). The central issue was this: Is nuclear power capable of being engineered and used safely?

This is a risk-management question. As will be discussed later, risk management and communication considers, among other topics, engineering and sound science assessments and management of the uncertainties of natural and artificial risks. It demonstrates how risk is not merely a communication matter, but one that involves all disciplines, including science, engineering, and management. Risk presumes an appropriate amount of precaution must govern the development and use of technology.

The Fukushima case reveals how, once a risk manifests itself, a crisis of some magnitude can—and often will—occur. Such crises can have three time-line stages: pre-crisis, which in the case of Fukushima included emergency management and crisis response planning and messaging; crisis event response, which as in the case of the BP blowout in 2010 (see Chapter 5) can go on for days, be harrowing, and challenge the credibility of one or more organizations' technical and managerial competence; and post-crisis.

This chapter explores the contexts of society and the content of the discourse relevant to private and public policy dialogue around issues, crisis, and risk. It examines SIM contributions to *strategic business management* (mission- and vision-driven C-Suite planning, positioning, policy development, and implementation), *issue monitoring, meeting or exceeding CSR standards*, and *issue communication*. Attention is focused on leading theories and research relevant to crisis communication and management: *apologia theory, image restoration theory (IRT), crisis and the rhetoric of renewal*, and *situational crisis communication theory (SCCT)*. The final section discusses risk management and communication, including the role of *sound science through the mental models approach (MMA), cultural theory of risk* (which justifies thinking of society as organizing for the collective management of risk), *sociopsychometric aspect of risk perceptions and evaluation*, and the quality of *risk management and communication infrastructures*.

Throughout the chapter, interconnections are noted regarding public relations theories explained in other chapters. Since the mid-1970s, issues management, crisis, and risk have been interdependent themes. Broadly, issues arise from crisis and risk. As they develop, they can grow out of crises and create them. Understanding risks helps to identify and understand crisis as risk manifested. When risks manifest, crisis occurs; then, issues are likely to arise, in order to reduce the likelihood of their recurrence. Issues can be created by what organizations do, but how they are resolved defines what actions an organization can use to gain the resources it needs to be successful. Thus, managements must understand issues and mitigate their harmful impact.

Public relations theory discusses how to help make organizations effective and societies good places to live and work. To make society more fully functioning, SIM, crisis management and communication, and risk management and communication must be interdependent. SIM is the foundation for understanding their relationship.

Issues and Issues Management

How issues management is conceptualized and theorized determines how it is practiced. Some see it as nothing more than public relations, or one of its subdisciplines. Others conceptualize it as a management discipline that subsumes public relations. It can promote and defend reputation and brand equity, as well as justify public policy engagement and outcomes. Less robust views limit SIM to government relations, issue monitoring, futures-based planning, or lobbying. Issues management is more than communication; it centers on strategic management, especially insofar as change management may be needed to resolve key issues and achieve legitimacy. Issues are points of contention concerning how management occurs and what it accomplishes. SIM can help management address and respond effectively and ethically to stakeholder challenges and interest alignments.

The Public Affairs Council champions public policy and reputation as SIM leverage points: "Issues management involves prioritizing and proactively addressing public policy and reputation issues that can affect an organization's success. Many large companies use issues management techniques to keep their external relations activities focused on high-priority challenges and opportunities" (Public Affairs Council, n.d.).

Pioneering issues management, Chase (1984) called it the new management science for dealing with activist criticisms that were casting doubt on standard management practices of the private and public sectors during the 1970s and 1980s. He was dedicated to helping "the person who sees things whole, the reader who is eager and anxious to identify, analyze, and place priorities on trends, and then to exert direct influence on events through issue action programing" (frontispiece).

Recognizing that corporate managements cannot control their own future, Davis and Thompson (1994) emphasized the legitimacy limits of management control: "Management's control within the firm is contingent on rules determined externally by state and federal governments, and the allocation of corporate control thus depends on political struggles among management, capital, and various governmental bodies" (p. 141).

At the macro-level, SIM is a management activity predicated on knowing, engaging, and achieving CSR standards through strategic budgeting, planning, and policy implementation guided by issue monitoring and communication. After carefully considering the array of topics being discussed in the SIM literature, Heath and Cousino (1990) identified the reasoning that defined the whole of SIM as resting on four integrated pillars: strategic management, issue monitoring, meeting stakeholder CSR expectations, and issue communication. In developing this model, they drew on an exhaustive literature review of management, futurism, communication, reputation, brand equity, activism, public affairs, and reputation. Executives emphasized that businesses must operate in the public interest. The four pillars of organizational success are fundamental to how well organizations reflectively understand threats to their preferred approach to operations, so that executives can maximize their ability to add CSR value to the communities in which they operate.

SIM was inspired by emerging sociopolitical issues that were causing grief—if not havoc—as management teams planned and operated in an era of extreme political and public policy turbulence. In the face of this turbulence, traditional approaches to public relations seemed clueless. Alternative paradigms were needed to develop systems and methodologies for scanning, identifying, analyzing, and responding to issues early in their life cycle. The assumption was that managements could defend or refine their strategic plans if they spotted issue trends early. This would allow them to correct their planning and operations in order to reduce criticism. Alternatively, it could allow business voices to engage with other voices before issues became carved in stone and beyond response and revision.

Pillar One: Strategic Management

Organizations, whether for-profit, nonprofit (nongovernmental organizations, NGOs), or governmental, require planning and operations that organize the material and symbolic resources they need to accomplish their missions, visions, and core values. This resource-dependency approach to management emphasizes that the struggle for legitimacy requires knowing which dynamic and contextual CSR standards judge private- and public-sector activities to be legitimate. Using CSR as a guidance system, managements frame mission and vision statements to be implemented by budgeting through the reinvention of change management that expresses core values. Alone, issue communication is insufficient to reconcile the organization with its stakeholders' expectations—a resource-dependency paradigm of management, organizational, and societal success. But issue communication can rhetorically engage in ways that collaboratively establish CSR norms and public policy guidelines through which managers plan.

Considering such tensions, Renfro (1993) featured the discipline's management contribution:

> The overriding goal of an issues management function is to enhance the current and long-term performance and standing of the corporation by anticipating change, promoting opportunities, and avoiding or mitigating threats. Attaining this corporate goal, of course, promotes the performance and standing of the corporate leadership, both within and outside the corporations, but this is secondary for issues management. (p. 107)

Born in an era when business was buffeted from every direction, SIM provided a strategic management rationale along with a communication rationale for how managements align their organizations with the norms and policies preferred in the communities in which they operate. SIM stakeholder participation could range between advocacy and accommodation.

Strategic management depends on how well executives plan and operate in the business (private-sector) and public-policy contexts in which each organization earns its legitimacy, its right to operate. Legitimacy depends on knowing and meeting CSR standards, which constantly change through strategic discourse. Discourse trends can be monitored.

Pillar Two: Issue Monitoring

Management must understand the conditions of legitimacy by monitoring issues: processes of scanning for issues, analyzing them, and prioritizing them in terms of their impact on the organization's ability to achieve its mission and vision. Issue monitoring and analysis need to be strategic; no entity can control issue trends and outcomes. They can narratively participate in the development of trends, their interpretation, and the creation of zones of shared meaning relevant to organizational success.

Strategic monitoring can be divided into sequential segments. Scanning entails looking for issues. Analysis is a complex process for understanding the nature of issues, the reasoning that sustains or challenges them, and the impact they can have on strategic management planning and operations. Tracking is trend analysis; the goal is to determine whether issues are gaining momentum, with more people engaged on a side and being convinced of its rightness. Analysis can inform organizational priority setting. Relevant to each of these stages—particularly the development of early-warning scanning—monitoring looks for potential risks and crises, and for voices that can bring them into the public sphere. It seeks to identify and analyze changing CSR standards.

Championing this theme, Jacques (2000, 2014) suggested that no organization can identify, track, and respond to every issue. It cannot afford to get sidetracked by issues identification, scanning, monitoring, and analysis, or it will default in the public policy process because it will try to do too much with every issue and accomplish too little with the ones that truly matter to it.

Some issues focus only or primarily on values; others center on scientific processes and technical facts that leave the realm of public discussion to be debated or negotiated in legislative, regulatory, or judicial chambers by experts working for companies, governmental agencies, and activist groups. The upshot of issue monitoring is knowing which stakeholder expectations constitute issue positions that are relevant to an organization's need for and right to acquire the resources it needs to operate. (More attention will be devoted to issue monitoring in Chapter 8.)

Pillar Three: Meeting Stakeholder CSR Expectations

The justification for issues management is that public policy debates set limits on and legitimize business (organizational) activities. Thus, voices engaged in dialogue contend over how and why businesses and other organizations should act, and how they should conduct themselves responsibly in order to be judged legitimate. (This theme was developed in Chapters 5 and 6 through discussions of neo-institutionalism.) Organizations define themselves and participate with others who co-define the acceptable powers of and limits on organizations. This approach to issues emphasizes the impact of stakeholder expectations on organizational legitimacy. A gap can exist between how and why organizations want to operate as they do within the boundaries of such expectations. Jaques (2010) correctly noted that *legitimacy* is "defined as a gap between actions of the organization concerned and the expectations of its stakeholders" (p. 437).

This view draws on Sethi's (1977) description of the legitimacy gaps—however large or small, whether actual or falsely attributed—that exist between the policy-driven actions of an organization and stakeholder expectations. What the organization does may please some but displease others. (Such gaps can be caused by crises or can themselves cause crises.) Thus, issues result, based on the legitimacy-gap logic, from actual or mistaken differences of fact, value, policy, identity, and identification.

Legitimacy depends on what an organization does, why it operates as it does, and who identifies or does not identify with it. CSR standards define an organization's right to operate in a particular way. The ethical implications of these standards are evaluative (moral legitimacy) and cognitive/pragmatic (financial/material legitimacy) (Golant & Sillince, 2007). The fundamental question underpinning this social productivity approach to CSR is whether organizations are responsible brokers of private and public interests. If they are, so goes SIM logic, they deserve the support of society; if not, resistance builds to correct offensive actions and misjudgments in order to resolve legitimacy gaps.

For this reason, SIM theory calls for continual stakeholder engagement. Like others who discuss stakeholders, de Bussy (2005, 2008, 2010) built on the seminal efforts of management scholar

Freeman (1984) and his colleagues (see Freeman & Gilbert, 1988; Freeman, Harrison, Wicks, Parmar, & de Colle, 2010). The connection between CSR, stakeholders, and legitimacy is simple: firms are societal entities enfranchised by the social contract, and so they must take seriously their "obligations to society" (Freeman & Gilbert, 1988, p. 89). As a foundation for understanding the need for and legitimizing influence of social capital, Freeman and Gilbert (1988) reasoned that "effective strategy will be formulated and implemented if and only if each player successfully puts himself or herself in the place of other players and endeavors to see the situation from the others' perceptions" (p. 91). This tension calls for effective stakeholder engagement in order to recognize, respond to, and solve risk challenges in ways that conform to or exceed stakeholder CSR expectations.

Which policies and actions are legitimate, and which are not? This question sets the parameters of the SIM playing field. Legitimacy is defined through issue-centered dialogue. It occurs within dynamic, interactive systems that strive for organic balance. Tensions between systems can be understood as being basic to the dynamics of social exchange. According to social exchange theory, systems constantly adjust to one another as reward/cost give and take. Through social exchange, actors calculate the costs of a relationship versus its rewards. Discourse focuses on the challenges of getting along with one another, whether as humans, businesses, governmental agencies, or activist NGOs. Critical theory imposes normative judgments as to the nature of issues and their impact on the quality of relationships.

No organization is an island unto itself; all are variously interdependent with complexes of stakeholders and stakeseekers. Thus, managerial and rhetorical acts assert organizations into a stakeholder marketplace seeking to achieve rewards and minimize relational costs. CSR frames such costs in terms of stakeholder/stakeseeker expectations. When organizations are managed in such a way that expectations are met, the relationship is positive. Violations raise relational costs to exceed rewards.

Pillar Four: Issue Communication

The strategic discourse processes vital to issue communication are discussed in depth in Chapters 5 and 6. Here, it suffices to generalize that stakeholder voices influence management decisions through the discourse that occurs in marketplace and public policy rhetorical arenas. Regulation, legislation, and judicial decisions shape how business is conducted, and how governmental agencies and nonprofits and NGOs are legitimatized to operate. Engagement raises and investigates issues.

What is an issue? Seminally, Chase (1984) defined it as "an unsettled matter which is ready for decision" (p. 38). Later, Wartick and Mahon (1994) isolated three themes regarding what constitutes an issue: controversy, expectation gaps, and impact.

The *disputation or controversy theme* assumes that issues are worthy of or demand discussion where voices express conflicting opinions as to which among several options is best.

On the theme of *expectation gaps*, Heath's (2006) rhetorical perspective treated an issue as a rhetorical problem seeking enlightened choice and problem solution. Thus, an issue is a contestable matter of fact, value (evaluation), policy, identity, or identification: "It is a difference of opinion that can result from or lead to a legitimacy gap. An emerging public policy issue attracts significant attention to the way an organization plans and operates" (p. 81). This view of issues points to what is contested and to the implications of the contest's resolution.

Jaques (2010) critiqued such definitions as passive; he championed the *impact (on management decision making) theme* as being more dynamic. This view:

provides a very clear statement that the focus is, and must be, on what is significant. While organizations face problems every day, of varying nature and importance, the great strength of the impact theme in issue definition is its emphasis that issue management is not a general-purpose problem-solving tool, applied to every dispute or gap in expectation, but is most appropriately employed when the impact is, or is likely to be, significant. (pp. 437–438)

All disputes and expectation gaps are more or less significant to the extent they affect what an organization wants and needs to do in order to accomplish its legitimate mission and vision.

These definitions introduce into SIM theory the following specific actions: (a) base an organization's strategic management on policies and procedures designed to use its business plan to achieve its mission and vision; (b) understand and work to meet or exceed relevant CSR standards by monitoring and analyzing issues; and (c) engage with others in society regarding the facts, values, policies, identities, and identifications relevant to power resource management. Thus, believing that large, even powerful organizations cannot completely shape issues to their will, the assumption is that they must participate in issues discussion and manage their responses to the outcomes of such engagement.

In terms of the Fukushima case, people tolerate or even applaud the use of nuclear power to generate electricity for various reasons, but its benefits can be compromised by system failures that allow radiation to harm workers or near neighbors. To minimize such violations, many disciplines must work together: management, engineering, operational safety, and emergency response.

Stakeholder theory reasons that strategic management must think reflectively from the outside in (Freeman, 1984; Freeman et al., 2010). By 1988, Freeman's stakeholder theory had become intertwined with ethics as the normative principle of strategic engagement (Freeman & Gilbert, 1988). By introducing layers of "ethics" into the fray, Frederick (1986; Frederick & Weber, 1990) differentiated responsiveness, responsibility, and rectitude, the latter being the highest ethical barrier to corporate adjustment to stakeholders' expectations. Leaders in operations science and management theory realized that a clear understanding of CSR was necessary in order to define the limits, tensions, and responsibilities of legitimate stakeholder participation (Heath, 2010; Kotler & Lee, 2005; Post, Preston, & Sachs, 2002). The logic of collaboration presumes that negotiation can achieve balance through social exchange.

Freeman's (1984) theory assumed engaged relationships between stakeholders and stakeseekers. Figure 7.1 combines stakeholder relations and CSR standards. This reasoning supports Ewing's (1987) rationale for SIM: "Issues management developed within the business community as an educational task aimed at preserving the proper balance between the legitimate goals and rights of the free enterprise system and those of society" (p. 5).

Meaning, shared and co-created, shapes power and the conditions of stake exchange (Heath, Motion, & Leitch, 2010; Leitch & Motion, 2010; Smudde & Courtright, 2010). Meaning centers on matters of fact (understanding of reality), identity/self (whether individual, organizational, or societal), and society/relationship (the dynamics of institutions for decision making and regulation). The key to the emergent, coherent, and conflicting meaning that operates in stakeholder/stakeseeker exchanges is based on premises that justify, guide, and constraint individual, organizational, and societal actions. Meaning expresses principles of social arrangement that are co-created, known, adopted, and enacted.

In the case of nuclear energy, spokespersons for the technology work to inform and convince key stakeholders that nuclear facilities can be constructed and operated in ways that meet the highest standards of safety. A crisis like that experienced by the Fukushima No. 1 (Daiichi) Plant disputes such safety claims. Thus, issues lead to crisis, which in turn raises further issues.

A stakeholder's influence derives from the power they exert. Their power derives from the stakes (power resources) they can grant or withhold. Consequently, Heath (2010) reasoned, stakeholder

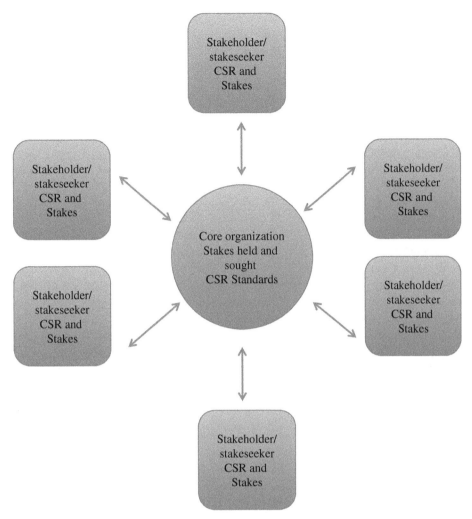

Figure 7.1 Multiple stakeholder/stakeseeker analysis. Based on Freeman (1984) and Heath and Palenchar (2009).

theory is inseparable from efficiency, power, risk, and control—key elements of power resource management. The engagement between participating stakeholders/stakeseekers focuses on premises regarding how resources are earned, held, and distributed. This reasoning was extended by de Bussy (2008): "The theory raises a highly contentious question: in whose interest should a business corporation or other type of organization be run?" (p. 4815).

Strategic management coupled to communication, according to de Bussy (2010), has been the rationale for stakeholder participation theory. In such matters, "Engaging with stakeholders should be one of the most important core competencies of public relations" (p. 127). This could not be the case if organizations were not stake-oriented. To this end, de Bussy featured stakeholder participation as dialogue—the engagement of organizations with stakeholders regarding the quality of relationship between them. The rationale for issue communication presumes that the co-creation of meaning guides and regulates private-sector activities: "*Genuine* dialogue involves each participant really having the others in mind and turning to them with the intentions of establishing a living, mutual relation" (p. 132).

As was argued in Chapters 5 and 6, good discourse can—depending on the public arena—drive bad discourse from the marketplace of ideas. Issue communication entails platforms of fact, evaluation, policy, and discussions of CSR, as well as reputation, brand equity, and identification. It is, at its best, capable of and focused on making society more fully functioning as an agency for collective decision making.

One lesson learned through discussions of issues management is that one or two cleverly worded press releases are unlikely to resolve an issue. The paradigm of issue communication is sustained argumentation, advocacy, contention, debate, engagement, accommodation, and collaboration—as discourse, dialogue, and rhetorically co-created meaning. Credibility and character are fundamental principles of effective issue communication. Public issue discussion can make societies better places to work and live.

An issue may arise when someone puts a fact into play that points to a problem or calls for a better solution than that which has been advocated. In the case of the Fukushima No. 1 (Daiichi) Plant, nature raised the issue of plant safety engineering. On the subject of such rhetorical problems, Campbell (1996) compared scientists, for whom "the most important concern is the discovery and testing of certain kinds of truths," to rhetoricians, who "would say, 'Truths cannot walk on their own legs. They must be carried by people to other people. They must be explained, defended, and spread through language, argument, and appeal'" (p. 3). From this foundation, Campbell reasoned, rhetoricians take the position "that unacknowledged and unaccepted truths are of no use at all" (p. 3). The rhetorical tradition is founded on matters of facts and value; rhetors assert and support propositions by demonstrating that one value perspective is better and more appropriate than another.

As this section concludes, it should be clear how legitimacy gaps motivate issue communication, but resolving such gaps may require change management. Because of safety design flaws and operations mistakes, the Daiichi Plant failed to mitigate the risk created by the tsunami. The company's reputation, as well as that of the nuclear industry as a whole, was brought into question. This case emphasizes how legitimacy depends on engineering, planning, budgeting, and operations. It demonstrates how CSR standards—safety, generically—are the major challenge to achieving legitimacy. At issue is the reputation of nuclear power, the engineers who design facilities, the management and personnel who operate them, and the government agencies that license them and monitor their operations. At issue, too, is the ability of the Daiichi Plant company to maintain the quality of relationship efficacy required for its legitimacy.

Around the world, the case raised issues. Can nuclear power be used safely to generate electricity? What design features and standards ensure maximum safety? As events begin to cascade, and dominos begin to topple, can the necessary means of risk mitigation be implemented? Are other sources of electricity better? Are plants properly regulated? These are operational, managerial, and public policy questions that will continue to be debated as unfinished matters.

In closing this section, several key points emphasize the nature of issues management and its role in public policy and reputational discourse. SIM requires both highly technical communication and communication that is friendly, comprehensible, and sensitive to the needs and interests of those who experience risk and crisis.

Crisis Management and Communication

Because of iconic events such as the Tylenol poisoning tragedy, crisis management and communication became a cottage industry in the last half of the twentieth century. Crisis inspires theory-driven, research-based conclusions, as well as best-practice prescriptions. This section features this research and theory, and is mindful of best practices.

Crisis occurs when risks manifest; for instance, when an organization makes an error in strategic management planning and operations that affects its stakeholders. In addition to mistakes, an organization may suffer a crisis if it is attacked, such as by product tampering, a security-system compromise, a customer-information hack, or a physical (terrorist) attack. Nature can create a crisis: earthquake, flood, fire, or weather-related power outages. Crisis can occur unpredictably, although some savvy expert or vigilant manager should usually have known that such an event or outcome could occur.

Crisis magnitude can range from a bad-news day to events that linger in societal memory for decades. Often, we think of crises as negative events, but they can also result in positive outcomes—as a rationale and motive for change management, based on lessons learned toward achieving renewal. Crisis offers threat and opportunity. It can result from allegations brought against an organization, correctly or falsely. It can demonstrate that an organization is stupidly bumbling, that it deserves to be criticized or even condemned.

Clear and factual communication can set the record straight and put a crisis to bed. It can harm competitive advantage and motivate political battles. It can result from differences of opinion regarding what activities fail to meet CSR standards. It can demonstrate that an organization failed to act in the public interest. Crisis management and communication can be a partner to emergency management. We can even imagine, particularly in a political sense, how organizations (and politicians) might manufacture "crisis" so that they can respond and solve a problem as part of a demonstration of their efficacy and societal value. Thus, nations go to war in response to "crisis" by "wagging the dog."

Often, crisis is too narrowly seen from the limited view of its impact on a focal organization—a managerial bias (Waymer & Heath, 2007). Theory, research, and practice should never ignore the impact a crisis has on people, other organizations, and even the environment.

Conceptually, crisis is likely to have three stages: pre-crisis, crisis event, and post-crisis. Pre-crisis communication can prepare people for and even avert a crisis; the impact can be minimized and mitigated through planning and preparation. The crisis event is the period when the crisis receives spotlighted attention. Post-crisis is tough to define. As already noted, the Daiichi Plant may still be in crisis years after the "event" occurred. The glare of the spotlight has lessened, but impact continues to ripple out into the community. The post-crisis period can become a narrative for public awareness, prevention, and lessons learned, in order to cope with another, similar event in the future.

Want a definition of crisis? Look around and you will find dozens. Emphasizing how a crisis is a risk manifested, Coombs (2007) observes that a crisis is "a sudden and unexpected event that threatens to disrupt an organization's operations and poses both a financial and a reputational threat" (p. 164). Crisis management is those "factors designed to combat crises and to lessen the actual damaged inflicted" (Coombs, 2010, p. 20). In this way, Coombs emphasizes one of the major truisms of this discipline: the best-managed crisis is the one prevented, the one that does not happen. That principle emphasizes the importance of vigilant proaction. Sound and responsible management practices are the best "defense" against crisis; the best option for crisis mitigation and response. "Crisis communication can be defined broadly as the collection, processing, and dissemination of information required to address a crisis situation" (Coombs, 2010, p. 20).

Seeger, Sellnow, and Ulmer (2010) add important dimensions to the understanding of crisis. Often, crisis response is seen as restoring the *status quo*—for instance, repairing an organization's image or reputation. That may be, but responses will be incomplete without change management; renewal is a best-case outcome of crisis. In their analysis, including emphasis on chaos as a human condition, Seeger et al. find "Renewal argues that communication processes are central to framing a prospective vision for how organizations may be reconstituted following a crisis" (p. 496).

Crisis can damage an organization's reputation. It can harm and even kill. For that reason, it is best to think broadly in order to understand the breadth of crisis, the dimensionality of harm, and the rich texts that readily or stubbornly enlighten publics regarding some condition or event.

One of the earliest developed theories was *corporate apologia as crisis communication*, a predominantly rhetorical approach (Coombs, 2009). This was founded on the classic rhetorical device, *apologia*. As Hearit (2006) observes, *apologia* reflects "the many ways individuals, organizations, and institutions try to 'save face' as they seek to extricate themselves from difficult straights" (p. vii). As such, "crisis researchers are wise to pay particularly close attention to the language used by those who would extricate themselves from their wrongdoing—try to uncover the lexicon of the lie" (p. vii). Message-centric approaches can presume that clever wording solves problems. *Apologia,* however rhetorically and ethically sound, does not preclude that lies and similar strategies do not occur during efforts to repair reputation. Persons well-grounded in rhetorical theory presume that public arenas become places where truth triumphs over lies.

Contrary to what some imagine to be the rhetorical approach, those schooled in rhetoric simply do not believe that public relations practitioners, using words carefully chosen, can with their magic wand make a reputation problem disappear or change shape. Hearit (2006), for that reason, advises us to realize that most crises are not the result of the effort of an external "psychopath," but are caused by a screw-up on the part of a responsible organization.

Hearit (2006) cautions against confusing *apologia* with apology. *Apologia* is a form of discourse that ancient Greeks and Romans explained as speech of defense. It is a traditional response to a rhetorical problem. "Apology is a newer term that, conversely, has just the opposite connotation." As Hearit has it, "*apologia* is a broad term that means to respond to organizational criticism by offering a vigorous and compelling defense" (p. 4; italics in the original). At heart, such defense can focus on the accuracy of criticism and on the rightness of an organization's policy and managerial character. It can address the failures, mistakes, false assumptions, and ill-conceived behaviors that led to crisis. As a means for defense, *apologia* is valuable to image, an organization's reputation and legitimacy, and "the degree to which corporate activities are congruent with the values of the social system in which they operate" (p. 12).

Out of this logic has grown various rhetorical topoi, or standardized, scripted responses, which Hearit (2006) illustrates as follows:

"We didn't do it."
"Counterattack"
"It's really not our fault."
"We promise not to do it again."
"Talk to our lawyers."

The response taxonomy that developed out of *apologia* includes strategies of denial, counterattack, differentiation, apology, and legal defense.

As we think about the Fukushima case, we should note that apology is vital to Japanese culture. It is both sincere and ritualistic. However, if a crisis is due to technical or management misjudgment, change is the only correction that can end it, especially when there is no doubt as to why it occurred. If a crisis account points to design flaws and operational errors, management is ultimately responsible for making corrections.

Apologia can be criticized for a managerial bias that focuses attention on the organization (its reputation) in the hot seat, and not on the publics affected by misjudgment. Those persons harmed or offended by corporate actions deserve sincere contrition, compensation, and corrective actions.

A second organization-centric approach, image restoration theory (IRT), was developed by William L. Benoit (1995). This approach presumes that wise strategic choices in messaging can restore or enhance a reputation as the outcome of crisis response. A crisis triggers a defense of an organization's reputation. Response options include denial, evasion of responsibility, reduction of the offensiveness of the event, and corrective action. The strategy is to select the one that will provide the most crisis defense, including asserting that the organization did not actually produce the alleged event—some other entity created it; it was not as serious as is asserted. If these options fail, mortification is available.

Thus, denial can shift blame. Responsibility can be evaded by employing several substrategies, including arguing that the offense resulted when the organization responded to provocation. Another option is to argue that insufficient information prevented management from fully assessing what actions were needed to avoid crisis. Blame can be shifted by advocating that the offense was accidental or the unfortunate result of good intentions leading to a bad but unintended outcome.

Offense can be reduced, IRT reasons, by bolstering the organization's reputation by highlighting the good it has done in the past (reputational CSR). The impact of the crisis can be minimized by pointing out how the allegation of offense is overblown. Other response strategies include differentiating the current act from other, similar ones. Transcendence advocates that a different interpretation of the act results in its more favorable/less unfavorable evaluation. Offense can be reduced by challenging those who claim a crisis exists or by compensation—giving something of value to assuage the perception of damage. Engaging in corrective actions (lessons learned) can reduce the likelihood of subsequent offense and further damage. Corrections should include the promise to change and improve, as well as to put into place policies that prevent crisis recurrence. The final option, mortification, entails asking forgiveness, admitting guilt, and expressing regret.

IRT assumes that each kind of crisis poses distinct rhetorical problems that require appropriate rhetorical responses. The challenge facing the crisis communicator is to know which responses are ethical and effective to end the crisis and restore the organization's reputation. Such theory presumes that careful, ethical, and strategic responses do little to address the consequences of an offense. For that reason, the strategies in part or in sum can fail to restore reputation or rebuild the relationship between the organization and its stakeholders.

The Fukushima case is relevant to this analysis. Crisis theory should consider how vigilant and cautious a nation, government, or industry needs to be in the face of disaster. As will be addressed in the next section, planning to predict, respond to, and protect interests in the event of a catastrophe is not easy. For instance, the 2011 earthquake's magnitude was extraordinary, as was the tsunami that followed. Together, they damaged a lot of property and human life. The engineering design and operation of the nuclear facility were insufficient to withstand their impact. Thus, one option would be to explain why this was the case and apologize by blaming nature rather than committing to higher operating and response standards at nuclear generating facilities. Such efforts are often confronted with an extraordinarily low probably event, despite its high consequence. As will be addressed below, risk management and communication rest on the logic of contestable standards of how safe is safe enough (Fischhoff, Slovic, Lichtenstein, Read, & Combs, 1978), as well as how fair is safe (Rayner & Cantor, 1987). By this logic, we highlight the interconnections between issues management and crisis and risk management and communication. The most ethical crisis response presumes that sound science must drive planning and operation, as well as help inform the cultural norms regarding ethical risk management.

Apologia is the strategy of defense. As the Fukushima crisis started and continued, spokespersons explained why the catastrophe had occurred and how stopping the leaks of radioactive materials was difficult. Statements emphasized the heroism of plant emergency-response personnel. But these IRT strategies were inadequate to address the magnitude of the crisis, its far-reaching damage, and the challenges of restoring the community and rebuilding the company's (and the industry's) reputation. A strategic messaging approach presumes that for every crisis, one or more response option is situationally relevant and capable of advocating a position that assuages offended parties. As such, IRT presumes that communication can override management misjudgment and key publics' feelings that their interests have been offended or trivialized. IRT may thus be too concerned with the interests of the offending organization and not fully capable of embracing community interests. Rhetorical and critical approaches to public relations recognize the limitations of standard response options that do not make matters right.

A third paradigm of crisis communication features the *rhetoric of renewal* (Seeger, Sellnow, & Ulmer, 2003; Seeger et al. 2010; Ulmer, Sellnow, & Seeger, 2006). Its molar concepts are uncertainty, chaos, and renewal. These concepts are relevant to risk management and therefore firmly connect crisis and risk. The key theme of the rhetoric of renewal is that a crisis is not over until "renewal" is achieved. It reflects these conditions as definitional: "a crisis may be defined as a specific, unexpected, non-routine event or series of events that creates high levels of uncertainty and a significant or perceived threat to high priority goals" (Sellnow & Seeger, 2013, p. 7). It emphasizes how crisis is more than a bad news day, threatening to publics, and conceptually attached to risk manifestation.

This theory has been developed and examined by using case studies of industrial fires, foodborne health and safety issues, and recurring floods. The research includes pre-crisis efforts such as emergency preparations and strategies to protect the integrity of the mass-production/mass-consumption foodstream. Its hallmark is post-crisis response, especially the need for lessons leading not to *status quo* restoration, but to renewal. Using uncertainty and chaos to inform the theory, the team argues that effective pre-crisis planning and communication and effective post-crisis efforts mitigate the impact of crisis events on an organization—and the victims (those actually or nearly harmed by the crisis events).

This theory features crisis response as depending on ethical (CSR) standards that the organization knew, understood, and used to guide its practices prior to the crisis. It emphasizes the quality of relationships between the focal organization, other participants in the crisis, and the victims. Was a collaborative and transparent planning/implementation effort in place before the crisis? Was the organization willing to shoulder rather than avoid or shift blame? Was the organization (or complex of organizations) able to engage in effective and ethical crisis communication at all stages of the event: pre-crisis, crisis event, and post-crisis (Ulmer et al., 2006)? Did the crisis discourse produce a compelling narrative? "Crisis creates a narrative space, a communication vacuum, or a meaning deficit that will be filled by stories told by those who experienced the crisis, crisis managers, journalists, and observers" (Seeger & Sellnow, 2016, p. 13). How the gaps in crisis narratives get filled is a daunting challenge for crisis managers and communicators (Heath, 2004).

This theory reasons that the cause of crisis is failed assessment of risk that allows uncertainty and chaos to overwhelm sound planning. It argues that strong, collaborative relationships foster community-wide, responsive communication and planning. Renewal through planned change management and effective communication can reduce the impact of a crisis and mitigate or prevent its recurrence. Key to this theme is that renewal cannot—typically—be achieved merely through communication. Crisis response as renewal requires careful attention to sound, reflective, and responsive changes in management policy and procedure, as well as improved communication.

One major contribution of renewal theory is that it focuses less on organizational reputation compared to other theories. Reputation may be harmed; credibility may be damaged. But restoration depends on agentic renewal, as Ulmer et al. (2009) summarize:

The discourse of renewal provides a different perspective to crisis communication than is presently examined in the research on Corporate Apologia, Image Restoration Theory, or Situational Communication Theory. Rather than protecting or repairing the image of the organization following a crisis, the discourse of renewal emphasizes learning from the crisis, ethical communication, communication that is prospective in nature, and effective organizational rhetoric. (p. 308).

This theory is forward looking. Ethical change is its hallmark.

A fourth approach to crisis communication is *situational communication theory*. Advanced by the work of Coombs and Holladay (see, e.g., 2010), this theory, based on attribution theory, has matured to be called *situational crisis communication theory (SCCT)*. Its attributional foundations have produced many themes that are valuable to crisis analysis. One is this, as it features the crisis management response employing recall: "The perception of the recall as socially responsible has the clearest application to communication" (Coombs, 2010, p. 38). Attribution theory has a long history in the research of psychologists who try to solve the puzzle of how humans come to know one another and deal with the uncertainty of not knowing—including efforts to reduce it—as a foundation for interpersonal communication and relationship development and dissolution.

Development of SCCT began in the mid-1990s. According to Coombs (2010), "The premise was very simple: crises are negative events, stakeholders will make attributions about crisis responsibility, and those attributions will affect how stakeholders interact with the organization in crisis" (p. 38). Thus, SCCT is audience-centered, focusing on their reactions to a variety of crisis strategic responses—the types of statements that affect their attributions regarding an organization's managerial reputation. It explains how audiences respond to what organizations did and said, do and say.

The theory presumes that "the nature of the crisis situation shapes audience perceptions and attributions" (Coombs, 2010, p. 38). In keeping with this reasoning, it features a two-step process. "The initial step is to determine the frame stakeholders are using to categorize the process" (p. 39). Understanding and researching crisis types advances its theoretical insights: (a) attributing the organization as victim (low crisis responsibility/threat); (b) attributing the event as accident (minimal crisis responsibility/threat); and (c) intentional (strong crisis responsibility/threat). By applying these attributed responsibility/threat frames, audiences respond predictably in ways that pose varying degrees of harm to the organization's reputation.

The second step depends on how attributions are affected by two intensifying factors: crisis history and prior reputation. Here, reputation is not so much the target of protection as likely to lead the perceiving audience to assess whether the organization is victim, the event is accidental, or management choices led to malfeasance. Attributions are likely to be different if audiences perceive a company to have a good crisis history rather than to be crisis-prone. They will depend on whether it is known/perceived to be responsible and responsive rather than characteristically dismissive, constantly shifting or placing blame, and unempathetic toward victims' interests.

Attributions made in these stages relate to behavioral intentions by audiences who witness and judge a crisis. If an organization has a good crisis history and a reputation for being responsive and empathic to those affected by a crisis, the audienc is likely to have favorable rather than unfavorable intentions. Positive attributions result in behavioral intentions (and behaviors) of support, forgiving, and hope for successful crisis resolution. Bad companies suffer the opposite response; audiences may long for them to go out of business and for C-suite culprits to go to jail: "They got what they deserved." Audience response will be different if a good company is ruthlessly attacked than if a whistleblower outs a bad company.

The theory can guide practitioners' response to crisis. For instance, "Expression of concern or sympathy, basic information on the crisis event, and any corrective actions to prevent a repeat of the crisis would qualify as adjusting information" (Coombs, 2010, p. 40). By this analysis, SCCT suggests three crisis response options: deny, diminish, or rebuild—plus the supplemental activity of reinforcing. "Reinforcing strategies try to add positive information about the organization by praising others (ingratiation) and/or by reminding people of past good works by the organization (bolstering)" (p. 41). By this reasoning, organizations that are more accommodating of publics who are affected by a crisis receive better attributional frames and better behavioral intentions than would result from lower levels of accommodation.

With reasoning such as this, SCCT is linked to best practices of organizational rhetoric (Coombs, 2009) and to contingency theory (Coombs, 2010). The link between contingency theory and SCCT features the ameliorative and mitigating effects of accommodation. Rhetorical theory features the logic of adjusting people to ideas and ideas to people—a rhetorical strategy popularized by Bryant (1953). For related discussions of contingency theory and rhetorical theory, see Chapters 4 and 5.

Narrative theory supports SCCT's attributional and response predictions. For instance, the child who falls without being warned may be comforted differently than that who falls after careful warning. "Oh, I'm so sorry" and "See what you get when you don't listen" scripts are amply available for crises. How a community's narrative regarding a crisis evolves and becomes "final" depends on different narrative frames employed by different publics. *Apologia* and IRT, by that reasoning, may overattribute how well stock responses can be employed universally toward a positive outcome in the presence of different publics. Companies and other organizations are accountable for their ability to know and implement appropriate narrative content that aligns their relationships and interests with those of their stakeholders (Heath, 2004).

As this section ends, the theories discussed shed light on the Fukushima crisis. Recall its three crisis focal points: earthquake, tsunami, and nuclear facility disaster. They are interconnected narratively. Several organizations are accountable, as are emergency communication (prior to, during, and after the event) and the technical response (during and after the event).

The event's magnitude and nature quickly made it a level of crisis where standard approaches were inadequate. A bad-news-day crisis is likely to be more manageable using *apologia* and IRT than one as extreme and complex as Fukushima. The event and the damage could not be denied. Natural causes could be blamed, but in our modern society, operational safety should be driven by science and technology; facility design and emergency response are supposed to understand and mitigate the forces of nature. So, even though the causes were "natural," this did not excuse the authorities who planned for, initiated the response to, and oversaw the crisis itself. The same rhetorical problem is also true for the BP case discussed in Chapter 5. Officials from the government and from the power company operating the nuclear facility apologized to community members. But China blasted Japan for not apologizing for failing to keep near-neighbors fully apprised of the dangers related to the release of radiation.

Renewal, driven by issues debates, offers positive recovery. One issue in this regard is the design standards of nuclear facilities. These break broadly into two topic areas, each of which is subject to technical, scientific, and community standards of safety debate. What preventative design and emergency response plans are necessary to prevent or mitigate a recurrent event? Relevant to the issue is the probability (a risk concept) that a similar event will occur—this only becomes greater with the rising water level due to climate change. Relevant as well is the issues debate in other countries (as well as within Japan) about the role of nuclear power, the safe design and operation of facilities, and the efficacy of emergency responses. Renewal is inevitable. Still, it is fortunate that a country and society so experienced with nuclear power and earthquakes led this issue debate. Its expertise increases the likelihood that community and technical efficacy will drive the renewal effort (Heath, Lee, & Ni, 2009; Roberto, Goodall, & Witte, 2009).

Attributions soon appeared, which were population- or culture-specific. Not everyone saw the event in the same way, or judged it with a single evaluative, attributional frame. If crisis history counts, perhaps no country is better prepared than Japan to understand and recover from such an event. However, the nuclear facility operators' credibility was strained because, in the view of the public, many response and recovery strategies had failed. Community patience frayed as technical efficacy seemed to fail the society.

Denial counted for naught. The strategy of diminishing had potential efficacy given scientists' understanding of the effects of radiation and their ability to treat as well as abate its effects. But the process took a long time, and the scientists' efficacy was sorely tested. Empathy and concern were voiced by the industry and by government. Reinforcing and renewal strategies were employed. These were interpreted, and behavioral intentions were generated, by people with high self-efficacy and high community efficacy to strengthen a resilient society.

Risk Management and Communication

Discussion of the Fukushima crisis highlights how the risk communication regarding that facility connected with the Three Mile Island nuclear event in the United States and the Chernobyl Plant in the Ukraine. This case illustrates the issue of how nations use energy to strengthen their economies and enrich their citizens' lives.

Risk communication and management studies and practices in the past 60 years grew out of what has become an increasingly technical and possibly more dangerous society (Palenchar, 2009). Even so, risk studies and mitigation/response practices are as old as human civilization. Risk communication, in human history, began when the first parent said, "I told you not to do that or you would hurt yourself." Risk is the harmful or beneficial consequence of actions and events whose occurrence and outcome magnitude is uncertain but consequential.

Wars, plagues, and natural disasters are timeless aspects of the human condition. Risk management and communication defines the response efficacy of societies. As a paradigm, that society which organizes best for the collective management of risk is most resilient and efficacious. Persons in societies that best manage risks survive/thrive proportionally better than do their less capable risk competitors. Reasoning of this sort has been supported by anthropology studies by Mary Douglas (1992) and the critical analysis of modern society by Ulrich Beck (1992, 1999).

Risks can occur naturally, as in the case of earthquakes and tsunamis, brush fires and tornadoes. They can result from human actions, as in the case of nuclear weaponry, nuclear power, chemical manufacturing, food safety, epidemics, and careless campers. They can result because of actions by others, such as identity thieves and manufacturers of harmful products.

Entities that create risk are called risk generators; what they do affects risk bearers. Those who intervene between risk generators and risk bearers are risk arbiters and risk mitigators. Dramaturgically, Palmlund (1992, 2009) defined the players in risk infrastructures as risk bearers, risk bearers' advocates, risk generators, risk researchers, risk arbiters, and risk informers. This analysis emphasizes risk bearers' interests (health, safety, and well being). The central question is to what degree the personae in the social risk drama work to understand, manage, and mitigate damage and fairly distribute the harms/benefits of risk.

Other risks occur because of people's personal choices, such as incautious sexual activity or the consumption of unhealthy foods. Use of tobacco and alcohol produces risks to their consumers as well as to others—as in the case of drunk driving and secondary smoke exposure. Personal risk includes driving while texting, but the driver is not only a personal risk generator, but also one who affects others—risk bearers. The list of interdependent risk roles goes on and on.

Culture as the normative for community and society is an essential problematic. Understanding the ways that societies create and operate through infrastructures to generate information helps risk mitigators evaluate that information and use it to create and implement risk management/mitigation policies, programs, and measures. Assessment of risks require sound science to understand their types, magnitudes, likelihoods of occurrence, causes and effects, mitigators, and bearers. Critical philosophy and sociology address the normative distribution of risk/reward ratios. To put it simply, the logics of risk assessment and management focus on knowing how safe is safe and determining whether risk reward, impact, and mitigation are unfairly distributed among the members of society (Fischhoff et al., 1978; Rayner & Cantor, 1987).

Four paradigms have emerged in the discussion, research, and practice of risk management and communication. One features sound science: the *mental models approach (MMA)* (Fischhoff, 1995; Morgan et al., 2002). The MMA expects scientists to shoulder the challenge of getting the data correct and assessing them properly in order to understand and assess risks, determine the degree to which each stakeholder group agrees with their interpretation, and narrow the gap between what the scientists know and what lay publics believe. This approach presumes societal and individual cost–benefit rationale for risk understanding and assessment (Starr, 1972).

MMA advocates champion the paradigm of risk communication anchored by scientific conclusions that may not be known, understood, or accepted by key stakeholders. The objective of risk communication, according to the MMA, is to narrow the gap by bringing stakeholders to understand and accept the conclusions of sound science. Aside from the problems inherent in scientists communicating with nonscientists, an additional obstacle occurs when stakeholders receive too much data, which they find difficult to interpret and base decisions upon in meaningful ways (Hadden, 1989). The MMA also wrestles with the problematics of conflicting and inconclusive results and inconsistent findings.

The second paradigm builds on the anthropology of Mary Douglas (1992). Her colleagues and protégés have advanced the *cultural interpretation of risk* (Rayner, 1992, Tansey & Rayner, 2009), which has also become known as a *risk society approach* to managing risk (Beck, 1992, 1999). It reasons that those potentially (and actually) affected by risks are empowered to ask "whose science and whose scientists?" This critical question, broadly and fundamentally applied, leads to a clash of cultural (narrative) perspectives that challenges the primacy of sound science as the singular rubric of risk communication. In part, this approach worries that business or government becomes privileged to determine what risks exists and the level or probability of occurrence and impact that is acceptable—and who is harmed. Such critical decisions can result in unequal and unfair distributions of risk in ways that short circuit stakeholder participation on matters of risk science and norms. This approach has long been seen as a decline of deference to the traditional corporate and scientific power structures of society; it presumes that elites knowingly but unfairly interpret and manage risks in the public interest (Laird, 1989). As such, critical risk understanding and allocation is not only a scientific matter, but also a sociopolitical one defined by political economy.

The third paradigm, called a *sociopsychometric approach* to risk (Sjoberg, 2000; Slovic, 1979; Slovic, Fischhoff, & Lichtenstein, 1987), features the attributional heuristics—often idiosyncratically sensitive to demographics—that are used to understand and assess recurring and predictable patterns of risk perceptions. These attributions are often idiosyncratic and predictive of the behavioral intentions that result from stakeholders' judgments of risk, the magnitude of the risk impact, and the identities of risk bearers who suffer risk harms disproportionate to their benefits. For instance, risks that are perceptually associated with dreaded consequences and delayed effects (e.g., cancer resulting from long-term exposure to a carcinogen) tend to be less tolerated than those associated with familiar activities (e.g., driving/riding in a car). It matters, according to this perspective, whether the risk bearers are children versus a different demographic category. Childhood cancer is socioemotionally different than any cancer of the elderly.

The fourth paradigm, an *infrastructural approach* (Heath, Palenchar, & O'Hair, 2009; McComas, 2010; Renn, 1992, 2009; Renn et al., 1995), reasons that stakeholder engagement requires varying degrees of deliberation that occurs and is enacted within democratic decision-making infrastructures. Risk-based analyses and decisions require collaborative decision making through public participation. Such participation brings together risk generators, mitigators, arbiters, and bearers to assess risks and craft appropriate corporate and public policy measures. This can only occur through fair and transparent stakeholder engagement within infrastructures that exist in communities. It may entail measures that help risk bearers, as well as the entire community, to achieve higher levels of risk response efficacy.

This view of risk communication and management combines reflective management, trust, and pre-crisis communication to achieve community efficacy. Citizens need and want to know about the risks they encounter and the measures that experts and communities are taking to prepare them to respond appropriately. This paradigm emphasizes the importance of emergency management planning and implementation to increase public safety.

As high-risk industries (e.g., petrochemical manufacturing) that engage in reflective management increase community risk response efficacy, they increase the extent to which they are perceived to be legitimate and supported by community goodwill (Heath & Lee, 2016). Applying the logic of the protective action decision model (PADM) (Lindell & Perry, 2012; see also Lindell & Perry, 2004), Heath, Lee, Palenchar, and Lemon (2018) reported that over time, a high-risk community can develop emergency response protocols and effectively use a cartoon spokes-character (Wally Wise Guy, a turtle that would go into its shell when threatened) to convince residents that they should know how to (and be prepared to—behavioral intention) shelter in place once alerted that they are at risk, likely due to a chemical release. Over time, the spokes-character can "nudge" compliance with expert risk response recommendations (Heath, Lee, & Lemon, 2019). Other examples of risk communication narrative mascots include Smokey the Bear, Sparky the Dog, Vince and Larry the crash test dummies, and Red Panda.

This working together, often called risk democracy, is not only ethical, but also effective for solving risk problems (National Research Council, 1989). It accepts the problematic of chaos and uncertainty—the ability to predict risks through probabilistic judgment, assess their impact (in terms of both rewards and costs/harms), determine which risk bearers suffer the risk, and calculate the magnitude of the impact should the risk manifest. As such, one of the logics of this analysis is that crisis (think in terms of the Fukushima case) occurs when risk manifests.

Each day, companies are at various levels of risk for industrial failure that could harm various bearers (e.g., employees, neighbors, customers). The crisis history (track record of effective risk management) and reputation (ability to know, prevent, and mitigate risk) is a relevant line of analysis here. As industries fail to exhibit the willingness and ability to understand, manage, and mitigate risk impact, advocates call for public policy changes: regulation, legislation, and judicial review—the stuff of issues management.

The theory of risk management and communication will continue to grow and advance understanding of how to manage and communicate for public interest legitimacy. Such analysis will necessarily rely on scientific methodologies and insights. It will depend on principles of rhetoric, democracy, and culture—foundations for stakeholder participation. It derives insights from the sociopsychometric aspects of risk perception and judgment. It transpires in various kinds and qualities of infrastructures that are rhetorical, dialogic, and even distorted to foster some interests to the disadvantage of others. It requires understanding of macrosystems of communication as well as the dynamics of public/constituency engagement.

Being culturally sensitive, different perceptions of risk, the fairness of risk distribution, magnitude, and various kinds of efficacy exist. Broad concepts are fundamental to the discipline and ripe for public relations theory, research, and practice. Key among these variables are control (organizational, community, and individual), trust, uncertainty related to risk tolerance, cost–benefit ratios, proximity to risk/perception of being a risk bearer, transparency, knowledge (expert, societal, and individual), and support for and opposition to organizations (ones that create, manage, and mitigate risks). Knowledge is a function of what experts know and lay people believe. Decisions are variously complex, leading to discussions of decision heuristics such as the precautionary principle (Maguire & Ellis, 2009).

Risk communication, especially to motivate protective actions, is often more "asymmetric" than "symmetric." In many contexts (types of risks), people are provided advisory messages designed to guide their operation of cars and other equipment and prepare them for severe weather, toxic/hazardous releases, and such. However symmetrical such communication might be during program development deliberations, once the need arises, messages prescribe and recommend actions to reduce the harm of risks. Parents are advised to have their children immunized. Careful and ethical risk assessment and planning is crucial to the development of expert efficacy, community efficacy, and individual efficacy: the elements of a resilient community.

Ongoing Research

Developing the logic of PADM, Lindell and Perry (2012; also Lindell & Perry, 2004) reason that when people experience threat, they want to learn what to do to reduce it. They engage in cognitive decision making in order to know what actions others—especially experts—recommend. The PADM links environmental and social cues, pre-decision processes (attention, exposure, and comprehension), and risk–decision perceptions (threat, alternative protective actions, and stakeholder norms) to determine whether they predict the behavioral intention to engage in protective-action decision making.

Arvai, Gregory, and McDaniels (2001) examine the quality of public participation in support of managing environmental and technical risks. Their research emphasize the participative efficacy of value-focused communication in helping citizens use value-driven questions to engage in risk assessment and management. It supported the contention that value-focused decision making leads to more thoughtful and better-informed risk management decisions when citizens interact with experts.

Seeger and Sellnow (2016) reason that a narrative paradigm can productively be applied to crisis and risk communication, especially as it may culminate in renewal. Renewal occurs as lessons learned change the narrative from a dysfunctional set of assumptions and programs to a "new and improved" management philosophy and plan of action.

Veil and Bishop (2014) examine the infrastructural role public libraries can play in enhancing community resilience through risk communication and management. Libraries can provide space (rhetorical arena) and access to risk communication discourse and technologies. They can be a repository for community information and disaster narratives. Planning and funding can give public libraries the tools required for prevention, response, and recovery.

Conclusion

Public relations researchers and practitioners, whether for businesses, nonprofits (including NGOs), or governments, play crucial roles in the collective management of risk. They have vast opportunity through the understanding of crisis management and communication to prevent crises, lower their impact, and move quickly to resilient renewal. Effective public relations research and practice are vital to the safety, health, and well being of affected stakeseekers who seek the stakes of safe products and communities, for instance. This line of reasoning champions the socially responsible role of public relations in society. Such value is critically trivialized when professional practice and research privilege the interest of one organization or entity to the detriment or even through the manipulation of others.

Organizations use issues management as a means for adjusting to CSR standards. Standards result as many voices compete to create a playing field where legitimacy and CSR are co-created through discourse. However, crisis occurs when operations fail to proceed as planned and risks manifest themselves. Thus, operational safety supports the issue of each community's support or opposition to nuclear power; crisis raises doubt about the ability to construct and operate facilities safely. Violations damage or even destroy a company's relationship with citizens.

Chapter Summary

The end of this chapter offers the opportunity to look back and see what key themes were addressed and what vocabulary should guide and motivate theory development, as well as your practice of public relations.

The essential theme of this chapter is that the robust interconnection of issues management, crisis, and risk contributes to the practical and ethical practice of public relations and its ability to serve society.

Key Terms

Community Resilience: The available response efficacy (expert, community, and individual) that increases effective prevention, response, and recovery from risk and crisis.

Corporate Social Responsibility (CSR): Balancing values and practices regarding how and why organizations want to operate as they do within the boundaries of stakeholder expectations.

Dramaturgical (Narrative) Approach: The idea that narratives provide interpretative texts, roles, themes, actors, and such, which in combination can maximize reward and minimize harm.

Issue-Driven Strategic Business Planning: The idea that managements recognize, understand, and acknowledge issue position constraints on business planning and implementation.

Legitimacy: The license to operate, based on the assumption that organizations serve a community need; legitimacy gaps exist when management practices and operations fail to meet stakeholders' CSR expectations. Legitimacy is a threshold concept that focuses attention on the alignment of interests and values between organizations and stakeholders.

Power Resource Distribution (Management): Within a community, hard and soft resources exist that can be acquired and managed for the interest of the few or the mutual benefit of many. Organizations are resource-dependent.

> *Precautionary Principle:* The balancing point between being cautious regarding some risk ("look before you leap") and the benefits or harms that result from it ("the early bird gets the worm"). The challenge of precaution is to avoid unintended consequences but not miss opportunities of innovation and renewal.
>
> *Resource Management:* The dynamics of strategic efforts made by organizations, communities, and individuals to acquire and use the resources necessary for individual and collective agency.

Discussion Questions

1 What is an issue? Can it be managed, and can organizations' responses to it be managed?
2 What rationales and strategies are needed for effective issue monitoring?
3 What is CSR and what role does it play in organizations' legitimacy, the legitimacy gaps they encounter, and their ability to gain the resources they need?
4 What are the foundational elements of issue communication? Why is it inherently dialogic and rhetorical?
5 What is crisis?
6 What variables and predictions are central to *apologia* theory?
7 What variables and predictions are central to IRT?
8 How and what do crisis response and the rhetoric of renewal add to the literature and practice of public relations?
9 What are the variables and predictions that are explored and advanced by SCCT? Why is the theory of attribution vital to this theory?
10 What is the rationale for thinking of the agency of a society as the collective management of risk?
11 What are the four dominant paradigms characterizing risk management and communication? Are they complementary or contrary to one another?
12 How do the topics of issues, crisis, and risk add to and draw from excellence/situational theory, contingency theory, rhetorical theory, and critical theory?

References

Arvai, J. L., Gregory, R., & McDaniels, T. L. (2001). Testing a structured decision approach: Value-focused thinking for deliberative risk communication. *Risk Analysis, 21*, 1065–1076.

Beck, U. (1992). *Risk society: Towards a new modernity*. London: Sage.

Beck, U. (1999). *World risk society*. Cambridge: Polity Press.

Benoit, W. I. (1995). *Accounts, excuses, and apologies: A theory of image restoration*. Albany, NY: State University of New York Press.

Bryant, D. C. (1953). Rhetoric: Its function and its scope. *Quarterly Journal of Speech, 39*, 401–424.

Campbell, K. K. (1996). *The rhetorical act* (2nd ed.). Belmont, CA: Wadsworth.

Chase, W. H. (1977). Public issue management: The new science. *Public Relations Journal, 32*, 25–26.

Chase, W. H. (1982). Issue management conference: A special report. *Corporate Public Issues and Their Management, 7*, 1–2.

Chase, W. H. (1984). *Issue management: Origins of the future.* Stamford, CT: Issue Action Publications.

Coombs, W. T. (1999). *Ongoing crisis communication: Planning, managing and responding.* Thousand Oaks, CA: Sage.

Coombs, W. T. (2007). Protecting organization reputations during a crisis: The development and application of situational crisis communication theory. *Corporate Reputation Review, 10,* 163–176.

Coombs, W. T. (2009). Crisis, crisis communication, reputation, and rhetoric. In R. L. Heath, E. L. Toth, & D. Waymer (Eds.), *Rhetorical and critical approaches to public relations II* (pp. 237–252). New York: Routledge.

Coombs, W. T. (2010). Parameters of crisis communication. In W. T. Coombs & S. J. Holladay (Eds.), *The handbook of crisis communication* (pp. 17–53). Malden, MA: Wiley-Blackwell.

Coombs, W. T., & Holladay, S. J. (Eds.) (2010). *The handbook of crisis communication.* Malden, MA: Wiley-Blackwell.

Davis, G. F., & Thompson, T. A. (1994). A social movement perspective on corporate control. *Administrative Science Quarterly, 39,* 141–173.

de Bussy, N. (2005). Applying stakeholder thinking to public relations: An integrated approach to identifying relationships that matter. In B. van Ruler, A. T. Vercic, & D. Vercic (Eds.), *Public relations metrics: Research and evaluation* (pp. 282–300). New York: Routledge.

de Bussy, N. (2008). Stakeholder theory. In W. Donsbach (Ed.), *International encyclopedia of communication* (pp. 4815–4817). Malden, MA: Blackwell Publishing.

de Bussy, N. (2010). Dialogue as the basis for stakeholder engagement: Defining and measuring the core competencies. In R. L. Heath (Ed.), *SAGE handbook of public relations* (pp. 127–144). Thousand Oaks, CA: Sage.

Douglas, M. (1992). *Risk and blame.* London: Routledge.

Ewing, R. P. (1987). *Managing the new bottom line: Issues management for senior executives.* Homewood, IL: Dow Jones-Irwin.

Fink, S. (1986). *Crisis management: Planning for the inevitable.* New York: ANACOM.

Fischhoff, B. (1995). Risk perception and communication unplugged: Twenty years of process. *Risk Analysis, 15,* 137–145.

Fischhoff, B., Slovic, P., Lichtenstein, S., Read, S., & Combs, B. (1978). How safe is safe enough? A psychometric study of attitudes towards technological risks and benefits. *Policy Sciences, 8,* 127–152.

Frederick, W. C. (1986). Toward CSR3: Why ethical analysis is indispensable and unavoidable in corporate affairs. *California Management Review, 28,* 126–141.

Frederick, W. C., & Weber, J. (1990). The values of corporate managers and their critics: An empirical description and normative implications. In W. C. Frederick & L. E. Preston (Eds.), *Business ethics: Research issues and empirical studies* (pp. 123–144). Greenwich, CT: JAI.

Freeman, R. E. (1984). *Strategic management: A stakeholder approach.* Boston, MA: Pitman.

Freeman, R. E., & Gilbert, D. R., Jr. (1988). *Corporate strategy and the search for ethics.* Englewood Cliffs, NJ: Prentice Hall.

Freeman, R. E., Harrison, J. S., Wicks, A. C., Parmar, B. L., & de Colle, S. (2010). *Stakeholder theory: The state of the art.* Cambridge: Cambridge University Press.

Friedman, S. M., Dunwoody, S., & Rogers, C. L. (Eds.) (1999). *Communicating uncertainty: Media coverage of new and controversial science.* Mahwah, NJ: Lawrence Erlbaum Associates.

Golant, B. D., & Sillince, J. A. A. (2007). The constitution of organizational legitimacy: A narrative perspective. *Organization Studies, 28,* 1149–1167.

Hadden, S. G. (1989). Institutional barriers to risk communication. *Risk Analysis, 9,* 301–308.

Hearit, K. M. (2006). *Crisis management by apology: Corporate response to allegations of wrongdoing.* Mahwah, NJ: Lawrence Erlbaum Associates.

Heath, R. L. (2004). Telling a story: A narrative approach to communication during crisis. In D. P. Millar & R. L. Heath (Eds.), *Responding to crisis: A rhetorical approach to crisis communication* (pp. 167–188). Mahwah, NJ: Lawrence Erlbaum Associates.

Heath, R. L. (2006). A rhetorical theory approach to issues management. In C. Botan & V. Hazleton (Eds.), *Public relations theory II* (pp. 63–99). Mahwah, NJ: Lawrence Erlbaum Associates.

Heath, R. L. (2010). Stakeholder participation. In J. J. Cochran (Ed.), *Wiley encyclopedia of operations research and management science* (Vol. 7, pp. 5115–5123). Boston, MA: John Wiley & Sons.

Heath, R. L., & Cousino, K. R. (1990). Issues management: End of first decade progress report. *Public Relations Review, 17*, 6–18.

Heath, R. L., & Lee, J. (2016). Chemical manufacturing and refining industry legitimacy: Reflective management, trust, pre-crisis communication to achieve community efficacy. *Risk Analysis, 36*, 1108–1124.

Heath, R. L., Lee, J., & Lemon, L. (2019). Narratives of risk communication: Nudging community members to shelter-in-place. *Public Relations Review, 45*, 128–137.

Heath, R. L., Lee, J., & Ni, L. (2009). Crisis and risk approaches to emergency management planning and communication: The role of similarity and sensitivity. *Journal of Public Relations Research, 21*, 123–141.

Heath, R. L., Lee, J., Palenchar, M. J., & Lemon, L. (2018). Risk communication emergency response preparedness: Contextual assessment of the protective action decision model. *Risk Analysis, 38*, 333–344.

Heath, R. L., Motion, J., & Leitch, S. (2010). Power and public relations: Paradoxes and programmatic thoughts. In R. L. Heath (Ed.), *SAGE handbook of public relations* (pp. 191–204). Thousand Oaks, CA: Sage.

Heath, R. L., & Nelson, R. A. (1986). *Issues management: Corporate public policymaking in an information society.* Beverly Hills, CA: Sage.

Heath, R. L., & O'Hair, H. D. (Eds.) (2009). *Handbook of risk and crisis communication.* New York: Routledge.

Heath, R. L., & Palenchar, M. J. (2009). *Strategic issues management: Organizations and public policy challenges* (2nd ed.). Thousand Oaks, CA: Sage.

Heath, R. L., Palenchar, M. J., & O'Hair, H. D. (2009). Community building through risk communication infrastructure. In R. L. Heath & D. H. O'Hair (Eds.), *Handbook of risk and crisis communication* (pp. 474–490). New York: Routledge.

Herman, S. (2016). Problems keep piling up in Fukushima. *VOA News,* February 17. Available from https://www.voanews.com/a/problems-keep-piling-up-in-fukushima/3194401.html (accessed May 20, 2020).

Jacques, A. (2000). *Don't just stand there: The do-it plan for effective issue management.* Melbourne: Issue Outcomes.

Jaques, T. (2006). Activist "rules" and the convergence with issue management. *Journal of Communication Management, 10*, 407–420.

Jaques, T. (2010). Embedding issue management: From process to policy. In R. L. Heath (Ed.), *SAGE handbook of public relations* (pp. 435–546). Thousand Oaks, CA: Sage.

Jaques, T. (2014). *Issue and crisis management: Exploring issues, crises, risk and reputation.* Melbourne: Oxford University Press ANZ.

Kotler, P., & Lee, N. R. (2005). *Corporate social responsibility: Doing the most good for your company and your cause.* Hoboken, NJ: Wiley.

Krimsky, S., & Golding, D. (Eds.) (1992). *Social theories of risk.* Westport, CT: Praeger.

Laird, F. N. (1989). The decline of deference: The political context of risk communication. *Risk Analysis, 9*, 543–550.

Leitch, S., & Motion, J. (2010). Publics and public relations: Effecting change. In R. L. Heath (Ed.), *SAGE handbook of public relations* (pp. 99–110). Thousand Oaks, CA: Sage.

Lindell, M. K., & Perry, R. W. (2004). *Communicating environmental risk in multiethnic communities.* Thousand Oaks, CA: Sage.

Lindell, M. K., & Perry, R. W. (2012). The protective action decision model: Theoretical modifications and additional evidence. *Risk Analysis, 32,* 616–632.

Maguire, S., & Ellis, J. (2009). The precautionary principle and risk communication. In R. L. Heath & H. D. O'Hair (Eds.), *Handbook of risk and crisis communication* (pp. 119–137). New York: Routledge.

McComas, K. A. (2010). Community engagement and risk management. In R. L. Heath (Ed.), *SAGE handbook of public relations* (pp. 461–476). Thousand Oaks, CA: Sage.

Morgan, M. G., Fischhoff, B., Bostrom, A., & Atman, C. J. (2002). *Risk communication: A mental models approach.* Cambridge: Cambridge University Press.

National Research Council. (1989). *Improving risk communication.* Washington, D.C.: National Academic Press.

Palenchar, M. J. (2009). Historical trends of risk and crisis communication. In R. L. Heath & H. D. O'Hair (Eds.), *Handbook of risk and crisis communication* (pp. 31–52). New York: Routledge.

Palmlund, I. (1992). Social drama and risk evaluation. In S. Krimsky & D. Golding (Eds.), *Social theories of risk* (pp. 197–212). Westport, CT: Praeger.

Palmlund, I. (2009). Risk and social dramaturgy. In R. L. Heath & H. D. O'Hair (Eds.), *Handbook of risk and crisis communication* (pp. 192–204). New York: Routledge.

Post, J. E., Preston, L. E., & Sachs, S. (2002). *Redefining the corporation: Stakeholder management and organizational wealth.* Stanford, CA: Stanford Business Books.

Public Affairs Council. (n.d.). Issues management. Available from http://pac.org/issues_management (accessed May 20, 2020).

Rayner, S. (1992). Cultural theory and risk analysis. In S. Krimsky & D. Golding (Eds.), *Social theories of risk* (pp. 83–115). Westport, CT: Praeger.

Rayner, S., & Cantor, R. (1987). How fair is safe enough? The cultural approach to technology choice. *Risk Analysis, 7,* 3–9.

Renfro, W. L. (1993). *Issues management in strategic planning.* Westport, CT: Quorum.

Renn, O. (1992). Concepts of risk: A classification. In S. Krimsky & D. Golding (Eds.), *Social theories of risk* (pp. 53–79). Westport, CT: Praeger.

Renn, O. (2009). Risk communication: Insights and requirements for designing successful communication programs on health and environmental hazards. In R. L. Heath & H. D. O'Hair (Eds.), *Handbook of risk and crisis communication* (pp. 80–98). New York: Routledge.

Renn, O., Webler, T., & Wiedemann, P. (Eds.) (1995). *Fairness and competence in citizen participation.* Dordrecht: Kluwer Academic.

Roberto, A. J., Goodall, C. E., & Witte, K. (2009). Raising the alarm and calming fears: Perceived threat and efficacy during risk and crisis. In R. L. Heath & H. D. O'Hair (Eds.), *Handbook of risk and crisis communication* (pp. 285–301). New York: Routledge.

Seeger, M. W., & Sellnow, T. L. (2016). *Narratives of crisis: Telling stories of ruin and renewal.* Stanford, CA: Stanford University Press.

Seeger, M. W., Sellnow, T. L., & Ulmer, R. R. (2003). *Communication and organizational crisis.* Westport, CT: Praeger.

Seeger, M. W., Sellnow, T. L., & Ulmer, R. R. (2010). Expanding the parameters of crisis communication: From chaos to renewal. In R. L. Heath (Ed.), *SAGE handbook of public relations* (pp. 177–190). Thousand Oaks, CA: Sage.

Sellnow, T. L., & Seeger, M. W. (2013). *Theorizing crisis communication.* Chichester: Wiley-Blackwell.

Sethi, S. P. (1977). *Advocacy advertising and large corporations: Social conflict, big business image, the news media, and public policy.* Lexington, MA: D. C. Heath.

Sjoberg, L. (2000). Factors in risk perception. *Risk Analysis, 20,* 1–11.

Slovic, P. (1979). Rating the risks. *Environment, 21,* 14–39.

Slovic, P., Fischhoff, B., & Lichtenstein, S. (1987). Behavioral decision theory perspectives on protective behavior. In N. D. Weinstein (Ed.), *Taking care: Understanding and encouraging self-protected behavior* (pp. 14–41). Cambridge: Cambridge University Press.

Smudde, P. M., & Courtright, J. L. (2010). Public relations and power. In R. L. Heath (Ed.), *SAGE handbook of public relations* (pp. 489–500). Thousand Oaks, CA: Sage.

Starr, C. (1972). Benefit–cost studies in sociotechnical systems. In National Research Council (Ed.),. In *Perspectives on benefit–risk decision making: Report of a colloquium* (pp. 17–42). Washington, D.C.: National Academies Press.

Tansey, J., & Rayner, S. (2009). Cultural theory and risk. In R. L. Heath & H. D. O'Hair (Eds.), *Handbook of risk and crisis communication* (pp. 53–79). New York: Routledge.

Ulmer, R. R., Sellnow, T. L., & Seeger, M. W. (2006). *Effective crisis communication: Moving from crisis to opportunity.* Thousand Oaks, CA: Sage.

Ulmer, R. R., Sellnow, T. L., & Seeger, M. W. (2009). Post-crisis communication and renewal: Understanding the potential for positive outcomes in crisis communication. In R. L. Heath & H. D. O'Hair (Eds.), *Handbook of risk and crisis communication* (pp. 302–322). New York: Routledge.

Veil, S. R., & Bishop, B. W. (2014). Opportunities and challenges for public libraries to enhance community resilience. *Risk Analysis, 34,* 721–734.

Wartick, S. L., & Mahon, J. F. (1994). Toward a substantive definition of the corporate issue construct: A review and synthesis of the literature. *Business and Society, 33,* 293–311.

Waymer, D., & Heath, R. L. (2007). Emergent agents: The forgotten publics in crisis communication and issues management research. *Journal of Applied Communication Research, 35,* 88–108.

8

Public Relations and Measurement Challenges

Introduction

This chapter brings together two of the key themes of public relations theory, research, and practice: (a) the role public relations plays in and on behalf of organizations and communities; and (b) how the impact of public relations can be measured—narrowly and broadly. In addressing matters relevant to measurement, it connects roles, strategies, programs, and theory-based predictions to measurable impacts or outcomes. The topics of role and impact, at whatever level of analysis, combine because measurement assumes that public relations can make a difference that can be measured. To that end, measurement also gives insights into the contextual challenges and constraints that call for public relations, affect its practice, and justify its societal value.

These points focus attention on the rationale and contexts for measurement. The reasons for measuring public relations impact can be either campaign-centric or strategic process-centric—the continuing efforts by public relations to adjust organizations to society. Campaigns tend to be functional and instrumental, highly pragmatic, and necessarily concerned about ethics. The assumption is that they are purposeful and outcome-driven, but so too is murder. The essential question is: Did a campaign achieve its goal? To that end, research may be used before a campaign to increase its likely impact. Excellence theorists caution against using research designed to gain outcomes in the name of self-interested pragmatism, or utilitarianism—the campaign outcomes will then continue that line of analysis.

The other rationale for measurement is that it is strategic and ongoing. It is not campaign-driven, but it might embrace various campaigns (or continuing strategic processes). This rationale focuses more on the long-term monitoring of opinions about and relevant to the strategic business planning of an organization, regardless of its type. Thus, oil and gas companies track public opinion on environmental issues, nonprofits monitor opinions on the arts, and government agencies monitor issues relevant to income and quality of life. The broad purpose is to be alert to and knowledgeable about issue trends that offer opportunities and pose obstacles.

Some professionals specialize in measurement. Organizations such as the Public Relations Society of America (n.d.) and the Institute for Public Relations (n.d.) provide resources, guidelines, protocols, and templates for successful and ethical measurement. These resources are not only comprehensive, but draw together top-line thinking by practitioners and academics. Today, major books are devoted to the topic, such as *A Practitioner's Guide to Public Relations Research, Measurement, and Evaluation*, by Donald W. Stacks and David Michaelson (2010; see also Stacks, 2011), and it is addressed in several entries in the *Encyclopedia of Public Relations*, second edition (Heath, 2013).

Public Relations Theory: Capabilities and Competencies, First Edition. Jae-Hwa Shin and Robert L. Heath.
© 2021 John Wiley & Sons, Inc. Published 2021 by John Wiley & Sons, Inc.

Pitches to clients often include discussions and explanations of how recommendations for professional services should and can lead to measurable outcomes. The question is frequently put in these simple terms: How can we move the needle? So, what's the needle, how can it be moved, how can that movement be measured, and is it ethical? Measuring ethics, as will be discussed in Chapter 9, adds another layer of assessment. The same question also occurs within companies when discussions of budgeting turn to how much funding the public relations department deserves. What financial and ethical value does it add to the organization?

These questions necessarily demand a definition of what public relations is and what it does. A publicity, promotion, reputation-building, and marketing-communication orientation has traditionally been the focus of measurement, including increased sales and even increased share value for publicly traded companies. Reputation can be measured in terms of attitude toward an organization, but it can also be extended as a measure of its corporate social performance (CSP). Community and employee relations have attitudinal and behavioral components. All of this becomes more complicated when we address the elements of shared meaning and operational legitimacy presumed by issues management, crisis, and risk. Relationship quality can be measured, but such measurement tends to be singular rather than multidimensional. What impact does a better reputation or stronger relationship have on various outcomes? So goes the challenge of measurement.

Measurement brings to mind the reality that definition, conceptualization, and theory are vital to understanding the discipline's strategic means, role, and impact. The extent to which it lacks a firm consensus regarding its definition and role on behalf of organizations and communities makes measurement difficult, even daunting—and perhaps ethically challenging. Legend has it that many public relations executives argue that what the discipline does cannot be measured. How then do they justify their budget requests? Sometimes, perhaps often, the fact that something does not happen is the mark of success—insofar as no crisis or controversy occurred. If theories do not agree on which themes and practices are most important and how they should be defined, then measurement will be imprecise, and perhaps impossible.

In the best of all worlds, measurement should build upon agreement regarding what public relations is, does, and produces. Even in that regard, while some theories and theorists downplay the importance of symbols and shared meaning, others feature these same concepts. Relationship and reputation are two broad lines of measurement analysis and purpose, but they too have ethical implications. And related disciplines plug away to define reputation, brand, identity, and image. A case in point is the large and growing body of work reflected in journals such as *Corporate Reputation Review*. Also, journals like *Corporate Communications: An International Journal* and others outside of communication like to address corporate social responsibility (CSR), with implications for marketing communication, reputation, and issues management.

Setting aside these theoretical challenges, it is safe to say as a starting point for this chapter that measurement is a simple topic to grasp, but fraught with complexities and tangles. Simply stated, measurement is an ordinary part of every person's life. Early on, children recognize the importance of key measures, especially those relevant to them: age, height, and weight. How old are you? How tall are you? How big are you? What grade are you in? People conceptualize and monitor their lives in terms of many such measures; age, wealth, attractiveness, likability, self-efficacy, morality, and ability are among the most common.

Measurement presumes some standard against which to assess some matter. Such assessment may be purely quantitative, but even that which is quantified can presume a qualitative difference. For instance, age is a measure of the length of time a person has lived. But there are milestones.

Children's ages are measured by the number of fingers they are taught to hold up; thus, they realize that more is "better." The ages of driving, drinking, and voting are important, as is the age of retirement.

Some people are "better" athletes than others. That can be measured through performance. Some run faster, score more points, and prevent their opponents from scoring. Who is more skilled?

Cooking/food channels remind us of the quantity and quality of ingredients. Viewers are told to what temperature to heat the oven and for how long they should cook their food. How far is it to work? What grade are you in at school? What's your GPA, SAT, GRE, GMAT? How much do you like studying public relations? How fast are you driving? How many miles per hour are legal when in a school zone? All of these matters entail measurements. Measurement is a routine, ordinary part of life.

Then, communication majors encounter "measurement" as part of their education and professional practice. Some are interested in their numbers of viewers, listeners, visitor hits, readers, users, followers, likes, and such. They may be interested in how many potential customers see their advertisements or how many friends share their posts.

However basic measurement is to communication, students and even practitioners often make the following statement: "I'm not good at math, so I'm in communication." Or, more self-efficaciously: "I'm good at communication, but not at math." Not only is "measurement" a concept meaningful to such statements, but they suggest that communication and math are opposed, even indifferent, to one another. They imply that the ability to write well, for instance, is unrelated to the ability to count and measure. However, the following theme is worth considering: One can't quantify one's abilities without empirical measurement, however crude. Agencies often tout total billings to demonstrate they are the agency of choice, for example.

Consider the following illustration. A recently graduated public relations professional has been asked to help prepare a public relations proposal. These are typical in agency work, and are prepared in response to a Request for a Proposal (RFP) by a prospective client. They allow the client to assess (measure) several features of the agency and its competence as it reviews proposals by different agencies. A similar logic exists when practitioners are asked to propose a public relations plan or program for management review and approval. The proposal is likely to state one or more objectives; these are derived from the RFP and are refined by the strategic thinking/best practices approaches of the agency/team. One objective might be to create awareness, another might be to increase understanding. Next, the proposal will address how awareness and understanding can be increased. What are the strategies, tactics, and tools the agency/team can bring to the project? Finally, the proposal is likely to feature measurement. How will awareness and understanding be measured?

This logic recalls the discussion in Chapter 2 regarding variables, concepts, and hypothesis testing. In this case, what is being tested is not a theory but a public relations plan, as part of the agency's ability to show what it can do, and how well (thereby justifying its proposed budget). This return-on-investment approach to management and strategic planning often catches newly graduated practitioners off guard. One can only imagine how common this sort of thinking is in the work of public relations practitioners. But public relations practice can be oriented to apply theory to solve problems that have measurable outcomes.

Measurement is also essential for research. As noted in Chapters 3–6, theory testing is a matter of measuring how and how well variables interact with one another. A quick review of research articles in leading journals such as *Public Relations Review* and the *Journal of Public Relations Research* suggests the kinds of hypotheses that are tested and the statistical measures used to assess the impact and interrelationship of different variables. What affects what? This is often a defining theme of social-scientific, positivistic research. Related to this topic, however, is the qualitative research typical of rhetorical and critical studies.

Measurement is vital to the practice of and research regarding public relations. For that reason, one can find agencies and even companies that explain how and what they measure. Professional associations such as the Institute for Public Relations create joint projects that bring academics and practitioners together to refine measurement protocols, strategies, tools, and valued outcomes. Some practitioners and agencies specialize in measurement, particularly in this era of big data and the ability (via statistical programs) to define an issue's prominence by the terms (and frequency of use) used in the strategic discourse around it (e.g., climate change).

With this foundation in mind, this chapter draws on the logics and protocols of measurement to justify and explain this process. It does so by looking at how various theories feature certain public relations challenges, offer advice on how to achieve valued outcomes, and thereby create a logic that brings best practices into a happy relationship with theory.

By the end of the chapter, readers should appreciate the principles of measurement, as well as its challenges. They should be aware of the liabilities involved in failing to measure. They should be convinced that any approach to measurement depends on which assumptions are made about public relations and the particular theory invoked to guide it. They should become alert to ethical considerations regarding what is measured, how, and to what ends.

Questions to Frame the Discussion of Measurement

- What is measurement, and how routine (and potentially complex) is it in daily life and professional practice?
- How does measurement relate to public relations theory, research, and best practices?
- Is the nature of measurement dependent on the kind of theory that is relevant to what is being measured and why?
- Is measurement contextual?
- Should measurement, however empirical, ever not include ethical assessment?

These questions should help students and practitioners be strategic in their thinking as they plan and execute public relations programs and philosophies. The discussion that follows is designed to make measurement a friendly and useful tool for students and practitioners who are math-averse, and even those who have been known to say, "What I do cannot be measured."

Key Themes

- Everything can be measured, but in different ways and for different reasons.
- Measurement is part of daily life.
- More commitment is made to measurement in professional practice than actually occurs.
- Measurement requires knowing what should be measured and how its measurement can be accomplished.
- Measurement depends on what needs to be known and understood, and how such understanding can be accomplished.
- Empirical measurement does not deny the need for ethical assessment.

Measurement Is as Measurement Does

In 1990, Walter K. Lindenmann observed, "Much has been written in recent years about the growing importance of research, measurement and evaluation in public relations" (p. 3). He wrote on this topic for years by combining practitioner and academic points of view. With Ph.D. in hand, he became Senior Vice President and Director of Research at Ketchum Public Relations in New York. That position helped him to see what had been done using what strategies to influence many opinions in a decade that witnessed a robust era in public relations research and measurement. Despite his sense that a lot was being said on measurement, he cautioned, "Yet, an examination of this literature does not give a clear picture of the full extent of how much research is being carried out by public relations practitioners, counselors, or academicians across this country" (p. 3).

This benchmark study added to and expanded what others had done or were doing to ascertain how popular measurement was at the time and how much of it was being conducted. Lindenmann observed that measurement was popular, but not widely conducted—especially with precision. Three-quarters of his national survey of public relations senior personnel revealed support for research and measurement. Less than a quarter disagreed with the statement that it was not well accepted as a necessary and "integral part of the planning, program development and evaluation process" (p. 5). Much assessment was casual and informal. The practitioners who participated in the survey believed that there was more lip service paid to research than was actually being conducted.

Lindenmann, like many others, preferred research that was methodologically and conceptually precise and therefore evaluatively utilitarian. The difference lies in knowing that, beyond just "I am driving fast in a school zone," your speedometer says exactly 32 miles an hour. If you don't know that precisely, the officer who writes you a ticket will provide an exact measure.

Measurement in Daily Life: Getting There on Time

To give measurement a friendlier feel, several *typical days* are featured throughout this chapter. The take away is that we all engage in measurement as part of our daily life, but we do not always realize how ordinary and routine it is or the constructive role it plays in our activities.

This section features several concepts, two of which are formative research and evaluative research. Formative research is used to understand some situation prior to undertaking some activity, including a public relations campaign or program. Evaluative research assesses whether goals were achieved, and why or why not.

Imagine that you and friends plan to drive approximately 300 miles to a major city for a concert. The concert is set to occur on a specific day and at a specific time. Being late would be a disappointment. Missing the concert entirely would be even more of a disappointment.

Is it reasonable that if you want to arrive at least 1 hour before the concert, you need to know the route you will take, the distance and travel time, and any factors that might affect your plan, such as the timing of meals, rest stops, traffic patterns, and parking congestion. This planning calls for *formative research.*

Such research might start with an examination of a map or route instructions, seeking the experiences of others who have made the trip, or logging into a navigation system. The point: Perhaps the group will decide to "wing it," but it is wise to have key details about the trip in order to increase the chances of being there at the desired time.

> During the trip, tracking and monitoring may occur. Perhaps the navigation system indicates how much longer the travel time and distance are. Perhaps someone checks the map and their watch, and calculates your progress. This requires assessing how far the group has traveled in how much time, and how far it has still to travel and how many hours remain until the concert.
>
> Because the planning was bad, the formative research inadequate, and the monitoring faulty, the group arrives two and a half hours late. Is it possible that evaluative research/measurement will occur as you figure out why the trip was a failure—and likely assign blame? Evaluative research is what occurs in order to measure outcomes and explain why they happened and for what reasons, including failure to meet goals.

Formative research is conducted prior to creating a program and used to guide its formulation and execution. Such efforts begin with the imagining or stating of one or more goals or objectives. A public relations goal might be to increase awareness of a product through publicity. It might be to provide information that a public wants in order to solve some problem. It might be to resolve a conflict, build a case that one policy position is better than another, or champion the identity of a population that seems to be marginalized by marketing or public policy discussion. It might be to build or repair a reputation. It might be to increase a community's sense of response efficacy in the face of a pending major storm. So, measurement always is contextually relevant to what needs to be known in order to be successful in accomplishing some goal.

For this reason, research can be—and often is—used to gain insights into what needs to be addressed in the development and execution of a public relations plan or program in order to achieve the desired or necessary objectives. This form of research is formative. *Formative research* entails the strategic application of a variety of tools in order to make decisions as the basis for developing and using public relations strategies. The counterpart of formative research is *evaluative research*, which is used—at intervals or after some campaign or program—to assess the efficacy of a public relations plan, tool, or tactic.

These broad concepts, when combined with measurement strategies, set the foundation for the systematic gathering of data in order to increase performance insight. For instance, the two types of research—formative and evaluative—can variously be used to track and monitor research. As a speedometer measures how fast a car is going, which may be formative or evaluative, it is also tracking and monitoring the "progress" of the driving. Another dimension, miles traveled, can be measured—tracked and monitored—by the odometer. And, eventually (or immediately, in many modern automobiles), miles per hour of travel (distance traveled divided by travel duration) and even miles per gallon can be determined evaluatively or monitored and tracked.

Thirty years ago, Lindenmann (1990) was able to report the good news that public relations measurement was becoming recognized as having substantial potential and benefit for practitioners (and academic researchers). Practitioners wanted to believe that measurement could be used to help them justify their employers' budgets and the worth of their consulting practices for clients. The bad news was "the acknowledgement by better than 9 out of every 10 PR professionals that research is still talked about much more in PR than it is actually being done" (p. 15).

Since that important study, many more articles, chapters, and books have discussed the importance of and methods for measurement. Advances in practice are driven by many factors. Some derive from the growth in theory. Theory helps practitioners understand what needs to be done in order to have successful public relations, and to document (formatively, evaluatively, and by tracking/monitoring) how well they are navigating the terrain on which they operate.

Pioneering research and measurement, Grunig (1983) advocated for the value of this tool, but he also realized—nearly a decade earlier than Lindenmann—that he was preaching to the choir. He mused, "Just as everyone is against sin, so most public relations people I talk to are for evaluation. People keep on sinning, however, and PR people continue not to do evaluation research" (p. 28). Much has changed since 1983. Measurement, theory, and research have become more interconnected, but one can imagine that the vision of these visionaries is still more on the horizon than they would have preferred.

As will be discussed in the next section, tools, techniques, and commitment continue to look toward and advocate—as well as guide—systematic, programmatic, and universal measurement.

Tools and Techniques

Rather than wandering in the dark, senior public relations practitioners have increasingly understood and appreciated the need to conduct measurement. They have learned to conduct and contract research as necessary. As such, tools and techniques are all important. Such tools might consist of complex surveys of employee, public, or stakeholder opinions, or they might be as simple as having citizens who attend a public hearing on environmental quality provide their responses to a few questions on a 3 × 5 card. This section features the tools and techniques useful for public relations measurement.

Measurement starts with a commitment to know what is being measured and the implications thereof. Measurement is more precise when the concepts and variables it makes use of enjoy a substantial amount of agreement or, ideally, consensus. Thus, public relations and measurement specialists should understand and share a sense of what public relations is, what it does, and what it requires. The implications of this will become more apparent in the sections that follow, in which discussion explicitly attaches measurement challenges to specific theories and strategies.

A survey by Judd (1990) found that practitioners make use of a number of different research techniques, including in-depth interviews, focus groups, formal clipping analysis, and public opinion surveys. Such tools seem to be driven by the recognized need on the part of companies and clients to understand the effectiveness of their programs. This understanding can increase the influence of a public relations department among management. Research is also important to help develop the knowledge base required for professional status. On this point, recall the discussion in Chapter 2 regarding how those in other professions bring research and theory to the table as they work to help increase organizational effectiveness and make societies more fully functioning.

Measurement in Daily Life: Knowing the Tools and Having Them Ready

Humans have developed many means of measuring all sorts of matters. There are numerous measuring instruments in a kitchen, as there are in a woodworker's shop.

In the earlier discussion of the trip to the concert, several tools were mentioned that are readily available for use by those who want to get "there" on time.

One can imagine having a map and a watch, and using the car's odometer and speedometer. Don't forget the gas gauge. More and more people are relying on navigation systems, whether built in to the car or downloaded to a cellphone. Other gauges might also help, such as the temperature gauge and the oil gauge, both of which monitor the car's "health." Travelers can also ask for directions, make corrections regarding previous directions, and discuss suggestions for alternative routes, especially if factors such as traffic and weather are affecting travel time.

Over the past several years, not only has the selection and use of measurement tools become more sophisticated, but so too has the purpose of measurement. DiStaso and Stacks (2010), for instance, note how accountability, transparency, and relationship quality have been added to the long and growing list of variables that humans like to measure. In addition to knowing what to measure, it is also important to know what tool to use in doing so. Over the years, public relations research "has shifted from the simple act of counting publicity materials to more sophisticated evaluations of public relations effectiveness" (p. 325).

Broadly, two categories of research protocols are available for measurement. One is qualitative, the other is quantitative. Qualitative research (especially relevant to rhetorical and critical theories) is guided by worldview themes. It might analyze the content of arguments on climate change, for instance, to determine whether conclusions are based on sound science or some other, less sound form of analysis. Such research tends to hold a template of preferred opinion or meaning up as a ruler to measure what is said and believed on some matter (recall the discussion of the mental models approach (MMA) to risk communication in Chapter 7). Case studies are a powerful form of qualitative research, for instance. Tools such as in-depth interviews and focus groups are important means for generating and assessing themes and their contents relevant to public relations. Qualitative research can even be conducted by applying the normative logics of the critical theory of public relations.

Some of the most important qualitative tools involve simply engaging in discussions with important publics and stakeholders, or reading the publications that they read. If they express opinions and issue-position preferences, knowing that and understanding why is crucial. Some critics of this method suggest that it is too "unscientific" to be useful. They also say that just because issue and opinion leaders hold positions, it does not mean their followers do as well. Making such critiques is likely to be folly, however.

Quantitative research depends on measures that are close-ended, forced choices. It relies on the ability to measure variables (e.g., attitudes) accurately and with such precision that numerical (statistical) analysis can be performed. Scales might, for instance, ask subjects/respondents to mark or state which number in a range (e.g., from 1 to 7) best represents their agreement/disagreement with each of a series of statements. This kind of research, measured numerically, ranges from reports of percentages to statistical analysis—some of which is extremely sophisticated.

Quantitative and qualitative research can be considered as opposites, and as qualitatively different. Some reason that the world is too complex, too chaotic, for the precise measures recommended by quantitative research. Others look at qualitative research as more of a hunch than sound social science. This battle will continue, but another way of looking at it is to realize that the two can be partners rather than enemies.

As practitioners are called upon to be problem solvers, counselors, and strategic thinkers, they should seek to use the most appropriate tool for each task at hand. Research to measure important aspects of public relations, like surgery, requires knowledge of the best, most appropriate strategy and tool for the purpose, and the competent and sophisticated use of the same.

Building toward the part of the chapter where specific public relations theories are brought into the discussion of measurement, we return to a topic raised in Chapter 2: the role of concepts and variables in strategic thinking. Here, the subject is how concepts and variables are foundational to measurement.

Variables and Concepts

This chapter is necessarily more suggestive than comprehensive in its treatment of measurement, public relations, and strategic and tactical problem solving. There is insufficient space here to discuss all aspects of the topic, which are considered more fully in many other venues. For instance, book-length discussions explain the operational connections between theory, concepts, variables, contexts, strategies, and forms of measurement and statistical analysis (e.g., Fawcett & Downs, 1986; Hocking, Stacks, & McDermott, 2003).

In this book, the purpose is to feature theory, and its contribution to ethical public relations—and to do so in a way that connects and justifies measurement as part of the puzzle. In keeping with this analysis, this section features the role of variables and concepts in the topic of measurement. Because of the need for brevity, it makes no pretense to discuss all those that are relevant to the topic. Previous chapters offer many of these, and set them in the context of different theories. Chapter 2 discussed them as the terms that support the development and measurement of theories. In fact, this entire book does not presume to be comprehensive. Each day, new concepts and variables are introduced into the discussion of public relations, and new connections are tested among these workhorses of theory. But once one understands the nature of concepts and variables and their relationships with one another, the world opens to continuing education on these matters.

Measurement in Daily Life: Knowing and Mastering the Variables

The story of our travelers to the concert continues. Elsewhere, variables relevant to that objective have been introduced. Relevant to the task are miles, miles per hour, miles per travel hour, hours traveled, hours remaining, distance traveled, and distance remaining. The weather introduces key variables relevant to road conditions: it might be dry, wet, slippery, or icy, or even have places where water is standing. Perhaps it is sunny, or foggy. Often, speed limits are affected by the time (night versus day). Different speed zones are typical. And traffic patterns are variable, as is the potentiality of encountering slow traffic because of an accident, a lost load from a truck, or some other obstacle to ordinary speeds.

Because different factors can affect the time of arrival, some concert goers might want to give themselves extra time in getting there, or even an extra day. How well the road is patrolled can slow traffic. How much of a risk taker the primary driver is can affect how much they are willing to drive in excess of the speed limit, and for how long.

Strategic performance operates in a matrix of multiple variables. All of these factors can affect whether the travelers will get there with time to spare, at the last minute—or not at all.

Best professional practices and sound theory supported by research build coherent approaches to professional practice by identifying variables and knowing how they affect one another, leading to successful and ethical outcomes—or not. That endeavor features the importance of cognition and perception. Measurement is a tool for understanding and assessing what people think, think about, and do—at least, plan to do—based on their thoughts, knowledge, attitudes, and decision-making and problem-solving skills. For that reason, the ability of a theory to guide practice—and provide the foundation for measurement—depends on its accuracy and comprehensiveness. If a theory has gaps, so will its advice and measurement.

Some variables are potentially universal to all contexts. Information is one. That core concept allows for measurement of how informed a population is on some matter, how badly/misinformed it might be, and how enduring or changeable is the use of certain information to draw conclusions. Information is a complex topic; so is information as a variable. Thus, to set a public relations goal of "sharing" information presumes lots of strategic options and measurement challenges.

As discussed in Chapter 3, for instance, situational theory uses three variables: desire for information, the ability to use that information to solve problems, and the ability to act in the face of constraint. Measurement of this theory focuses on how much and why people communicate: their problem recognition, level of involvement, and constraint recognition as a precursor to being active communicators who seek information and attend to it, as well as processing and sharing it.

Information and evaluation-based decision making are often modeled as KAB: knowledge creates attitudes, which motivate behavior. Is it possible that, situationally, the model is BAK: the desired behavior leads to the formulation or selection of the attitudes most likely to achieve it, and thus to the knowledge most likely to support those attitudes? Is this called rationalization? Also, tons of research suggest that modest, rather than robust, predictions can be made using KAB (Valente, Paredes, & Poppe, 1998). For instance, a buyer might "know" which product is best, but not buy it—perhaps it costs too much, perhaps it is sold at a store of which the buyer disapproves. A sales person might reinforce its sales appeal, or totally sink the deal: "I was really turned off by the clerk." And so it goes.

Relationship quality has been an important variable over the past 20–25 years. Strategically, is it an independent, mediating, or outcome/dependent variable? How much does the question depend on various contexts? Does the examination of relationships focus only on that between an organization and a public, or does it include those between different organizations and between different publics? If relationship quality is important, what makes a relationship a positive factor in public relations, rather than a negative factor? How should relationship quality be measured? That is a recurring measurement challenge. The topic of relationships and public relations is featured in Chapter 11.

What is a crisis? Is it serious, or merely a passing bad news day? Does an apparent benefit (or loss) affect a person's willingness to risk—to take a risk or make a risky decision? Does more key and relevant information affect the risk decision? Does the magnitude of the risk manifested—the number of people killed, for instance—affect the magnitude of the crisis that results? Is a minor leak from a pipe carrying crude oil of the same magnitude of crisis as the *Deepwater Horizon* blowout in the Gulf of Mexico—a crisis that haunts BP and the oil industry even today?

Reputation, image, and brand equity are key variables, especially for issues, crises, and risks. They can affect conflict management and public policy battles, as was mentioned in Chapter 7. Crisis can hurt reputation. Issues can grow into or from beliefs that one or more organizations are not legitimately committed to public health and environmental quality. Do organizations with better reputations weather crises—at least for a while—better than those with bad ones?

Discussions such as this, fraught with implications for strategic public relations, can go on and on. Such is the nature of the field, based on an understanding of variables and their interactions—and the implications of those interactions for desirable and ethical public relations outcomes.

As discussed in Chapter 2, variables are essential to strategic thinking and behavior, but they become more useful when driven by the sort of generalized thinking that is capable of theory. Theory makes the workhorse variables pull as a team, rather than being independent and uncoordinated. With that thought in mind, the next section engages in a closer discussion of the connections between measurement and theory.

Another key development in measurement is the recent emphasis on capabilities as a measure of public relations department, agency, and professional performance. Discussions of measurement tend to feature issues discussion, theme development, relationship quality, crisis impact, risk response impact, and such: measuring the opinions of publics and stakeholders/stakeseekers. Shifting focus to consider capabilities, a research team (Fawkes et al., 2018) identified some communication, organizational, and professional capabilities that are measurable and, when implemented ethically, increase an organization's ability to align strategies, purposes, and values. The detailed compilation of capabilities can be measured to assess individual, group, and company abilities to communicate proactively across a full range of platforms and technologies. Capabilities, appropriately implemented, can facilitate relationships, build trust, and enhance reputation with internal and external stakeholders and communities. Capability assessment supports the ability to serve as a valued counselor and trusted advisor, to offer organizational leadership, and to develop individual and group capabilities. One important capability is that needed to implement and use formative and evaluative research/measurement. What capabilities are needed, are they available, and can they be brought to bear ethically?

Theory and Best Practices

How measurement is conducted depends on the theoretical foundations at play. For instance, as emphasized in Chapter 2, some theories depend on the logics of variable analytical research. Recall how that chapter defined a variable: a concept that takes on different values. A variable is a concept that, because it changes, can be measured. Thus, a message can contain/convey a lot of or a little information. Chapters 3 (excellence) and 4 (contingency) discuss theories that depend heavily on well-defined and carefully measured variables, and on researchers' ability to measure the interactions between and among them.

So, one approach to measurement, as reflected in the theories featured in this book, is through variable analytic analysis. This approach translates into how those theories inform best practices. In short, one or more variables, given the conditions requiring public relations, can be predicted to affect various other variables, including outcomes. Thus, it can be argued that high-quality relationships lead to reduced criticism. Two measurable concepts in that statement are "high" and "reduced." Researchers can measure the interaction between relationships and criticism.

A second broad approach to measurement results from the discussion in the other two major theory chapters: Chapters 5 (rhetorical) and 6 (critical). These still discuss concepts (and variables), but they do so both in a more abstract qualitative way and in a manner less likely to result in precise measurement. Meaning and critical judgment and discourse processes and outcomes are essential measurement touch points. Chapters 5 and 6 feature ideas, co-created meaning, narratives, terministic frames, ethics, norms, and qualitative insights into different situations and ethical engagement.

The best parallel to ideas in terms of measurement is "public opinion," or the "opinions of various publics." Simply stated, Chapters 5 and 6 contend that public relations results from and leads to the creation of ideas than can agentically bend organizations to serve community interests rather than self-interests. Both chapters, at the societal level, reason that not one voice but many engage in creating, championing, and debating ideas. How ideas come about depends on the infrastructures of society, as well as on the strength of ideas as proposed. Such strength, according to constitutive theory, depends not only on what is said and how, but also on the interpretative frames of those who engage in the dialogue, affecting it and being affected by it.

By that reasoning, we can measure contests of fact: "Is global climate change occurring, and does human activity (including industry) affect it?" That is a quite global or macro-level question. They can get more specific: "Does business (or industry) X treat its customers fairly?" And, even more specifically: "Does business X treat me fairly?"

Relevant specifically to the themes explored in this current chapter, measurement can be either quite neutral or heavily evaluative, based on the terminology used to measure some matter. For instance, public opinion—the opinions held by some publics—judges "chemicals in the food stream" and "processed foods," and even "fat," as variously negative, neutral, or positive. Each of these terms can be measured for its impact, using agree/disagree measures, as issues communication debate/advocacy and even collaborative decision making relevant to industrial food processing. Fat in a scientific sense can be defined in neutral terms, but in discussions of food safety/health it may be loaded with positive/negative evaluation. Thus, even though the topics discussed in Chapter 7 do not depend heavily on precise measurement, they emphasize how shared meaning and aligned interest strengthen the quality of judgments, evaluations, and such—all of which translate into measurements of public opinion, self-interest, and public interest.

Measurement is contextual. This important principle must guide the explanation, application, and theoretical approaches to this topic. As expressions of context, at least three focal points for measurement have developed and become refined over the years, in many disciplines, including economics and sociology. Such analysis becomes more meaningful and precise if caution is given to each of several levels of measurement analysis: macro, micro, and meso.

A macro level would focus on the impact of the profession as a profession. Simply asked, does public relations have an impact on society? If so, what is that impact, and how strong is it? Micro-analysis is quite specific: it is the smallest unit of analysis. A macro-analysis—the highest or most general level of analysis—of climate change might include many levels of micro-analysis. Meso levels of analysis fit between macro and micro levels. They might be specific systems (part of macro systems and consisting of micro systems), such as species or types of fish living in water of different temperatures.

In terms of public relations, the concept of a fully functioning society focuses attention of society as a macro variable and supra system. It consists of meso-level clusters, such as types of business, single-issue nongovernmental organizations (NGOs), and governmental (also by level) agencies arranged by specific issues. Micro-analysis can include specific debates, their content, the data that support each position, and the professional integrity of various individuals and organizations engaged in the controversy. Such battles might turn on the differences between "global warming" and "human causes of climate change."

To apply both a multidimensional approach to measurement and a contextual one, the next four subsections integrate the discussion of measurement with the four major theories of public relations featured in this book (see Chapters 3–6). As such, theory can help inform measures applied to determine an organization's effectiveness—which can be agentically self-serving; it can also examine how well organizations, through public relations, make society more agentic. As will be examined in the following subsections, each of the theories focuses on different concepts and treats them in unique ways. This uniqueness leads to different formative and evaluative assessments.

Excellence Theory

Excellence theory features the theme that public relations can make organizations more excellent and that excellent organizations lead to excellent public relations and communication management. This theory further features the roles that public relations plays, the quality of the organizations in which it occurs and which it serves, and the qualitative impact of their relationships with publics. As excellence is the central theme, measurement features the conditions of excellence and the results or benefits of having excellent organization–public relationships (OPRs). It builds on the theme that people are problems solvers, that they join and share identity based on that reality, and that they communicate to solve problems. Publics want information; they want to be effective problem solvers. Thus, measures address the following questions:

- What roles do public relations professionals play in their organizations, or as consultants? Are they part of an organization's decision-making process? Can they bring to bear a range of options, from management planning to strategies, programs, tools, and tactics? Are they problem solvers and counselors or program implementers?

- Is the communication between an organization and its publics one-way or two-way, symmetrical or asymmetrical?
- What is the quality of an organization's relationship with its publics? Does the organization earn goodwill by how it adjusts to its publics? What changes in the nature of its OPRs would strengthen the linkages the organization needs for success?
- On important topics, what problems do publics recognize, how high is their level of involvement, and what constraints do they recognize regarding the solutions?
- As publics seek, use, and share information, what referent criteria do they use to solve problems? Are these criteria ones that have worked in the past? Are they appropriate and useful in solving the problem at hand? Are new criteria needed?
- How do levels of involvement, problem recognition, and constraint recognition affect the information publics want in order to solve problems and make decisions? How and what do they communicate among themselves under these circumstances?
- Are OPRs producing a positive reputation for the organization and supporting collaborative conflict resolution?

Given the explicit importance of OPRs to this theory, brief attention will be given here to how relationships can be measured. Such measures are important, as Kang and Yang (2010) demonstrated, in connecting OPR outcomes and elements of the persuasion model (see earlier): relationship quality interacts positively with awareness, attitude, and behavioral intention.

Huang (2001) applied OPR scales featuring control mutuality (agreement as to rightful and reciprocal influence), trust (willingness to rely on one's partner in vulnerable, uncertain circumstances), relational satisfaction (feeling favorable to one another), relational commitment (belief that the effort to maintain a relationship leads to rewards), and favor/face (an Eastern culture dimension: social benefits that one party pays to another, and are reciprocated).

Jo's (2006) study of a manufacturer–retailer relationship featured trust (credibility), commitment (enduring desire to maintain the relationships), satisfaction (distribution or rewards and responsibilities), control mutuality (rightful power to influence one another), face and favor (social dignity), and personal network (connecting networks that are satisfyingly unique and exclusive to those in the relationship).

Investigating situational crisis communication theory (SCCT), Brown and White (2011) examined the impact of OPR and the attribution for crisis responsibility (by crisis response strategy: scapegoating, justifying, apologizing, or reminding). They found "significant differences in the attribution scores among students with positive and negative relationships for the scapegoating, justification, and apology strategies" (p. 87). Crisis responsibility attribution was affected by relationship quality and crisis response strategy.

Contingency Theory

Rather than presuming a preference for a particular communication style (direction and style, i.e., asymmetry/symmetry), contingency theory reasons that management and public relations practices are best when they are contingent—adjusted to each situation. Part of such contingency depends on the degree and kind of agreement/disagreement between an organization and a public. Thus, depending on the context and purpose, the communication style employed might be more accommodation or more advocacy.

- Which contingency variables help identify the most salient factors in a given situation for bringing about the best positioning, leading to a resolution, to the solving of some problem in mutual interest?
- Of the many factors—as many as 87—relevant to making such decisions, which best predict a favorable outcome?
- Does communication based on the factors selected lead to resolution?
- If not, should it be adjusted so that the response is either more accommodative or more advocative?
- Does the organization become locked into one response option that makes it inflexible to adjust to the operant contingencies?
- Presuming a multifactorial influence on contingency, are these factors relevant to a specific, desirable outcome: a public's perception of its power, potential threats to the organization, organizational characteristics, economic concerns, experience levels of public relations practitioners, individual characteristics such as tolerance of uncertainty, or personal ethics?
- What factors predict an accommodative approach, and in the specific situation, do they achieve resolution?
- Given that organizations have multiple publics, are different degrees of accommodation or advocacy more or less effective with each?

Rhetorical Theory

Rhetorical theory features shared meaning to justify the need for and value of different discourse strategies in response to each unique rhetorical problem in relevant rhetorical arenas regarding rhetorical situations. This theory presumes that language defines physical and social reality, injects factual content and moral judgment into issue discussions, and can lead all parties to mutually satisfying answers to rhetorical problems. It reasons that people want to make enlightened choices which solve problems and that strategic discourse can accomplish this outcome. Its most basic value is that humans live together in various states of association, identification, identity, conflict, accommodation, advocacy, information sharing, and all other forms of propositional discourse. These constructs also have relevance for the nature and quality of relationships and discourse processes, which depend on how they are understood and enacted terministically. Such discourse can improve relatedness.

- What voices (stakeholders/stakeseekers) are engaging on some matter of public policy, organizational policy, or reputation? Who is saying what, in what way, with whom, and with what impact?
- What facts, values/evaluations, policies, identities, and identifications are being contested? Is the substance of the discourse based on good reasons, and how it is used to support and oppose various positions?
- In that regard, what rhetorical problems are being addressed, by what voices, with what discursive strategies, and to what impact?
- What voices are most credible, and in the opinion of which audiences, publics, or stakeholders?
- What issue signals, issue emergence, issue positions, issue priorities, and issue impacts need to be understood to determine the status of the debate on contested matters?
- Are some voices being amplified and others muted? If so, does this distort the quality of the discourse? In what ways?
- What choices are being featured, and are the arguments for them sufficient to enlighten them?

- Is advocacy being used to intimidate or enlighten choice? Are voices inviting inspection and evaluation of the propositions set forth?
- Are terministic screens emerging that make society a better place to live and work?
- Do these terministic screens support narratives that make society more fully functioning— leading to a collective "happily ever after"?
- Do the discursive strategies help build a sense of community?
- Is the discourse trend advancing society, making it more fully functioning, or merely advancing some interests to the potential or actual disadvantage of others?

Critical Theory

However subjective the measures relevant to rhetorical theory, those for critical theory may be more so. Critical theory reasons that language is never neutral, ideology counts, value judgments are vital, and empirical measures are difficult to create and use. Because of its belief that positivism is limited, it assumes that qualitative assessment is the best measure for critical judgment.

The foundations of measurement for the critical theory of public relations arise from issues relevant to norms. Power (power/knowledge) is one. Critical theorists are keenly interested in the ability to identify and assess the amount of power each key player has and how that becomes embedded in the language of and influence over decision making.

Another measure is the engagement quality of the discourse arena. Do all voices have appropriate access to each arena and the decisions made in it? One assumption, for instance, is that language and discourse processes can marginalize some voices and even deny their influence. Critical theorists worry that the more powerful exert more influence, which allows them to keep their power and even gain more of it. Measures of power are connected with the access key voices have to the infrastructures of a community. They are also connected with the way power is formulated and applied through the language of the discourse.

- What hegemonies are at play, and is the management of the important organizations cognizant of them as part of their reflective management in ways that lead to and benefit from stakeholder engagement?
- What interests are at play in public relations and organizational management philosophies, practices, and processes?
- Do deep pockets (elite agency) distort discourse and privilege certain interests to the disadvantage of others?
- Does dialogue embrace and encourage voices or mask the absence of some and the marginalization of others?
- How is legitimacy conceptualized and invoked in instances of problem solving and relationship development?
- Is decision making collaborative, the product of engagement?
- Is community advanced through discourse or invoked as a weapon to bias arguments against a collective interest?
- Do the conditions of discourse meet the standards of comprehensibility, truth, sincerity, authenticity, and moral rightness?
- Are the worldviews reflected in discourse genuinely supportive of or in conflict with one another?

- Is power masked or apparent? How is it conceptualized, distributed, and rewarded in each political economy?
- Are publics instrumentalized for the interest of the agency of an organization, or do they voice views that are given due and empathic consideration by reflective management?

Issues, Crisis, and Risk

Issues management, along with crisis and risk communication and management, contextualizes measurement challenges and methodologies reflected in the four theories just discussed.

- What legitimacy gaps exist, why, and to what consequence? How can they be lessened, or increased?
- What standards of CSR do stakeholders expect organizations to meet? Are they perceived to meet these standards? Is there a legitimacy gap, and if so, what needs to be done and said to narrow it?
- Is management reflective? Does it know and appreciate the challenges posed by conflicting standards of CSR? Does it learn by issue monitoring?
- Do the voices engaged in issue discussion focus appropriately on the challenges of fact, value, policy, identity, and identification?
- Depending on the nature of the crisis and the theory applied, do the strategies, tactics, and tools used in response restore/repair image/reputation?
- Does a gap exist between scientists' and lay audiences' understanding of risk (MMA)? What type and content of discourse reduces that gap, if any?
- Do organizations' positions on risks protect and promote risk bearers' interests and concerns in a way that fairly distributes risk/reward ratios?
- Does risk decision making and communication gain appropriate insight into key audiences' psychodemographic assessments of risk in ways that fairly advances all parties' safety?
- Do the institutions/infrastructures in which risks are discussed allow full participation and exhibit a genuine commitment to addressing and resolving concern for safety?

As discussed in Chapter 7, strategic issues management requires issue monitoring, which is a unique approach to measurement. Arguably, monitoring requires five integrated processes: identification, scanning, tracking, analysis, and priority setting.

- Identification requires "spotting" an issue and naming it. How it is named and framed is important to knowing who is discussing it, why, how, with whom, and to what outcomes.
- Scanning (surveillance, as a radar scope signals what is being seen) requires vigilant observation, often by issue-content experts, in order to observe and understand where each in an array of issues fits. Computer programs can help "scanners" to determine by key word analysis the importance, in cluster form, of terms that are associated with one another in a particular discourse.
- Tracking is time- and path/trajectory-oriented monitoring. Over time, is discussion increasing, are voices joining or leaving the arena, is content changing, are values focusing responsibility and harm, and are other changes occurring?
- Analysis again requires topic expertise. As medical researchers and epidemiologists raised concerns about the impact of smoking on health, experts were called on to "analyze" the quality of the discussion, its fact basis, and its health implications. Analysis can focus on content, but also on implications. What changes in business planning and operations will be required as the

issue "matures"? Will customers stop buying products based on the discourse? Will competitors gain advantage? Will restrictions increase operating standards?

- Priority setting is the result of the other steps and can lead to the development of rhetorical positions on issues, increasing resources used, changing the priorities of resource applications, taking advantage of opportunities, or minimizing the actions that fuel stakeholder threats.

Publicity and Promotion, Reputation, and Image/Brand Equity

Publicity and promotion have received very little attention in this book, although they have often been in the background of several discussions. The analysis in this section is augmented by the discussion of capabilities just presented. Such practices, purposes, and strategic processes often define public relations, and justify its role in organizational success. "Publicity" refers to practitioners' ability to gain favorable attention for an organization and its products, services, or personnel—especially senior managers. "Promotion" refers to a sustained publicity campaign. Thus, with regard to the discussion on attitudes and behaviors, publicity and promotion—often in conjunction with advertising and marketing—seeks to achieve what has been called "advertising equivalency." That concept is not universally appreciated, nor are its measures universally agreed upon, but in essence the notion is that publicity can do what advertising does but at less cost and with third-party commentary, which can add credibility to its message. The key concepts in publicity and promotion are awareness, knowledge, attitudes, and behaviors, each of which can be measured.

- Using tools such as press releases and events, can public relations gain media attention for an organization and its products, services, or personnel?
- Can it achieve such visibility by gaining column inches, electronic media moments/time, or social media impact? How many eyes are likely to see the comments or ears to hear them? Thus, what is its reach?
- Does the coverage include favorable comments by reporters and editorialists?
- Does it provide information, create attitudes, and motivate behavior intentions that eventually lead to purchases, uses, or other tangible and desirable responses?
- Since such measures may have social media relevance, general commentators and marketing/advertising and public relations personnel work to establish social media metrics. Following is a list of social media metrics relevant to the role of public relations practitioners: visits/hits, friends/followers, shares/likes/retweets, engagement, sentiment, share of voice, hits on recruiters' profiles (contextualized to human resources), job applicants through LinkedIn, and impressions/sales leads (Neill & Moody, 2015). The measurement questions at the moment minimally ask for frequency count by measure.
- Social media applications are adding to the complexity of measurement. The challenge is to connect reach to behavioral outcomes, connect metrics to communication strategies, derive meaningful measures that drive customer behavior, and understand how all of this strengthens brand, obtains user demographic and preference profiles, connects reputation and customer behavior, and measures credibility. It is necessary in this regard for public relations personnel to show return on investment (DiStaso, McCorkindale, & Wright, 2011).

Brief attention has been given in this section to social media, not only in an attempt to look to the future, but also to indicate the measurement challenges associated with publicity and promotion.

Cases Relevant to Measurement

Rather than use one major case in this chapter, it seems best to offer a few short ones that ask readers to apply their knowledge of measurement. Addressing the following cases may require revisiting sections and topics in other chapters.

Case 1: What measurement challenges are involved and what techniques are advised in determining customer satisfaction with a bank that brands itself as favoring small businesses as customers? Can the comparative impact of banking products be compared to customer satisfaction with bankers' knowledge, ability, and customer care?

Case 2: Critics are offended by an automobile company's manipulation of mileage (MPG) reports as a brand feature. Should the company advocate in its defense or accommodate to the critics' claims? What factors should answer that question and how can the success of the contingent response be measured?

Case 3: During the financial crisis of 2008, big banks in the United States argued that they needed to be bailed out because they were "too big to fail." What measures can be used to assess how well this rhetorical claim addressed the rhetorical problem, "should the U.S. government bail out the big banks"? Given that General Motors also asked for a bail-out, what rhetorical claims were used and were they proved right or wrong by the government's response?

Case 4: Several U.S. states have changed their requirements for voter registration, reducing opportunities to vote and requiring documentation to verify the person at the poll is who they say they are. This last measure includes the requirement that a voter must show picture identification of a specified kind. Such measures are presented to the public, and debated in legislatures, as a means for reducing voter fraud. What critical theory measures should be used to assess the ability of such legislation to strengthen the democratic process?

Case 5: A country decides to engage in a branding campaign to convince travelers that it is a desirable place to visit. It uses placed television advertisements, publicity and promotion, and social media efforts to this end. What measures should it use to determine whether the money spent is beneficial to its citizens?

Case 6: Shortly after the Obama administration passed the Affordable Care Act, critics began to point to its flaws, and even gave it the mocking name "Obama Care." Its creation and implementation, as well as its impact on the economy and public health, have been the focus of continuing issues debate. Some might even call it a crisis. Members of Congress, commentators, reporters, and ordinary citizens have all engaged in "public relations" for and against the program. Does one theory best explain how you would approach defense or attack of the Act? How would you measure the impact of supporters' and critics' discourse and dialogue?

Conclusion

Measurement flows from a firm idea regarding what public relations is and what it contributes to the success of individuals and organizations, as well as how it advances the quality of society, making it a better place to live and work. Measurement is natural and normal, not some strange or frustrating requirement imposed to make the lives of practitioners more difficult. However, critics who argue against a functional and instrumental approach to the practice of public relations assert that pragmatism can too easily be the prevailing standard of the practice.

As planning is essential to public relations, so too is measurement. Planning presumes outcome impacts and resources are applied to solve problems and overcome challenges. Measurement indicates whether and what impact is occurring, and why. In this way, measurement in public relations is as normal as monitoring the speed at which we drive. It is a test of our ability to practice skillfully, legally, and ethically.

Addressing such challenges should convince the student that measurement is not simple, not easy, and has ethical implications. To add to the difficulty, beyond merely counting something such as hits, likes, or retweets, it must first be determined which variables are best to measure and how to measure them. A tool such as an interview or a focus group might be a good choice, perhaps based on the use of a questionnaire. These factors, plus the challenges of statistical analysis, can bring to bear on measurement some very sophisticated knowledge. All of that is too detailed to include here, but it is not irrelevant to the subject under debate. This, then, becomes another challenge for students who want to add to their toolbox of theory-based professional skills.

Chapter Summary

As an additional challenge, students are encouraged to revisit the many cases discussed in other chapters (some are already restated at the end of this chapter). These cases will challenge them to use their knowledge of theory and measurement to develop a measurement plan. What approaches and assumptions should practitioners take to measure the conditions requiring and potential for achieving success in each case? This sort of exercise continues and reinforces a central theme of this chapter: measurement is important, driven by theoretical assumptions, and as vital to the profession as is monitoring one's speed while driving in a school zone.

The purpose of this chapter is to introduce students to the logics and challenges of public relations measurement. It uses relevant terminology and highlights books and articles that provide insights useful to accomplishing this task ethically and effectively. It features some concepts that run throughout communication and psychology, such as awareness, visibility, knowledge, attitude, behavioral intention, and behavior. It demonstrates how the ideas featured by each of the theories discussed can help in measurement.

If it is successful, the chapter should also convince students that no matter how hard it is to measure public relations impact and ethics, the integrity of the practice depends on that ability. It is part of the service to employer and client, but more importantly, it is a means for making public relations an ethical, normative, functional, structural, strategic, and otherwise valued profession that can help organizations succeed and communities benefit.

Discussion Questions

1 What is measurement? Why is it valuable to human activities, including public relations?
2 What are the advantages and pitfalls of measurement?
3 How important are variables and concepts to measurement? Why are knowledge, attitude, and behavioral intent—even behavior—routine logics of a measurement plan?
4 Is measurement contextual? In various contexts, how important is it to start by knowing the outcome that an organization favors?
5 What are the unique concepts, variables, factors, and measurement challenges of excellence theory?

> **6** What are the unique concepts, variables, factors, and measurement challenges of contingency theory?
>
> **7** What are the unique concepts, variables, factors, and measurement challenges of rhetorical theory?
>
> **8** What are the unique concepts, variables, factors, and measurement challenges of critical theory?
>
> **9** What are the unique concepts, variables, factors, and measurement challenges of issues management, crisis communication, and risk communication?
>
> **10** What are the unique concepts, variables, factors, and measurement challenges of publicity and promotion?
>
> **11** How is social media measured? What changes might it bring to public relations practice and measurement?

References

Brown, K. A., & White, C. L. (2011). Organization–public relationships and crisis response strategies: Impact on attribution of responsibility. *Journal of Public Relations Research*, *23*, 75–92.

DiStaso, M. W., & Stacks, D. W. (2010). The use of research in public relations. In R. L. Heath (Ed.), *SAGE handbook of public relations* (pp. 325–337). Thousand Oaks, CA: Sage.

DiStaso, M. W., McCorkindale, T., & Wright, D. K. (2011). How public relations executives perceive and measure the impact of social media in their organizations. *Public Relations Review*, *37*, 325–328.

Fawcett, J., & Downs, F. (1986). *The relationship of theory and research*. Norwalk, CT: Appleton Century Crofts.

Fawkes, J., Gregory, A., Falkheimer, J., Gutierrez-Garcia, E., Halff, G., Rensburg, R., ... Wolf, K. (2018). *A global capability framework for the public relations and communication management profession*. Huddersfield: University of Huddersfield.

Grunig, J. E. (1983). Basic research provides knowledge that makes evaluation possible. *Public Relations Quarterly*, *28*, 28–32.

Heath, R. L. (Ed.) (2013). *Encyclopedia of public relations* (2nd ed.). Boston, MA: Cengage Learning.

Hocking, J. E., Stacks, D. W., & McDermott, S. T. (2003). *Communication research* (3rd ed.). Boston, MA: Allyn & Bacon.

Huang, Y. H. (2001). OPRA: A cross-cultural, multiple-item scale for measuring organization–public relationships. *Journal of Public Relations Research*, *13*, 61–90.

Institute for Public Relations. (n.d.). IPR Measurement Commission. Available from http://www.instituteforpr.org/ipr-measurement-commission (accessed May 20, 2020).

Jo, S. (2006). Measurement of organization–public relationships: Validation of measurement using a manufacturer-retailer relationship. *Journal of Public Relations Research*, *18*, 225–248.

Judd, L. R. (1990). Importance and use of formal research and evaluation. *Public Relations Review*, *16*, 17–28.

Kang, M., & Yang, S.-U. (2010). Mediation effects of organization–public relationship outcomes on public intentions for organizational supports. *Journal of Public Relations Research*, *22*, 477–494.

Lindenmann, W. K. (1990). Research, evaluation and measurement: A national perspective. *Public Relations Review*, *16*, 8–16.

Neill, M. S., & Moody, M. (2015). Who is responsible for what? Examining strategic roles in social media management. *Public Relations Review*, *41*, 109–118.

Public Relations Society of America. (n.d.). Measurement resources: Guidance for qualifying public relations' impact on business outcomes. Available from https://apps.prsa.org/Intelligence/BusinessCase/MeasurementResources (accessed May 20, 2020).

Stacks, D. W. (2011). *Primer of public relations research*. New York: Guilford Press.

Stacks, D. W., & Michaelson, D. (2010). *A practitioner's guide to public relations research, measurement, and evaluation*. New York: Business Expert Press.

Valente, T. W., Paredes, P., & Poppe, P. R. (1998). Matching the message to the process: The relative ordering of knowledge, attitudes, and practices in behavior change research. *Human Communication Research, 24*, 366–385.

9

Public Relations and Ethical Challenges: Being a Saint, Not a Sinner

Introduction

Humans moralize their identities, lives, interactions, relationships, and dealings with one another. This need for morality leads to religion, provokes philosophical discussions, justifies laws, fosters codes of personal and professional behavior, and structures contracts, including social contracts. Morality, as a means for enacting trust in human relationships, invariably becomes part of professions' brands and guides professional activities. For these reasons, considerations of public relations theory and practice would be incomplete without a thorough discussion of what ethical challenges the profession faces and what core values can support its moral development. Ethical judgment does not apply only to communication, but also to management issues, such as counseling. It informs and guides organizational strategic planning and plan implementation and evaluation.

Ethics is relevant to all aspects of public relations professionalism, especially considerations of who practitioners influence internally as they counsel and how morally they serve many interests externally. The study of ethics is a means for improving the moral functionality of the profession and for strategic moralizing of its role in society. Such principles refine how it is taught. Learning and refining a sound set of ethical principles is important to students' education (Austin & Toth, 2011; DiStaso, Stacks, & Botan, 2009). The reputation of the profession is improved by how it is practiced, and how it is practiced improves general and specific perceptions of its reputation for ethical performance.

As such, performance standards/codes for the profession must be pragmatic, global, and increasingly sensitive to the opportunities and threats of social media (Black, 2008). Can public relations be the corporate conscience that organizations require (Bowen, 2008)? Given the paradoxes and entanglements of ethics and resource management, should one ask whether more moral organizations gain more resources than less moral ones (Heath & Waymer, 2019)? Do profits corrupt? Do organizations instrumentalize publics and stakeholders as a means of gaining advantage? Practitioners are often assumed to put their clients' interests before those of others.

The incentive to raise the ethical standards of the profession comes from the widely held perception that public relations is inherently an unethical practice, largely because of its functional dysfunctionality. That may be more myth than fact, but perception counts, especially when critics say that public relations is "spin," stonewalling, slippery wording, the telling of untruths, and friendly lying (Callison, Merle, & Seltzer, 2014). Rather than being transparent, many believe, public relations has mastered opaqueness.

Public Relations Theory: Capabilities and Competencies, First Edition. Jae-Hwa Shin and Robert L. Heath.
© 2021 John Wiley & Sons, Inc. Published 2021 by John Wiley & Sons, Inc.

Practitioners are known to be gatekeepers capable of controlling the flow of information from and to an organization; suspicions mount about their power and their being rewarded for craftiness, rather than their ethics. Critics believe that the wordsmithing ability of practitioners is such that they can seem to be telling some profound truth while actually dealing in falsehoods. To support such stereotypes (brands?), research reveals that survey participants use positive terms to describe practitioners' personality and intellectual traits but negative ones to describe their ethics (Callison et al., 2014).

As noted in Chapter 1, some believe public relations is the work of the devil. Professionals are called upon to enact moral and functional constructs such as transparency. However contextual such guidelines are, transparency, for instance, is a constructive part of efforts to build or restore trust and reduce reputational risk (Auger, 2014). But how do stakeholders know whether organizations are actually transparent or only seemingly so (Christensen & Langer, 2009)?

The devil metaphor has a parallel in Fawkes' (2012) insightful parsing of ethical challenges, competing views on ethics, and the dysfunction of pasting ethics on to functions. Her case study features the need for practitioners (academics and students) to develop an archetypal identity that approaches ethical dilemmas not by a servile application of a code of ethics, by supposing that functions can either be ethical or not, or by meeting some high moral challenge that is too complex and rigorous for daily use by busy professionals, but through the tension of the saints/sinners archetype; as that tension forces moral dilemmas back on to the moral judgment of each professional's self-identity—"be a saint"—it centers on the balance between personal ethical satisfaction and the comfort achieved by knowing that choices serve the good of society, however complex that may be.

One reason for this opinion is the general sense among practitioners and academics that the role of public relations is to make organizations effective—or more effective—at all ethical costs. That incentive can require not telling the truth, telling something other than the truth, shifting the lens to obscure the truth, or portraying false statements as though they were true. It can entail twisting the truth to make it seem false, and making falsehoods seem true. Thus, the classic battle between flacks (practitioners) and hacks (journalists): they can't live with each other, they can't live without each other.

This chapter discusses the ethics and ethical challenges associated with standards of professionalism. It is mindful of research findings such as those by DiStaso et al., (2009) that practitioners and educators aspire to ensure that students receive an education that places "more emphasis on research, ethics and strategic planning as the field moves from a low-paid technical emphasis toward a much better paid strategic planning and research emphasis" (p. 254). It recalls theory from previous chapters. It points to the richness of discussions of public relations ethics. It gives students the opportunity to consider ethical challenges and quandaries by reflecting on cases— decisions and circumstances—relevant to public relations.

As much as the chapter sets out key aspects of public relations ethics, it is also mindful of how this material can advance the well being of organizations and public relations professionalism by providing details that help managers serve as ethics counsels for the organizations they represent (Bowen, 2008). It is mindful of survey findings pointing to the importance of developing moral character and moral reasoning and integrating them with professional skills (Erzikova, 2010). It suggests the importance of exploring the role of ethics in public relations program evaluation (Place, 2015)—an extension of Chapter 8.

By the end of the chapter, readers should understand ethics and public relations, various theories of ethics, the connections between ethics and public relations theories, and the challenges of ethical decision making. To that end, it brings together the theory and context of ethical challenges in a way that allows readers to test their ethical decision-making abilities and moral principles. It emphasizes how practitioners should not only understand ethics but be able to articulate positions on ethical choices—to explain and justify their positions in ways that reflect their moral core in order to convince others both inside and outside of their organizations.

Questions to Frame the Discussion of Ethical Challenges

- How and why is ethics central to professionalism in general, and to public relations specifically?
- How do standards of best practice, codes of professionalism, principles of corporate social responsibility (CSR), reflective management, and commitment to communitarianism shape public relations ethics?
- Do the four theories of public relations featured in this book (excellence, contingency, rhetorical, and critical) address ethics as fundamental to the practice? What ethical insights are valued by each?
- Three well-defined philosophies—pragmatism, utilitarianism, and deontology—have become part of the literature on public relations. What is the key theme of each regarding ethics, and how does it advance the morality of the profession, if at all?
- In what ways are ethical considerations central to issues management, crisis management and communication, and risk management and communication? In this regard, how does CSR bring ethics into reputation and policy choices?
- Are promotion and publicity so inherently flawed that they can never be practiced in a truly ethical manner?

Key Themes

- Professions develop ethical standards and establish codes to guide practice in a manner that is responsible to clients, employers, and society.
- The professional ethics of public relations addresses how best practices can be understood as being connected to those ethical standards by which professionals serve the good of society.
- Ethical principles are not random considerations and conclusions; they grow from an understanding of the standards and requirements of CSR, reflective management, and communitarianism.
- Public relations theory, because of the need for professionalism, should consider and add ethical clarity to the practice.
- Moral decision making can have pragmatic, utilitarian, and deontological implications. Practitioners and academics contest and examine these philosophies in order to set high standards of public relations practice and strategic management.
- Ethics is an underpinning of issues management's commitment to achieving legitimacy through reflective strategic planning, knowing and meeting CSR standards, monitoring issues (including those vital to value-driven moral reasoning), and engaging in morally responsible dialogue and engagement.
- Crisis often focuses on ethical choices and mistakes.
- Risk management and communication addresses how safe is safe and how fair is safe—key moral concerns.
- Publicity and promotion are often the aspects of the profession that receive the most criticism as being ethically challenged. They can be used to help people solve problems by making enlightened choices, or they can frustrate such choices.

Ethics and Public Relations: Theory and Professional Practice

Ethical judgment fundamentally addresses whose interest the profession serves; to whom are professionals accountable? It focuses on the integrity of professionals as the profession's enactors; what moral value do they add to society? Such inquiry can move from asking the broad question, is public relations ethical, to focusing more on what it is that the profession does (what should it do, how, why, and on whose behalf) to add moral value to the agency of society. Zoch, Supa, and VanTuyll (2014) surveyed the *New York Times* during the early part of the twentieth century to learn how the paper defined and evaluated the practice. Their study found that it accurately described the media and tactics used by the profession but doubted the moral rationale for its practice.

Working to develop the philosophy of public relations, L. Grunig (1992) emphasized how prominently such philosophy required discussion of "ethical issues, the nature of practitioners' moral reasoning, public and social responsibility, and ideology and values" (p. 75). Her philosophy rested on Kant's aspiration that human lives should be worthy of happiness. In public relations, balanced, symmetrical relationships offer one means of achieving such outcomes through communitarian commitment. Moral reasoning is a focused consideration of the nature and hierarchy of responsibility more than of rights. Responsibility expresses a commitment to serve the interests of others. That is true for all true professions, including medicine, accounting, engineering, financial planning, agriculture, public health, and architecture. It is true of social activism, such as environmentalism, civil and human rights advocacy, and community change management.

In the face of ethical criticism, academics and practitioners have called for codes of ethics and improved moral decision making to strengthen the managerial role of public relations. A focus on ethics can encourage practitioners to bring to bear a set of ethical principles higher than those of people engaged in the management of organizations (Holtzhausen, 2011). Does public relations serve the community, especially if its role is to help management "plan strategies and tactics to manage the relationships" between an organization and its publics (Valentini, Kruckeberg, & Starck, 2012)? This irony hangs heavy on the discipline and those who work to advance it. The responsibility to avoid instrumentalizing publics and stakeholders serves others but can foster the interest of organizations, too. Professionals have to overcome the widespread belief that public relations can only be the ethical conscience of an organization in the same way that a fox can protect a chicken house. The goal of public relations ethics is to proactively search for moral responsibility, rather than reactively defending the profession and its clients.

In public relations, best practices, codes of ethics, and commitments to CSR are important aspects of professionalism. But codes may not count as much as personal characteristics that are dedicated to moral reasoning. Ethical leadership depends on a practitioner's personal ethics, interpersonal behaviors, and ability to articulate ethical standards (Lee & Cheng, 2011).

Professionals wrestle with knowing and applying the ethical standards required for *best practices*. What ethical standards, for instance, should guide strategies, functions, tactics, and other best practices typical of public relations? Questions regarding the ethics of daily practice address topics such as deception, fullness of explanation, transparency, word choice, visual presentations, accurate portrayal, and fairness. Best practices consider the ethics of when (and when not), what, how, and with whom to communicate. Such challenges draw attention to the potentiality that theory is so general that it either does not adequately guide practice or allows practitioners the flexibility to justify questionable professional choices.

One transition point between a practice and a profession is the ability to consider and bring about the highest ethical behavior of practitioners as its positive brand. But focusing narrowly on a professional brand should not obscure the core ethical challenges, as ethics—moral codes—can become pasted on to a profession in a defensive, reactive manner. Any robust, inclusive debate over professional ethics must necessarily focus on the clash over interests; a profession becomes morally richer when it is not limited to imposing ethics on its functions or to arguing that its preferred strategic processes, functions, tactics, and purposes somehow are inherently ethical. A philosophy of professional ethics must embrace such matters but approach them proactively rather than reactively. Instead of being inspired and guided by "don'ts" and "nevers," the profession should aspire toward sound, proactive moral judgment. For instance, is the ethic "don't lie" the same as "tell the truth"?

To spark thought and discussion on key aspects of public relations ethics, this book provides some narrative ethical dilemmas. The cases offered in other chapters encourage readers to think about and apply the material presented therein. As is often the case in public relations classes, each "ethical challenge" poses a moral dilemma—a narrative that forces ethical choice (Eschenfelder, 2011).

Ethical Challenge

Imagine that you have been asked to prepare a draft of a press release for your employer, a division of a multinational manufacturing company that produces specialty parts for the automobile industry. Management believes it is necessary to close a branch located in a small town that depends heavily on the jobs and business it provides. The company can manufacture the parts produced there more cheaply abroad, and it is losing market because its customers are buying from overseas suppliers. What ethical considerations need careful consideration, based on public relations best practices, as you prepare this draft?

The ethics of when (and when not), what, and how to communicate are among the many broad ethical themes vital to professional social responsibility. Based on an extensive literature review, Boynton (2002) concluded that professionalism centers on "trait-related definitions of professionals as well as the emerging power-based approach to understanding professions" (p. 230). As professionals, what traits are typical of practitioners, and do they relate to the sorts of ethics they prefer and practice? Are such traits means by which saints can be separated from sinners?

One of the traits typical of practitioners is the strategic ability to craft messages. Another is the monitoring of issue trends, including changing norms. Another still is the understanding and appreciation of the public interest (aligned interests with publics and stakeholders) and of the interests of different organizations as they relate to and align (or conflict) with one another. One more trait is the ability to understand how public relations adds value to organizations and to the societies in which it operates. Professionalism presumes that practitioners will serve and do good for others.

Professionalism and ethics are connected by the principle that each profession is expected, as part of its rationale for existence, to add value to society—what Brunner (2015; see also L. Grunig, 1992) called "civic professionalism." This is done through what the profession knows and how it brings that knowledge to bear on matters of organizational and public importance. As Boynton (2002) summarizes the literature on the topic, "Public relations traditionally has drawn on the concept of professionalism to show a responsible commitment to society and to reinforce credible image" (p. 232). On such matters, as the rhetorical tradition concludes, character counts—and perhaps becomes more universally defined and implemented through codes of conduct.

Such codes are typical of professions, and in some instances even become the basis for accreditation, licensing, and peer review. As one of the leading professional public relations associations, the Public Relations Society of America (PRSA, n.d.) has developed and promulgated a series of updated codes of ethics. It sees the creation of such documents as part of its responsibilities, along with the monitoring of the performance of those who aspire to be professionals and the advocacy of principles to advance the credibility of the profession and its commitment to the good of society. (See also the International Public Relations Association [IPRA] Code of Athens, Watson, 2014.)

The PRSA Code addresses the following topics: advocacy, honesty, expertise, independence, loyalty, and fairness. It is committed to the free flow of information and competition for resources. The PRSA Member Code of Ethics Pledge includes the following commitment:

> To conduct myself professionally, with truth, accuracy, fairness, and responsibility to the public; To improve my individual competence and advance the knowledge and proficiency of the profession through continuing research and education; And to adhere to the articles of the Member Code of Ethics 2000 for the practice of public relations as adopted by the governing Assembly of the Public Relations Society of America.

As penalty for failure to adhere to these ethical principles, a PRSA member can lose their membership and accreditation.

Codes advocate the need to be well educated in all aspects of the profession and to continue such education. Knowledge of the codes governing one's profession is integral to the accreditation process and to professional standards. Such codes may be part of an agency's or organization's explicit conditions of practice. They help individuals to make ethical choices concerning both individual and organizational performance.

Codes are a tool for implementing a profession's ethical judgment, but they have their limitations. They have the force of shifting responsibility from the individual to the group, especially when some penalty is to be suffered for not following them or for following them incorrectly. And, their application is limited by the difficulty of their interpretation in the real world. Knowing such limitations, Holtzhausen (2015) called "for the rejection of universal codes of ethics of professional organizations in favor of individual, responsible ethical decision-making, which will be determined by the specific environment and situation of the practitioner" (p. 769). Even as codes exist, professionals (and students) should regularly discuss what they mean, how they can be implemented, and whether they truly elevate ethical practice.

A third category of ethics vital to professionalism is CSR. After World War II, a general social movement arose to scrutinize the extent to which industry, nonprofits, and government actually

---

Ethical Challenge

In the PRSA Code, several key terms are important for public relations professionals. Imagine that you have been assigned to gather photographs (which includes commissioning a photographer to take more) of a company for which you work as part of its presentation in print and on the company intranet, social media, and website. Your boss says that the pictures should present an image of a highly successful company—one that is clean and modern, and whose employees are happy workers. The boss says, "Avoid any pictures that show older equipment, older facilities, and employees who are not beaming with happiness for their jobs." As you prepare your task, with reference to the PRSA code, what ethical concerns do you have? Should these be discussed with your boss? If so, how?

served purposes that could be deemed to be socially responsible. This era was intent on moralizing itself. The topic of "social" as a key theme in this discussion is important because one standard of CSR calls for organizations—especially businesses—to be "nice." As a nice neighbor, a company might be expected to help fund community activities, such as Little League and youth soccer teams. It is also expected to act responsibly; to be responsible to others' interests as it is to its own. As such, elite CSR organizations set the standards—as stakeholder expectations—regarding what moral and pragmatic actions and norms justify ethical responsibility (Heath & Waymer, 2019).

The topic of community relations becomes controversial when industry is expected to solve social issues that some believe are best left to government and nonprofits, such as tackling crime and poverty. This approach to CSR can include supporting public school programs, especially those designed to foster reading or the study of science. Some call for companies to meet this level of social responsibility in order to be seen as being good neighbors. Thus, the highest level of corporate responsibility is being a *reflective and responsive neighbor*. By this standard, companies are called on to consider the interests of others as equal to their own (Heath & Ni, 2010).

Ethical Challenge

Imagine that you are asked to design a CSR communications program for a local business that is part of a multinational beverage (soft drink) company. As much as the company is successful, it has its critics, who claim its products contribute to obesity. One component of the company's CSR program is the enhancement of the quality of life in the local community. Would you consider creating and obtaining funding for a multipurpose/multi-activity community recreation area? What should such a facility be named? How should it be managed? How might its cost be sold to other businesses, area nonprofits, and civic associations as a joint community project? Should the facility feature your company's name? If so, in what way? What ethical considerations are important to keep in mind as you plan and propose this community relations project? When management decides to include video of individuals participating in the company-sponsored fitness program, what body types should be featured?

Standards of responsibility (being reflective and responsive) challenge organizations—especially businesses—to know and comply with standards relevant to fairness, equality, safety, and environmental quality—even sustainability. These standards have substantial implications for a business' reputation, but they are the contested substance of public policy debates. The question is, who sets and enforces CSR standards (Ihlen, Bartlett, & May, 2011)? This relates to many other important topics, including that of legitimacy—long the foundation of issues management.

Ethical Challenge

Imagine that you have been asked to prepare a management policy document for a very large banking and financial services company. The senior management team has been challenged to develop a policy position regarding the kind of regulation it deems best and most appropriate for the banking and financial services industry. Some other companies in the industry would prefer as little regulation as possible. They believe that merely providing banking and financial services constitutes the industry's legitimacy by serving the public interest. You believe, as do critics of the industry, that extravagant executive bonuses and minimal regulation actually endanger the autonomy of the industry over the long run. What ethical theme would you propose to define and justify your company's and the industry's legitimacy?

The effort to know and adjust to others' expectations is made complex by additional decision criteria. One problem is the profound differences of opinion among any organization's stakeholders regarding what is socially—morally—responsible. What is "ethical" to some might be "unethical" to others. Thus, any theory or approach to ethics must acknowledge the paradox of multiple voices, interests, and nuances of ethics regarding CSR legitimacy. Otherwise, the process is limited in what it can contribute to the discussion of ethics in public relations.

Just being responsive to the preferences of one or more other voices in a community of interest may be inadequate. Frederick (1986) made that point in his discussion of CSR by differentiating the ethics of three R's: responsibility, responsiveness, and rectitude. Limiting a stance on CSR to either of the former two can be less "ethical" than seeking a standard of the third, rectitude. Merely accommodating to or adjusting to others' preferences might be strategically wise, but it does not necessarily comply with the highest moral standards.

For that reason, Frederick called on managements "to act with rectitude, to refer their policies and plans to a culture of ethics that embraces the most fundamental moral principles of humankind" (p. 136). The pursuit of those fundamental moral principles is never easy, and merely adjusting to the preferences of one or more public or stakeholder may not be enough. For that reason, the continuing discussion of CSR helps frame the challenge, but sees it also as a discourse-based work in progress (Ihlen et al., 2011). Understanding the culture of ethics at play in each community, as well as nationally and globally, is daunting, but that is the specific challenge confronted by the role of CSR in public relations ethics.

Ethical Challenge

Your company (and, by implication, industry) is faced with a challenge by a human rights activist group. The issue is one of pay, working conditions, and worker rights. Gender is a key aspect. Your company, like many others, does not own its own manufacturing facilities, but uses ones located in countries that allow them to operate as what critics call "sweatshops." These facilities hire only young women, who are paid a wage that is 20% greater than the average for women in these countries. Dorms are provided so that the women are close to their work. They are encouraged, in part by their national and ethnic cultures, to be hard-working, quiet, and loyal. The work they perform is tedious, routine, and held to high quality standards. One of the complaints by the human rights group is that both the work culture and the dorm culture prevent or limit social time. This, the critics charge, leads to health problems, low morale, and even suicide. You have been asked to investigate these charges and make recommendations to management, which it can use to define and monitor the working conditions of its supplier companies. What ethical challenges do you consider and propose to solve?

In this way, CSR is central to how organizations perform and how they are judged by various and even competing stakeholders' ethical standards and legitimacy expectations. The best performing organizations are capable of managing stakeholders' interests, and can become known for that. Such strategic management requires a commitment to distributive justice and reciprocity, both of which are vital to building trust (Harrison, Bosse, & Phillips, 2010). Thus, CSR is central to organizational ethics, and therefore is the fodder of strategic planning by public relations (and other) professionals. A basic question is whether an organization helps make the communities in which it operates more fully functioning. How does it add to that functionality, and how well? Does the level of CSR it achieves earn it the right to operate, the approval of stakeholders to gain resources by what it does and says? CSR, therefore, is a normative rationale for organizational enactment.

For these reasons, the topic of reflective management is intimately connected to the ethics of public relations (Holmstrom, 2010). Ethics discussions realize that the practice can be compromised by standards and actions that are not reflective.

Central to this discussion is the locus of interest—whose and what interest(s)? One view of management is that company policy is good (pragmatic) if it achieves the company's mission and vision. This standard of modernity, largely based on efficient and rational business practices, was the foundation for management ethics until the post-World War II era. That era spawned the CSR movement, whereby public policy constraints were justified over business practices that offended the expectations of key stakeholders.

The CSR movement arose from broad and robust critical discussions of business ethics, a topic that public relations practitioners and academics eventually joined. The key theme of reflective management is that business planning and policy (management decision making) necessarily interrogate and respond to the moral expectations and resource interests of various stakeholders (Freeman, 1984). This line of reasoning has become vital to issues management, as well as corporate reputation and relationship management.

Ethical Challenge

Imagine you work for a public relations firm counseling several companies that are jointly proposing the construction of a major pipeline. This pipeline will carry raw hydrocarbons to refining and manufacturing facilities. Its construction and operation will provide much-needed jobs, and therefore are supported by labor. State governments have mixed views because they are being pressured by environmental groups. Both the construction and the operation of the pipeline could harm the environment, especially should a rupture occur, which would damage aquifers, habitats, city water sources, and farmland. Industry claims that it can operate safely. Local communities need the jobs and taxes, and the nation needs energy at competitive prices. Given that multiple stakeholders are involved, and in an effort to know and implement reflective management, what ethical principles do you believe are important for your agency to propose?

Communitarianism reflects the principles and practices by which an organization can earn goodwill and demonstrate devotion to the good of a community in which it operates. Communities of interest include those that are or might be affected by the organization's presence. Communitarianism is an important topic in critical theory, and it is friendly to rhetorical theory because it presumes that high-quality, deliberative, and trust-building discourse adds value to and makes society more fully functioning. It is also relevant to the principles of balance, interdependence, and systems harmony that are championed by systems theory.

A central theme of communitarianism is the ethical standard that, each day and in every way, management (and the organization it enacts) must earn the right to operate by how it serves the communities in which it is present (Starck & Kruckeberg, 2001; see also Coombs & Holladay, 2011).

Communitarianism calls on management to consider the ethics of what makes its organization a good place to work, and to plan and operate in ways that help make each community of interest more fully functioning, a better place to live. Connecting these dots, Heath (2006) concludes:

> Public relations is a piece of some whole. The challenge is to continue to search to discover the whole and public relations' place in it. One view of that whole is the nature of society and, consequently, the constructive and destructive roles public relations can play to that end. (p. 110)

Steyn and Niemann (2014) leverage that conclusion to provide a normative framework that balances enterprise strategy, shared governance, and global sustainability.

Enterprise strategy is that which managements use to seek organizational success. Such a strategy is always enacted in the context of societal expectations, values, and norms, which are the foundations of shared governance. For that reason, strategic management's enterprise strategy— including its use of public relations—is always within the normative empowerment and constraint of societal expectations.

Ethical Challenge

Your management works on the proposition that a company is supposed to generate profit, pay as little in tax as possible, provide salaries and benefits that are competitive, and operate safely enough to avoid legal and regulatory problems. Anything more than that violates the principles of the free-market system, which are increasingly shaped by global supply chains and markets. What arguments would you use to defend and define the communitarian ethics that each company should implement to make society more fully functioning? Would you propose meetings by which you can understand and respond to stakeholders whose opinions and preferences exhibit varying degrees of conflict and controversy over the matter? Should your organization sponsor, support, and respond to citizens advisory committees (CACs)? What ethical challenges should be identified in a paper written to help management understand and appreciate each community in which it operates?

As the discussion proceeds in this chapter, it will flesh out these themes, reflect on how well theories of public relations address ethics, and pose ethical quandaries relevant to professional best practices. The next section examines the four theories featured in this book to learn how each views ethics of organizational performance and the professional practice of public relations.

Ethics and Public Relations Theories

Each of the four theories featured in this book takes a position on the ethics of public relations. One of the challenges to the reputation and role of the profession is to demonstrate and justify its ability to add value, and to do so in ways that aspire to the highest ethical standards. For that reason, ethics should be an inherent aspect of public relations theory.

Excellence theory stresses the need for public relations managers to be part of the "dominant coalition" so that the opinions of publics and stakeholders can be brought to bear on organizational planning, policy, and performance. Knowing these opinions, and being committed to ethics of excellence, senior public relations officers can integrate ethical decision making (corporate conscience) with planned strategic behavioral adjustment. That adjustment can achieve harmony between the organization and its publics—but systems theory's view of such adjustment is aethical, driven by adjustment but not an inherent ethical system. This thinking grounds the organization's adjustive ability to create, strengthen, and repair relationships in order to achieve publics' and stakeholders' goodwill.

Symmetry is applauded as inherently consistent with excellence and social responsibility. It is claimed to be normatively superior to other communication management options. Symmetry is discussed as idealistic because it is assumed to be consonant with the highest ethical standards. Such idealism must also be realistic. As a key to the implementation of practical ethics, excellence theorists are committed to discussing and validating moral principles. Out of this ethical discourse should arise a culture of rule-based behaviors that reflect the normative assumptions of excellence and social responsibility (J. Grunig, 1992).

Excellence theorists strive to develop *"an ethical framework for public relations practitioners to use as they participate in strategic management"* (Grunig & Grunig, 2008, p. 341; italics in original). Central to meeting this challenge is the ability to move public relations from a buffering to a bridging function. Ethical decision making is vital to such bridging; it presumes the means and rationale for organizations to adjust themselves to ethical worldviews wherever they operate.

Advancing this point, Bowen (2007) reasoned that "Ethics is a single excellence factor and the common underpinning of *all* factors that predict excellent public relations" (p. 275; italics in original). Working for an ethics that helps inform excellence theory, Bowen continued, "Moral philosophy is the theory of ethics, and it is used to reinforce the understanding and applicability of ethics in public relations theory and practice" (p. 275). For Bowen, excellence theory's bridging ability explains how community and organizational moral judgment are brought together. The logic of deontology, Immanuel Kant's principles of moral philosophy, Bowen concluded, add ethical foundations to excellence because of their commitment to rationality and transcendentalism, the law of autonomy, the categorical imperative, dignity and respect, duty, and intention—the core of moral good will. The categorical imperative, the centerpiece of this reasoning, proposes that good moral judgment is that which, because of its insights to moral decision making, should become a universal law. In contrast to utilitarianism, deontology calls on humans to be moral agents and not merely to serve the interests of some particular members of a community.

Ethical Challenge

Your company's mission and vision statement expresses a commitment to managerial excellence. To that end, it strives for mutually beneficial relationships with its stakeholders and seeks to provide information that helps customers and employees solve problems relevant to the company's policies, products/services, and quality of life impact on the community in which it operates. You realize that stakeholders are often pretty self-interested. Critics of the company's shareholders' dividend policy complain that some profits are spent to support special school programs in music and science. They argue that senior management's compensation is too generous. Community environmental activists, meanwhile, complain that the company has a sizable carbon footprint. These and other continuing complaints strain the quality of the relationship between the company and the community in which it operates. What ethical principles help you know whether management is excellent, whether communication with publics and stakeholders is asymmetrical or symmetrical, and whether control is mutual?

Such joining of dialogue and two-way symmetry, Theunissen and Noordin (2012) claim, may uncritically see the two paradigms as interchangeable. What makes dialogue ethically unique, drawing on the influence of Martin Buber, is the role or quality of "between"—how dialogue bridges and empowers I and Thou. This normative goal challenges management's desire for control because it presumes the potential rightness of opinions that conflict with its preferred issue positions. Thus, dialogue presumes a union of control between parties and the norm of self-governance, and self-generated pursuit of social truth. Excellent interpretations of relationship quality emphasize that an organization needs to be willing and able to demonstrate that it can change policies based on interaction with publics.

Contingency theory features the virtue of conflict resolution through a strategic, contingent balance of advocacy and accommodation. It presumes that leaders should not use a single, boiler-plated approach to problem solving and conflict resolution, but rather should draw from an arsenal of strategies those which seem most likely to be effective and ethical in a given situation. Instead of adopting a single public relations strategy—namely, symmetry or control mutuality—as the ethically superior approach to public relations, contingency theorists champion an open-minded search for alternative means to achieve ethical outcomes. Contingency theory reasons that practitioners should, and do, select wisely and ethically, as well as strategically, from options on a continuum contingent to the conditions present in each specific public relations moment.

According to this theory, practitioners and critics alike operate out of personal ethics. This drives the choices they make, both individually and collectively. It informs the contingent choices between advocacy and accommodation as they seek the collaborative resolution of conflict (Pang, Jin, & Cameron, 2010).

Ethical Challenge

Imagine that you are asked to design a planning and policy document, with colleagues from human relations (HR), regarding employee compensation. Your company, like others inside and outside of the industry, typically pays women marginally lower salaries and wages. Studies indicate that women typically take more leave time, more parental leave time, and more uncompensated leave time. This is true not only for women with younger and school-aged children, but also for those with elderly parents and relatives. Most such women provide a second, rather than a primary, income. Health insurance costs are higher for women, and in fact your company is considering both higher co-pays and reduced health insurance coverage as part of maintaining profitability. The HR members of the team provide policy research and development. You are asked to offer ethical insights and to develop the messaging used to explain and justify the company's compensation policy to employees. Assuming that compensation is eternally a matter of conflict, do you prefer more of an accommodative approach or more of an advocacy one in the communication plan? What ethical considerations drive your counsel and message design?

Rhetorical theory has been challenged as being ethically deficient since its inception in ancient Greece. The rhetorical heritage has wrestled with many ethical challenges, especially as some theorists began a systematic critique of the ethical relativism—utilitarianism—of rhetorical strategies. Plato began that critique with a sweep of his intellectual hand; he rejected rhetoric, in preference for dialectic, as being a mere art, like cookery. He was frustrated by the fact that a case could be won by flaunting truth and justice.

Finding an ethical position that balances the concerns of excellence theory regarding persuasion and the enduring heritage of rhetorical theory, Edgett (2002) stressed the inherent compatibility of ethics, rhetoric, advocacy, and persuasion. Rather than seeing rhetoric as a means to control persuasive influence, she emphasized the ethical responsibility of putting information, opinions, values, policy positions, and such into play for the good of society. Self-governance requires input from many voices championing different points of view. The form of communication *per se* is not as relevant to ethical judgment as is the quality of the form—what it can achieve in service of the community. Rhetoric does not inherently equate to falsehood, and in fact can be used by one voice to challenge the substance of the discourse of others. Advocacy is ethically desirable for the following reasons: societal need for public evaluation of ideas, priority setting based on input from many voices, sensitivity to the protection of rights, confidentiality when morally responsible, veracity, reversibility (reversing the target of the message so that the source takes on, in a reflective manner, the role of recipient, or message target), validity, visibility, respect, and consent. Such ethical standards are foundational to rather than imposed on the rhetorical heritage.

That sort of thinking was incentive for Aristotle and Isocrates to clarify and strengthen rhetoric's connection to ethics. This Aristotle did in his interdependent treatises on rhetoric, ethics, and politics. He challenged rhetoric to be public, based on fact and sound reasoning, and to reflect high moral standards of character as the normative ability to serve the community. Similarly, Isocrates reasoned that rhetoric is the essential means by which people demonstrate their capacity to meet the test of citizenship needed to achieve self-governance. As citizens are inspired to serve their own interests, they should realize that such service is inseparable from service to collective interests, which in turn serve individual interests. That reasoning features the rhetorical principle that for dialogue to be effective and ethical, each participant (including organizations) must be good and virtuous—a theme that has pedagogic advantages (Stokes & Waymer, 2011).

With the addition of Martin Buber's appeal for an enriching "between" as the norm of dialogue, Theunissen and Noordin (2012) featured the unpredictability of where dialogue agonistically leads. True dialogue is not purposeless discourse or that which does not advance and defend premises; it is more a search for collective insight, rather than a means for achieving a predetermined outcome—especially one that satisfies the need by management to control opinions. The ethics of discourse is its agonistic exploration, a principle that is comfortable to the rhetorical and critical conditions of public relations (Ihlen & Heath, 2019).

For rhetorical theorists, good character is a means by which individuals and organizations influence discourse as a moral duty to society. With such interest in character, rhetorical theory has long pondered the traits and strategies that enhance or confound the perception of credibility and legitimacy. Being able to demonstrate good character—associating an organization with good values—is central to playing a constructive role in discourse. Discourse can contest whether each individual and organization exhibits good character and aligns interests.

Rhetoric acknowledges monologue but sees substantial merit in the corrective impact of discourse: statement and counter-statement. On many matters, but perhaps none more than ethics, discourse is a means by which ideas and positions, principles and policies, are subjected to public scrutiny based on the ideal that discourse produces superior outcomes. For that reason, emergent strategic process is important to rhetorical engagement, but process alone is inconsequential. The consequence of discourse as advocacy and counter-advocacy is the examination and testing of ideas and shared meaning on matters of ethics. The ideas that survive the test of discourse, and the vocabulary in which they are expressed, become the sources and resources of power. Power is the agonistic rationale for how people live in varying degrees of harmony and disharmony based on what they perceive, the identities and identifications that are at play, and the quality of society that results.

Broadly, the substance and rationale of discourse is the public consideration of propositions of fact, value, policy, identity, and identification. Moral philosophy guides strategic discourse. Through deliberative infrastructures and language resources, the norms of interest alignment are achieved so that society can be fully functioning. Public relations ethics grows from the quality of enactment by each organization, and from the ability of discourse to reveal and vet fact and value and to unite through collective policy making. Through the ethics of rhetoric, interests become known, weighed, and aligned.

Rhetorical theory centers on the ethics of fairness. The theory and praxis of rhetoric require ethical principles on individual and societal levels. Such analysis investigates the virtue of *fairness* as a moral principle (Ihlen & Heath, 2019). The concept of *rhetorical citizenship* (Kock & Villadsen, 2012) includes the *moral obligation* of caring (Theunissen, 2018). Agonistic theory appreciates *conflict as a productive motive* (Mouffe, 2013).

Rhetoric is a relational concept—one that defines the quality of relationships, as the quality of fairness defines relationship quality. Rhetorical acts contribute ethical judgment to strategic processes that legitimately serve collective interests above self-interests or as the fair adjustment of self-interests to one another. Individual and collective standards of ethics influence discourse processes with the spirit of fairness.

Pearson (1990) provided support for such ethical contributions of rhetorical theory as he contrasted the ethical implications of how systems theory can lead to an emphasis on functionalism versus an emphasis on interdependency. Rather than presuming the ethical superiority of a specific functional paradigm, Pearson reasoned that practice and theory should prefer a structure that advances "communicative and collaborative decision-making processes and the role it might play in mediating the tensions among interdependent social systems" (p. 232).

Agonism is paradigmatic of ethical rhetoric. Featuring both the classical origins of rhetoric and the ontology of the process, Davidson (2016) observed that "central to agonism is the idea that protagonists perform openly in public, seeking to win acclaim and admiration" (p. 148). He drew on Hornig's work (1993) to emphasize how "the value of classical agonism is its commitment to open public discourses that are able to contest closure and domination by a single or overlapping forces" (p. 148).

Ethical Challenge

Imagine that you are an advocate for the rhetorical theory of public relations. Knowing that, you realize that your management and your company's critics often believe that you should be able to monologically win every battle, and craft messages that always favor your interests while seeming—only seeming—to foster the interests of all. You aspire to help your organization and others to make society a better place to live—more fully functioning—through the quality of discourse on an array of important matters. Even though you are committed to helping to achieve the best ideas through discourse, you know that as a public relations practitioner you are suspected of engaging in sham, spin, and other forms of trickery in order to help your company win and stakeholders to lose. What ethical principles do you champion to make yourself and your company good, or of high character? How can you seek to use the best facts (fairly interpreted), the best values, the wisest policies, and communitarian identification? Presuming that power is in language, and language shapes power resources, how do you shape and voice company positions so that they advance the public interest? Can your reasoning be reflected in the company's CSR statement?

Critical theory is inherently connected to competing sociopolitical ideologies and ethically critical preferences regarding power, privilege, interest priority, and the public sphere. This theory warns that language, however seemingly neutral, is the primary means by which humans impose power constraints on one another and privilege some interests over others. The theory also champions the virtue of dialogue in the public arena, as opposed to monologue or to dialogue that gives voice only to privileged interests (Edwards & Hodges, 2011). With these themes in mind, it is easy to see how ethics is not something added on or brought into critical public relations, but is fundamental to it.

Critical theory requires insights into how language shapes people's sense of reality, their identities, and their relationships. Those who create ideas, policies, plans, and message content for public relations efforts should, it reasons, be insightful and sensitive to the power resources that are shaped and deployed through word choice. Beyond the ethics of clarity, critical theory reasons that, over time, key terms become the playground for ethically good or bad judgments and actions.

For that reason, the greatest ethics challenge might be how to explain what a term such as "sustainability" means for an organization's business plan. It is simplistic to merely commit an organization to helping achieve "sustainability" without exploring and explaining how that commitment can be achieved by, for instance, the organization's efforts to reduce its carbon footprint. It is important to consider the ethics of timing. Is it sufficient for coal-using utility companies to be committed to clean coal technology by 2050? The key is that policy, planning, and execution of the business plan are never neutral but are fraught with ethical challenges that require insights from many perspectives in order to craft an ideologically rich and reflective terminology by which to conduct business—and enrich communities.

Relevant as well is how each organization engages in ongoing dialogues. Does internal rhetoric lead it to be a better place to work, and does external rhetoric provide insights that help people collectively? Instead of making such decisions behind locked doors or in special sessions with limited participation, what ethical challenges are important to ensuring that all sides of an important issue are voiced, heard, and given due regard?

Ethical Challenge

Imagine that you are involved in the public relations publicity and promotion program for a major automobile manufacturer that brands itself as being at the cutting edge of automobile safety and sustainability through wise and ethical resource development. You are aware of the controversy over the health implications of bisphenol A (BPA): some scientists argue that the chemical, widely used in plastics, can have adverse health effects, especially on children. You notice that each new car your company produces comes equipped with nice plastic drinking glasses branded with the company's name and logo. You discover that these glasses contain BPA. You work to find a company that provides drinking glasses made from agricultural products, and lobby to have it supply your glasses in the future. You advocate that they come with the statement, "BPA free." You write a blurb for the CSR section of your company's website stating its sustainability and health commitments. Your CEO receives a curt statement from a plastics trade association challenging your efforts as not understanding sound science, caving in to environmental radicals, and creating an image problem for plastics, which are major components of automobiles. The key line in the letter from the trade association is that "plastic must be branded as safe, energy efficient, and recyclable." What are the ethics of your response and your company's position on the matter?

In these ways, the major theories of public relations offer insights regarding ethical challenges and solutions. Some ethical standards are inherent to these theories. Some ethics are imported to strengthen their normative stances. As part of this dialogue, the next section features three ethical theories and explores their implications for public relations.

Ethical Theories and Public Relations

Public relations theorists draw upon philosophers for their understanding of ethics. The challenge is to know what each of the philosophies of ethics offers, what its strengths and weaknesses are. A related challenge is to couple such understanding with the role and practice of public relations in order to elevate the ethical counseling and communicative performance of the profession.

At least three approaches to ethics are found explicitly and implicitly in the practice and theory of public relations: pragmatism, utilitarianism, and deontology. These are not the only ethical themes available for public relations theory and practice, but they seem most relevant. Time will tell whether other ethical perspectives will gain prominence.

Pragmatism was a popular theory primarily in the early years of the twentieth century. It was of great appeal in the United States, which is touted as the hotbed of pragmatism. It was advanced through the writings of Charles Sanders Pierce, William James, John Dewey (whose influence on public relations theory has been featured in other chapters), and George Santayana.

Pragmatism reasons that theory and experience combine to achieve intelligent practice through informed and skilled problem solving. This is often used to help teach principles of strategic message design; the process of reflective thinking leads to systematically superior decisions. It presumes that well designed and skillfully executed messages help targeted publics address and reflectively solve problems. For that reason, it offers a rationale for persuasive discourse, including advertising and publicity/promotion.

Pragmatism's approach to ethics is that the best solution to a problem is also likely to be the most ethical. Best can be efficient, clean, quick, and effective. Although pragmatism is often slighted as offering little insight into ethics, it nevertheless is central to important decisions. None is more telling, perhaps, than the ethical justification for the dropping of nuclear bombs on Japan, in order to reduce the civilian and military casualties that would have resulted had the war continued. In matters of medical therapy, treatment that is efficient and effective can best meet the test of ethics. As regards public relations, excellence's commitment to symmetry has pragmatic value, as does rhetoric's commitment to reflective thinking through public discourse. Contingency theory presumes that the best tactics are those contingent on context to achieve desirable outcomes. Hence, pragmatism's ethics focus on the instrumental quality of actions needed to solve problems.

Utilitarianism, a philosophy of consequentialism, reasons that the consequences or outcomes of an act are instrumental to determining its moral worth. This ethic has been used to justify the free market, but it can also be used to justify social-movement challenges to free-market economics. The value of a consumer good, service, or even labor can be the result of free and fair market exchange. Perhaps the ethic might be expressed this way: "we get what we pay for." Or: "we are worth what we earn."

The corrupting aspect of utilitarianism is the logic that the ends justify the means. (Pragmatism reasons that means lead to good ends.) By that standard, a "factually challenged" statement might, at least for a while, abate the wrath of critics. But will it stand the test of time? Also, in marketing, goods can be sold by pricing them higher (even if the quality is not higher) on the assumption that people work from the utilitarian premise that we get what we pay for. If we pay more, we get more!

Deontology, its champions advocate, is the highest form of moral philosophy. As an exemplar of deontology, Bowen (2010) has contended that the ethical practice and societal role of public relations is duty-based; that theme reflects a normative ethic. This approach to moral philosophy presumes that practitioners—any professionals, for that matter—serve ethically through their recognition of the duty to do good. In contrast to the duty to do good, deontology argues, pragmatism and utilitarianism are based on what works and on whether ends justify means.

Devoting much of her work to strengthening the ethical underpinnings of excellence theory by exploring deontology, Bowen (2007) saw consideration of "the ethical, the moral, and the good to be the essential components of excellence" (p. 275). And, she added, "none of the principles of excellence can be studied without, at the least, an admonition to implement them ethically in practice" (p. 275).

For that reason, either someone in public relations or a separate ethics officer is needed in the executive suite who is knowledgeable of what can be done through excellent public relations to make an organization excellent and thereby worthy of goodwill. Bowen advised this perspective in sum: "Deontology sees the duty of the organization to consider the perspective of publics as one driving force behind the ethical imperative of relationship maintenance" (p. 287).

On that analysis, duty as worthy service is paramount to deontology. Another essential factor is "good," the normative standard of seeking truth, creating knowledge, and bettering the home, the workplace, and society (Bowen, 2010). These themes can serve as the rationale for programmatic strategies, fundamental to organizational and societal cultures, that foster as well as result from duty and good. Such moral principles capable of guiding public relations include the following:

- collaborative or integrative decision making;
- listening and appreciating;
- social value and meaning as the liberating forces of willed choice;
- dialogue and responsiveness as engagement;
- management of competition and conflict as means for just resource distribution;
- responsibility, the duty of taking the right action for the right reasons; and
- autonomy, basing judgment on principle rather than mere self-interest.

To bring such principles to bear on management decision making and public relations best practices, practitioners should be authentic, consistent, and reflective. Perhaps the key is not to focus on the interests of any one organization as "something," but to see them as part of "something" larger (Bowen, 2010).

Excellence theory features this normative principle as the rationale for symmetry. Contingency theory postulates that such reasoning guides choices along the accommodation–advocacy continuum in conflict resolution. Rhetorical theory sees it as the culture for dialogue-produced enlightened choice. Critical theory sees it as requiring the ongoing analysis of discursive power and agency.

Ethical Challenge

In light of the themes of pragmatism, utilitarianism, and deontology, reconsider the ethics conclusions you drew on any or all of the ethical challenges found earlier in the chapter.

Imagine that you have been asked to help revise your organization's mission and vision statement for public relations so that it reflects the best core values. You have been asked to prepare this statement by your boss, who knows and appreciates that you studied public relations theory, including ethics. You may assume that you are employed in an agency, a company, a nonprofit, or a government agency. First, are there ethical challenges that differ based on the type of organization you work at? Second, what five principles are most central to defining and explaining the ethics portion of a unit or organization's mission and vision statement in the twenty-first century?

Considerations such as those made in previous sections highlight themes relevant to issues, crisis, risk, and publicity and promotion. The next section provides a brief opportunity to address these different aspects of public relations and the ethics specific to each one.

Issues, Crisis, Risk, and Publicity and Promotion

Ethics is essential to the management of issues, the resolution of crisis, and the management and communication of risk—especially expert, self, and community efficacy. In fact, a case can be made that ethics is "the" central efficacy theme, especially as it relates to CSR, legitimacy, safety, fairness, equality, and environmental quality. This section briefly reviews these topics with special attention to ethics. It also looks at publicity and promotion.

Issues Management

Bowen (2010) reasoned that issues management is functionally able and committed to bring ethics and moral philosophy into the service of public relations. Issues management has historically addressed how and why legitimacy and CSR are key pillars of issues management and discourse-based self-governance (see Heath & Palenchar, 2009). A centerpiece of the ethical challenge of issues and strategic management is the legitimizing or delegitimizing frames of CSR. Operant narratives contextually frame the operant CSR standards stakeholders use to assess the legitimacy of corporate management strategic planning and operations as well as strategic issue communication processes. What is done is never independent of the ethical question of why it is done. Such is the moral case for what an organization says and the communicative potential of its observable actions (McLeod et al., 2018). However, "ethics are difficult to ascertain and understand since they are abstract, riddled with biases, constantly evolving, and inherently nested across levels of analysis" (McLeod, Payne, & Evert, 2016, p. 440).

Key to understanding how issues are managed is the way they are framed and the ethical justification for such framing (Hallahan, 1999). Given that framing is a co-construction of social reality, "a *frame* limits or defines the message's meaning by shaping the inferences that individuals make about the message" (Hallahan, 1999, p. 207; italics in original). Frames can be of several kinds (e.g., semantic or story), and can express either a positive or a negative valence about the issue in question. Issue communication, especially as rhetoric, employs rhetorical elements such as "because," "since," and "so," which can frame the thematic trajectory of issues interpretation and debate.

Framing is not "merely" a matter of the style of expression. It is "a *cognitive heuristic* or rule-of-thumb that guides decisions in situations involving uncertainty or risk" (Hallahan, 1999, p. 208; italics in original; see also Kahneman & Tversky, 1979). It is not simply the purview of organizational communicators (rhetors) making strategic and ethical choices, but is fundamental to management decision making (Bayster & Ford, 1997). Within these cognitive and managerial processes, framing is a matter of defining situations, assigning attributes (evaluative elements, as in the case of attitudes), favoring choice options and actions (in the face of risk and uncertainty), interpreting issues, and expressing responsibility. Such frames occur in many contexts, including news reporting and commentary (Hallahan, 1999).

Issues management was conceived in an era characterized by sharp criticism of business and government. Grassroots voices demonstrated the importance of understanding and achieving legitimacy, and so meeting stakeholder CSR expectations. From its inception, strategic issue(s) management (SIM) featured strategic business planning (best discussed as reflective management), CSR legitimacy battles, issue monitoring (in order to know and understand the status of issue debates), and communication. Thus, ethics is central to issues management—not only the process of engagement, but also the content of public policy battles. For instance, one of the themes of the 1970s continues today based on the molar concept of fairness: What is a fair wage, fair carbon footprint, fair executive compensation, or fair tax burden?

Ethical Challenge

Knowing that perceptions of fairness are central to human judgment and approval, what ethical principles would you use to help an organization engage ethically in a debate in which that concept was central?

Crisis Management and Communication

Earlier in the book, crisis was discussed in terms of risk manifestation. As an example, the arrest of a customer for shoplifting can go wrong if an innocent person is badly treated. Executives—another example—can prosper handsomely from incentive bonuses at just the time that a company is causing financial harm to its workers, customers, and the general public/economy. The list continues, and experts on crisis communication advocate strategies for reputation restoration and renewal in such cases. They know that one or more accounts of an alleged crisis are needed by an organization under public scrutiny. Central to the design and delivery of messages relevant to discussions of crisis is the moral imperative to tell the truth, not avoid blame, and serve the public interest. Emphasizing this point, Bowen and Zheng (2015) conclude that "Ethics should be foremost among the considerations of an organization's reputation and a primary factor of successful crisis management" (p. 40).

Ethical Challenge

If you presume that in matters of crisis response, "the truth will eventually be known," what first ethical principle would you use to devise a crisis response plan for your organization? How should that principle be stated as a communication policy? In making such decisions, what value is offered by pragmatism, utilitarianism, and deontology?

Risk Management and Communication

Among the most important issues in risk management and communication are these: What degree of safety in some matter is safe enough? When is any standard of safety fair? The mental models approach (MMA) to risk features the centrality of sound science in the making of such decisions, often using probabilities as standard measures. Critical theorists call for normative judgment about the thoughts and interests of risk bearers and their culturally sensitive judgment of safety and fairness. The sociopsychometric view of risk finds that different perceptions of risk likelihood and safety are basic to human nature, and therefore central to risk discourse and policy. Finally, the infrastructural approach presumes dialogue on these matters must occur where experts, risk creators, and risk bearers—along with advocates—are brought together in collaborative decision making and self-governance.

Ethical Challenge

Knowing that CACs have become popular and are demonstrably efficacious in risk management and communication, what ethical positions would you use in developing a program to create one or more on specific risk topics? A CAC typically consists of an array of types of citizens, including those who express an interest in how a company operates, city officials responsible for health and safety, elected officials, and health and safety experts working for a particular company.

Publicity and Promotion

Publicity and promotion rely on discourse to help people make enlightened choices. This could include decisions about business products and services, but it might also include donorship to the arts, animal rights, and public broadcast, for instance. One ethical complaint about publicity and promotion is that they can actually frustrate their own goal, often by obscuring truth. They can lead people to think one thing when something else is actually the case.

Publicity and promotion are not always founded on the goal of aligning interests between organizations and stakeholders. Such communication tools should seek moral alignment rather than biasing decisions to favor some interests at the disadvantage of others.

Ethical Challenge

If you believe that one of the goals of publicity and promotion is to connect the identity of an organization (product or service) and the identity of a public, what ethical differences are there if the organization is a government agency, a business, or a nonprofit? From what you have learned, what ethical principle should guide your publicity and promotion programs?

As noted earlier, the four topics in this section (issues, risk, crisis, and publicity and promotion) can be viewed either as tools or as the defining rationale for public relations. Be that as it may, this section is designed to help the reader be aware of the pervasive role ethics plays in all aspects of the profession. Professionals are wise to keep ethical challenges in mind.

Conclusion

This chapter is devoted to the theme that no profession enjoys a positive status if it does not continually consider the ethics of its role and its professionals in society and the ethical quality of the tools of its trade. That principle is vital for medicine, engineering, accounting, social work, architecture—the list goes on. Ethics and ethical challenges are the big battleground on which is contested the identity of a profession, its legitimacy in society, and the means by which it accomplishes what it does.

Ethics is not an auxiliary topic or an afterthought in the discussion and practice of public relations. It is central to its practice, to its role in society, to the (continuing) education of its students and professionals, and to the creation, development, and purpose of its professional associations.

As such, public relations can find itself at times being too defensive. It is often expected to do what solid professionals believe it ethically ought not to do. Rather than being systematic in their ethical thinking and planning, practitioners may rely on their "gut." And they may allow their egos and earnings to corrupt their professional judgments. This is not unique to public relations. But as the profession seeks to be trusted—to operate in the public trust—it needs ethical grounding. To that end, this chapter has explored many themes relevant to the theories, practices, roles, contexts, and ethical thinking required of the public relations professional's worldview.

Chapter Summary

Ethics is vital to every profession. It is a means of justifying its role as a servant of society. Each profession takes its identity from how it is perceived to ethically serve others. The range of its scope and purpose, from counseling senior managements to making media responses, is constantly subjected to ethical scrutiny. For that reason, the discussion of public relations professionalism depends on how its ethics is studied and the purpose of that discussion. Senior practitioners need to model ethical behavior and discuss ethical challenges with junior members (Lee & Cheng, 2011). And all must shoulder the responsibility of institutionalizing ethics into the organizations for which they work, and among their coworkers (Fitzpatrick, 1996).

As was asked in Chapter 1: What is public relations, and what role does it play? One ancient and continuing theme is that it can help make organizations and individuals successful. The question, then, is whether the means of its effectiveness meet the highest ethical standards. More recently, the discussion has added the theme that ethical consideration is needed if public relations is to help make a community an effective place for organizations to succeed, as argued by neo-institutionalism.

Theories of public relations feature ethics, both centrally and as an added form of analysis. Excellence theory draws primarily on symmetry, as a systems feature, for its rationale of ethics. It reasons that behavioral adjustment through symmetry is the central ethical requirement of all excellent organizations. Contingency theory wrestles with the ethics of preferring advocacy or accommodation—or some combination thereof—as the means for ethically resolving conflict through public relations. The rhetorical tradition has for centuries featured the challenge of ethics for "speakers" and has argued that ethics (ethos) is central to the substance and text of discourse and the credibility of all voices that strive to enlighten choices through discourse. Critical theory is a theory of ethics. It seeks to bring ethics into discussions of power, meaning, knowledge, and discourse.

Several ethical perspectives have played and continue to play a role in the discussion of public relations. Three are featured in this chapter: pragmatism, utilitarianism, and deontology. In all three, the question is raised: What choices are ethically superior to others, and why?

Given the contextual nature of public relations, the chapter discusses issues, risks, crisis, and publicity and promotion. Each of these topics is relevant not only to the role of professionals in public relations, but also to the profession's ethical performance. Ethics is central to the management of issues, which, based on management planning and enactment, must meet operant CSR standards in order for plans, policies, and implementations to be legitimate.

Risks are decisions whose outcome is uncertain, where the benefits are presumed to be best when they outweigh the harms. How risk-relevant discourse plays out in society has ethical implications regarding the fundamental decisions about how safe is safe, how fair is safe, and how well the rewards of risk are balanced against the costs.

Crisis puts organizations and individuals in the hot seat. Discourse plays many roles, but one is to participate in collective ethical decisions as to whether wrongdoing has occurred and, if so, what best can be done to put matters right.

Publicity and promotion, strategic and functional hallmarks of the profession, presume individuals are problem solvers who want to make enlightened choices concerning products, services, nonprofit support, places of employment, and so forth. Long is the tradition that in these and other professional programs and strategies, spin, sham, deceit, diversion, and other self-serving strategies and programs are the stock-in-trade of public relations. Vital to the professional service of public relations, publicity and promotion must be informed by ethics if the profession is to enjoy such status in society.

In matters of ethical professional practice, public relations is no different than the practice of law, medicine, accounting, financial management, engineering, fire and police protection—the list goes on and on. The task is to know, achieve, and hold one another accountable for the ethical standards that bring approval to the profession.

In terms of public relations, ethical judgment focuses on the morality of strategies, functions, tactics, and purposes. It addresses what practitioners do, how they counsel, what they refuse to do, and how the organizations they represent aspire to meet legitimizing CSR standards.

Key Terms

Deontology: Moral philosophy that stresses the importance of moral responsibility, the duty to do good.

Ethics: Moral norms that can improve the strategic processes and functions of public relations.

Ethics Counsel: A key value-based role of public relations practitioners in strategic planning processes, capable of elevating the ethical judgment of planning and management, as well as communication.

Pragmatism: The moral philosophy of judging outcomes by means; achieving intelligent practice through informed and skilled problem solving.

Transparency: Maximum openness by organizations regarding the information desired by stakeholders as they assess their ethical judgment.

Utilitarianism: The moral philosophy that the ends justify the means.

Discussion Questions

1 What roles can codes of ethics play in the profession? What do they contribute to ethical practice? Can focus on the effectiveness of the functions of the practice obscure and confound practitioners' sound moral judgment?

2 What competing views exist on ethics, such as the role of codes of conduct, pragmatism, utilitarianism, deontology, and moral identity?

3 Why are CSR standards and communitarian principles vital to the ethics of public relations?

4 What ethical themes define excellence theory, contingency theory, rhetorical theory, and critical theory? What ethical principles does each address, and how does this advance the professionalism of public relations?

5 If issues management is a test of organizational legitimacy, what role does ethics play?

6 How can crisis management and communication be judged by pragmatism, utilitarianism, and deontology?

7 If risk depends on knowing how safe is safe and how fair is safe, why is it ethically important that risk communication be situationally dialogic as well as monologic?

8 How can the ends of publicity and promotion be ethically corrupting?

9 What do moral principles such as openness, authenticity, and transparency have to do with public relations?

References

Auger, G. A. (2014). Trust me, trust me not: An experimental analysis of the effect of transparency on organizations. *Journal of Public Relations Research, 26*, 325–343.

Austin, L. L., & Toth, E. L. (2011). Exploring ethics education in global public relations curricula: Analysis of international curricular descripts and interviews with public relations educators. *Public Relations Review, 37*, 506–512.

Bayster, P. G., & Ford, C. M. (1997). The impact of functional classification schema on managerial decision processes. *Journal of Managerial Issues, 2*, 187–203.

Black, J. (2008). An informal agenda for media ethicists. *Journal of Mass Media Ethics, 23*, 28–35.

Bowen, S. A. (2007). The extent of ethics. In E. L. Toth (Ed.), *The future of excellence in public relations and communication management: Challenges for the next generation* (pp. 275–297). Mahwah, NJ: Lawrence Erlbaum Associates.

Bowen, S. A. (2008). A state of neglect: Public relations as "corporate conscience" or ethics counsel. *Journal of Public Relations Research, 20*, 271–296.

Bowen, S. A. (2010). The nature of good in public relations: What should be its normative ethic? In R. L. Heath (Ed.), *SAGE handbook of public relations* (pp. 569–584). Thousand Oaks, CA: Sage.

Bowen, S. A., & Zheng, Y. (2015). Auto recall crisis, framing, and ethical response: Toyota's missteps. *Public Relations Review, 41*, 40–49.

Boynton, L. A. (2002). Professionalism and social responsibility: Foundations of public relations ethics. In W. B. Gudykunst (Ed.), *Communication yearbook 26* (pp. 230–265). Mahwah, NJ: Lawrence Erlbaum Associates.

Brunner, B. R. (2015). What is civic professionalism in public relations? Practitioner perspectives—A pilot study. *Public Relations Review, 42*, 237–239.

Callison, C., Merle, P. F., & Seltzer, T. (2014). Smart friendly liars: Public perception of public relations practitioners over time. *Public Relations Review, 40*, 829–831.

Christensen, L. T., & Langer, R. (2009). Public relations and the strategic use of public relations. In R. L. Heath, E. L. Toth, & D. Waymer (Eds.), *Rhetorical and critical approaches to public relations II* (pp. 129–153). New York: Routledge.

Coombs, W. T., & Holladay, S. J. (2011). *Managing corporate social responsibility: A communitarian approach.* Hoboken, NJ: Wiley-Blackwell.

Davidson, S. (2016). Public relations theory: An agonistic critique of the turns to dialogue and symmetry. *Public Relations Inquiry, 5*, 145–167.

DiStaso, M. W., Stacks, D. W., & Botan, C. H. (2009). State of public relations education in the United States: 2006 report on a national survey of executives and academics. *Public Relations Review, 35*, 254–269.

Edgett, R. (2002). Toward an ethical framework for advocacy in public relations. *Journal of Public Relations Research, 14*, 1–26.

Edwards, L., & Hodges, C. E. M. (2011). *Public relations, society & culture: Theoretical and empirical explorations.* New York: Routledge.

Erzikova, E. (2010). University teachers' perceptions and evaluations of ethics instruction in the public relations curriculum. *Public Relations Review, 36*, 316–318.

Eschenfelder, B. (2011). The role of narrative in public relations ethics pedagogy. *Public Relations Review, 37*, 450–455.

Fawkes, J. (2012). Saints *and* sinners: Competing identities in public relations ethics. *Public Relations Review, 38*, 865–872.

Fitzpatrick, K. (1996). The role of public relations in the institutionalization of ethics. *Public Relations Review, 22*, 249–258.

Frederick, W. C. (1986). Toward CSR3: Why ethical analysis is indispensable and unavoidable in corporate affairs. *California Management Review, 28*, 126–141.

Freeman, R. E. (1984). *Strategic management: A stakeholder approach.* Boston, MA: Pitman.

Grunig, J. E. (Ed.) (1992). *Excellence in public relations and communication management.* Hillsdale, NJ: Lawrence Erlbaum Associates.

Grunig, L. A. (1992). Toward the philosophy of public relations. In E. L. Toth & R. L. Heath (Eds.), *Rhetorical and critical approaches to public relations* (pp. 65–91). Hillsdale, NJ: Lawrence Erlbaum Associates.

Grunig, J. E., & Grunig, L. A. (2008). Excellence theory in public relations: Past, present, and future. In A. Zerfass, B. van Ruler, & K. Sriramesh (Eds.), *Public relations research: European and international perspectives and innovations* (pp. 327–347). Wiesbaden: VS Verlag.

Hallahan, K. (1999). Seven models of framing: Implications for public relations. *Journal of Public Relations Research, 11*, 205–242.

Harrison, J. S., Bosse, D. A., & Phillips, R. A. (2010). Managing for stakeholders, stakeholder utility functions, and competitive advantage. *Strategic Management Journal, 31*, 58–74.

Heath, R. L. (2006). Onward into more fog: Thoughts on public relations' research directions. *Journal of Public Relations Research, 18*, 93–114.

Heath, R. L., & Ni, L. (2010). Community relations and corporate social responsibility. In R. L. Heath (Ed.), *SAGE handbook of public relations* (pp. 557–568). Thousand Oaks, CA: Sage.

Heath, R. L., & Palenchar, M. J. (2009). *Strategic issues management: Organizations and public policy challenges* (2nd ed.). Thousand Oaks, CA: Sage.

Heath, R. L., & Waymer, D. (2019). Elite status talks, but how loudly and why? Exploring elite CSR micro-politics. *Corporate Communications: An International Journal, 24*, 232–247.

Holmstrom, S. (2010). Reflective management: Seeing the organization as if from the outside. In R. L. Heath (Ed.), *SAGE handbook of public relations* (pp. 261–292). Thousand Oaks, CA: Sage.

Holtzhausen, D. R. (2011). *Public relations as activism: Postmodern approaches to theory and practice.* New York: Routledge.

Holtzhausen (2015). The unethical consequences of professional communication codes of ethics: A postmodern analysis of ethical decision-making in communication practice. *Public Relations Review, 41*, 769–776.

Honig, B. (1993). *Political theory and the displacement of politics.* Ithaca, NY: Cornell University Press.

Ihlen, O., & Heath, R. L. (2019). Ethical grounds for public relations as organizational rhetoric. *Public Relations Review, 36*, 59–62.

Ihlen, O., Bartlett, J. L., & May, S. (Eds.) (2011). *The handbook of communication and social responsibility.* Malden, MA: Wiley-Blackwell.

Kahneman, D., & Tversky, A. (1979). Prospect theory: An analysis of decision under risk. *Econometrica, 47*, 263–291.

Kock, C., & Villadsen, L. S. (2012). Introduction: Citizenship as a rhetorical practice. In C. Kock & L. Villadsen (Eds.), *Rhetorical citizenship and public deliberation* (pp. 1–10). Philadelphia, PA: Penn State University Press.

Lee, S. T., & Cheng, I.-H. (2011). Characteristics and dimensions of ethical leadership in public relations. *Journal of Public Relations Research, 23*, 46–74.

McLeod, M. S., Payne, G. T., & Evert, R. E. (2016). Organizational ethics research: A systematic review of methods and analytical techniques. *Journal of Business Ethics, 134*, 429–443.

McLeod, M. S., Moore, C. B., Payne, G. T., Sexton, J. C., & Evert, R. E. (2018). Organizational virtue and stakeholder interdependence: An empirical examination of financial intermediaries and IPO firms. *Journal of Business Ethics*, *149*, 785–798.

Mouffe, C. (2013). *Agonistics: Thinking the world politically*. London: Verso.

Pang, A., Jin, Y., & Cameron, G. T. (2010). Strategic management of communication: Insights from the contingency theory of strategic conflict management. In R. L. Heath (Ed.), *SAGE handbook of public relations* (pp. 17–34). Thousand Oaks, CA: Sage.

Pearson, R. (1990). Ethical values or strategic values? The two faces of systems theory in public relations. *Public Relations Research Annual*, *2*, 219–234.

Place, K. (2015). Exploring the role of ethics in public relations program evaluation. *Journal of Public Relations Research*, *27*, 118–135.

Public Relations Society of America. (n.d.). PRSA Code of Ethics. Available from https://www.prsa.org/ethics/code-of-ethics (accessed May 20, 2020).

Starck, K., & Kruckeberg, D. (2001). Public relations and community: A reconstructed theory revisited. In R. L. Heath (Ed.), *Handbook of public relations* (pp. 51–60). Thousand Oaks, CA: Sage.

Steyn, B., & Niemann, L. (2014). Strategic role of public relations in enterprise strategy, governance and sustainability—A normative framework. *Public Relations Review*, *40*, 171–183.

Stokes, A. Q., & Waymer, D. (2011). The good organization communicating well: Teaching rhetoric in the public relations classroom. *Public Relations Review*, *37*, 441–449.

Theunissen, P. (2018). Philosophy and ethics of engagement. In K. A. Johnston & M. Taylor (Eds.), *The handbook of communication engagement* (pp. 49–60). Medford, MA: John Wiley & Sons.

Theunissen, P., & Noordin, W. N. W. (2012). Revisiting the concept "dialogue" in public relations. *Public Relations Review*, *38*, 5–13.

Valentini, C., Kruckeberg, D., & Starck, K. (2012). Public relations and community: A persistent covenant. *Public Relations Review*, *38*, 873–879.

Watson, T. (2014). IPRA Code of Athens—The first international code of public relations ethics: Its development and implementation since 1965. *Public Relations Review*, *40*, 707–714.

Zoch, L. M., Supa, D. W., & VanTuyll, D. (2014). The portrayal of public relations in the era of Ivy Lee through the lens of the *New York Times*. *Public Relations Review*, *40*, 723–732.

10

Publics, Stakeholders, and Other Voices

Introduction

"Public relations" is a combination of the two terms "public" and "relationship." Understanding the term "public" is basic to defining the discipline of public relations. "Public" is the focus of this chapter, while the closely related concept of "relationship" is discussed in Chapter 11. The here discussion begins with a careful assessment of the reason why the concept of public or publics has become a key part of the discipline, and how it fits with other key concepts utilized in public relations theories.

During much of the twentieth century, the term used to describe the "target" of public relations was "public opinion." But how did one measure public opinion from a public relations standpoint? The media relations bias undergirding public relations theory and practice presumed that public relations messages needed to be placed in the standard media: newspapers, radio, and television. Other channels were also relevant, but the mass dissemination of messages was the common assumption of the practice, with a visceral sense that effective public relations conducted through standard media channels affected public opinion.

Although public opinion was a well-established concept, it was given a central place in communication studies and practices in 1922 with the publication of Walter Lippmann's *Public Opinion*. Lippmann wrote that "because the pictures inside people's heads do not automatically correspond with the world outside," the concept of public opinion serves as an organizing system that provides for individuals "the picture of themselves, of others, of their needs, purposes, and relationships" (Lippmann, 1922, pp. 18–19). This suggests the interconnectedness of what people think and how they act in a democracy, but it presents the manufacture of consent as a problem. Lippmann proposed that a professional "specialized class" of individuals would use "the art of persuasion" to help guide the public in the formation of its opinions. Lippmann's concept of public opinion led practitioners and educators to envision the practice in the following way: if media shape people's thoughts, which affect how they act in a democracy, then public relations professionals are needed to influence the media, and accordingly to influence public and private policy trends. The problem is that this model implies that public relations operates in the service of good leaders—something that the experience in Europe in the 1930s and 1940s demonstrated was not always the case.

It thus became clear that middle opinions, as defined by a bell curve, may not be the most important criteria by which organizations are judged. The role of dissent and uneasiness with established opinions was recognized during the second half of the twentieth century. Thus, the idea developed that the concept of public opinion was not monolithic, but rather a conglomeration of multiple publics, each competing to offer the best interpretation of reality—what was on this

Public Relations Theory: Capabilities and Competencies, First Edition. Jae-Hwa Shin and Robert L. Heath.
© 2021 John Wiley & Sons, Inc. Published 2021 by John Wiley & Sons, Inc.

multiple public's mind. Typical of such trends, Rawlins and Bowen (2004) presumed that "in modern public relations, there is no such thing as 'a general public'" (p. 718). The concept took on even more important dimensions as other terms were introduced to describe and differentiate multiple publics, such as "stakeholders," "markets/customers," "activists," "supporters," "opponents," "followers," and eventually something as vague as "voices." As Rawlins (2006) noted, the interchangeable use of terms such as "public" and "stakeholder" represented misperception of the distinction. Use of the term "stakeholder" to describe individuals or groups who own, work for, support, or have an interest in an organization derived from business management theory in the early 1960s. According to Freeman (1984), "stakeholder" referred to a group broader than the concept of "shareholder," which was limited to a financial stake, and further suggested that the concerns of a more expansive definition of "interest group" possessed legitimacy. He contended that almost anyone associated with an organization could be considered a stakeholder depending on the context, and that an organization's management had a moral responsibility to consider the interests of *all* actual and potential stakeholders. This chapter, for these reasons, notes that "public" served as a shorthand for the persons with whom an organization wanted and needed to communicate. That concept became a convenient term for public relations planning and measurement. The paradigm thus emerged: What segment of the public, or a public, should an organization communicate with? This logic led to an analysis of types of publics, segmentations, prioritization, and other heuristics for guiding the practice of and research into public relations.

This chapter thus traces the evolution of the concept "public" from ancient perspectives situating it in relation to the political arena. It considers mass perspectives emphasizing group consciousness, as well as situational views based on analysis of social and psychological factors. It examines some other perspectives that tackle the question of how group participation or identity emerges from discrete, individual beliefs and expressions. One prevailing strain of thought holds that publics are defined by shared symbolic meanings—cultural threads or *memes* that are shared by being presented, adapted, and re-presented in ever evolving forms—resulting in the formation of a group identity and interest advocacy that is constantly shifting. The chapter attempts to unpack these concepts of publics and the various conceptualizations of those persons with whom public relations practitioners need to engage. By its conclusion, readers should understand the power and problematic of deciding which conception is best for understanding publics, stakeholders, and voices, especially in evolving media environments.

Questions to Frame the Discussions of Publics

- What are some definitions of "public" in public relations?
- Can you differentiate the concepts of "the public," "publics," "stakeholders," and "voices"? What are the differences and similarities among these concepts?
- Compare and contrast different perspectives defining the "public" in public relations. What are the differences and similarities among these perspectives?
- What are some characteristics of the "public" in public relations? What are their roles in the relationship with an organization in a given society?
- What are some different types of publics?
- How is a public developed around an issue from the situational perspective, assuming that "public" is issue-dependent?
- How has globalization or technology affected or changed the notion of "public"?

Key Themes

- The concept of "public" emerged from a monolithic to a multiple conceptualization from a number of different perspectives.
- The public sphere stands in contrast to the private sphere.
- "Public" is issue-dependent through a cycle of issue development.
- Publics can be measured by psychological and behavioral variables in a given situation.
- Democracy, the press, and institutions that allow individuals to express themselves freely are central to the modern concept of "public."
- Stakeholders are an expansive collection of groups or individuals with an interest in an organization.
- A fully functioning society can be inclusive of multiple stakeholders and voices, whether they are powerful, marginalized, or voiceless.

What Is a/the Public?: A Historical Perspective

Generically, "public" stands in opposition to the term "private." Thus, "public" refers to matters that are revealed, open to, or shared with others, whereas "private" denotes things that are personal, cloistered, and often self-oriented. "Public" can refer to policies and norms that have meaning and significance for general audiences, whereas "private" tends to involve matters of particular and individual relevance, even as applied to business. One early definition is offered by the icons of public relations theory and practice, Cutlip and Center (1971, p. 128):

> A *public* is simply a collective noun for a group—a group of individuals tied together by some common bond of interest—and sharing *a sense of togetherness*. It may be a small group or a large group; it may be a majority group. Ogle defines a *public* as "any group of two or more persons who demonstrate in any manner whatever that they are conscious of group solidarity."

To further understand the term "public," it is useful to review its history. It is derived from the Latin term *publicus*, defined in an 1879 Latin dictionary as meaning "of or belonging to the people, State, or community; that is done for the sake or at the expense of the state; public, common" (Lewis & Short, 1879). *Publicus* is a contraction of the term *populicus* or *populous*, meaning "of the people." As the origin of the word suggests, ancient Greeks and Romans were among the first to posit the idea of a public. Because of their views on politics and rhetoric, Greek and Roman civic bodies granted citizens—members of the public—certain proscribed privileges. Chief among them was the right to vote and to engage in debate. Although citizenship was limited by class and status, the ancient model established the concept of democracy, defined as the right of an individual to participate in civic life. The ancient conception presumed that those with greater power resources historically have tended to have greater representation in public life—an assumption that has continued to hold force to this day.

The first use of the term "public" in English emerged in about 1500, with a meaning very close to the original Latin definition. In medieval times, the idea of a public was conceived according to a strict hierarchy: at the top was the church, followed by nobles, landowners, and finally the disenfranchised. While the opinions and interests of religious leaders and lords were considered important, those of the common people, known as "vassals," were not. Only members of the elite classes

Case Study: Fracktivism

Is the general public a single entity bound together by shared values and aspirations, or a collection of multiple or competing groups joined by their interests? Can a public exist in the absence of counterpart individuals or organizations? How do publics seek to build legitimacy and power? Does dialogic engagement with organizations promote an improvement of social values and standards? Are publics sometimes more interested in calling attention to themselves, playing devil's advocate, and building support than in solving problems for the good of society? Also, do organizations simply feign interests in the positions outlined by activists with the cynical goal of "coopting" their position to better limit or defeat it as public debate unfolds (Coombs & Holliday, 2007, p. 11)?

These questions were posed by a series of films released in the 2010s. The documentary *GasLand* (2010) focuses on communities in the rural Western United States, where hydraulic fracturing (fracking) is used to extract natural gas. In some instances, farmers who leased their land for fracking discovered that their water supplies became polluted. In one iconic scene, a man lights his tapwater on fire as evidence of seeping methane gas.

In response to the pro-environmental message promoted in *GasLand*, filmmakers Phelim McAleer, Ann McElhinney, and Magdalena Seigieda made *FrackNation* (2013) to reveal "fracking facts suppressed by environmental activists" (FrackNation, n.d.). McAleer pointed out that instances of water being lit on fire occurred before the fracking began. Additionally, the Independent Petroleum Association of America chronicled a scene-by-scene critique of perceived inaccuracies in *GasLand*, and even made a documentary film entitled *TruthLand* (2012) to debunk its narrative and argue that fracking provides more economic benefit than harm.

Finally, *Promised Land* (2013), a narrative film starring Matt Damon, focuses on a company's attempts to secure mineral rights from farmers in order to conduct fracking on their land. It follows the company's campaign to influence the community using deceptive tactics.

Together, these films evoke or represent different or competing publics, each with vested interests born out of a particular socio-political outlook centered on the issues of economic vitality, global warming, and corporate responsibility. Environmentalists and those negatively affected by natural gas drilling contend that the societal and environmental harm resulting from fracking outweighs its economic benefits. This is the perspective advocated in *GasLand*, and in *Promised Land* in a more subtle manner. On the other side, *TruthLand* and *FrackNation* represent groups with a vested interest in natural gas production, arguing that environmentalist misrepresents the facts about fracking. In particular, the plot of *Promised Land* hinges on an environmentalist named Dustin Noble who tells landowners the story of how fracking destroyed his family's farm in Nebraska. The landowners later learn that the energy company attempting to buy their land hired Noble to fabricate this story: it intended to demonstrate that activists were untrustworthy and thus discredit the environmental movement. The conclusion of the film reveals that the company has deceived the landowners by exploiting the gap between the goals of activists and its own goals by feigning concern, coopting their position, and seeking to undermine their legitimacy (Coombs & Holliday, 2007).

Each of these films was intended to affect public opinion and policy on drilling. Ultimately, while *GasLand* and *Promised Land*, critical of the fracking industry, raised concerns voiced by a range of publics, they seem to have had little long-term impact on policy. For example, a rule against fracking on federal lands initiated by the Obama administration was blocked by a federal judge, who stated that hydraulic fracking was not subject to federal regulation. The Environmental Protection Agency (EPA) under the Trump administration has upheld this ruling, and has also backed off on enforcement of regulations such as the Clean Water Act.

were given the authority to participate in civic life from the standpoints of economics, politics, and culture. This view began to change slowly from about the twelfth century as growing economic power among a rising merchant class and landless knights presented challenges to the strict hierarchy. This emerging public sought avenues to have its opinions and interests expressed, such as through the establishment of the Knights of Malta and the Masons.

During the Enlightenment in the eighteenth century, the concept of "public" underwent a significant change. Powerful merchants, followed by tradesmen and small landowners, and eventually property-less serfs, demanded reform, as expressed through political and intellectual revolution. This Enlightenment public comprised the reading public, whose numbers were swelling at a rapid pace. Enlightenment values led to experiments in modern democracy—a form of government rooted in discourse and the expression of public opinion. Jürgen Habermas (1989) proposed that the period was marked by the open exchange of ideas in places such as taverns and coffee houses, which he linked to the public sphere. Habermas identified two dimensions to the public sphere: the literary and the political. While it was conceived as a physical space in the early years, the rising status of media meant that the public sphere became an increasingly virtual space. Freedom of association was its defining characteristic. It was a place where "private people come together as a public ... to engage [public authorities] in a debate over the general rules governing relations in the basically privatized but publicly relevant sphere of commodity exchange and social labor" (Habermas, 1989, p. 27).

For Habermas, the public sphere was both prerequisite and essential to the survival of democracy. However, with the rise of industrial capitalism, its democratic nature collapsed under the weight of consumerism and authoritarianism. It lost its independence. Later critics argued that Habermas' conception of the late-eighteenth-century democratic public sphere was overly idealistic, failing to account for the masses of impoverished and illiterate publics excluded from participation. The public sphere served as a discursive space where issues of mutual interest were discussed and public opinions were formed. Mass media provided both an outlet and an incubator for such opinions.

Walter Lippmann (1922) argued that the creation of the public operated in an imaginary space. In that space, the media facilitated people's need to create "pictures in their heads" based on secondary as opposed to direct experience (p. 3). Lippmann emphasized that individuals relied on experts and opinion leaders for guidance. Hallahan (2000) described Lippmann's view as related to the perils of industrial capitalism, social atomization, and the "division of labor and estrangement from others," leading to a disinterest in public affairs (p. 502).

"Public(s)" as the Central Term in Public Relations

At a foundational level, the term "public" has a high degree of ambiguity and thus is often used as a catchall to describe the "target" or mission of public relations. This raises a crucial question: Does public relations exist because there are publics, or does a public exist because of public relations? From the 1960s through the 1980s, most public relations scholars sided with the situational-organizational camp, conceiving of the public strictly in relation to organizations. This is a result of the historic development of the field, which as Karlberg (1996) noted, has its roots in "a commercial management function—a means of influencing consumer value and behavior, of cultivating markets, of corporate image control and issue management" (p. 266).

Grunig and Hunt (1984) stressed the role of organizations as generators of messages and that of the public as receivers. The situational theory of publics (STP) sought to explain why particular publics recognize and pay attention to particular messages at particular times. Situational theory scholars suggested that publics do not exist in the absence of a defining issue or problem. In this conception, a group that constitutes a public forms and organizes around a specific issue or agenda in relationship to organizations. To better target their messages, organizations define, segment, and prioritize publics according to their level of engagement or awareness of an issue.

Taking a more independent and self-empowering view of publics, Vasquez and Taylor (2001) described them as a "population of individuals involved in civic affairs under all circumstances" (p. 140). Leitch and Neilson (2001) summarized the critical perspective of publics as "groups of individuals participating in the public sphere" (p. 131). They voiced concern with the perspective of the situational-organizational view that "publics are treated as organizational artifacts or constructs" which "appear to come into existence only when an organization identifies them as publics" (p. 128). Leitch and Motion (2010) called this a "highly simplistic model" because it denied the possibility of defining a public unless it engaged with an organization (p. 100). Following Habermas's (1989) conception of the public sphere, they proposed instead that publics exist in empowered and self-defining ways and are not the tools of organizational public relations (Leitch & Motion, 2010, p. 101).

Publics are often defined as "stakeholders," or a group of individuals bound together by a "bond of interest or concern and who have consequences for an organization" (Newsom, Turk, & Kruckeberg, 2004, p. 90). These individuals are not necessarily directly connected to that organization. Organizational activities have an impact on society, and a variety of stakeholders have influence on an organization. As will be seen later in this chapter, "stakeholder" may not be synonymous with "public," although it might augment the term, or even replace it.

Reexamination of the Concept of "Public"

In recent years, scholars have begun to abandon the micro-level focus on strategic communication with active publics in an organizational context and to reexamine some of the assumptions about what constitutes a public, how they come into being, how best to understand them, and what significance this understanding has for the practice of public relations in a society. Botan and Soto (1998) noted that the "organization-centered perspective dominant in public relations and organizational communication scholarship" has come at the expense of a sophisticated understanding of the public (p. 23). Vasquez and Taylor (2001) expressed concern that "for all the importance placed on the creation, maintenance, and adaptation of organization-public relationships, the term public is one of the most ambiguous concepts in the field's vocabulary" (p. 139). Leitch and Motion (2010) reiterated the lack of contextualization or complexity in the understanding of the public in public relations theory (p. 100). Others, such as Botan (1993), Broom, Casey, and Ritchey (1997), Hallahan (2000), Kruckeberg (2006a), Pearson (1987), and Porter (1992), have agreed and made inroads into the topic by borrowing from other disciplines such as semiotics, sociology, psychotherapy, poststructuralism, and discourse analysis.

Grunig and Repper (1992) defined publics narrowly as stakeholders who have "become more aware and active" on the same interest (p. 125). According to this organizational perspective, publics come into being *only* in response to particular situations that arise in relationship to organizations. A public does not exist in the absence of either an active or a latent status: "A public, a market, or any other segment of the population exists only because [a public relations] practitioner uses a theoretical concept to identify it" (p. 129). Organizations instigate the communicative process, and publics exist as targeted receivers of these messages. Accordingly, publics can accept or reject messages depending on their degree of alignment with their interests. The primary distinction is between active and latent publics, or those with some relationship to a particular organization and those with a potential for a relationship. This view builds on Dewey's argument that "each issue or problem creates its own public" (Cutlip & Center, 1971, p. 128).

In contrast, taking a cultural perspective, Kruckeberg and Vujnovic (2010) emphasized how the concept of a general public remains important to the practice of public relations despite the functionalist approach to defining publics according to a segmented model and from an organizational perspective. Their view suggests that organizations are created and sustained by the consent of publics—something that is constantly renegotiated through interaction and communication. Others, such as Cancel, Mitrook, and Cameron (1999), reasoned that publics and organizations engage in dynamic relationships based on power differences, which are much more complex than simply striving for coordination of an organization and its publics. The contingency approach gives equal footing to the public in a strategic continuum between advocacy and accommodation. Both an organization and its publics are strategic entities, changing their stances and moving on a continuum with a variety of strategic choices. This approach presumes the dynamic and contingent relationships among multiple publics.

The dynamic interaction between an organization and its publics is also addressed by the semiotic and rhetorical approaches offered by Heath (2010), Pearson (1987), and Porter (1992). These authors broadly defined publics according to their relationship to the communicative and meaning development processes. Leitch and Neilson (2001) suggested that individuals could simultaneously occupy a multiplicity of subject positions and thus constitute a variety of publics at any given time. Based on the logics of social construction, publics are defined as individuals with collectively shared interpretations of reality. Such varied approaches present a challenge to traditional models of conceiving of publics as one-dimensional receivers of organizational messages.

Case Study: The Inflamed Public and "Destruction of the Tea"

Faced with bankruptcy, the British East India Company persuaded the British Parliament to pass the Tea Act in 1773. This allowed the company to sell tea directly to American colonists without paying taxes in England. This, however, threatened to undercut the profits of American tea merchants, who were benefitting from smuggling. Spearheaded by American mercantile interests, colonists boycotted British tea and convinced many shipping agents along the American seaboard to resign their commissions. But in Boston and a few other American ports, English shipping agents remained in place. On December 16, 1773, a group of about 150 American patriots calling themselves the Sons of Liberty boarded three ships in Boston harbor and threw chests of tea overboard, in what would become known as the Boston Tea Party.

The nascent press publicized these events. Stories were reported in cities such as Philadelphia, Baltimore, and Charleston, where patriots began to emulate the actions of the Sons. Passions were further inflamed when King George III issued the so-called Coercive Acts or Intolerable Acts in retaliation for Bostonians' refusal to pay for the destroyed cargo. These acts closed the port of Boston, allowed American subjects to be tried in England, reduced self-government in the colony, and provided for quartering of British troops in American residences. This was followed in 1775 by the Stamp Act and the Boston Massacre, in which five protesters were killed and six were injured by British Redcoats.

Cutlip (1995) framed these events as "propaganda" by the Americans and saw them as antecedents for modern public relations. Key to this analysis was his careful parsing of the "publics" at play during the years leading up to and continuing through the American War for Independence:

> The 20-year struggle from 1763 to 1783 that brought the United States its nationhood was sustained by a small group of revolutionaries who struggled uphill against great odds, against the strong pro-British loyalties of many influential citizens, and against the apathy of most citizens who were occupied with the hard tasks of life in a primitive country. These revolutionaries were among the first to demonstrate the power of an organized, articulate minority carrying the day against the unorganized, apathetic majority of citizens. (p. 17)

This telling paragraph features the "organized few" as an array of competing "publics." Some of these "publics" included organizations such as the colonial government, the British Parliament, radical anti-British colonists (or patriots), colonists sympathetic to British rule (or Tories), and citizens of Great Britain who held differing opinions about the colonial problem. The British Crown faced a divided parliament and conflicting opinions at home and in the colonies ranging from outrage to apathy. Discourse and power struggles were the fodder for the contest of alliance, allegiance, opposition, and indifference.

By staging a colorful and successful protest, a contingent of merchants incited an activist movement replete with a David and Goliath narrative and a memorable rallying cry: "No taxation without representation!" A sizable number of colonists were sympathetic to British rule, however. Even Benjamin Franklin was of the opinion that England should be recompensed for the loss of the tea. But the theatrics generated popular support for the patriot cause, magnified by the agency of the relatively recent innovation of mass-circulation newspapers.

This analysis emphasizes how well competing publics were organized and institutionalized in the events surrounding the Boston Tea Party. Individuals were rhetorically and discursively defining themselves, creating allegiances, and straining relationships. Dialogic voices were shaping ideas and obtaining adherence. Supportive publics of some organizations and institutions were opposing the publics of others. The idea of self-government appealed to a small group of radicals, such as John Adams, who wrote in his journal in 1773, "This Destruction of the Tea is so bold, so daring, so firm, intrepid and inflexible, and it must have so important Consequences." With the support of a vocal and partisan press and an emerging visual culture disseminated through popular engravings, the tide began to turn in favor of the patriots.

Theories of Publics

Historical definitions raise many thorny issues around attempts to define "the public." Are we referencing an ideal public—a well-informed, thoughtful, and deliberative body acting in the group interest—or a more inclusive one—an undifferentiated mass that is all too often unregulated and unruly? Is the public a single entity or a multiplicity of entities? Is it defined according to aligned, shared interests or by heterogeneity? Does an issue define the public or does a public define the issue? Does a public exist without an organization? These questions will be examined in this section among competing perspectives of publics in the context of public relations theories.

Mass Perspectives

Pioneering sociologists such as Lippmann (1925) and Dewey (1927) theorized that the public constituted an extended group of individuals who shared some common values and beliefs. Blumer (1946) differentiated between a "mass" as "an aggregation of people who are separate, detached, anonymous" and the public, which has some issue that brings it together (pp. 186–187). In assessing Blumer's contribution, Hallahan (2000) called this a "symbolic community" or a "group of people who share a common set of symbols and experiences" (p. 502).

In a public relations context, the mass perspective has concentrated on identifying key characteristics of the public that affect the decision-making process. Some of the earliest work in this direction focused on the political process. Lippmann (1922) analyzed elections against the frame of an unsophisticated public, ill-educated or ill-equipped to make informed decisions about candidates or issues in an increasingly complex political landscape. He worried about the potential for demagogues to employ propaganda techniques to hoodwink naive voters into accepting dubious propositions. Beneath Lippmann's perspective is a deeply cynical assessment of the American citizen and the future of democracy. Does the public require an elite group to define and organize it? Lippmann (1922) proposed that a professional class of men would take a lead in swaying public opinion—or, as he called it, "manufacturing consent" (p. 248).

At the other end of the spectrum, Habermas (1989) worried that wealthy elites were dominating the political process, using glittering generalizations and appeals to patriotism and nationalism to enlist the support and manufacture the consent of the bourgeoisie. He put his faith in the opposing forces created by the working class, or proletariat, who would eventually overthrow the hegemony of the capitalist's control of the political process. The public sphere, in Habermas's ideal sense, was an arena in which ideas could be debated on their respective merits.

The mass perspective offered by Lippmann and Habermas posits an enduring state of consciousness. This view of the public is rather one-dimensional and generalized, ascribing to it characteristics that may have a basic explanatory value *en masse* but little place for individual difference, psychological factors, or transformations in evolving situations.

Public Interest

From the outset, public relations has been connected with the public interest. Bernays (1928) defined the social value of public relations in terms of the avoidance of advocating on behalf of "unsocial or harmful movements or ideas" (p. 199). During the 1950s, textbooks defined the public interest as paramount, governing every aspect of what a public relations professional "writes or says or causes others to write or say" (Stephenson & Pratzner, 1953). The Public Relations Society of America (PRSA) included "honoring our obligation to serve the public interest" as one of its six core values (PRSA, n.d.), because organizations have an impact on society as a whole (Ulrich, 1995).

While there is some agreement that the public interest represents "advocacy that communicates truthful, socially responsible ideas and information that otherwise might fail to gain public attention and consideration" and that one-way advocacy is unethical, the concept is often defined in vague and abstract terms (Stoker & Stoker, 2012, p. 34). A more rigorous definition of public interest is offered through reference to political science and philosophy. Thomas Hobbes (2017), for example, linked the public interest to the social contract, arguing that individuals surrender some of their individual rights in the name of the greater good of society. Likewise, Jean-Jacques Rousseau (2002) contended that the public interest represented the exercise of "the general will" or "common interest" of a collection of people (p. 170).

Lippmann (1955) took these conceptions of public interest cynically, noting the ability of people to manipulate or distort facts in the name of self-interest. Dewey (1927) was more optimistic about how the public interest was served by open, democratic discussion, which allowed individuals to evaluate the merits of particular viewpoints. Public relations, in Dewey's conception, "would promote democratic processes of debate, discussion, and persuasion and encourage public inquiry through the truthful dissemination of facts and research" (Stoker & Stoker, 2012, p. 39). The problem of balancing individual interests with public interests, according to Stoker and Stoker (2012), is addressed by appeal to "superior interests," which are defined as "deeper, enlightened interests" that are both "personal and public in nature" and "promote authenticity, moral responsibility, and accountability" (p 40). Thus, superior interests recognize both the values and rights of the individual and what is good for the community. Recognizing how public relations might advance superior interests depends, to a large degree, on a faith in the moral development of individual practitioners.

Organizational and Situational Perspectives

Organizational and systems perspectives assume that publics are defined in relation to the organizations with which they come into contact. These views presume that the public exists and is to be understood as the result of communicative actions within the framework of an organization or a system. Each public exists as an "artifact" of the process of interaction with an organization, or a particular public does not exist prior to engagement with organizations. While organizations are construed as real entities with specific goals and interests, organizational theory is less precise about specifying the needs and interests of its publics (Grunig & Hunt, 1984). Grunig and Repper (1992) proposed that publics are defined in response to "the involvement of people in situations and their perceptions of situations and not from internal needs" (p. 135).

STP identifies some of the social-psychological traits that distinguish publics, while rejecting the mass perspective that these traits are enduring. Mass traits are important in organizational theory only to the degree that they are useful or functional in a given public relations context. Geographic, demographic, and psychographic commonalities—categories familiar in the mass perspective— are used to identify segments of the public as they relate to the strategic goals of the organization in a given situation. Situational theory sidesteps the question of the enduring characteristics or state of consciousness that defines publics, but suggests an aggregate of multiple publics circumscribed by a specific issue at hand, or a micro focus on discrete incidents.

STP depends on three independent variables: problem recognition, level of involvement, and recognition of constraints. A public does not exist until it recognizes an issue. During the *problem recognition* phase, publics perceive that there is a problem: "People perceive that there are obstacles in a situation that limit their ability to do anything about the situation" (Grunig, 1997, p. 10). This is followed by *level of involvement*, as a measure of how likely an individual will be to understand and engage in a public relations message based on social-psychological variables, which are often used for segmenting publics. The final independent variable, *recognition of constraints*, is a recognition of the factors that constrain their involvement. Limiting factors may be physical, such as a lack of access to communication channels, or psychological, such as a perception of powerlessness in the face of a large organization.

These three variables are used to define publics as individuals that collectively perceive a problem, recognize their limits to act upon it, and appreciate the utility of participating actively in finding a solution. Efforts to confront the issue of handgun violence offer an example of these independent variables in action. First, a mass shooting renews public recognition of the problem, leading to a general call for some action. Following this, the limits of a grassroots campaign are discussed, such as the recognition that powerful lobbying groups are working against gun control. One's level of involvement depends, to a large degree, on whether or not one is a gun owner, whether or not one has been affected by gun violence, or whether or not one has had some other form of personal involvement in the issue.

STP also proposes two dependent variables, information seeking and information processing, since publics select information as they solve problems. As Case (2012) indicated, "Ideally, what we would really like to know is how people go about seeking (or avoiding) information in a *generic* way, free of specific contexts like heart disease or car purchases" (p. 12). The former variable focuses on whether or not individuals—and, by extension, publics—actively engage in active communication behaviors. People who are actively engaged in *information seeking* are regarded as active publics. On the other hand, *information processing* is defined as a more passive activity. Although they may not do so intentionally, passive audiences can still act on messages disseminated through communication channels. Communicative behaviors are systematic and dependent on individual cognitive resources (Grunig, 1997).

Problem solving depends on the level of communicative activeness or passivity in information acquisition, transmission, and selection. As one moves toward actively solving problems, one learns to apply more systematic and specific information-processing behaviors. *Information permitting* is related to the acceptance of information in the context of problem solving. This behavior can be reactive or passive, although active problem solvers both permit and seek information. *Information forefending* refers to the tendency for audiences to judge the relevance of information by discriminating or measuring its utility for problem solving. *Information sharing* is passive information giving or sharing of information reactively, while *information forwarding* is active information dissemination for problem solving with others. Kim and Grunig (2011) refined STP to emphasize that the motivation of problem solving is a crucial variable, labeling their new version the situational theory of problem solving (STOP) and stressing a focus on communication about a given situation. STP extends into STOP by integrating information seeking (active) and information processing (passive) into *information acquiring*, information forefending (active) and information permitting (passive) into *information selecting*, and information forwarding (active) and information sharing (passive) into *information transmitting* (Kim & Grunig, 2011).

Public relations, from organizational and situational perspectives, has sought to reach diverse publics by identifying the specific beliefs and behaviors that characterize various subgroups. This technique is known as segmentation. Segmentation is a process of differentiating not only opinions, but also the "perceptual, cognitive, and motivational antecedents" that predisposed subgroups to behave in particular ways in relation to a specific issue or problem (Kim, Ni, Kim, & Kim, 2012, p. 144). The goal is to augment organizational effectiveness by lowering costs and to garner support from stakeholders (Kim, Ni, & Sha, 2008).

Strategic communications have tended to segment the public into active and passive groups, defined as engaged or target publics and latent or nonpublics. A nonpublic is disinterested and has no consequence to an organization. A latent pubic may have bearing on an issue, but it has not been made aware of it and has not acted in a communicative sense. An aware public has perceived the problem, but has not acted on it. Finally, an active public engages issues in an organized manner and is pursing resolution.

Strategic communications is inclined to regard the relationship between an organization and its public as adversarial or at least problematic. Active publics, whose actions may have some consequences, are the major concern, and thus the practice of public relations frequently has been conceived of as conflict management, presupposing that an active public is bound to have goals that

Defining Characteristics of Public(s)
In public relations program planning and evaluation, the characteristics of publics can be discussed as follows (Smith, 2017, p. 66–67):

- *Distinguishable:* A recognized organization or formal group.
- *Homogenous:* Sharing common traits and features.
- *Important and powerful:* Having significant impact on an organization.
- *Large enough:* Warranting strategic attention and possible use of media.
- *Accessible:* Reachable and able to interact and communicate with an organization.

compete with an organization's own. However, as Hallahan (2000) noted, latent or inactive publics may also have relevance to the practice of public relations (p. 499). He defined inactive publics as those with low levels of involvement and knowledge, are argued they may be aroused to interest—and become an active public—to the degree that they recognize that an organization is relevant to them (p. 511). Thus, public relations efforts should be extended to arouse interest among inactive publics.

Activists and Activism

Activism has been defined as the "process by which groups of people exert pressure on organizations or other institutions to change policies, practices, or conditions the activists find problematic" (Smith, 2005, p. 5), and activists as a collection of people who seek to "solve collectively a problem that they feel they have in common" (Toch, 1965, p. 205). Activism may be spontaneous, generated around an emergent incident, such as the shooting of an unarmed individual, or institutionalized, such as the activities of environmentalists engaged in a protracted campaign. Activists use rhetoric and imagery that mixes emotional and rational appeals in an effort to establish credibility and trust.

While activism has ancient origins, it is most closely linked to the rise of democratic societies and industrialization. Not all activism results in positive changes—the rise of Nazism in Germany and of Maoism in China began as a call for social change by members of their respective societies. Rooted in the social movements of the nineteenth century, such as the abolition and women's rights movements, activism has been a prominent feature of social and political life in the United States since the Progressive Era of the 1920s and the Civil Rights movement of the 1950s and 1960s. Activism in a corporate setting grew out of the environmental movement in the late 1960s, spreading to a host of issues including labor relations, biotech, and climate change. While public relations professionals have tended to be employed by organizations to respond to and often counter activists' demands, nonprofits such as the Sierra Club, the National Rifle Association, and the Southern Poverty Law Center use public relations strategies and tactics to advocate their positions and sway public opinion and policies.

Like other activists, shareholder activists put pressure on companies to change their policies or behavior, but they have a direct financial stake in the company that they can use to leverage change. In this way, they possess a "formal power" over the company that outside organizations do not. As Weber, Rao, and Thomas (2009) put it, activist shareholders are "activists in suites" rather than "activists in the streets" (p. 106). A subset of shareholder activism has been defined by Lee and

Lounsbury (2011) as "social shareholder activism," the concerns of which extend to issues of corporate responsibility beyond a company's fiscal health (p. 156). Uysal and Tsetsura (2015) argued that by engaging social shareholder activists, organizations can secure "legitimacy in society, which, in turn, will contribute to their well-being and prosperity" (p. 211). While Grunig (1992) tended to regard the activist public as a hindrance to the efficient functioning of an organization and a threat to its goals, Holtzhausen (2007) argued that activists played a crucial and often positive role in defining organizational goals and missions—one that privileged the interests of ordinary, often marginalized people. This critical view focuses on the role of public relations in a society beyond organizational context. It follows the call by Bourdieu and Accardo (1999) for attention to the "multiplicity of coexisting, and sometimes directly competing, points of view" (p. 3). It represents a justification for the constructive role of corporations and contributions to the "fully functioning society" described by Heath (2018). By extension, it provides a justification for the role of public relations in serving the interest of stakeholder publics and the betterment of society as a whole.

Case Study: Activist Group in Action—Strategic Communication of Live Action

Based in Arlington, Virginia, Live Action has been among the most vocal organizations targeting abortion in the United States. It has launched an aggressive and effective attack on organizations such as the National Organization of Women, and has sought to influence the public at a grassroots level. Using press releases and op-ed accounts, one of its major goals is to counter a perceived mainstream media support of abortion advocates, or a woman's right to choose. Live Action particularly targets Planned Parenthood, which it accuses of engaging in "corruption and illegal activities" including "rampant sexual abuse cover up, racism, [and] the willingness to assist sex traffickers" (Armstrong, 2015).

Many of its approaches are reasoned, based on moral objections similar to those presented by Catholic organizations. It argues that abortion is a sin and cannot be condoned in a civilized society, any more than murder. Other approaches are sensational, such as posting a hidden video recording of an exchange between a counselor and a patient at a Planned Parenthood clinic that paints the organization as crass and amoral. Sensationalism and inflammatory rhetoric have the appeal of shock value, but can sometimes incite the organization's supporters to extreme acts of violence.

Live Action's approaches are strategic in the sense that it presumes multiple publics and seeks to reach them through various channels. The organization has made use of traditional press releases, appearances on cable news networks, and social media engagement. Its goal is ambitious: "to expose abuses in the abortion industry and advocate for human rights of the pre-born, using new media to education and mobilize both local and national audiences" (Redmond, 2013). For example, in order to influence the youth market, it tweeted a link to the British indie band Daughter's song, "Lifeforms," about the pain of abortion. To exert influence in the political arena, it posted a link to a blog outlining the testimony of Planned Parenthood employees before the Delaware legislature regarding the organization's misdeeds. It also linked to a summary of a research study linking abortion to a higher suicide rate in Finland. Planned Parenthood has largely avoided direct confrontation with Live Action by not mounting an aggressive, direct defense.

Amid this tangle of rhetoric, it is easy to lose sight of what constitutes the public interest. On the surface, Live Action appears to be a relatively small organization with an appeal among a limited public. However, by using various approaches and through strident engagement with Planned Parenthood, it has emerged as a leading voice in the abortion debate.

Agenda-Building Perspectives

Agenda building is defined as "the process by which demands of various groups in the population are translated into items vying for the serious attention of public officials" (Cobb, Ross & Ross, 1976, p. 126). Cobb and Elder (1971) distinguished between two types of agendas: the public and the formal. Issues that are of general concern to the populace and believed to require action on the part of elected officials or government agencies constitute the public agenda. The formal agenda refers to issues that have been brought forth and are in process of consideration by an administration or other officials. Agenda building focuses on public participation in civic matters, and is used principally to examine democratic societies. This perspective focuses on issue development as a key concept. Like STP, the agenda-building perspective generally focuses on the processes by which publics become aware of and participate in political conflicts. However, rather than focusing on the relationship of the public to an organization, it concentrates on describing how and, to a degree, why publics participate in the political process.

The agenda-building perspective gives primacy to publics. It suggests that they drive the democratic process by bringing forth issues that politicians then act upon. The *a priori* construction of a public is thus seen as sustaining organizations, such as the government. This seems very close to the presumptions of the U.S. Constitution that government exists to serve the public, rather than the other way around. By contrast, organizational theory presumes that publics are either undefined, unimportant, or non-existent in the absence of institutions. The difference is subtle, but crucial.

This is not to suggest that agenda building regards all publics as equally important. Cobb and Elder (1983) identified four specific subsets based on their relation to issues. First, specific public-identification groups engage the political process out of sympathy for particular, sometimes narrow interests. Second, specific public-attention groups are interested in particular issues but are not necessarily aligned with any particular groups. Third, mass public-attentive groups tend to have a general interest in a wide range of issues and to wield influence over other members of the public. Fourth, mass public-general groups tend to be neither informed nor active in politics. The interaction of these groups—especially the first three—expands political discourse and is essential to its very structure.

Cobb et al. (1976) provided three models for interaction between publics and government representatives. First, the outside initiative model suggests that publics work though nongovernment groups to capture the attention of decision makers. Campaigns waged by Black Lives Matter offer a good example of this model. Second, the mobilization model proposes that publics are enlisted to support issues originating within the political arena. Public opinion is crucial, as in the case of efforts to repeal the Affordable Care Act. Third, the inside initiative model suggests that government entities introduce issues without great effort to enlist public support. Passing a bill to build a bridge that benefits a small number of individuals or special interests is an example of this.

Agenda building is a useful theoretical perspective for the analysis of publics and their interaction with media, as well as their influence within democratic political systems. It is also useful in the sense that it offers an explanation of the dynamics of communication between publics and institutions. However, its scope and area of inquiry may be too limited to serve as a general theory of publics as they relate to public relations.

Organic Perspectives

Some organizations have come to recognize that all publics are interconnected, like the parts of a living organism, and thus it is crucial to treat each public as important from the organic perspective (Kruckeberg & Vujnovic, 2010). According to earlier work by Kruckeberg (2006a), "Western models of public relations center on the organization and its interests as the hub from which the 'spokes' of an organization's communication and relationships radiate outward to satellites of stakeholders" (p. 8). By contrast, he argued, the organic model "recognizes that each organization is only one part of the social system ... an organization's responsibility [is] to *all* members of society" (p. 8). At the heart of the organic perspective, there is the belief that an organization seeks harmony with its publics. It presumes that organizations bear a "social responsibility toward benign publics"—whereas strategic communication focuses on conflict management, with the presupposition that "the world is evil" (Kruckeberg & Vujnovic, 2010, p. 121).

The organic perspective thus constructs publics according to an ideological worldview that is nevertheless utilitarian in the sense that it accounts for the ever-increasing globalization and homogeneity rooted in the expansion of mass media, education, transportation, new media, and technology. In many ways, the organic perspective is the polar opposite of Lippmann's (1922) cynical view of an ignorant, ill-informed, and lazy public. For Kruckeberg and Tsetsura (2004), globalization and technology have broken down the traditional notions of the public and the private and fundamentally altered journalism and public relations. They asked, "is today's communication 'revolution' more accurately a 'reformation' in which each person can be his or her own journalist within a global milieu of interactive multimedia?" (p. 85).

Death of the Concept of the Public in Public Relations, or a New Beginning

Whereas the idea of "public" implies a group of people organized around a central issue or problem (Dewey, 1927), the definition of "audience" is more associated with a particular media channel or physical event. As Schrøder and Gulbrandsen (2018) contend, audience is "an imaginary grouping of strangers" (p. 42). With the advent of print media in the fifteenth century and of electronic media in the 1920s, the definition of what constitutes an audience was expanded and complicated. The boundaries of time, space, and access expanded exponentially. The advent of social media in the mid-2000s necessitated a further reconceptualization. Notably, the concepts of "gatekeeper," "sender," "receiver," and "audience" became progressively blurred. The Internet was hailed as a similar revolution a decade earlier, but for the most part the online platforms of the 1990s and early 2000s lacked a crucial component—the ability to crowd-source diverse publics at a massive scale in "real time" and to receive nearly instantaneous feedback along a continuum ranging from the latent to the activist segments, both supportive or opposed.

Distinguishing between the publics that count for an organization is not straightforward in an age of instant communication. The revolution in networking and transportation technology has led to a protracted demise of the concept of the pubic in public relations practice and theory. While revolutionary channels such as social media offer great promise for public relations to define and reach publics in a sophisticated, effective, and engaging manner, they also complicate the identification of a strategic public from among an "infinite number of volatile publics" (Kruckeberg & Vujnovic, 2010, p. 117).

The focus on the segmentation of publics into active, latent, and passive groups advocated by adherents of strategic public relations seems to be less useful than it once was, given this multiplicity of voices. Kruckeberg and Vujnovic (2010) argued not so much that the public has perished, but that the traditional conception of publics has reached the end of its useful life. They also suggest that the very concept of the public man or woman is rapidly giving way to a focus on private social relationships, referring to Sennett's (1992) assertion that "*Public man ... has become private man*, whose interests extend as far as does his selfish need for self determination" (p. 123). The communication revolution has led to the destruction of meaningful public-sphere discourse as conceived by Habermas (1989). In its place, private concerns and social relationships, which were once off-limits, have become the core of public life (Sennett, 1992).

The issue is further complicated by the practice of "astroturfing," or presenting organizational messages as though they come from individuals or grassroots public groups. Distinguishing the spontaneous from the calculated has become increasingly difficult. Social media has served as a skeptical corrective to self-interested official accounts, but it also raises troubling issues about fake news and credibility. This has significant implications for the practice of public relations. The profession must come to terms with the new social conception of the public. As already discussed, Kruckeberg (2006a, 2006b) has argued for an organic theory of public relations based on social responsibility and the awareness that one is a global citizen. Social media holds promise in this regard, yet at the same time it threatens to undermine the concept of social responsibility as individuals may be subject to manipulation by algorithms that advance politically motivated communication or to the lure of narrow and often purely private interests.

What is clear is that the traditional concept of multiple publics defined by their place within segmented categories has become less meaningful as technology has allowed individuals and interest groups to circumvent, undermine, and outmaneuver the best-laid public relations plans. Web 2.0 has equalized and empowered a multiplicity of publics relative to their counterpart organizations. Social media has put them on a level playing, at least in a rhetorical sense (Kent, Sommerfeldt, & Saffer, 2016). New media provides the potential for the voiceless to have a voice, "empowering previously silenced, unacknowledged, or marginalized groups" (Maples, 2008, p. 13).

Case Study: Social Media Activism—#BlackLivesMatter

Black Lives Matter (BLM) represents one of the most powerful online activist movements to emerge from a social media context. In the wake of the acquittal of George Zimmerman for the shooting of the unarmed black teenager Trayvon Martin on July 13, 2013, it originated with a Facebook post by Alicia Garza that concluded "black lives matter." Fellow activists Patrisse Cullors and Opai Tometi reposted the phrase as a hashtag and worked to mobilize a movement. A succession of other shootings of black men by police, notably John Crawford, Eric Garner, and especially Michael Brown in Ferguson, Missouri, helped crystallize support (Boniulla & Rosa, 2015).

The social media content, identified by the hashtag #BlackLivesMatter, helped frame the activists' goals, insert them into the media agenda, and coordinate activities such as marches, sit-ins, and other forms of protest. Hashtags represent a form of "distributed framing" that allows social media audiences to identify issues, ascertain significance, and add their own commentaries, voices, or meanings (Ince, Rojas & Davis, 2017). Social media has facilitated the exponential amplification of ideas, whether well-conceived and profound or offhand and ill-advised. Hashtags also allow dissenters to offer rhetorical challenges. According to a survey by the Pew Research Center, the hashtag #BlackLivesMatter appeared more than 30 million times between 2013 and July 2018, or more than 17,000 times a day (Anderson, Toor, Rainie & Smith, 2018).

BLM created a diverse range of stakeholders and voices—not all of whom are sympathetic to the movement. Alternative hashtags such as #AllLivesMatter and #BlueLivesMatter offer a form of subversion of its narrative proposed. According to the Pew Research Center, only 4 in 20 Americans surveyed supported BLM, although 65% of African-Americans were sympathetic. Slightly more than a third of respondents admitted to not understanding BLM's goals (Anderson et al., 2018).

The same study found that more than two-thirds of Americans believe that social media campaigns are effective in defining and sustaining social movements such as BLM (Anderson et al., 2018). As Lovejoy and Saxon (2012) suggest, BLM engaged in the communicative functions associated with disseminating information, defining community, and motivating action. Edrington and Lee (2018) concluded that BLM has been effective in informing stakeholders, but less so in building community over time and offering a consistent call to action. The Pew study found that 71% of respondents believed that social media provided the illusion of real engagement—a kind of virtual engagement that has little impact on real events or injustices (Anderson et al., 2018). However, people of color were more likely to believe it offered an effective channel for engaging in political action injustices (p. 4).

BLM has faced criticism for having few identifiable leaders and a lack of clear agendas or action items. Such decentralization translates into democratic participation, but also results in a diffusion and dilution of core messages. Kim Hunter, CEO of Lagrant Communication, argued that BLM has the power of a grassroots organization but lacks a "systematic, procedural, and defined" approach to communication (Daniels, 2016). A major issue is that the group seems to lack leadership and an identifiable "face" to associate with it. Negative stories and misperceptions about BLM are difficult to counter without coordinated communication. While the hashtag #BlackLivesMatter establishes a rallying point to activate stakeholders on social media, the challenge has been to overcome negative perceptions, identify clear messages, and leverage outrage into effective action. As Fay Ferguson, CEO of transcultural communication at Burrell, suggested, BLM needs to move from hashtags and social media presence to "a unified structure around the organization to help control content and messaging, because anyone can put their spin on it right now" (Daniels, 2016).

Stakeholder Engagement Perspectives

The term "stakeholder," describing individuals or groups who own, work for, support, or have an interest in an organization, comes from business management theory of the early 1960s. In a historical sense, it derives from the definition of "shareholder," or a person with an interest in a company and the ability to hold management accountable for its actions (Freeman, 1984, p. 41). The terms "stakeholder" and "public" are frequently used interchangeably. Rawlins (2006) defines stakeholders in an organizational context and publics in the context of their relationship to messages (p. 1).

Freeman (1984) stated that "stakeholder" refers to a broader group than "shareholder," which is limited to those with a financial stake in an organization. A stakeholder is "any group or individual who is affected by or can affect the achievement of an organization's objectives" (p. 46). Organizations are contingent on the presence of stakeholders for their very survival (Freeman & Reed, 1983). According to Freeman (1984), almost anyone associated with an organization can be considered a stakeholder, depending on the context. He argued that an organization's management has a moral responsibility to consider the interests of all actual and potential stakeholders. This conception, based on ethical principles, is known as multifiduciary stakeholder theory—as opposed to a stakeholder theory rooted in a strategic approach. However, Freeman's critics have pointed out that a multifiduciary approach is not necessarily any more or less ethical than a strategic one (Goodpaster, 1991). An organization's managers do not always behave less ethically, nor are their motivations any less self-interested, than third-party stakeholders—and vice versa. The term "stakeholder" is highly contested and fluid, contingent on various assumptions made by theorists. Miles (2015) demonstrated that while "stakeholder" is a problematic term, the theory can be classified as a single model through recognition of the boundaries defined in various disciplines.

Publics, on the other hand, are *sui generis*. According to Grunig and Repper (1992), they "arise on their own and choose the organization for attention" (p. 128). For Carey (1997), the term "public" is linked to specific and particular groups: "the term pubic (active audience) encompasses any group of people who are tied together, however loosely, by some common bond of interest or concern and who have consequence for an organization" (p. 94). Willis (2015) is critical of this organizational bias toward stakeholders in general, arguing that the "inability to confront issues around organizational power" represents a "blind spot" in the conception of how public relations conceives of and interacts with stakeholders (p. 225). He perceived a tendency within organizations toward inaction and non-engagement with stakeholders, which constitutes a "sugar-coated hostility" (p. 222). This passive-aggressive stance, often presented as an attempt to engage in mutually-beneficial dialogue, disguises hegemonic and "privileged organizational interests" (Edwards, 2006, p. 229).

Stakeholder engagement implies active participation of both organizations and their constituents (Buchell & Cook, 2013; Jelen-Sanchez, 2017). Open communication with publics represents a "leap" from mere recognition that this is the ethical position to take, and implies that dialogue will become "a driving force for change" (Garcia & Garraz, 2010, p. 197). L'Etang, Lugo-Ocando, and Amad (2011) pointed to the moral obligation that organizations have to engage fairly with their stakeholders. Crucial to this perspective is the co-creational aspect of the process, whereby all sides "agree to shared meanings, interpretations, and goals" (Heath, 2014, p. 93). Heath (2014) led the call for greater stakeholder engagement as a force for change, describing it as a commitment to real community building and calling for public relations to "serve the co-creation of narratives that make society fully functioning" (p. 93).

The pragmatic part of engagement involves acknowledgement of the power relations among diverse stakeholders (Johnston, 2014). Cunliffe (2009) described the nature of power relations embedded in stakeholder engagement as "the privileging of certain groups and the marginalization of others," while at the same time stressing that relational interaction implies a moral component of "social and organizational experience" (p. 409). Many ethical, "high-quality," and mutually beneficial engagements between stakeholders and organizations occur, but it is wrong to assume that exclusive, irresponsible, deceptive, discriminatory, asymmetrical, and immoral interactions are uncommon (Greenwood, 2007, p. 322).

Dialogue is crucial to establishing and maintaining stakeholder engagement, conceived as both mass and interpersonal communication (Kent & Taylor, 2002; Heath, Toth, & Waymer, 2009). Theories ranging from organizational to rhetorical approaches propose that engagement fosters relationships. Taylor and Kent (2014) found that much of what passes for dialogic engagement is in fact one-way communication presented from the organizational perspective masquerading as an opportunity for stakeholder engagement. Macnamara (2012) called out the assumption that dialogue gravitates toward symmetrical relationships between organizations and stakeholder publics based on agreement and that mutual benefit is undercut by power differentials and "dark dialogues" that "nullify dialogue and inhibit engagement by stakeholders" (Willis, 2015, p. 221). As O'Byrne and Daymon (2014) concluded in their discussion of citizen investors as a stakeholder group, "engagement has a moral dimension and suggest that our application of the concept of engagement has been enriched by including consideration of responsibility and irresponsibility" (p. 470).

Conclusion

Public relations, in its formative years, focused on influencing public opinion. During the late 1950s, public relations professionals began to acknowledge that the mass perspective was insufficient because publics were not monolithic entities, and that various stakeholders had interests in different issues.

By the early 1990s, as public relations theory came of age, the organizational-situational perspective came to dominate, stressing the strategic role of organizations as disseminators of messages and publics as their receivers. The goal was to refine and target messages to publics according to their level of engagement.

However, organizations were neither more or less primary nor less self-interested than publics. An organization has a moral responsibility to consider the interests of all its actual and potential stakeholders. Recognizing the multiplicity of publics and serving the public interest in a broader context necessarily means acknowledging the power imbalances that exist among competing voices. By the early 2000s, many scholars had begun to question the organization-centric view of publics, and turned to what Leitch and Neilson (2001) termed "new relevant bodies of social and cultural thought" (p. 127). They suggested that relationships between organizations were dynamic and shifting. Scholars such as Heath (2012) defined publics from a rhetorical perspective according to communicative action and ascription of meanings—in other words, as socially constructed entities. Others, such as Holtzhausen (2007) and Hallahan (2000), demonstrated how multiple and even marginalized publics had a significant and often positive impact on organizations. Kruckeberg and Vujnovic (2010) offered a more optimistic view, in which organizations embraced a "social responsibility toward benign publics" (p. 121). This view is embedded in theories of stakeholder engagement, which hold that publics are groups that arise spontaneously and are defined by their common interests. Active and authentic engagement of both stakeholders and organizations is a moral obligation (Johnston, 2014). Dialogue has been seen as a panacea (Kent & Taylor, 2002; Heath et al., 2009), allowing diverse parties to engage on a level playing field. However, dialogue does not necessarily imply erasure of power differences, nor are the actors necessarily operating in everyone's best interests (Willis, 2015).

Chapter Summary

Public relations arose in the early twentieth century from a unified view of the public as a mass, and sought to assess public opinion. The first serious academic work conducted after World War II drew upon organizational theory and interpersonal communication processes, proposing a model of senders (organizations) and receivers (audience). The interest in assessing the effectiveness of organizations' communication efforts continued through the 1990s.

In the late 1990s and early 2000s, scholars began to embrace a multidisciplinary conception of publics that took into account social, political, economic, ideological, and cultural aspects. They considered publics as co-equal with organizations in terms of co-creating meaning. Rather than seeing publics as active or latent entities to be acted upon by public relations messages from organizations, scholars illuminated how individuals and groups constituting multiple publics and voices engaged in participatory and democratic communication processes contributing to a fully functioning society. Recent conceptions of publics consider how dialogue works to help ensure that multiple views of different power groups are represented. The era of social media and mobile communication makes possible greater dialogue and more authentic relationships, but public relations efforts have not yet utilized the potential of the stakeholder engagement made available by new media. A more inclusive conception of publics should be based on dialogue, awareness that one is a global citizen, and a sense of responsibility to various stakeholders, whether they be powerful or marginalized.

Key Terms

- *Active Public:* Discusses and acts on a shared issue. The group organizes to respond to the problem.
- *Activist Public:* Takes a leading role in the communication process. Often holds strident and entrenched views.
- *Audience:* People who are grouped by their use of a particular communication medium.
- *Aware Public:* Shares an issue but isn't organized to discuss or act on it. The group recognizes the problem.
- *Constraint Recognition:* The extent to which people perceive there are impediments to their ability to act. The greater their perception of the obstacles, the less likely they are to seek information or to act upon it.
- *Fully Functioning Society:* Rests on the presumption that people as agents engage in discussion and other forms of discourse to make decisions that align with their individual and collective interests. A central proposition is that the goal of discourse is to maximize the collective quality of society as a whole, instead of serving the interests of specific individuals or groups. The collective choices made by the community at large are superior in both a pragmatic and an ethical sense to those made by individual or specific interests. The theory of a fully functioning society runs counter to the organization-centric position insofar as it proposes that the purpose of institutions is to serve the community at large.
- *Information Processing:* An active communication behavior in which a person attempts to locate and make sense of data or evidence. People who engage in information seeking are considered active publics.

- *Information Seeking:* A passive activity in which individuals make sense of data or evidence that comes to them without proactive effort.
- *Involvement:* The extent to which people align themselves to a situation. The more people think they are engaged in a situation, the more likely they are to seek information and not see impediments.
- *Latent Public:* Shares an issue with an organization but doesn't recognize that situation or its potential. The problem is there, but the public is not aware.
- *Market:* A consumer public with similar demographics targeted for financial interaction to support an organization's bottom line.
- *Nonpublic:* Doesn't share any issues with an organization, and is therefore of no significance to it. No problem is recognized or exists, so there are no effects.
- *Passive Public:* Does not seek information but still receives it. Not actively engaged.
- *Problem Recognition:* Actively looking for information or, if information comes, actively processing it.
- *Stakeholder:* An individual or group that has a stake or interest in the relationship with an organization, and thus is affected by or can affect decisions made by it.

Discussion Questions

1 How can you define a public? What are some similar terms, and what are the differences among them?
2 Do think that a public is a singular entity or multiple groups? Why?
3 What are the stages of public development, assuming that publics are issue-dependent?
4 The concept of public is associated with self-interest and is often activated by a triggering event. Explain these concepts.
5 Name and describe the characteristics involved in various stages of publics, such as latent, aware, active, and activist.
6 How do multiple publics, with their conflicting interests, play a role in public relations? Give an example.
7 Discuss four different perspectives on publics in public relations. How are they different or similar?
8 What is the role of media in the formation of a public from an agenda-building perspective?
9 How has social media changed the definition of publics?
10 How can public relations help enhance a high-quality dialogue and facilitate a fully functioning society?

References

Anderson, M., Toor, S., Rainie, L., and Smith, A. (2018). Activism in the social media age. Pew Research Center. Available from https://www.pewinternet.org/2018/07/11/activism-in-the-social-media-age (accessed May 20, 2020).

Armstrong, P. (2015). Is it wrong to lie to Planned Parenthood? *Catholic News & Inspiration*, August 19. Available from http://www.pattimaguirearmstrong.com/2015/08/were-makers-of-undercover-videos-wrong.html (accessed May 20, 2020).

Bernays, E. (1928). *Propaganda*. New York: Routledge.

Blumer, H. (1946). Collective behavior. In A. M. Lee (Ed.), *New outlines of the principle of sociology* (pp. 170–222). New York: Barnes & Noble.

Boniulla, Y., & Rosa, J. (2015). #Ferguson: Digital protest, hashtag ethnography, and the racial politics of social media in the United States. *American Ethnologist, 42*(1), 4–17.

Botan, C. H. (1993). Introduction to the paradigm struggle in public relations. *Public Relations Review, 19*, 107–110.

Botan, C. H., & Soto, F. (1998). A semiotic approach to the internal functioning of publics: Implications for strategic communication and public relations. *Public Relations Review, 24*, 21–44.

Bourdieu, P., & Accardo, A. (1999). *The weight of the world—Social suffering in contemporary society* (trans. P. P. Ferguson). Cambridge: Polity Press.

Broom, G. M., Casey, S., & Ritchey, J. (1997). Toward a concept and theory of organization– public relationships. *Journal of Public Relations Research, 9*, 83–98.

Buchell, J., & Cook, J. (2013). Sleeping with the enemy? Strategic transformations in business–NGO relationships through stakeholder dialogue. *Journal of Business Ethics, 113*, 505–518.

Cancel, A. C., Mitrook, M. A., & Cameron, G. (1999). Testing the contingency theory of accommodation in public relations. *Public Relations Review, 24*, 171–198.

Carey, J. W. (1997). Communications and economics. In E. S. Munson & C. A. Warren (Eds.), *James Carey: A critical reader* (pp. 60–75). Minneapolis, MN: University of Minnesota Press.

Case, D. O. (2012). *Looking for information: A survey of research on information seeking, needs, and behavior*. Bingley: Emerald Group.

Cobb, R. W., & Elder, C. D. (1971). The politics of agenda-building: An alternative perspective theory. *Journal of Politics, 33*(4), 892–915.

Cobb, R. W., & Elder, C. D. (1983). *Participation in American politics: The dynamics of agenda-building*. Baltimore, MD: Johns Hopkins University Press.

Cobb, R. W., Ross, J. K., & Ross, M. H. (1976). Agenda building as a comparative process. *American Political Science Review, 70*(1), 126–138.

Coombs, W. T., & Holliday, S. J. (2007). *It's not just PR: Public relations in society*. Malden, MA: Blackwell.

Cunliffe, A. L. (2009). The mass, the public and public opinion. In S. J. Armstron & C. V. Fukami (Eds.), *The SAGE handbook of management learning, education, and development* (pp. 405–418). London: Sage.

Cutlip, S. M. (1995). *Public relations history: From the 17th to the 20th century, the antecedents*. Hillsdale, NJ: Lawrence Erlbaum Associates.

Cutlip, S. M., & Center, A. H. (1971). *Effective public relations*. Englewood Cliffs, NJ: Prentice-Hall.

Daniels, C. (2016). Experts: Black Lives Matter's decentralized structure is holding it back. *PR Week*, July 15. Available from https://www.prweek.com/article/1402521/experts-black-lives-matters-decentralized-structure-holding-back (accessed May 20, 2020).

Dewey, J. (1927). *The public and its problems*. Athens, OH: Swallow Press.

Edrington, C. L., & Lee, N. (2018). Tweeting a social movement: Black Lives Matter and its use of Twitter. *Journal of Public Interest Communications, 2*(2), 289–306.

Edwards, L. (2006). Rethinking power in public relations. *Public Relations Review, 32*(3), 229–231.

FrackNation. (n.d.). About us. Available from http://fracknation.com/about (accessed May 20, 2020).

Freeman, E. R. (1984). *Strategic management: A stakeholder's approach*. Boston, MA: Pitman.

Freeman, R. E., & Reed, D. L. (1983). Stockholder and stakeholders: A new perspective on corporate governance. *California Management Review, 25*(3), 88–106.

Garcia, E. G., & Garraz, T. S. (2010). Making things happen: The role of communication in strategic management: A case study on banking industry. *Comuncación y Sociedad, 23*(2), 179–201.

Goodpaster, K. E. (1991). Business ethics and stakeholder analysis. *Business Ethics Quarterly*, *1*(1), 57–73.

Greenwood, M. (2007). Stakeholder engagement: Beyond the myth of corporate responsibility. *Journal of Business Ethics*, *74*, 315–327.

Grunig, L. A. (1992). *Activism: How it limits the effectiveness of organizations and how excellent public relations departments respond. Excellence in public relations and communication management.* Hilldale, NJ: Lawrence Erlbaum Associates.

Grunig, J. E. (1997). A situational theory of publics: Conceptual history, recent challenges and new research. In D. Moss, T. MacManus, & D. Verčič (Eds.), *Public relations research: An international perspective* (pp. 3–46). London: ITB Press.

Grunig, J. E., & Hunt, T. (1984). *Managing public relations.* New York: Holt, Reinhart & Winston.

Grunig, J. E., & Repper, F. C. (1992). Strategic management, publics and issues. In J. E. Grunig (Ed.), *Excellence in public relations and communication management.* Hillsdale, NJ: Lawrence Erlbaum Associates.

Habermas, J. (1989). *The structural transformation of the public sphere: An inquiry into a category of bourgeois society* (trans. T. Burger and F. Lawrence). Cambridge, MA: MIT Press.

Hallahan, K. (2000). Inactive publics: The forgotten publics in public relations. *Public Relations Review*, *26*, 499–515.

Heath, R. L. (2010). Mind, self, and society. In R. L. Heath (Ed.), *Handbook of public relations* (pp. 1–4). Thousand Islands, CA: Sage.

Heath, R. L. (2012). Western classical rhetorical tradition and modern public relations: Culture of citizenship. In K. Sriramesh & D. Verčič (Eds.), *Cultural and public relations: Links and implications* (pp. 25–41). New York: Routledge.

Heath, R. L. (2014). Public relations role in engagement: Functions, voices, and narratives. Paper presented at the Engagement as Strategy, Theory and Practice: ICA Preconference 2014. Seattle, WA, May 22.

Heath, R. L. (2018). Fully functioning society. In R. L. Heath & W. Johansen (Eds.), *The international encyclopedia of strategic communication II* (pp. 641–649). Boston, MA: Wiley-Blackwell.

Heath, R. L., Toth, E., & Waymer, D. (2009). *Rhetorical and critical approaches to public relations II.* New York: Routledge.

Hobbes, T. (2017). *Leviathan.* London: Penguin.

Holtzhausen, D. R. (2007). Activism. In E. L. Toth (Ed.), *The future of excellence in public relations and communication management: Challenge for the next generation* (pp. 357–379). Mahwah, NJ: Lawrence Erlbaum Associates.

Ince, J., Rojas, F., & Davis, C. A. (2017). The social media response to Black Lives Matter: How Twitter users interact with Black Lives Matter through hashtag use. *Ethic and Racial Studies*, *40*(11), 1814–1830.

Jelen-Sanchez, A. (2017). Engagement in public relations discipline: Themes, theoretical perspectives and methodological approaches. *Public Relations Review*, *43*, 934–944.

Johnston, K. A. (2014). Public relations and engagement: Theoretical imperatives of a multidimensional concept. *Journal of Public Relations Research*, *26*(5), 381–383.

Karlberg, M. (1996). Remembering the public in public relations research: From theoretical to operational symmetry. *Journal of Public Relations Research*, *8*, 263–278.

Kent, M., & Taylor, M. (2002). Toward a dialogue theory of public relations. *Public Relations Review*, *28*, 21–37.

Kent, M. L., Sommerfeldt, E. J., & Saffer, A. J. (2016). Social networks, power, and public relations: *Tertius iungens* as a cocreational approach to studying relationship networks. *Public Relations Review*, *42*, 91–100.

Kim, J. N., & Grunig, J. E. (2011). Problem solving and communicative action: A situational theory of problem solving. *Journal of Communication, 61*(1), 120–149.

Kim, J. N., Ni, L., & Sha, B. L. (2008). Breaking down the stakeholder environment: Explicating approaches to the segmentation of publics for public relations research. *Journalism & Mass Communication Quarterly, 85*(4), 751–768.

Kim, J. N., Ni, L., Kim, S. H., & Kim, J. R. (2012). What makes people hot? Applying the situational theory of problem solving to hot-issue publics. *Journal of Public Relations Research, 24*(2), 144–164.

Kruckeberg, D. (2006a). An "organic model" of public relations: The role of governments, civil organizations (CSOs) and corporations in developing and guiding social and cultural policy to build and maintain community in 21st-century civil society. Conference talk, Municipal Social Policy and Publics: Realities and Perspectives, Ulan-Ude City, Buryatia, Russia, June 30–July 1.

Kruckeberg, D. (2006b). The role of ethics of community-building for consumer products and services: With some recommendations for new-marketplace economies in emerging democracies. In C. H. Botan & V. Hazelton (Eds.), *Public relations II* (pp. 485–497). Mahwah, NJ: Lawrence Erlbaum Associates.

Kruckeberg, D., & Tsetsura, K. (2004). International journalism ethics. In A. S. de Beer & J. C. Merrill (Eds.), *Global journalism* (4th ed., pp. 84–92). Boston, MA: Pearson, Allyn & Bacon.

Kruckeberg, D., & Vujnovic, M. (2010). The death of the concept of publics (plural) in 21st century public relations. *International Journal of Strategic Communication, 4*, 117–125.

Lee, M. P., & Lounsbury, M. (2011). Domesticating radical rant and rage: An exploration of the consequences of environmental shareholder resolutions on corporate environmental performance. *Business and Society, 50*, 155–188.

Leitch, S., & Motion, D. (2010). Publics and public relations: Affecting change. In R. L. Heath (Ed.), *The handbook of public relations* (2nd ed., pp. 127–138). Thousand Oaks, CA: Sage.

Leitch, S., & Neilson, D. (2001). Bringing the public into public relations: New theoretical frameworks for the practice. In R. L. Heath (Ed.), *Handbook of public relations* (pp. 127–138). Thousand Oaks, CA: Sage.

L'Etang, J., Lugo-Ocando, J., & Amad, J. A. (2011). Ethics: Corporate social responsibility, power and strategic communication. In Ø. Ihlen, J. Bartlett, & S. May (Eds.), *The handbook of communication and corporate social responsibility* (pp. 170–187). Hoboken, NJ: Wiley.

Lewis, C. T., & Short, C. (1879). *A Latin dictionary: Founded on Andrew's edition of Freund's Latin dictionary*. Oxford: Clarendon Press.

Lippmann, W. (1922). *Public opinion*. New York: Harcourt Brace, Jovanovich.

Lippmann, W. (1925). *The phantom public*. New York: Harcourt Brace, Jovanovich.

Lippmann, W. (1955). *Essays in the public philosophy*. Boston, MA: Little, Brown.

Lovejoy, K., & Saxton, G. D. (2012). Information, community, and action: How nonprofit organizations use social media. *Journal of Computer-Mediated Communication, 17*(3), 337–353.

Macnamara, J. (2012). *Public relations: Theories, practices and critiques*. Frenchs Forest, NSW: Pearson.

Maples, C. J. (2008). Giving voice: The use of interactive theatre as professional development in higher education to reduce alienation of marginalized groups. Ph.D. dissertation, University of Missouri-Columbia.

Miles, S. (2015). Stakeholder theory classification: A theoretical and empirical evaluation of definitions. *Journal of Business Ethics, 142*(3), 437–459.

Newsom, D., Turk, J., & Kurkeberg, D. (2004). *This is PR—The realities of public relations* (8th ed.). Belmont CA: Wadsworth/Thomson Learning.

O'Byrne, S., & Daymon, C. (2014). Irresponsible engagement and the citizen investor. *Journal of Public Relations Research, 26*, 455–473.

Pearson, R. (1987). Decoding corporate discourse: semiotics and the analysis of organizational texts. Paper presented at the International Communications Association Conference, Montreal, Quebec.

Porter, M. (1992). The environment of the oil company: A semiotic analysis of Chevron's "people do" commercials. In E. Toth & R. Heath (Eds.), *Rhetorical and critical approaches to public relations*. Hillsdale, NJ: Lawrence Erlbaum Associates.

PRSA. (n.d.) Ethics for an evolving profession. Available from https://www.prsa.org/aboutprsa/ethics/codeenglish#MemberStatement (accessed May 20, 2020).

Rawlins, B. L. (2006). Prioritizing stakeholders for public relations. Institute for Public Relations. Available from https://instituteforpr.org/prioritizing-stakeholders/ (accessed May 20, 2020).

Rawlins, B. L., & Bowen, S. A. (2004). Publics. In R. L. Heath (Ed.), *Encyclopedia of public relations* (pp. 718–721). Thousand Oaks, CA: Sage.

Redmond, M. (2013). Profiles on the right: Lila Rose. Political Research Associates. Available from https://www.politicalresearch.org/2013/09/04/profiles-right-lila-rose (accessed May 20, 2020).

Rousseau, J. J. (2002). *The social contract and the first and second discourses*. New Haven, CT: Yale University Press.

Schrøder, K. C., & Gulbrandsen, I. T. (2018). Audience. In R. L. Heath & W. Johansen (Eds.), *The international encyclopedia of strategic communication I* (pp. 41–49). Boston, MA: Wiley-Blackwell.

Sennett, R. (1992). *The fall of the public man*. New York: W. W. Norton & Company.

Smith, M. F. (2005). Activism. In R. L. Heath (Ed.), *Encyclopedia of public relations* (pp. 5–9). Thousand Oaks, CA: Sage.

Smith, R. D. (2017). *Strategic planning for public relations* (5th ed.). New York: Taylor & Francis.

Stephenson, H., & Pratzner, W. F. (1953). *Publicity for prestige and profit*. New York: McGraw-Hill.

Stoker, K., & Stoker, M. (2012). The paradox of public interest: How serving individual superior interests fulfill public relations' obligation to the public interest. *Journal of Mass Media Ethics*, *27*, 31–45.

Taylor, M., & Kent, M. L. (2014). Dialogic engagement: Clarifying foundational concepts. *Journal of Public Relations Research*, *24*(5), 384–398.

Toch, H. (1965). *The social psychology of social movements*. Indianapolis, IN: Bobbs-Merrill.

Ulrich, P. (1995). Business in the nineties: Facing public interest. In P. Ulrich & C. Sarasin (Eds.), *Facing public interest: The ethical challenges to business policy and corporate communications* (pp. 1–8). Dordrecht: Kluwer Academic Publishers.

Uysal, N., & Tsetsura, K. (2015). Corporate governance on stakeholder issues: Shareholder activism as a guiding force. *Journal of Public Affairs*, *15*(2), 210–219.

Vasquez, G. M., & Taylor, M. (2001). Research perspectives on "the public". In R. L. Heath (Ed.), *Handbook of public relations* (pp. 139–145). Thousand Oaks, CA: Sage.

Weber, K., Rao, H., & Thomas, L. G. (2009). From the streets to the suites: How the anti- biotech movement affected German pharmaceutical firms. *American Sociological Review*, *74*(1), 106–127.

Willis, P. (2015). Public relations, passive aggression and critical social auditing: Reflections on organisational inaction in stakeholder engagement. *Journal of Public Affairs*, *15*(3), 220–226.

11

Public Relations and Relationships

Introduction

The relationship is a central construct in public relations. Like the concept of "publics," the operational definition of the term "relationships" used by public relations scholars has suffered historically from a lack of rigorous and agreed-upon definitions. As Heath (2005) noted, the conception of public relations contains an internal paradox. On one hand, the term "public" suggests openness and transparency. On the other, the terms "relations" and "relationships" suggest private connections distinguished by closure, exclusion, or privacy. There is a certain tension between the group and Interpersonal communications (IPC) in the dynamic between organizations and stakeholders (Stoker, 2014). Only in recent years have the preconceptions and assumptions about what relationships means to public relations been the focus of intense study.

Since the mid-1980s, a number of studies have examined relationships in terms of definition or measurement, yet the definition, dimensions, and characteristics of relationships in public relations is still a matter of ongoing discussion and debate. For at least a quarter century, the organization–public relationship (OPR) and relationship management as a functional enterprise have been a central focus of the discipline. However, scholars recently recognized that OPR perspectives have tended to privilege the interests of the organization over those of the public, which has been largely conceived of as a monolithic body to be acted upon by public relations practitioners (Kelleher, 2015; Sweetser, English, & Fernandes, 2015; Sweetser & Kelleher, 2016). The public's role in defining the relationship was marginalized, yet it is important to understand how the public played a role the communication process and pointed to the important role of antecedents. OPRs are complicated phenomena—"moving targets" on one hand, and filled with contradictions and constantly negotiated shifts in attitudes and behaviors on the other (Sweetser & Kelleher, 2016, p. 217). As Stoker (2014) argued, the objective model of managing relationships by public relations practitioners is a paradoxical endeavor that risks exerting "control over public values, opinions, and behaviors" (p. 352). Considering two-way symmetrical dialogue leading to mutually beneficial relationships, he continued: "No guarantee exists that the public will reciprocate unless coerced" (p. 352).

The managerial-centric perspective of relationships, which dominated scholarship between the 1990s and early 2000s, focused on short-term relations between organizations and constituents arising out of specific problems. The nature of such relationships is conditional, and endures only so long as there is an issue that requires attention. However, care should be taken not to overstate the limited focus of the symmetrical perspective; Grunig and his followers acknowledged the contradictions and paradoxes inherent in the concept of mutual benefit given the relative power

Public Relations Theory: Capabilities and Competencies, First Edition. Jae-Hwa Shin and Robert L. Heath.
© 2021 John Wiley & Sons, Inc. Published 2021 by John Wiley & Sons, Inc.

differences of organizations and publics, reflecting an organization-centric approach (Grunig, Grunig, & Ehlring, 1992; Grunig and Repper, 1992).

More recently, a more nuanced approach has focused on the conception of public relations as a collaboration among multiple stakeholders (Avidar, 2017; Kent & Taylor, 2002). Heath (1997) defined "stakeholder" in terms of having a stake in the outcome or operation of an organization, or in "anything—tangible or intangible, material or immaterial—that one person or group has that is of value to another person or group" (p. 28). The emphasis on relationship management, which led to an organization-centric approach, was challenged beginning in the early 2000s by a co-creational model that emphasized a multifaceted conception of publics and centered on relationship building, relationship maintenance, and dialogue. As Heath (2013) put it, the "myopic focus" on one public at a time, as well as the assumption that relationships are inherently positive, should be replaced by analysis of how relationships are "co-defined and negotiated discursively" (p. 426). Although Grunig (1989) acknowledged the importance of stakeholder engagement, some of the topics that have emerged as central to the discussion of relationships include an examination of communication networks, rhetorical and discursive approaches such as examination of the role of conversational voice, the building of civil society, the impact of social media on relationships, corporate social responsibility (CSR), activism, and critical theory (Milam & Heath, 2014). This chapter will address the history and current status of these ongoing discussions and the future direction of research and practice in the study of relationships.

Questions to Frame the Discussion of Relationships

- What are some of the competing definitions of relationships in OPRs?
- What are some variables be associated with defining or measuring OPRs?
- Can you explain OPRs from a changing continuum?
- Can you define OPRs in relation to the democratic process?

Key Themes

- OPRs may be defined from different perspectives beyond individual variables and measurements.
- Theories of relationships have moved from an organization-centric perspective to one that focuses on dialogic co-creation of meaning with stakeholders, as a result of shared signs, symbols, outlooks, perceptions, and behaviors.
- From an organizational perspective, OPRs measure relationships from perceptual and attitudinal variables in order to create managerial relational outcomes.
- OPRs are multidimensional, complex, contextual, and contingent on multiple publics that change over time.
- OPRs focusing on CSR conceive of themselves as part of a democratic process.

Definitions of Relationships

The Oxford English Dictionary defines "relationship" as "the way in which two or more concepts, objects, or people are connected or the state of being connected," or "the way in which two or more people or organizations regard and behave toward each other" (www.oed.com). Such definitions emphasize the connectedness that arises out of association, coercion, convenience, or necessity.

Relationships have two components: perceptual and behavioral. The perceptional component refers to how people and groups view their connection to one another. The behavioral one is used to describe what actions individuals and groups take as a result of exchange. Public relations scholars have attempted to account for both perceptual and behavioral components, taking into account attitudes and opinions about a particular relationship, as well as its demonstrable effects. Theorists have sought to understand the conditions that lead to the formation of relationships, their maintenance, their outcomes, and their relative quality.

In recent years, relationships have begun to be forged and conceptualized on both an actual and a virtual level. With the rise of social media, it is possible to form relationships that include a great deal of direct communication with people with whom one has never interacted on a face-to-face basis.

Relationships form as a result of shared signs, symbols, outlooks, perceptions, and behaviors. Scholars have described these basic points of intersection as "worldviews." West and Turner (2000) concluded that a shared worldview "provides people with a lens for seeing and making sense of the world they inhabit" (p. 60). Interaction results from shared worldviews, and, over time, relationships develop through familiarity (Burleson & Kunkel, 1994).

The conditions that govern the formation of a relationship are known as antecedents. Intuition and research have suggested that similarities and shared worldviews are among the most important preconditions governing relationship formation. Both internal and external factors affect this process. For example, should an organization make the internal decision to alter its mission statement, it would likely alienate some publics while gaining the support of others. Once formed, relationships evolve again as the result of internal and external factors. Scholars have referred to this evolution in terms of "turning points" (Baxter & Bullis, 1986). Being able to accurately predict when a turning point will occur, under what conditions it will become manifest, and what effects it will have on stakeholders is a significant area of research and of crucial importance to the practice of public relations.

Researchers have categorized relationships according to their properties. The most common means of assessment involve scales that measure qualities which positively or negatively affect the formation, endurance, enhancement, or dissolution of relationships. In the field of psychology, research has focused on the conditions governing the client–patient relationship based on perception measured by relational scales. For example, according to Broom, Casey, and Ritchey (1997), relationships are formed "when parties have perceptions and expectations of each other when one or both parties need resources from the other, when one or both parties perceive mutual threats from an uncertain environment, or when there is either legal or voluntary necessity to associate" (p. 17). IPC scholars have developed relational scales to measure dimensions such as satisfaction, trust, and commitment. These scales have been adopted an amended to serve the needs of public relations scholars.

History of Conceptualizing Relationships

The study of relationships as a key construct in public relations can be traced back to the early 1950s. Most of the early work was rooted in IPC research and psychology. It focused on the development of relationships between individuals, positing the idea that interactions could be described according to various relational characteristics and dimensions (Watson, 2012).

By the early 1970s, scholars such as Cutlip and Center (1971) had begun to suggest the application of interpersonal relationship dimensions to OPRs. Although many argued that there were crucial differences between interpersonal relationships and OPRs, the theoretical underpinnings pioneered by interpersonal scholars—more recently cast as a dialogic and co-creational model with the goal of symmetrical communication—emerged as a dominant strain in public relations research on relationships.

In 1984, Ferguson published a seminal article suggesting public relations scholars should make the OPR itself the focus of study in public relations, as opposed to analyzing relationship outcomes or byproducts. Ferguson's "relational approach" represented a "turning point in public relations scholarship" (Sweetser & Kelleher, 2016, p. 217). Scholars such as Cutlip, Center, and Broom (1985) thus suggested that relationship management should be brought to the foreground in both public relations practice and theory. They called for an approach that focused on building relationships based on common interests and the achievement of mutually beneficial goals. Broom and Dozier (1990) suggested that fostering mutual benefit was a crucial goal of public relations initiatives.

Following the lead of IPC scholars, Grunig et al. (1992) and Hon and Grunig (1999) argued that public relations scholars and practitioners should focus on perceptions held by organizations and individuals. They contended that it was important to strategically measure dimensions such as trust, reciprocity, commitment, mutual legitimacy, openness, and satisfaction. Their goal was to enhance the symmetrical relationship between publics and organizations by fostering mutual understanding, agreement, and satisfaction. They commenced two decades of research that attempted to quantify the characteristics of relationships.

Broom et al. (1997) proposed that researchers should focus on three aspects of relationships: antecedents, concepts or properties, and consequences. Antecedents are the perceptions, motives, and other conditions that lead to the formation of a relationship. Concepts are the interactions or communications that define or are associated with relationships. Consequences are the effects or outputs that affect the environment or situation as the result of a relationship. Of these dimensions, Ledingham (2003) and Bortree (2011) argued that antecedents have been the most important and the most overlooked in the theory of relationships.

For the most part, scholars have focused on two aspects: concepts and consequences. As a result, there has been a tendency to measure relationships in terms of outcomes and outputs. Broom and Dozier (1990) and Grunig and Hunt (1984) stressed the role of process indicators (e.g., number of press releases) and outcome indicators (e.g., whether or not target audiences retained the message). A crucial problem, identified by Grunig and Huang (2000), is that both tend to concentrate on the assessment of one-way effects.

Since the mid-2000s, much of the scholarship on OPR has highlighted the importance of CSR (Botan & Taylor, 2004). Wilson (2004), for example, stated that public relations should "facilitate positive communication between an organization and its publics" by enhancing and underscoring "a public perception of what has come to be called corporate social responsibility" (p. 136). Broadly, these initiatives have been categorized under the rubric of OPR studies.

The renewed emphasis on the study of relationships has reinvigorated, defined, and helped to justify the discipline of public relations. While most agree that building and maintaining positive, open, and mutually beneficial connections between organizations and publics in the long term is at the heart of the discipline, scholars have disagreed on the approaches that are best suited to understanding and facilitating the development of relationships. Heath (2013) described the predominance of OPR perspectives in public relations, calling it the "magic elixir for improving public relations theory and practice" (p. 426). Terms like "trust," "loyalty," "commitment," and "transparency" have been used to define OPRs as conceived by theorists and practitioners. However, a crucial problem in OPR research is how cumbersome is the process of assessing and measuring multiple variables—to say nothing of determining which are the most salient. Sweetser and

Kelleher (2016) called for the establishment of "a brief measure through which to understand OPR" (p. 228). In particular, they pointed to the significance of how conversational voice and communicated commitment correlate with how an organization is perceived. They argued that, in this way, it is possible to meaningfully assess the correlation between organizational actions and stakeholder attitudes. However, recent work on OPRs has been highly contested, as have terms such as "common interest," "mutual understanding," and "shared goals."

Furthermore, Heath (2013) argued against the instrumental view that dominated OPR research in the 1990s and early 2000s, endorsing instead a view that accommodates the discursive, linguistic, cultural, interpretive, and subjective dimension (p. 427). Publics co-create symbolic form and meanings that are characterized by ambiguity and constant renegotiation. From this point of view, an OPR hinges on the specific culture and context from which it arises and the theater in which it takes place. Ideally, OPRs lead to mutually beneficial relationships, in which individuals help co-create meaning and organizations are "committed to empower and serve the community," leading to a more "fully functioning society" (Heath, 2013, p. 430). This discursive conception of OPR, in which meanings are negotiated, is conceived as a set of multiple and overlapping organizations–others relationships (OsOsRs).

A Definitional Crisis: The Managerial Perspective

As already indicated, the concept of "relationships" is crucial to the understanding of public relations theory. Together with understanding the "public," an appreciation of "relationships" conditions our approach to the discipline. Yet, also as with "publics," engagement with a robust theoretical definition of "relationships" has largely been ignored. Among public relations scholars, there seems to have been little consensus about the goal of public relations as it pertains to understanding relationships. On the surface, it is curious that the discipline should not have a strong definitional sense of such a foundational term. Broom et al. (1997) argued that "the absence of a fully explicated definition precludes the development of valid operational measures of organization–public relationships and limits theory building in public relations" (p. 83).

As with the concept of the public, relationships in public relations tend to be defined by organizations, and how they interact with others. As a result, scholars are often left with tautological definitions. Center and Jackson (1995) wrote of the goal of public relations practice that: "The proper term for the desired outcome of public relations practice is public relationships" (p. 2). Public relations is thus the practice of establishing relations with the public. The standard approach to measuring such relationships has been to conduct surveys to measure the perception of them. Thus, while the functional relationship between an organization and the public—and the measurement of short-term outcomes and outputs—has received a great deal of attention, the theoretical underpinnings of the term "relationship" remain ill-defined.

From the standpoint of an organization—especially from the perspective of top management—the ability to define, quantify, and predict outputs and outcomes over time is essential to the very survival of public relations as a discipline. Hon and Grunig (1999) argued that the ability to understand relationships determined the value of public relations to an organization as a whole. They contended that scholars of public relations had made progress in measuring "the relatively short-term *outputs* and *outcomes* of specific public relations programs, events and campaigns," but that no benchmarks or theories existed to measure "the success or failure of long-term *relationships* stemming, in part from public relations effort" (Hon & Grunig, 1999, p. 2). Grunig et al. (1992) defined relationships in relation to IPC:

Researchers and practitioners could use any of these concepts to measure the quality of the strategic relationships of organizations, but we suggest that the following are most important: reciprocity, trust, credibility, mutual legitimacy, openness, mutual satisfaction, and mutual understanding. (p. 83)

An organization's interest in strategic communication—driven by the bottom line—has often outweighed the need for a general theory of relationships where they cannot be quantified or turned to profit. Krukeberg (2000) commented: "in its symmetrical models, public relations is, itself, highly value-laden and ideological with a concomitant set of professional beliefs and world-views" (p. 155). This worldview is often driven by the exigencies of business practices. As Heath (2013) suggested, significance, meaning, and practice "becomes contextualized through the nature of the organization as the dominant entity, especially, one might argue, through the service of public relations, which is, or as it is, managerial-centric" (p. 12).

With the emphasis that Grunig et al. (1992) placed on the strategic nature of relationships, normative public relations practice has thus focused on measuring the qualities of a relationship, or its byproducts, as opposed to the nature of the relationship itself, in the short term. As Pavlik (1987) noted, the dependence on surveys as a principal working method privileges the perspectives of individuals, making them the unit of analysis, rather than the characteristics of the relationship itself. As tempting as it is to accept the theoretical constructs offered by the scholars carrying out such surveys, their explanatory value may be limited, as it is not confirmed through rigorous observation. Hon (1998) wrote: "No one described experimental research designs whereby a strong case could be made for causal inferences between public relations activities and specific outcomes" (p. 130).

A large portion of OPR research appears designed to justify the discipline of public relations and secure its place within an organization's dominant coalition. As Ki and Shin (2006) wrote, "relational perspectives shift the validation of public relations initiatives from measures of communication output to measures of behavioral outcomes, thus providing a basis for evaluating public relations effectiveness" (p. 194). These authors surveyed 38 articles on OPR published between 1985 and 2004 and found "little consensus regarding the definition or measurement of OPR" (p. 194). As may be expected, excellence theory was a dominant theoretical construct, accounting for more than half of the articles looking at OPRs from a managerial perspective. Reliance on IPC scholarship for a definition of "relationships" prevailed. About half of the articles offered suggestions about relationship management strategies. Outcomes and antecedents accounted for nearly 80%, with satisfaction, commitment, trust, mutual understanding, and control mutuality being the dominant outcome variables.

Ki and Shin (2006) concluded that scholars tended to overlook the dynamism inherent in OPRs and needed to work toward building common definitions and a common terminology. Contingency theorist such as Cancel, Cameron, Sallot, and Mitrook (1997) focused on the dynamism of organizations, arguing that environmental conditions play a role in whether an organization takes a stance of accommodation or advocacy. The contingent, multiple, and longitudinal nature of OPRs has been gaining increasingly more attention from scholars.

Rethinking OPRs

As already noted, the categories developed by scholars of interpersonal relationships have been borrowed by public relations researchers and refined to suit the specific qualities of the OPR. As Coombs (2001) stated, "[r]elationships will remain center stage in public relations" (p. 113). Public relations, in its infancy, focused on message dissemination and persuasion, and often failed to account for the interactive, dynamic, and transitory nature of relationships—a nature that has evolved over time. OPR has been seen as a corrective, focusing on "the effective and efficient management of the organization–public relationship based on common interests and shared goals, over time, to engender mutual understanding and mutual benefit" (Ledingham, 2003, p. 184). For example, Ki and Nekmat (2015) reiterated the importance of relationship management, but showed that the relation between the perceived quality of an organization's efforts to manage relationships (organizational impressions as well as "bottom-line outcomes") and its behavior intention was indirect (p. 696).

As it became clear that it best served organizations' interests to enter into a dialogic relationship with stakeholders as co-equal partners, public relations theory and practice began to reflect this new reality (Johnston, 2014, 2018; Taylor & Kent, 2014). The concept of engagement with multiple publics and stakeholders, particularly in the era of social media, emerged as a central theoretical concept presaging the reconceptualization of public relations (Dhanesh, 2017; Jelen-Sanchez, 2017). Botan and Taylor (2004) had pointed the way to the central importance of engagement and the "co-creational perspective" (p. 93). Stakeholder engagement in public relations can be conceived as a means of manipulation, but also as a means of encouraging socially responsible outcomes (Johnston, 2018).

The idea that organizations are best served by listening to the concerns of stakeholders, engaging in "authentic involvement" and dialogue on an equal footing, and aligning their practices to the needs of publics has become an operative paradigm governing the practice of public relations (Johnston, 2014, p. 381). Taylor and Kent (2014) described authentic dialogue as characterized by propinquity, or openness to engagement with stakeholders; these concepts were conceived in equally generous terms. Johnston (2014) argued that involving stakeholders in decision-making processes contributed to the perception of organizational legitimacy.

The concept of open dialogue, as advocated by scholars ranging from Taylor, Kent, and White (2001) to Sweetser et al. (2015), advocates a transparent exchange between organizations and publics, as this holds the potential for ethical interactions and authentic "community building" (Vujnovic & Krukeberg, 2015, p. 331). Many organizations have embraced the concept of social responsibility and taken proactive steps to anticipate public needs and aspirations. While the bottom line still governs decisions behind the scenes and the balance of power is generally tipped in the favor of those organizations with the greatest political and economic power, OPR has moved in the direction of including publics.

An ideal, sketched out by Vujnovic and Krukeberg (2015), is of organizations as being part of the larger community, as opposed to the "hub of the universe," and further being "equally concerned about stakeholders' relationships with one another as with stakeholders' relationship with the organization" (p. 334). However, proclamations about its commitment to open and transparent dialogue may represent an organization's attempt to conceal a hidden agenda (Glaser, 2012). O'Byrne and Daymon (2014) proposed that organizations' public relations efforts are rarely focused on informing citizen stakeholders of their rights and responsibilities as owners of large companies. The concept of stakeholder engagement includes an ethical commitment to multiple publics, but O'Byrne and Daymon (2014) found that "public relations perpetuates a hierarchical distinction within the discrete but amorphous stakeholder group of shareholders" that is often unethical, irresponsible, and discriminatory (p. 469).

This is not to suggest that scholars, often working at the margins of public relations theory, have not proposed alternative explanations of how relationships function in a public relations context. In the mid-2000s, some challenged the assumption that the strategic management of relationships by organizations was the most effective and ethical course of public relations practice. The movement beyond a dyadic focus on OPR has gradually crystallized as public relations became enmeshed in larger, interconnected networks of social relationships. Strategic communication is informed by the view that "there is no such thing as a 'nonrelevant' public" (Sommerfeldt & Kent, 2015, p. 249).

Huang and Zhang (2013) found that researchers on OPR in the first decade of the twenty-first century had begun to move beyond reliance "more on intuition than meticulous conceptualization and rigorous methodology" (p. 85) and toward an elusive approach involving "dynamic and process oriented methodologies" that was "multi-dimensional in conceptualization and require[d] a multi-indexed approach" (p. 87). They identified two major strains of research. The first focused on "relational outcome by exploring it as a dependent variable or as a relationship characteristic that mediates various effects on public relations practice including digital communications, crisis communicative strategy, and relationship cultivation strategy" (p. 86). The second defined "OPR from the perspective of the public's attitudes toward an organization" (p. 86). Interestingly, these authors found that recent scholarship has emphasized the perspective of the public as opposed to that of the organization by a margin of nearly two to one.

OPR remained a dominant perspective through the early 2010s, refined by attention to the conceptualization of relationship variables—particularly attributes such as trust, intimacy, and control (Gelso & Carter, 1985; Millar & Rogers, 1987). Scholars have begun to describe relationships in terms of the subjective and objective components used by IPC scholars and psychologists. For example, the distinction between transference or displacement and real relationships between counselors and patients has been incorporated into public relations research (McAllister-Spooner & Kent, 2009). Research into interorganizational relationships is based on resource dependency and exchange theories; for example, how attributes such as necessity, asymmetry, reciprocity, and desire for legitimacy allow organizations to develop and thrive (Sommerfeldt, 2011).

The ecological approach, suggested by the early work of Cutlip and Center (1952), has contended that relationships are at their root an exchange of information and resources, and are negotiated through the communicative process to result in fragile balance between interested parties. For the most part, these alternatives focus on general theories of the nature of relationships between individuals, organizations, publics, and institutions at different levels, as opposed to organizational or situational relationships.

Case Study: Dialogic Approach—Hey Baby vs. Stop at Two

The dialogic approach represents an emerging area of public relations theory development. According to Grostedt (1997), this approach emphasizes the role of the public as "active, interactive, and equal participants of an ongoing communication process" (p. 39). The dialogic approach is relational in the sense that it seeks to understand the beliefs and interests of publics as antecedent to entering into a relationship, and models communication outreach efforts on skills such as listening and providing feedback in "a user friendly way" (Grostedt, 1997, p. 39). Ledingham and Bruning (2000) suggested that public relations efforts be harmonized with key members of the public by experimenting with multiple approaches with the goal of building long-term relationships.

In theory, this goal seems transparent and laudable. In practice, cultivating harmonic and consonant views can be difficult and complicated. According to Baxter and Bullis (1986), relationships between organizations and publics are reconceptualized at key moments, which they call "turning points." These moments may be positive, such as helping harmonize with publics and build long-term relationships, but they can equally lead to negative outcomes, where a public begins to "withhold resources and even attacking the organization" (Coombs, 2001, p. 112). The reasons for this are often ideological, based on perceived differences in worldviews and goals. According to Krukeberg (2000), public relations "not only represents ideologies; rather, in its symmetrical models, public relations practice is, itself, highly value-laden and ideological with a concomitant set of professional beliefs and worldviews" (p. 155).

This is what happened in Singapore in the wake of a government campaign to encourage couples to have children. Like many prosperous countries, Singapore faces a rapidly declining birthrate—down to 1.14 per couple in 2018, from 1.82 in 1980. Prime Minister Lee Hsien Loong has led the campaign to encourage couples to marry early and procreate, following on from the Baby Bonus scheme established by his predecessor, Goh Chok Tong, in 2001. His government has offered incentives such as cash payments of up to S$12,000 per child, generous maternity-leave benefits, preferential treatment in public housing, and subsidized fertility treatments. Lee is particularly concerned with the rising tide of immigration, due to the demand for labor. "If we go on like that," he said in a recent speech, "this place would fold up because there will be no original citizens to form the majority." The government sponsors a website called Hey Baby, dedicated to "building a supportive environment for Singaporeans to form families and raise children" and outlining incentives contained in the Marriage & Parenthood Package 2013. It also seeks to engage potential couples via a Facebook page.

The attempt to engage in dialogic communication has fallen flat, however. Seow Ting Lee (2013) found that the government-sponsored Facebook initiative has been marked "with little realization of the social networking site's dialogic principles." There are three chief reasons for this. First, rising prosperity since the 1980s has led many young people to rank having children as a low priority. Second, Prime Minister Lee Kuan Yew, the current prime minister's father, launched a campaign in the 1970s encouraging couples to "Stop at Two" children, and going so far as to encourage sterilization. This led to a "turning point" in the relationship between the government and publics that has proven resilient. Third, Singaporeans have the prevailing perception that raising a child is expensive. Actual costs are estimated at 20% higher than in the United States. A study conducted by the Singapore Management University suggested that women in Singapore ranked higher than American or European women in the pursuit of materialism. They also outnumber men in college graduation rates and make up almost 45% of the workforce. Even with generous subsidies and messages tied to Confucian values regarding the importance of family, the government of Singapore has yet to find a means of engaging couples in a public relations campaign based on meaningful dialogue and taking into account antecedent factors contributing to delayed marriage and a low birthrate.

Case Study: Virtual Relationships—Online Dating to Consumer Outrage

Technology has transformed the nature of relationships in the past two decades. Online portals and social media have allowed people to meet and interact from remote locations and to connect with others around the world. Content- and subject-specific sites cater to groups with similar, often narrow interests, such as fans of Kim Kardashian, Apple products, or antique locomotives. Facebook, Twitter, and other social media sites allow users to customize a personal profile with the expectation of forming relationships with people who share similar interests, concerns, beliefs, attitudes, and expectations. Organizations have used integrated campaigns built around social media to establish dialogue and build relationships on multiple platforms

(Shin, Pang, and Kim, 2015). The pace of virtual social interaction has been accelerated by the use of mobile devices such as smartphones and tablets. For many, online relationships offer advantages over physical ones, including lower cost and immediate access from any location. In 2013, the number of 19-year-olds with drivers' licenses dropped to 69%, compared to 87.3% a decade earlier (Beck, 2016). Although the economic downturn and other factors may offer a partial explanation for this astonishing change, the ubiquity of virtual relationships is a significant contributing factor. Increasingly, and especially for younger members of society who have grown up on the Web, the distinction between face-to-face interactions and virtual relationships has blurred.

Developing relationships is one of the motivating factors behind forming and maintaining virtual relationships. Online dating sites now number in the hundreds. Among the largest are Match.com—the first Internet dating site, launched in 1995—and eHarmony. Many cater to specific demographic groups, such as Christian Mingle, ManHunt, and JDate. Most are subscription services, but OKCupid, Grindr, and Plenty of Fish offer free options. Research has suggested that relationships formed in the virtual space can be more enduring and of higher quality than those resulting from face-to-face encounters. A study published in the *Proceedings of the National Academy of Sciences* and funded by eHarmony found that 35% of 20,000 survey respondents had met their partners online, and that those who did reported a 2% lower rate of divorce than those who met through other means (Reich, 2013). However, it is important to remember that the Internet has blurred the lines between private and public behavior in the context of relationships. A post on a social media site created in the spirit of intimate conversation can assume permanence in the public sphere.

OPR research, which has traditionally focused on short-term communication effects, has begun to examine how relationships are built and maintained over time (Bruning & Lambe, 2008). Scholars have called for a focus on the quality of relationships, as well as their characteristics as measured by variables. On another dimension, organizations are tapping into the world of virtual relationships. Shin, Carithers, Lee, Graham, and Hendricks (2012) analyzed the Facebook pages of Fortune 500 corporations during the rise of corporations' use of online and social media in the mid-2000s. As an example, as of mid-August 2013, the Facebook page My Coke Rewards had more than 380,000 "likes" and hundreds of comments on every post. Many of these comments took the form of complaints about the inability to redeem rewards or expressions of frustration about the limitations imposed by the rewards programs, but the company made efforts to redress these issues through mediation addressed directly to aggrieved stakeholders.

Organizations can also misjudge the nature of relationship-building and -maintaining efforts. In 2017, Pepsi Cola and Kendall Jenner drew fire for a commercial that coopted imagery associated with protests over police shootings of unarmed African Americans. In 2018, Dolce & Gabbana was criticized for a commercial depicting a Chinese model struggling to eat spaghetti with chopsticks. In each case, the campaigns were seen as tone-deaf by many consumers—and each went viral, prompting thousands of tweets, blog posts, and YouTube responses. Although the companies' reputations were damaged, a series of email apologies and promises to take corrective action helped defuse the situation. However, the crisis communication response strategy failed to engage a significant number of outraged stakeholders, missing the opportunity to harness diverse social media channels such as blogs and Twitter to interact directly with consumers. On the front end, they could have anticipated or gauged consumer opinions before launching their campaigns; in the wake of the controversy, they could have answered the charges of insensitivity though timely interaction on Facebook and other online venues.

IPC Theories of Relationships

IPC emerged as a distinct discipline in the 1970s. A subgenre of the field of communications, borrowing some key concepts from psychology and sociology, it focuses on the exchange of information between people. A central premise is the notion of dyadic communication, defined as a two-part relationship between sender and receiver, which may be either individuals or groups. According to Burleson (2010), IPC has "a radical lack of consensus about fundamental conceptual matters" as well as a lack of a stable definition (p. 145). He noted that some scholars have defined the basic concepts in varying terms, from the idea that IPC is conditioned by the quality of communication and the closeness of the relationship (Bebbe, Bebee & Redmond, 2002), to an emphasis on the roles of sender and receiver within a nexus of mutual activity (Trenholm & Jensen, 2008), to any form of exchange between individuals "regardless of the relationship that they share" (Guerrero, Andersen, & Afifi, 2007, p. 11).

The situation is analogous to that of the concept of relationships in public relations, where there is no clear consensus about what OPRs are or how they should be measured. Burleson (2010) noted that it is crucial for theorists to share a common understanding of IPC because "it is maximally effective at producing knowledge when its practitioners form a community around shared understandings of the objects of study, relevant questions about these objects, and research exemplars focused on those objects" (p. 47).

As outlined by Burleson (2010), among the earliest understandings was the situational perspective, based on an analysis of context. Variables such as proximity of communicators, number of communicators, channels used, and types of feedback (but not necessarily the quality of the feedback) are the units of analysis used by its followers. Although criticized for presenting a rather static and structuralist approach to communications, the situational perspective continues to have relevance in IPC scholarship (Trenholm & Jensen, 2008). It has informed the variable-based analyses that have dominated theories of OPR in public relations. Normative OPR and IPC both focus on the quantitative rather than qualitative aspects of communication within relationships. Burleson (2010) noted that "the situational view equates a face-to-face conversation between a postal clerk and a customer with a conversation between a pair of longtime lovers" (p. 148).

In contrast, the developmental perspective of IPC, which has only recently been embraced in public relations, focuses on the quality of relationships, making a distinction between personal and impersonal interactions. The theory is developmental in the sense that it postulates that IPC moves from impersonal to personal along a continuum depending on the level of involvement (Berger, 2005). As Burleson (2010) contended, the developmental perspective emphasizes that personal relationships are considered more significant than impersonal ones (p. 149).

The interactional perspective defines IPC according to the effect that communication has on behavior patterns. It considers all forms of communication as interpersonal, regardless of the nature or conditions of the interaction, focusing instead on influence and on "mutual adjustments" to behavior (Cappella, 1987). Normative OPR in public relations has tended to treat relationships as essentially impersonal. Burleson (2010) criticized the interactional perspective as "overly broad" (p. 150), citing Delia, O'Keefe, and O'Keefe (1982): "interaction is not the same as communication" (p. 159).

Public relations scholars have incorporated IPC concepts into theory building. Grunig and Huang (2000) suggested that public relations theory could derive "analogues" from IPC. He "appropriated" dimensions based on IPC work and included openness, which in contemporary parlance might be conceived as transparency, writing that "disclosure can produce more symmetry in the distribution of power" than maintaining secrets (Grunig & Huang, 2000, p. 37). As an example, assurance may be translated in the public relations concept of legitimacy. Grunig et al. (1992) argued that recognizing the legitimacy of publics was a crucial factor in building relationships. The concept of networking is akin to the public relations process of identifying active publics that are significant stakeholders in OPR. Of especial importance is the concept of control mutuality, defined by Stafford and Canary (1991) as "the degree to which partners agree about which of them should decide relational goals and behavioral routines" (p. 224).

Ferguson (1984) predicted the intersection of public relations theory with this IPC concept, defining it as the distribution of power in relationships. Control mutuality, according to Grunig and Haung (2000), operates on a continuum from situations in which one party possesses no power to co-equal partnerships. In most cases, a degree of power asymmetry exists: in organizational–public contests, the balance usually favors the organization, because of the difference in distribution of resources. However, the strength of the relationship may be measured by the perception of a sense of control mutuality expressed by both parties.

Grunig and Haung (2000) also adopted IPC concepts of relational trust, satisfaction, and commitment. In earlier work, Grunig et al. (1992) had argued that trust, or "the belief that others will not exploit one's goodwill," was central to the maintenance of OPRs over the long term (p. 44). Ledingham (2003) argued that perceptions of trust and satisfaction were most significant to the effectiveness of public relations practice and should therefore be the central focus of study. Attempting to manipulate the relational factors of control mutuality, trust, satisfaction, and commitment for one's own benefit, Grunig and Huang (2000) argued, would "lead to relational dissatisfaction and misunderstanding" (p. 37). Instead, they suggested using coorientational measures such as those proposed by Broom (1977) to assess first-, second-, and third-party perceptions of relationship according to the four IPC factors.

Missing from the equation is the significant role of symbols, messages, meaning, intention, and relative quality of communication. The message-centered approach, as defined by Burleson (2010), is "a complex, situated social process in which people who have established a communicative relationship exchange messages in an effort to generate shared meanings and accomplish social goals" (p. 151). Burleson (2010) defined messages as "a set of behavioral expressions, typically consisting of shared symbols, which are produced in an effort to convey some internal meaning" (p. 151). He defined meanings as "internal states (thoughts, ideas, beliefs, feelings, etc.) that communicators seek to express or convey in a message and interpret a message as expressing or conveying" (p. 151). Although messages and their interpretation have a conventional aspect, termed "denotative," the process of reaching agreement on shared meaning is contingent on the context, or connotative, aspect.

As Burleson (2010) noted, the communicative act does not occur in a vacuum, but is designed to accomplish larger social goals that entail the formation and maintenance of relationships. At the level of specific research, IPC examination of relationships has focused on measuring individual-level characteristics based on relationship scales, from which the variables used by public relations scholars to research OPR were derived. Common points of intersection include research on issues such as commitment, satisfaction, trust, similarities, control mutuality, expectations, personal commitment, calculation of benefit, and exchange relationships. Each of these variables has been studied, in one form or another, by scholars of IPC as well as by OPR public relations scholars.

Moreover, Bruning, Castle, and Schrepfner (2004) pointed out that "interpersonal communication relationship principals cannot be applied directly to the organization-public context," citing research by Ledingham, Bruning, and Wilson (1999). Coombs (2001) wrote that a relational approach drawing on the body of IPC research provides "an excellent resource for understanding and coping with the organization-stakeholder relationships" (p. 113), but yet "holds great promise for future applications to public relations" (p. 114), which suggests measuring the perceptions of individuals about relationships with organizations as distinct from perceptions of individuals about their relationship to other individuals.

Relational and Social Capital

Communication between individuals and groups depends on the exchange of relational or social capital. Putnam (1994) defined social capital in terms of relationships, as "the features of social organizations such as networks, norms, and social trust that facilitate coordination and coopera-tion for mutual benefit" (p. 665). An emerging strain of research suggests how public relations can facilitate building social relationship structures that benefit both individuals and groups, including organizations (Sommerfeldt, 2018). Taylor (2011) suggested how putting relationships at the center of the practice of strategic communication could augment social capital and lead to a society that functions more fully. This has emerged as a new paradigm, challenging the earlier emphasis on an OPR relationship management perspective.

By building relationships and facilitating the co-creation of meaning, public relations holds the promise of enhancing civil society, making democracy more robust, and empowering marginal-ized groups (Taylor & Doerfel, 2005). An emphasis on social capital allows the assessment of both the structure and the quality of relationships, as well as accommodating a conception of relation-ships as a series of interconnected networks (Sommerfeldt, 2013b; Yang, 2018). Using public rela-tions strategies and tactics, organizations cultivate relationships to build social capital within the marketplace of ideas. Successful organizations establish network partners within civil society to "leverage the potential of each group" (Taylor & Doerfel, 2005, p. 122). This builds a stronger, more egalitarian, and more ethical civil society, defined as "the process of interactions that lead to rela-tionships, build trust and create social capital" (Taylor, 2009, p. 77). Effective strategies for strength-ening relationships include openness, sharing of tasks, assurance, and access.

Sommerfeldt (2018) contended that trust is the most significant variable associated with social capital; without it, "low levels of civic engagement" result (p. 5). With trust, the social capital rela-tionship cultivation has the consequence of strengthening outcomes through strategies such as information exchange, cooperation, bonding, and bridging (Burt, 2001; Doerfel & Taylor, 2004; Putnam, 2000; Sommerfeldt, 2013b; Taylor & Doerfel, 2003). Bonding, according to Putnam (2000), is a form of social capital that usually takes place within homogenous groups and serves to tighten cohesiveness. Bridging, on the other hand, generally occurs among individuals and groups that are weakly linked, but likewise serves to build or enhance group solidarity (Sommerfeldt, 2018).

Public Relations as Engagement in a Fully Functioning Society

The fully functioning society theory (FFST) proposes that public relations can play a key role in building community by helping individuals engage with organizations through fostering commu-nication. The currency by which engagement transpires is relational capital, defined as "the per-ceived value or worth of the relationship between organizations and stakeholders" (Johnston & Lane, 2018, p. 634). The concept is related to social capital: the "features of social organization such as trust, norms, and networks that can improve the efficiency of society by facilitating coordinated action"; in other words, things that contribute to collective trust (Putnam, Leonardi, and Nanetti, 1993). For Yang and Taylor (2013), social capital may be transformed into relational capital when it is situated within a network of interactions, and thus serve to build and maintain community. For Saffer (2016), relational capital is akin to goodwill, and can function as a means of compensating for power differences among individuals and organizations. Relational capital can also be used to mend relationships and restore trust with dissatisfied or marginalized publics (Waymer, 2013).

From the standpoint of OPR, organizations that build strong relational capital reinforce legitimacy and commitment to the social good. Relational engagement over long periods, as a means of building relational capital, is correlated to greater stakeholder trust (Ledingham & Bruning, 1998). Relational engagement occurs over time, as opposed to episodically, and takes place on an informal and interpersonal basis (Johnston & Lane, 2018). Through repeated interactions, ideally in situations where stakeholders and organizations negotiate and co-create meanings, relational engagement leads to the creation and reinforcement of relational capital "by creating and curating narratives, interaction, and sentiment that positively support the organization and its activities" (Johnston & Lane, 2018, p. 641).

Social network analysis (SNA) represents an attempt to understand how individuals are connected to other people, groups, and network systems (Sommerfeldt & Taylor, 2015; Taylor, 2011). According to Kent, Sommerfeldt, and Saffer (2016), it seeks to describe how organizations and stakeholders interact in public relations settings. Following Burt (1992), a central concept focuses on the concept of structural holes, or the "communicative gaps between organizations and other groups and organizations" (p. 93). Entities that connect groups and serve to "broker the flow of information between people and control the form of the projects that bring people together, from opposite sides of the hole" gain power and received benefits (Burt, 1998, p. 8). While structural holes raise the specter of gaining unethical advantage, the presumption is that public relations professionals in such situations do not exploit their position for asymmetrical purposes and become *tertius gaudens*, or a "third who benefits," at the expense of the negotiating parties (Burt, 1992, p. 32).

Sommerfeldt and Yang (2017) examined the relationship between public relations, dynamic social networks, and social movement organizations in the context of the evolution of strategic issues management (SIM). They found support for the contention that network diversity, characterized by a "broad and diverse assemblage of weak ties," led to more effective outcomes because of a nimbleness of communication and a lack of state or organizational censorship (Sommerfeldt & Yang, 2017, p. 833). By broadening the range of constituents, activist social movement organizations in particular could amplify their message because if was framed as collective rather than personal action.

To make society more fully functioning, public relations should have a role in the democratic process. For Taylor (2010), this means that it should help "create (and re-create) the conditions that enact civil society" (p. 7). The instrumental view of public relations, which focuses on the management of relationships by organizations, often runs counter to the definition of public relations as unfettered "communication and exchange of ideas to facilitate change" (L'Etang, 2008, p. 18). Public relations conceived as a means of advancing organizational goals in a competitive marketplace is not necessarily conducive to advancing democratic engagement with multiple publics. On the other hand, theorists of deliberative democracy have proposed that public relations can generate and distribute social capital in ways that facilitate open and inclusive debate, leading to decisions that represent multiple stakeholder interests (Dryzek, 2000, 2009; Edwards, 2016). Presenting arguments on a level playing field, grounded in respect for ethics and transparency, holds the promise of fostering democratic engagement that serve the public interest and leads to a "more fully functioning society" (Heath, 2013, p. 420). In an ideal situation, every stakeholder with an interest in the issue would be involved and communication would be transparent (Edwards, 2016). Organizations that use public relations in a socially responsible manner, with the goal of enhancing civil society, are more likely to achieve long-term goals of fostering goodwill and enhancing reputation (Sommerfeldt, 2013b).

Intermediaries

Public relations scholars have pointed to the significant and often overlooked role of intermediaries in the process of relationship building and maintenance. Intermediaries act to mediate the communication between organizations and their stakeholders. According to Frandsen (2018), their role includes defining boundaries and collective identity, managing reputation, exercising political influence, and acting as a source of information (p. 1). Intermediaries do not act directly on the part of either organization or stakeholder, but serve to mediate the process. Frandsen and Johansen (2015) distinguished between intermediaries that were closely linked to specific organizations or stakeholders and those that did not have a formal relationship, such as government agencies or the media.

As discussed in Chapter 10, Freeman (1984) wrestled with the issue of how a stakeholder without a direct stake in an organization could wield influence. He proposed that certain parties could act as intermediaries or influencers. Freeman expanded on this idea in the following decade, proposing that stakeholders were divided among two groups: primary or definitional and secondary or instrumental (Freeman, Harrison, and Wicks, 2007). Phillips (2003) likewise distinguished between normative and derivative stakeholders. Fassin (2010) suggested that there were three groups: stakeholders, stakewatchers, and stakekeepers. His stakeholder may be likened to Freeman's primary stakeholder; stakewatchers includes groups like unions that monitor the activities of an organization; and stakekeepers are groups that have responsibility for oversight but no direct interest in a particular organization, such as media outlets and government regulators. Friedman and Miles (2006) noted that both organizations and stakeholders had their own respective intermediaries, but found structural asymmetries between the relative power exercised by organizations and constituents.

From a cultural critical perspective, Bourdieu (1984) proposed that a set of cultural intermediaries are involved in negotiation of the symbolic economy, such as tastemakers, advertising account executives, critics, and lifestyle gurus. L'Etang (2008) included public relations practitioners in this list. Likewise, Deephouse and Heugens (2009) proposed that information intermediaries serve as gatekeepers, setting the agenda on social and political issues.

Current Status and Future Directions for Building Theories of Relationships

The OPR model has stressed that organizations can improve efficiency by adopting communication strategies designed to maximize mutual satisfaction between them and their stakeholders or stakeseekers. This has been a useful model for resolving conflicts and mitigating the challenges posed by activist groups from a strategic perspective. From an organizational perspective, OPR or SIM holds the prospect of being a "magic elixir," as suggested by Heath (2013), insofar as it offers a theoretical basis for building relationships between organizations and publics with the goal of maximizing satisfaction and building mutual trust.

Measuring supposedly "valid operational variables" in relationships, such as trust, control mutuality, openness, similarity, agreement, accuracy, and commitment, offers a testable means of measuring the interaction between organizations and publics (Broom et al., 1997; Ledingham, 2003). However, as Chung, Lee, and Heath (2013) recently argued, these models are insufficient to explain the fullness and complexity of relationships. They were particularly critical of the emphasis on the analysis of ill-defined relationship variables that are used to model public relations theory and research:

> Over the years since the 1990s, conceptualization in public relations research has focused more on taxonomies of relational variables with little sensitivity to the contextualization of those variables. As is evident in the interpersonal communication literature, the speculation about lists of variables that differentiate relationship qualities is often similar to a dog chasing its tail. Many variables are proposed by various theorist but those that truly differentiate the enactment of successful from unsuccessful relationships continue to be more speculative than definitive. (Chung et al., 2013, p. 3)

Instead, they argued for a more parsimonious approach focused on relational attributes that are "conceptually designed to account for, as modeled, substantial and valuable variance to predict outcome variables" (p. 3). In other words, they selected a limited number of variables that fit the specific situation rather than a "one-size" model based on an array of variables such as that proposed by Waters and Bortree (2012). Chung et al. (2013) argued for a focus on "relationship quality rather than product marketing as a key to brand equity" (p. 4). They proposed that relational attributes such as motivations and experiences are more powerful predictors of customers' favorable assessments than product or brand attributes. In other words, assessment of relational attitudes and relationship quality is positively correlated to customer motivation and behavior. Put more simply, the contextual aspect of relationship variables matters.

Heath (2013) proposed a deep engagement with IPC theory and a rigorous examination of the role of discourse and rhetoric in building comprehensive public relations theories of relationships. He followed Kuckenberg (2000) in his general criticism of OPR studies as ideologically laden and centered on the organizational perspective, to the detriment of consideration of the role of the public in the communication process. Strategic communications or the situational perspective, he suggested, has a bias toward the managerial perspective, with public relations envisioned as "a tool by which managers/supervisors accomplish various outcomes" (p. 13). Establishing relationships with the public are thus seen as a necessary byproduct of achieving institutional goals and interests first and foremost. Any ambiguity—much less activist dissent—is to be avoided. In the end, Heath (2013) argued for a social exchange approach, one in which organizations and publics are seen as co-equal partners, working to "more creatively to co-define and negotiate relationships" (p. 15). These publics are not so much unified as multiple and constantly shifting; not so much OPRs as of "OPsRs" or "OsPsRs."

Heath (2013) thus proposed a reconceptualization of the entire theoretical construct. Rather than focusing on OPRs, which suggests a message–receiver model organized along a unified chain of discrete communication processes and privileging the sender over the receiver, he proposed conceiving of the theoretical enterprise as OsPsRs. This reconceptualization suggests the multiplicity and dynamic nature of relationships, positing "that organizations have relationships with one another as well as all the constellations of stakeholders/stakeseeker combinations that make up the relevant fabric (network complexity and political economy) of society" (p. 4). He countered what he perceived to be OPRs' reductive focus on relationship variables such as mutual satisfaction, trust, and commitment to an approach that recognizes that relationships "are complex, multidimensional, multilayered, and subject to motivation for conflict and aggression" (p. 2). Heath (2010) had earlier argued that "as a paradigm, relationship management must address the reality of opposing perspective" (p. xiii). Publics are multiple and their opinions evolve. Likewise, organizations often count as constituents of other organizations, which are affected by their decisions, as in the case of the 2011 BP oil spill, which sent reverberations throughout the industry. Ki and Shin (2006) had earlier proposed that a dynamic conception of OPRs at multiple levels over time offers promise as a research direction. Based on the contingency theory of accommodation, their research suggested that the stance that an organization takes is based on a wide array of environmental and internal factors and is subject to change as the situation evolves. Thus, OPRs are both dynamic and contingent.

To account for the multiplicity and complexity of relationships, Heath (2013) proposed a theoretical foundation that incorporates resource dependency theory, social exchange theory, IPC research, and linguistics and critical theory. The power dimensions of relationships, Heath argued, is an area that has been largely overlooked in OPR theory. Heath (2013) also cited Conrad and Haynes (2001) discussing how power relationships are negotiated through the symbolic aspects of communication.

OPR strategies focus primarily on positive relationships and do not reach to questions of legitimacy (Heath, Waymer, & Palenchar, 2013). Heath (2013) contended that the fundamental questions facing public relations practitioners and theorists involve power dynamics and the nature of OPRs, particularly on a corporate level: "is the community presumed and defined to serve the corporation or is the corporation committed to empower and serve the community?" (p. 17). Put another way, "legitimacy is not predicated on efficiency but on discursively enlightened choice" (p. 16). He argued forcefully from the perspective of resource dependency and social exchange theory that legitimacy is "the foundation dimension of relationships" (p. 19).

Conclusion

Scholars have argued that public relations theory should shift away a from functionalist effort to manage relationships, as though stakeholders were something that organizations should act upon, to efforts to build and maintain relationships in a global context. As Brønn (2018) suggested, public relations has gradually abandoned the view that managing communication on behalf of organizations is its primary goal, in preference of one that emphasizes building high-quality relationships for the greater good. Vujnovic and Krukeberg (2015) have argued that rather than drawing on social and behavior science, public relations theorists should "embrace a holistic ecological community worldview as well as an 'ecological conscience' in their relationship building and maintenance efforts" (p. 345). This reflects a shift in interest among many theorists toward the cultural dimensions associated with relationships. The ecological approach represents a challenge to the assumption that terms such as "mutual satisfaction" are universal goals in all contexts: "The most basic concepts may be the ones most vulnerable to cultural assumptions, yet these are the ones that warrant the most attention and scrutiny because of their potential impact" (Zaharna, 2015, p. 205)

Heath (2013) surmised that the concept of OPR was central to public relations but remained problematic because its fundamental "dimensions and assumptions" had not been fully "explored by scrutinizing out intellectual maps" (p. 426). At the most basic level, it is not clear whether the concept posits "public" as a single body in relationship to organizations, or whether it sees publics as multiple entities. If publics are multiple, how do they interact with one another and how are their relationships entangled? OPR research has focused on its role as an independent variable leading to specific outcomes such as building brand loyalty or fostering reputation and goodwill. For public relations practitioners, OPR emerged as a tool that managers could use to achieve outcomes deemed positive for their organizations.

The question is best framed not in terms of cost–benefit analysis embedded in OPR and strategic communications, but thorough a rigorous analysis of the rhetoric and terminology used around relational communications in the interest of establishing a moral and ethical foundation for public relations. Relationships, Heath (2013) argued, consist of a complex web of discursive texts within a rhetorical framework. Tensions as well as agreements are implied in the terms used to describe relationships: "wife, husband, friend, neighbor, colleague, client ... owner, fan, customer, competitor, trade association, government oversight and such" (p. 20). These terms not only provide benchmarks against which one can measure relationships, but are crucial in enacting and constituting them. As Stoker (2014) contended, "the common denominator in the sequence of events from establishing, having, and building a relationship is the continual act of relating through shared values, interests, and communication" (p. 354).

Returning to Ferguson (1984), it is crucial to the future of public relations research and theory to pay close attention to OPRs. To date, however, the narrow variables and corporate-centric focus of much of the scholarship on relationships have been an impediment to robust theory development. As Heath (2013) argued, a "dialogic, discursive, rhetorical approach to such matters adds the rich insights that grow from the ideal that however measured and enacted, relationships are textual, multidimensional, multilayered, and complexly interrelated" (p. 21).

Chapter Summary

The concept of "relationships" is at the heart of public relations. It is thus ironic that there has been so little agreement about its meaning and definition. Scholars have attempted to provide a rigorous definition of "relationships" since the mid-1980s, focusing on how publics are oriented to organizations. It has been defined as a connection between two or more concepts, ideas, or people; in the case of the later, it arises through shared symbols and rhetoric, outlooks, or behaviors. The ability to understand the nature and development of relationships is of crucial importance to the practice and theory of public relations.

The scholarly understanding of relationships in public relations may be traced to theories of interpersonal relationships (Cutlip & Center, 1971). By the early 1970s, relationships in public relations were defined as OPRs. The focus was on both dialogue and a co-creational model. Ferguson (1984) was instrumental in placing the OPR at the forefront of public relations theory. Much theoretical work was aimed at specifying the quantitative measurement of three aspects of OPR: antecedents, properties, and consequences.

This organizational bias, represented most tellingly by the theory of situational management pioneered by James Grunig, has dominated much of the public relations theory of the last four decades. Under the rubric of pursing mutual benefit, public relations theory centered on the functional strategies and tactics used to bring the relationships between publics and organizations into alignment in pursuit of mutual benefit. Thus, organizations were encouraged to seek symmetrical relationships because they were postulated to be the most efficient and ethical forms of communication. Public relations researchers developed valid operations measures that could predict the long-term success or failure of strategic relationships between organizations and their publics (Hon & Grunig, 1999).

In recent years, more nuanced approaches have emerged that consider a broad range of economic, political, and social differences. While the concepts of mutual benefit and symmetrical communication appear on the surface to be reasonable and laudable goals, researchers such as Heath (1997) have noted that organizations and publics are not necessarily on a level playing field, owing to power differences between them. Thus, there is a new emphasis on seeing organizations as part of a larger community, rather than as isolated centers of their own universes (Vujnovic & Kruckeberg, 2015, p. 334). This has led to the emergence of new strains of public relations theory, such as resource dependency theory, the ecological approach, the rhetorical approach, and particularly the dialogic approach. Each attempts to examine the active role of publics in the development and maintenance of relationships. Stakeholders operate as active participants in the communicative process, as opposed to passive agents there to be acted upon by organizations, as suggested in situational management theory (Grostedt, 1997).

Sommerfeldt (2013a) argued for a role for public relations in helping build social capital by engaging in dialogue as a mean of forging relationships based on trust in order to build community. Following on the trend toward dialogic approaches and analysis of power differentials, SNA has been used to examine the interactions between individuals and groups, and the outcomes that result. It shares some common operational definitions with the situational approach, but places more emphasis on the dialogic, co-creational aspects of the relationships between organizations and publics (Heath, 2006; Kent et al., 2016). The related concept of social exchange theory likewise proposes that organizations and publics can operate as co-equal partners (Heath, 2013). However, building community based on dialogue and trust requires attention to advocacy and discourse on the one hand and ethics on the other. It brings up the issue of legitimacy and reputation, whereby an organization must demonstrate that it is both committed and empowered to serve a community of stakeholders (Heath et al., 2013).

Key Terms

- *Antecedents:* Perceptions, motives, needs, and behaviors posited as preconditions, contingencies, or causes in the establishment of relationships.
- *Commitment:* Maximal efforts at maintaining an ongoing relationship. Includes continuance commitment—the dedication to continuing a certain line of action; and affective commitment—an effective or emotional orientation to an entity.
- *Consequences:* Outputs that have the effect of changing the environment goal states of an organization.
- *Control Mutuality:* The degree to which parties agree mutual goals and behavioral outcomes.
- *Intermediaries:* Agents acting as go-betweens who do not serve either an organization or its stakeholders, but facilitate the dialogue between them.
- *Interorganizational Relationships:* The relatively enduring transactions among or between an organization its environment.
- *Legitimacy:* Aspects of interorganizational relationships that allow the appearance of agreement with prevailing norms, and expectations.
- *Organization–Public Relationship:* The state that exists between an organization and its key publics, where the actions of one entity affect the economic, social, political, and cultural well being of the other.
- *Organizations–Others Relationships (OsOsRs):* The idea that relationships are complex, and consist of a constellation of stakeholders and organizations interacting as a network and in multiple ways.
- *Reciprocity:* The cooperation, and coordination among parties.
- *Relationship Properties:* Recurrent patterns of relational events.
- *Satisfaction:* Encompasses affection and emotion.
- *Stability:* The relative predictability of relationships in situational or environmental uncertainty.
- *Trust:* The belief that others will maintain goodwill.

Discussion Questions

1 How can we define OPRs? What are some different perspectives on this matter?
2 Why are relationships at the heart of the practice and theory of public relations?
3 What are the foundations of OPR research? What is its historical origin?
4 How do perspectives on relationships in other fields shape your understanding of them in public relations?
5 What is the role of variables in defining OPRs?
6 Why is it more important to measure public relations outcomes than public relations outputs when developing or maintaining relationships with publics?
7 Which relational outcomes are most important when measuring the quality of an organization's strategic relationships of organizations? Why?
8 In what way is the role of communication—as a symbolic relationship—imperative to understanding the relationships between clients and publics?
9 Ethics, CSR, and legitimacy have been discussed as a part of relationship studies. Why do or don't they matter?
10 What are some concerns and criticisms around OPR research? Discuss the future direction of relationship studies.
11 How do we define relationships in a public relations context?
12 What are the leading perspectives on relationships in public relations?
13 How are relationships measured at individual, organizational, and societal levels?
14 What are the current agendas and issues in OPR research?

References

Avidar, R. (2017). Public relations and social business: The importance of enhancing engagement. *Public Relations Review*, *43*, 995–962.

Baxter, L. A., & Bullis, C. (1986). Turning points in developing romantic relationships. *Human Communication Research*, *12*(4), 469–493.

Bebbe, S. A., Bebee, S. J., & Redmond, M. V. (2002). *Interpersonal communication: Relation to others.* Boston, MA: Allyn & Bacon.

Beck, J. (2016). The decline of the driver's license. *The Atlantic*, January 22. Available from https://www.theatlantic.com/technology/archive/2016/01/the-decline-of-the-drivers-license/425169 (accessed May 20, 2020).

Berger, C. R. (2005). Interpersonal communication: Theoretical perspectives, future prospects. *Journal of Communication*, *55*, 415–447.

Bortree, D. S. (2011). Mediating the power of antecedents in public relationships: A pilot study. *Public Relations Review*, *37*, 44–49.

Botan, C. H., & Taylor, M. (2004). Public relations: The state of the field. *Journal of Communication*, *54*(4), 645–661.

Bourdieu, P. (1984). *Distinction: A social critique of the judgement of taste*, trans R. Nice. Cambridge, MA: Harvard University Press.

Brønn, P. S. (2018). Relationship management. In R. L. Heath & W. Johansen (Eds.), *The international encyclopedia of strategic communication* (pp. 1–11). New York: John Wiley & Sons.

Broom, G. M. (1977). Coorientational measurement of public issues. *Public Relations Review*, *3*, 110–119.

Broom, G. M., Casey, S., & Ritchey, J. (1997). Concept and theory of organization-public relationships. *Journal of Public Relations Research, 9*, 83–98.

Broom, G. M., & Dozier, D. M. (1990). *Using research in public relations: Applications to program management.* Englewood Cliffs, NJ: Prentice-Hall.

Bruning, S. D., Castle, J. D., & Schrepfer, E. (2004). Building relationships between organizations and publics: Examining the linkage between organization–public relationships, evaluations of satisfaction, and behavioral intent. *Communication Studies, 55*(3), 435–446.

Bruning, S. D., & Lambe, K. E. (2008). Linking worldview, relationships attitudes, and behavioral outcomes: Implications for the study and practice of public relations. *Journal of Promotional Management, 14*, 139–151.

Burleson, B. R. (2010). The nature of interpersonal communication: A message-centered approach. In C. R. Berger, M. E. Rotloff, & D. R. Roskos-Ewoldsen (Eds.), *The handbook of communication science* (2nd ed., pp. 145–163). Thousand Oaks, CA: Sage.

Burleson, B. R., & Kunkel, A. W. (1994). The socialization of emotional support skills in childhood. In G. R. Pierce, B. R. Sarason, & I. G. Sarason (Eds.), *Handbook of social support and the family* (pp. 105–140). New York: Plenum.

Burt, R. S. (1992). *Structural holes: The social structure of competition.* Cambridge, MA: Harvard University Press.

Burt, R. S. (2001). Structural holes versus network closure as social capital. In N. Lin, K. Cook, & R. S. Burt (Eds.), *Social capital: Theory and research* (pp. 31–56). New York: Aldine De Gruyter.

Burt, R. S. (1998). The gender of social capital. *Rationality and Society, 10*, 5–46.

Cancel, A. E., Cameron, G. T., Sallot, L. M., & Mitrook, M. A. (1997). It depends: A contingency theory of accommodation in public relations. *Journal of Public Relations Research, 9*(1), 31–63.

Cappella, J. N. (1987). Interpersonal communication: Definition and fundamental questions. In C. R. Berger & S. H. Chafee (Eds.), *Handbook of communication science* (pp. 184–238). Newbury Park, CA: Sage.

Center, A. G., & Jackson, P. (1995). *Public relations practices: Management case studies and problems* (5th ed.). Englewood Cliffs, NJ: Prentice Hall.

Chung, Y. G., Lee, J., and Heath, R. L. (2013). Public relations aspect of brand attitudes and customer activity. Unpublished manuscript. Used with permission.

Conrad, C., & Haynes, J. (2001). Development of key constructs. In F. M. Jablin & L. L. Putnam (Eds.), *The new handbook of organizational communication: Advances in theory, research, and methods* (pp. 47–77). Thousand Oaks, CA: Sage.

Coombs, W. T. (2001). Interpersonal communication and public relations. In R. L. Heath (Ed.), *Handbook of public relations* (pp. 105–114). Thousand Oaks, CA: Sage.

Cutlip, S. M., & Center, A. H. (1952). *Effective public relations.* Englewood Cliffs, NJ: Prentice Hall.

Cutlip, S. M., & Center, A. H. (1971). *Effective public relations* (4th ed.). Englewood Cliffs, NJ: Prentice-Hall.

Cutlip, S. M., Center, A. H., & Broom, G. M. (1985). *Effective public relations.* Englewood Cliffs, NJ: Prentice-Hall.

Deephouse, D. L., & Heugens, P. P. (2009). Linking social issues to organizational impact: The role of infomediaries and the infomediary process. *Journal of Business Ethics, 86*, 541–553.

Delia, J. G., O'Keefe, B. J., & O'Keefe, D. J. (1982). The constructivist approach to communication. In F. E. X. Dance (Ed.), *Human communication theory: Comparative essays* (pp. 147–191). New York: Harper & Row.

Dhanesh, G. S. (2017). Putting engagement in its PRoper place: State of the field, definition and model of engagement in public relations. *Public Relations Review, 43*, 925–933.

Doerfel, M., & Taylor, M. (2004). Network dynamics of interorganizational cooperation: The Croatian civil society movement. *Communication Monographs, 71*(4), 373–394.

Dryzek, J. (2000). *Deliberative democracy and beyond: Liberals, critics, and contestations.* Oxford: Oxford University Press.

Dryzek, J. (2009). Democratization as deliberative capacity building. *Comparative Political Studies, 43*(11), 1379–1402.

Edwards, L. (2016). The role of public relations in deliberative systems. *Journal of Communication, 66,* 60–81.

Fassin, Y. (2010). A dynamic perspective in Freeman's stakeholder model. *Journal of Business Ethics, 96*(Suppl. 1), 39–49.

Ferguson, M. A. (1984). Building theory in public relations: Interorganizational relationships. Paper presented at the annual convention of the Association for Education in Journalism and Mass Communication, Gainesville, FL.

Frandsen, F. (2018). Intermediaries. In R. L. Heath & W. Johansen (Eds.), *The encyclopedia of strategic communication.* New York: John Wiley & Sons.

Frandsen, F., & Johansen, W. (2015). Organizations, stakeholders, and intermediaries: Towards a general theory. *International Journal of Strategic Communication, 9*(4), 253–271.

Freeman, R. E. (1984). *Strategic management: A stakeholder approach.* Boston, MA: Pitman.

Freeman, R. E., Harrison, J. S., & Wicks, A. C. (2007). *Managing for stakeholders: Survival, reputation, and success.* New Haven, CT: Yale University Press.

Friedman, A. L., & Miles, A. (2006). *Stakeholders: Theory and practice.* Oxford: Oxford University Press.

Gelso, C. J., & Carter, J. A. (1985). The relationship in counseling and psychotherapy: Components, consequences, and theoretical antecedents. *The Counseling Psychologist, 13*(2), 155–243.

Glaser, E. (2012). PR: The industry that likes to be heard but not seen. *New Statesman,* August 27. Available from https://www.newstatesman.com/culture/culture/2012/08/pr-industry-likes-heard-not-seen (accessed May 20, 2020).

Grostedt, A. (1997). The role of research in public relations strategy and planning. In C. L. Caywood (Ed.), *The handbook of strategic public relations and integrated communications* (pp. 34–59). New York: McGraw-Hill.

Grunig, J. E. (1989). Symmetrical presuppositions as a framework for public relations theory. In C. Botan & V. Hazelton (Eds.), *Public relations theory* (pp. 17–44). Hillsdale, NJ: Lawrence Erlbaum Associates.

Grunig, J. E., & Huang, Y. H. (2000). From organizational effectiveness to relationship indicators: Antecedents of relationships, public relations strategies, and relational outcomes. In J. A. Ledingham & S. D. Bruning (Eds.), *Public relations as relationship management: A relational approach to the study and practice of public relations* (pp. 23–53). Mahwah, NJ: Lawrence Erlbaum Associates.

Grunig, J. E., & Hunt, T. (1984). *Managing public relations.* New York: Holt, Rinehart & Winston.

Grunig, J. E., & Repper, F. C. (1992). Strategic management, publics, and issues. In J. E. Grunig (Ed.), *Excellence in public relations and communication management* (pp. 285–325). Hillsdale, NJ: Lawrence Erlbaum Associates.

Grunig, L. A., Gruing, J. E., & Ehlring, W. P. (1992). What is an effective organization? In J. E. Grunig (Ed.), *Excellence in public relations and communication management* (pp. 65–90). Hillsdale, NJ: Lawrence Erlbaum Associates.

Guerrero, L. A., Andersen, P. A., & Afifi, W. A. (2007). *Close encounters: Communication in relationships* (2nd ed.). Thousand Oaks, CA: Sage.

Heath, R. L. (1997). *Strategic issues management: Organizations and public policy challenges*. Thousand Oaks, CA: Sage.

Heath, R. L. (2005). Public relations. In R. L. Heath (Ed.), *Encyclopedia of public relations* (Vol. 2, pp. 679–684). Thousand Oaks, CA: Sage.

Heath, R. L. (2006). Onward into more fog: Thoughts on public relations' research directions. *Journal of Public Relations Research*, *18*(2), 93–114.

Heath, R. L. (2010). *The SAGE handbook of public relations*. Thousand Oaks, CA: Sage.

Heath, R. L. (2013). The journey to understand and champion OPR takes many roads, some not yet well travelled. *Public Relations Review*, *39*, 426–439.

Heath, R. L., Waymer, D., & Palenchar, M. J. (2013). Is the universe of democracy, rhetoric, and public relations whole cloth or three separate galaxies? *Public Relations Review*, *39*(4), 271–279.

Hon, L. C. (1998). Demonstrating effectiveness in public relations: Goals, objectives, and evaluation. *Journal of Public Relations Research*, *10*, 103–135.

Hon, L. C., and Grunig, J. E. (1999). Guidelines for measuring relationships in public relations. Available from https://www.instituteforpr.org/wp-content/uploads/Guidelines_Measuring_Relationships.pdf (accessed May 20, 2020).

Huang, Y. H., & Zhang, Y. (2013). Revisiting organization–public relations research over the past decade: Theoretical concepts, measures, methodologies, and challenges. *Public Relations Review*, *39*, 85–87.

Jelen-Sanchez, A. (2017). Engagement in public relations discipline: Themes, theoretical perspectives and methodological approaches. *Public Relations Review*, *43*, 934–944.

Johnston, K. A. (2014). Public relations and engagement: Theoretical imperatives of a multidimensional concept. *Journal of Public Relations Research*, *26*, 381–383.

Johnston, K. A. (2018). Engagement. In R. L. Heath & W. Johansen (Eds.), *The international encyclopedia of strategic communication* (pp. 1–9). Boston, MA: Wiley-Blackwell.

Johnston, K. A., & Lane, A. B. (2018). Building relational capital: The contribution of episodic and relational community engagement. *Public Relations Review*, *44*, 633–644.

Kelleher, T. (2015). Everybody's job? Managing public relations in the age of social media. In E. J. Ki, J. N. Kim, & J. A. Ledingham (Eds.), *Public relations as relationship management: A relational approach to the study and practice of public relations* (2nd ed., pp. 281–305). New York: Taylor & Francis.

Kent, M., & Taylor, M. (2002). Toward a dialogue theory of public relations. *Public Relations Review*, *28*, 21–37.

Kent, M. L., Sommerfeldt, E. J., & Saffer, A. J. (2016). Social networks, power, and public relations: *Teritus iungens* as a cocreational approach to studying relationship networks. *Public Relations Review*, *42*, 91–100.

Ki, E. J., & Nekmat, E. (2015). Decomposing impressions from attitude in relationship management outcomes. *Journal of Promotion Management*, *21*, 685–702.

Ki, E. J., & Shin, J. H. (2006). Status of organization–pubic relationship research from an analysis of published articles, 1985–2004. *Public Relations Review*, *32*, 194–195.

Kruckeberg, D. (2000). Public relations: Toward a global profession. In J. A. Ledingham & S. D. Bruning (Eds.), *Relationship management: A relational approach to the study and practice of public relations* (pp. 145–157). Mahwah, NJ: Lawrence Erlbaum Associates.

Ledingham, J. A. (2003). Explicating relationship management as a general theory of public relations. *Journal of Public Relations Research*, *15*(2), 181–198.

Ledingham, J. A., & Bruning, S. D. (1998). Relationship management in public relations: Dimensions of an organization–public relationship. *Public Relations Review*, *24*, 55–65.

Ledingham, J. A., & Bruning, S. D. (2000). A longitudinal study of organization-public relationship dimensions: Defining the role of communication in the practice of relationship management. In J. A. Ledingham & S. D. Bruning (Eds.), *Public relations as relationship management* (pp. 55–69). Mahwah, NJ: Lawrence Erlbaum Associates.

Ledingham, J. A., Bruning, S. D., & Wilson, L. J. (1999). Time as an indicator of the perceptions and behavior of members of a key public: Monitoring and predicting organization–public relationships. *Journal of Public Relations Research, 11*, 167–183.

Lee, S. T. (2013). Beautifully imperfect: Using Facebook to change a population's attitudes toward marriage. *Public Relations Review, 38*(3), 515–517.

L'Etang, J. (2008). *Public relations: Concepts, practice, and critique*. London: Sage.

McAllister-Spooner, S. M., & Kent, M. L. (2009). Dialogic public relations and resource dependency: New Jersey community colleges as models for web site effectiveness. *Atlantic Journal of Communication, 17*, 220–239.

Milam, J. M., & Heath, R. G. (2014). Participative democracy and voice: Rethinking community collaboration beyond neutral structures. *Journal of Applied Communication Research, 42*(4), 366–386.

Millar, F. E., & Rogers, L. E. (1987). Relational dimensions of interpersonal dynamics. In M. E. Roloff & G. R. Millar (Eds.), *Interpersonal processes: New directions in communication research* (pp. 117–139). Newbury Park, CA: Sage.

O'Byrne, S., & Daymon, C. (2014). Irresponsible engagement and the citizen investor. *Journal of Public Relations Research, 26*(5), 455–473.

Pavlik, J. V. (1987). *Public relations: What research tell us*. New Delhi: Sage.

Phillips, R. (2003). *Stakeholder theory and organizational ethics*. San Francisco, CA: Berrett-Koehler.

Putnam, R. D. (1994). Tuning in, tuning out: The strange disappearance of social capital in America. *Political Science and Politics, 28*(4), 664–683.

Putnam, R. D. (2000). *Bowling alone: The collapse and revival of American community*. New York: Simon & Shuster.

Putnam, R. D., Leonardi, R., & Nanetti, R. (1993). *Making democracy work: Civic tradition in modern Italy*. Princeton, NJ: Princeton University Press.

Reich, A. (2013). Online dating leads to higher marriage satisfaction, lower divorce rates: Study. *The Huffington Post*, June 4. Available from http://www.huffingtonpost.com/2013/06/04/online-dating-leads-to-hi_n_3384721.html (accessed May 20, 2020).

Saffer, A. J. (2016). A message focused measurement of the communication dimension of social capital: Revealing shared meaning in a network of relationships. *Journal of Public Relations Research, 38*(3–4), 170–192.

Shin, J. H., Carithers, H., Lee, S., Graham, M., & Hendricks, N. (2012). The current trends in social media usage at corporations: Analysis of Facebook fan pages of Fortune 500 companies. In J. Hendricks & H. N. Al-Deen (Eds.), *Social media and strategic communication* (pp. 62–79). New York: Palgrave Macmillan.

Shin, W., Pang, A., & Kim, H. J. (2015). Building relationships through integrated online media: Global organizations' use of brand web sites, Facebook, and Twitter. *Journal of Business and Technical Communication, 29*(2), 184–220.

Sommerfeldt, E. J. (2011). Activist online resource mobilization: Resource building features that fulfill resource dependencies. *Public Relations Review, 37*(4), 429–431.

Sommerfeldt, E. J. (2013a). The civility of social capital: Public relations in the public sphere, civil society, and democracy. *Public Relations Review, 39*, 280–289.

Sommerfeldt, E. J. (2013b). Networks of social capital: Extending a public relations model of civil society in Peru. *Public Relations Review*, *39*, 1–12.

Sommerfeldt, E. J. (2018). Social capital. In R. L. Heath & W. Johansen (Eds.), *The international encyclopedia of strategic communication* (pp. 1–8). New York: John Wiley & Sons.

Sommerfeldt, E. J., & Kent, M. L. (2015). Civil society, networks, and relationship management: Beyond the organization–public dyad. *International Journal of Strategic Communication*, *9*(3), 235–252.

Sommerfeldt, E. J., & Taylor, M. (2015). A social capital approach to improving public relations' efficacy: Diagnosing internal constraints on external communication. *Public Relations Review*, *37*(3), 197–206.

Sommerfeldt, E. J., & Yang, A. (2017). Relationship networks as strategic issues management: An issue-stage framework of social movement organization network strategies. *Public Relations Review*, *43*, 829–839.

Stafford, L., & Canary, D. J. (1991). Maintenance strategies and romantic relationship type, gender, and relational characteristics. *Journal of Social and Personal Relationships*, *8*, 217–242.

Stoker, K. (2014). Paradox in public relations: Why managing relating makes more sense than managing relationships. *Journal of Public Relations Research*, *26*, 344–358.

Sweetser, K. D., English, K., & Fernandes, J. (2015). Super PACs and strong relationships: The impact of digital interaction on the political organization-public relationship. *Journal of Public Relations Research*, *27*(2), 101–117.

Sweetser, K. D., & Kelleher, T. (2016). Communicated commitment and conversational voice: Abbreviated measures of communicative strategies for maintaining organization–public relationships. *Journal of Public Relations Research*, *28*(5–6), 217–231.

Taylor, M. (2009). Civil society as a rhetorical public relations process. In R. Heath, E. L. Toth, & D. Waymer (Eds.), *Rhetorical and critical approaches to public relations II* (pp. 76–91). Mahwah, NJ: Routledge.

Taylor, M. (2010). Public relations in the enactment of civil society. In R. L. Heath (Ed.), *The SAGE handbook of public relations* (pp. 5–16). Thousand Oaks, CA: Sage.

Taylor, M. (2011). Building social capital through rhetoric and public relations. *Management Communication Quarterly*, *25*(3), 436–454.

Taylor, M., & Doerfel, M. L. (2003). Building interorganizational relationships that build nations. *Human Communication Research*, *29*(2), 153–181.

Taylor, M., & Doerfel, M. L. (2005). Another dimension to explicating relationships: Measuring inter-organizational linkages. *Public Relations Review*, *31*(1), 121–129.

Taylor, M., & Kent, M. L. (2014). Dialogic engagement: Clarifying foundational concepts. *Journal of Public Relations Research*, *26*(5), 384–398.

Taylor, M., Kent, M. L., & White, W. J. (2001). How activist organizations are using the Internet to build relationships. *Public Relations Review*, *27*, 263–284.

Trenholm, S., & Jensen, A. (2008). *Interpersonal communication* (6th ed.). New York: Oxford University Press.

Vujnovic, M., & Krukeberg, D. (2015). Conceptualization, examination, and recommendations for a normative model of community-building for organizations managing change using new media. In E.-J. Ki, J.-N. Kim, & J. Ledingham (Eds.), *Public relations as relationship management: A relational approach to the study and practice of public relations* (2nd ed., pp. 330–348). New York: Routledge.

Waters, R. D., & Bortree, D. S. (2012). Advancing relations management theory: Mapping the continuum of relationship types. *Public Relations Review*, *38*, 123–127.

Watson, T. (2012). The evolution of public relations measurement and evaluation. *Public Relations Review*, *38*(3), 390–398.

Waymer, D. (2013). Democracy and government public relations: Expanding the scope of "relationship" in public relations research. *Public Relations Review*, *39*(4), 320–331.

West, R. L., & Turner, L. H. (2000). *Introducing communication theory: Analysis and application.* Mountain View, CA: Mayfield.

Wilson, L. J. (2004). Building employee and community relationships through volunteerism: A case study. In J. A. Ledingham & S. D. Bruning (Eds.), *Public relations as relationship management* (pp. 137–144). Mahwah, NJ: Lawrence Erlbaum Associates.

Yang, A. (2018). Relationships. In R. L. Heath & W. Johansen (Eds.), *The international encyclopedia of strategic communication* (pp. 1–15). New York: John Wiley & Sons.

Yang, A., & Taylor, M. (2013). The relationship between t eh professionalization of public relations, societal social capital and democracy: Evidence from a cross national study. *Public Relations Review*, *39*(4), 257–270.

Zaharna, R. S. (2015). Beyond individualism—Collectivism divide to relationalism: Explicating cultural assumptions in the concept of "relationships.". *Communication Theory*, *26*(2), 190–211.

12

The Role of Public Relations Professionals and Leadership Challenges

Introduction

As noted in previous chapters, public relations was established as a distinct field in the early twentieth century. However, serious research into the precise roles adopted by public relations professionals is a relatively recent phenomenon, and it has continuously evolved with changing media environments. This chapter explores the rise of specialized functions and roles ascribed to public relations professionals, particularly how practitioners have been conceived historically and how they have arisen as professionals. The trend has been an evolution in the role of the public relations professional from technician to manager, or social change agent. Some topics of concern have included role or function, leadership, ethics, professionalism, image and reputation, the role of education, gender equality or diversity, and status within organizations. The place of public relations in the larger context of society—particularly its role in creating a more fully functioning society—has emerged as a major concern among scholars in the last decade. Many of these issues play out on a micro level, but each touches on the meso and macro levels of the relationship between organizations, stakeholders, and the position of public relations both within an organization and relative to society as a whole.

The distinctive or defined role of public relations as a profession is of comparatively recent vintage. Grunig and Hunt (1984) proclaimed that although the function of public relations was "as old as civilization, the profession itself was defined only in the early twentieth century" (p. 14; see also Cutlip, 1994; L'Etang, 2004). As Yaxley (2012) summarized, "during the first decades of the 20th century, public relations had succeeded in becoming a full-time job, and at least in the U.S., training courses had been introduced and a professional association was established" (p. 404). She traced the origin of the discipline to pioneers such as Ivy Lee and Edward Bernays in the United States and to government bureaucracies in the United Kingdom around the time of World War I. Lee's "Declaration of Principles" (1906) is cited as "the starting point of modern public relations" (Hiebert, 1966, p. 12), while Bernays (in a career that spanned nearly 80 years) was involved in each of the five processes that L'Etang (2004) details as necessary in order for an occupation to achieve the status of a profession: (a) emergence of the full-time occupation; (b) establishment of the training school; (c) founding of professional associations; (d) political agitation directed towards the protection of the association by law; and (e) adoption of a formal code (Yaxley, 2012, p. 403).

The growth of public relations as a profession has depended on the establishment and refinement of the categories used to define and distinguish it. This necessarily embodies a refined sense

Public Relations Theory: Capabilities and Competencies, First Edition. Jae-Hwa Shin and Robert L. Heath.
© 2021 John Wiley & Sons, Inc. Published 2021 by John Wiley & Sons, Inc.

of what differentiates it from advertising, journalism, marketing, and other closely related fields. If broad categories are used to define the role and value of public relations, its function faces the threat of becoming imprecise at best and meaningless at worse. On the other hand, if the terms used to define it are too narrow, they offer a distorted view that fails to capture the fullness and specialization of the work done by public relations professionals.

Some scholars have addressed the similarity or integration of adjacent areas. Ha and Ferguson (2015) described the "conceptual vagueness of public relations and marketing functions" in many contexts, while Moriarity (1994) chronicled instances where public relations functions were performed by other departments, such as human resources or legal teams, and Nath and Bell (2016) argued for the positive benefits of the integration of marketing and public relations departments. However, others have been concerned about a loss of the distinctiveness and identity of the field. As Coombs and Holladay (2012) noted, "[i]f everything is public relations then public relations itself is nothing" (p. 348). They argued that definitions had been dominated by "corporate-centric approaches" at the expense of the contribution of activists, whose efforts had been "mimicked and co-opted by corporate public relations" (p. 347). Together with a growing number of other scholars, they called for a more inclusive definition that took into account the contribution of activists and other stakeholders working outside the corporate world (Ciszek, 2017; Holtzhausen, 2012; Taylor, Kent, & White, 2001; Wolf, 2018).

Public relations has been increasingly linked to strategic communication among stakeholders. Defined in a general sense as "the purposeful use of communication by an organization to fulfill its mission," strategic communication also "implies that people will be engaged in deliberate communication practice on behalf of organizations, causes, and social movements" (Hallahan, Holtzhausen, van Ruler, Verčiĉ, & Sriramesh, 2007, p. 7). Strategic communication is an organized, planned, and enacted process designed to help organizations, causes, or social movements reach tangible goals (Holtzhausen & Zerfass, 2015). It adopts an integrative approach to reach internal and external publics, drawing on the strengths and talents of multiple disciplines within an organization, and focuses on long-term goals (Falkheimer, Heide, Nothhaft, von Platten, Simsonsson, & Andersson, 2017). It is not concerned exclusively with meeting financial targets, but looks also at risk management, reputation, and social responsibility. The so-called Triple Bottom Line suggests that strategic communication also relates to "stakeholder inclusiveness, corporate governance and sustainability" (Steyn & Niemann, 2014, p. 171).

"Strategic communication" has become a catch-all term used to describe a variety of activities without specifying the difference in roles and functions among professionals operating under its rubric. Falkheimer et al. (2017) found that organizations' members generally are clear about the importance of strategic communication, but have less understanding of the role of strategic communication professionals. To counter this, Frandsen and Johansen (2015) focused on the strategic role of communication professionals as part of the dominant coalition involved in the strategy development. A dominant coalition is a group of people inside or external to an organization who have decision-making powers over it (Ni & Izzo, 2018). White (2018) defined the decision-making process as a process of strategic choice made by empowered individuals within an organization based on external and internal relationships. In this conceptualization of public relations, the strategist role supersedes that of the communication manager and is distinguished from the technical function traditionally assigned to public relations professionals (Steyn, 2018). The term "public relations" seems still to be preferred to—or at least more prevalent than—"strategic communication," because it more accurately describes the goal of establishing and cultivating relationships with stakeholder publics.

Questions to Frame the Discussion of Public Relations Professionals and Leadership Challenges

- What are some of the skills and competencies required for public relations professionals to be effective?
- What are some ethical standards or professional norms specific to the public relations profession?
- How do you distinguish public relations professionals from other professions according to their respective roles and functions?
- How would you compare the role of public relations professionals within an organization and in society?
- What is the role of public relations professionals from a strategic communication perspective?
- Have the roles of public relations professionals changed in new and social media environments?
- Are the roles of public relations professionals different across diverse cultures or countries?
- How do diversity factors such as gender and race come into play in the public relations profession?

Key Themes

- There are various sets of public relations professional competencies, along with ethical standards and professional norms suggested by professional associations.
- There are various managerial and technician roles, and public relations professionals strive to encroach into the managerial ones in order to make public relations efforts effective and successful.
- Public relations is often connected to the broader field of communication, and its roles overlap with other functions such as marketing and crisis communication.
- The role of public relations has recently been defined as a form civic professional communication, contributing to democracy and making society more fully functioning by augmenting the social capital of various stakeholders through engagement in dialogue as a means of forging relationships based on a shared sense of community.
- The role of public relations professionals has evolved through new media environments, and its emphasis seems to vary across different organizations and cultures.
- Such factors as gender and race have played a significant role in the public relations profession.

Case Study: Complicit?—The Ethical Dilemma of Sarah Huckabee Sanders

The role of the public relations professional often represents a delicate balance between satisfying the demands of the client, serving the public interest, and staying true to professional and ethical guidelines. White House Press Secretary Sarah Huckabee Sanders worked for President Trump from May 2017 through June 2019. Her job was complicated by his wild oscillations and inconsistent and sometimes false statements. On occasion, she responded by uncritically repeating his obvious falsehoods, stretching credibility with her statements. For example, she claimed that President Trump's nickname for Senator Elizabeth Warren,

"Pocahontas," was not intended to be disrespectful and was not meant as a slur. This violates not only ethical guidelines and professional standards, but the primary job description of the press secretary: to fully and impartially communicate the truth to the public who elected the president through interaction with the free press (Wilkie, 2017).

Sanders was not alone in her acceptance of President Trump's statements. In 2017, his first press secretary, Sean Spicer, defended his statement that his inauguration was the largest in history despite the evidence to the contrary. This led advisor Kellyanne Conway to claim that Spicer was not lying, but providing "alternative facts." This perspective was reinforced in August 2018 by the president's lawyer, Rudy Giuliani, stating that there were different versions of the truth. Backed into a corner, Giuliani claimed: "truth isn't truth" (Abramson, 2018).

On the other hand, it is possible to defend Sanders' stances. In many ways, she was doing the job that had been given to her in representing the views, messages, and brief provided by her employer. Has she been unfairly singled out for representing the views of her client? She has stated that the forces of resistance to Trump were out to get her, hanging on her every word waiting for the slightest misstep. On June 22, 2018, for example, she was asked to leave a restaurant in Lexington, Virginia because the owner, Stephanie Wilkinson, disagreed with her advocacy of the president (Selk, 2018).

The Public Relations Society of America (PRSA) Code of Ethics states that honesty and fairness are the cornerstones of professional practice. However, the code also states that public relations professionals should be faithful and loyal to the clients that they represent and to society as a whole. This collision between the obligation to serve the interests of the public and the obligation to serve one's client is readily apparent in Sanders' navigation of the difficult position of White House Press Secretary. Still, at times she overstepped the boundaries. For example, she defended Trump after he banned CNN reporter Jim Acosta from the White House Press Room in November 2018. And if the goal of the White House Press Secretary is to interact effectively with the press, it is probably not the wisest course of action to repeat the president's opinion, as Sanders did in late October 2018, that the press is "the enemy of the people." Although she did not give precise reasons for her departure, Sanders resigned her position at the end of June 2019. She holds the distinction of being one of the longest-serving cabinet members in the Trump administration (Rogers & Baker, 2019). Two days after the announcement of her resignation, the PRSA issued a statement calling on the White House to select a new press secretary "who can conduct frequent and informative briefings, and work productively with the press ... [to] help build trust and faith among the citizenry" (PRSA, 2019).

Emergence as a Distinct Profession

One of the ways that professionalism has been defined is through the establishment of explicit guidelines that individuals must submit to in order to be considered part of the profession. Professional organizations set boundaries and define the nature of the work undertaken by their members. According to Powell and DiMaggio (1991), a professional organization is characterized by the creation of "normative rules" about what constitutes acceptable behavior and what is considered aberrant. Those who adhere to these rules are rewarded, while those who fail to do so are punished (p. 71). According to L'Etang (2004), the first modern public relations professional organizations arose in the United States and Britain after the end of World War II. By the mid-2010s, there were public relations professional organizations in more than 60 countries (Yang & Taylor, 2014, p. 511). However, not everyone agrees that the presence and proliferation of professional organizations alone means that public relations is a distinct profession, nor is there broad agreement about the nature and characteristics of professional standards among practitioners and theorists (Bernays, 1980; Bivins, 1993; Ehling, 1992; Sallot et al., 1998; Falkheimer et al., 2017; Fawkes, 2014; Grunig, 2000; Ha & Ferguson, 2015; Kim & Reber, 2009; L'Etang, 2004).

A second way to define public relations as a profession is through educational requirements. Thus, Kruckeberg (1998) defined it as "as a distinct professional occupation requiring a specific professional curriculum of study" (p. 245). In the same year, the National Communication Association (NCA) undertook a study to determine what proficiencies were most cited by top-ranked programs in connection to recruitment for public relations students, identifying writing skills and business acumen in its results (Stacks, Botan, & Turk, 1999). Similarly, the Commission of Public Relations Education took a broad and synthetic view of the topics that should concern public relations students, finding they ranged from research methods to understanding of information technologies and globalization (DiStaso, Stacks, & Botan, 2009). Coordinating and balancing academic practice with practical and short-term organizational goals has been a persistent challenge (Todd, 2009; Wright & Turk, 2007). The lack of a consensus definition of what constitutes public relations consulting is one example of the need for clear guidelines and standards (Röttger & Preusse, 2013). Another is the lack of a common professional frame of reference or framework to bind public relations activities together (Hallahan, 1993). In recent years, there has been broad consensus that augmenting the integration of public relations to technological and social innovations wrought by online communication should be at the heart of pedagogy (Kent, 2013; Kent & Saffer, 2014; Kent & Taylor, 2002; Kinsky, Freberg, Kim, Kushin, & Ward, 2016; Moreno, Navarro, Tench, & Zerfass, 2015).

Some scholars, such as Grunig and Hunt (1984), have argued that public relations has emerged as a distinct and mature profession. Others have discussed the field as being in the process of staking out its own territory. Wylie (1994) argued that public relations is well on the way to becoming a genuine profession in every sense, but claimed that "it will not get there through self-anointment, or self-proclamation" (p. 3). Ehling (1992) noted that this was due to negative public perceptions, and that public relations was generally regarded as "an unsavory activity committed to cluttering the mass media with the debris of pseudo-events and phony phrases leading to channels of communication being corroded with cynicism and credibility gaps" (p. 457). Grunig (2000) acknowledged that recognition as such by members of the general public was a prerequisite of professionalism: "Most people seem to view public relations as mysterious hidden persuaders working for the rich and powerful to deceive and take advantage of the less powerful" (p. 23). Cameron, Sallot, and Weaver-Lariscy (1996) concurred that public relations practitioners had not yet reached the status of professionals. Sallot, Cameron, and Weaver-Lariscy (1997) noted that public relations practitioners were divided on what constituted professional standards, indicating that consensus had yet to be reached. Likewise, they found that public relations practitioners tended to view their peers as less professional than themselves, demonstrating the third-person effect: "[t]here is very little consensus regarding professional standards among professionals in public relations and practitioners in the flied seldom accurately perceive how their peers view professional standards" (p. 10).

Roles of Public Relations Professionals

Serious research into the roles played by public relations professionals is a recent development. Broom and his colleagues have argued that roles can be circumscribed according to a limited number of categories, typically including the negotiator, policy advisor, brand officer, internal communication facilitator, technical service provider, and press agent (Broom & Dozier, 1986; Broom & Smith, 1979). The negotiator is involved with both technical issues and strategic management functions. The policy advisor is also a management function and is involved with risk assessment and the identification of opportunities within the field of communication. The brand officer is usually involved with external communication and focuses on customer interactions. The internal communication facilitator maximizes the communication relationships between employees. The technical service provider offers advice and performs tasks on behalf of the client, operating much like a tradesperson. Finally, the press agent is concerned with devising messages for external audience.

Although they may differ slightly, there is general agreement that roles can be designated according to a limited number of categories that take into account whether they are engaged in internal or external communications and the degree to which they fall into the managerial or technical realms. Managerial roles are connected to interaction with the dominant coalition—whether this is located in the C-suite of a major corporation or among powerful stakeholders who exercise control from outside the company—whereas technical roles are generally not deeply involved in organizational functions and are often excluded from the processes of planning and assessment (Neill, 2014; Ni & Izzo, 2018). However, the typologies associated with these distinct functions have been largely supplanted as the binary conception of public relations has fallen out of fashion (Johansson & Larsson, 2015; Moss, Newman, & DeSanto, 2005). Although public relations professionals are still rarely part of the dominant coalition at large organizations, their role has gradually evolved from that of a technician concerned with functional and operational tasks to one of manager, operating at a more reflective and synthetic level (Johansson & Larsson, 2015; Tench & Moreno, 2015).

Broom and Dozier (1986) identified four broad role categories that public relations professionals can perform: (a) expert prescriber; (b) communication facilitator; (c) problem-solving process facilitator; and (d) communication technician. There is broad consensus that the communications technician is the lowest level, providing for an organization "the specialized skills needed to carry out public relations programs ... concerned with preparing and producing communications materials for public relations efforts" (Broom, 1982, p. 18). A little further up the chain, the communication facilitator serves as a "'go between' or information broker" in the relationship between the organization and its relative publics (Toth, Serini, Wright, & Emig, 1998, p. 146). The problem-solving process facilitator works in close harmony with the management team, but their role is largely limited to public relations problems as opposed to general management issues; they operate "as the authority on both public relations problems and their solutions" (Broom, 1982, p. 18). At the highest level, the communication facilitator assumes even greater authority within the management structure. They serve as a member "of the management team, guiding others through a rational problem-solving process that may involve all parts of the organization in the public relations planning and programming process" (p. 18).

Vieira and Grantham (2014) linked the various roles played by public relations practitioners to the Beurer-Zullig classification system, commonly used in Europe (see Beurer-Zullig, Fieseler, & Meckel, 2009). As with other models, the first two roles in the Beurer-Zullig—negotiator and advisor—are linked to the managerial function identified as crucial to the practice of advance public relations. In contrast, the brand officer, internal communicator, and press agent are relegated to the technical function. Vieira and Grantham (2014), like most commentators who have followed the classification systems advanced by Dozier and Broom (1995), agree that the managerial function is of a higher order than the technical roles played by public relations professionals. One crucial difference is that American public relations practitioners seem to have a greater degree of overlap between managerial and technical functions than their European counterparts (p. 67).

The Manager vs. Technician Dichotomy

The role of public relations professionals has been tied to the terms used by organizational communications for a number of years. The organization role is preeminent in the definition of Cutlip, Center, and Broom (1985): "management function that identifies, establishes and maintains mutually beneficial relationships between organizations and the public on whom its success or failure depends" (p. 4). Broom (1982), Broom and Dozier (1986), and Broom and Smith (1979) were instrumental in defining public relations in terms of the organizational contribution that they make, as well as establishing a hierarchal typology of roles: expert prescriber, communication facilitator, problem solver, and communication technician.

Dozier and Broom (1995) surveyed the literature of the preceding decades and concluded that public relations roles had been conceived as sharply divided between the manager and the technician. They argued that the "technical tasks" were of a lower order than those accorded to the manager, who was involved in "strategic decision-making" (p. 5). By contrast, the technician essentially executed "decision[s] made by others" (p. 4). In other words, the communications manager was a leader and the technician a follower. Those involved in "managerial role enactment" experienced increased job satisfaction and the perception that they were part of the senior management team (p. 7). This view has been supported by Cutlip, Center, and Broom (2006), who distinguished between the "communication technician" and the "expert advisor." The technician, on Cutlip's account, acts "most often without knowing the original motivation or expected results" (p. 43), whereas the expert advisor is "an authority in identifying public relations problems and solutions" (p. 46).

Level of experience may be a more salient measure. Dozier and Broom (1995) found that number of years of professional experience was the dependent variable and that roles, whether managerial or technical, had a degree of inevitability or permanence. Their research supported the idea that professional experience was the most important determinant of whether one held a particular role, what salary one received, and what level one occupied within the organizational hierarchy. They assumed that the managerial role was preferable to the technical one, not only in terms of remuneration, but also in terms of status within the organization. Interestingly, however, a fax poll conducted in the early 1990s suggested that most practitioners preferred working on the technical aspects of public relations as opposed to enacting managerial roles (Dozier & Broom, 1995). In fact, only 4 of 170 respondents stated that "working with top management" was their top preference (Dozier & Broom, 1995, p. 21). By contrast, Rentner and Bissland (1990) surveyed 649 members of the PRSA and International Association of Business Communicators (IABC) and found that those engaged in management functions were more "happy with both their jobs overall and most facets of them" compared to technicians (p. 955). This disparity suggests mixed views among public relations professionals related to their roles.

Although Dozier and Broom (1995) tended to make a hard and fast distinction between manager and technician, they admitted that there was a great deal of overlap between the two roles; although they differed, they were not mutually exclusive.

Some other scholars have argued that the assigned roles fail to capture the fullness or degree of overlap in public relations functions. Culbertson (1991), for example, contended that the very concept of "roles" was suspect, particularly the bifocal perspective that proposed practitioners fell into one role or another. Instead, he argued for a fluid concept that was subject to process and change. Toth et al. (1998) argued that the distinction between manager and technician remained dominant in public relations, reinforcing the finding that professional experience was the key predictor of whether or not one served in a managerial capacity. However, they contended that roles were malleable and "constantly in process" (p. 145). The overlap between managers and technicians was supported by research by Cameron et al. (1996). Johansson and Larsson (2015) put it bluntly, finding that "the simple dichotomy between managers and technicians cannot be used to understand the breadth of and real nuances in the responsibilities of personal holding managerial level positions in public relations" because "the reality of modern organizational live and functional responsibility is simply far too complex" (p. 136).

Work Categories and Professional Competencies

Scholars have attempted to categorize the work done by public relations practitioners and the professional competencies—known as knowledge, skills, and abilities (KSAs)—required of them. The PRSA's Universal Accreditation Board (UAB), for example, identifies 12 work categories and 10 KSAs.

According to Sha (2011), the UAB work categories are as follows:

1) *Account/client management:* Focus on relationships.
2) *Strategic planning:* Focus on reputation management.
3) *Public relations program planning:* Researching and implementing tactical and strategic plans.
4) *Project management:* Designing and implementing a project.
5) *Media relations:* Identifying, pitching, developing, and placing stories and managing publicity.
6) *Social media relations:* Designing and maintaining social networks across platforms.
7) *Stakeholder relations:* Establishing and maintaining partnerships with internal and external constituents.
8) *Issues management:* Preparing for potential crises.
9) *Crisis management:* Reacting to crises.
10) *Internal relations/employee communication:* Management of in-house communications.
11) *Special events:* Organizing conferences, meetings, and other events.
12) *Community relations:* Outreach efforts with multiple stakeholders.

While its professional competencies are:

1) *Planning and implementing programs:* Including researching, managing, and evaluating programs.
2) *Ethics and law:* Understanding and applying moral principles and legal issues.
3) *Communication theories:* Understanding and applying theoretical models.
4) *Business literacy:* Knowledge and application of organizational issues and trends.
5) *Management skills:* Leadership and problem-solving abilities.
6) *Crisis communication management:* Planning, implementing, and evaluating crisis communication strategies.
7) *Media relations:* Synthetic knowledge of media networks.
8) *Efficient use of information technology:* Understanding communication channels.
9) *History and issues in public relations:* General understanding of past and current concepts of public relations.
10) *Advanced communication skills:* Ranging from building consensus to negotiating in a contested environment.

Meanwhile, the IABC tests the following competencies: goal setting, general management skills, audience research, written communication, verbal communication, developing communication plans, managing internal communications, budgeting, media relations, ethics, project management, problem-solving skills, business culture, time management, evaluation, managing external communications, developing communication programs, and technology (Sha, 2011, p. 6). As is clear, there is a large degree of overlap between what is tested by the PRSA and what is tested by the IABC. Additionally, two major international public relations organizations offer similar but slightly different definitions and lists of roles: the International Public Relations Association (IPRA) and the Global Alliance for Public Relations and Communications Management.

Although professionalism has been defined according to specific competencies that entail specific shared skills and knowledge, Bentele and Szyszka (1995) argued that public relations practitioners need both quantifiable and specific competencies and nonquantifiable, unspecific abilities connected with a broad knowledge and understanding of the world, together with qualities such as empathy, discretion, judgment, and moral sensibility. Dagenais (2002) offered a typical survey of the professional knowledge required of public relations practitioners: awareness of the organization, knowledge of the public, attention to the environment, and understanding of research methods. Others have stressed the personal qualities necessary to success. Black (2003) identified a good sense of humor, the ability to handle pressure, creativity, organization, curiosity, confidence, practicality, energy, toughness, a down-to-earth attitude, focus, and a strong sense of ethics (pp. 21–25)—qualities she noticed also apply to many other professions (p. 21). Wilcox and Cameron (2011) focused on personal qualities specific to public relations: (a) skillful use of language; (b) creativity; (c) persuasiveness; (d) interest in problem solving; and (e) ability to present effectively (p. 84). Morris and Goldsworthy (2008) suggested the ideal personality of public relations practitioners, with a list of attributes ranging from the ability to be realistic and rational to the ability to charm stakeholders and create a sense of mystery about the process of creativity (p. 88).

Gender and Diversity Issues

As noted by Cutlip (1994), the early history of public relations includes few women. He pointed to a handful of exceptions, including Elizabeth "Bessie" Tyler, notorious for her role working on behalf of the Ku Klux Klan, and Doris Fleishman, a noted practitioner and wife of Edward Bernays. As Yaxley (2012) contended, pioneering women were not only largely invisible in the field, but were not expected to pursue public relations with the same vigor as their male counterparts. Nor was their role within the profession accorded a great degree of seriousness. For the most part, women involved in public relations were confined to roles that capitalized on their perceived skills and interests, such as promoting household goods and women's fashion (pp. 404–405). Furthermore, Aldoory and Toth (2002) reported that women usually earned less than men in performing similar functions.

As with other fields in the humanities and social sciences, research and commentary on the role of women in public relations has witnessed a major increase in interest over the last three decades. Women's presence in the profession has seen a progressive demographic shift over the same period. The ratio of women to men working in the field increased from 25% in 1968 (Cutlip et al., 1985) to 66% in the early 1990s (Jacobson & Tortorello, 1992). Dozier and Broom

(1995) stated that, at the time of their writing, 59% of public relations professionals were women, although men still tended to possess more years of experience in general and to hold positions of greater responsibility within an organization. They explained this as the "consequence of sex discrimination" (p. 7). A survey conducted by Toth et al. (1998) revealed increasing numbers of women involved in public relations. In 1990, 58% of respondents were male and 42% were female. Five years later, 36.5 were male and 63.5 were female. According to the U.S. Bureau of Labor Statistics, women accounted for 63.5% of public relations practitioners in 2017. Interestingly, nearly 60% of those described their role as that of manager (U.S. Department of Labor, 2018). It is telling that, in 1979, women made 76% of the salary of men, accounting for factors such as educational level, years of experience, and other mitigating factors (Dozier & Broom, 1995, p. 15)—and by the early 1990s, the disparity had hardly changed (p. 17). According to surveys conducted by Women in PR, the salary gender gap between men and women in the United States remained at $6,072 in 2017 (Women in PR, 2017).

For the most part, the top jobs at top firms, as described in a piece for the *Atlantic*, were until recently dominated by men (Khazan, 2014). Perhaps the image of the public relations bunny is still in force. Khazan (2014) quoted Jennifer Pan, writing for the *Jacobian*:

> [T]he dismissal of the publicist as a corporate shill or a purveyor of a kind of false consciousness that interferes with the otherwise unsullied work of the journalist not only reifies a gendered hierarchy of labor, but additionally eclipses the primacy of emotional labor for all workers under neoliberalism.

Gender equality is linked to educational attainment. A higher number of women are earning advanced degrees. This is true in public relations as in many other majors in social sciences and the humanities. Given the educational advantage they hold, it comes as something of a surprise that the perception of women in the field is not better. Despite their advantages, women have failed to advance because they do not fit into organizational culture, and their male counterparts still prevail in some quarters (Dozier, Grunig, & Grunig, 1995). The "velvet ghetto" or "glass ceiling," which sees women relegated to lower-level functions, has remained an operative concept (Aldoory & Toth, 2002; Cline, Masel-Walters, Toth, Turk, & Johnson, 1986; Creedon, 1991; Golombisky, 2015; Toth & Cline, 1990; Toth & Grunig, 1993; Vardeman-Winter & Crowe, 2018). On the other hand, some have argued that public relations offers a unique career choice for women because they tend to favor working collaboratively and engaging in social functions to a greater degree than men (Perkins, Phillips, & Pearce, 2013). Some argued from a feminist perspective that society should change to accommodate the perspectives of women (Gilligan, 1982). Others contended that practical steps such as the formalization of mentoring relationships would improve the situation (Tam, Dozier, Lauzen, & Real, 1995).

As with other fields, feminist theory has presented a challenge not only to public relations' male-dominated bent, but to the normative view that it is adequately characterized by symmetry, equality, positivism, and functionalism (Aldoory & Toth, 2002; Benhabib, 2013; Gilligan, 1982; Golombisky, 2015). Dozier and Broom (1995) noted that the male gender was positively related to managerial roles at the expense of women. They further found that "gender salary discrimination" was persistent in the field (p. 7). However, at the same time, they contended that—as of the early 1990s—the "relationship between gender and predominant manager role enactment is not statistically significant once the influence of professional experience is controlled" (p. 16). According to their research, women possessed an average of 11.1 years of experience, versus 16.1 years for men. They concluded that "gender discrimination has lessened, but is still present" (p. 18). Toth et al. (1998) contended that men earned more than women even though they performed the same roles (p. 147). Toth and Grunig (1993) showed that women were working in both managerial and technical roles—or, more often, in roles that overlapped between managerial and technical—for less money than men. They further demonstrated that women were more often viewed as technicians within the organizational structure than their male counterparts, even though they performed similar functions. Hon (1995) contended that this led to a perception among female public relations professionals that they were working in a "male-dominated work environment" and that their opportunity for advancement was limited despite their skills or accomplishments. Interestingly, Weaver-Lariscy, Sallot, and Cameron (1996) demonstrated that men perceived greater role equality in public relations than did women, and believed that salaries were similarly equitable.

As with gender, age, race, cultural background, and other issues of diversity and inclusion have been major topics of public relations research in the last three decades. As Ravazzani (2018) discussed, diversity management emerged as a topic of public relations and communication management scholarship in the 1980s. Three aspects were central: (a) what personal attributes distinguish individuals; (b) how diversity is constituted and understood in the workplace; and (c) what diversity factors, including intersectionality, are understood as most salient in given situations (Qin, Muenjohn, & Chhetri, 2014). Organizations have engaged diversity as a matter of ethics, but also as on eof employee productivity, efficiency, satisfaction, commitment, and development (Ravazzani, 2018).

Professionalism

The role of the public relations professional has progressed through a variety of models, including propaganda, press agentry, advocacy, communications management, relationship building, and social responsibility. Throughout its relatively brief history, the definition of standards has been a contentious subject, although what constitutes a profession has been defined in a general sense by numerous scholars, such as Elliot (1972):

> The list covers familiar ground—a specialised skill and service, an intellectual and practical training, a high degree of professional autonomy, a fiduciary relationship with the client, a sense of collective responsibility for the profession as a whole, an embargo on some methods of attracting business and an occupational organization testing competence, regulating standards and maintain discipline. (p. 5)

The definition of professionalism in public relations has occupied the attention of many scholars (Bernays, 1923; Cutlip et al., 2006; Heath & Bowen, 2006; Wilcox, Ault, & Agee, 1989), and there is some general agreement that an intellectual tradition, ethical standards, practical skills, and a form of certification are necessary (Cutlip, Center, & Broom, 1994). The emphasis on definitions is particularly characteristic of U.S. practice, where public relations has perhaps the longest and most robust history. Marston (1968) was among the first to define the profession in a systematic manner. Among the features he identified were: (a) practical competence; (b) body of knowledge; (c) self-awareness; (d) control of access; (e) requirement for continued education; and (f) support for research. Grunig and Hunt (1984) suggested similar characteristic features distinguishing the profession: (a) membership organization or accreditation process; (b) norms, values, and a code of ethics; (c) intellectual tradition and knowledge base; (d) specialized education; and (e) practical skill set. Similarly, Nelson (1994) defined it according to five criteria: (a) values; (b) membership in professional organizations; (c) agreed upon ethics and professional norms; (d) intellectual tradition; and (e) technical skills. In addition to a code of ethics, Cameron et al. (1996) added a sense of altruism and an emphasis on public service. Other recent studies have grouped the standards of professionalism in public relations as a whole into the following general topics: (a) ethical standards; (b) social responsibility; (c) technical skills; (d) educational criteria; (e) accreditation or licensing; (f) inclusion of public relations within an organization's dominant coalition; (g) providing a unique and essential service; and (h) objectivity or seeing the larger picture (see Meyer & Leonard, 2014, p. 377).

The gradual increase in emphasis on issues of social responsibility and public service since Grunig and Hunt's (1984) definition is striking. On one hand, it represents a recognition of the ethical dimension associated with professionalism. On the other, the trend toward social responsibility is connected with the globalization of public relations practice. Globalization brings a renewed sense of professional responsibility to one's community. As the mission statement of the Global Alliance has it, the goal of the organization is to "raise its professional standards all over the world" (Global Alliance for Public Relations and Communications Management, 2016). According to Meyer and Leonard (2014), the Stockholm Accords of 2010, followed closely by the Melbourne Mandate of 2012, "signal a final departure from a tactical orientation in defining the scope of the professional field and emphasize the issues of sustainability and governance" (p. 379). Put another way, these two agreements represent a consensus acknowledgment that public relations professionals have an ethical responsibility to serve the public sector as well as the individual organizations for which they work.

Cameron et al. (1996) summarized the debate over professionalism thus: "Some would argue for more interest, while others claim that introspective research is simply 'navel-gazing' or unnecessary when true respect is accorded a profession" (p. 44). Even given a comprehensive list of standards related to the professional practice of public relations, including educational background and training, management skills, technical skills, research strategies, accountability and ethics, accreditation and licensing, gender and racial equality, budgeting, the place of the public relations professional within the organizational chart, and salaries, they would still "challenge the assumption that professional standards have yet been defined, much less achieved" (p. 44). Issues such as trust and credibility are still major issues facing public relations professionals.

Gitter and Jaspers (1982) found that public relations professionals fared poorly in terms of public perceptions when compared with members of other professions, such as sales, accounting, and social work. They concluded that "trust in public relations is still badly needed" (p. 31). By contrast, Judd (1989) found that public relations professionals believed that they performed in the interest of the public, exercising social responsibility at the expense of personal gain—even when they believed that their peers did not. Wright (1978) suggested that the work environment sometimes constrained public relations professionals: "public relations counselors want to be more professional than their present positions will allow" (p. 28). According to Pieczka (2000), functioning effectively as a practitioner "is not only a matter of knowing what the right solutions are, but convincing others about the legitimacy of these solutions and the professional's right to deal with the problem in the first place" (p. 214). She concluded that the "self-obsession may sometimes verge on the farcical, but it is an important sign of the process of creation and public reaffirmation of expertise" (p. 231). The profession has been unable to demonstrate its worth to those on the outside: "critics argue that public relations has yet to achieve professional status and exits only as a trade or skilled technical communication activity" (Bowen, 2009, p. 403).

Public relations as a profession has suffered reputational and identity crises in part because of a suspicion that it is driven by organizational interests and in part because of misunderstandings concerning the work and role of practitioners. A typical perception is that it is somehow "less ethical, less credible, and less transparent than journalism" (Coombs & Holladay, 2012, p. 350). While it is true that public relations in some contexts has been used to for immoral purposes, such as the furthering of coercion, most practitioners today link their role and professional identity to ethical and moral codes. A great deal of literature on the subject of roles tackles the issue of enhancing the reputation of the profession. This may be in part because of the negative image held by individuals in other fields, which constrains opportunities to exercise strategic communication management on par with other executives.

Despite the negative stereotypes and sense of insecurity about the role of public relations among practitioners, the criteria for establishing it as a profession—intellectual rigor or a defined body of scholarly literature, an established course of study, an accrediting or governing agency, and a code of ethics—seem to have been met. Public relations is an established major at hundreds of colleges and universities across the country. Organizations such as the PRSA and IABC provide accreditation for professionals and a code of ethics, and the body of scholarship on the field is established and broad.

Practical Experience vs. Academic Education

Public relations practitioners tend to value experience over education as a major determinant in one's success in the field (Stacks et al., 1999). Coman (2008) wrote that "the stereotype widespread within the guild according to which experience is more important than knowledge gained in academic environment" (p. 89). Many practitioners failed to recognize the value of any educational experience that goes "beyond the technical level" (Wright & Turk, 2007, p. 575). Stacks et al. (1999) found that practical skills topped the list of competencies that practitioners sought in hiring public relations staff. These included writing, experience, and communication skills. In particular, a strong portfolio of past works was a determining factor in whether or not a particular individual would be hired.

This perspective recalls the perception of the enhanced status of public relations professionals involved in management as opposed to technical functions. Turk (1989) suggested an engagement with practical business experience in public relations education. Baskin (1989) argued that public relations students lack practical understanding of skills ranging from managerial and organizational to contextual and environmental. In a similar manner, Bowen (2003) found that public relations faculty and professional organizations tended to do "a lax job of communicating [the field's] core responsibilities and activities to new and potential university majors" (p. 199). She contended that public relations should do a better job of communicating its close ties to business culture and management and its strategic communication functions, in order to compete directly with business schools for potential students (p. 210). In a survey of the literature on the need for integration of theory and practice, Moreno, Tench, and Okay (2017) found that there was a wide gap between "recommendations and adherence and between educational outcomes and market labor needs" (p. 111).

At the other end of the spectrum, many academics engaged in graduate education have stressed the importance of theory and principles in public relations education and practice (Gibson, 1987; Toth, 2006; van Ruler, 2003), but many of these same scholars and educators actually teach practical skills at the expense of theory, as revealed by a survey conducted by Benigni and Cameron (1999). Of 99 faculty members, only 33 required students to read communication theory texts as part of a class's curriculum. Similarly, Stacks et al. (1999) found that public relations professors rated practical skills (e.g., writing news releases) higher than mastery of theoretical concepts. Part of the difficulty, as suggested by Latchaw, Allen, and Ogden (2009), is that public relations theory remains underdeveloped in comparison to other fields. Peck (2004) put it bluntly, claiming that most theoretical writing on public relations has offered a "mish-mash of interpretations" or has "dumbed-down" sophisticated arguments (p. 343).

Public relations theory still has a number of defenders, who stress the importance of revamping the curriculum to include engagement with public relations theories, as well as general social science and humanities theories. For example, the PRSA Commission on Public Relations Education recommends "a liberal dose of coursework in business and the behavior sciences" (Latchaw et al., 2009, p. 4). Gibson (1987) and Toth (2006) advocated a liberal education for public relations professionals, with the hope of yielding practical benefits. Stacks et al. (1999) contended that theory is necessary to designing effective campaigns and communication strategies. Mukherjee (2008) offered a more specific example, where an awareness of cultivation theory advanced a practitioner's ability to understand the formation of "opinions and perceptions of the masses to cultivate attitudes, beliefs and notions about products, services, and people" (p. 1). Likewise, Miller and Kernisky (1999) contended that the spiral of silence, as advanced by Elisabeth Noelle-Neumann in the 1970s, can provide practitioners with a means of understanding why minority opinions do not find a voice for fear of becoming socially ostracized.

Licensing vs. Accreditation

An area of particular contention has been whether or not to license public relations professionals. A number of commentators have argued for licensing along the lines of architects or members of the medical or legal professions, with Bernays the most vocal: in a series of articles published primarily in *Public Relations Quarterly*, he argued that licensing would bring a level of accountability to the field that accreditation could not supply (1977, 1980, 1983, 1987, 1992, and 1993). Licensing, which is compulsory and enforced by law or government decree, enforces ethical standards, enhances credibility, and provides sanctions against those who violate the dictates of the licensing board (Broom, 2009). While Forbes (1986) is among the several scholars and practitioners who have argued for the licensing of public relations professionals, Nolte (1980) and Lesly (1986) are among those who have disagreed with the idea. A handful of countries do mandate licensing for public relations practitioners, including Panama, Nigeria, Brazil, Peru, and Puerto Rico. Romania has recently established strict guidelines, with the Romanian Classification for Occupations (2013) outlining the specific responsibilities required of public relations practitioners, including to "create and manage the public image of institutions, companies, political parties and organizations, NGOs, etc." and "mediate conflicts and consult for negotiations" (Palea, 2014, p. 18).

As early as 1964, the PRSA devised an accreditation program for public relations professionals. By the mid-1970s, researchers such as McKee, Nayman, and Lattimore (1975) had perceived a marked effect on the self-assessment of professionalism among practitioners. However, their perception among those outside the field still had a long way to go. By the early 1980s, there was a divide in opinion as to the best way to improve the status of public relations practitioners, as identified by the PRSA Task Force on the Stature and Role of Public Relations. There was a call in the United States and Europe for a more robust accreditation process. The PRSA's Future of Public Relations Committee stated that three of the seven steps to improving the professional standing of public relations were focused on such a process. The formation of the UAB in the early 2000s bolstered the process of obtaining and maintaining the status of Accreditation in Public Relations

(APR). The IABC offered a similar accreditation process, known as the Accredited Business Communicator (ABC). Likewise, the Chartered Institute of Public Relations provided an accreditation certificate for members on a voluntary basis, known as the Chartered Practitioner. Accreditation is most popular in the United States, with the greatest number of public relations practitioners holding an APR coming from there. Sha (2011) conducted research on whether accreditation provides tangible benefits to those who possess it, and found that it does make a difference regarding work categories and professional competencies.

Dozier and Broom (1995) contended that experience rather than accreditation was the most significant factor in whether or not a public relations practitioner practiced managerial or higher-level functions as a professional. Berger, Reber, and Heyman (2007) argued that the diversity of experience was more significant than merely the number of years. They found that accreditation was not a key factor cited by practitioners as leading to a successful career. However, Sha (2011) found that accredited practitioners did register differences in the degree of engagement with higher-level functions compared with nonaccredited practitioners in 7 out of 12 work categories— account management, strategic planning, program planning, project management, stakeholder relations, issues management, and crisis management—and 7 out of 10 professional competencies, including strategic planning, ethics and legal issues, communication theory, business literacy, and advance communication skills. Although the survey conducted by Sha (2011) indicated that level of experience made some difference, "accreditation status *does* make a significant difference in the extent to which practitioners engage in specific work categories in public relations even when the effects of age and experience are controlled" (p. 8). The same holds true in general for professional competencies.

Hogan (1983) argued that licensing would prove to be an ineffective method of improving professional practice because of inefficiency and the inadequate means of enforcing violations. Bernays (1992), on the other hand, argued that it would improve the public perception of public relations professionals and enhance their credibility within the marketplace. Voluntary accreditation, Bernays argued, can demonstrate that one possesses the necessary skills and knowledge to practice ethical public relations, but lack of accreditation does not necessarily mean that one does not possess these skills and knowledge. Organizations such as the PRSA have opposed licensing in favor of voluntary accreditation. Wright (1981) found that those accredited by the PRSA were perceived as having a greater degree of professionalism than their nonaccredited peers.

Ethics

As discussed in previous chapters, ethics is one of the major themes connected with the role and function of public relations practitioners. The field has faced many challenges with regard to image, whether among journalists, media representations, members of the general public, or the scholarly and professional community. Wright (2004) narrated the story of the response to a presentation on ethics in public relations given by a young faculty member in Toronto, Canada:

> The first question was asked by a very senior and extremely well-known journalism professor who took the opportunity to criticize "anyone who would even consider using the words public relations and ethics in the same paragraph." The news-editorial icon insisted public relations and ethics was an oxymoron and then ranted and raved for several minutes and concluded by asking the author if the next research project he might work on would be "ethics and the mafia." (p. 1)

Wright (2004) concluded that such views are not only rampant, but widely tolerated within the academy.

From the moment of the field's definition in the early twentieth century, practitioners and theorists have linked public relations to an ethical dimension. Bernays (1928) argued for its social value, claiming that it was unethical for practitioners to engage in "unsocial or harmful movements or ideas" (p. 199). Both public relations practitioners and educators routinely cite ethical issues as a major concern of public relations professionals (Bowen, 2007; Holtzhausen, 2012; Pieczka & L'Etang, 2001; Ryan & Martinson, 1988).

Today, ethics is an institutionalized part of practice that is linked closely to the role and identity of public relations practitioners. The PRSA Member Code of Ethics calls for members to "serve the public interest by acting as responsible advocates for those we represent," and further to adhere to "our obligation to serve the public interest." The Member Code of Ethics Pledge calls for members "To conduct myself professionally, with truth, accuracy, fairness, and responsibility to the public" (PRSA, 2000).

However, what constitutes ethical standards has been the subject of much debate and discussion, particularly in the 1980s and 1990s, when professional roles were under discussion. Public relations practitioners often has no clear idea of what ethics, the public interest, or social responsibility actually was, and only a vague sense of "the complexities of an obligation of service in the public interest" (Bivins, 1993, p. 3). The "public interest" is not explicitly defined, and it is left largely to individual members to distinguish the dimensions of advocacy on part of a client versus the interest of the public at large. Newsom, Scott, and Turk (1992) contended that "personal ethics ultimately govern the quality of professional performance" among public relations professionals (p. 40). Not everyone agrees that there is a consensus about what constitutes superior moral interests versus individual ones. Martinson (1996) was concerned that public relations professionals were ill equipped to make ethical or moral decisions.

In contrast, Stoker and Stoker (2012) argued that practitioners could engage in ethical public relations by appealing to "superior individual interests" and taking into account communitarian moral values or participating in John Dewey's conception of the "Great Community" (pp. 31, 35). This view presupposes that practitioners will behave ethically; Stoker and Stoker (2012) argued that it is in their best interest—as well as that of their clients—to do so.

Harrison (1990) concluded that public relations textbooks did an inadequate job, for the most part, of describing and defining ethics. He noted that 97% of the respondents to a survey sent to nearly 200 schools that taught public relations as listed in the PRSA directory agreed that "ethics is important for students." Further, a widely adopted public relations text, *Public Relations: Strategies and Tactics* by Wilcox et al. (1989), offered multiple cases and examples, as well as a synthetic definition of public relations ethics:

> Ethic refers to the value system by which a person determines what is right or wrong, fair or unfair, just or unjust ... Some people may make decision and judge the actions of others based upon absolutist Judeo-Christian principles. Others may rely upon such ethical orientations as secular humanism ... The range in ethical considerations comprises a basic part of public relations. (pp. 117–118)

It is notable that the authors placed the burden of determining what is ethical on individual beliefs, as opposed to the establishing requirements for a universal code of ethics. Perhaps because of the indeterminacy of established standards, Bowen (2009) noted that public relations students often had a poor concept of the ethical dimension of the field. She found that they frequently "omitted ethics" from discussion of the principal functions of public relations (p. 405), tending instead to describe it "in terms of deception" (p. 407).

Krukeberg (1996) has been among the most vocal proponents for a universal code of ethics applicable to public relations practitioners. He noted that such a code should be sensitive to regional and cultural differences, yet robust enough to ensure a degree of uniformity among practitioners. An enforceable code of ethics is one of the watermarks of professionalism, and the perception that public relations professionals follow such a code is necessary to improving their image (Cutlip et al., 1994; Day, Dong, & Robins, 2001; Shamir, Reed, & Connell, 1990). In discussing Korean practitioners' self-perceptions, Jeong (2011) pointed out that a code of ethics would need to be both explicit and practical, so that the field could "establish standards and guidelines that would minimize practitioners' ethical dilemmas" (p. 101).

Corporate social responsibility (CSR) is a major theme in the debate over ethics in public relations. Heath and Ryan (1989) were among the first to call for the integration of social responsibility into the code of ethics adopted by public relations practitioners. They pointed to the crucial role played by public relations professionals within organizations in acting as ethical guardians and helping the dominant coalition exercise greater moral authority. Heath and Palenchar (2009) continued to argue that ethical standards served the interest of organizations in the sense that demonstrating corporate responsibility was good for the bottom line. He wrote that "by achieving high standards of corporate responsibility through fostered mutual relationships, issues managers can attract stakes and avoid costly conflicts" (p. 134). Kim and Reber (2009) demonstrated that public relations practitioners' attitudes toward social responsibility were linked to their self-assessed perception of professionalism in a survey of nearly 300 members of the PRSA.

A common charge is that public relations subverts, undermines, or unfairly skews the democratic process and sacrifices the public interest for narrow corporate goals. According to Miller and Dinan (2007), public relations helps to "to ensure that liberal democratic societies do not respond to the will of the people and that vested interests prevail" (p. 11). Rim and Kim (2018) recently tested public evaluations of CSR activities and found that preexisting skepticism about a company's altruism was the strongest predictor of whether or not members of the public exercised a negative response to efforts to repair corporate reputation and build a reservoir of goodwill.

Heath (2007) noted that there exists a tension in normative excellence model approaches, which dominate the ethical approaches adopted by many public relations firms, insofar as they advocate symmetrical relationships on one hand and advocacy in the interest of the client on the other. Scholars such as Fitzpatrick and Bronstein (2006) and Porter (2010) also argued that the conception of ethics in public relations should acknowledge that advocacy, debate, asymmetry, and persuasion play an important but often overlooked role, given the free-market condition under which public relations firms conduct business. Fawkes (2012) argued that the symmetrical, functionalist model has been promoted in emerging economies and strongly informed the code of ethics advanced by the Global Alliance (p. 867). Ethics and values constellate differently in different cultures, and despite a call for a universal, global code of ethics, reaching consensus on what this would be has proven notoriously difficult. Fawkes (2012) thus perceived two distinct strands in the discussion of professional ethics. The first, which he termed "functionalist," conceives of "professional ethics as embodying the profession's commitment to social value and also offering a protection for ignorant client." The second, the "revisionist" strand, which includes post-modernists, post-structuralists, and feminists, sees "professional ethics as empty and self-promotional" (p. 866). Fawkes (2012) linked the former stance to utilitarian or Kantian approaches and the latter to Marxist analyses of class, Habermas's theories of discourse ethics, postcolonial approaches, feminist perspectives, and Jungian approaches—characterized by the identification of archetypes and recognition of group psyches, whose "values will constellate differently in different cultures" (p. 868).

Public Relations Leadership

Scholarship on leadership communication has been focused on the connections between personal traits, individual skills, and leadership effectiveness (Aldoory & Toth, 2004; Bass, 1985; Johansson, 2018; Men, 2014b; Men & Stacks, 2014). Much of the work was conducted under the auspices of organizational psychology and industrial management theory and had a normative, mechanistic, or functionalist bias. In the 1980s and 1990s, an interest in the relationship between leaders and those whom they led emerged, with an emphasis on measuring conversational exchanges between leaders and followers (Graen & Uhl-Bien, 1995). The model focused on transmission, whereby leaders transmitted a message, which was received by their followers. Transformational leadership, in contrast to transactional leadership with its focus on day-to-day progress towards organizational goals, examines how followers are transformed by charismatic or visionary leaders who promote interactive, caring, encouraging, and inspirational communications (Bass, 1998; Hackman & Johnson, 2004; Men, 2014a).

In recent years, scholars have criticized the visionary model as lacking consistent measurement scales and failing to establish strong correlations between cause and effect (Johansson, 2018). Tompkins (1984) rejected the functionalist view of organizations and communication as distinct elements and proposed that organizations are socially constructed entities, constituted by communication (p. 660). Leadership thus involves sensemaking, as both leaders and followers frame the terms of discussion and interpret subtle shades of meaning (Smircich & Morgan, 1982). The management of meaning, or of facilitating and guiding the sensemaking process, is a key role of leaders (Johansson, 2018). The constitutive view of communication suggests that interaction between leaders and followers is dynamic and circular, without necessitating a hierarchy of leaders and followers in terms of creating meaning. This co-creational view suggests that meaning is enacted through dialogic and contextual processes (Barge & Little, 2008). In this regard, the strategic framing of issues and activities, together with decision making, become a key leadership role (White, 2018). Storytelling, or creating an "ordering narrative" that builds common identity among employees, is another tactic associated with effective leadership (Johansson, 2018, p. 12). "Discursive leadership" involves interaction and dialogue designed to socially construct meaning through interaction between the leader and team members (Johansson, 2018, p. 9). The theory of communicative leadership proposes that leadership is defined and created through the enactment of strategic communication processes. The ideal communicative leader "engages employees in dialogue, actively shares and seeks feedback, practices participative decision making, and is perceived as open and involved" (Johannson, Miller, & Hamrin, 2014, p. 155). Outcomes of communicative leadership include building trust, augmenting employee engagement, fostering employee empowerment, improving the well being of employees, and promoting organizational effectiveness.

Meng and Berger (2013) argued that public relations leaders are crucial to achieving organizational effectiveness by making strategic choices and engaging in ethical practice. They pointed out that no agreed-upon definition of public relations leadership had emerged. Scholars such as Berger and Meng (2014), Bowen (2009), Meng and Berger (2013), Murphy (2011), and Northouse (2013) had examined the various definitions of leadership germane to public relations leadership. Martinelli and Erzikova's (2017) conducted a study specifically dedicated to the evolution of leadership in the public relations profession. Berger and Reber (2006) noted that the future direction of public relations practice was closely tied to the competencies and actions of leaders. While there is little sound evidence for the effectiveness of leadership practices such as executive coaching or 360° feedback (Day, Fleenor, Atwater, Sturm, & Mckee, 2014), conceiving of leadership as a wide-ranging, contextual, and ongoing process of development that includes mentoring appears to hold the most promise (Eby et al., 2013). Nath and Bell (2016) mounted an argument for the integration of marketing and public relations departments under a common leader to "enhance the synergy across multiple customer touch points that come from integration" (p. 646).

As a process of development, the integrated model of public relations leadership focuses on personal and cultural dimensions (Berger & Meng, 2014; Northouse, 2013). These include insight into self, propensity toward collaboration, ethical capacities, relationship-building capacities, environmental awareness, skill at communication management, and strategic decision-making abilities. Berger and Meng (2014) argued that the most important of these was strategic decision-making, because it represented a higher-order enactment of public relations acumen in the widest variety of situations and contexts. Cross-cultural research provided the salience of skills and abilities aligned to specific contexts, although patterns of leadership development appeared to be shared (Martinelli & Erzikova, 2017). For example, Luo and Jiang (2014) found that public relations managers at a Chinese telecommunication conglomerate were effective in using their strategic decision-making skills to gain access to the dominant coalition. However, because they failed to engage different employee constituencies using transformational leadership techniques, the results were disastrous. Men (2014b) found that transformational leadership characterized by symmetrical communication and particularly face-to-face interaction positively affected employee satisfaction. Compared to task-oriented or transactional leaders, transformational leaders expressed genuine concern for their employees and motivated them to prioritize the needs of the organization over short-term, self-interested goals (Jin, 2010). Transformational leaders thus inspire employees to report greater satisfaction with their organization (Men, 2014b).

Case Study: The PRSA, Ethics, and the Resignation of Tony Franco

In 1986, Anthony M. Franco resigned the presidency of the Public Relations Society of America (PRSA), as well as his membership, amid an investigation by the Securities & Exchange Commission (SEC) into his sale of stock holdings. He had allegedly used his knowledge of the acquisition of a Detroit department store to turn a profit. Although Franco admitted no wrongdoing, the perception of unethical behavior dogged him until his death in 2002.

The case is still referenced frequently when discussing the PRSA's position on ethics. Many commentators argued that Franco had an ethical responsibility to share with members the details of the SEC investigation, which was pending when he was elected. Franco claimed that he had sought the advice of PRSA counsel and it was recommended to him to keep quiet as the case was still under arbitration. David Ferguson, former president of the PRSA, commented that whether or not Franco was in the wrong, it mattered little because it was a private matter. This did not sit well with others (Fitzpatrick, 2002).

In addition to the ethical question, what disturbed PRSA members was that the letter announcing Franco's resignation failed to mention its cause. This led a writer for the Associated Press to comment, "The public relations business seems to be having trouble relating to the public" (Associated Press, 1986). As a result of the debacle, the PRSA took a renewed interest in its code of ethics, adding four additional clauses to its statement of principles.

However, having a code of ethics is no guarantee that one will behave in a moral fashion. As the Franco case illustrates, the advice of counsel can overrule ethical codes that are ultimately unenforceable except insofar as one can be excluded from membership. Franco's resignation put an end to the PRSA's investigation of his behavior, since its bylaws allowed official scrutiny only of active members. As has been argued by many scholars, membership in the PRSA or any other professional organization is no guarantee that one is either professional or ethical.

More than 30 years later, it appears as though the fallout from the Franco case is still affecting the organization. Candidates for office are guarded when answering questions about their views on personal ethics and past behaviors out of concern that their statements could be misinterpreted should a controversy such as the Franco case arise. While Franco lost his reputation, he avoided further sanctions from a public relations accrediting body by resigning. As some have argued, the case illustrates the ultimate inability of membership organizations such as the PRSA to provide meaningful, enforceable ethical guidelines that have ramifications beyond mere dissociation.

Global Perspectives on the Roles of Public Relations Professionals

Globalization is defined as complex sets of interconnecting networks among various nations with distinct social, cultural, and economic backgrounds (Sriramesh, 2009). Sriramesh (2009) pointed to the primary forces driving globalism: reduction of trade barriers, acknowledgment of international issues such as environmentalism, and a rapid increase in technological means of communication and information dissemination. The role of public relations professionals varies greatly around the world, contingent on the space that they occupy in a given context. Yang and Taylor (2014) assessed the rise of professional associations globally. Their study suggests that less developed nations tend to adopt models of practice and theory from more developed ones and that the development of global public relations networks shares "common structural, institutional, and culture features of public relations professions across nations" on a global scale (p. 523). While regional differences have tended to remain intact, there is a general move toward the development of international networks based on models common to affluent, Western countries—notably the United States and European nations (pp. 525–526).

On the other hand, Halff and Gregory (2014) found a paradigm that differed from Western models operating in Asian public relations contexts, showing support for "alternate voices and polyphony" in their meta-analysis (p. 399). A country's unique history and cultural dimensions affect public relations practice there. For example, the "corporate expert system" that dominates Western public relations is hybridized with local practices (Halff & Gregory, 2014, p. 405). Modella, Moreno, and Navarro (2017) examined contextual variables such as freedom of the press, market conditions, and the political system in their study of Latin American conceptualizations of public relations professionalism and professionalization. They found that while practitioners were optimistic about trends in education and ethics, they were less hopeful where it came to establishing the professional legitimacy of public relations within the marketplace. Similarly, Niemann-Struweg and Meintjies (2008) chronicled efforts to define public relations professionalism in South America, finding that infighting between the governing body and practitioners presented an untenable situation.

The Global Alliance emerged as a driving force in bringing public relations professionals from diverse nations into alignment. It also provided "third party validation of [national associations'] own efforts to position and legitimize the profession and the sharing of knowledge across boundaries" (Valin, Gregory, & Likely, 2014, p. 652). Gregory and Fawkes (2019) undertook a major study with partner organizations on seven continents, resulting in 11 synthetic statements describing the state of the profession in the current global context. The Global Alliance supports the global capabilities framework with a conglomeration of professional organizations on all inhabited continents. This framework includes the following goals:

1) To align communication strategies with organizational purpose and balance.
2) To identify and address communication problems proactively.
3) To conduct formative and evaluative research to underpin communication strategies and tactics.
4) To communicate effectively across a full range of platforms and technologies.
5) To facilitate relationships and build trust with internal and external stakeholders and communities.
6) To build and enhance organizational reputation.
7) To provide contextual intelligence.
8) To provide valued counsel and be a trusted advisor.
9) To offer organizational leadership.
10) To work within an ethical framework on behalf of the organization, in line with professional and society's expectations.
11) To develop self and others, including continuing professional learning. (Gregory and Fawkes, 2019, p. 9)

While these views were generally and widely shared, Gregory and Fawkes (2019) found "minor, but significant, variations between countries' capability sets, particularly concerning the social role of public relations and in the use of terminology" (p. 11).

As with the push toward increasing globalization, the sharing economy upends the traditional creation of stable and coherent relationships between organizations and stakeholders that has been the purview of public relations practitioners. The sharing economy created a large degree of ambiguity about what constitutes an organization, which public relations is not well equipped to address. Halff and Gregory (2016) noted that the sharing economy has three characteristics: first, it means granting temporary access to otherwise unused or under-used resources; second, it is marked by planned disintermediation between providers, consumers, and a third party; and third, it depends on the integration and sharing of technological resources such as social media and mobile platforms. On the surface, this would seem to short-circuit the role of public relations; however, Halff and Gregory (2015) argued that public relations professionals assume the role of "an expert who communicates about communication" (p. 10), and thus, the central role of public relations will emerge as the steward of meta-communication, framing the terms without particularly engaging in the communication itself.

Evolving Roles of Public Relations Professionals in New Media Environments

Public relations professionals have expressed strong agreement that the influence of traditional news media is waning and "new media are changing the way public relations is practiced" (Wright & Hinson, 2014, p. 14). Among the vexing questions facing public relations professionals is what role they should play in designing and implementing an organization's social media presence. Does social media represent a revolution in the way organizations and publics interact, or is it more rightly characterized as a new channel for engaging in traditional networking? Kent (2013) proposed that social media represented a powerful new communication technology capable of fostering democratic ideals and real connections; however, he worried that it also led to insularity and isolation, implying that "social media are a tool that can be used better" (p. 344).

Despite the promise of dialogic models of online and social networks facilitating equal participation in the public sphere, leading to the spread of democratic ideals, there is the suspicion that the "Old Boy's Club" is somehow lurking in the background, ensuring that meaningful network communication takes place only among those who are invited (Toledano & Maplesden, 2016, p. 721). However, public relations practitioners and researchers have maintained the faith that technological innovation will help public relations enhance its engagement with constituents, stakeholders, and stakeseekers.

Lee, Sha, Dozier, and Sargent (2015) found that the skills associated with engagement with social media tended to be found among younger practitioners, who often occupy technical roles. Although they cautioned against viewing this as a predictor of role enactment as either technician or manager, Vieira and Grantham (2015) pointed to the necessity of updating competency with technological skill sets such as social media communication as a prerequisite to moving up the ladder of strategic management in public relations. Kim and Johnson (2009) and Wright and Hinson (2014) demonstrated that employers rate social media skills highly. Luo, Jiang, and Kulemeka (2015) demonstrated that leaders who engaged in social media management gained power by exerting "upward" influence among their peers (p. 167). Likewise, Neill and Moody (2015) documented how proficiency in social media increased not only the marketability of public relations practitioners, but also their status within an organization. They outlined nine strategic roles associated with social media management: "(1) internal collaborator, (2) policy maker, (3) policing, (4) technology tester, (5) communication organizer, (6) issues manager, (7) relationship analyzer, (8) master of metrics, and (9) employee recruiter" (p. 112). Toledano and Maplesden (2016) proposed that social media holds the promise of establishing and supporting "genuine social networks" in which "genuine community dialogue" may prosper, uncorrupted by "organizational interventions that undermine true democracy" (p. 721).

The strategic management of social media, and how this is integrated into an organization's communication program, has emerged as a key role associated with public relations practitioners. Charest, Bouffard, and Zajmovic (2016) demonstrated how managers plan strategy around social media and in order to promote a global approach to interacting with audiences thereon. They outlined this role against the backdrop of building and maintaining stakeholder trust, stressing the importance of a monitoring or "listening strategy" followed by a content strategy aimed at reaching target audiences (p. 532).

Public Relations Professionals Serving the Public Interest

Public relations in its infancy was indistinguishable from press agentry and publicity. As Hallahan (2018) noted, Ivy Lee preferred the term "publicity" or "publicist," while Bernays (1980) favored "public relations counselor." Cutlip and Center (1978) contended that the goal of public relations was to "influence opinion" through communication (p. 1). Nearly a decade later, Cutlip et al. (1985) offered a definition of public relations that has continued to hold sway: it is a "management function that identifies, establishes, and maintains mutually beneficial relationships between an organization and the various public on whom its success of failure depends" (p. 1). The managerial or functional approach exemplified by Grunig and Hunt (1984) dominated the 1980s through the early 2000s. This approach betrays an organization-centric view, with a bias toward the operation of corporations, often at the expense of the needs and interests of their stakeholder publics. As Hallahan (2018) argued, such an organizational bias often occludes the fact that "public relations can be practiced by any public entity, including social movements, loosely knit grassroots activist groups, and public figures such as political candidates or entertainment celebrities who promote themselves or their brand" (p. 3).

As discussed earlier, public relations practitioners serve both as communicators, which is often linked to the technical function, and as counselors, which is linked to the managerial one as part of the dominant coalition (Bernays, 1923; Grunig, 2006; Hallahan, 2018; Lee, 1925; Neill, 2014). This dual role is the reason that public relations practitioners may be seen as boundary spanners, interacting with external publics not served by others within an organization. They serve as intermediaries between external publics and an organization's management. They are positioned to protect reputation and trust by outlining potential threats to "*intangible assets* or *symbolic capital*" (Hallahan, 2018, p. 5).

Scholars have argued for a role of public relations in helping build social capital through engaging in dialogue as a means of forging relationships and building community (Hallahan, 2013; Heath, 2006; Ihlen, 2013; Kruckeberg and Stark, 1998; Sommerfeldt, 2013). Public relations can be connected to the role "concerned with issues and values that are considered publicly relevant, which means relating to the public sphere" and contribute to the public good by fostering democratic engagement of disparate parties (Jensen, 2001, p. 134). Dialogic engagement undertaken in the spirit of mutuality, openness, and honesty is central to the practice of democracy (Kent & Taylor, 1998; Kent & Taylor, 2002). Democratic, dialogic engagement leads the way toward the creation of a "more fully functioning society" (Heath, 2006). It does not necessarily run counter to organizational goals, because inclusiveness and transparency based on the exchange of rational arguments increases the likelihood of bringing audiences into collective agreement (Leitch & Motion, 2010; Sommerfeldt, 2013). However, Cardwell, Williams, and Pyle (2017) suggested that effective management of internal stakeholder relationships "is a prerequisite to successful external relationships" (p. 161) and that internal organizational dynamics often prove to be an impediment to establishing meaningful dialogue with stakeholders.

Critical approaches to public relations scholarship, often informed by social theorists such as Habermas (1996), have focused on theoretical examinations of the ways in which corporations subvert the public interest in order to advance their own private agenda. The state has often enlisted public relations to support hegemony:

> [P]ublic relations is engaged in the exercise of symbolic power and can be viewed as an instrument of social control wherein practitioners are complicit in helping powerful corporate or political clients impose their political, cultural, and social beliefs and values on society through the public's tacit, hegemonic acceptance of their legitimacy. (Hallahan, 2018, p. 12)

Public relations is seen as a tool of the powerful, whether for the advancement of narrow and selfish corporate interests to the detriment of society or in support of an imperialist exploitation of people from disadvantaged regions. Habermas (1996) cautioned that deliberation in a democratic public sphere should be free from coercion or undue influence of vested interests and should incorporate the perspectives of multiple stakeholders affected by the issue under discussion. Chambers (2009) warned against the manipulation of public opinion through government and corporate public relations efforts that offer "pseudo-preferences" of the public (p. 328). Critical scholars presume that the public possesses greater legitimacy than corporations, and is more inclined to act in a socially responsible manner.

Edwards (2016) contended that it is possible for public relations to intervene in ways that create social capital which empowers a wide range of constituents, thereby connecting organizations with activists and other stakeseekers in support of deliberative democracy (p. 61). Thus, relationships built through public relations efforts can be based on the exchange of ideas—which is fundamental to an effective democracy—and can serve to encourage positive and empowering transformations (L'Etang, 2008). Democratic engagement takes place in formal and informal "dynamic decision-making arenas that address societal decisions," known as deliberative systems (Edwards, 2016, p. 67). The task of public relations professionals is to ensure that different segments of the public are represented in the deliberative process. Dryzek (2009) suggested they encourage pluralism by framing the diversity of potential interests in a given discussion. Public relations thus helps establish the legitimacy of various constituent stakeholders in the process of deliberative engagement (Heath & Waymer, 2009). This recasts its role as a positive force for encouraging the social good, enhancing the social capital of diverse constituents, stakeholders, or stakeseekers, and making society fully functioning (Edwards, 2016; Heath, 2006). Brunner (2016) pointed to civic professionalism—defined as the merging of professional communication practice with an examination of ethics and the public good.

Conclusion

The role of public relations professionals has undergone a series of transformations since the establishment of the field more than a century ago. Research into the precise roles played by practitioners dates to the 1970s, and has focused on definitions, work competencies, the status of public relations professionals within an organization or in society, roles in related fields such as journalism, questions of accreditation and licensing, diversity, leadership, interplay with culture and technology, and the future of the field. It has centered on the distinction between technician and manager, as well as the quest for status as part of the dominant coalition (Broom & Dozier, 1986; Broom & Smith, 1979; DeSanto & Moss, 2004; Johansson & Larsson, 2015). There is a general agreement that public relations professionals can serve roles ranging from technician to manager, and there is a degree of overlap in their functions that is subject to process and change. Educational requirements and specific curricula represent further means of defining roles. The balance between practical and academic skills taught to public relations students has been an ongoing area of debate, as has the adoption of common professional standards (Kruckeberg, 1998). A range of competencies are required of public relations professionals, from technical communication skills such as designing and writing press releases to leadership, analytical, strategic, and problem-solving abilities (McKinney, 2018).

The definition of professionalism as it applies to public relations has been the subject of a great deal of research. Standards are closely related to the development of the field in the United States, which maintains hegemony over practice and theory. Public trust in practitioners remains low and stereotypes persist, and the introduction of licensure or accreditation is seen as a means of bolstering reputation and credibility. Organizations such as the Public Relations Society of America (PRSA) have called for a more robust process for assuring competencies in a public manner; however, the debate over whether this should be through licensing, accreditation, or some other method remains active.

Ethics remains a major theme of research. It has been a hot topic from the onset, as seen in Bernays' (1928) argument that the social value of public relations is connected to the public's perception that it avoids engagement with movements that are harmful or antisocial. But public relations practitioners have not always had a clear sense of what constitutes ethical behavior and social responsibility (Bivins, 1993). The debate over functionalist definitions of ethics as loyalty to clients versus not harming society has in recent years collided with revisionist concepts of ethics as being sensitive to the perspectives a broader class of individuals and cultures (Fawkes, 2012). Scholars have challenged the idea that public relations should primarily serve the interests of organizations. A renewed interest in how it increases dialogue, access to the public sphere, and democratic participation is evident in scholarship aimed at making society fully functioning. Scholars such as Heath (2006), L'Etang (2008), and Hallahan (2018) have argued that public relations has an ethical responsibility to take into account the views and outlooks of a variety of stakeholders and stakeseekers.

Closely related to ethics are issues of diversity and gender (Aldoory & Toth, 2004; Ravazzani, 2018). Where they were once excluded from all but supporting roles, women now make up a majority of public relations practitioners (Khazan, 2014). The number of minorities in public relations roles is likewise increasing. Intersectionality, or the combination of identity statuses, has become an emerging area of scholarship (Vardeman-Winter, Tildall, & Jiang, 2013). Perceptions of unequal empowerment persist, however, and white males still hold most upper-level jobs (Golombisky, 2015; Vardeman-Winter & Crowe, 2018).

The rise of globalism and multiculturalism has wrought many changes, notably bringing a threat to the hegemony of American and Eurocentric culture. It is beginning to be recognized that a homogenous and homophilious approach to communicating with constituents is not sufficient for an increasingly diverse environment, especially when coupled with the evolving new media and technological landscape. The role of public relations professionals within organizations, causes, and social movements is thus increasingly complex and diverse.

Chapter Summary

The role of the public relations practitioner has undergone a transformation over the years, characterized by enhanced professional status, refined social practices, genuine reflection on and maintenance of professional standards, the establishment of consensual ethical norms, a rigorous focus on ethical practice, and increasing emphasis on its benefit to society as a whole. The practice of public relations is ancient, although definition of the field as a distinct endeavor and specification of the roles that it plays in society are of comparatively recent vintage. Public relations has been scrutinized with academic rigor since the last quarter of the twentieth century. The emphasis on ethics, enhancement of professionalism, and overcoming stereotypes and negative opinions associated with propaganda and press agentry has been an ongoing issue, while the quest for status as a recognized professional has consumed much of the scholarly discussion.

Public relations roles have been circumscribed for a number of years by an emphasis on the relationship between organizations and practitioners. As public relations professionals strived for acceptance and a place within the dominant coalition, the focus in theory from the 1920s through the 1990s was on their evolution from technical communication specialists to managers involved in strategic decision making. Research during the 1980s and 1990s sought to categorize the specific roles, personal qualities, and professional competencies required of practitioners, with an emphasis on managerial functions such as expert prescriber and problem-solving facilitator. The aim was to link public relations to general management functions, as encapsulated in Cutlip et al.'s (1985) definition.

Examination of curricula for aspiring public relations professionals and the debate over licensure versus accreditation have been the focus of recent research and theoretical development associated with public relations scholarship. The issue of practical experience versus mastery of theoretical concepts is ongoing, with most scholars arguing that a balance between the two is most productive. Scholars have also tended to side with the call for accreditation as opposed to professional licensing. Krukeberg (1996), for example, promoted the concept of an explicit code of ethics, while Heath and Ryan (1989) were among the most vocal proponents of social responsibility as part of such a code.

Diversity, gender, and global issues have come to the forefront of public relations research and practice in the last two decades. While women have tended to have a large representation in the field, most top public relations management positions are still held by men. Similarly, white people far outnumber members of minority groups in terms of public relations representation in the dominant coalition. A majority of minority public relations practitioners have experienced discrimination and believe that they have been relegated to low-level functions and limited to performing menial tasks (Applebaum & Ford, 2005; Sha & Ford, 2007). Likewise, there is a general trend toward less developed countries adopting their practice and theory from the United States, and the Eurocentric perspective has dominated in global settings.

Public relations has been increasingly defined as strategic communication, with complex and multiple disciplinary identities assumed by public relations professionals. Recent theoretical developments that embody the rhetorical perspective and cultural and critical approaches have emphasized the role that public relations professionals play in CSR, co-creating meaning with various constituents, stakeholders, and stakeseekers, facilitating meaningful dialogue between competing interests, and making society more fully functioning. The question of how organizations can empower publics is largely a matter of who controls the rhetoric and discourse (Botan, 1997; Heath, Motion, & Leitch, 2010; Vardeman-Winter & Crowe, 2018).

Key Terms

Accreditation: Professional submission to a set of guidelines outlined by a regulating body. Accreditation is currently voluntary in the United States.

Dominant Coalition: Those individuals who make decisions and provide leadership in an organizational context

Glass Ceiling or Velvet Ghetto: The tendency for women to be involved in more technical functions, while men have more managerial roles. Women are often relegated to middle-management and find it difficult to rise above this level. They are also more likely than men to suffer during periods of economic downturn.

Licensing: Regulation of a professional that is compulsory and enforced by law or government decree. Currently, there is no licensing requirement for public relations professionals in the United States.

Managerial Role: Often, the managerial position is an authority in identifying problems and providing solutions through its decision-making power. Managerial roles oversee people and craft communication strategy and tactics for building, maintaining, and improving relationships with stakeholders.

Professional Competences: The knowledge, skills, and abilities required for individuals working in a specific field. For public relations, these include categories such as financial and account management, media relations, social media competency, writing and communication ability, and stakeholder and crisis management.

Professionalism: Public relations professionals work in the public interest in a larger nexus beyond organizational purpose and transcend a "technician mentality" or careerist mindset. They are not hired guns who say whatever the client or organization wants them to, but abide by a well-defined code of ethics.

Role Enactment: The encroachment of public relations professionals into the dominant coalition or managerial positions. Public relations professionals strive to be a part of the dominant coalition in order to make public relations efforts more effective and successful. There are obvious links between managerial role enactment and income: those in managerial positions get paid more, most of the time. There is no empirical evidence that professional experience is linked to income.

Technician Role: The technician undertakes their role most often without knowing the reason or the expected results. They are a follower, just as the communications manager is a leader. Technical roles are considered less sophisticated than managerial ones and are paid less accordingly.

Discussion Questions

1 What skills and knowledge are required of public relations professionals?
2 How has the role of public relations professional changed, especially in the new media environment?
3 Do you think the role of public relations professional varies across cultures and countries?
4 What competencies are required of public relations professionals?
5 What is the difference between the managerial and technician roles of the public relations professional?
6 How does the role of public relations professional differ at organizational versus societal levels?
7 Do you agree or disagree with licensing and accreditation?
8 What are some ethical guidelines for public relations professionals?
9 What are some professional norms and standards for public relations professionals?
10 What are some gender and diversity issues facing the profession?

References

Abramson, J. (2018). Rudy Giuliani has turned out to be a dangerous liability for Trump. *The Guardian*, August 5. Available from https://www.theguardian.com/commentisfree/2018/aug/05/rudy-giuliani-liability-trump (accessed May 20, 2020).

Aldoory, L., & Toth, E. L. (2002). Gender discrepancies in a gendered profession: A developing theory for public relations. *Journal of Public Relations Research*, *14*, 103–126.

Aldoory, L., & Toth, E. L. (2004). Leadership and gender in public relations: Perceived effectiveness of transformational leadership styles. *Journal of Public Relations Research*, *16*, 157–183.

Applebaum, L., and Ford, R. (2005). Multicultural public relations practitioner survey. Available from https://www.ccny.cuny.edu/prsurvey (accessed May 20, 2020).

Associated Press. (1986). Public relations society gets bad PR. *AP News*, September 26. Available from https://www.apnews.com/2d1e5d3c9e3a15701a22b5e0034252b8 (accessed May 20, 2020).

Barge, J. K., & Little, M. (2008). A discursive approach to skillful activity. *Communication Theory*, *18*(4), 505–534.

Baskin, O. W. (1989). Business schools and the study of public relations. *Public Relations Review*, *15*(Spring), 25–37.

Bass, B. M. (1985). *Leadership and performance beyond expectations*. New York: Free Press.

Bass, B. M. (1998). *Transformational leadership: Industry, military, and educational impact*. Mahwah, NJ: Lawrence Erlbaum Associates.

Benhabib, S. (2013). *Situating the self: Gender, community and postmodernism in contemporary ethics*. New York: Routledge.

Benigni, V. L., & Cameron, G. T. (1999). Teaching PR campaigns: The current state of the art. *Journalism & Mass Communication Educator*, *54*(2), 50–60.

Bentele, G., & Szyszka, P. (Eds.) (1995). *PR-Ausbildung in Deutschland Entwicklung Bestandsaufnahme und perspecktiven*. Oplanden: Westdeutcher Verlag.

Berger, B. K., & Meng, J. (Eds.) (2014). *Public relations leaders as sensemakers: A global study of leadership in public relations and communication management*. New York: Routledge.

Berger, B. K., & Reber, B. H. (2006). Finding influence: Examining the role of influence in public relations. *Journal of Communication Management*, *10*(3), 235–249.

Berger, B. K., Reber, B. H., & Heyman, W. C. (2007). You can't homogenize success in communication management: PR leaders take divers paths to top. *International Journal of Strategic Communication*, *1*, 53–71.

Bernays, E. L. (1923). *Crystallizing public opinion*. New York: Boni & Liveright.

Bernays, E. L. (1928). *Propaganda*. New York: H. Liveright.

Bernays, E. L. (1977). Four steps toward enhancing the future of public relations. *Public Relations Quarterly*, *22*(2), 26.

Bernays, E. L. (1980). Viewpoint: Gaining professional status for public relations. *Public Relations Quarterly*, *28*(1), 20.

Bernays, E. L. (1983). Viewpoint: The case for licensing PR practitioners. *Public Relations Quarterly*, *28*(1), 32.

Bernays, E. L. (1987). Viewpoint: Words subject to change without notice: Let's legally define public relations. *Public Relations Quarterly*, *29*(2), 6–9.

Bernays, E. L. (1992). Securing the future of public relations. *PR Update*, *2*(1), 8–9.

Bernays, E. L. (1993). The future of public relations: Is licensing the answer? *Journal of Corporate Public Relations*, *3*, 8–10.

Beurer-Zullig, B., Fieseler, C., & Meckel, M. (2009). Typologies of communicators in Europe. *Corporate Communication: An International Journal*, *14*(2), 158–175.

Bivins, T. H. (1993). Public relations, professionalism, and the public interest. *Journal of Business Ethics*, *12*, 117–126.

Black, C. (2003). *The PR practitioner's desktop guide*. London: Thorogood.

Botan, C. H. (1997). Ethics in strategic communication campaigns: The case for a new approach to public relations. *Journal of Business Communication*, *34*(2), 188–202.

Bowen, S. A. (2003). "I thought it would be more glamorous": Preconceptions and misconceptions among students in public relations principles course. *Public Relations Review*, *29*, 199–214.

Bowen, S. A. (2007). The extent of ethics. In E. L. Toth (Ed.), *The future of excellence in public relations and communication management: Challenges for the next generation* (pp. 275–298). Mahwah, NJ: Lawrence Erlbaum Associates.

Bowen, S. A. (2009). All glamour, no substance? How public relations majors and potential majors in an exemplar program view the industry and function. *Public Relations Review*, *35*, 402–410.

Broom, G. M. (1982). A comparison of sex roles in public relations. *Public Relations Review*, *8*(3), 17–22.

Broom, G. M. (2009). *Cutlip & Center's effective public relations*. Upper Saddle River, NJ: Prentice-Hall.

Broom, G. M., & Dozier, D. M. (1986). Advancement for public relations role models. *Public Relations Review*, *12*(1), 37–56.

Broom, G. M., & Smith, G. D. (1979). Testing the practitioner's impact on clients. *Public Relations Review*, *5*, 47–59.

Brunner, B. R. (2016). What is civic professionalism in public relations? Practitioner perspectives—A pilot study. *Public Relations Review*, *42*, 237–239.

Cameron, G. T., Sallot, L. M., & Weaver-Lariscy, R. A. (1996). Developing standards of professional performance in public relations. *Public Relations Review*, *22*(1), 43–61.

Cardwell, L. A., Williams, S., & Pyle, A. (2017). Corporate public relations dynamics: Internal vs. external stakeholders and the role of the practitioner. *Public Relations Review*, *43*, 152–162.

Chambers, S. (2009). Rhetoric and the public sphere: Has deliberative democracy abandoned mass democracy? *Political Theory*, *37*(3), 323–350.

Charest, F., Bouffard, J., & Zajmovic, E. (2016). Public relations and social media: Deliberative or creative strategic planning. *Public Relations Review*, *42*, 530–538.

Cisczek, E. L. (2017). Public relations, activism and identity: A cultural-economic examination of contemporary LGBT activism. *Public Relations Review*, *43*(4), 809–816.

Cline, C. G., Masel-Walters, L., Toth, E. L., Turk, J. V., & Johnson, N. (1986). *The velvet ghetto: The impact of the increasing percentage of women in public relations and organizational communication*. San Francisco, CA: IABC Research Foundation.

Coman, C. (2008). Instituţioinalizare şi profesionalizare in relaţiile publice din România. *Revista română de comunicare şi relatii publice*, *12*, 89–99, cited and translated in Palea, A. (2014). The public relations professional: Elements of identity. *Professional Communication and Translations Studies*, *7*(1–2), 17–22

Coombs, W. T., & Holladay, S. J. (2012). Privileging an activist vs. a corporate view of public relations history in the U.S. *Public Relations Review*, *38*(3), 347–353.

Creedon, P. J. (1991). Public relations and "women's work": Toward a feminist analysis of public relations roles. In J. E. Grunig & L. A. Grunig (Eds.), *Public relations research annual* (Vol. *3*, pp. 67–84). Hillsdale, NJ: Lawrence Erlbaum Associates.

Culbertson, H. M. (1991). Role taking and sensitivity: Keys to playing and making public relations roles. In L. A. Grunig & J. E. Grunig (Eds.), *Public relations research annual* (Vol. *3*, pp. 37–64). Hillsdale, NJ: Lawrence Erlbaum Associates.

Cutlip, S. M. (1994). *The unseen power: Public relations, a history*. Hillsdale, NJ: Lawrence Earlbaum Associates.

Cutlip, S. M., & Center, A. H. (1978). *Effective public relations*. Upper Saddle River, NJ: Prentice-Hall.

Cutlip, S. M., Center, A. H., & Broom, G. M. (1985). *Effective public relations* (6th ed.). Englewood Cliffs, NJ: Prentice-Hall.

Cutlip, S. M., Center, A. H., & Broom, G. M. (1994). *Effective public relations* (7th ed.). Englewood Cliffs, NJ: Prentice-Hall.

Cutlip, S. M., Center, A. H., & Broom, G. M. (2006). *Effective public relations* (9th ed.). Upper Saddle River, NJ: Pearson/Prentice-Hall.

Day, K. D., Dong, Q., & Robins, C. (2001). Public relation ethics: An overview and discussion of issues for the 21st century. In R. L. Heath (Ed.), *Handbook of public relations* (pp. 403–409). Thousand Oaks, CA: Sage.

Day, D. V., Fleenor, J. W., Atwater, L. E., Sturm, R. E., & Mckee, R. A. (2014). Advance in leaders and leadership development. *Leadership Quarterly, 25*, 63–82.

DeSanto, B., & Moss, D. (2004). Rediscovering what PR managers do: Rethinking measurement of managerial behavior in the public relations context. *Journal of Communication Management, 9*(2), 179–196.

DiStaso, M. W., Stacks, D. W., & Botan, C. H. (2009). State of public relations education in the United States: 2006 report on a national survey of executives and academics. *Public Relations Review, 35*(3), 254–269.

Dozier, D. M., & Broom, G. M. (1995). Evolution of the manager role in public relations practice. *Journal of Public Relations Research, 7*(1), 3–26.

Dozier, D. M., Grunig, L. A., & Grunig, J. E. (1995). *Manager's guide to excellence in public relations and communication management*. Mahwah, NJ: Lawrence Erlbaum Associates.

Dryzek, J. (2009). Democratization as deliberative capacity building. *Comparative Political Studies, 42*(11), 1379–1402.

Eby, L. T., Allen, T. D., Hoffman, B. J., Baranick, L. E., Sauer, J. B., Baldewin, S., et al. (2013). An interdisciplinary meta-analysis of the potential antecedents, correlates, and consequences of protégé perceptions of mentoring. *Psychological Bulletin, 139*, 441–476.

Edwards, L. (2016). The role of public relations in deliberative systems. *Journal of Communication, 66*, 60–81.

Ehling, W. P. (1992). Public relations education and professionalism. In J. E. Grunig (Ed.), *Excellence in Public Relations and Communication Management* (pp. 439–464). Hilldale, NJ: Lawrence Earlbaum Associates.

Elliot, P. (1972). *The sociology of professions*. New York: Herder & Herder.

Falkheimer, J., Heide, M., Nothhaft, H., von Platten, S., Simsonsson, C., & Andersson, R. (2017). Is strategic communication too important to be left to communication professionals? Managers' and coworkers' attitudes toward strategic communication and communication professionals. *Public Relations Review, 43*, 91–101.

Fawkes, J. (2012). Saints and sinners: Competing identities in public relations ethics. *Public Relations Review, 38*, 865–872.

Fawkes, J. (2014). *Public relations ethics and professionalism: The shadow of excellence*. New directions in public relations & communication. London: Routledge.

Fitzpatrick, K. (2002). Evolving standards in public relations: A historical examination of PRSA's codes of ethics. *Journal of Mass Media Ethics, 17*(2), 89–110.

Fitzpatrick, K., & Bronstein, C. (2006). *Ethics in public relations: Responsible advocacy*. Thousand Oaks, CA: Sage.

Forbes, P. S. (1986). Why licensing is an opportunity for public relations. *Public Relations Review, 12*(4), 9–11.

Frandsen, F., & Johansen, W. (2015). The role of communication executives in strategy and strategizing. In D. Holtzhausen & A. Zerfass (Eds.), *The Routledge handbook of strategic communication* (pp. 229–243). New York: Routledge.

Gibson, D. (1987). Public relations education in a time of change: Suggestions for academic relocation and renovation. *Public Relations Quarterly, Fall*, 25–31.

Gilligan, C. (1982). *In a different voice*. Cambridge, MA: Harvard University Press.

Gitter, A. G., & Jaspers, E. (1982). Are PR counselors trusted professionals? *Public Relations Quarterly, 27*(Winter), 38–31.

Global Alliance for Public Relations and Communications Management. (2016). Who we are. Available from https://www.globalalliancepr.org/who-we-are (accessed May 20, 2020).

Golombisky, K. (2015). Renewing the commitments of feminist public relations theory from velvet ghetto to social justice. *Journal of Public Relations Research, 27,* 389–415.

Graen, G. B., & Uhl-Bien, M. (1995). Relationship-based approaches to leadership: Development of leader-member exchange (LMX) theory of leadership over 25 years: Applying a multi-level multi-domain perspective. *Leadership Quarterly, 6*(2), 219–247.

Gregory, A., & Fawkes, J. (2019). A global capability framework: Reframing public relations for a changing world. *Public Relations Review, 45,* 1–13.

Grunig, J. E. (2000). Collectivism, collaboration, and societal corporatism as core professional values in public relations. *Journal of Public Relations Research, 12,* 23–48.

Grunig, J. E. (2006). Furnishing the edifice: Ongoing research on public relations as a strategic management function. *Journal of Public Relations Research, 18*(2), 151–176.

Grunig, J. E., & Hunt, T. (1984). *Managing public relations.* New York: Holt, Rinehart & Winston.

Ha, J. H., & Ferguson, M. A. (2015). Perception discrepancy of public relations functions and conflict among disciplines: South Korean public relations versus marketing professionals. *Journal of Public Relations Research, 27,* 1–21.

Habermas, J. (1996). *Between facts and norms.* Cambridge: Polity Press.

Hackman, M. Z., & Johnson, C. E. (2004). *Leadership: A communication perspective* (4th ed.). Long Grove, IL: Waveland.

Halff, G., & Gregory, A. (2014). Toward an historically informed Asian model fo public relations. *Public Relations Review, 40*(3), 397–407.

Halff, G., & Gregory, A. (2015). What is public relations to society? Toward an economically informed understanding of public relations. *Public Relations Review, 41,* 719–725.

Halff, G., & Gregory, A. (2016). Understanding public relations in the "sharing" economy. *Public Relations Review, 43,* 4–13.

Hallahan, K. (1993). The paradigm struggle and public relations practice. *Public Relations Review, 21,* 123–136.

Hallahan, K. (2013). Community and community building. In R. L. Heath (Ed.), *Encyclopedia of public relations* (2nd ed., pp. 166–169). Thousand Oaks, CA: Sage.

Hallahan, K. (2018). Strategic communication. In R. L. Heath & W. Johansen (Eds.), *International encyclopedia of strategic communication* (pp. 1463–1486). Hoboken, NJ: Wiley-Blackwell.

Hallahan, K., Holtzhausen, D., van Ruler, B., Verčiĉ, D., & Sriramesh, K. (2007). Defining strategic communication. *International Journal of Strategic Communication, 1*(1), 3–35.

Harrison, S. L. (1990). Ethics and moral issues in public relations curricula. *Educator, 45*(3), 32–38.

Heath, R. L. (2006). Onward into more fog: Thoughts on public relations' research directions. *Journal of Public Relations Research, 18,* 93–114.

Heath, R. L., & Bowen, S. A. (2006). The public relations philosophy of John W. Hill: Bricks in the foundation of issues management. *Journal of Public Affairs, 2*(4), 230–246.

Heath, R. L. (2007). Management through advocacy: Reflection rather than domination. In J. E. Grunith, E. L. Toth, & L. A. Grunig (Eds.), *The future of excellence in public relations and communication management.* Mahwah, NJ: Lawrence Erlbaum Associates.

Heath, R. L., Motion, J., & Leitch, S. (2010). Power and public relations: Paradoxes and programmatic thoughts. In R. L. Heath (Ed.), *The SAGE handbook of public relations* (pp. 191–204). Thousand Oaks, CA: Sage.

Heath, R. L., & Palenchar, M. J. (2009). *Strategic issues management: Organizations and public policy challenges* (2nd ed.). Los Angeles, CA: Sage.

Heath, R. L., & Ryan, M. (1989). Public relations' role in defining corporate social responsibility. *Journal of Mass Media Ethics, 4*(1), 21–38.

Heath, R. L., & Waymer, D. (2009). Activist public relations and the paradox of the positive. In R. Heath, E. Toth, & D. Waymer (Eds.), *Rhetorical and critical approaches to public relations II* (pp. 194–215). New York: Routledge.

Hiebert, R. E. (1966). *Courtier to the crowd: The life story of Ivy Lee: Distinguished founder of modern public relations.* Ames, IA: Iowa State University Press.

Hogan, D. B. (1983). The effectiveness of licensing: History, evidence, and recommendations. *Law and Human Behavior, 7*(2–3), 117–138.

Holtzhausen, D. (2012). *Public relations as activism: Postmodern approaches to theory and practice.* New York: Routledge.

Holtzhausen, D., & Zerfass, A. (2015). Strategic communication: Opportunities and challenges of the research area. In D. Holtzhausen & A. Zerfass (Eds.), *The Routledge handbook of strategic communication* (pp. 3–17). New York: Routledge.

Hon, L. C. (1995). Toward a feminist theory in public relations. *Journal of Public Relations Research, 7,* 27–88.

Ihlen, Ø. (2013). Social capital. In R. L. Heath (Ed.), *Encyclopedia of public relations* (2nd ed., pp. 838–839). Thousand Oaks, CA: Sage.

Jacobson, D. J., & Tortorello, N. J. (1992). Seventh annual salary survey. *Public Relations Journal, 48,* 9–21.

Jensen, I. (2001). Public relations and emerging functions of the public sphere: An analytical framework. *Journal of Communication Management, 6*(2), 133–147.

Jeong, J. Y. (2011). Practioners' perceptions of their ethics in Korean global firms. *Public Relations Review, 37*(1), 99–102.

Jin, Y. (2010). Emotional leadership as a key dimension of public relations leadership: National survey of public relations leaders. *Journal of Public Relations Research, 22,* 159–181.

Johansson, C. (2018). Leadership communication. In R. L. Heath & W. Johansen (Eds.), *The international dictionary of strategic communication.* Chichester: John Wiley & Sons.

Johansson, B., & Larsson, L. (2015). The complexity of public relations work: PR managers in the public and private sector in Sweden. *Nordicom Review, 26,* 125–139.

Johannson, C., Miller, V. D., & Hamrin, S. (2014). Conceptualizing communicative leadership—A framework for analyzing and developing leaders' communication competence. *Corporate Communication: An International Journal, 19*(2), 147–165.

Judd, L. R. (1989). Credibility, public relations and social responsibility. *Public Relations Review, 15*(2), 34–40.

Kent, M. L. (2013). Using social media dialogically: Public relations role in reviving democracy. *Public Relations Review, 39*(4), 337–345.

Kent, M. L., & Taylor, M. (1998). Building dialogic relationships through the world wide web. *Public Relations Review, 24*(3), 321–334.

Kent, M. L., & Taylor, M. (2002). Toward a dialogic theory of public relations. *Public Relations Review, 28*(1), 21–37.

Kent, M. L., & Saffer, A. J. (2014). A Delphi study of the future of new technology research in public relations. *Public Relations Review, 40*(3), 568–576.

Khazan, O. (2014). Why are there so many women in public relations: The field is nearly two-thirds female. Is it because of a lack of better options—Or is it, in fact, the best possible option? *The Atlantic,* August 8. Available from http://www.theatlantic.com/business/archive/2014/08/why-are-there-so-many-women-in-pr/375693/ (accessed May 20, 2020).

Kim, E., and Johnson, T. (2009). Sailing through the port: Does PR education prepare students for their profession? 12th annual international public relations research conference, Miami, FL.

Kim, S. Y., & Reber, B. H. (2009). How public relation professionalism influences corporate social responsibility: A survey of practitioners. *Journalism & Mass Communication Quarterly, 86*(1), 157–174.

Kinsky, E. S., Freberg, K., Kim, C., Kushin, M., & Ward, W. (2016). Hootsuite University: Equipping academics and future PR professionals for social media success. *Public Relations Education, 2*(1), 1–18.

Krukeberg, D. (1996). Transnational corporate ethical responsibilities. In H. M. Culbertson & M. Chen (Eds.), *International public relations: A comparative analysis* (pp. 81–92). Mahwah, NJ: Lawrence Erlbaum Associates.

Kruckeberg, D. (1998). The future of PR education: Some recommendations. *Public Relations Review, 24*(2), 235–248.

Kruckeberg, D., & Stark, K. (1998). *Public relations and community: A reconstructed theory*. Westport, CT: Praeger.

Latchaw, J., Allen, C., & Ogden, D. (2009). Public relations professionals as shapers of public information: The role of theory in their education. *Similie, 9*(1), 18–27.

Lee, I. L. (1925). *Publicity: Some of the things it is and is not*. New York, NY: Industries Publishing Co.

Lee, N. M., Sha, B. L., Dozier, D. M., & Sargent, P. (2015). The role of new public relations practitioners as social media experts. *Public Relations Review, 41*, 411–413.

Leitch, S., & Motion, J. (2010). Publics and public relations: Effecting change. In R. L. Heath (Ed.), *Sage handbook of public relations* (pp. 99–110). Thousand Oaks, CA: Sage.

Lesly, P. (1986). Why licensing won't work for public relations. *Public relations review, 12*(4), 3–7.

L, Etang, J. (2004). *Public Relations in Britain: A history of professional practice in the 20th century*. Mahwah, NJ: Lawrence Earlbaum Associates.

L, Etang, J. (2008). *Public relations: Concepts, practice, critique*. London: Sage.

Luo, Y., & Jiang, H. (2014). Effective public relations leadership in organizational change: A study of multinationals in mainland China. *Journal of Public Relations Research, 26*, 134–160.

Luo, Y., Jiang, H., & Kulemeka, O. (2015). Strategic social media management and public relations leadership: Insights from industry leaders. *International Journal of Strategic Communication, 9*(3), 167–196.

Marston, J. (1968). Hallmarks of a profession. *Public Relations Journal, 24*(7), 8–10.

Martinelli, D., & Erzikova, E. (2017). Public relations leadership development cycle: A cross-cultural perspective. *Public Relations Review, 43*, 1062–1072.

Martinson, D. L. (1996). 'Truthfulness' in communication is both a reasonable and achievable goal for public relations practitioners. *Public Relations Quarterly, 41*, 42–45.

McKee, B. K., Nayman, O. B., & Lattimore, D. L. (1975). How PR people see themselves. *Public Relations Journal, 31*(11), 47–52.

McKinney, D. B. (2018). Communication departments. In R. L. Heath & W. Johansen (Eds.), *The International Encyclopedia of Strategic Communication* (pp. 1–5). Chichester: John Wiley & Sons.

Men, L. R. (2014a). Strategic internal communication: Transformational leadership, communication channels, and employee satisfaction. *Management Communication Quarterly, 28*(2), 264–284.

Men, L. R. (2014b). Why leadership matters to internal communication: Liniing transformation leadership, symmetrical communication, and employee outcomes. *Journal of Public Relations Research, 26*(3), 256–279.

Men, L. R., & Stacks, D. (2014). The effects of authentic leadership on strategic internal communication and employee–organization relationships. *Journal of Public Relations Research, 26*, 301–324.

Meng, J., & Berger, B. (2013). An integrated model of excellent leadership in public relations: Dimensions, measurement, and validation. *Journal of Public Relations Research, 25,* 141–167.

Meyer, A. L., & Leonard, A. (2014). Are we there yet? En route to professionalism. *Public Relations Review, 40,* 375–386.

Miller, D., & Dinan, W. (2007). Public relations and the subversion of democracy. In W. Dinan & D. Miller (Eds.), *Thinker, faker, spinner, spy: Corporate public relations and the assault on democracy* (pp. 11–20). London: Pluto Press.

Miller, D. P., & Kernisky, D. A. (1999). Opportunity realized: Undergraduate education within departments of communication. *Public Relations Review, 25*(1), 87–100.

Modella, J. C., Moreno, A., & Navarro, C. (2017). Professionalization of public relations in Latin America: A longitudinal comparative study. *Public Relations Review, 43,* 1084–1093.

Moreno, A., Navarro, C., Tench, R., & Zerfass, A. (2015). Does social media usage matter? An analysis of online practices and digital media perceptions of communication practitioners in Europe. *Public Relations Review, 41*(2), 118–141.

Moreno, A., Tench, R., & Okay, A. (2017). Re-fuelling the talent tank. A quantitative study of key deficiencies, future needs, and life-long learning needs of communication management professionals in Europe. *Communication & Society, 30*(3), 109–127.

Moriarity, S. E. (1994). PR and IMC: The benefits of integration. *Public Relations Quarterly, 3,* 38–44.

Morris, T., & Goldsworthy, S. (2008). *PR—A persuasive industry? Spin, public relations, and the shaping of the modern media.* London: Palgrave Macmillan.

Moss, D., Newman, A., & DeSanto, B. (2005). What do communication managers do? Defining and refining the core elements of management in a public relations/corporate communication context. *Journalism and Mass Communication Quarterly, 82,* 873–890.

Mukherjee, M. (2008). Stalagmite theory in public relations. *India PR Blog.* Cited in J. A. Latchlaw, C. Allen, and D. Ogden (2009). Public relations professionals as shapers of public information: The role of theory in their education. *Studies in Media & Information Literacy Education, 9*(1), 1–15.

Murphy, S. E. (2011). Providing a foundation for leadership development. In S. E. Murphy & R. J. Reichard (Eds.), *Early development and leadership: Building the next generation of leaders* (pp. 3–37). New York: Routledge.

Nath, P., & Bell, M. (2016). A study of the structural integration of the marketing and PR functions in the C-suite. *Journal of Marketing and Communications, 22*(6), 626–652.

Neill, M. (2014). Building buy-in: The need for internal relationships and informal coalitions. *Public Relations Review, 40*(3), 598–605.

Neill, M. S., & Moody, M. (2015). Who is responsible for what? Examining strategic role in social media management. *Public Relations Review, 41,* 109–118.

Nelson, R. A. (1994). The professional dilemma. *PR Update,* Nov., 1.

Newsom, D., Scott, A., & Turk, J. (1992). *This is PR: The realities of public relations* (5th ed.). Belmont, CA: Wadsworth.

Ni, L., & Izzo, D. A. (2018). Dominant coalition. In R. L. Heath & W. Johansen (Eds.), *The international encyclopedia of strategic communication* (pp. 1–7). Chichester: John Wiley & Sons.

Niemann-Struweg, I., & Meintjies, C. (2008). The professionalism debate in South Africa. *Public Relations Review, 34*(3), 224–229.

Nolte, L. (1980). Let's forget licensing. *Public Relations Quarterly, 25*(2), 14.

Northouse, P. G. (2013). *Leadership: Theory and practice* (6th ed.). Thousand Oaks, CA: Sage.

Palea, A. (2014). The public relations professional: Elements of identity. *Professional Communication and Translations Studies, 7*(1–2), 17–22.

Peck, L. A. (2004). Foolproof or foolhardy? Ethical theory in beginning reporting texts. *Journalism & Mass Communication Educator, 58*(Winter), 243–363.

Perkins, S., Phillips, K. W., & Pearce, N. A. (2013). Leader do matter—But when does their gender matter too? KellogInsight from Kellog School of Management, Northwestern University. Available from https://insight.kellogg.northwestern.edu/article/leaders_do_matterbut_when_does_their_gender_matter_too (accessed May 20, 2020).

Pieczka, M. (2000). Objectives and evaluation in public relations work: What do they tell us about expertise and professionalism? *Journal of Public Relations Research, 12*(3), 211–233.

Pieczka, M., & L, Etang, J. (2001). Public relations and the question of professionalism. In R. L. Heath (Ed.), *The handbook of public relations* (pp. 223–235). Thousand Oaks, CA: Sage.

Porter, L. (2010). Communicating for the good of the state: A post-structuralist polemic on persuasion in ethical public relations. *Public Relations Review, 36*, 127–133.

Powell, W. W., & DiMaggio, P. J. (1991). *The new institutionalism in organizational analysis.* Chicago, IL: University of Chicago Press.

PRSA. (2019). PRSA statement on White House Press Secretary role. Available from https://web.archive.org/web/20190729013455/https://www.prsa.org/prsa-statement-on-white-house-press-secretary-role/ (accessed May 20, 2020).

PRSA. (2000). Ethics for an evolving profession. Available from http://www.prsa.org/aboutprsa/ethics/codeenglish/ (accessed May 20, 2020).

Qin, J., Muenjohn, N., & Chhetri, P. (2014). A review of diversity conceptualization: Variety, trends, and a framework. *Human Resources Development Review, 13*(2), 133–157.

Ravazzani, S. (2018). Diversity management. In R. L. Heath & W. Johansen (Eds.), *The international encyclopedia of strategic communication* (pp. 1–13). Chichester: John Wiley & Sons.

Rentner, T. L., & Bissland, J. H. (1990). Job satisfaction and its correlates among public relations workers. *Journalism & Mass Communication Quarterly, 67*(4), 950–955.

Rim, H., & Kim, S. (2018). Dimensions of corporate social responsibility (CSR) skepticism and their impacts on public evaluations toward CSR. *Journal of Public Relations Research, 28*(5–6), 248–267.

Rogers, K., and Baker, P. (2019). Sarah Huckabee Sanders leaving White House at the end of the month. *The New York Times*, June 13. Available from https://www.nytimes.com/2019/06/13/us/politics/sarah-sanders-leaving-white-house.html (accessed May 20, 2020).

Röttger, U., & Preusse, J. (2013). External consulting in strategic communication: Functions and roles within systems theory. *International Journal of Strategic Communication, 7*, 99–117.

Ryan, M., & Martinson, D. L. (1988). Journalists and public relations practitioners: Why the antagonism? *Journalism Quarterly, 62*, 131–140.

Sallot, L. M., Cameron, G. T., & Weaver-Lariscy, R. A. (1997). Professional standards in public relations: A survey of educators. *Public Relations Review, 23*(3), 197–216.

Sallot, L. M., Cameron, G. T., & Weaver-Lariscy, R. A. (1998). Pluralistic ignorance and professional standards: Underestimating professionalism of our peers in public relations. *Public Relations Review, 24*(1), 1–19.

Selk, A. (2018). The owner of the Red Hen explains why she asked Sarah Huckabee Sanders to leave. *The Washington Post*, June 25. Available from https://www.washingtonpost.com/news/local/wp/2018/06/23/why-a-small-town-restaurant-owner-asked-sarah-huckabee-sanders-to-leave-and-would-do-it-again/ (accessed May 20, 2020).

Sha, B. L. (2011). 2010 practice analysis: Professional competencies and work categories in public relations today. *Public Relations Review, 27*, 187–196.

Sha, B. L., & Ford, R. L. (2007). Redefining "requisite variety": The challenge of multiple diversities for the future of public relations excellence. In E. L. Toth (Ed.), *The future of excellence in public relations and communication management: Challenges for the next generation* (pp. 381–398). Mahwah, NJ: Lawrence Erlbaum Associates.

Shamir, J., Reed, B. S., & Connell, S. (1990). Individual differences in ethical values of public relations practitioners. *Journalism Quarterly, 67*(4), 956–964.

Smircich, L., & Morgan, G. (1982). Leadership: The management of meaning. *Journal of Applied Behavioral Science, 18*(3), 257–273.

Sommerfeldt, E. J. (2013). The activity of social capital: Public relations in the public sphere, civil society, and democracy. *Public Relations Review, 39*(4), 280–289.

Sriramesh, K. (2009). A theoretical framework for global public relations research and practice. In K. Sriramesh & D. Verčič (Eds.), *The global public relations handbook: Theory, research, and practice* (2nd ed., pp. 42–63). Florence, KY: Routledge.

Stacks, D. W., Botan, C., & Turk, J. V. (1999). Perceptions of public relations education. *Public Relations Review, 25*, 9–28.

Steyn, B. (2018). Strategist role (public relations/communication). In R. L. Heath & W. Johansen (Eds.), *The international encyclopedia of strategic communication* (pp. 1–18). Chichester: John Wiley & Sons.

Steyn, B., & Niemann, L. (2014). Strategic role of public relations in enterprise strategy, governance and sustainability—A normative framework. *Public Relations Review, 40*, 171–183.

Stoker, K., & Stoker, M. (2012). The paradox of public interest: How serving individual superior interests fulfill public relations' obligation to the public interest. *Journal of Mass Media Ethics, 27*, 31–45.

Tam, S. Y., Dozier, D. M., Lauzen, M. M., & Real, M. R. (1995). The impact of superior–subordinate gender on the career advancement of public relations practitioners. *Journal of Public Relations Research, 7*(4), 259–272.

Taylor, M., Kent, M. L., & White, W. J. (2001). How activists organizations are using the internet to build relationships. *Public Relations Review, 27*(3), 263–284.

Tench, R., & Moreno, A. (2015). Mapping communication competencies for European practitioners: ECOPSI an EU study. *Journal of Communication Management, 19*(1), 39–61.

Todd, V. (2009). PRSSA faculty and professional advisors "perceptions of public relations curriculum, assessment of students" learning, and faculty performance. *Journalism and Mass Communication Educator*, Spring, 71–90.

Toledano, M., & Maplesden, A. (2016). Facilitating community networks: Public relations skills and non-professional organizers. *Public Relations Review, 42*, 713–722.

Tompkins, P. K. (1984). The functions of human communication in organization. In C. C. Arnold & J. W. Bowers (Eds.), *Handbook of rhetorical and communication theory* (pp. 659–719). Boston, MA: Allyn & Bacon.

Toth, E. L. (2006). On the challenge of practice informed by theory. *Journal of Communication Management, 10*(1), 110–111.

Toth, E. L., & Cline, C. G. (1990). *Beyond the velvet ghetto*. San Francisco, CA: IABC Research Foundation.

Toth, E. L., & Grunig, L. A. (1993). The missing story of women in public relations. *Journal of Public Relations Research, 5*, 153–175.

Toth, E. L., Serini, S. A., Wright, D. K., & Emig, A. G. (1998). Trends in public relations roles: 1990–1995. *Public Relations Review, 24*(2), 145–163.

Turk, J. V. (1989). Management skills need to be taught in public relations. *Public Relations Review, 15*(1), 38–52.

U.S. Department of Labor. (2018). Women in the labor force: A databook. BLS Reports: Bureau of Labor Statistics. Available from https://www.bls.gov/opub/reports/womens-databook/2018/home.htm (accessed May 20, 2020).

van Ruler, A. (2003). Four basic communication strategies, beyond the borders of traditional public relations practice. *All Academic Research*. Available from http://citation.allacademic.com/meta/p_mla_apa_research_citation/1/1/2/0/4/p112043_index.html (accessed May 20, 2020).

Valin, J., Gregory, A., & Likely, F. (2014). The Global Alliance for Public Relations and Communication Management: Origins, influence, issues, and prospects. *Public Relations Review, 40*, 639–653.

Vardeman-Winter, J., & Crowe, S. (2018). Empowerment. In R. L. Heath & W. Johansen (Eds.), *The international encyclopedia of strategic communication* (pp. 1–10). Chichester: John Wiley & Sons.

Vardeman-Winter, J., Tildall, N., & Jiang, H. (2013). Toward intersectional theory of public relations. In R. L. Heath (Ed.), *Handbook of public relations* (2nd ed., pp. 223–235). Thousand Oaks, CA: Sage.

Vieira, E. T., & Grantham, S. (2014). Defining public relations roles in the U.S.A. using cluster analysis. *Public Relations Review, 40*, 60–68.

Vieira, E. T., & Grantham, S. (2015). Determining factors leading to strategic management practitioner roles. *Public Relations Review, 41*, 544–550.

Weaver-Lariscy, R. A., Sallot, L., & Cameron, G. T. (1996). Justice and gender: An instrumental and symbolic explication. *Journal of Public Relations Research, 8*, 107–121.

White, J. (2018). Decision making. In R. L. Heath & W. Johansen (Eds.), *The international encyclopedia of strategic communication* (pp. 1–11). Chichester: John Wiley & Sons.

Wilcox, D. L., Ault, P. H., & Agee, W. K. (1989). *Public relations: Strategies and tactics* (2nd ed.). New York: Harper and Row.

Wilcox, D. L., & Cameron, G. T. (2011). *Public relations: Strategies and tactics* (10th ed.). New York: Pearson.

Wilkie, K. (2017). White House's Sarah Huckabee Sanders says "Pocahontas" is not a racial slur. *CNBC*, November 27. Available from https://www.cnbc.com/2017/11/27/white-houses-sarah-huckabee-sanders-says-pocahontas-is-not-a-slur.html (accessed May 20, 2020).

Wolf, K. (2018). Power struggles: A sociological approach to activist communication. *Public Relations Review, 44*(2), 308–316.

Women in PR. (2017). Women in PR USA releases global gender pay gap annual survey results. Available from https://womeninpr.com/women-in-pr-usa-releases-global-gender-pay-gap-annual-survey-results/ (accessed May 20, 2020).

Wright, D. (1978). Professionalism and the public relations counselor: An empirical analysis. *Public Relations Quarterly, 23*, 26–29.

Wright, D. (1981). Accreditation's effect on professionalism. *Public Relations Review, 7*(1), 48–61.

Wright, D. K. (2004). Examining the existence of professional prejudice and discrimination against public relations. Paper presented at the Association for Education in Journalism and Mass Communication, Toronto, Canada.

Wright, D. K., & Hinson, M. D. (2014). An updated examination of social and emerging media use in public relations practice: A longitudinal analysis between 2006 and 2014. *Public Relations Journal, 8*(2), 1–35.

Wright, D. K., & Turk, J. V. (2007). Public relations knowledge and professionalism: Challenges to educators and practitioners. In E. L. Toth (Ed.), *The future of excellence in public relations and communication management: Challenges for the next generation* (pp. 571–588). Mahwah, NJ: Lawrence Erlbaum Associates.

Wylie, F. (1994). Commentary: Public relations is not yet a profession. *Public Relations Review, 20*(1), 1–3.

Yang, A., & Taylor, M. (2014). A global perspective on public relations professionalism: Mapping the structure of public relations associations' international networks. *Journalism & Mass Communications Quarterly, 91*(3), 508–529.

Yaxley, H. M. L. (2012). Exploring the origins of careers in public relations. *Public Relations Review, 38*, 399–407.

13

Current Trends and Issues in Building Public Relations Theories

Introduction

Public relations has been evolving in its practice and theory, just like any other academic discipline. Since first defined in the early twentieth century, it has suffered from a crisis of identity, uncertain about its intellectual origins and commitments, how to find the balance between theory and practice, and how to define its relationship to disciplines such as communication, business, sociology, and psychology (Zerfass, Verĉiĉ, Nothhaft, & Werder, 2018). Public relations scholars have long been concerned about its theoretical underpinnings. Ferguson (1984) raised a perennial concern over the state of public relations theory and suggested that the field had progressed little in the way of systematic theory building, based on a survey of articles published in *Public Relations Review*. Morton and Lin (1995) conducted a similar survey of the literature and found that the majority of articles focused on professional issues, to the detriment of theory building. On a brighter note, Sallot, Lyon, Acosta-Aluru, and Jones (2003) showed that topics which identified theory building as a major purpose had increased from 4% to nearly 20% over the two decades between the publication of Ferguson's study and their own. More recently, Cernicova (2016) has characterized the multichannel, multidisciplinary, and "ever-evolving" nature of public relations in the early twenty-first century as involving "(re)interpretation, (re)invention of the profession, practices, instruments and uses" (p. 6). On this view, theory has assumed a growing role in public relations research since the beginning of the twenty-first century.

One of the most robust areas of debate among public relations theorists is how the profession and practice best serve the interests of organizations and of society. While most scholars concur that establishing relationships between organizations and publics is a central goal, the nature of what constitutes authentic dialogue on a co-equal footing and what constitutes mutual interest is hotly debated. On one hand, researchers who subscribe to a normative view informed by excellence theory have contended that it is most efficient and rational that organizations enact communications that benefit both the public *and* themselves by employing public relations strategies and tactics as catalysts tipping the balance toward win–win situations (Grunig, 2006; Grunig, Grunig, & Dozier, 2002). At the opposite end of the ideological spectrum, scholars informed by critical theory have examined the role of public relations as a means of perpetuating hegemonic control of dominant coalitions composed of organizations and the political infrastructure, to the advantage of the powerful at the expense of the powerless and disadvantaged (Dutta, 2006; Leitch & Neilson, 2001; L'Etang & Pieczka, 2006). The goal of such critical and rhetorical analysis is to improve public relations practice in order to bring all voices out and make society more just, democratic, and fully functioning (Hallahan, 2018; McKie & Heath, 2016).

Public Relations Theory: Capabilities and Competencies, First Edition. Jae-Hwa Shin and Robert L. Heath.
© 2021 John Wiley & Sons, Inc. Published 2021 by John Wiley & Sons, Inc.

Scholars have called for a sociological approach to building public relations theory via qualitative research (Hallahan, 2018). L'Etang (2014), for example, is highly critical of public relations methodology that is rooted in a functionalist approach, arguing instead for historical research into public relations within a societal context. Everett and Johnston (2012) similarly contended that researchers should pay more attention to an ethnographic approach to public relations, defined as building "descriptive inferences about the influence of an organization's culture on its social ecology" (p. 522). In contrast to the functionalist or managerial perspective that has dominated research to date, this societal view is more encompassing and based on the role of public relations as it fits within society in general. Wehmeier (2009) noted that excellence theory has been challenged in recent years by approaches that range from rhetorical theory (Benoit, 1997; Heath, 2001) to critical theory, based on the work of sociologist such as Jürgen Habermas, Pierre Bourdieu, and Michel Foucault (Burkart, 2004; Curtain and Gaither, 2005; Holtzhausen, 2002; Roper, 2005). Each of these theories seeks to redefine the role of the public in the practice of public relations, whether through an analysis of stakeholder perceptions or by assessing the significance of power differences, stakeholder activism, and corporate social responsibility (CSR).

Like other academic disciplines, public relations is in the process of moving from a modernist approach, marked by emphasis on quantification and scientific management of communication, to a global perspective that emphasizes the democratic participation of a wide range of stakeholders around the globe, who are empowered with tools and channels designed to foster dialogue and communicative action (Wehmeier, 2009). Public relations practice is a process that Gregory and Halff (2017) have described as "deliberative disintermediation" (p. 7), shifting from actively managing communication with the goal of engineering consent to serving as and for communication intermediaries or facilitators. Underlying this perspective is the constitutive role of communication, which privileges context:

> Organizations exist only in so far as their members create them through discourse. This is not to claim that organizations are "nothing but" discourse, but rather that discourse is the principle [sic] means by which organization members create a coherent social reality that frames their sense of who they are. *(Mumby & Clair, 1997, p. 181)*

A variety of interdisciplinary strands of thought, including economic and social changes—notably, the impact of globalization and technology—have been the driving forces behind this shift in orientation. This chapter traces key recent themes, emerging interests, and areas of development. Crucially, the impact of new media and technologies and the diminished economic, social, and political power of traditional media have changed the practice and theoretical orientation of public relations, as have reconceptualizations of political, cultural, social, and economic boundaries.

Questions to Frame the Discussion of Current Trends and Issues

- What are some of the most significant topics of current interest in public relations practice, theory, and education?
- How can different theoretical approaches to framing public relations (e.g., excellence theory, contingency theory, rhetorical theory, critical theory, etc.) explain the evolution of public relations practice?
- What are some likely future directions of public relations practice, theory, and education, based on your observations?

- How have new media and technologies influenced public relations theory and practice?
- How does the dimension of culture play a role in public relations practice currently? Do you think public relations theory and practice will vary across different cultural settings?
- Do you think that theoretical exploration is useful for public relations students in preparing for their future careers?

Key Themes

- Diverse public relations theoretical frames seek to explain public relations practice from different angles. As a body, they supplement one another to fill lacunae through a process of critical examination.
- Public relations theories have emerged and changed over time, following the evolving nature of public relations practice (e.g., new media engagement in different cultural settings).
- It is an ongoing endeavor to build more solid and better public relations theories in order to guide professionals, researchers, and students in their practice, research, and education.

Case Study: It's Never OK—The Hard and Fast Limits of Cultural Appropriation

On April 20, 2016, Snapchat introduced a Bob Marley filter to celebrate "Weed Day." Notwithstanding the criticism of reducing the reggae icon's achievements to a marijuana-smoking meme, the company apparently failed to recognize how the filter was in essence encouraging participants to engage in a form of digital blackface. Blackface, originating with the minstrel shows of the 1840s, involved a generally white musician darkening his or her skin for a performance, and remained in vogue through the early 1930s. Most notably, white performer Al Jolson played a black character in the early talkie picture, *The Jazz Singer* (1927). Following World War II, blackface gradually fell out of favor, and by the 1970s it was condemned generally as a racist display. When confronted with messages that pointed out its rather obvious blunder, Snapchat doubled down on its support the filter: "The lens we launched today was created in partnership with the Bob Marley Estate, and gives people a new way to share their appreciation for Bob Marley and his music." To give added emphasis to their intent, they added: "Millions of Snapchatters have enjoyed Bob Marley's music, and we respect his life and achievements" (Bradley, 2016).

It would be easy to chalk up Snapchat's decision as a momentary indiscretion and expect that the young social media company known for pushing the envelope of good taste would learn its lesson. But a few months later, Snapchat introduced a "yellowface" lens that caricatured Asian features with slanted eyes and large buckteeth. Again, its response to criticism was tone-deaf: "This anime-inspired lens has already expired and won't be put back into circulation." Many were quick to point out that anime characters generally have radically different features than those found in this filter, which bore closer resemblance to propaganda posters issued when the United States was at war with Japan. Instead of acknowledging its mistake, the company argued that "Lenses are meant to be playful and never to offend" (Meyer, 2016).

From a public relations point of view, Snapchat could hardly have made more missteps. First, it failed to acknowledge products that were racially insensitive. Rather than engaging in dialogue with its stakeholders, it sidestepped the issue with diversion messages about how much it appreciated achievement or how its audience misunderstood its intent. Second, it repeated its mistake in a second case. Third, it never issued a *mea culpa* for either incident, much less offered authentic expressions of remorse. Finally, it missed the opportunity to bolster its reputation by issuing or reiterating its commitment to racial and global diversity. The company could have announced initiatives to ensure hiring across broad demographic ranges. Presented with a golden opportunity to engage with audiences, capitalize on a teachable moment, and build a reservoir of goodwill, Snapchat instead insulted its public with disingenuous messages followed by silence. One only wonders when the next such incident will take place.

The example presented by Snapchat represents one of the pitfalls of embracing multicultural and global themes in promotional campaigns without careful consideration of all their implications and ramifications. The creators of the Bob Marley meme apparently did not consider the possibility of unintended messages, such as recalling the painful history of blackface or appropriating reggae culture in a flippant manner. Although it was not nearly as blatantly racist and offensive as other memes that have circulated recently, such as "El Negro de WhatsApp," the range of connotations suggested by the "Weed Day" filter is problematic (Matamoros-Fernández, 2020). While edgy humor can be interpreted as good fun by some audience members, disseminating messages connected with cultural identity can easily lead down the path of becoming offensive to others. In promoting a form of digital blackface, followed by one of yellowface, Snapchat failed to recognize the power of Mumby and Clair's (1997) contention that organizations create and frame their identity through dialogue with stakeholders. While the company may have reached a certain demographic group, the Bob Marley campaign risked alienating members of the global audience and further truncating the potential for encouraging co-equal and democratic participation of multiple stakeholders. Most damning of all, Snapchat seemed tone deaf to the responses of its constituents and repeated its misstep.

Meta-Analyses of Theory Development

An ongoing problem facing theory development in public relations is the lack of basic agreement about the definition of the field itself, its goals, and its orientation to society (Russell & Lamme, 2016). Historically, public relations has been synonymous with propaganda, press agentry, and publicity. More recently, the attempt has been made to rebrand it under the rubric of "strategic communications" (Hallahan, Holtzhausen, Van Ruler, Verčič, & Sriramesh, 2007; Nothhaft, Werder, Verĉiĉ, & Zerfass, 2018; Werder, Nothhaft, Verĉiĉ, & Zerfass, 2018). The challenge has been to distance public relations from "managerial abstractions," or at least balance the organizational orientation with the interests of publics in order to allow stakeholders to exercise agency—especially the input of multiple factions (Brown, 2015, p. 3; Edwards, 2012; Heath, Coombs, Edwards, Palenchar, & McKie, 2015a, 2015b; Zerfass et al., 2018). As Heath et al. (2015b) questioned, is public relations "really about organizational communication" or is the field transitioning from a "corporate centric perspective to a more fully functioning society perspective" (pp. 708, 711)? Their answer was the latter, insofar as the "epistemological, methodological, and axiological battle lines are blurring" (Heath et al., 2015b, p. 711), and public relations scholars are embracing the diverse perspectives and theoretical sophistication that have been transforming other social science fields.

Kim, Choi, Reber, and Kim (2014) analyzed trends in public relations scholarship as reflected in the titles of articles published in *Public Relations Review* between 1975 and 2011 and the *Journal of*

Public Relations Research between 1989 and 2011. They used semantic network analysis to identify "paired associations based on shared meanings" and determine trends based on distinctive keywords (p. 117). In the 1970s and 1980s, they found, "research, role, evaluation, theory, campaign and value" were predominant keywords. In the 1990s, "crisis, education, ethics, issue, strategy, culture and news" were the most common. In the 2000s, "crisis, effect, analysis, strategy, study, relations, organization, media, and case" emerged, together with new terms such as "website," "social media," "blog," and "Internet" (p. 117). In addition, they noted a marked increase in the number of articles on public relations in countries apart from the United States during the 1990s and 2000s. Globalization, an emphasis on online communications, and a focus on crisis and strategy emerged as predominant trends in public relations research. Heath et al., 2015b suggested that the historic focus on public relations as a management function had become conflated with public relations in corporations, and that "public relations in agency, nonprofit or activist settings" had been neglected. Pasadeos, Berger, and Renfro (2010) confirmed these findings and echoed the same three emerging areas: new technology, particularly social media; crisis communication; and international or global public relations. Reaching agreement about operationalized definitions of public relations and the issue of professionalism remains an ongoing concern among scholars today (Hallahan, 2018).

There is a general agreement that in the last two decades excellence theory, as pioneered by James E. Grunig, has dominated the field and has been used as a theoretical framework for researchers with a wide range of orientations (Kim et al., 2014; Pasadeos et al., 2010; Sallot et al., 2003). In tandem with this approach, while the situational theory of publics has cast a long shadow over public relations theory for the past three decades, the organization–public relationship (OPR) has been an area of ongoing concern, as discussed in Chapters 3, 10, and 11. Huang and Zhang (2013) reviewed recent literature, noting criticism of OPR as "being informed more by intuition than meticulous conceptualization and rigorous methodology" (p. 85). They reviewed major public relations journals, using keyword searches related to OPR, and identified two predominant clusters. First, a group of OPR studies based on relationship measurement scales developed by Hon and Grunig (1999) saw OPR as "a dependent variable or as a relationship characteristic that mediates various effects of public relations practice" (Huang & Zhang, 2013, p. 86). Second, a cluster of articles based on the proposition of Bruning and Ledingham (1999) "define OPR from the perspective of the public's attitudes toward an organization" and "treat OPR as an independent variable and to explore its effects on the public's attitudes, evaluations, and behaviors" (Huang & Zhang, 2013, p. 86). Further, a growing number of OPR studies were found centered on international contexts, particularly China, Taiwan, and South Korea. The managerial or business-centric approach to public relations has had profound implications for the field.

Public Relations as Strategic Communication

Strategic communication has recently gained attention as a distinct discipline, but one fiercely protective of its interdisciplinary roots and orientation (Hallahan et al., 2007; Nothhaft et al., 2018; van Ruler, 2018). It remains a contested concept, but it has been defined from an organizational perspective as "coordinated actions, messages, images, and other forms of signaling or engagement intended to inform, influence, or persuade selected audiences in support of national objectives" (Paul, 2011, p. 3). The Public Relations Society of America (PRSA) defines public relations as "strategic communication process that builds mutually beneficial relationships between organizations and their publics" (Cernicova, 2016, p. 5). Scholars have echoed this definition, further describing strategic communications as "purposeful use of communication by an organization to fulfill its mission," which implies that it is "a means of advancing the goals of an organization at the expense of the needs of stakeholder and publics except as they pertain to shaping their behavior in ways that help achieve organizational goals" (Hallahan et al., 2007, pp. 3–4), "the major intended and emergent initiatives taken by general managers on behalf of owners, involving utilization of resources to exchange the performance of firms in their external environments" (Nag, Hambrick, & Chen, 2007, p. 942), or "a set of managerial decisions and actions of an organization that can be used to facilitate competitive advantage and long-run superior performance over other organizations" (Kong, 2008, p. 283). There is little room in such definitions for the interests and perspectives of publics and stakeholders.

Strategic communication can serve a variety of goals and audiences. Volk and Zerfass (2018) contended that it should remain focused on the goal of bringing stakeholders into alignment, whether they were internal or external. Holtzhausen and Zerfass (2015) argued that it should further democratic participation by inviting a wide range of stakeholders—"the ultimate aim of strategic communication is to maintain a healthy reputation for the communication entity in the public sphere" (p. 5).

The concept associated with strategic communication can be shorthand for "communication for any actor to serve the interests of any constituency," as opposed to a specific theoretical perspective with specific research objects and goals (Zerfass et al., 2018, p. 488). It is at its core an interdisciplinary approach that involves many actors at many levels (Werder et al., 2018). As a general principle, it is a process characterized by complexity and importance, one that requires expert knowledge, intelligence, and skill (Zerfass et al., 2018). Zerfass et al. (2018) traced four strains of meaning. First, strategic communication is used interchangeably with integrated communication, or a combination of strategies and tactics from disciplines such as marketing, public relations, and political communication (Heath & Johansen, 2018). Second, strategic communication is conceived as a decisional and goal-oriented activity, rather than a secondary, supportive one (Steyn, 2003). Third, strategic communication is used in a national context as a form of deterrence—a kind of "information warfare," in place of actual weapons (Graham, 2017). Finally, "strategic communication" is used as an alternative name for "public relations," in part to circumvent the negative associations linked to the historical definition of the latter as centering on media relations and persuasion (Heath, 2010). Translating the term "public relations" into many other languages changes its meaning and sometimes brings unintended connotations—for example, the German translation "Öffenlichkeitsarbeit" can variously mean work with the public, for the public, or in public view, depending on the context (Zerfass et al., 2018, p. 490).

The movement toward strategic communication has followed on the heels of the revolution in communication technology. Specifically, social media has necessitated a more integrated approach based on being more strategic than tactical (Plowman & Wilson, 2018). According to the White House (2010), strategic communication is the "synchronization of words and deeds and how they will be perceived by selected audiences, as well as (b) programs and activities deliberately aimed at communicating and engaging with intended audiences" (p. 2). However, professionals engaging in strategic communication and organizational decision makers cannot completely control the message, nor are they the only ones who set the terms of the discussion. Communication and interaction are multivocal and complex, and "all kinds of actors shape the organization through his or her strategic communication role in the organization" (Aggerholm & Thomsen, 2015, p. 175), embracing the "complexity and interconnectedness of the relationships between organizations and stakeholders" (O'Connor & Shumate, 2018). This echoes Heath, Waymer, and Palenchar's (2013) description of organization–stakeholder relationships as "complex, multidimensional, and multilayered," and calls for robust theories to fully account for them (p. 426).

Forecasting Trends in the Practice of Public Relations

In the early 2010s, the PRSA provided forecast trends for the field of public relations on the forum PRsay, and predicted that digital platforms would become increasingly important and that public relations professionals would play a key role in helping decision makers understand how to use them. It foresaw the convergence of public relations, marketing, and information technology, message integration across channels, the blurring of media channels, and the rise of so-called "brand journalism." It also predicted that the increased pace of globalization would present challenges to public relations professionals. Later, the USC Annenberg Center for Public Relations issued "The Holmes Report 2017 Global Communication Study" to assess the most pertinent issues facing the field. A survey of PRSA members identified the most important trends as digital storytelling (88%), social listening (82%), social purpose (71%), big data (70%), behavioral research (65%), artificial intelligence (43%), fake news (36%), and virtual reality (35%). While "fake news" was thus seen as relatively unimportant, 60% of respondents agreed that the balance between the amounts of revenue brought in by public relations firms from earned media versus paid or branded content would only increase. Similarly, about half of those surveyed believed that the public would increasingly not distinguish between paid and earned media.

Vujnovic and Krukeberg (2018) proposed that among the major challenges facing the practice of public relations was the unequal distribution of resources as a byproduct of the increase in global capitalism and acceleration of technology. They noted that "considerable forces for de-globalization have been unleashed," citing examples such as "Brexit, nation-states' attempts to relieve the pressure of massive immigration, and widespread recognition of the economic challenges and disparities that are being blamed on globalization" (p. 1). Public relations practitioners are increasingly faced with political challenges to globalization that include coverage of isolationist and nationalist rhetoric, together with xenophobia, the spread of misleading information, and even open expressions of hate speech endorsed by political leaders in societies that were previously noted for their openness and support of egalitarian and democratic principles.

The Identity and Image of Public Relations

As suggested throughout this and other chapters, public relations has had an ongoing identity and reputational crisis since it first emerged as a profession and a discipline in the early twentieth century. While not the most significant frontier of research, issues of identity, image, and reputation are part of the ongoing theoretical development of the field. Many scholars have noted the irony that a profession devoted to presenting a positive image of its clients has such difficulty maintaining one for itself (Brody, 1992; Henderson, 1998; Jo, 2003; Spicer, 1993). Much of the bias is territorial insofar as it originates in a professional setting. For example, Kopenhaver (1985) found that journalists believed that the profession of public relations was inferior to their own. Spicer (1993) found that 83% of print journalists surveyed connected the public relations profession with negative values such as lack of ethics, lack of trust, and deceptiveness. Jo (2003) concurred that negative values were attached to the term "public relations."

The media portrayal of individual public relations practitioners and of the field as a whole is marked by "consistent negative themes" (White & Park, 2010, p. 319). Recurrent stereotypes include public relations as spin, damage control, engaging in trivial activities, manipulation, propaganda, obfuscation, deceptive, lying, and institutional advocacy at the expense of the public interest. Henderson (1998), for example, found that the media portrayal of public relations was negative 85% of the time, and that only 5% of occasions were aligned with definitions offered by the PRSA. These themes, White and Park (2010) argued, are repeated so often in the media that they become "stock frames" that drown out more balanced assessments. Still, White and Park (2010) found that the use of negative terminology in the media did not necessarily correlate with public perceptions in general. Their survey found that, in general, "respondents regard public relations as an important activity that benefits society by providing information and that it moves an organization forward" (p. 323). The respondents disagreed with statements such as "public relations is a non-substantive activity" and "public relations is an organization's attempt to hide or disguise something" (p. 321). This suggests that the public's assessment or judgment of value of the field does not necessarily correspond to the media portrayal. Halff and Gregory (2015) suggested that public relations research may contribute to the negative evaluation of the field, observing that more studies are devoted to the harm caused by the profession than to its benefits. Even if not openly hostile to the advancement of a co-creational model—what Heath (2006) called a "fully functioning society"—public relations often positions itself as, at best, a useless appendage.

Bowen (2009) concluded, "public relations has been unsuccessful in demonstrating its worth" (p. 403), citing Stacks, Botan, and Turk (1999)'s survey showing that 85% of public relations practitioners and educators disagreed or strongly disagreed with the statement, "the general public understands what public relations is" (p. 27). Professionals, educations, and students perpetuate and reinforce stereotypes and misconceptions and are thus "undermining their own credibility and the future credibility of the field" (Bowen, 2009, p. 409). Public relations as a field is thus "self-constraining" and "self-limiting" (p. 409). Demonstrating its value has become a major strain of emerging research. Bowen (2009) further argued that the positive functions of public relations—including "issues management, public affairs, acting a liaison in internal relations, community relations and corporate social responsibility, acting as an ethical conscience, financial relations, activist and advocacy or NGO communication, coalition building, relationship management, and policy analysis"—are overshadowed by media portrayals and even by a self-deprecating attitude among professionals, educators, and practitioners (p. 409).

The image of public relations professionals on film has likewise been predominantly negative. Miller (1999) examined 67 movies and 51 works of fiction produced across several decades, noting that primarily negative themes emerged, such as "shallow but loveable," willing to "lie and cheat both for personal career advancement and on behalf of their clients," and "guided by whatever they think will satisfy their employer" (pp. 8–10). However, Miller also found positive values, such as confidence, skill, personableness, and even trust. While public relations practitioners were frequently presented in a positive light on network news, the occupation itself, seen in a cultural context, was associated with negative values that could border on criminality (Keenan, 1996).

However, the image of public relations seems to be improving, with many arguing for the positive value of the profession in a broad social sense (Spicer, 2000). For example, the portrayal of public relations practitioners on film became gradually more positive over the years between 1996 and 2008 (Ames, 2010). Ames (2010) concluded that "the image of the practitioner has improved, with negative stereotypes decreasing in kind, frequency, and virulence," and that "PR works is now considered more valuable and its processes are better understood" (pp. 168, 169).

Critique of the profession has come from scholars outside of the field. Miller and Dinan (2007) offered a damning assessment:

Public relations was created to thwart and subvert democratic decision making. Modern public relations was founded or this purpose and continues to be at the cutting edge of campaigns to ensure that liberal democratic societies do not respond to the will of the people and that vested interests prevail. (p. 11)

Snow (2003) and Stauber and Rampton (1995) are among those who have leveled the antidemocratic charge. Such a perspective has resonance with those who believe that corporate hegemony raises an ideological barrier to the free exercise of democracy. Logan (2014) traced the historical connection between public relations and the assault on democracy to the Industrial Revolution in the late nineteenth century, and particularly the rise of corporations in the early twentieth. In its infancy, public relations concentrated on the production and dissemination of messages that mirrored the corporate voice, and was thus ideologically suspect. As faith in corporations as a "necessary, natural and benevolent" part of society waned, so too did trust in the motive behind the public relations profession (p. 661).

New Media and Technology as a Force for Change

The advent of new technologies and the increasing global orientation of the field are two evolving factors and crucial areas of research and theory building addressed in this chapter. Technology has changed the landscape of public relations practice and called for a necessary reexamination of theories (Kent & Taylor, 2002; Macnamara, 2010; Wright and Hinson, 2015; Tusinski, 2017). The Internet and social media are comparatively recent phenomena, the former dating to 1991 and the latter to the mid-2000s. Not surprisingly, Ye and Ki (2012) found that while Internet usage constituted the subject matter of about 30% of the articles in 28 public relations and communication journals between 1992 and 1999, 44.3% of those claimed to use a theoretical framework but no theory predominated, with only 7.8% using dialogic theory and 7% using excellence theory. Duhé (2015) similarly found that only 14% of articles on new media published between 1981 and 2014 could be considered as having a theoretical orientation. She pointed to a "notable lack of pickup and continuing investigation" of the insights in the seminal research conducted by Kent and Taylor (1998) and Kent, Taylor, and White (2002). Ye and Ki (2012) found that scholarship between 1992—a year after the Internet first appeared—and 2009—coinciding with the rise of social media—tended to focus on quantitative analysis at the expense of sophisticated theoretical frameworks. Morton and Lin (1995) added that public relations research was characterized by "a steady increase in articles using quantitative methods" (p. 338). With the dialogic features of the Internet and social media, Ye and Ki (2012) suggested that "greater attention in public relations scholarship should be paid to audiences and stakeholders who are not only recipients of organizations' communication but active communicators themselves" (p. 426).

The rise of the digital era has wrought fundamental changes in the way organizations reach audiences, with "visuality and screen culture [becoming] the dominant coalition of persuasion" (Brown, 2015, p. 105). According to Kent (2014), there was an increase in interest in technology in the decade between 2004 and 2014; by the early 2010s, it had emerged as one of the top three topics in articles submitted to *Public Relations Review* (p. 1). However, most analyses of social media have focused on relatively narrow concerns, and little in the way of a general or synthetic theory of the impact of technology has emerged. Scholars have had something of an obsession with particular platforms and channels, such as Twitter and Facebook, as opposed to "public relations, communication, and stakeholder/public" (Kent, 2014, p. 1). Kent argued that technology such as social media has not so much revolutionized the practice and study of public relations as added a new (albeit powerful) arsenal of tools to the age-old issue of communication between organizations and publics. The focus, he contended, should be on engaging the broad range of public relations theory and practice, as well as addressing "real world problems and meet the needs of stakeholder and publics" (p. 1). An early believer in the promise of technology to transform how information was is disseminated and how public relations was practiced, Kent (2013) also noted that "the Internet has not lived up to its hype, especially as it pertains to public relations" (p. 337).

Interactivity, driven progressively by the Internet, social media, and the rapid proliferation of mobile devices, has been termed "the biggest evolution in the History of PR" (Solis, 2008). Macnamara (2010) predicted that Web 2.0, which revolves around social media, heralds an era of "open interactivity" taking place "through conversation, collaboration, and creativity harnessing collective intelligence" (p. 27). The Internet provides a number of opportunities to engage with stakeholders along the lines of dialogic principles (Kent & Taylor, 1998), with social media defined as "a collection of Internet-based tools that enhance communication though openness and interactive capabilities" (Sadeghi, 2012, p. 126). Interactivity, from the perspective of building OPRs or co-creating meanings among multiple constituents, may be described as the fostering of symmetrical relationships in which both organization and public witness tangible and mutual benefits, or as engaging with stakeholders and bringing together different or conflicting views.

A common refrain among scholars is that social media as a public relations tool is being exploited with mixed results or without taking advantage of its full potential. For instance, McAllister-Spooner (2009) contended that public relations professionals and their organizations rarely exploit the interactive potential of new technologies. Their research mostly considered interactivity as a function of the Internet, remaining tied to a model that favored the dissemination of information over the assumption of shared authority and dialogic principles. Still, as Kent and Taylor (1998) argued, current research has by and large chronicled the ways in which social media has failed to reach its potential as a form of communication in which the give and take between organizations and stakeholders—or the public—occurs on an equal footing (Aragón & Domingo, 2014, p. 559). Sommerfeldt and Yang (2018) surveyed the incredible rise of research addressing the dialogic principles outlined by Kent and Taylor (1998). They agreed that "computer mediated communication is now an indispensible part of public relations practice," representing the "potential of dialogic communication," but worried that the "dialogic promise" of digital media as a public relations tool was being largely unfulfilled (p. 60).

Lurking beneath the hyperbole is the cynical view that organizations engage in interactivity only insofar as it affects the bottom line (Aragón & Domingo, 2014, p. 560). In other words, companies interact with their publics only to the degree to which they can see a positive return on the investment of capital and time—and only so long as they can maintain some control over the process. In this regard, technologies such as social media platforms become symbols of an organization's progressive or youthful approach, rather than being approached as avenues toward quality interactions. In other words, the appearance of being innovative and the willingness to encourage interactivity are merely means of achieving strategic goals set and controlled by the organization. Such a cynical view privileges the formal aspects of the technological platform and user perceptions of modernity over the substance of the relationship (Kelleher, 2009). Verčič, Verčič, and Sriramesh (2015) concluded that research on digital, social, and mobile media by and large adopted a functionalist viewpoint and concentrated on media relations as opposed to "holistically addressing all aspects of the media" (p. 147).

Public relations scholarship has seen a gradual shift "from usability studies regarding the mechanics of a particular medium to studies of how use of a particular platform leads to a change in one's emotive states" (Duhé, 2015, p. 162). Together with the rise of social media, new forms of relationship have emerged. The collaborative or sharing economy has been defined as a reconfiguration of the concept of ownership, whereby resources are defined by temporary access negotiated among members of a community (Halff & Gregory, 2017). While one possible outcome is that there will be no place for public relations, since the sharing economy proposes to short-circuit the traditional need for gatekeepers, an emerging line of theory advocated by scholars such as Miller (2016) and Belk (2014) proposes that the role of public relations be reconceived to resemble that of a coach or mentor. Public relations professionals would thus foster "deliberative disintermediation," or a process of facilitating communication among community members whereby the "act of communication itself will define community" (Gregory & Halff, 2017, pp. 7, 9). Meta-communication, or communicating about the processes of communicating, is both the goal and the outcome of such a renewed role.

Dialogical Theory

Dialogic theory, in public relations often identified with Kent and Taylor (1998, 2002), has emerged as an important paradigm, especially in relation to online communication. The dialogic approach is connected intimately with ethics: "It is morally right to establish and maintain communication relationships with all publics affected by organizational action and, by implication, morally wrong not to do so" (Pearson, 1989, p. 329). It was defined with five features:

> mutuality, or the recognition of organization–public relationships; propinquity, or the temporality and spontaneity of interactions with publics; empathy, or the supportiveness and confirmation of public goals and interests; risk, or the willingness to interact with individuals and public on their own terms; and finally, commitment, or the extent to which an organization gives itself over to dialogue, interpretation, and understanding in its interactions with publics. (Kent & Taylor, 2002, pp. 24–25)

The intellectual foundations of dialogic theory are rooted in Habermas's (1981) theory of communicative action and Michel Foucault's inquiries into the nature of power (Burkart, 2004). Broadly, dialogic theory posits a consensus-based model of public relations on the one hand (Holtzhausen, 2002; Kent & Taylor, 2002), and questions the field's complicity in power-control on the other. It is the predominant methodological framework used to analyze Internet and social media communication in a public relations context. Although it is a somewhat basic explanatory mechanism, given the multiplicity of issues surrounding the diverse communication forms made possible by the rise of social media (Cho & Khang, 2006), "no new theory had [previously] been developed to explain Internet phenomena in communication, marketing, and advertising"(Ye & Ki, 2012, p. 424).

Dialogic theory is well weaved into strategic communication and tied to crisis communication. Kim, Avery, and Lariscy (2009) pointed to a growing number of crisis communication studies based on strategic communication and dialogic theory. In contrast to the general trend toward quantitative studies, crisis communication is an area with a large number of qualitative ones. Defined as "strategic dialogic communication and relationship building process" (Coombs, 2012, p. 459), the crisis communication model builds on the concept of strategic communication and dialogic theory. For example, message strategies have been analyzed in relation to level of democratic participation (White & Radic, 2014).

Globalization and Multicultural Approaches

Scholars and professionals have questioned whether universal principles exist in public relations practice across cultures as the field continues to grow during the twenty-first century. With the waning influence of the hegemony of the U.S. and, to a slightly lesser degree, European model of economic predominance, the assumption that public relations based on Western models is not only the most efficient but also the most ethical option in all situations is coming into question. Taken together with the concurrent decline of implementation of the excellence model in public relations practice that follows the dominant coalition of business interests, new paradigms have begun to emerge (Vujnovic & Krukeberg, 2018). A combination of social, economic, cultural, and political trends has transformed the field (Valentini, Kruckeberg, & Stark, 2016). For public relations, the challenge of forging a theory to accommodate globalization is linked to the issue of geographic diversity and sharpening distinctions, as opposed to understanding the ways in which social and economic life is undergoing processes of integration (Holtzhausen, 2011; L'Etang, 2012; Rittenhofer and Valentini, 2015; Sison, 2014; Sriramesh and Verčič, 2003; Valentini et al., 2016). The problem, as Kent and Taylor (2011) have argued, is to understand that culture is not a straightforward set of practices, but rather a continuum marked by simultaneous interactions with multiple regional and global identities.

Valentini et al. (2016) identified four distinguishing characteristics of globalization: internationalization, liberalization, Westernization, and deterritorialization. This formulation is both postcolonial and postmodern, in the sense that multiple symbolic and environmental factors affect the way in which people interact (Brown, 2012; Radford, 2012). In other words, the ground is constantly shifting. Such shifts primarily involve the availability of information, which in turn affects the definition and formation of community. With instantaneous access to unprecedented levels of news, information, and other intelligence without the constraint of borders, the potential for the definition and formation of publics is unprecedented and unpredictable. However, seemingly unfettered access to information has a dark side. It can lead to a loss of privacy, the threat of constant surveillance, fragmentation, tribalism, skepticism, and a lack of trust (Valentini et al., 2016). The supposed transparency and trust in organizations facilitated by public relations practitioners takes on a new meaning when a sizable percentage of the public believes that all information coming from the government or industry is suspect. Instead of narrowing the gulf between modernity and traditionalism, the process of globalism is to some degree accentuating the conflict in many parts of the world (Simandi, 2006). Activist groups employ public relations strategies and tactics, disrupting the traditional role of public relations as a means of facilitating mutually beneficial relationships as boundary-spanning instruments of benevolent organizations (Berger, 2005; Holladay and Coombs, 2013; Valentini and Kruckeberg, 2011). Public relations theory on globalism is punctuated with idealistic predictions of the potential for "promoting fruitful and constructive interactions among corporations, NGOs/civil organizations, and governments" (Valentini et al., 2016, p. 242). Embracing such a paradigm shift shall doubtless be attended by a difficult and uncertain period of transition in an era when the word "globalism" is used by so many leaders as shorthand for imperialism and oppression.

Molleda and Laskin (2005) presented an overview of public relations scholarship in international contexts between 1990 and 2005. Their analysis of 647 articles and book chapters published in 10 academic journals, 12 academic books, and 5 professional journals using 97 categorical variables showed that 38% of scholarly articles focused on Europe, 28% on Asia, 6% on Oceania, 5% on North America, 4% on Latin America, and a little more than 2% on Africa (p. 15). The articles were categorized into four types: introspection, practice-application, theory development, and contextualized research. Introspective articles most often centered on the profession (20%), pedagogy (10%), and history (7%); practice-application related to social issues management (8%), the implementation of programs or campaigns (8%), and comparative or single-country contextualized research (10%); theory-development articles focused on comparative or single-country contextualized research (10%), excellence or symmetrical communications (4%), organizational communications (4%), and ethics or social responsibility (4%); and contextualized-research articles centered on culture (12%), media (8%), the political environment (5%), and the socioeconomic climate (5%) (pp. 17–18). Trade articles (n = 244) devoted to international issues were most prevalent in the early years, peaking in 1991, shortly after the collapse of the Soviet Union. Once again, Europe predominated, representing 32% of the articles published; however, 23% of articles featured more than one region. Africa (9%) and Latin America (6%) were better represented than in scholarly articles (p. 25). Not surprisingly, there were a high number of introspective articles focused on the profession (26%) and pedagogy (10%), as well as practice-application topics on the implementation of programs or campaigns (15%), contextualized research (24%), and organizational communication (11%). Theory development was uncommon, with only 1% of articles focused on ethics and social responsibility and 1% on critical or cultural theories (p. 27). Book chapters (n = 169) showed a similar pattern to that of academic journal articles. The highest concentration (38%) focused on Europe, while 24% centered on Asia, and 12% looked at more than one region. Interestingly, Africa (11%) and Latin America (9%) were better represented, in line with articles published in trade magazines (p. 32).

Verčič, Verhoeven, and Zerfass (2014) surveyed practitioners in 43 European countries and identified five primary concerns: "linking business strategy and communication, coping with the digital evolution and social web, building and maintaining trust, dealing with the demand for more transparency and corrective action, and dealing with the speed and volume of information flow" (p. 142). As with public relations in the United States, European public relations has been broadly conceived as centered on management (Wehmeier, 2009, p. 266). There are regional and cultural differences, however. For example, Palea (2014) found that public relations professionals in Romania held linguistic and professional competence to be the most valued trait for a practitioner, with a mixed assessment for the definition of ethical behavior (p. 21).

Xu and Huang (2016) surveyed scholarship on Asian public relations between 1995 and 2013 and found significantly increased scholarly productivity, eclectic approaches, internationalization, an intensive focus on quantitative analysis, and a "dearth of theoretical frameworks" (p. 548). Of 162 articles examined, they found 111 used explicit theoretical conceptualizations, representing an "extraordinary growth and impact both regionally and globally" (p. 550). They also noted that most theoretical contributions represented the adaptation of a Western model to an Asian context. The most common theories were four models of public relations (10.8%), framing (6.3%), relationship management (5.4%), contingency theory (5.4%), Hofstede's cultural dimensions (4.5%), situational crisis communication theory (4.5%), and excellence theory (4.5%). Interestingly, their survey of the literature suggests a decline in the dominance of excellence theory and a rise in the "heterogeneity of public relations research itself" (p. 559). Still, they concluded that the scope of research in Asia itself was comparatively narrow and focused on application—testing and applying existing theories in a new context—as opposed to advancing the construction of new and emerging theories.

Molleda and Laskin (2005) confirmed that international collaborations were rare, constituting "17 percent of book chapters, one tenth of academic publications and only three percent of trade publications were authored by researchers or professionals from more than one country" (p. 41). Less surprising is that most international public relations scholarship originated in the United States, and that the United States and United Kingdom were the regions most often researched, followed by Europe and Asia. Molleda and Laskin (2005) pointed out that there was something of a marginalization of international scholarship, noting that it was "disappointing" from an ethno-centric perspective to consider that "when a U.S. scholar studies public relations practices in the United States, we do not even attempt to call it an international research," but "if an Australian scholar writes an article about public relations practices in Australia, we would not be surprised to see it published in [the] international section of the journal" (p. 43). Countering this perspective, Ki and Khang (2005) pointed to the rising number of international authors and the increasing attention given to both local non-Western and global topics between 1995 and 2004.

Jain, De Moya, and Molleda (2014) provided an updated overview of international public relations during the period 2006 through 2011. They examined 200 articles published in 12 journals, using the same four categorizations of scholarship as Molleda and Laskin (2005): introspective, application-practical, theory development, and contextualized research. Three leading journals predominated—*Public Relations Review*, *Journal of Mass Communications*, and *Journal of Public Relations Research*—accounting for 89% of the total number of articles focusing on international issues (p. 596). Among the most striking changes was the increased number of articles focused on Africa (n = 63), making it the most studied region in international public relations. This was followed by Europe (n = 60), Asia (n = 55), North America (n = 25), Australia and Oceania (n = 14), and Latin America (n = 8). Following the findings of Molleda and Laskin (2005), most articles were about a single country, with only 18% being cross-cultural and only 5% that could be counted as global in scope (Jain et al., 2014, p. 596). As with scholarship in the United States, excellence theory or symmetrical communication models constituted the principal framework for those coded for theory development, accounting for 19% of the sample. Similarly, 58% of the sample overall relied primarily on literature generated in the United States, while 22% used non-U.S. literature (p. 596). Issues management, risk communication, and critical or cultural theories were also used, but there were very few that related to gender studies, ethnic issues, or social theories. Even fewer focused on issues such as activism, legal environments, and regulation. While the emergence of Africa as a viable topic for research is applauded, Jain et al. (2014) noted that Latin America remained a region that was seriously underrepresented in public relations research, and that these lacunae point "to an opportunity for the development of this research stream" (p. 597).

The rise of emerging markets has had a profound effect on the conception of public relations. For example, Chang and Lin (2013) showed how public relations in China has gradually transformed the propagandistic model that predominated during the Cultural Revolution into one of public diplomacy. This is not to say that the role of the state is any less significant nor that governance of the media is any less constraining, only that public relations in China represents the exercise of "soft power" (p. 450). In many emerging markets, especially those with a history of authoritarianism, the distinction between propaganda and public diplomacy is often a fine one. In China, the issue of censorship continues to be troublesome. China shares with other emerging markets issues that have been tied to public relations since the founding of the discipline, including charges of bribery of journalists, crony capitalism, and favoritism. Many of these issues are political in nature, but public relations is implicated in the sense that it has been harnessed to vested interests and the concomitant projection of a favorable opinion. As Chang and Lin (2013) suggested, one of the principal goals of public relations as practiced in China has been to "repair international relations" (p. 451). With the rise of the 24-hour news cycle and a constantly transforming media landscape that is truly global in nature, the challenges and opportunities in international relations have become all the more urgent.

European public relations has evolved largely on the model of that in the United States and United Kingdom. The European Communication Monitor (Zerfass, Verĉiĉ, Verhoeven, Moreno, & Tench, 2015) conducted a survey of more than 2,000 professionals involved in public relations or strategic communication working in 41 countries to identify the most significant trends over the next 3 years. When asked to pick three issues that respondents believed would be most significant to the practice, 42.9% identified "linking business strategy and communication," followed by "coping with the digital revolution and the social web" (37.2%), "building and maintaining trust" (36.6%), "matching the need to address more audiences and channels with limited resources" (33.4%), and "dealing with the speed and volume of information flow" (31.9%). Although it is clear that in Europe public relations is conceived as a strategic and management function and is closely tied to corporate communications, a substantial number of respondents identified issues that suggest the importance of establishing a symmetrical relationship with stakeholders. Two factors, "dealing with the demand for more transparency and active audiences" (24.4%) and "dealing with sustainable development and social responsibility" (16.3%), received a substantial number of endorsements (Zerfass et al., 2015, p. 40). Interestingly, while "liking business strategy and communication" and "building and maintaining trust" were identified as relatively stable concerns between 2008 and 2015, "coping with the digital revolution and social web" peaked in importance in 2011, at about 55%, before falling to just over 30% in 2014, then slowly beginning to rise again (p. 43). When asked whether face-to-face conversations were effective means of organizational listening, 90.7% agreed, compared to 56.2% who agreed that "social media communication is an effective technique to understand and engage stakeholders" (p. 60).

Moreno, Zerfass, Tench, Verčič, and Verhoeven (2009) identified the interaction of "business strategy and communication, sustainable development, and social responsibility" as the most significant emerging challenge (p. 81). While the link between business, strategy, and communication remained a fairly constant concern among communication professionals, other top issues such as corporate responsibility and transparency witnessed a gradual decline. "Dealing with the demand for more transparency and active audiences" fell from a high of 35% in 2011 to 25% in 2015 (Zerfass et al., 2015, p. 43). Even more surprisingly, "Dealing with sustainable development and social responsibility" fell from 42% in 2008 to 16.3% in 2015 (p. 43). The issue of CSR seems to have emerged as a leading issue, only to have declined somewhat in the wake of the global financial crises of 2008. Moreno et al. (2009) speculated that the emphasis on CSR had a utilitarian motivation, "i.e. as an instrument for obtaining economic profit" linked to reputation management and bolstering a corporate profile (p. 81). The identification of social media as a major challenge among European public relations professionals seems to have declined somewhat between 2008 and 2015. Although 63.4% of European professionals noted that social media monitoring was a regular part of their job in 2015, "dealing with the digital revolution and social web" was rated as declining as a top emerging trend (Zerfass et al., 2015, p. 61).

Deconstructionism and Diversification

Public relations, unlike many related field, has been slow to adapt postmodernism, deconstructivism, ideological critiques, and other emanations of critical theory that have transformed theoretical discussions in other disciplines. For example, Habermas's (1984) theory of communicative action, which has had a major impact in such adjacent fields as media studies, cultural studies, and sociology, is little discussed outside of a handful of public relations scholars (Brown, 2015; L'Etang, 2008). The bulk of theoretical perspectives defining public relations have reinforced and reified the "hegemony of dominant corporations over their environment" (Halff & Gregory, 2015, p. 719). Weaver (2016) expressed surprise that the impact of Karl Marx's writing had barely touched public relations theory, even as scholars began to embrace critical theory in public relations. As an artifact of the recent interest in developing a critical theory of public relations, the concept of power is being discussed as a function and structure, as social construction, as discursive, as symbolic, as knowledge, and in connection to resource management theory (Heath et al., 2015a, p. 705).

Hazelton and Kennan (2000) and L'Etang (2004) are among the newer voices who do draw upon sociologists, literary critics, and philosophers associated with deconstructionism, postmodernism, and critical theory. More recently, McKie and Xifra (2014) have documented the explosion of international contributors to both theory and practice, calling the trend "diversification history" (p. 670)—although it can be difficult to find one's way within the diverse environment. A field of inquiry related to critical studies is postcolonial theory, which centers on issues of race and national origin and offers an implicit critique of the hegemony of Western culture (Munshi, 2005). Pal and Dutta (2008) were among the pioneers in this line of inquiry, demonstrating how the managerial bias implied in public relations practice marginalizes subaltern groups, particularly minorities and those in third-world countries, and reinforces the hegemonic framework of first-world capitalism.

Heath (2006) argued that "public relations is a piece of some whole" and "the challenge is to continue to search to discover the whole and public relations' place in it," (p. 110) reminding public relations researchers that the task is made all the more challenging because there is little agreement about its goal or process. Although theory may by its very nature be "partial, perspectival, political, and contested" (May & Mumby, 2005, p. 278), McKie and Heath (2016) argued that "public relations as a holistic configuration is greater than the sum of its parts in being able to respond appropriately to changing environments" (p. 303) and thus has the potential to contribute to uncertainty reduction.

Public relations research has pointed to the "need for strategic information, analytic insights and anticipatory approaches through analysis and intelligence capabilities for taking decisions in the domain of communication and managing relationships with key stakeholders and publics" (Arcos, 2016, p. 269). Embracing the concept of multiple intelligences helps provide insight into the human condition, and "connecting public relations and intelligences" can be used in strategic ways to "make society more fully functioning" (McKie & Heath, 2016, p. 303). Public relations driven by strategic intelligence can be brought to bear on advancing "shared insights and collective benefits" (p. 304). The problem lies in the question of who decides what is in the public good: Enlightened individuals or benevolent organizations? Or is the risk of a malevolent but intelligent "agentic elite" willing to push antidemocratic principles to its own benefit too great?

One answer is based on an economic argument. Public relations is a "social institution that helps mitigate market imperfections and consequently both increases the efficiency with which society's resources are allocated and increase the changes for more market participants to derive value out of economic transactions" (Halff & Gregory, 2015, p. 720). The role of public relations is to build trust, which maximizes the "efficient allocation of society's resources" (p. 720). Yet, this model is idealistic in the sense that it proposes that organizations and publics will behave rationally to further their mutually best interests. As the reemergence of nationalism in politics across the globe has demonstrated, the potential for misuse of communication is all too real: "propagandistic public relations increases information asymmetry, prevents market efficiency from increasing and reduces net aggregate wealth because of the cost involved in a spiral of competitive signaling" (p. 723). In other words, market efficiency is, as the critical theorists would argue, offset by the unequal distribution of power that leads to an unequal allocation of resources, most often in the direction of powerful organizations over a subaltern public, the members of which surrender consent through the exercise of false consciousness developed and manipulated by the use of unethical public relations.

McKie and Munshi (2005) presented a forceful argument for paying attention to the theories that were emerging on the periphery of public relations research and theory building. After deconstructing the dominance of practice based on U.S. models and theories built on the excellence model, they suggested embracing "fresh theoretical perspectives" that were emerging from "diverse writers from many different nations and regions, as a watershed in the quest to give voice to divergent perspectives" (Heath, 2001). Public diplomacy, economic diplomacy, and business diplomacy models of public relations have also emerged in recent years (Morgensen, 2017). The former is concerned principally with the establishment and maintenance of political relationships and policy through strategic communication (Pamment, 2018). Economic and business diplomacy focuses on "establishing and sustaining long-term positive relationships" in an effort to "create legitimacy in a foreign business environment" by interacting with "foreign governments and non-governmental stakeholders" (Rüel & Wolters, 2016, p. 569). Both public and economic diplomacy are aimed at engaging in purposeful and strategic communication that is goal-oriented. Cultural diplomacy is seen as an exercise in soft power, and is used to foster mutual understanding or for more contested purposes such as spreading mistrust, sowing confusion, spreading propaganda, or engaging in "information warfare" (Pamment, 2018, p. 7). Public relations is a crucial component in all such diplomacy because corporate organizations are concerned with public opinion and "being perceived as legitimate" (Morgensen, 2017, p. 612).

Movement Toward Interdisciplinary Perspectives

As public relations has been increasingly defined as strategic communication, even though the term has not been fully institutionalized nor agreed upon, the role of practitioners has changed (Diggs-Brown, 2011; Coombs & Holladay, 2015; Frandsen & Johansen, 2017; Falkheimer, Heide, Northhaft, von Platen, Simonsson, Andersson, 2017; Hallahan, 2018; O'Conner & Shumate, 2018). Zerfass et al. (2018) stated that strategic communication is "fuzzy, and not properly defined" (p. 487). Still, it represents an attractive, integrated, interdisciplinary outlook that encompasses insights from fields ranging from advertising and marketing to organizational communication and artificial intelligence. Heide, von Platen, Simonsson, and Falkheimer (2018) argued that it is "an ambition to break down the silos surrounding closely related communication disciplines" (p. 452). A case in point is the breakdown of the traditional separation of marketing and advertising from public relations. One example is the convergence between public relations and marketing messages disseminated on platforms such as Twitter. It is often unclear whether a message is designed to foster the establishment of relationships and the building of goodwill or to meet the needs of consumers and satisfy their demands for products or services. As another example, the rise of native advertising has complicated the traditional relationship between paid media and earned press. The intermixing of functions has been the cause of conflict as much as collaboration. As Ha and Ferguson (2015) concluded, overlap between reputation management—traditionally the role of public relations professionals—and promotion in a pragmatic or short-term sense can either have "positive synergy effects" or lead to role conflict and perceptual discrepancy (Reid, 2005).

Network Theory

The movement toward interdisciplinary perspective has led many public relations theorists to view the traditional organization-centric conception of public relations, advocated most strongly by James Grunig and John Ledingham, as outdated. Insights drawn from fields ranging from sociology to information science have suggested that network theory might profitably be applied instead. According to the influential text *The Rise of the Network Society* (Castells, 2000), a network is a "set of interconnected nodes ... the relative importance of a node does not stem from its specific feature but from its ability to contribute to the network goal" (p. 3). Once of its central goals is the creation and negotiation of social capital arising from the connections among individuals and organizations (Bourdieu, 1986). A key insight is that individuals and groups are defined according to the relationships into which they enter, whether direct or indirect. Contexts include "interpersonal face-to-face relations, collocated or virtual team projects, joint ventures, collaborative partnerships, and membership in professional organizations" (Matni & Stohl, 2018). Organizational networks can be advocating or adversarial, and can originate within or outside of group boundaries. Relational characteristics of network organizations include multipelxity, or the overlap and sharing of multiple relationships; homophily, or the degree to which members share values, beliefs, and stances; and strength of link, or the ways in which members communicate and reciprocate (Matni & Stohl, 2018).

Network theory aligns with the call by many public relations researchers—notably Kruckeberg and Stark (1998), Stark and Kruckeberg (2001), Sommerfeldt (2013), Heath et al. (2013), and Hallahan (2013)—to more fully integrate the practice of public relations into diverse sets of communities, and society as a whole. The ideal role for a public relations practitioner is to forge and maintain social networks, thus building community and fostering an "efficient society, as it leads to less conflict and more satisfied citizens" (Ihlen, 2013, p. 838). Heath et al. (2013) argued that public relations is central to the sustenance of networks because of the role it plays in "obtaining, processing, and outputting information between organizations and individuals" (p. 605). In this regard, Hallahan (2013) described three roles for public relations practitioners: community involvement, community nurturing, and community organizing. Community involvement entails defining and strengthening the network relations that already exist in a community. Community nurturing involves an organization sponsoring activities that encourage the formation of meaningful and vital relationships within a community. Community organization entails creating relationships that define new communities (Hallahan, 2013, pp. 168–169). Heath et al. (2013) argued that public relations is central to the sustenance of networks because of its role in "obtaining, processing, and outputting information between organizations and individuals" (p. 605). A model of public relations based on network theory implies the potential for moving toward greater voice and democratic participation. This suggests an expanded role for the profession, situating it as a driver of social justice in what Taylor (2010) termed a "fully functioning society," composed of co-equal communities within a civil society (p. 9). As Yang and Taylor (2013) contended, "[w]hen public relations reflects an educated, ethical relationship building function, then the profession of public relations contributes to the accumulation of social capital and democratic process" (p. 269). Public relations interventions can foster "deliberative democracy" based on "dialogue rather than demagoguery" (Edwards, 2016, p. 61). The idea that public relations contributes to society as a whole, as opposed to serving the interests of an organization first and foremost, can be logically extended to give the profession a role in "check[ing] the power of the state and maintain[ing] the social infrastructure" (Sommerfeldt, 2013, p. 280). Heath et al. (2013) also made a strong argument for a supportive role for public relations in democracy, leading ultimately to a more fully functioning society. This new role is in keeping with the call by Kent and Taylor (1998), and reiterated by Kent (2013), to use social media in a more responsive manner that is "genuinely social and committed to the democratic ideals of public relations" (Toledano & Maplesden, 2016, p. 713).

Future Directions for Research, Practice, and Education

Public relations is ever changing and seems perpetually to oscillate between being at a crossroads and facing a crisis. As Everett and Johnston (2012) noted, an "unresolved but continuing challenge in public relations theory is identification of the nature of public relations itself and the consequent imperatives for practice" (p. 523). Two broad traditions have informed theory building. The first is the management perspective, represented by excellence theory, which holds that public relations is essentially about managing relationships between organizations and publics. According to Grunig and Hunt (1984), "management of communication" and the establishing of symmetrical or mutually beneficial relationships is the goal (p. 6). The 2009 Delphi Study, an examination of international trends in public relations, confirmed the assumption that the field is conceived broadly as a management function, informed by theories of relationship and communication management (Wehmeier, 2009, p. 266). However, it is clear that the perspective of the organization—often presupposed as a commercial, for-profit, or corporate entity—has precedence and that the benefit can and should be measured in economic terms: the bottom line. At the opposite end of the spectrum, the sociological view holds that the ideal goal is to position "public relations research more broadly as a cultural and ideological practice engaged in complex inter-cultural processes and pulling back from technocratic concerns" (L'Etang, 2006, p. 39). This view aligns with stakeholder theory and power-control perspectives, which assume that organizations exercise power over publics in asymmetrical ways and devalue the significance of individual actor in favor of organizational imperatives (Curtain & Gaither, 2005; Dutta, 2009; Roper, 2005). Critical theory, and rhetorical and sociological perspectives, as major strains of recent theory crafting on public relations, suggest that pluralism has become the new normal. The interdisciplinary nature of sociological theories has, at the most idealistic end of the spectrum, led to the conception of the discipline as contributing to a "fully functioning society" in ways that are, at present, difficult to quantify (Heath, 2006, p. 96). These two strains are reflected in current areas of theory development. Crisis, issue, reputational, and strategic communication theories tend to suggest that organizations can and should control their communication for their own benefit. Theories focused on CSR, sociological approaches, and the unequal distribution of power are aligned with the organizational role and "its relationships to life worlds and the public sphere as part of a broad sociocultural enterprise" (L'Etang, 2006, p. 39).

The divide between theory and practice continues to be salient for practitioners and educators. Wright and Turk (2007), for example, found that public relations practitioners dismissed the value of theory as taught in college and university programs, failing to see the value in coursework "that goes beyond the technical level" (p. 405). On the other hand, scholars have argued that public relations education should be grounded in broad concepts, notably ethics (Pratt & McLaughlin, 1989; Verwey, Benecke, & Muir, 2017). This reflects the view of Pearson (1989) that public relations should by necessity be based on ethical communication among all parties involved in a given issue. It recalls too the position of Grunig and Hunt (1984) that symmetrical communication is the foundation of ethical public relations—though they argued that the organizational interest is at the center and that communication with publics is measured by the degree to which building relationships "constrain[s] or enhance[s] the ability of an organization to meet its mission" (p. 55). According to Kent and Taylor (2002), the dialogic approach is considered "more ethical" only insofar as the playing field is leveled by giving organizations and stakeholders equal voice, and actors can enter into discussion based on "principles of honesty, trust, and positive regard for the other rather than simply a conception of the public as a means to an end" (p. 33).

More recently, Verwey et al. (2017) argued for public relations education that takes into account recent scholarship on power differences as outlined in postmodern work. This perspective is related to that of Holtzhausen (2015), who admonished public relations educators to counter the uncritical acceptance whereby practitioners reproduce the political and social values of their clients at the expense of the broadly conceived interests of stakeholders. McKie and Willis (2015) contended that pluralistic education should emphasizes a reflective approach to the cognitive and behavioral aspects of public relations theory and practice, as well as leadership and ethics. Likewise, Saffer (2018) proposed that the introduction of value-added theory to public relations education aims to discover how collective behavior is manifested through an examination of the beliefs and motives of individuals and groups, and to guide them to band together and undertake collective actions for or against a cause.

Conclusion

As with any field, public relations is continuously evolving in practice and in theory. Yet, it has been particularly self-conscious concerning its relationship to related fields and the need to distinguish itself by a robust theoretical framework. Since the 1980s, articles and books lamenting the lack of theory building in public relations have proliferated. However, the self-reflective concern about how the profession serves society may be taken as a healthy and productive development. The managerial perspective suggests that public relations enacts communication between organizations and publics that is ethical and efficient, producing mutually beneficial outcomes. The sociocritical approach suggests that public relations can help balance the benefits accrued by the moneyed and powerful against those of the poor and powerless.

Meta-analyses in the 2000s and 2010s demonstrated that public relations scholarship has moved from a focus on evaluation of practice in the United States to look at issues of crisis, strategy, and ethics in a global setting (Kim & Weaver, 2002; Kim et al., 2014). Likewise, the predominant theoretical constructs have shifted from excellence theory and the relationship measurement scale from an organizational perspective (Hon & Grunig, 1999) to contingency theory, rhetorical theory, critical theory, stakeholder theory, and network theory from a sociological point of view. The focus has moved from an analysis of practice in the United States to look at other countries, notably South Korea, China, and Taiwan, but also Eastern European and African nations. Public relations has been increasingly defined as strategic communication, or the "deliberate and purposive communication that a communication agent enacts in the public sphere on behalf of a communicative entity to reach set goals" (Holtzhausen & Zerfass, 2015, p. 284). In strategic communication, the public relations practitioner is reconceived as a "communication agent," suggesting an integrated role within an organization oriented toward the outcome. This redefinition indicates how the profession has embraced the theoretical perspectives of related fields such as organizational communication, business administration, sociology, and psychology. The focus on goal-oriented communication and the realities of the competitive marketplace in terms of both economic viability and social relevance have necessitated integration and coordination among various communication agents both within and outside of an organization (Zerfass et al., 2018).

Public relations as strategic communication shifts the emphasis from a tactical and supportive role to one that is more integrated with the decisional process of an organization's dominant coalition (Volk & Zerfass, 2018). On the other hand, virtually all communication between organizations and stakeholders, regardless of who is sending or receiving the messages, may be considered part of strategic communication (Heide et al., 2018; Winkler & Etter, 2018). In a public relations context, strategic communication takes place in more narrow confines. Communication management occurs as a process of one- and two-way communication, according to the resources invested by both organization and stakeholder, and with regard to intangible assets such as reputation, social capital, and degree of trust (Zerfass et al., 2018). One conception of strategic communication is based on establishing true dialogue and focused on building networks dedicated to the co-creation of meaning (Hallahan et al., 2007; Kent & Taylor, 2002).

This is as incompatible as it may seem. As Holtzhausen and Zerfass (2015) observed, "there is place for both a functionalist and an emerging strategic process in organizations, which depends on transformational and visionary leadership and broad stakeholder participation" (p. 9). While the meanings associated with the rebranding of public relations as either strategic or integrated communication have various iterations, the move suggests that it may be conceived as communication that is undertaken deliberately. This view was challenged by van Ruler (2015), who argued for an agile, responsive, and transformational conception of strategic communication with less attention to planning and goal-oriented process. Furthermore, contemporary public relations calls upon a variety of disciplines and approaches, is integrated with other functions within an organization, shares languages and methods that can be justified, and avoids the negative associations that have dogged it historically (Hallahan et al., 2007; Nothhaft et al., 2018). "Strategic communication" is not simply another way of saying "public relations," but represents a rethinking of how the discipline is practiced. A public relations initiative combining "strategic intent" with stakeholder agency or choice is one way of leveling the power difference between publics and organizations (Russell & Lamme, 2016, p. 746).

As signaled by Heath's *Handbook of Public Relations* (2001), a number of fresh theoretical perspectives have emerged from scholars working in diverse contexts and geographic regions. Dialogic theory (Kent & Taylor, 1998, 2002) is one significant paradigm, transitioning from an organizational perspective to a consensus-based model that accords a balance of power between stakeholders and organizations. Another key trend is the rise of sociological perspectives such as ethnographic and ecological theories and, notably, ideological critiques and critical theory. While public relations "was created to thwart and subvert democratic decision making" (Miller & Dinan, 2007, p. 11) and may be considered either as a useless appendage or as a tool for exercising control over the environment and maintaining hegemonic power (Bowen, 2009), Heath et al. (2013) envisioned it as serving the public good, contributing to a "fully functioning society."

Technology has transformed the landscape of public relations, just as it has changed society. Interest in new technology, social media, and mobile devices has increased steadily among researchers, although there has been a dearth of synthetic theoretical approaches (Kent, 2014; Ye & Ki, 2012). Kent (2014) in particular criticized the unfulfilled potential of technology as having failed to bring about the expected revolution in public relations theory and practice. Sommerfeldt and Yang (2018) likewise suggested that the dialogic promise of digital media was largely unfulfilled, although the revolution in Internet and mobile technology still has the potential to provide greater and more democratic access to communication platforms, leading to public empowerment.

Together with the revolution in communication technology, the other major trend is the increasing homogenization, internationalization, and deterritorialization that has affected perceptions of national and geographic boundaries. Global approaches have challenged the assumption that a public relations based on Western models is necessarily the effective and ethical. Valentini et al. (2016) suggested that a paradigm shift is underway, and that future interactions hold "fruitful and constructive" promise (p. 242). However, the transition may equally be attended by interactions based on coercion, deceit, asymmetry, and oppression (Dutta, 2012). The recent history of public relations in second-world and emerging markets has shown mixed results, but scholars with perspectives ranging from the strategic management of communication to a postmodern critique of the effects of globalism have remained optimistic that the development of synthetic theories of public relations will benefit society as a whole.

Chapter Summary

The direction of theoretical research in public relations is multivalent and continuously evolving. However, there are some notable threads that bind the discussion together. The field is still concerned about measuring relationships based on communication, and the primary interest has shifted from assessing how it can benefit a given organization to how it can benefit multiple stakeholders and contribute to society as a whole. Studies of strategic communication on behalf of organizations remain relevant, however, particularly where they emphasize crisis, issue, risk, and conflict management, CSR and good citizenship, and ethical and professional principles. The rise of engagement or interactivity, which helps assess public relations in the age of social media, holds a yet unrealized promise of providing equal voice and representation to organizations and stakeholders, allowing them to operate on a leveled playing field.

Public relations is experiencing rapid growth both professionally and in academia, and one often encounters students who desire to learn hands-on skills or techniques rather than theories and methods. Many expect ready answers to problems or a kind of unambiguous "roadmap" to help them in facing issues. The question is how they can be (a) guided to understand that theories and research methods are important prerequisites to understanding and solving problems; (b) taught to link theories and practice in service of future research and professional enhancement; and (c) shown how theories and research methods are applicable to real-world situations. Moreover, how do we link theories and practice in an ever-changing environment?

Key Terms

- *Dialogic Theory:* The development and maintenance of mutual relationships with stakeholders based on open discussion and interaction among individuals and organizations from their respective orientations.
- *Engagement:* Authentic and meaningful interaction among individuals or between individuals and organizations.
- *Fully Functioning Society:* The proposition that individuals and groups engage in dialogue, debate, and discourse to reach a decision that is enlightened and contributes to the betterment of their communities and of society as a whole.
- *Interactivity:* The give and take of communication among distinct parties. Often shorthand for engagement with stakeholders in digital or social media settings.
- *Network Theory:* A social scientific approach to the diversity of linking symmetrical and asymmetrical relationships among multiple individuals and communities, with an emphasis on optimizing communication processes and finding solutions to problems in intergroup settings.
- *Strategic Communication:* Integrated and coordinated efforts to interact with audiences with the goal of informing them about or persuading them to change their attitudes and behaviors related to particular issues.

Discussion Questions

1 What have been the main concerns and discussions of interest in the trends of public relations over time?
2 How have practice and theories evolved together?
3 From your standpoint, what are the current issues in public relations theory-building?
4 How would you apply some existing or emerging theoretical or conceptual frames to explain the evolution of public relations practice?
5 What will be the future directions of public relations theory building from your point of view?

References

Aggerholm, H. K., & Thomsen, C. (2015). Strategic communication: The role of polyphony in management team meetings. In D. R. Holtzhausen & A. Zerfass (Eds.), *The Routledge handbook of strategic communication* (pp. 172–189). New York: Routledge.

Ames, C. (2010). PR goes to the movies: The image of public relations improves from 1996 to 2008. *Public Relations Review, 36*, 164–170.

Aragón, E. P., & Domingo, D. (2014). Developing public relations 2.0: practitioners' perceptions on the implementation of interactive communication strategies. *Public Relations Review, 40*, 559–561.

Arcos, R. (2016). Public relations strategic intelligence: Intelligence analysis, communication, and influence. *Public Relations Review, 42*(2), 264–270.

Belk, R. (2014). You are what you can access: Sharing and collaborative consumption online. *Journal of Business Research, 67*, 1595–1600.

Benoit, W. L. (1997). Image repair discourse and crisis communication. *Public Relations Review, 23*(2), 177–186.

Berger, B. K. (2005). Power over, power with, and power to relations: Critical reflections of public relations, the dominant coalition, and activism. *Journal of Public Relations Research, 17*, 5–28.

Bourdieu, P. (1986). The forms of capital. In I. Szeman & T. Kaposy (Eds.), *Cultural theory: An anthology* (pp. 81–93). Oxford: Wiley-Blackwell.

Bowen, S. (2009). All glamour, no substance? How public relations majors and potential majors in an exemplar program view the industry and function. *Public Relations Review, 35*, 402–410.

Bradley, D. (2016). Snapchat defends Bob Marley 4/20 filter from blackface accusations. *PRWeek*, April 20. Available from https://www.prweek.com/article/1392067/snapchat-defends-bob-marley-4-20-filter-blackface-accusations (accessed May 20, 2020).

Brody, E. W. (1992). We must act now to redeem PR's reputation. *Public Relations Quarterly, 37*(3), 44.

Brown, R. E. (2012). Epistemological modesty: Critical reflections on public relations thought. *Public Relations Inquiry, 1*(1), 89–105.

Brown, R. E. (2015). *The public relations of everything: The ancient, modern and postmodern dramatic history of an idea.* New York: Routledge.

Bruning, S. D., & Ledingham, J. A. (1999). Relationship between organizations and publics: Development of a multi-dimensional organization-public scale. *ublic Relations Review, 25*(2), 157–170.

Burkart, R. (2004). Consensus-oriented public relations (COPR): a conception for planning and evaluation in public relations. In B. van Ruler & D. Verčič (Eds.), *Public relations in Europe: A nation-by-nation introduction to public relations theory and practice* (pp. 446–452). Berlin/New York: Mouton De Gruyter.

Castells, M. (2000). *The rise of the network society: Information Age: Economy, society, and culture.* New York: Wiley-Blackwell.

Cernicova, M. (2016). Redefining "public relations" in the 21st century. *Professional Communication and Translation Studies, 9*, 3–6.

Chang, T.-K., & Lin, F. (2013). From propaganda to public diplomacy: Assessing China's international practice and its image, 1950–2009. *Public Relations Review, 40*, 450–458.

Cho, C. H., & Khang, H. (2006). The state of Internet-related research in communication, marketing, and advertising: 1994–2003. *Journal of Advertising, 35*(3), 143–163.

Coombs, W. T. (2012). *Ongoing crisis communication: Planning, managing, and responding* (3rd ed.). Thousand Oaks, CA: Sage.

Coombs, W. T., & Holladay, S. (2015). CSR as crisis risk: Expanding how we conceptualize the relationship. *Corporate Communication: An International Journal, 20*(2), 144–162.

Curtain, P. A., & Gaither, K. T. (2005). Privileging identity, difference, and power: The circuit of culture as a basis for public relations theory. *Journal of Public Relations Research*, *17*(2), 91–115.

Diggs-Brown, B. (2011). *Strategic public relations: An audience-focused approach*. Boston, MA: Wadsworth.

Duhé, S. (2015). An overview of new media research in public relations journals from 1981 to 2014. *Public Relations Review*, *41*, 153–169.

Dutta, M. J. (2006). U.S. public diplomacy in the Middle East. *Journal of Communication Inquiry*, *30*, 102–124.

Dutta, M. J. (2009). On Gayatri Spivak: Theorizing resistance: Applying Gayatri Charkavorty Spivak in public relations. In Ø. Ihlen, B. van Ruler, & M. Fredricksson (Eds.), *Public relations and social theory* (pp. 278–300). New York: Routledge.

Dutta, M. J. (2012). Critical interrogations of global public relations. In K. Sriramesh & D. Verčič (Eds.), *Culture and public relations: Links and implications* (pp. 202–218). New York: Routledge.

Edwards, L. (2012). Defining the "object" of public relations research: A new starting point. *Public Relations Inquiry*, *1*(7), 7–30.

Edwards, L. (2016). The role of public relations in deliberative systems. *Jouranl of Communication*, *66*(1), 60–81.

Everett, J. L., & Johnston, K. A. (2012). Toward an ethnographic imperative in public relations research. *Public Relations Review*, *38*, 522–528.

Falkheimer, J., Heide, M., Northhaft, H., von Platen, S., Simonsson, C., & Andersson, R. (2017). Is strategic communication too important to be left to communication professionals? Managers' and coworkers' attitudes towards stragetic communication and communication professionals. *Public Relations Review*, *43*, 91–101.

Ferguson, M. A. (1984). Building theory in public relations: Interorganizational relationships as a public relations paradigm. Paper presented at the Public Relations Division, Association for Education in Journalism and Mass Communication Annual Convention, Gainesville, FL.

Frandsen, F., & Johansen, W. (2017). Strategic communication. In L. Lewis & C. Scott (Eds.), *International encyclopedia of organizational communication* (pp. 2250–2258). Boston, MA: Wiley-Blackwell.

Graham, P. (2017). *Strategic communication, corporatism, and eternal crisis*. New York: Routledge.

Gregory, A., & Halff, G. (2017). Understanding public relations in the sharing economy. *Public Relations Review*, *43*, 4–13.

Grunig, J. E. (2006). Furnishing the edifice: Ongoing research on public relations as a strategic management function. *Journal of Public Relations Research*, *18*(2), 151–176.

Grunig, J. E., & Hunt, T. (1984). *Managing public relations*. New York: Holt, Rinehart & Winston.

Grunig, L. A., Grunig, J. E., & Dozier, D. M. (2002). *Excellent public relations and effective organizations: A study of communication management in three countries*. Mahwah, NJ: Lawrence Erlbaum Associates.

Ha, J. H., & Ferguson, M. A. (2015). Perception discrepancy of public relations functions and conflict among disciplines: South Korean public relations versus marketing professionals. *Journal of Public Relations Research*, *27*(1), 1–21.

Habermas, J. (1984). *Theory of communicative action*, trans. T. McCarthy. Cambridge: Polity.

Halff, G., & Gregory, A. (2015). What is public relations to society? Toward an economically informed understanding of public relations. *Public Relations Review*, *41*, 719–725.

Halff, G., & Gregory, A. (2017). Understanding public relations in the "sharing economy". *Public Relations Review*, *43*, 4–13.

Hallahan, K. (2013). Community and community building. In R. L. Heath (Ed.), *Encyclopedia of public relations* (2nd ed., pp. 166–169). Thousand Oaks, CA: Sage.

Hallahan, K. (2018). Public relations. In *The international encyclopedia of strategic communication* (pp. 1–16). Hoboken, NJ: John Wiley & Sons.

Hallahan, K., Holtzhausen, D., Van Ruler, B., Verčič, D., & Sriramesh, K. (2007). Defining strategic communication. *International Journal of Strategic Communication, 1*(1), 3–35.

Hazelton, V., & Kennan, W. (2000). Social capital: Reconceptualizing the bottom line. *Corporate Communications: An International Journal, 5*(2), 81–86.

Heath, R. L. (2001). A rhetorical enactment rationale for public relations: The good organization communicating well. In R. L. Heath (Ed.), *Handbook of public relations* (pp. 31–50). Thousand Oaks, CA: Sage.

Heath, R. L. (2006). Onward into more fog: Thoughts on public relations' research directions. *Journal of Public Relations Research, 18*(2), 93–114.

Heath, R. L. (2010). *The SAGE handbook of public relations* (2nd ed.). Thousand Oaks, CA: Sage.

Heath, R. L., & Johansen, W. (Eds.) (2018). *The international encyclopedia of strategic communication*. Hoboken, NJ: John Wiley & Sons.

Heath, R. L., Waymer, D., & Palenchar, M. J. (2013). Is the universe of democracy, rhetoric, and public relations whole cloth or three separate galaxies? *Public Relations Review, 39*(4), 271–279.

Heath, R. L., Coombs, W. T., Edwards, L., Palenchar, M. J., & McKie, D. (2015a). Using the Encyclopedia of Public Relations as a springboard for something new. *Public Relations Review, 41*, 703–713.

Heath, R. L., Coombs, W. T., Edwards, L., Palenchar, M. J., & McKie, D. (2015b). Shaping the field: Bob Heath and the two volumes of the Encyclopedia of Public Relations. *Public Relations Review, 41*, 703–713.

Heide, M., von Platen, S., Simonsson, C., & Falkheimer, J. (2018). Expanding the scope of strategic communication: Towards a holistic understanding of organizational complexity. *International Journal of Strategic Communication, 12*(4), 452–468.

Henderson, J. K. (1998). Negative connotations in the use of the term "public relations" in the print. *Public Relations Review, 24*, 45–54.

Holladay, S. J., & Coombs, W. T. (2013). Public relations literacy: Developing critical consumers of public relations. *Public Relations Inquiry, 2*(2), 125–146.

Holtzhausen, D. R. (2002). Towards a postmodern research agenda for public relations. *Public Relations Review, 28*(3), 251–261.

Holtzhausen, D. R. (2011). The need for a postmodern turn in global public relations. In N. Bardhan & C. K. Weaver (Eds.), *Public relations in global cultural contexts* (pp. 140–167). New York: Routledge.

Holtzhausen, D. R. (2015). The unethical consequences of professional communication codes of ethics: A postmodern analysis of ethical decision-making in communication practice. *Public Relations Review, 41*(5), 769–776.

Holtzhausen, D. R., & Zerfass, A. (2015). Strategic communication: Opportunities and challenges. In D. R. Holtzhausen & A. Zerfass (Eds.), *The Routledge handbook of strategic communication* (pp. 3–17). New York: Routledge.

Hon, L. C., and Grunig, J. E. (1999). Guidelines for measuring relationships in public relations. Available from https://www.instituteforpr.org/wp-content/uploads/Guidelines_Measuring_Relationships.pdf (accessed May 20, 2020).

Huang, Y. H. C., & Zhang, Y. (2013). Revisiting organization-public relations research over the past decade: Theoretical concepts, measures, methodologies, and challenges. *Public Relations Review, 39*, 85–87.

Ihlen, Ø. (2013). Social capital. In R. L. Heath (Ed.), *Encyclopedia of public relations* (pp. 140–145). Thousand Oaks, CA: Sage.

Jain, R., De Moya, M., & Molleda, J. C. (2014). State of international public relations research: Narrowing the knowledge gap about the practice across borders. *Public Relations Review, 40,* 595–597.

Jo, S. (2003). The portrayal of public relations in news media. *Mass Communication and Society, 6,* 397–411.

Keenan, K. (1996). Network television news coverage of public relations: An exploratory census of content. *Public Relations Review, 22*(3), 215–231.

Kelleher, T. (2009). Conversational voice, communicated commitment, and public relations outcomes in interactive online communication. *Journal of Communication, 59*(1), 172–188.

Kent, M. L. (2013). Using social media dialogically: Public relations role in reviving democracy. *Public Relations Review, 39,* 337–345.

Kent, M. L. (2014). Rethinking technology research and social media. *Public Relations Review, 40,* 1–2.

Kent, M. L., & Taylor, M. (1998). Building dialogic relationships through the World Wide Web. *Public Relations Review, 24*(3), 321–334.

Kent, M. L., & Taylor, M. (2002). Toward a dialogic theory of public relations. *Public Relations Review, 28,* 21–37.

Kent, M. L., & Taylor, M. (2011). How intercultural communication theory informs public relations practice in global settings. In N. Bardhan & C. K. Weaver (Eds.), *Public relations in global cultural contexts: Multi-paradigmatic perspectives* (pp. 50–76). New York: Routledge.

Kent, M. L., Taylor, M., & White, W. J. (2002). The relationship between Web site design and organizational responsiveness to stakeholders. *Public Relations Review, 29*(1), 63–77.

Ki, E.-J., and Khang, H. K. (2005). The status of public relations research in the leading journals between 1995 and 2004. Paper presented at the Association for Education in Journalism and Mass Communication at San Antonio, TX.

Kim, S. T., & Weaver, D. (2002). Communication research about the Internet: A thematic meta-analysis. *New Media & Society, 4,* 518–538.

Kim, S. T., Avery, E. J., & Lariscy, R. W. (2009). Are crisis communicators practicing what we preach? An evaluation of crisis response strategies analyzed in public relations research from 1991 to 2009. *Public Relations Review, 35*(4), 446–448.

Kim, S. Y., Choi, M.-I., Reber, B. H., & Kim, D. (2014). Tracking public relations scholarship trends: Using semantic network analysis on PR journals from 1975 to 2011. *Public Relations Review, 40,* 116–118.

Kong, E. (2008). The development of strategic management in the non-profit context. Intellectual capital in social service non-profit organizations. *International Journal of Management Reviews, 10*(3), 281–299.

Kopenhaver, L. L. (1985). Aligning values of practitioners and journalists. *Public Relations Review, 11*(1), 34–42.

Kruckeberg, D., & Stark, K. (1998). *Public relations and community: A reconstructed theory.* New York: Praeger.

Leitch, S., & Neilson, D. (2001). Bringing publics into public relations: New theoretical frameworks for practice. In R. Heath (Ed.), *Handbook of Public Relations* (pp. 127–139). Thousand Oaks, CA: Sage.

L'Etang, J. (2004). *Public relations in Britain: A history of professional practice.* Mahwah, NJ: Lawrence Erlbaum Associates.

L'Etang, J. (2006). Public relations and propaganda: Conceptual issues, methodological problems, and public relations discourse. In J. L'Etang & M. Piecska (Eds.), *Public relations: Critical debates and contemporary practice* (pp. 23–40). Mahwah, NJ: Lawrence Erlbaum Associates.

L'Etang, J. (2008). Writing PR history: Issues, methods and politics. *Journal of Communication Management, 12*, 319–335.

L'Etang, J. (2012). Thinking about public relations and culture: Anthropological insights and ethnographic futures. In K. Sriramesh & D. Verčič (Eds.), *Culture and public relations: Links and implications* (pp. 218–237). New York: Routledge.

L'Etang, J. (2014). Public relations and historical sociology: Historiography as reflexive critique. *Public Relation Review, 40*(4), 654–660.

L'Etang, J., & Pieczka, M. (2006). *Public relations: Critical debates and contemporary practice.* Mahwah, NJ: Lawrence Erlbaum Associates.

Logan, N. (2014). Corporate voice and ideology: An alternative approach to understanding public relations history. *Public Relations Review, 40*(4), 661–668.

Macnamara, J. (2010). Public relations and the social: How practitioners are using, or abusing, social media. *Asia Pacific Public Relations Journal, 11*, 21–39.

Matamoros-Fernández, A. (2020). "El Negro de WhatsApp" meme, digital blackface, and racism on social media. *First Monday, 25*(1). Avaialable from https://firstmonday.org/ojs/index.php/fm/article/view/10420/8325 (accessed May 20, 2020).

Matni, Z., & Stohl, C. (2018). Organizational networks and strategic communication. In *The international encyclopedia of strategic communication* (pp. 1–10). Hoboken, NJ: John Wiley & Sons.

May, S., & Mumby, D. K. (2005). *Engaging organizational communication theory & research: Multiple perspectives.* Thousand Oaks, CA: Sage.

McAllister-Spooner, S. M. (2009). Fulfilling the dialogic promise: A ten-year reflective survey on dialogic Internet principles. *Public Relations Review, 35*(3), 320–322.

McKie, D., & Heath, R. (2016). Public relations as a strategic intelligence for the 21st century: Contexts, controversies, and challenges. *Public Relations Review, 42*, 298–305.

McKie, D., & Munshi, D. (2005). Tracking trends: peripheral visions and public relations. *Public Relations Review, 31*, 453–457.

McKie, D., & Willis, P. (2015). Advancing tendencies? PR leadership, general leadership, and leadership pedagogy. *PR Review, 41*, 628–635.

McKie, D., & Xifra, J. (2014). Resourcing the next stages in PR history research: The case for historiography. *Public Relations Review, 40*(4), 669–675.

Meyer, R. (2016). The repeated racism of Snapchat. *The Atlantic*, August 13. Available from https://www.theatlantic.com/technology/archive/2016/08/snapchat-makes-another-racist-misstep/495701/ (accessed May 20, 2020).

Miller, D., & Dinan, W. (2007). Public relations and the subversion of democracy. In W. Dinan & D. Miller (Eds.), *Thinker, faker, spinner, spy: Corporate public relations and the assault on democracy* (pp. 11–20). London: Pluto Press.

Miller, K. (1999). Public relations in film and fiction: 1930 to 1995. *Journal of Public Relations Research, 11*(1), 3–28.

Miller, S. (2016). First principles for regulating the sharing economy. *Harvard Journal on Legislation, 147*, 149–202.

Molleda, J. C., & Laskin, A. (2005). *Global, international, comparative and regional public relations knowledge from 1990 to 2005: A quantitative content analysis of academic and trade publications.* Gainesville, FL: Institute for Public Relations.

Moreno, A., Zerfass, A., Tench, R., Verčič, D., & Verhoeven, P. (2009). European communication monitor: Current developments, issues and tendencies of the professional practice of public relations in Europe. *Public Relations Review, 35*(1), 79–81.

Morgensen, K. (2017). From public relations to corporate public diplomacy. *Public Relations Review*, *43*, 605–614.

Morton, L. P., & Lin, L. (1995). Content and citation analysis of public relations review. *Public Relations Review*, *21*, 337–349.

Mumby, D. K., & Clair, R. (1997). Organizational discourse. In T. A. Van Dihk (Ed.), *Discourse as structure and process* (Vol. *2*, pp. 181–205). London: Sage.

Munshi, D. (2005). Postcolonial theory and public relations. In R. L. Heath (Ed.), *Encyclopedia of public relations* (Vol. *2*, pp. 631–631). Thousand Oaks, CA: Sage.

Nag, R., Hambrick, D. C., & Chen, M. (2007). What is strategic management really? Inductive derivation of a consensus definition of the field. *Strategic Management Journal*, *278*, 935–955.

Nothhaft, H., Werder, K. P., Verĉiĉ, D., & Zerfass, A. (2018). Strategic communication: Reflection on an elusive concept. *International Journal of Strategic Communication*, *12*(4), 352–366.

O'Conner, A., & Shumate, M. (2018). A multidimensional network approach to strategic communication. *International Journal of Strategic Communication*, *12*(4), 399–416.

Pal, M., & Dutta, M. J. (2008). Public relations in a global context: The relevance of critical modernism as a theoretical lens. *Journal of Public Relations Research*, *20*(2), 159–179.

Palea, A. (2014). The public relations professional: Elements of identity. *Professional Communication and Translation Studies*, *7*, 17–22.

Pamment, J. (2018). Public diplomacy. In R. L. Heath & W. Johansen (Eds.), *The international encyclopedia of strategic communication*. Hoboken, NJ: John Wiley & Sons.

Pasadeos, Y., Berger, B., & Renfro, B. (2010). Public relations as a maturing discipline: Notes on research networks. *Journal of Public Relations Research*, *22*(2), 136–158.

Paul, C. (2011). *Strategic communication: Origins, concepts, and current debates*. Santa Barbara, CA: Praeger.

Pearson, R. (1989). A theory of public relations ethics. Unpublished doctoral dissertation, Ohio University.

Plowman, K. D., & Wilson, C. (2018). Strategy and tactics in strategic communication: Examining their intersection with social media use. *International Journal of Strategic Communication*, *22*(12), 125–144.

Pratt, C. B., & McLaughlin, G. W. (1989). Ethical inclinations of public relations majors. *Journal of Mass Media Ethics*, *4*(1), 68–91.

Radford, G. P. (2012). Public relations in a postmodern world. *Public Relations Inquiry*, *1*(1), 49–67.

Reid, M. (2005). Performance auditing of integrated marketing communication (IMC) actions and outcomes. *Journal of Advertising*, *34*(4), 41–51.

Rittenhofer, I., & Valentini, C. (2015). A practice turn to global public relations: An alternative approach. *Journal of Communication Management*, *19*(1), 2–19.

Roper, J. (2005). Symmetrical communication: Excellent public relations or a strategy for hegemony? *Journal of Public Relations Research*, *17*(1), 69–86.

Rüel, H., & Wolters, T. (2016). Business diplomacy. In C. M. Constantinou, P. Kerr, & P. Sharp (Eds.), *The SAGE handbook of diplomacy* (pp. 564–576). London: Sage Publications Ltd.

Russell, K. M., & Lamme, M. O. (2016). Theorizing public relations history: The roles of strategic intent and human agency. *Public Relations Review*, *42*, 741–747.

Sadeghi, L. (2012). Web 2.0. In M. Lee, G. Neeley, & K. Stewart (Eds.), *The practice of government public relations* (pp. 125–140). Boca Raton, FL: CRC Press.

Saffer, A. J. (2018). Value-added theory. In R. L. Heath & W. Johansen (Eds.), *The international encyclopedia of strategic communication* (pp. 1–10). Hoboken, NJ: John Wiley & Sons.

Sallot, L. M., Lyon, L. J., Acosta-Aluru, C., & Jones, K. O. (2003). From aardark to zebra: A new millennium analysis of theory development in public relations academic journals. *Journal of Public Relations Research*, *15*, 29–90.

Simandi, F. A. (2006). The United Arab Emirates Youths (EAEU) between modernity and traditionalism. *International Journal of Sociology and Social Policy*, *26*(3/4), 172–184.

Sison, M. D. (2014). Public relations beyond borders: Future directions. *Asia Pacific Public Relations Journal*, *14*(1/2), 1–3.

Snow, N. (2003). *Information war: American propaganda, free speech and opinion control since 9/11*. New York: Seven Stories Press.

Solis, B. (2008). PR 2.0: Putting the public back in public relations. Blog post, April 8. Available from http://www.briansolis.com/2008/04/pr-20-putting-public-back-in-public/ (accessed May 20, 2020).

Sommerfeldt, E. J. (2013). The civility of social capital: Public relations in the public sphere, civil society, and democracy. *Public Relations Review*, *39*, 280–289.

Sommerfeldt, E. J., & Yang, A. (2018). Notes on a dialogue: Twenty years of digital dialogic communication research in public relations. *Journal of Public Relations Research*, *30*(3), 59–64.

Spicer, C. H. (1993). Images of public relations in the print media. *Journal of Public Relations Research*, *3*, 47–67.

Spicer, C. H. (2000). Public relations in a democratic society: Value and values. *Journal of Public Relations Research*, *12*(1), 115–130.

Sriramesh, K., & Verčič, D. (2003). *The global public relations handbook: Theory, research and practice*. Mahwah, NJ: Lawrence Erlbaum Associates.

Stacks, D. W., Botan, C., & Turk, J. V. (1999). Perceptions of public relations education. *Public Relations Review*, *25*, 9–29.

Stark, K., & Kruckeberg, D. (2001). Public relations and community: A reconstructed theory revisited. In R. L. Heath (Ed.), *Handbook of public relations* (pp. 51–59). Thousand Oaks, CA: Sage.

Stauber, J., & Rampton, S. (1995). *Toxic sludge is good for you: Lies, damn lies, and the public relations industry*. Monroe, ME: Common Courage Press.

Steyn, B. (2003). From strategy to corporate communication strategy: A conceptualization. *Journal of Communication Management*, *8*(2), 168–183.

Taylor, M. (2010). Civil society as a rhetorical public relations process. In R. Heath, E. L. Toth, & D. Waymer (Eds.), *Rhetorical and critical appraoches to public relations II* (pp. 76–91). Hillsdale, NJ: Lawrence Erlbaum Associates.

Toledano, M., & Maplesden, A. (2016). Facilitating community networks: Public relations skills and non-professional organizers. *Public Relations Review*, *42*, 713–722.

Tusinski, K. (2017). Trends in public relations: Exploring the role of ethics as it relates to social media and crisis communication. *Journal of Media Ethics*, *32*(1), 61–66.

Valentini, C., Kruckeberg, D., & Stark, K. (2016). The global society and its impact on public relations theorizing: Reflections on major micro trends. *Central European Journal of Communication*, *2*, 229–246.

Valentini, C. D., & Kruckeberg, D. (2011). Public relations and trust in contemporary global society: A Luhmannian perspective of the role of public relations in enhancing trust among social systems. *Central European Journal of Communication*, *4*(1), 91–107.

van Ruler, B. (2015). Agile public relations: The reflective communication scrum. *Public Relations Review*, *41*(2), 187–194.

van Ruler, B. (2018). Communcation theory: An underrated pillar on which strategic communication rests. *International Journal of Strategic Communication*, *12*(4), 367–381.

Verčič, D., Verhoeven, P., & Zerfass, P. (2014). Key issues of public relations in Europe: Finding from the European Communications Monitor, 2007–2014. *Revista Internacionale de Relaciones Publicas, 4*(8).

Verčič, D., Verčič, A. T., & Sriramesh, K. (2015). Looking for digital in public relations. *Public Relations Review, 41*, 142–152.

Verwey, S. D., Benecke, R., & Muir, C. (2017). Purpose and practice: Educating PR professionals for the future. Paper presented at the 2017 PRISA Conference. *Communication, 36,* 67–78.

Volk, S. C., & Zerfass, A. (2018). Alignment: Explicating a key concept in strategic communcaiton. *International Journal of Strategic Communication, 12*(4), 433–451.

Vujnovic, M., & Krukeberg, D. (2018). Globalization. In R. L. Heath & W. Johansen (Eds.), *The international encyclopedia of strategic communication* (pp. 1–9). Hoboken, NJ: John Wiley & Sons.

Weaver, C. K. (2016). A Marxist primer for critical public relations. *Media International Australia, 160*(1), 43–52.

Wehmeier, S. (2009). Out of the fog and into the future: Directions of public relations, theory building, research, and practice. *Canadian Journal of Communication, 34,* 265–282.

Werder, K. P., Nothhaft, H., Verĉiĉ, D., & Zerfass, A. (2018). Strategic communication as an emerging interdisciplinary paradigm. *International Journal of Strategic Communication, 12*(4), 333–351.

White, C., & Park, J. (2010). Public perceptions of public relations. *Public Relations Review, 36,* 319–324.

White, C., & Radic, D. (2014). Comparative public diplomacy: Message strategies in countries in transition. *Public Relations Review, 40*(3), 459–465.

White House. (2010). National framework for strategic communication. Available from https://www.hsdl.org/?abstract&did=27301 (accessed May 20, 2020).

Winkler, P., & Etter, M. (2018). Strategic communication and emergence: A dual narrative framework. *International Journal of Strategic Communication, 12*(4), 382–398.

Wright, D. K., & Hinson, M. D. (2015). Examining social and emerging media use in pubic relations practice: A ten-year longitudinal analysis. *Public Relations Journal, 9*(2).

Wright, D. K., & Turk, J. V. (2007). Public relations knowledge and professionalism: Challenges to educations and practitioners. In E. L. Toth (Ed.), *The future of excellence in public relations and communication management: Challenges for the next generation* (pp. 571–588). Mahwah, NJ: Lawrence Erlbaum Associates.

Xu, J., & Huang, G. (2016). Mapping public relations scholarship in Asia: A longitudinal analysis of published research, 1995–2014. *Asian Journal of Communication, 26*(6), 458–465.

Yang, A., & Taylor, M. (2013). The relationship between the professionalization of public relations, societal capital and democracy: Evidence from a cross-national study. *Public Relations Review, 39*(4), 257–270.

Ye, L., & Ki, E. J. (2012). The status of online public relations research: An analysis of published articles in 1992–2009. *Journal of Public Relations Research, 24,* 409–434.

Zerfass, A., Verĉiĉ, D., Nothhaft, H., & Werder, P. (2018). Strategic communication: Defining the field and its contribution to research and practice. *International Journal of Strategic Communication, 12*(4), 487–505.

Zerfass, A., Verĉiĉ, D., Verhoeven, P., Moreno, A., and Tench, R. (2015). European communication monitor: Creating communication values through listening, messaging, and measurement. Results of a survey of 41 countries. A study conducted by the European Public Relations Education and Research Association (EUPRERA) and the European Association of Communication Directors (EACD) supported by partner PRIME Research International and media partner Communication Director Magazine. Available from http://www.communicationmonitor.eu/wp-content/uploads/2018/03/ECM-2015-Results-ChartVersion-European-Communication-Monitor-Trends-Strategic-Communication-Management-Corporate-Communication-Public-Relations-PR.pdf (accessed May 20, 2020).

Index

Public Relations Theory: Capabilities and Competencies, First Edition. Jae-Hwa Shin and Robert L. Heath.
© 2021 John Wiley & Sons, Inc. Published 2021 by John Wiley & Sons, Inc.